PODIATRIC OFFICE MANAGEMENT AND PROCEDURES

Podiatric Office Management and Procedures

Peggy Kane, P.M.A.C.
New Smyrna Beach, Florida

Barbara S. Schlefman, D.P.M.
Diplomate, American Board of Podiatric Surgery
Fellow, American College of Foot Surgeons
Past President, American Association for Women Podiatrists
Faculty, The Podiatry Institute
Private Practice
Tucker, Georgia

Nancy Sinnott Vickers, B.M.
Manager, Medical Book Division
The Podiatry Institute
Tucker, Georgia

Foreword by E. Dalton McGlamry, D.P.M.

The Podiatry Institute
Tucker, Georgia

Mosby Year Book
St. Louis Baltimore Boston Chicago London Philadelphia Sydney Toronto

Mosby
Year Book
Dedicated to Publishing Excellence

Sponsoring Editor: James F. Shanahan
Assistant Editor: Joyce-Rachel John
Associate Managing Editor, Manuscript Services: Deborah Thorp
Senior Production Assistant: Maria Nevinger
Proofroom Manager: Barbara Kelly

Mosby-Year Book, Inc.
11830 Westline Industrial Drive
St. Louis, MO 63146

1 2 3 4 5 6 7 8 9 0 CL MV 96 95 94 93 92

Library of Congress Cataloging-in-Publication Data
Kane, Peggy.
Podiatric office management and procedures / Peggy Kane, Barbara Schlefman.
p. cm.
Includes bibliographical references and index.
ISBN 0-8016-6316-4
1. Podiatry. 2. Podiatry—Practice. I. Schlefman, Barbara.
II. Title.
[DNLM: 1. Office Management. 2. Podiatry—methods. 3. Podiatry—
-organization & administration. WE 890 K16p]
RD563.K26 1991
617.5'85—dc20 91-38928
DNLM/DLC CIP
for Library of Congress

CONTRIBUTORS

Karen Allred, P.M.A.
Loganville, Georgia

James L. Bouchard, D.P.M.
Diplomate, American Board of Podiatric Surgery
Fellow, American College of Foot Surgeons
Faculty, The Podiatry Institute
Private Practice
Roswell, Georgia

Brenda Britt, P.M.A.C.
Office Manager
Office of Dr. A. Louis Jimenez
Snellville, Georgia

Pat Burt
President, Medical Delinquency Management, Inc.
Loganville, Georgia

Bradley D. Castellano, D.P.M.
Faculty, The Podiatry Institute
Private Practice
Fort Myers, Florida

Raymond G. Cavaliere, D.P.M.
Fellow, American College of Foot Surgeons
Assistant Professor
Division of Surgical Science
New York School of Podiatric Medicine
Faculty, The Podiatry Institute
Private Practice
New York, New York

Thomas J. Chang, D.P.M.
Resident, Northlake Regional Medical Center
Tucker, Georgia

Luke D. Cicchinelli, D.P.M.
Resident, Northlake Regional Medical Center
Tucker, Georgia

Stephen V. Corey, D.P.M.
Consultant, National Naval Medical Center
Faculty, The Podiatry Institute
Private Practice
Decatur, Georgia

Lois F. Downey, J.D.
Law Offices of Parker, McCay, and Criscuolo, P.C.
Marlton, New Jersey

Michael S. Downey, D.P.M.
Associate Professor and Chairman
Department of Surgery
Pennsylvania College of Podiatric Medicine
Philadelphia, Pennsylvania
Fellow, American College of Foot Surgeons
Faculty, The Podiatry Institute

Gary S. Fields, D.P.M.
Diplomate, American Board of Podiatric Surgery
Fellow, American College of Foot Surgeons
Private Practice
Carrollton, Georgia

Harry Goldsmith, D.P.M.
President, American College of Podiatrics Medical Review
Fellow, American College of Foot Surgeons
Private Practice
Downey, California

A. Louis Jimenez, D.P.M.
Faculty, The Podiatry Institute
Private Practice
Snellville, Georgia

Peggy Kane, P.M.A.C.
New Smyrna Beach, Florida

Birdi Kribs, P.M.A.
Office Manager
Peachtree Podiatry Group
Tucker, Georgia

D. Scot Malay, D.P.M.
Assistant Professor
Department of Surgery
Pennsylvania College of Podiatric Medicine
Philadelphia, Pennsylvania
Co-Director of Podiatric Education
North Philadelphia Health System
Faculty, The Podiatry Institute

Dennis E. Martin, D.P.M.
Private Practice
North Charleston, South Carolina
Faculty, The Podiatry Institute

Terence M. McElgun, D.P.M.
Associate, American College of Foot Surgeons
Private Practice
Garden City, New York

E. Dalton McGlamry, D.P.M.
Diplomate, American Board of Podiatric Surgery
Past President, American Podiatric Medical Association
Faculty, The Podiatry Institute
Private Practice
Tucker, Georgia

Rebekah C. McGlamry, B.A.
Tucker, Georgia

Thomas J. Merrill, D.P.M.
Associate Professor of Surgery
Barry University, School of Podiatric Medicine
Miami Shores, Florida
Diplomate, American Board of Podiatric Surgery
Faculty, The Podiatry Institute

Stephen J. Miller, D.P.M.
Diplomate, American Board of Podiatric Surgery
Fellow, American College of Foot Surgeons
Faculty, The Podiatry Institute
Private Practice
Anacortes, Washington

Aaron C. Olson, D.P.M.
Diplomate, American Board of Podiatric Surgery
Fellow, American College of Foot Surgeons
Private Practice
Bismarck, North Dakota

Alfred J. Phillips, D.P.M.
Residency Research Director
North Carney Hospital
Dorchester, Massachusetts
Faculty, The Podiatry Institute
Private Practice
Scituate, Massachusetts

A.R. Pitts, Jr., D.P.M.
Private Practice
Valdosta, Georgia

T.E. Pitts, D.P.M.
Resident, Northlake Regional Medical Center
Tucker, Georgia

Deborah Rogers
Co-Owner, DR Software
Marietta, Georgia

Laurence G. Rubin, D.P.M.
Private Practice
Richmond, Virginia

Stuart J. Ruch, D.P.M.
Co-Owner, Ruch Orthotic Labs
Diplomate, American Board of Podiatric Surgery
Fellow, American College of Foot Surgeons
Pekin, Illinois

Barbara S. Schlefman, D.P.M.
Diplomate, American Board of Podiatric Surgery
Fellow, American College of Foot Surgeons
Past President, American Association for Women Podiatrists
Faculty, The Podiatry Institute
Private Practice
Tucker, Georgia

Miriam Y. Smalley
Financial Coordinator
Office of Dr. James L. Bouchard
Roswell, Georgia

Lynn M. Smith, M.S.E.D.
Executive Assistant
Office of Dr. Thomas F. Smith
Augusta, Georgia

Thomas F. Smith, D.P.M.
Fellow, American College of Foot Surgeons
Diplomate, American Board of Podiatric Surgery
Acting Chief, Veterans Administration Medical Center
Faculty, The Podiatry Institute
Private Practice
Augusta, Georgia

Heidi Stapp, P.M.A.C.
Miami, Florida

Mickey D. Stapp, B.S. (Pharm)
Fourth Year Student
Barry University School of Podiatric Medicine
Miami Shores, Florida

George R. Vito, D.P.M.
Faculty, The Podiatry Institute
Private Practice
Macon, Georgia

Caroline Welch, P.M.A.C.
Past President, American Society of Podiatric Medical Assistants
Tucker, Georgia

James E. Zelichowski, D.P.M.
Fellow, American College of Foot Surgeons
Private Practice
Alpharetta, Georgia

Richard J. Zirm, D.P.M.
Private Practice
Coeur d'Alene, Idaho

FOREWORD

Changes in podiatric medicine and surgery are occurring at a remarkable rate. The changes challenge the practicing podiatrist and his staff to try to stay current amid such technical evolution. But as important as the technical changes are, the administrative and socioeconomic changes are even more of a challenge. The editors of this book, along with their contributing authors, have performed a great service with this volume by teaching the podiatrist and his/her staff to adapt to the changes occurring within the profession.

Peggy Kane, P.M.A.C., has managed a podiatry practice for many years and has worked both in patient care and in the administrative area of the practice. Kane has coordinated seminars in podiatric practice organization and has published several books on podiatry for the assistant.

Barbara Schlefman, D.P.M., is an experienced podiatrist, an excellent surgeon, an accomplished teacher of podiatric practice, and a respected author.

Special recognition goes to Nancy Vickers of the Podiatry Institute who served as the authors' editor and coordinator of the textbook.

The material in this book has been drawn from the annual seminars in office administration and patient care presented by the Podiatry Institute.

The podiatry assistant and the podiatrist who is trying to improve the organization of his/her office will find the book most useful. Many of the skills presented find equal application by podiatrists and podiatric assistants.

I congratulate the editors and the authors on the completion of this outstanding work.

E. Dalton McGlamry, D.P.M.
Chief Executive Officer
The Podiatry Institute
Tucker, Georgia

PREFACE

Many textbooks and reference books are available for the student, trainee, and practitioner of podiatric medicine and surgery. New entries into the field and revisions of standard texts are appearing with increasing frequency, reflecting the evolution of the specialty and advances in the diagnostic and therapeutic options available to the practicing podiatrist. Many of these books are excellent, but there remains a gap in practical information available to and for the podiatric assistant. This is curious, given the equally noticeable evolution of the podiatric assistant from front office staffer to invaluable member of the diagnostic, therapeutic, and organizational team. There remains the need for a comprehensive, practical reference that blends the sheer variety of front and back office procedures required of the modern podiatric assistant in a manner equally useful in educational and clinical settings.

Podiatric Office Management and Procedures has attempted to meet that need. It has been written and produced for the modern podiatric assistant, the student, and the podiatric practitioners who train them. It is intended to serve as a useful, accessible reference for application to the daily operation of the podiatric office practice. We have attempted to produce a comprehensive book for the variety of circumstances likely to be faced by the podiatric assistant on any given day, and have focused on the unique front-office and clinical demands placed on the modern podiatric assistant.

The education, training, and staffing of the modern podiatric assistant is inherently varied and increasingly complex. We hope that *Podiatric Office Management and Procedures* has met its goal of presenting the spectrum of podiatric assisting procedures in a manner useful to all members of the podiatric medical and surgical practice.

Peggy Kane, P.M.A.C.
Barbara Schlefman, D.P.M.
Nancy Sinnott Vickers, B.M.
The Podiatry Institute
Tucker, Georgia

CONTENTS

SECTION I

Overview

1

The Profession of Podiatry

Rebekah C. McGlamry, B.A.

EARLY BEGINNINGS

Foot problems have plagued mankind from the earliest of times. Hippocrates (460–377 B.C.) described clubfoot and detailed the treatment that is fundamentally still used today.[1]

As civilization progressed, so did the knowledge and practice of physicians. During the Renaissance, intellectual and scientific inquiry began to burgeon. Barber-surgeons began practicing their trade in the 15th century and gained experience by treating wounds on the battlefields of central Europe. Anatomy lessons, learned from early writings, took on added significance as dissection of human cadavers in the 1500s added knowledge and corrected some of the errors in the earlier anatomy literature.

Corns were described in a scientific dissertation in 1686 by Johannes Reinhardus Fuchs.[2] In 1769 a book was published by Dufour of Paris that not only covered the common corn but also had information on verruca and nail care.

David Low of London published a book in 1785 entitled *Chiropodologia*. Low took most of his material from a book published earlier by Nicholas Laurent Laforest of Paris who had been chirurgeon pedicure to Louis XVI, but Low gave no credit to Laforest for his earlier work. The term *chiropodologia*, created by Low, was derived from Greek words meaning hand, foot, and study. The corn cutters of London and Edinburgh adopted this designation and became the chiropodists of the 19th century. The numbers of practitioners increased in England as the profession grew, and chiropody offices appeared in London and other English cities by 1840.

PODIATRY (CHIROPODY) IN THE PREPROFESSIONAL PERIOD IN THE UNITED STATES

Although the United States was quite independent of England, customs and information continued to funnel to the New World; therefore, it is not surprising that chiropodists appeared in the United States.

In the beginning, traveling practitioners went from town to town, and by the 1830s, many persons began to make the rounds of the larger cities and called themselves "corn doctors." In 1843 John Littlefield opened an office in New York, and in 1850 Richard N. Westervelt, later first president of the Pedic Society, joined Littlefield. Littlefield was the first practitioner in New York to use the term *chiropodist*.[3]

The first book on chiropody to appear in the United States was the English text of Lewis Durlacher. It was published in Philadelphia by Lea & Blanchard in 1845, the same year that the London edition was published. This book undoubtedly introduced the formal profession of chiropody to America. In 1860 Issacher Zacharie (1827–1900) authored the first American book on chiropody, *Surgical and Practical Observations on the Diseases of the Human Foot*, published in New York. Unfortunately, Zacharie took credit for material that he compiled from Eisenberg and from Durlacher of England.[4] A colorful character, Zacharie was the chiropodist of President Abraham Lincoln.

FIRST PROFESSIONAL GROUP OF CHIROPODISTS IN THE UNITED STATES

Before 1895 a true field of chiropodial practice did not exist in the United States. Barbers, shoemakers, and masseurs did most of this work with no specific knowledge or training. In 1895, a small group of practitioners in New York established what was the first society of chiropodists, the Pedic Society of New York. It was not until 1907 that the group published the first issue of its journal *Pedic Society Items*. There was no British journal or formal society of chiropodists in Britain at that time. British chiropodists probably subscribed to the *Items* from the early years.

In 1912, 35 prominent chiropody practitioners met in London and founded the National Society of Chiropodists. This group had exchanged correspondence and information with the American group from the early 1900s.

When the Pedic Society of New York was organized, it was done so with its own board of examiners. From 1895 to 1912 the issuing of certificates to practice, upon examination, was entrusted to this society.[5]

DEMAND FOR BETTER TRAINING AND EDUCATION BY PROFESSIONAL ORGANIZATIONS

In the 1860s Peter Kahler, having moved from his native Germany, was in Scranton, Pennsylvania, and advertised his shop as the largest boot and shoe establishment in Luzerne County. He made a pair of boots for President Lincoln and slippers for Mrs. Lincoln. By 1882 a booklet was issued in New York entitled *Dress and Care of the Feet* and on the title page was "Dr. P. Kahler." Another business had been started with no date attributed to it, but this new business was advertised as Dr. P. Kahler's Sons' School of Surgical Chiropody. This correspondence school, founded by Charles Otto, one of Dr. Peter Kahler's sons, required a period of study covering "three months' time," and granted a diploma "provided the student passes the required first examination." If the student did not pass the first examination, the course took 6 months. However, a diploma did not guarantee passing the New York State licensure examination.[6]

The Kahlers' school was not the only correspondence course available to persons wishing to become chiropodists; a Professor Rohrer offered a handbook to prepare students for the state examinations and included the subjects of anatomy, physiology, chemistry, therapeutics, minor surgery, and bandaging. Professor Rohrer's booklet could be ordered for $2.00 from his Institute of Beauty Culture in New York City.

In 1910 the Franco-American College, Inc., Chiropody and Beauty Culture, was listed under the same address in Philadelphia as "Rohrer's School of Beauty Culture" but with Madam L. Honauer as proprietor. In 1918 Louise Honauer was listed under "Chiropodist" in the city directory. In addition, other schools in Philadelphia, Chicago, and New York advertised training in chiropody.

The members of the New York Society (already organized in 1895) recognized the need for professional training and education. Matters of clinical and professional interest to the members had been appearing in *Pedic Items* since its inception. Chiropody's role, even then, in the treatment of diabetes and its relationship to the medical profession became evident.

At that time the New York Pedic Law defined chiropody as the surgical treatment of abnormal nails, removal of all superficial excrescences on the hands and feet (such as corns, warts, or callosities), and the treatment of bunions, but with no right to make incisions involving the structures below the true skin.[7] Now was the time for formal education of chiropodists to come to the forefront.

The Pedic Society of New York, now with 166 members, began to seek proper educational facilities (with physicians as chief instructors) and for Board of Regents examinations for all future candidates.[8] The Pedic Society went to Secretary of the New York State Board of Medical Examiners Maurice J. Lewi, M.D., for help in drafting a new chiropody bill. The bill was drafted and passed by the state legislature and took effect in September 1912. Under this bill licensing of chiropodists passed to the State Board of Medical Examiners. The Pedic Society was made the rule-making body for the profession and entitled to privileges such as those of the medical, dental, and veterinary societies of the state. Educational standards for new practitioners were set, and accreditation required graduation from a chiropody school headed by a medical practitioner. Dr. Lewi was persuaded to become the new president of the School of Chiropody of New York, which would grant the Master of Chiropody degree after a 1-year, full-time course. A 1-year completion of high school was the prerequisite for admission, but plans were formulated to advance this requirement to a high school diploma by 1918.

Increase in Education and Professional Levels

Chiropody groups began to form in other states in the early 1900s, although the New York Pedic Society was the only formally organized society for the first 10 years of its existence. In 1906 New Jersey and Massachusetts formed professional organizations, and Pennsylvania and Connecticut began their professional groups soon after.

In 1911 *Pedic Items* took the cue from James Richardson Bennie, a partner in one of Philadelphia's two leading chiropodial offices and a member of the Chiropody Society of Pennsylvania. An article printed in October 1911 presented a plan for advancing the profession by organizing into a national group. Letters were sent out to practitioners all over the country, and *Pedic Items* pushed the creation of such a group.

FORMAL ORGANIZATION OF THE NATIONAL ASSOCIATION OF CHIROPODISTS

The first meeting of the National Association of Chiropodists (NAC) was held at the LaSalle Hotel in Chicago on July 1, 1912. Approximately 225 chiropodists were present, but only 118 signed the registration book. Temporary officers were elected, and Alfred Joseph, editor of the *Pedic Items,* was elected as the first president pro tem. The 118 chiropodists who signed the registration book were from 12 different states, quite a remarkable response since there were probably fewer than 1,000 practitioners in the United States at the time.[9] On the second day of the meeting several scientific papers were read, and New York was chosen as the convention city for 1913.

Development and Maturation of the Profession

Now that the NAC was in existence, standards began to be developed for the regulation of the profession. The NAC began to interest itself in professional problems relating to the recruitment of podiatrists, foot health of school children, foot clinics for the indigent, and relations with shoe manufacturers. Education and upgrading standards for the profession of podiatry (chiropody) became one of the higher goals of the association. The first school (the New York school, which eventually became the M.J. Lewi School of Chiropody) had been in existence since 1911, even before the NAC was formed.

The first clinic was started in New York in 1910. Joseph P. Solomon, through his own energy and much of his own resources, secured from the New York State Board of Charities a charter for the People's Pedicure Clinic. This was an outgrowth of free treatment sessions conducted once a week by several leading New York City chiropodists. The People's Pedicure Clinic expanded from two nights a week to five nights a week and served poor people of the neighborhood in a dispensary on Washington Square, probably the first free foot clinic in the United States. In the fall of 1912 under the influence of Dr. Maurice J. Lewi, the clinic was moved to the 125th Street building of the School of Chiropody, which was to become the first institute. The New York school therefore had formal education plus the added advantage of a clinic in which the students might be trained. The professional school year consisted of 8 months for the day course and 2 years for the night course. In 1924, under pressure from the NAC Council on Education, night classes were abolished, and the day course was extended to 2 full years.[10] M.J. Lewi, M.D., president of the New York school, worked out curriculum and studies along the lines of the medical schools.

There were approximately ten schools teaching chiropody by 1921. Five or six appeared to be bona fide nonprofit educational enterprises. Standards for entrance requirements for schools of chiropody continued to rise, and curricula and faculty standards were also raised. By that time 21 states had passed statutes regulating the practice of chiropody/podiatry. In 1921 the Council on Education of the NAC had worked out a standard of curricula. In the years following, the five major schools were established along these lines, quite a far-sighted accomplishment for a national organization only 9 years old.

The Illinois College of Chiropody and Orthopedics was founded in the fall of 1912 by William M. Scholl, M.D., in Chicago. The college became the Illinois College of Chiropody in 1916, the Illinois College of Podiatry in 1962, and the Scholl College of Podiatric Medicine in 1981.

The California College of Chiropody was founded in 1914 and became the California Podiatry College in 1962. In 1969 it was renamed the California College of Podiatric Medicine and is located in San Francisco.

The Ohio College of Chiropody was founded in 1916 and originally located in downtown Cleveland. The name of the college was changed to Ohio College of Podiatry in 1963 and to Ohio College of Podiatric Medicine in 1969.

The Pennsylvania College of Podiatric Medicine was chartered in 1960 to begin a new podiatry college in Philadelphia. The name Philadelphia College of Chiropody was changed to Pennsylvania College of Podiatry in 1964 and, in 1969, to Pennsylvania College of Podiatric Medicine.

In 1982 the College of Podiatric Medicine and Surgery became the third college established within the University of Osteopathic Medicine and Health Sciences, Des Moines, Iowa.

Barry University of Miami, Florida, a private institution, established a School of Podiatric Medicine in 1985.[11]

Extinct Schools of Chiropody/Podiatry

Temple University in Philadelphia had a School of Chiropody that began in 1915. Temple closed out two of its colleges in 1958: chiropody and theology.

Middlesex College of Chiropody in Boston opened in 1916. This college failed to meet the Council on Education accreditation requirements in 1927 and was never recognized throughout its existence. It closed in 1941–1942.

The Beacon Institute of Podiatry was chartered in Boston in 1930. Its graduates were licensed to practice only in Massachusetts, and the school was disbanded in the early 1950s.

Northwestern College of Chiropody of Minneapolis is known only by an announcement that appeared in the *Northwest Pedic News* for 1917. This college evidently was in existence for only 2 years.

The Georgia College of Chiropody/Podiatry, Atlanta, was opened in 1930 on the premises of the Southern College of Pharmacy. In spite of the good will of the profession, the school became a casualty of the depression in 1935.

The Colorado College of Podiatry opened in Denver about 1927. It closed in 1938 because of failure to meet the NAC Council on Education standards.

The Von Schill Memorial College of Chiropody and Pedic Surgery opened in 1930 in Chicago. It was later known as the Northwestern Institute of Foot Surgery and Chiropody. In 1933 the institution was renamed Northwestern Institute and was apparently recognized but "without classification." Northwestern never regained accreditation. Although described as closing in 1945, Northwestern issued catalogs and commencement announcements as late as 1959.

The Chicago College of Chiropody and Pedic Surgery was founded in 1932 but closed in June 1962 after withdrawal of accreditation by the Council on Accreditation of the NAC.[12]

THE JOURNAL AS AN OFFICIAL ORGAN OF THE NATIONAL ASSOCIATION OF CHIROPODISTS (PODIATRISTS)

Until 1920, *Pedic Items* was owned and operated by Alfred Joseph, who served as its first editor.

However, in January 1921 it was renamed the *Journal of the National Association of Chiropodists and Pedic Items* and became the official publication of the Association. The year 1921 also marked the beginning of the work of Joseph's successor, E. Kenneth Burnett, who served as editor until 1930.[13] Dr. Joseph Lelyveld succeeded Dr. Burnett upon the latter's retirement. The content of the journal was broadened to reflect the happenings of the society, clinical and theoretical problems of podiatry-chiropody, and room for the officers of the NAC to informally discuss the aims and problems of the organization.

According to a 1937 editorial, the journal had three functions: "...first, to present scientific information; second, to spread the news of the organization and its activities; third, to bind the affiliated societies together and to make the individual feel the warm interest of the national association."[14]

Dr. William J. Stickel assumed the editorship of the journal in 1942 when he became the Executive Secretary of the National Association of Chiropodists. He held this position until his death in 1955.

Dr. Abe Rubin became editor of the journal in 1955. This began a period of major changes for the profession and the association. Chiropody became podiatry, and the National Association of Chiropodists became the American Podiatry Association (APA) in 1957. Major progress began as significant changes were made in prescription practice, including narcotic privileges, surgery, and health insurance, which benefited the podiatrist's patients. The journal carefully recorded the changes and growth of the profession. In 1970 Dr. Rubin left Washington to assume the leadership of the Ohio College of Podiatric Medicine, and Louis G. Buttell became the managing editor.

In January 1973, Dr. E. Dalton McGlamry became the acting senior editor, and in June 1973 he was appointed senior editor by the APA Board of Trustees. Special editors in 18 fields of specialization were appointed in addition to a group of general editors. Dr. McGlamry resigned as editor of the journal in 1983 and was followed by Dr. Michael Burns. In June of 1987 Dr. Thomas M. DeLauro became senior editor of the *Journal of the American Podiatric Medical Association.*

These editors have contributed greatly to the profession of podiatry. Medical knowledge, scientific advances, and creative reconstruction of the human body have come to the forefront in podiatry as in all medical professions. The profession of podiatry has vigorously moved ahead, and the *Journal of the American Podiatric Medical Association* documented as well as advanced these crucial scientific ideas and results.

In 1984 the House of Delegates of the APA voted to officially change the name of the organization to the American Podiatric Medical Association (APMA). Consequently, the journal changed its name to the *Journal of the American Podiatric Medical Association.*

GROWTH OF THE ASSOCIATION SIMULTANEOUSLY WITH GROWTH OF THE PROFESSION

The APMA has developed and matured as the journal came along to document these changes. The NAC came into being in 1912. Dr. Alfred Joseph was elected as its first president. There were six officers and ten members of the Board of Directors. Interestingly enough, two of these original board members were female practitioners.

Past presidents of the association are as follows[15]:

- 1912–1913: Alfred Joseph, New York
- 1913–1917: Earnest C. Stanaback, Newark, NJ
- 1917–1918: Harry Parker Kenison, Boston
- 1918–1920: Edwin Kenneth Burnett, New York
- 1920–1921: Harry P. Clifton, Baltimore
- 1921–1923: Walter V. Ramsburg, Minneapolis
- 1923–1924: Ernest Graff, New York
- 1924–1926: Walter V. Ramsburg, Minneapolis
- 1926–1928: Frank E. Hayden, Boston
- 1928–1930: Max S. Harmolin, Cleveland
- 1930–1932: Joseph Lelyveld, Rockland, Mass
- 1932–1934: George W. Scherer, Jr., Los Angeles
- 1934–1936: Albert Owen Penney, Washington, D.C.
- 1936–1938: G. Earle Whitten, Oakland, Calif
- 1938–1940: Charles E. Krausz, Philadelphia
- 1940–1941: Gus T. Dowling, Atlanta
- 1941–1942: Ralph W. Dye, Sandy Lake, Pa
- 1942–1943: Edward P. Durkin, Chicago
- 1943–1944: Harry W. Weinerman, Brooklyn, NY
- 1944–1946: John D. Walker, Hartford, Conn
- 1946–1947: Walter P. Fields, Nashville, Tenn
- 1947–1948: Leo N. Liss, San Francisco
- 1948–1949: Fred W. Isaacs, Durham, NC
- 1949–1950: Floyd Frost, Toledo, Ohio

- 1950–1951: Lester A. Walsh, Midland, Tex
- 1951–1952: Edward C. Stivers, Louisville, Ky
- 1952–1953: Max Speizman, Wilkes-Barre, Pa
- 1953–1954: Stewart E. Reed, Des Moines, Iowa
- 1954–1955: Walter C. Gigerich, Hot Springs, Ark
- 1955: honorary—Morse K. Upshaw, Sr., Jackson, Miss
- 1955–1956: Ralph E. Fowler, Detroit
- 1956–1957: Felton O. Gamble, Tucson
- 1957–1958: Jonas C. Morris, Audubon, NJ
- 1958–1959: George E. Guenzler, Freeport, Ill
- 1959–1960: Marvin W. Shapiro, Toledo, Ohio
- 1960–1961: Marvin D. Marr, Cedar Rapids, Iowa
- 1961–1962: Robert Shor, Los Angeles
- 1962–1963: Benjamin C. Mullens, Binghamton, NY
- 1963–1964: Earl G. Kaplan, Detroit
- 1964–1965: James A. Conforti, Bedford, Ohio
- 1965–1966: Edwin N. Barron, Little Rock, Ark
- 1966–1967: Douglas T. Mowbray, Waterloo, Iowa
- 1967–1968: Irving Yale, Ansonia, Conn
- 1968–1969: Clarence Bookbinder, Burlingame, NJ
- 1969–1970: Charles R. Turchin, Washington, D.C.
- 1970–1971: Lawrence G. Lefler, Fremont, Neb
- 1971–1972: Ernest M. Weiner, New York
- 1972–1973: E. Dalton McGlamry, Atlanta
- 1973–1974: Charles H. Johnson, Riverside, Calif
- 1974–1975: Irvin O. Kanat, Detroit
- 1975–1976: John R. Graham, Decatur, Ill
- 1976–1977: H. Darrel Darby, Huntington, WVa
- 1977–1978: Joseph R. Ordile, Ft. Worth, Tex
- 1978–1979: Theodore H. Clarke, Kokomo, Ind
- 1979–1980: William F. Munsey, Worthington, Ohio
- 1980–1981: Robert A. Guidice, Gainesville, Fla
- 1981–1982: Herbert Rothfeld, Hyattsville, Md
- 1982–1983: Arthur E. Helfand, Philadelphia
- 1983–1984: Charles W. Bradley, Burlingame, Calif
- 1984–1985: Jerry D. Brant, Jacksonville, Ill
- 1985–1986: Richard H. Lanham, Jr., Jeffersonville, Ind
- 1986–1987: Kove J. Schwartz, Newington, Conn
- 1987–1988: David A. Stone, Hollywood, Fla
- 1989–1990: Eric R. Hubbard, Long Beach, Calif

These professional men gave of themselves unstintingly during their terms of office. As all phases of medicine faced legislation, insurance problems, public awareness, and growth pains, so did the APMA.

When Dr. Stickel became executive director of the Association in 1942, the offices of the APMA (then the NAC) were in the Cavalier Apartments in Washington, D.C. The Stickels' home was the adjoining apartment. In the 1940s the entire staff of the association consisted of Dr. Stickel and three office assistants. In 1953 a suitable building was found for the headquarters. Property at 3301 Sixteenth Street, Washington, D.C., was bought for \$60,000. Extensive renovations were accomplished, and the move to the new headquarters was made in 1954.

In 1955 at the death of Dr. Stickel, who served as the first executive secretary of the association, Dr. Abe Rubin was appointed to this position. At that time, the association secretary was also the editor of the journal.

Seward P. Nyman, D.P.M., came into the Washington office of the APMA in the early 1960s. After serving as convention chairman and taking on other responsibilities, Dr. Nyman was appointed executive secretary in 1964. Dr. Abe Rubin continued his duties as editor of the APMA journal. Dr. Nyman served in the capacity of executive director as the national headquarters staff grew in proportion to the duties and responsibilities imposed upon it by the House of Delegates of the APMA.

In 1969 the APMA headquarters moved from its first office building on Sixteenth Street to a beautiful headquarters building at 20 Chevy Chase Circle. At this time, the administrative staff numbered 4, and the supporting staff grew to 11.

In 1980, after the death of Dr. Nyman, Norman L. Klombers, D.P.M., became the executive director of the APMA. Dr. Klombers, who had 2 years' experience at headquarters as Director of Scientific Affairs, served as executive director until 1989. In 1988 the APMA purchased and moved to a larger, better-equipped building located at 9312 Old Georgetown Road, Bethesda, Maryland.

Late in 1989 Mr. Frank J. Malouff, M.S.H.A., was appointed Executive Director of APMA. Mr. Malouff, who is the first nonpodiatrist to become Executive Director of the APMA, has an executive staff of seven. The support group staff numbers have also increased.

The elected officials of the APMA are now listed as officers: president, president-elect, vice president, treasurer, and the retiring president. There are ten members of the Board of Trustees. In 1990 these included two laypersons, or nonpodiatrists. One member of the Board of Trustees for the year 1989–1990 is a female podiatrist.

INTENSIVE CHANGES BRINGING A NEW IMAGE TO PODIATRY

During the 1920s, podiatry was a small profession interested mainly in corns, calluses, ingrowing nails, and the sale of arch supports. Any advancements were the results of forward-thinking individual practitioners who worked out new procedures and theories.

Another thrust came in the 1940s, when it was realized that correct orthopedic taping could help many foot defects and alleviate pain. The use of x-ray equipment for diagnostic purposes began to be widespread in the mid 1940s.

In the 1950s the profession realized that surgery was a necessary adjunct to podiatric care. It was also in this time frame that internal medications began to be directed at local pathology.

In the late 1960s another stage of development came into being with the field of biomechanics. By the end of the sixties, biomechanical demands were being combined with surgical corrections. This brought about the wider spread of knowledge, construction, and use of orthotic devices.

Concurrently, Blue Shield and Medicare, government support for colleges of podiatric medicine, and an increase in the profession's legal scope forcefully advanced the profession of podiatry.[16] With more and better ways of treatment, podiatry started to develop sophistication and affluence. More modern equipment evolved, and the podiatrist became more adept at treating patients. The advancing knowledge and training along with the availability of better-trained assistants meant better care for the patients of podiatric physicians.

SURGERY AND HOSPITAL AFFILIATIONS

Podiatric surgery took a giant step forward in 1942 when the American College of Foot Surgeons was organized. Douglas T. Mowbray, D.S.C., of Waterloo, Iowa, served as its first president. This organizing group initiated the original rigid requirements for membership, including oral and written examinations. The objectives of the college were as follows[17]:

> To promote the art and science of podiatry as embodied in all phases of foot surgery. To disseminate among its members and the podiatry profession in general, all knowledge of foot surgery...To encourage and maintain the highest professional standards among its members, who shall constantly strive to develop advanced techniques in foot surgery.

Podiatric surgery progressed rapidly with the opening in 1956 of Civic Hospital in Detroit, the first podiatry hospital in the United States. The hospital was the fruit of the labors of many practitioners in the Detroit area. With the excellent surgical facilities of the hospital, a podiatric residency program was begun. These first residents received a 1-year program of intensive training in anesthesiology, dermatology, emergency work, hospital protocol, medicine, neurology, orthopedics, pathology, physical medicine, physical rehabilitation, podopediatrics, radiology, and surgical and trauma techniques.

The first residency program that required 3 years was begun in 1969 at Doctors Hospital in Tucker, Georgia. The first residents had completed their first year of residency elsewhere and came to the Tucker program for their second and third years. All three years are now completed at Northlake Regional Medical Center (formerly Doctors Hospital).

The number of podiatric residencies continues to increase, with residencies being established across the United States. The colleges and the Council on Education are continually seeking new surgical training programs for graduating podiatric students.

POSTGRADUATE AND CONTINUING EDUCATION TRAINING

It is to the credit of the APMA that since its beginning continual effort has been made to upgrade practice, raise standards, and make continuing education available to its members. Specialty groups originated that continue to update and disseminate information to its members. These include surgery, podopediatrics, biomechanics, podiatric sports medicine, podiatric dermatology, geriatrics, and others.

The Council on Podiatry Education was created in 1918 by a constitutional provision. Since 1921, the Council on Education has presented a report at the annual meeting of the parent association except during the World War II years. From 1943 to 1950 no report was made by the Council on Education because the student body was seriously depleted by the draft.

In 1951 the Council on Education of the APA was accepted by the U.S. Office of Education as the sole accrediting agency for podiatry education. In 1972 a Podiatry Section was formally established in the American Public Health Association.

The growth of the profession developed a need for assistants with training that was different from that of a general medical assistant. In the early 1960s articles began appearing in the literature about the importance of well-trained office assistants. A committee of the association was established to develop appropriate standards. In 1964 the American Society of Podiatric Assistants (ASPA) was formed. In the early 1970s 1-year programs to train assistants were established at Pennsylvania College of Podiatric Medicine; Essex Community College, Maryland; and Jefferson Community College in Kentucky. When these programs were abandoned, primarily for financial reasons, the ASPA stepped into the breach through its journal, which included scientific articles, and through holding certifying examinations.[18] Successful candidates who took the examination were awarded a Podiatry Assistant's Certificate. Zelda Walling Vicha, a long-term officer of the ASPA, was a driving force in the organization of this group. A scholarship has been established in her name that is now given to a fourth-year female podiatry student. The ASPA has its own officers, board of directors, and scientific sessions and meets concurrently with the APMA annual meeting.

EMERGENCE OF PODIATRY FOR THE FUTURE

Over the years the APMA, like any other professional organization, has had spurts of growth and some setbacks. However, the APMA has become a strong and viable advocate for the profession. In 1987 the APMA celebrated its official 75th anniversary. The increase in residencies for graduating fourth-year students is an ongoing task, and postgraduate training is more sophisticated. Because relicensure in many states requires additional continuing education credits, scientific writings, seminars, and study courses continue to become available. Podiatric medical literature is mushrooming to fill the need for good podiatric medical materials written by podiatrists.

Podiatry and its professional association have a right to be proud of their accomplishments. They face the future with confidence and are prepared, along with other medical disciplines, to face the challenges of providing care in a changing world of health care. Podiatry is actively engaged in providing the best medical attention available for the foot ailments of the American public.

REFERENCES

1. Krausz CE: Early foot care, in Holloway LM (ed): *A Fast Pace Forward.* Philadelphia, Pennsylvania College of Podiatric Medicine, 1987, pp 1–2.
2. Krausz CE: Early foot care, In Holloway LM (ed): *A Fast Pace Forward.* Philadelphia, Pennsylvania College of Podiatric Medicine, 1987, p 4.
3. Westervelt RH: First president of the first pedic society in the world. *Pedic Items* 1907; 1:9.
4. Dagnall JC: The English influence on the beginnings of American podiatry, In Holloway LM (ed): *A Fast Pace Forward.* Philadelphia, Pennsylvania College of Podiatric Medicine, 1987, p 7.
5. Anonymous: Working for the tip. *Pedic Items* 1908; 1:19.
6. Krausz CE: The Kahlers: Tis a great feat to fit feet, in Holloway LM: *A Fast Pace Forward.* Philadelphia, Pennsylvania College of Podiatric Medicine, 1987, p 23.
7. Cohen I: Chiropody (paper read at a meeting of the Queen City Council, Royal Areanum, April 29, 1903). *Pedic Items* 1911; 2:28.
8. Lerner HJ: Steps in the development of the profession of podiatry, as noted in its professional journal. *J Am Podiatr Assoc* 1974; 64:281.
9. Krausz CE: A history of our national association. *J Am Podiatr Assoc* 1962; 52:629–632.
10. Holloway CE: The schools are established, in Holloway CE (ed): *A Fast Pace Forward.* Philadelphia, Pennsylvania College of Podiatric Medicine, 1987, p 53.
11. Gibley CW: History of podiatric medical education—An update. *J Am Podiatr Med Assoc* 1987; 77:404–418.
12. Holloway LM: Education 1920–1941, in Holloway CE (ed): *A Fast Pace Forward.* Philadelphia, Pennsylvania College of Podiatric Medicine, 1987, pp 76–77.
13. Mehl J: Journal of the American Podiatry Association: A history through its editors. *J Am Podiatr Assoc* 1974; 64:298–301.
14. Lelyveld J: Selecting an editor. *J Natl Assoc Chiropod* 1937; 27:22.
15. Holloway LM: Quo vadis? in Holloway LM (ed): *A Fast Pace Forward.* Philadelphia, Pennsylvania College of Podiatric Medicine, 1987, pp 141–177.
16. Hymes L: History of modern operative podiatry. *J Am Podiatr Assoc* 1974; 64:365–371.
17. Kaplan EG: The last fifty years: A historical review of podiatric surgery. *J Am Podiatr Assoc* 1974; 64:346–356.
18. Holloway LM: Women and minorities in the profession, in Holloway LM (ed): *A Fast Pace Forward.* Philadelphia, Pennsylvania College of Podiatric Medicine, 1987, pp 132–138.

2

The Podiatry Assistant in the Practice of Podiatry

Rebekah C. McGlamry, B.A.

THE NEED FOR ASSISTANTS

In the early years of the profession of podiatry, assistants were not needed because practice was simple and complications were few. As podiatry matured and practitioners became more proficient and sophisticated, the need for office personnel developed. The first podiatry assistant probably did nothing more than handle the phone and clean the treatment room between patients.

When simple surgeries began to be done in the office, the needs of the podiatrist changed. Better patient records needed to be kept, and often a second pair of hands was needed to help the office surgery move more swiftly and easily. Podiatrists delegated more and more duties to the assistant who, in turn, received more training.

With the appearance of modern equipment, the business office had an increase in paperwork: reappointments, scheduling of specific treatments or surgeries, and billing.[1] Obviously, a well-trained assistant was a valuable asset. Lectures were set up for the assistant, and special courses became available.

EARLY TRAINING OF ASSISTANTS

The value of a well-trained assistant was recognized as the podiatrist increased his practice in volume as well as scope. Teaching and training articles began to be written for the podiatry office assistant. Some of the earlier tasks given to assistants were making plantar impressions of the foot, taking and developing x-ray films, and applying most types of physical therapy.

Interviewing the patient was no longer a simple matter of obtaining demographic information. Now the podiatrist or his assistant took detailed medical backgrounds. The patient had to be evaluated as to circulatory, neurologic, and medical status.

In the 1960s a committee of the American Podiatry Association was established to develop appropriate standards for a podiatry assistant.

ESTABLISHMENT OF A FORMAL ORGANIZATION

In 1964 the American Society of Podiatric Assistants (ASPA) was formed in Oklahoma City.[2] At this time assistants (mostly young women) felt the need to band together to share knowledge and training. Four assistants from the southwestern area of the country, with a great deal of encouragement and assistance from four podiatrists, organized the fledgling group. These four young women were Zelda Walling Vicha, Margaret

Heidecker, Hindy Cohen, and Dolores Marshall Bowdler. The charter membership came from five states.[3]

The goals of the group were to work, study, and learn together to enhance the professional knowledge of the podiatric assistant. The meetings of the group, whether local, state, or national, were composed of lectures and training sessions to further this aim. The ASPA now has units in all 50 states.

In the 1970s, 1-year training programs for assistants were started at Pennsylvania College of Podiatric Medicine, Essex Community College in Maryland, and Jefferson Community College in Kentucky. These programs were abandoned after several years primarily because of financial reasons.

The ASPA has tried to fill this breach through its *Journal of the American Society of Podiatric Medical Assistants,* which includes scientific articles specifically for the podiatry assistant and references for the society's certification program.

The society is directed by four elected officers, the executive director, and an elected board of trustees. Three additional members of the board are doctors of podiatric medicine.

CERTIFICATION OF PODIATRY ASSISTANTS

As the society grew, certifying examinations were developed and given. Successful completion of the examination was rewarded by a designation of podiatric assistant, certified (PAC). In 1984, this designation was changed to podiatric medical assistant, certified (PMAC). A certified assistant must formally apply and then attend a meeting of the society at which the examination for certification is given. Recertification is required each year. An assistant may acquire the necessary continuing education credits for recertification by attending accredited courses given at meetings of the society, which are held in conjunction with American Podiatric Medical Association (APMA) affiliated meetings throughout the country. Assistants may also earn credits by writing articles and answering the examination questions that are published periodically in the journal specifically for recertification credits.

THE JOURNAL OF THE AMERICAN SOCIETY OF PODIATRIC MEDICAL ASSISTANTS

The official publication of the assistants' group is called the *Journal of the American Society of Podiatric Medical Assistants,* which is published quarterly. A subscription to the journal is included in the dues paid by members. The journal contains news of the organization, board and committee reports, as well as information concerning certification and recertification. Articles of interest to podiatric assistants are included. Examination sites, dates, and study guides are also printed regularly.

SCHOLARSHIP FUND

The society established a scholarship fund originally to assist a student at one of the established programs, but after these programs ended, the fund was awarded to a fourth-year female podiatry student. Monies for this fund are raised by the assistants' groups and by private donation. The scholarship fund is named the Zelda Walling Vicha Scholarship Fund for Ms. Vicha who was a long-term officer and who later became the first official executive secretary of the ASPA.[4]

REFERENCES

1. Hymes L: History of modern operative podiatry. *J Am Podiatr Assoc* 1974; 64:364–372.
2. Executive Director's Report. *J Amer Soc Podiatr Med Assist* 1989, October, p 9.
3. Vicha ZW: History. Presented at the 19th Annual Meeting of the American Society of Podiatric Assistants, Chicago, August 13–15, 1982, p 1.
4. Holloway LM: *A Fast Pace Forward.* Philadelphia, Pennsylvania College of Podiatric Medicine, 1987, p 135.

SECTION II

Front Office Procedures

3

Policies and Procedures for the Podiatric Office

Peggy Kane, P.M.A.C.

The purpose of a personnel policies and procedures manual is to prevent misunderstandings. This manual should simply and clearly tell employees what is expected from them and what they can expect from the employer. Small irritations over policies can often become large problems. There are important issues that need to be clarified with employees. Many times it is taken for granted that they understand. New employees, in particular, are often left to gather information about policies as best they can. Policies and procedures that are clearly stated and universally understood will help prevent costly and time-consuming employee turnover.

This chapter will cover general guidelines for hiring, discipline, review, and termination. A sample policies and procedures manual is also included.

HIRING PROCEDURES AND REGULATIONS

Prior to employing an individual, be certain to ensure uniformity in the application. Verify that a job description has been written and is up to date. The job description should include a description of duties and responsibilities, qualifications, salary range, and performance standards. The business manager may write job descriptions with the doctor's approval. After the job description has been approved, then the hiring cycle may begin. The qualifications that are listed in the job description as being necessary must be directly related to the successful performance of the job.

The business manager should first review all applications that are currently on file. If a suitable person is not available from past applications, a recruiting effort should begin. An advertisement can be written and submitted to a local newspaper or given to an employment agency.

The business manager should review all applications received, conduct preliminary phone interviews, and then schedule appointments to further screen qualified applicants. After these applicants have been screened, the best two or three should be scheduled for an interview with the doctor and business manager for final selection.

Interview questions must be job related. The interviewer should not ask any questions concerning or pertaining to race, color, religion, sex, age, or national origin.

The actual hiring of an individual should be done by the business manager of the practice. On the first day of employment, all personnel and financial records should be prepared, and a copy of the personnel policies and procedures manual should be reviewed and given to the employee by the business manager. The first day should be set aside for familiarization with the responsibilities of the other employees of the practice and how they relate to the new employee's duties.

Temporary and Part-Time Employees

There will be occasions when a practice will be required to employ temporary and/or part-time employees. These employees may assist with duties that require part-time effort such as a file conversion, month's end statements, bookkeeping, or transcribing.

Most employers do not provide benefits such as sick leave, vacation pay, or insurance to employees who work fewer than 24 hours per week. Part-time employees may be hired, as needed, to work less than the standard work week. The salary level should be in accordance with the position filled and prorated to the number of hours worked.

Temporary employees may be hired as substitutes or to assist in heavy work loads. They are usually utilized for no longer than 3 months unless employment is extended by mutual agreement. Salary for temporary employees should be commensurate with the salary level for the position being filled. If a temporary employee is retained on a permanent basis, the time served on a temporary basis is usually considered to have been part of the employee's probationary period. Temporary employees are entitled to workmen's compensation insurance as dictated by the laws of the state. Temporary employees are not entitled to leaves of absence, severance pay, vacation, holiday, sick pay, or group insurance.

Probationary Period

As each new employee is hired, most policies state that employment is on a probationary basis for the first 90 days. The employee's work is evaluated, and an attitude assessment is made. The employee is not expected to know everything about the job in 90 days; rather, this time is used to determine whether the employee is suited to work in a health care environment. The employer as well as the employee will use this time to determine how well the employee can adapt to the job and its responsibilities. Training and guidance should be given to the employee during this time to help develop the necessary skills. The employee should be encouraged to seek additional help if it is needed during this probationary period.

Near the end of the probationary period, a formal meeting should be planned to discuss the work performance. At that meeting the employee should be advised of permanent employment. If dismissal is necessary, either during or upon completion of the probationary period, the employee should be asked to work for a period of 2 weeks to allow time to find a replacement. In a few instances, however, termination may be immediate. If termination occurs anytime within the first 90 days of employment, severance pay should not be given.

Vacation leave or sick pay is not granted during the probation period. Upon attaining permanent status, the appropriate amount of accrued vacation and sick leave is credited to the employee for each month on probation. Probationary employees terminated prior to attaining permanent status are not paid for any accrued vacation pay.

DISCIPLINE

Discipline is to correct rather than punish. Good discipline is the kind of control that makes punishment unnecessary. Good control of employees is the mark of a good supervisor. Because discipline is a means to an end, it is better to be more concerned with end results than with discipline.

It is strongly recommended that disciplinary procedures include written warnings and a step-by-step process if the procedure may eventually result in the employee being suspended, discharged, or losing a promotion. If supervisors have been fair and consistent in disciplinary actions, a complete and accurate record of all incidents will protect them from unwarranted charges.

There are two basic forms of discipline. One form is informal control. This control works well because the employees have a high level of respect for the supervisor. They know that the supervisor is fair and conscientious in handling affairs. This is the most desirable kind of control. The other form of discipline is a formal disciplinary procedure with forms of misconduct and punishment prescribed and posted. Work rules must be enforced by the supervisor. Rules without enforcement are worse than not having any rules at all. It is well to establish detailed work rules and policies for the guidance of management, to ensure fair and equal treatment for all members of staff. Work rules and policies should be covered in a policy manual.

There are five typical options of disciplinary actions:

1. Employee counseling or oral reprimands.—The employee is counseled by a supervisor to eliminate possible misunderstanding and explain proper conduct.
2. Written reprimand.—The employee receives written notice following repeated minor offenses. The written reprimand is to make certain that the employee is fully aware of the misconduct and what is expected to avoid a recurrence.
3. Written warning.—The employee receives written notice following serious misconduct or repeated minor offenses. The purpose is to make certain that the employee understands the seriousness of the misconduct and the fact that further misconduct will most likely result in discharge.
4. Disciplinary time off without pay.
5. Discharge.—The employee is discharged as a result of serious offenses or as the final step in an accumulation of minor offenses.

WAGES

Good employee relations cannot be ensured by high wages alone. People work for reasons other than salary. Poor performance, however, is almost guaranteed by substandard wages.

Employees look to the practice and the salary you provide for their very substance. Salary levels must be fair. More importantly, your employees need to know that someone is paying attention to salary levels. Employees want to know that improved performance is worthy of increased wages. Salaries should also be compared with the other practices in the area.

The federal government has a minimum wage law, as do several states. Every employer needs to conform to that law, to the provisions of the Fair Labor Standards Act concerning overtime, and to other laws and regulations that affect the employment of personnel.

According to federal law, overtime rates must be paid to nonexempt employees for hours worked in excess of 40 hours in a regularly scheduled pay period of 7 consecutive days. Some states require the payment of overtime pay for any day in which an employee works more than 8 hours. Check your state laws. The overtime rate is 1½ times the employee's regular hourly rate of pay. You are only required to pay overtime for hours actually worked; therefore, during weeks when holiday pay is received, that time can be excluded from hours actually worked. Sick leave and vacation time taken during the week are not counted as hours worked when calculating for overtime pay.

Employees appreciate regular salary review sessions at a predetermined time each year. This avoids unnecessary and untimely pressure from employees. A productive salary review session should have the following criteria:

1. Advance planning to determine budget allocations and proposed increases
2. Regular scheduling so that the employee knows when to expect the review
3. Private, highly confidential session on a one-to-one basis
4. Review of performance and rewarding improved performance with increased wages or a bonus

The employee also needs to be reminded of upward opportunities, either by salary range or improved job responsibilities, title, and scope.

Careful consideration should be given to a cost-of-living wage increase policy. Employees may come to expect an increase every year based solely on the inflation rate.

Bonuses should be awarded for outstanding performance and should be issued when extra effort is completed. Employees should understand that bonuses and special awards are irregular and are not guaranteed by the season of the year, tenure, or any other factor.

Above all, be sure to keep accurate records. It is not just good business—it is the law.

PERFORMANCE REVIEW

All employees need to know where they stand with their work. They especially need to be thanked and praised for tasks well done. After the probationary period and again at a 6-month to 1-year interval, all employees should be reviewed privately to ensure a high performance level. A proper review requires preparation. Some of the essential components of a successful review session are as follows:

1. Schedule sessions regularly.
2. Ensure privacy.
3. Use the job description to review all the employee's tasks. Compliment tasks well done, and offer suggestions for improvement as needed.
4. Listen to the employee talk about the job. Ask for suggestions for improvements.
5. Conclude with positive points and praise.

If regular performance reviews are provided for all employees, they will soon develop a different feeling and attitude about their work.

All areas of discussion should be documented and kept in the employee's folder. It is particularly important to document notations about substandard performance that could necessitate termination. "Fairness" necessitates progressively more severe discipline prior to termination. If supervisors have warned the employee and documented those warnings, they can never be accused of not having issued fair warning.

TERMINATION

Some employees will have to be terminated. The employee should be notified of termination privately. If proper documentation and notification of warnings and disciplinary action have been maintained, a lengthy explanation as to why the employee is being terminated should not be necessary.

The employee should not remain in the practice after termination. It is a good policy to pay 2 weeks' severance pay and allow the employee the time to seek other employment.

When terminating an employee you should also do the following:

1. Review group insurance, conversion privileges, and any other pertinent employee benefits.
2. Reclaim all keys and other practice property.
3. Arrange for distribution of the final pay check.
4. Carefully document the entire process in the employee's record.

When an employee notifies the supervisor of an intention to quit, the supervisor should request a resignation letter for the employee's file. A termination interview should be arranged to gain insight into the reason for leaving, whether it is salary, working hours, or personnel problems. This interview may help prevent future employees from quitting.

All employees should be aware of any acts that would result in immediate termination. Examples of these acts are as follows:

1. Violation of confidential information
2. Embezzlement
3. Fraudulent forgery of documents (prescriptions, ledger cards, or patient records)
4. Illegal use of controlled substances
5. Abusive treatment of patients (physical contact, foul language)
6. Felony conviction that would affect the practice

SAMPLE POLICIES AND PROCEDURES MANUAL

The following is a sample of an office policies and procedures manual. Individual office circumstances will dictate the need for different policies. However, the main topics of working hours, absences, holidays, vacations, and the previously discussed topics of hiring, discipline, review, wages, and termination should be included in each manual.

Office and Working Hours

In order to provide proper staff coverage for all practice activities, all employees should know their personal working hours, and these should always be followed unless previous arrangements have been made and discussed with the supervisor.

You are expected to be at work on time. Your normal work week will consist of a 40-hour week, and you are needed every minute. A time card is expected to be filled out daily and turned into the business manager at the end of the week. Those who are eligible for overtime will have it noted on the time card.

Tardiness is unacceptable. We expect to pay you well for the time you work, but likewise, we expect you to work the time for which you are being paid. It is just as important to return from breaks and lunch promptly as it is to arrive on time in the morning.

If for any reason you cannot report to work on time, telephone as far in advance of your starting time as possible. State why you will be late or absent.

Rest Periods

There will be a short break in the middle of the morning and the middle of the afternoon. These are given to allow you to refresh yourself. A staggered schedule allowing normal patient flow will ensure fairness to all.

Similarly, you will be entitled to an unpaid lunch period daily so that you may comfortably enjoy your midday meal. If the office does not close for a lunch period, it is necessary to stagger individual lunch periods so that the office is properly covered. You are encouraged to leave the premises to properly enjoy your lunch period. You must clock out and clock in again after your lunch period.

Overtime

Overtime work may be necessary from time to time, depending largely on the number of patients requiring care. When necessary, overtime will be authorized in advance by the business manager.

Absence Due to Weather Conditions

Employees who are absent from work due to adverse weather conditions may work additional hours within that work week as directed by the business manager to make up the time missed. If circumstances prevent the employee from making up the time, the employee may charge the time missed to personal days off. Time charged this way will be in minimum increments of 1 whole day.

There are times when the employer will allow you to work a shorter day but will pay you for your normal week. These "breaks" will be allowed at the employer's convenience.

Temporary Hardship—Working Hours

If at any time your working hours present a temporary hardship, discuss the problem with the business manager. Usually these problems can be worked out to the satisfaction of all concerned. Repeated unsatisfactory attendance, including tardiness or leaving early, may be cause for disciplinary action, including discharge.

Holidays

A listing of any paid holidays will be given to new employees at the time of hiring. In the health care field, the day before and the day following holidays are very busy; therefore it is essential that the office be fully staffed.

An observed holiday that occurs during an employee's vacation shall not be counted as vacation time. If any of the holidays fall on a Saturday or Sunday, it will be discussed at the beginning of the year as to what the holiday policy will be, and any proposed changes will be posted in advance.

Vacations

Paid vacations are provided in recognition of past service. Your vacation will be arranged as nearly as possible to the time you desire. Vacations will accrue as follows:

- 0–1 year of service: 1 week's vacation
- 1–5 years of service: 2 weeks' vacation
- 5 or more years of service: 3 weeks' vacation

Thus personnel with less than 1 full year of service on the first of January will receive 1 week's vacation. Personnel who have completed 1 full year of service on the first of January will receive 2 weeks' vacation each year. Personnel who have completed 5 full years of service or more by the first of January will receive 3 weeks' vacation each year. Vacation time accrues but may not be taken during probation.

All vacation time must be taken by December 31st of each year. Vacation time must be taken in minimum increments of 1 week unless unusual circumstances prevail and arrangements have been made far enough in advance. Pay in lieu of vacation taken will not be granted.

Employees are asked to schedule their vacations at least 2 months in advance of the time they desire to take it. Employees with the longest length of service will be given preference in the scheduling of vacation time. Full-time salaried employees will be paid their regular salary while on vacation.

Advanced Payment on Earned Salary

Advance payment on earned wages or salaries may be paid in an emergency or when an employee's regular pay falls within her vacation or leave of absence. Except in cases of emergency, requests for advance payment on wages or salaries must be made at least 1 week in advance.

Paychecks Lost

Employees are responsible for their paychecks after they have been issued. Checks lost or otherwise missing should be reported to the business manager so that a stop payment order may be initiated and a replacement check issued. The employee will be responsible for the stop payment charge.

Leave of Absence

A leave of absence will not be considered until personal days, vacation, and other benefit days are used. Maternity leave will begin and end on the basis of a physician's written statement regarding the employee's ability to work. Beginning with the fifth month of pregnancy, the employee is required every month to provide the business manager with her physician's statement regarding her ability to work and the anticipated duration of her ability to work. A maternity leave of absence will not exceed 3 months following childbirth. An employee may not accept other employment while on a maternity leave of absence. An employee will be reinstated to her former or a similar position when returning from her leave.

Sick Leave

To establish a sensible policy for the office, set guidelines that take into account the following:

1. Eligibility
2. Amount of sick pay allowed
3. Annual number of days allowed
4. Carryover
5. Exceptions
6. Evidence of illness

If an injury is due to an accident on the job, you must report the accident to the business manager as soon as it happens to be eligible for sick pay benefits.

Personal Days

A possible alternative to sick days is to allow for personal days each year. The employee can then take a day off without any particular excuse or reason. There are two advantages to a personal day policy: the employees do not have to lie about being sick to get a day off, and the employee is more likely to give advance warning of the absence.

Jury Duty

The law states that an employee must be given time off to serve on jury duty.

Voting

Some states require the employee to receive time off to vote.

Funerals

The reasonable amount of time for attending a funeral for a full-time employee shall be a maximum of 3 days off with pay, as determined by the business manager. Funeral leave is not compensable when you are on vacation or on leave of absence.

Personal Appearance

We all want to look our best, but it is especially important when working in a medical practice to look professional. Patients expect more from you than from the average person. It is essential, therefore, that extra care be taken to live up to these expectations.

Uniforms

Uniforms are required. The standard uniform (in color or white) should be clean, neat, and ironed. Shoes should be white and spotlessly clean. Pants suits may be worn as uniforms provided that they are worn in good taste. All pants suits must be opaque material with tunics.

Makeup

Makeup should be used conservatively. Perfume and cosmetics should never be overwhelming, particularly in a medical office.

Hair

Hair should be above the collar of the uniform. It should be clean and well groomed.

Cleanliness

Personal body cleanliness is essential. Frequent bathing and the use of an effective deodorant are important to all with whom you come in contact and especially to the patient who does not feel well. Hands and nails require special attention and should be kept scrupulously clean. Fingernail length should not interfere with normal work.

Jewelry

Jewelry is out of place with a uniform. The abundant use of costume jewelry should be avoided. Rings should not interfere with normal work.

Smoking

It is difficult to structure a rigid policy on smoking in the office. A compromise policy that encourages reduced smoking but allows it in certain places at certain times is best.

4

Communication

Brenda Britt, P.M.A.C.

The word communicate is defined in Webster's dictionary as "to make known." Clear communication between the doctor, the patient, and the assistant is a must for a successful podiatric office.

The patient first communicates with the doctor by telephone through a member of the office staff. The importance of answering the telephone in a prompt, pleasant, and courteous manner cannot be overemphasized. It is important to speak clearly and to listen carefully. Never put a patient on hold and then forget to promptly return to the call. If you do not know the answer to a specific question, refer the call to a person who does.

Certain information is vital in scheduling appointments, particularly with new patients. Determine what kind of problem the patient is having and then determine how serious the problem is and how quickly he must be seen. It is good practice to see new patients within 2 days of the initial call. Ask whether they prefer a morning or afternoon appointment. All new patients should also be reminded to bring a list of any medication they are taking.

When patients are scheduled, sufficient time must be allowed for each procedure per number of rooms. A general guide is as follows:

New patients	45 minutes
Postoperative patients	30 minutes
Ingrown toenails	45 minutes
Verruca	45 minutes
Mosaic verrucae	1 to 1½ hours
Nail and verruca checks	15 minutes
Fractures	45 minutes
Maintenance patients	20 minutes

This is just an approximation and may be different for each office, but a similar schedule will help with the patient flow and communication.

When making an appointment for a new patient, it is important to review the policies regarding payment, especially if it is expected at the time of service. If the office accepts assignment from Medicare, let the patients know that they will be expected to pay the 20% copayment. Many patients will ask the charge for an initial office visit. If a fee is quoted, let the caller know this fee does not include x-rays or other procedures that may need to be performed. If the office files insurance claims on certain surgical procedures, it is important to ask the patient to bring insurance information to the office. Never turn away a patient with financial difficulties without checking with the office manager or doctor first. There are always exceptions to payment policies when there are extenuating circumstances. To build a good podiatric practice, the assistant must be flexible.

Occasionally, a patient will call and ask for fees for a specific procedure. These people are called "shoppers." They may have called several other podiatry offices to find the cheapest fee. It is never a good policy to quote fees over the phone. Without an examination, fees cannot be accurately determined. Once you quote a fee, the patient will expect this to be the total charge.

Many problems can be handled by phone. If the office has more than one employee, it should be decided who is responsible for each specific area. The receptionist can then direct calls to the appropriate person. This serves the patient well and keeps the communication in the office flowing smoothly.

Every office should have a routine for seeing patients. All patients should sign in, and new patients should be given the appropriate forms to be filled out. The waiting room should be neat and stocked with current reading material. Pamphlets regarding different podiatry problems should also be available. A bulletin board in the waiting room introducing the doctor and staff is an effective way to communicate information to the patient.

Occasionally, no matter how carefully patients are scheduled, the patient flow can come to a standstill, and the waiting room fills with patients. Here again, communication is the key. If the patients are given an explanation as to the delay, most of them will understand.

When a new patient enters the treatment room, the assistant's first job is to put him at ease. After introducing yourself to the patient, complete a history and physical. During this time an assistant can find out background information on the patient that can help to distract him if an injection or other painful procedure needs to be done.

With an established patient, check your information sheet and progress notes before entering the room. Know why he is being seen and make an effort to recall something personal about the patient to make him feel important and welcome. You represent your doctor, and your attitude can cause the patient to want to return if they have future problems.

Good intraoffice communication is vital to the success of your organization. The front office assistant must know what is expected in scheduling, collections, answering the phones, and handling patients. The back office assistant, who works side by side with the doctor and patient, has a different set of responsibilities. Since they work so closely together, the doctor-assistant relationship needs to be one of mutual respect and trust. Good communication can help build this relationship.

After working with the doctor, many procedures will become routine. It is a good idea to know the instruments and tapes required by the doctor. When time permits, list on a 3 × 5-in. card the different supplies needed for each procedure so that the next time the procedure is performed all the supplies can be on hand. These cards can also be used to train other assistants. It is also important for assistants to learn medical terminology so that they can communicate with the doctor on a professional level.

Staff meetings can be beneficial to a podiatry office. Whether you only have the doctor and yourself or a large staff, it is important to set aside time to discuss problems, review policies, and set goals. Staff meetings should be scheduled and held at approximately the same time on a weekly or monthly basis. During the staff meeting, suggestions or complaints can be offered, and new ideas can be discussed. Frequently personnel problems and misunderstandings can be worked out. Staff meetings are a method of communicating in a positive manner. Such a forum cuts down on turnover and promotes teamwork among employees.

Dealing with insurance companies can be an exacting and time-consuming job. With the many different rules and regulations, it is important that as much information as possible be obtained. All surgical patients must have their insurance coverage confirmed prior to surgery. Make sure that a current insurance card with phone numbers for precertification and benefits is on file. Usually a second number must be called for benefit information. Note in the patient's chart all conversations with the insurance company's representatives, including their full name. If a second opinion is required, inform the doctor. This information may be needed at a later date if problems arise when the claim is submitted. Gathering such information and writing it down may avoid any delays in payment.

Podiatrists perform many surgical procedures. The podiatrist is often on staff at several hospitals, each with its own different admitting policies, surgery scheduling, and x-ray procedures. Know whom to call and what information will be needed for each hospital. Most hospitals have a directory with listings of the different departments. If you have never booked a patient for surgery or scheduled a computed axial tomography (CAT) scan, ask questions when talking with hospital personnel. Even though you may never meet these people, you will have frequent phone contact with them, and they can help you be a more effective assistant.

Good communication with patients, staff, hospitals, and the podiatrist is an essential part of an effective podiatric practice.

5

Patient Relations

Aaron C. Olson, D.P.M.

First impressions are lasting impressions, especially in the patient-doctor relationship. Doctors and their staff have a relatively brief period of time in which to set the tone and make the best impression on the patient. Those brief encounters can make or break a practice. This chapter will review some of the tenets that will help in establishing good patient rapport.

The front office staff needs to personify friendliness and treat new and returning patients as though they were best friends or family. Instill in the staff the need to treat patients like their own parents or relatives, and this will be the basis for a good, trusting relationship.

Cheerfulness should be a key word in the office. There should be no glass partitions or total separation between the patients and staff. The front office staff should look up and greet all patients who enter (by name if possible) in the warmest manner possible.

The reception area should be kept looking its best. Pick up newspapers, magazines, and children's toys as needed. If the carpeting and/or furnishings are getting worn, have them replaced or reupholstered. Nothing conveys the message of a worn-out practice more than a worn-out waiting room. Rotate wall hangings and pictures for a change of pace and a new look. Patients perceive a tired-looking waiting room as meaning that the doctor and his equipment are outdated.

Reading material in the waiting room is also important. Daily newspapers make good reading. Offering current magazines, newspapers, and specialty catalogs are good standbys. Catalogs can be obtained at no cost by placing the office address on various mailing lists. Another good item to have in the waiting area is several cookbooks that provide a varied source of recipes and recipe cards for those patients who want to copy a recipe.

At the initial visit the staff must establish rapport with the patient in order to build an ongoing relationship. Patients should meet the staff members who will be assisting them and should know who is responsible for insurance problems, appointment scheduling, and treatment questions. The staff members must then be proficient in their responses and treatment of the patient. A nurse or assistant who needs to constantly check with the doctor to verify answers or instructions does not instill confidence in the patient. Soon the patient will only want to talk to the doctor because the assistant does not appear to know what she is talking about. Even the most routine answers will not be accepted by the patient when provided by auxiliary personnel. When the assistant has been "tuned out," any attempt to utilize her for patient education or even to reiterate the doctor's instructions will be negated. When the doctor and assistant have a specific office protocol and a means of handling different problems and treatments, the patient is secure and will respond equally well to the doctor and assistant.

The front office staff needs to communicate with the back office staff. Writing simple notes about questions, problems, or personal information relayed by the patient goes a long way in streamlining office function. The patient will feel that the staff cares and communicates about him. Something as simple as not having to answer the same questions twice shows that someone was listening. If a patient tells the front office that she has a large sore corn on her fifth toe that's rubbing in her shoe, that information should be written on a note and attached to the chart. When the assistant picks up the chart or checks the appointment sheet and escorts the patient to an examination room she can state: "Your fifth toe is bothering you. Does it rub in all shoes or just certain ones?" This is preferable to asking why she is here today only to have the patient say "Well, I told the girl out front, didn't she tell you about me?" Short notes should also be used to convey information of a personal nature to the doctor, (i.e., son gets married next month). This information helps the patient feel at home.

The returning patient is like a friend coming home. Return patients who are present for prophylactic nail care are ones who can truly become good friends and should be treated as such. Remember that return and ongoing patients are also a prime source for new patient referrals. Word of mouth is still one of the best means of acquiring new patients. Each time a patient returns, let him know what is new in the office. If a new staff person, new treatment plan, or new equipment has been added, let him know. Never assume that these people know everything about what a podiatrist does. Never give the impression that a podiatrist only treats toenails and corns. These patients must be reminded that a podiatrist also treats bunions, warts, sports injuries, etc.

A new patient office brochure has many functions and can help detail the office policies, provide a tool to market the practice, and familiarize the new patient with staff members who will be helping them. If the new patient visit is scheduled well in advance of the appointment date, it is a good idea to send the patient a brochure prior to the appointment along with a patient information form to be completed and returned on the appointment date. Patients seem to appreciate the information, and having the medical intake form completed prior to coming in saves in-office time. If this cannot be accomplished routinely, the receptionist should provide each new patient in the office with a brochure and remind the patient to take the time to read it. The office brochure should contain office information showing hours and days open, emergency numbers, staff names and positions, financial policies, a brief office history, and any special services offered. The brochure may also detail whether the podiatrist or staff members are available for speaking engagements. Inclusion of pictures of the staff and doctor are appropriate, but this is personal preference. Remember that this practice brochure can and should be used in instances other than just new patients. It is a strong promotional tool that can be distributed at health fairs, speaking engagements, and other promotions.

In podiatry the key to a good practice is to educate, educate, and educate. The public does not always perceive all the areas that are covered by the podiatrist and the necessity of ongoing follow-up care.

It is important to invest in the staff members' ongoing training. The staff should be current and capable. In order to achieve this end, the staff must be well trained. It is especially important for staff members who work with Medicare, Medicaid, and insurance to be current in the latest changes and regulations. When an assistant says to a patient "I was just at a Medicare seminar, and I know we need to file this differently," it shows that the office is up to date. These investments will never be regretted.

Since education is of the utmost importance, the doctor should provide volumes of information in many forms for the patient. Having patient handouts *written by the doctor and specific for his own office* is one of the best patient education tools. The generic materials that are available should be used as a supplement to the office-produced materials. No patient should leave the office without informational brochures. Leaving these brochures in the waiting room for patients to pick up is good but is not the most effective. The doctor or nurse should provide the patient with material specific to his medical problem. There are many uses for these informational handouts, both inside and outside of the office.

An in-house video is a good source of material for patient education. A patient can view this material while sitting in the treatment room waiting for the doctor. This helps take the edge off "waiting time." It also reinforces what the doctor has been trying to teach the patient. It is a good idea to document this information in the chart notes. This is a readily acceptable means for a patient to get the needed podiatric education. Make sure that all videos are previewed in their entirety. The information and pictures within the video should accurately convey the views and philosophy of the individual doctor.

Occasionally a patient becomes angry or upset with the staff or the podiatrist for a variety of reasons. Insurance complications are a big source of frustration. Assist the patient in dealing with insurance companies. Resubmit claims even before a patient requests it if it can be determined that the reimbursement or denial was made improperly. Another step in the insurance cycle is to appeal. Even after payment is received from the insurance company, appeal anything questionable, and keep the patient apprised of what is being done. Medicare patients and Medicare supplemental insurance are one of the prime sources of problems. The use of any materials printed by Medicare is the first step in helping the patient understand his coverage. Highlight portions of this material that explain noncovered services and coinsurance, and explain that Medicare pays only 80% of the "allowed charge." Using Medicare's own materials to explain helps defuse some of the problematic situations. Be sure to freely give out the local Medicare's toll-free number so that the information you provide can be substantiated.

Another source of patient frustration is the cost of services and the patient's availability of funds to pay for services. Make certain that the office charges are in line with those in the community, and make sure that the patient is aware of the charges without any surprises. If the cost of services warrants it, work out budget plans for the patient so that he can make monthly payments to take care of his financial obligations.

A patient's perception that he is not receiving the services he is paying for can cause alienation. *Itemizing* services and restating what each item means both reduce any questions in this regard. Explaining each item on a bill alleviates questions. Having each item listed on a billing statement separately also reduces questions. When a problem is not clearing up or there is no perception of improvement, the patient can also feel that he is not getting the services he is paying for. In this instance, the doctor and nursing staff need to reassure the patient and demonstrate how far the patient has come. Pictures or charted size of ulcers is a means of illustrating to the patient his progress. The nurse's assistance in educating the patient becomes crucial at this point.

A minor irritation that can sometimes grow to major proportions is the late appointment. Waiting in the doctors' office, no matter how nice the surroundings, is the main gripe of patients. It is sometimes unavoidable. However, if the office is habitually late for appointments, the schedule needs to be modified, or additional assistants need to be hired. If the office is behind schedule, explain why. If the office is extremely behind, sending a patient a written apology and a card for an ice cream cone or a similar simple token is a nice gesture. Or send a card for "Immediate Treatment on your Next Visit." When the patient comes in at the next visit and presents the card, usher him into the next open room. Anything that can be done to minimize "the wait" improves patient relations.

When confronting an angry patient, it is essential to defuse the situation. Remain calm, and never get ruffled or angry yourself. Talking in low tones can sometimes get the patient to lower his tone. Remove the patient from earshot of patients in the waiting room, if at all possible. Use an empty treatment room, the doctor's private office, or a separate business office to confer with the patient. *Listen to the problem.* Many times the problem with the doctor and the office is minimal, and all that is needed is to listen to the complaints. When the irate dissertation is completed, then work to explain the office's position. Address the issues that can be resolved. Whatever the problem, there are steps that can be taken to eliminate or alleviate it. Tell the patient what you will do to help resolve the problem, and then be sure to follow through.

The reasons patients become angry are most often the reasons the patient leaves the doctor's practice: insurance problems, staff conflicts, conflicts with the doctor, money and costs, lack of confidence in the quality of work, failure to provide perceived services, and long waits for appointments. Those circumstances that are under the office's control should be addressed before they become a problem. Most can be treated as a practice ailment and alleviated.

Patient follow-up is one of the keys to successful patient relations. After every new patient is seen, one of the nursing staff should phone within 2 to 3 days of the patient's visit to check on progress and to ask whether there are any more questions that the patient might have and forgot to ask at the appointment. The staff member should notate this information on the chart and do further follow-up if the unanswered questions were ones to which she could not give a response. It is a good idea to check on all patients who have received in-office treatment within 2 days of their appointment to ask for the same information.

Building good patient relations is an ongoing task in the podiatric office. Taking the time to make the patient feel comfortable will go a long way toward building a solid practice.

6

Public Relations and Marketing

Aaron C. Olson, D.P.M.

Recalls are the backbone of the practice. It is imperative that the patient return to your practice, whether for routine follow-up or new problems. A simple, but complete recall system should be set up and followed. Merely telling the patient that he should return in 2 or 6 months will not suffice. Patients are great procrastinators and will put off returning for follow-up, ongoing, or preventive care until something acute occurs.

Prior to exiting your office, the patient should set the appointment for the next visit even if it is a year away. A variety of systems will work. Decide what works best for your individual office. Any system from computer tracking to individual card systems filed by the month can work. If the patient refuses to set an appointment, you must still be able to remind that patient of those visits. By logging all unappointed visits into the first of the month during which they should make a reappointment and by sending recall notices 1 week prior to the beginning of the month to remind them of the upcoming need for an appointment, you may be able to get 25% to schedule without a staff member calling them. An alternative is to set a date and time. Send a card telling them that this time period has been set aside for them but if there is a conflict they should call you to reschedule. Obviously patients do not always like to schedule very far in advance. Many complaints will arise regarding patients not knowing what they will have planned 6 months in the future. Simply informing them that this is a reminder and that they can change it as needed seems to handle the question for most patients.

Referrals are important to the practice. Sources of referrals may include doctors, other allied medical fields, patients, and staff. Doctors on your referral list should receive a follow-up immediately on any patients they send to your office. Follow-up by personal letter is better than a form letter. Gifts for the doctor's office or staff are also in order. Flowers can be sent to nurses at other offices or to the office in general of doctors who have been ongoing referral sources. Shoe shines make nice "gifts" for the busy referring doctor. Send a gift certificate for this service as a reminder of the type of health care provided by your office.

The doctor needs to keep in touch with the medical community and be visible to remind them of his presence. He must ask for referrals. He should send letters to auxiliary medical personnel as well. His letters to these sources should advise them of new techniques learned, new studies done, new procedures, new office equipment, etc. This educates the medical community and keeps the doctor's name in mind.

When patients refer someone to the office, *always* send a thank-you note. Have a place on the new patient information sheet that tells whether the patient is a referral and who referred him. A good practice builder is to send a thank-you note to the patient for one referral. If the same patient refers three new patients, send flowers to the referring patient. If a patient refers ten patients, send a gift certificate for a dinner at a local restaurant. Devise a system with which you feel comfortable, and assign a staff person to keep a log or file card system for all referrals in order to follow up appropriately.

At some point, if the patient referral base is low, the office may want to consider adopting some sort of incentive to get patients to refer new patients. The staff and the doctor should ask the patient to refer any family or friends who may have similar problems. A simple statement such as "Anyone else who has a problem with their feet, we would like to help them too" is sufficient.

Staff members are another source of referrals. The staff should have business cards and should be encouraged to hand these out often. A good incentive is to reward the staff member who referred the new patient.

In seeking wider referral bases, do not overlook tapping into health maintenance organizations (HMOs); preferred provider organizations (PPOs); city, county, and public health nursing services; senior centers; wellness centers; and various support groups and associations for diabetes or arthritis. Target these for in-service education and/or screenings, but *do not charge for these services.*

Local health fairs and community health services should be utilized to promote the practice. Providing a foot screening with a minimal diagnosis and suggestions has proved to be a good way of attracting new patients. Remember that the primary purpose is exposure. Do not charge for your services in speaking engagements. Remember to have sign-up sheets at these and to send "free" information and newsletters later on.

Nursing staff in-services and senior center talks are all part of the art of practice building and increasing the referral base. Remember to use all your handouts to distribute information from your office. Get a list of names and addresses of all those present at the talk. Send letters thanking them and telling them that if there are further questions they would like answered to be certain to call.

A source of referrals and publicity for the office is the yellow pages of the phone book. It is somewhat expensive advertising, but it should be done and done well. Hire professional help, if necessary, to design this piece. One of your largest market audiences can be through this one source. The advertisement should be professional and should convey exactly what services the office provides.

There are currently a wide variety of phone books from various companies. It is costly for small businesses to advertise in all of these phone books. However, it is a good practice to advertise in all of them. You have no way of knowing which of the books is favored by which segment of the population, and it is impossible to try to second-guess.

Provide many thoughtful comforts for your patients in the office. Have a set of scrubs available that the patient can borrow when a cast is going to be put on. Provide a phone (with a long distance governor on it) in the waiting room for patients to make personal calls while they wait. Pens and pretty writing paper in the reception room make the wait seem shorter. Make sure that there are crayons and coloring books in each treatment room for the children who have accompanied a parent to the office. Provide coffee, tea, and cookies or doughnuts in the waiting room. Make sure that the office is decorated for holidays. Television and/or videos in the waiting room help entertain the patients and families as they wait. The list is limited only by your imagination.

Many practices send birthday cards, sympathy cards, and get-well cards to all their patients. These cards can be purchased in large quantities and should be addressed by hand. Many practices also send Christmas and Hanukkah cards to all patients who have had surgery in the last year, all new patients from the past year, and all patients seen routinely. Holiday cards can also be sent to referring doctors and medical groups.

If you are new to an area, it may be a good idea to start a newsletter to educate people. You can also buy a newsletter and alter it to individual needs. This newsletter can be mailed out or sent out as a tag along with billings. If the office is one of the first to provide this service in your community, then invest in it. If everyone is printing a newsletter, it should be discontinued.

On occasion we have given school tours and talks at school. Start by offering to give a talk for the class of a staff member's child. The class can tour the office, have refreshments, and go home with lots of handouts. This helps the children learn what a podiatrist does and also informs the parents of the existence of the office.

Foot Health Month lends itself easily to promotion. Utilize the advertising materials available through the national association. These materials are professionally produced and represent a minimal investment. We have also had poster contests that have been well received by local youths and patients' families.

Give away items during Foot Health Month; also encourage people who stop in to visit the office. Usually you can convince local stations to carry some public service–type announcements during this time period, particularly if you are already investing in some purchased time.

Signage is the public's first view of you. Always

make sure that it is well done, highly visible, and tasteful. The newspaper is another advertising media that has been used a lot in the past. It can be utilized for promotions of special health issues.

Television is a possible advertising medium. Some practices have had excellent results from the sizable part of the population who are unaware that there is such a thing as a foot doctor. The third medium available is radio. Some practices have a somewhat higher success rate than others. This medium can be useful for community service spots and sponsoring of local sporting events for the high schools in smaller areas.

Bulk mailings are another source of advertising and patient education. Bulk mailings are easy to do but are sometimes difficult to target to the appropriate market. Higher response rates can be expected if you can specifically target the neighborhood or suburb in which the office is located and follow up personally. The mailing piece should center on the fact that the practice is located right in their "backyard" and relies on their local support. It is also successful if you ask people to stop in to visit and perhaps pick up a free giveaway. Usually this is hard work for low rewards. The maximum return on bulk mail is generally 10%, with the average running at 2% to 5%. You can purchase mailing lists from mailing houses and local consulting firms that can target population segments and households within a market area. These mailing lists might be useful if you have not developed your own.

Scheduling open houses or patient appreciation days is a good way to show off new facilities, new equipment, new services, and new associates. Open houses can also be used to thank patients, celebrate years in business, or celebrate a grand opening. You can schedule one set of programs for patients and a separate type of affair for the medical/business community. If the goal is to attract new patients, you need to do more promoting and offer some draw other than just the open house (free food, door prizes, or entertainment). You could plan a party just for patients who have referred others to you. The ideas are only limited by your imagination. The Patient Appreciation Day is gaining favor in practice management circles as a means of reminding the past patient of your ongoing presence and repaying patients for their years of working with you. Yours can be as large or small as you wish to design it.

Make the office available for occasions other than strictly office functions. Provide a conference or meeting room for local groups. This is excellent exposure for the practice. Hold an open house for a local cause, and help promote this other organization. A good choice is the local diabetes or arthritis association.

Make the office available for local artists to display their works on a rotating basis. This promotes the artists, gives the office new and constantly changing decor, and brings a new clientele base in contact with the staff members. You can arrange this service through a local arts group or arts council.

Patient surveys can be used as a means of determining patient complaints and compliments about the office. This can be a good basis for making positive changes in the office. The survey should be short for the best response, and anonymity must be maintained. Several short surveys over a period of time are better than any lengthy ones. If the survey is mailed out, the return rate should be expected to be low. The best way to get answers is to have the survey completed while the patient is in the office and have him drop the card in a box in the waiting room. This gives the patient something to do while waiting and ensures a high response rate.

Offer a shoe talk service for local managers and sales personnel of shoe stores. Bring them to your office early on a Saturday morning, provide a continental breakfast, and give a presentation on shoe gear. Demonstrate what the office needs from the store when they send a patient. Use a slide presentation on general foot problems to familiarize the sales staff with the scope of a podiatrist's practice. Encourage them to bring samples of shoes to the meeting, and answer all their questions. Distribute your business cards and shoe gear handouts, urge them to contact the office with ongoing questions at any time, and then be available to them. They will be an excellent referral source.

A single one of these techniques will not work on its own as a means for building a practice; however, finding a combination of ideas and techniques can have a great impact on the image of the podiatric office.

7

Medical-Legal Concerns of the Podiatric Medical Assistant

Lois F. Downey, J.D.

There is a perception—right or wrong—among the public and the medical community that we, as a society, are encountering a medical malpractice crisis. Plaintiffs' attorneys have, by using a variety of methods, communicated to the public that bringing any type of lawsuit is easy and requires little or no personal cost. Plaintiffs' attorneys have convinced their clients that we are not even addressing "malpractice" any more since that term seems to imply an "evil" or "malicious" attempt to injure patients by medical professionals. Rather, the plaintiff-patient is convinced that his case is justified merely because of a bad result. Even those of us who routinely defend medical professionals have replaced the term "malpractice" with "negligence." Thus, the patient is not timid to sue his doctor or those who assist him. Finally, the publicization of million-dollar jury awards results in the belief that for every award one hears about, there must be ten others, thus making litigation appear to be the golden road to financial opportunity.

No one advocates that all medical negligence suits are without merit. However, the great majority of them are leading some insurance companies to implement policies that provide that all lawsuits will be defended through trial to a jury verdict. This eliminates the plaintiff's opportunity to pursue an out-of-court settlement for a suspicious claim, but in turn, it forces the medical defendant to vigorously defend defenseless claims, thereby increasing the possibility of adverse media exposure. Moreover, the jousting described above takes its toll on the professional. The loss is not just dollars and cents. It also acts as a magnifying lens to expose "warts" and injure reputations, it cleverly manipulates the professional into questioning his abilities, and undermines his confidence with other patients, and in a good many cases, it acts as a personal affront that affects the personal life of the professional.

The effects of medical negligence suits are reduced or eliminated through efforts to prevent lawsuits. The podiatric medical assistant is an important part of the scheme for prevention. An awareness of the common elements that can lead to a negligence claim is very important. Specifically, the podiatric medical assistant's activities involving hands-on medical assistance, entries on the patient's chart, telephone or face-to-face conversations with the patient or the patient's family and friends, and the disclosure of information about the patient to anyone, including the patient himself, all expose the podiatric medical assistant and podiatrist to liability if they are performed incorrectly, inadequately, or without a certain degree of professionalism.

THE ASSISTANT AS AGENT

It is not difficult to understand that anything that the podiatric medical assistant says or does at the direct request and/or supervision of the podiatrist is imputed to the doctor because the law has determined the assistant, in that instance, to be an agent of the doctor. In other words, the assistant is a conduit through which the works of the podiatrist are performed. In this way, the podiatrist is legally liable for the verbal and physical conduct of the assistant. But what about the daily duties undertaken by the podiatric medical assistant without direct instruction by the podiatrist? Generally in every state, where the podiatric medical assistant says or does something to further the interests of the podiatrist and therefore is authorized by the doctor in either a medical or administrative function (in areas such as the care and treatment of the patient to promote healing or well-being or the collection of overdue bills), these actions will also be imputed to the podiatrist. This is not to say that podiatric medical assistants will never be held personally responsible for their actions. If the assistant does or says something beyond the scope (outside the realm) of the job, then the law interprets the conduct as not authorized by the podiatrist, and the assistant will be held liable for the results of that conduct. For example, a podiatric medical assistant who calls a patient an unflattering name with the intent to injure the patient's reputation will be personally liable for any injuries resulting from that action.

Generally, podiatric medical assistants may perform a wide spectrum of duties limited only by the doctor for whom they work. Thus, the podiatric medical assistant may debride nails, prepare a patient for casting, perform redressings and paddings, take a medical history, or perform laboratory technical functions such as developing x-ray films or preparing a specimen for the laboratory. In all of these activities, the assistant is seen as the agent of the doctor. Poor performance on the part of the assistant is imputed to the podiatrist. These activities, if done incorrectly, expose the podiatric medical assistant as well as the doctor to liability should a patient be injured as a result of the activity. It is unclear whether the podiatric medical assistant will be held to the same standard of care as the podiatrist when the harmful conduct was something usually performed by the podiatrist, as in the case of nail debridements. It would be highly unlikely that a court would be convinced by a defense argument that the quality of nail debridement expected of a podiatric medical assistant should be less than that of a podiatrist.

It is vital, therefore, that podiatric medical assistants receive adequate training if their function is to include actual medical assistance. The teaching of proper technique could be left to the employer, but the podiatrist may not take the time required to ensure thorough instruction. Resorting to outside educational programs may be necessary. Nonetheless, the most important thing to remember is that assistants should never do anything for which they have not been properly and adequately trained. It is far better for the assistants to simply excuse themselves from the presence of the patient and inform the doctor that they cannot do the activity as instructed than to risk causing injury to the patient and increase the risk of a lawsuit. Good office practice dictates that the podiatrist ensure that his assistants receive this training from himself, another trained assistant, or outside sources.

It is important that the podiatrist find out whether the particular state in which he practices delineates the scope of the podiatric medical assistant's practice so that the assistant is not engaging in unapproved conduct. Such conduct that results in injury to the patient—whether or not caused by malpractice—is difficult if not impossible to defend. Delegating professional responsibilities to an assistant who is not qualified by training, experience, or licensure to perform them will result in disciplinary action for the podiatrist as well.

COMPREHENSIVE RECORD KEEPING IS NECESSARY

Accurate charting is a *must!* The statute of limitations for malpractice actions is generally 2 years. Some legal exceptions permit an even longer period of time. For example, in almost all states, children (minors) may wait until they have reached the age of 18 years before the 2-year statute of limitations begins, so they may bring a lawsuit at age 20 even though the alleged act of malpractice occurred at 5 years of age. The doctor and the podiatric medical assistant's only ability to remember the patient and the care and treatment she received is usually after a review of the chart.

This is because one may have seen literally hundreds of patients since this particular patient. Contrary to this, the plaintiff-patient, in addition to those family members and friends to whom she complained, will recall or allege to recall everything that was said and done in great detail. To counter the plaintiff-patient's seemingly accurate and vivid account of her treatment, the only ammunition is the chart, which, if done correctly, should provide the podiatric medical assistant and the doctor with a specific recollection of the plaintiff-patient's problems, treatment, and resulting condition. Accurate chart keeping is the *key* to a good *defense!* Thus, the entries should be complete so that the treatment rendered to the patient appears to flow in a logical sequence. Well-kept records will permit the preparer to reconstruct the events of several years ago and explain to the jury why certain actions were or were not undertaken.

When making an entry, the podiatric medical assistant should state observations of events or notes of conversations in the present tense. For example, upon entering the waiting room, the assistant observes the patient ambulating without crutches when the podiatrist's order after the last office visit indicates that the patient is to be non–weight bearing. The podiatric medical assistant should immediately, or as soon as possible, write in the chart "Patient *enters* the office ambulating without assistance of other persons or crutches." Similarly, if the cast appears to have been abused, note on the chart "Cast *is* scratched, broken, dirty, or wet." If the patient or those accompanying him tell the assistant information such as the patient is not keeping his cast dry, is not doing his exercises, or is not taking his medication, then note it in the chart as well as *who* related the information.

When blood pressure, temperature, and/or other vital sign information is taken, always record the data in the chart. There is a school of thought among physicians that "normal" findings are not noted in the chart, which leaves one to accept the doctor's word 2 years down the road that he distinctly remembers that all appropriate tests were performed and the results were in normal limits. This may be reasonable to expect of an emergency room physician where failure to take the time to record "normal" findings is in the patient's interest. However, when possible, "normal" findings should be recorded in the chart. Doing so will effectively counter the plaintiff-patient's argument that the tests were never performed or important data were inadvertently omitted from the chart. One can see the strength of the plaintiff-patient's argument when one considers that the podiatric medical assistant may have spent a scant 5 minutes with her to take a history and perform a physical examination, thus leaving the jury with the impression that the disputed test could not have been performed given the lack of time.

All data received from outside laboratory sources should be included in the medical records. Not only does this act as backup documentation for the laboratory result in the event that the laboratory loses the information, but it also gives the reviewer the impression that the doctor was aware of the laboratory result before rendering further treatment to the patient.

Meticulous documentation is essential when the patient is noncompliant and fails to return for follow-up care. The legal question that arises is whether the podiatrist has discharged or abandoned the patient. A patient who suffers an untoward result because she fails to return to the office for follow-up care may claim that her podiatrist abandoned her and can bring a lawsuit against him.

If a patient fails to show up for a routine office visit, a telephone call to that patient and documentation of the new appointment as well as the reasons for the missed appointment should be made by the assistant. Failure to return for the reappointment date should result in a telephone call with documentation of the conversation. Caution would also support a certified letter, return receipt requested, indicating that the two office visits have been missed and that although it is unknown at the time whether she is suffering from any podiatric problems, it is suggested that she make an office visit at her earliest possible convenience.

Patients who fail to show up for office visits for postoperative care, management of infection, diabetic foot care, etc., require a more conservative, well-documented approach. The initial telephone call should advise the patient of the importance of follow-up care in addition to that previously mentioned, and this conversation should be recorded on the chart. If the patient misses a second appointment, a certified letter (return receipt requested) should be sent that sets forth information that would advise the patient as to the severity of her condition, the need for follow-up care, and the potential risks and complications that may occur without follow-up care. A telephone call should be made to reschedule the missed appointment with documentation of the conversation. Failure to return for a third visit necessitates a second certified letter that, if appropriate, should inform the patient that if her foot is not examined by a professional, then she is putting herself at risk to various factors such as gangrene, amputation, immobility, etc. This final "doomsday" letter should indicate that the patient must see a medical professional and, if she will not return to the office, she must contact a podiatrist in her area. This doomsday letter should be a balance between the notice of the severity of the condition and the need to do something, but it should stop short of describing the patient's condition as emergent and that the office will send an ambulance for her. The purpose of all of these letters is to inform the patient that her failure to act appropriately with regard to her condition may lead to risks and complications that she may not have otherwise experienced.

Needless to say, copies of all such letters should be stored in the patient's file. It is important that these letters establish to the jury at a trial that the physician adequately informed the patient of the potential for problems because of the patient's failure to follow up with the physician and that the patient has knowingly placed herself in jeopardy of suffering complications. In such a case, the podiatrist will be able to establish that he neither abandoned nor prematurely discharged the patient and therefore is not legally responsible for her problems.

Even if the comprehensive medical records do not jolt the podiatric medical assistant's memory to permit testifying at a deposition or trial about her involvement in the treatment of the plaintiff-patient, most states permit the records themselves to be admitted into evidence if the records are properly authenticated. Authentication requires the podiatric medical assistant, as the preparer of the chart, to testify that entries to the chart were made contemporaneously with the event they describe, that at the time of the recordation the entry was true and correct to the best of her knowledge, and that no later alteration to the chart has occurred.

Some doctors dictate their office notes and have them typed into the chart. Podiatric medical assistants do not normally dictate their entries. Instead, they usually handwrite them. Clean, clear, legible notes help the reviewer, especially the jury, to easily read the chart. This is important for two reasons. First, a neutral party such as the jury will naturally draw the inference from clear, legible notes that the doctor and the assistant are organized and know what they are doing. Illegible entries often leave the reviewer with the impression that the medical professional does not want anyone to be able to read his notes and, therefore, has something to hide. Second, where the medical defendant cannot testify independently of the medical records so that the medical record must be admitted into evidence, the doctor's defense hinges on the jury's ability to read the chart to understand why the defense has relied upon it.

Without legible, complete medical records, the case is reduced to testimony from the plaintiff-patient who claims to have complete and total recall about his treatment and the inadequacy thereof and from the defendant podiatric medical assistant and/or other medical personnel who cannot recall their treatment of the plaintiff-patient and cannot even rely upon the medical records to support their belief that they did not create an error in judgment or an omission. Obviously, the chances for a plaintiff's verdict in such a situation are great.

NEVER CHANGE, ALTER, OR MODIFY CHART ENTRIES

An important subissue to good record keeping concerns altering the entries in the patient's chart. *Never* change or otherwise destroy entries on the patient's chart or other medical documents. Most hospitals have a policy establishing how errors on the record are to be treated. This policy usually includes an additional note in the chart dated as of the date that this correcting note is being written that indicates what the error was. Errors that are written in the chart contemporaneously with the entry should be crossed out by a single line through the statement (so that even though the entry has been crossed out it can still be read), dated, and initialed at that time. It cannot be emphasized enough that to change or somehow delete a prior entry makes an otherwise defensible claim into one that may well be so difficult to defend that an out-of-court settlement may be immediately pursued. Even if the alteration is done for a perfectly good reason, the plaintiff's lawyer will try to establish that the assistant is attempting to hide something, thus placing the assistant's and doctor's credibility on the line. This warning is particularly crucial once a claim has been made or a lawsuit filed. Thus, even if the podiatric medical assistant clearly remembers what transpired during a particular office visit of the patient and desires to enter additional information on the chart, he should not do so because such action will be twisted by the plaintiff's attorney and used against the podiatrist and the assistant.

As stated above, entries on the patient's chart should be made contemporaneously with the treatment or when the conversation occurs. This, we hope, permits the chart to be a reflection of what has occurred rather than a document prepared in anticipation of a lawsuit. As mentioned above, although physicians may dictate their office notes and the transcription of the notes may not occur until 48 to 72 hours later, it is taken for granted that the physician dictated his note at the time the event occurred and did not interfere with the transcription or alter what was dictated prior to the transcription of the note, thus giving it the same stature as having been contemporaneously created with the event. Late additions to the chart will only be viewed as a reaction to a negative change in the patient's condition and the possibility that litigation may ensue.

BE CAREFUL AND PROFESSIONAL IN CONVERSATIONS

The podiatric medical assistant must be careful about what is said or done when working with a patient, especially when there is a risk that the patient may misunderstand, misconstrue, or mischaracterize what has been said. Objectivity and professionalism are key. Avoid being judgmental. While this may seem obvious, the assistant could unintentionally violate this tacit professional rule during the solicitation of the patient's social history. The podiatric assistant may know that it is unhealthy to smoke or drink too much alcohol. In an offhand and casual manner, the assistant could inadvertently express personal judgment by stating to the patient that she ought to "stop smoking" or "cut back on her alcohol intake." Although these examples may hardly constitute the basis for a lawsuit, they are the demonstrable steps toward further and potentially more damaging judgmental statements.

It should be fairly obvious that the podiatric medical assistant should not criticize the podiatrist's technique, judgment, and skill in the presence of the patient. The patient may believe that the assistant has just informed her that malpractice has occurred. Furthermore, telling a patient that her surgical result was not as good as if the assistant's employer had performed the surgery or stating that the podiatrist "would not have done it that way" will also be interpreted as an opinion that malpractice by another health care professional has been committed even if such interpretation was not the intent of the assistant. The podiatrist knows that criticism of earlier medical treatment by another health care professional does not promote the health and well-being of the patient. Instead, it can actually result in anxiety, distrust, and anger on the part of the patient toward the former doctor, the podiatrist, and the podiatric profession. Additionally, the patient may become difficult, refuse to follow instructions, and constantly request the podiatrist to promise to testify against the former physician should a lawsuit result. The caution maintained by the podiatrist should also be borne by the podiatric assistant. Avoiding critical comments in the presence of the patient means being nonjudgmental when dealing with the patient.

Avoiding speculation or making statements that are judgmental and not based upon one's personal knowledge while attempting to fully respond to legitimate and sincere questions and concerns of the patient can be very difficult. Podiatric medical assistants by their very nature, if not by their job description, are helpful individuals and may make statements involving judgment or speculation in the belief that they will make the patient feel better. Patients who are anxious or apprehensive about impending treatment may not comprehend or closely listen to what the podiatric medical assistant has to say. A better approach is to strictly adhere to the doctor's instructions. The assistant should only discuss the treatment that the doctor will perform in general terms and leave the patient to discuss specifics with the doctor. If the podiatrist requests that the assistant tell the patient more detailed information such as the alternatives to treatment and the risks associated with each alternative, the medical assistant must be sure that his communication with the patient is complete and record the discussions in the chart.

Documentation of the alternatives and risks discussed should be made on the patient's chart. Documentation is helpful where state law requires that a health care professional obtain the patient's "informed consent" prior to instituting treatment. Informed consent is defined as permission by the patient to undergo the recommended treatment after the health care professional has disclosed all of the alternatives and risks that a reasonable person would deem important in the making of his decision. Most states require an informed consent. Therefore, if the podiatrist has instructed the podiatric medical assistant to explain the alternatives and risks to the patient, failure to do so adequately may result in legal liability. Documentation of the discussion of alternatives and risks supports the doctor's defense that the patient did provide her informed consent prior to the implementation of the treatment.

The same advice applies to directions or cautions that the podiatric assistant provides to the patient or his family: document it on the chart. Be specific—remember objectivity. As mentioned before, if the patient or anyone with the patient tells the podiatric medical assistant something of medical significance such as the patient's failure to follow instructions or a recent fall or other trauma, the assistant should make an entry in the chart and identify from whom the information came. The importance of the documentation will be seen when, years later at trial, the patient testifies in direct contradiction to the record. The record is viewed by the jury as an objective piece of evidence more worthy of credence than the testimony of the plaintiff-patient, which may be understood to be subjective and/or self-serving.

Finally, the assistant should never refer the patient to another health care provider, whether podiatric or not. Should the referral doctor cause the patient injury through incompetent or substandard care, the assistant and the podiatrist for whom he or she works could be legally liable for those injuries. The patient could sue the podiatrist—and the assistant working as his agent—for negligent referral. This means that the patient is claiming that the assistant knew or *should* have known that the referral doctor was incompetent or would likely render substandard care and therefore the assistant and the podiatrist are responsible for the patient's injuries.

NEVER RELEASE INFORMATION ABOUT THE PATIENT WITHOUT AUTHORITY

Most podiatric medical assistants perform administrative duties in the office. In addition to maintaining patient charts, setting up patient appointments, and taking care of the billing, the assistant may be responsible for handling inquiries with regard to the patient's records or x-ray films. In most states, the release of medical records is controlled by statute due to privacy concerns. However, in some states there is no statute that prevents a treating physician from disclosing information about the patient without the patient's consent. Nonetheless, the best practice is to never release records, even to the patient personally, without an authorization executed by the patient permitting the release of the records. Even if the request for the records or x-ray films comes from the patient's lawyers, insist on an appropriate authorization. Releasing medical records without first obtaining the patient's permission can result in a lawsuit against the doctor or medical facility for either a breach of privacy or invasion of privacy. If there is no authorization, insist on a court order commanding that the patient's records be released.

However, most states acknowledge that when a patient files a medical negligence suit against her doctor and/or the doctor's assistants, the patient is deemed to have placed her care and treatment or the nature and extent of her resulting injury at issue. In those instances, the doctor on behalf of himself or his assistant may be permitted to release the patient's medical records to his professional liability insurance carrier or his defense lawyer without obtaining the patient's prior authorization. Nonetheless, an overabundance of caution will not result in an oppressive burden, and therefore, in the absence of a court order signed by a judge or the patient's executed authorization, the podiatric medical assistant or the podiatrist should consult with the doctor's personal attorney prior to the release of the medical records. In any event, do not ignore a request for records because many statutes require responses to the request.

Of course, medical emergencies do occur, and a hospital or another health care professional may require a review of the patient's records in order to provide immediate treatment to the patient. It is a good idea in such an emergency situation that the assistant or podiatrist obtain an authorization for the release of the records from a member of the patient's family.

CONCLUSION

The prevention or reduction of medical malpractice claims and lawsuits merely requires careful and thoughtful conduct on the part of the health care professional. It is not an onerous burden to be careful and complete. Daily living requires that citizens decrease their risk of liability toward one another with conduct such as shoveling one's sidewalk, maintaining one's automobile, and not engaging in physically harmful activity. The podiatric medical assistant must be careful about what is said to the patient. The assistant must be objective and professional and should avoid judgmental statements or offering information beyond the expertise or authority of an assistant. Significant events, problems, and information obtained from whatever source should be documented. Unfortunately, even the most careful podiatric medical assistant may be the subject of a lawsuit. Therefore, since the lawsuit will usually refer to conduct that occurred nearly 2 or more years ago, it is crucial to the defense of that lawsuit that the medical records be neat, legible, comprehensive, and most of all, accurate without alterations. Proper documentation will allow podiatric medical assistants to reconstruct their involvement in the patient's care and treatment in order to properly prepare a defense to the allegations of negligent medical care.

8

The Telephone and the Receptionist

Karen Allred, P.M.A.

The telephone is a vital business tool that connects you with patients. How effectively the telephone is handled can make a major difference in a medical practice.

The office must have a sufficient number of phone lines since the telephone is used for so many purposes. Some of these functions include scheduling appointments, collecting past due accounts, consultations, referrals, and postoperative follow-up. One telephone line is not adequate even in a small practice. A busy phone line discourages potential patients. Always have at least one phone line available exclusively for incoming calls. A separate line should be dedicated to outgoing calls. This line should be used by your office staff to make outside calls without interfering with important incoming calls.

INITIAL OFFICE CONTACT

The initial office contact is made by telephone. This first phone call should effectively open the lines of communication between the office and the patient. A patient's first impression of the office is formed by his or her treatment during this phone call. The telephone should be answered before the third ring. It should be answered politely and professionally in a well-modulated voice.

When the patient visits the office, the receptionist should reinforce the original good impression by treating the patient in a pleasant and courteous manner. Maintaining a good disposition throughout the day is the key to an effective receptionist. It takes a special person with the qualities of patience, poise, a sense of humor, and a positive attitude to handle the responsibilities of the telephone-receptionist position. You may have to employ several people before you find someone who possesses the ability to communicate effectively with patients on the telephone and in the office.

Initial appointments are usually made over the telephone. The employee scheduling these appointments must be efficient, thorough, quick, and considerate of the patient's time. Give new patients your name when making the appointment so that they will feel more comfortable upon arrival at the office and less like strangers. Always confirm the appointment by repeating the details to the patients: calling them by name; repeating the day, date, and time; and mentioning the doctor's name who will be treating them. This is one way to ensure that there are no misunderstandings.

This call is a good opportunity to inform the patient about office policy pertaining to payment for treatment, filing insurance claims, and missed appointments. Be sure to obtain both home and work phone numbers from the patient in case you have to reschedule the appointment.

CANCELLATIONS, RESCHEDULING, AND MISSED APPOINTMENTS

Cancellations and rescheduling should always be documented on the chart in a timely manner. A simple notation of "N/S" for no show or the reschedule date entered on the appropriate chart at the end of the day will save the office staff a great deal of paperwork. It also could be crucial evidence in the event of a malpractice case if the patient was negligent in returning for postoperative visits. Cancellations and rescheduling should also be reported to the other staff members during the day.

It is very important to document all missed appointments (M/A). The patient should be contacted within 24 hours to ascertain the reason for the M/A and to reschedule the appointment. Note each attempt to call on the chart. After the patient is reached, detail the conversation on the chart. Such documentation is necessary for proper record keeping.

SCHEDULING TELEPHONE TIME

A busy doctor must have time set aside in his daily schedule to return or instigate phone calls. Certain patient calls must be handled by the doctor. Communication with a referring doctor, both before and after examination of the patient, is extremely important. A telephone call and a follow-up letter to the referral doctor for inclusion on the patient's chart is good practice. Discuss scheduling telephone time with the doctor. It will assist him in utilizing his time more productively.

PERSONAL TELEPHONE CALLS

There will always be a need for personal phone calls in an office. Individual office policy sets limits on these calls. It is the responsibility of the receptionist to prioritize incoming personal calls. Calls to the doctor should go through unless you are instructed differently. Personal telephone calls to the employees should be handled according to policy. As a general rule, personal telephone calls should be handled during lunch or break time, except in an emergency. If there is no clear-cut telephone policy governing personal use of the office phone, serious phone abuse problems may develop.

PATIENT TELEPHONE CALLS

A good receptionist should be able to analyze patient phone calls and direct them to the proper department. If it is necessary to have the call returned, certain information needs to be communicated to the patient as well as to the recipient of the call. Patients should be told why the person they are calling is not available and be given an approximate time that their call will be returned. A duplicate phone message pad can be used to note the patient's name, phone number, and a concise reason for the call, legibly written. This duplicate record helps in tracing information from previous calls and assists the receptionist in confirming that the calls have been returned as promised. Pulling the patient's chart, repeating the phone number, taking accurate messages, and confirming that calls are returned are ways a good receptionist contributes to an efficiently run practice.

The emergency patient needs to be handled with special care. The receptionist should be able to distinguish between a real or imagined emergency. A condition afflicting a patient for several months can seem like an emergency on Friday afternoon. Usually such an "emergency" can wait until Monday. Reassuring the patient that a doctor will be on call over the weekend will often alleviate the patient's apprehension. Experience will help the receptionist in classifying a true emergency. After consultation with the doctor or his assistant, the emergency patient can be instructed to report to the office or emergency room, whatever is deemed most appropriate. Remember that the receptionist is not a doctor and should not make medical judgments. If there is any doubt, refer immediately to the podiatrist.

Good relationships with patients are good business. A courteous, caring receptionist is your best defense against disruptive or disgruntled patients. Sometimes a problem patient is just lonely and needs someone to talk to. As long as it does not interfere with your responsibilities, taking a few minutes to listen to someone can make a loyal patient out of a problem one.

When dealing with an angry or belligerent patient, it is imperative to establish the problem. Sometimes the receptionist can resolve minor misunderstandings on the phone. More complex problems need to be referred to the department or staff member involved in the dispute. Get as much background information as possible from the patient, and then relay the details to the proper staff member.

The telephone and the receptionist have a significant impact on a medical practice. It is imperative to employ a competent, caring person as the receptionist. A good receptionist provided with an adequate telephone system can contribute significantly to the success of a medical practice.

9

Appointments

Miriam Y. Smalley, P.M.A.

I. Flexible Formats
II. Call List
III. Computer-Generated Appointment Schedule

An increasingly competitive professional environment demands efficient office operation to achieve success. Many management techniques can be utilized to upgrade an office and anticipate the future needs of a practice that range from streamlining routine procedures to purchasing in bulk. Often these methods can improve productivity and stabilize cash flow. In a podiatrist's office, one simple adjustment can enhance every other effort: instituting a well-planned appointing and recall system. It is one of the most straightforward methods for increasing productivity.

Controlling your appointment book translates into several office improvements: good communication between doctor, staff, and patient; optimum use of space and equipment; and the efficient scheduling of everyone's time. A good appointing system makes these improvements possible.

Good appointing has three beneficiaries. First, the patients are spared long waits in the office. Efficient appointing procedures and well-scheduled visits ensure satisfied patients who are likely to remain loyal. Second, the doctor benefits by being able to concentrate on delivering care without the distraction of scheduling glitches. Finally, staff members are provided with the right information at the right time to do their jobs well. At all levels, good appointing is the key to productivity.

Once adopted, a good appointing system becomes the foundation for countless other improvements. Good appointing practices enhance record keeping. It provides a way to communicate information to the staff setting up treatment rooms. Standards of care and service can be readily monitored. A streamlined system makes it easier to find extra time in a daily schedule filled with tightly planned procedures and routines. Skillful management of the appointment book keeps everyone productive and every space fully utilized. Once a good appointing system is in place, it becomes the only way to run a practice.

The variety of health services available in the marketplace has made today's patients cost-conscious consumers. An efficiently operated podiatric office that values the patients' time in addition to providing quality care projects a positive image that increases business in this competitive environment.

A well-organized appointment book gives you more flexibility to accommodate patients. Good appointing methods call for setting aside a block of time each day to allow for emergency care without disrupting regularly scheduled appointments. Many offices do not require emergency time every day, and this extra time can often be utilized by standby patients on your call list.

Since every practice is unique, appointing methods should be tailored to the individual office's needs to maximize their usefulness.

It is important that one person control the appointment book and establish a system to complement the needs of the practice. This primary person may not make all appointments or block time for emergency cases, but she should be responsible for training the staff on proper appointing procedures and tracking the overall system for accuracy and efficiency.

The importance of placing one individual in charge of the appointing plan cannot be overemphasized. Improper scheduling results in chaos. Only trained personnel should make appointments. Follow-ups, routine checkups, and emergency cases should be channeled through the system to ensure that productivity is maintained and patients are efficiently served. Training key staff members to operate an effective appointment system requires providing them with a working knowledge of procedures practiced in the office. Knowing what kind of preparation and how much time is required for each procedure will enable them to accurately assess the patient's needs.

Equipped with this knowledge, personnel are able to schedule adequate time for a procedure during the initial telephone call or, in the case of a follow-up visit, before the patient leaves the office. With an efficient system in place the doctor is freed from involvement in scheduling decisions for specific patients. Occasionally when the doctor needs to become involved, a good appointing system has the flexibility to accommodate that need and the stability to maintain the flow in other areas.

A well-trained staff that understands procedures and time strictures forms a cohesive group that respects one another. When everyone works toward a common goal, it translates into productivity.

FLEXIBLE FORMATS

A single appointment book format would be inadequate to meet the needs of a wide variety of professional offices. Practices vary not only in size but also in the way services are delivered. What these offices have in common is the need for a streamlined appointing system.

Many appointment books are set up in a single or multicolumn format. They feature everything from a column per day to four or more columns per day per office. You can choose a dated or undated style to suit your needs.

A frequently used form is the dated appointment page divided into 10- or 15-minute intervals. Month, day, and year appear at the top. The single-column format works well for practices with one doctor on staff. The multicolumn format allows you to schedule several doctors on the dated page or set aside one column for additional information. Columns can be assigned by other definitions as well.

It is possible to adapt the pages of today's appointment book to almost any system that works. It is important to be flexible enough to create the kind of appointing system that makes a discernible difference in your office operation.

Survey the practice and discuss ideas with the staff. Review the current appointing system to identify strengths and weaknesses. Comparisons are important as you outline what you want from a new system geared toward productivity and improved communication. Rely on your staff to outline weaknesses, and make suggestions for refining the appointing system. Their input can be crucial to its success.

As previously mentioned, plan to set aside a block of time for emergencies. It provides the flexibility needed to gain control of your appointment book. Blocking emergency time is another effective marketing essential. It allows you to respect the preappointed patients' time as well as accommodate last-minute and emergency patients.

Review available resources like personnel, space, and equipment required for performing various procedures. Booking appointments at set times each week for new patients, routine care, and complex procedures helps to streamline the work flow. With careful monitoring, assigned time blocks can become the model of efficiency in your office.

The appointment book is the front line of patient information for your office. Each appointment slot should contain the patient's name, home and work phone numbers, and a brief description of the scheduled procedure or treatment. There are many other ways to utilize the appointment book in your practice. To double-check on the recall process, mark appointments with different-colored pencils denoting the need for a reminder card or telephone call. You can also use the appointment book to keep notes on no-shows and cancellations. Include any information that is relevant to the people who use the book for planning and as a complete record of the day's schedule.

It is essential to understand the working patterns of each care provider. Develop a reference list of procedures and times, and update it periodically. Communication is essential between care providers and appointment personnel. While there is room for individual differences, they cannot be allowed to severely hinder productivity.

Place a premium on accuracy in the appointment book. This is the main source of information transferred to the appointment lists of the day's schedule and distributed among treatment rooms and doctors. At the same time, it is a permanent record of a "day in the practice" and, as such, has legal standing.

CALL LIST

Every professional office should maintain a current call list with the names and numbers of patients to contact when appointment slots become open. The main objective of a good appointment system is to keep the practice as busy as possible with few idle hours or empty rooms. When an appointment opens up or an emergency hour is not needed, a good call list helps you book the space quickly.

List the names of patients who need a routine examination or treatment but, because of unpredictable schedules, prefer to book appointments on short notice. The list should contain information on the service requested, the time preferred for an appointment, and both work and home phone numbers. This list is a gold mine of opportunity when you are faced with cancellations or no-shows.

The term "call list" is also used in some offices to describe a list for contacting patients after treatment to check their progress. In either case, the call list puts you in touch with patients and demonstrates your interest and concern for their needs.

COMPUTER-GENERATED APPOINTMENT SCHEDULE

Offices that are computerized usually have the capability of programming the computer to make appointments, thereby eliminating the need for an appointment book. There are advantages and disadvantages of computerization.

The computerized system can be programmed with the time, date, and type of appointment at 10- or 15-minute intervals. The person making the appointment enters the patient's name and nature of the visit in a specific time slot. The appointment schedule can be printed and distributed at the beginning of the workday. Using the computer to make appointments provides scheduling that is organized and easily read.

The primary disadvantage is the expense and availability of computer equipment. When using the computer for appointments, the office will need a terminal and printer dedicated to that function exclusively. Appointments cannot be made if the computer is being used for other tasks, and this results in long waits by the patient for service. In the event of a power failure, you would not know what your schedule was on any given day or be able to make future appointments. In short, use of the computer for setting appointments may not be practical for every office.

In summary, efficient appointing has a positive effect on the practice and the patients. The practice operates under an effective system that utilizes the entire staff's time efficiently. Patients know that their health is being carefully monitored and their time is respected. From appointments to call backs, going by the book does make a difference.

BIBLIOGRAPHY

1. Palmer DM, Hanna S: *The Telephone Handbook for Medical and Dental Practices*. Aurora, Colo, Palmer Associates, 1989.

10

Scheduling Surgery

Birdi Kribs, P.M.A.

Scheduling surgery for a patient is an aspect of the medical practice where attention to detail is extremely important. The physician, patient, hospital, and insurance company all depend on you to ensure that the process proceeds smoothly.

Once the patient has elected to undergo surgery, he will rely on you to handle the scheduling of the surgery, the scheduling of the preoperative tests, and the communication with the insurance companies. Remember that the patient may be anxious about the upcoming surgery. Treat him with care and concern.

The physician will detail the type of surgical procedure to be performed, the approximate time required for the surgery, and whether the surgery will be outpatient, inpatient, or an A.M. admittance. Explain this information to the patient. Ask the patient for his preference for surgery dates, and work as closely as possible to these dates. Check the physician's personal calendar, his existing surgery schedule, and his office schedule for any conflicts. If necessary, discuss alternate dates with the patient until a mutually acceptable date is selected.

After you and the patient have agreed upon a date, immediately phone the hospital operating room staff and request that specific surgical date. Once the date of surgery has been confirmed on the telephone, give the operating room the pertinent information on the patient including the patient's name, age, and phone number; surgical procedure; which foot the surgery will be performed on; whether the patient will be an A.M. admittance, inpatient, or outpatient (AM, IP, or OP); the approximate time required for the surgery; and the surgeon's and attending physician's names.

After securing the surgery date with the operating room, phone hospital admissions and give them the patient's date of admission; name and address; birth date; the date for laboratory tests, history, and physical; and the surgeon's and attending physician's names.

Inform the patient about the necessary preadmission laboratory tests, x-ray studies, and the history and physical examination. Each hospital has specific rules governing when the patient needs to have these tests performed. Be familiar with these rules, and schedule the patient accordingly. Determine that the patient understands the purpose and importance of these procedures.

Schedule the history and physical examination with the attending physician's office. Make sure that the attending physician's office has all pertinent information including the time the patient will be at the hospital to have the examination performed. Explain to patients that the attending physician will perform the examination to determine that they are medically stable for the proposed surgery. As you perform each step in this scheduling process, always be sure to notate the name of each person you speak with, the date, phone number, and any information given to you.

Give the patient a detailed map and a photograph of the hospital. Make sure that the patient has thorough directions to the hospital, including

A

OFFICE NAME

PHYSICIAN'S NAME

INSTRUCTIONS FOR OUT-PATIENT SURGERY

HOSPITAL NAME
ADDRESS
PHONE

PATIENT NAME ______________________________

DATE OF LAB WORK ______________ TIME ______________

DATE OF SURGERY ______________ TIME ______________

Do not eat or drink ANYTHING within (8) hours prior to reporting for your lab work.

You must have your lab work done (2) two days prior to your scheduled surgery, between the hours of ________

You will need to report to the hospital at __(time)__ on __(date)__ for surgery.

Please remember to supply all insurance information to the office and the hospital prior to your surgery.

If you have any problems or questions, please contact ______________ at our office (phone number).

B

OFFICE NAME

PHYSICIAN'S NAME

INSTRUCTIONS FOR IN-PATIENT SURGERY

HOSPITAL NAME
ADDRESS
PHONE

PATIENT NAME ______________________________

DATE OF ADMISSION ______________ TIME ______________

DATE OF SURGERY ______________ TIME ______________

________ You are to be admitted as an "AM Admit" (the same day as surgery). Please go to the hospital at __(time)__ on __(day)__ for your lab tests and history & physical exam.

REMEMBER TO NOT EAT OR DRINK ANYTHING AFTER MIDNIGHT THE NIGHT BEFORE YOUR SCHEDULED SURGERY.

________ You are to be admitted to the hospital as an "In-patient" prior to your surgery. Please go to the hospital at __(time)__ on __(date)__ to be admitted. Your lab tests and history & physical examination will be performed the day of your admission.

Please remember to supply all insurance information to the office and the hospital prior to your surgery.

If you have any problems or questions, please contact ______________ at our office (phone number).

FIG 10–1.
A and **B,** sample written instructions for outpatient and inpatient surgery. The report dates for both the preoperative testing and the surgery are indicated on the form.

the address and telephone number. Write down the time the patient should be at the hospital for preadmission testing and for surgery (Fig 10–1,A and B). Give the specific location where the patient should report.

Make a copy of the patient's insurance card. Call the insurance company to verify coverage and benefits. Determine whether precertification and/or a second opinion is necessary, and follow up on these additional requirements.

Most offices require a surgical deposit that is due before the surgery is performed (Fig 10–2). A 20% deposit will cover most of the patient's liability, other than the deductible. Take this time to explain what the "usual and customary" charges are. Make a note of all surgery deposits as they are received.

Explain to the patient the specific restrictions for eating and drinking. Also detail any specific restrictions for the particular surgery. Reiterate the importance of following these instructions *exactly*. Give the patient written instructions, and then verbally read over these written preoperative instructions (Fig 10–3). Always be sure to leave nothing to chance. Answer all questions and explain all information in detail.

Schedule an appointment for the patient to meet with the podiatrist in the office for the presurgical consultations. At this time the patient should review the surgical consent form and sign

OFFICE NAME

PHYSICIAN

SURGERY ASSIGNMENT

(DEPOSIT)

PATIENT NAME ______________________________

DATE OF SURGERY ______________________________

SURGICAL PROCEDURES:

1. ______________________________
2. ______________________________
3. ______________________________
4. ______________________________

APPROXIMATE SURGICAL FEE ______________________________

20% DUE BEFORE SURGERY IS PERFORMED ______________________________

10% DUE BEFORE SURGERY IS PERFORMED (MEDICARE) ______________________________

I UNDERSTAND THAT I AM RESPONSIBLE FOR ALL CHARGES FOR SERVICES RENDERED TO ME BY Physician's Name AND I AGREE TO PAY ALL OUTSTANDING BALANCES NOT COVERED BY MY INSURANCE CARRIER.

____

SIGNATURE (INSURED OR AUTHORIZED PERSON)

____

WITNESS (YOUR OFFICE)

PHYSICIAN NAME

FIG 10–2.
Each patient should sign a surgical deposit form prior to the surgery.

OFFICE NAME

PHYSICIAN

Please read the following instructions carefully. Ask questions about any instructions that you do not understand or need clarified.

______ 1. Notify your physician of any cuts, scrapes, or infected areas that develop on your foot or leg the week prior to surgery.

______ 2. Do not eat or drink ANYTHING after midnight the night before your scheduled surgery. Do not drink coffee the morning of surgery: not even toast is permissible. You must have an absolutely empty stomach unless otherwise directed by your physician.

______ 3. Do not cut your toenails the night before surgery.

______ 4. Notify your physician if you develop any signs or symptoms of illness. The physician should be made aware of any sore throat, earache, abdominal illness, or fever that may occur during the week before surgery.

______ 5. Discuss with your physician any plans regarding your anticipated activity following your surgery.

______ 6. Make arrangements for someone to drive you home following surgery. You will not be permitted to drive yourself.

______ 7. ____

It is important that you understand and follow these instructions. Failure to follow these instructions may result in a postponement of the surgery.

Thank you for your cooperation.

FIG 10–3.
Patients should receive preoperative instructions in both oral and written forms. Use a form similar to this to serve as written instructions.

it. Give the patient an opportunity to ask any additional questions. Make sure that the patient has your business card so that he may contact you if needed. Escort the patient to the door, and remind him to telephone with any questions or concerns that he might have.

After all arrangements have been made, mail all of the patient's information to the hospital admissions office. This information also needs to be mailed to the attending physician's office. All written information should be given to the podiatrist. Double-check to make sure that his schedule reflects the surgery.

You will perform the same steps with an out-of-town patient. This patient will usually report to the office on the day prior to the surgery. Handle all scheduling steps over the telephone, and mail the surgical forms and instructions to the patient. Make sure that you provide self-addressed envelopes, and indicate clearly which forms need to be signed and returned to the office.

When scheduling surgery, it is important to remember to make sure that the patient clearly understands all instructions. Document all conversations, keep copies of all forms on file, and maintain attention to detail. These steps will help the scheduling process run smoothly.

11

Computerization of the Podiatry Office

James L. Bouchard, D.P.M
Deborah Rogers

Computers are becoming prevalent in podiatric offices. Medical software has been designed specifically to help a practice operate more efficiently. Many office functions can be performed quickly and accurately with the aid of a computer and specific software.

The staff of most computerized podiatry offices will agree that a computer can make your office more efficient (Fig 11–1). One of the essential elements in a successful podiatric practice is a well-organized and efficient office. Computers have the main advantage of storing large amounts of information such as correspondence, insurance, billing, practice analysis, and record keeping in a small, readily accessible area (Fig 11–2). However, a computer is not a cure-all for the podiatry office that is disorganized and inefficient. It is essential that a highly motivated, well-trained, and efficient office staff be maintained.

DO YOU NEED A COMPUTER?

There are many factors that determine whether or not a computer system will be advantageous for your particular office. Warning signs that computerization of your office may increase efficiency are that insurance work is behind schedule, collections are behind, statements are not being sent out on a regular basis, too much time is being spent on paperwork, office expenses are increasing, offices are in more than one location or have multiple doctors, practice analysis and statistical information regarding the practice are not available, office storage is a problem, or the practice lacks demographic and statistical information.[1]

Cost-effectiveness is another important factor in considering whether or not to computerize your office. The cost of the hardware itself is only a small portion of the initial investment in computerizing the medical office. Hardware refers to the computer, keyboard, monitor, and printer (Fig 11–3,A and B). In addition to the costs of the hardware, there are many other expenses that will be incurred including software (the programs that run the computer), maintenance agreements and extended warranties, training of staff and support, and paper and supplies.

Computerization of the average podiatry office can range from several thousand dollars to $50,000 or $60,000 depending upon the number and type of hardware and software and the specific needs of the individual office (Fig 11–4).

FIG 11–1.
A computer is not a cure-all for the disorganized and inefficient office.

There are several alternatives to directly purchasing a computerized system for the office. One major alternative is to lease the equipment, which could spread the payments out over a period of years. Another alternative to purchasing or leasing

FIG 11–2.
Computers store large amounts of information necessary for completing day-to-day routine and repetitive tasks in the podiatry office.

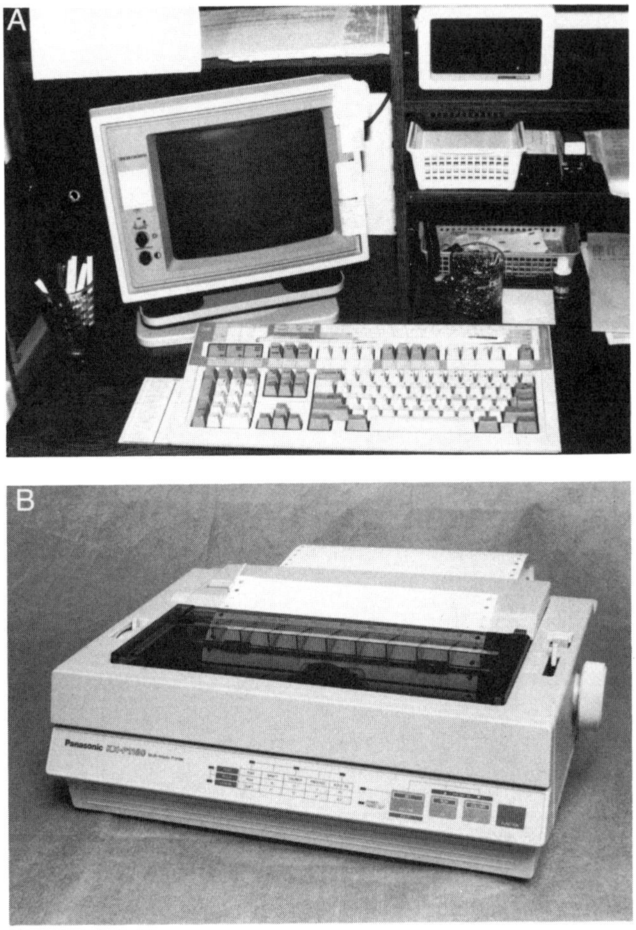

FIG 11–3.
A, computer hardware may consist of the computer, keyboard, and monitor. **B,** this typical printer is also considered to be part of the computer hardware. More recently, higher-quality printers such as a laser printer are available.

is to use one of the various computer service bureaus. These bureaus handle processing of office information by contract, usually on a monthly fee basis depending on the amount of time the user utilizes the service. There are many advantages and disadvantages to purchasing, leasing, or utilizing service bureaus. The needs of each office vary greatly and must be evaluated on an individual basis.

In the final analysis, it should be determined whether the computer will increase office efficiency and office revenues. In general, most practices that have effectively computerized their offices agree that productivity is increased, expenses are reduced, and accounts receivable and collections are improved simply because day-to-day routine functions are readily managed with a computer system. The computer can provide more information in a relatively short period of time

FIG 11–4.
Software is a term that refers to the specific programs that run the computer. They vary in price according to their capabilities.

and assist in making decisions for planning and development of the podiatry practice.

HOW DO YOU COMPUTERIZE THE PODIATRY OFFICE?

Once the decision has been made to computerize the podiatry office, a lot of time, effort, and research will be necessary in choosing the right computer system to meet your present office needs. It is not unusual when computerizing the office to observe anxiety and resistance to change from the staff. This is particularly true when dealing with computers because of the often-confusing computer language and new terminology (Fig 11–5).

One of the best ways to avoid this confusion is to assign one member of the staff who has leadership abilities to be a computer administrator. The major function of the computer administrator is to obtain as much information and research about hardware, software, and various computer consultants in order to assist in computerizing the office.

One of the preliminary steps in selecting a computerized system for the office is to investigate and consult with various computer representatives. Most sales representatives are willing to demonstrate the actual software and hardware in your office with hands-on experience. This is an excellent method for reviewing and selecting the computer software and hardware best suited to your individual office needs. It is essential for the individuals who will be working on the computer to be at these meetings to get a basic understanding of computers as well as the applications of computer software.

Another possible avenue to consider when computerizing the podiatry office is to hire a computer consultant to analyze your practice needs. A consultant can be a valuable asset; however, he can also be costly.

Another effective method to investigate computerization of the podiatry office is to discuss and visit with another podiatry office that has already been computerized. The computer administrator can determine the pros and cons of a particular

FIG 11–5.
Computer terminology and computer language may be confusing to the first-time user.

system as it is actually being used in an office setting. One of the best recommendations for software and hardware is word of mouth or a personal recommendation by an office.

It is very important to work with a reputable software and computer representative who is sensitive to your specific office needs and willing to take the time to answer your questions. If your office is working with a representative who is reluctant or unable to answer your specific questions, then you should be very cautious and skeptical about his service. Choose a computer representative you can comfortably work with during the necessary installation and training sessions.

It is important to train at least two employees in each office to operate the computer in the event of employee illness or absence. This will ensure that there is always an employee available to perform the day-to-day functions in the office or train others without any loss of continuity in patient care.

SOFTWARE FOR THE PODIATRIC OFFICE

Today, most of a practice's computerization is concentrated on patient billing, insurance billing, and accounts receivable. Most software can prepare the bills, keep track of outstanding claims, and produce aged accounts receivable reports, but that is just the beginning. There are many software programs that can be selected to assist with many areas of the practice.

Billing

Insurance billing is tedious. Computers automate insurance and patient billing, thus resulting in more accurate bills and faster payment. Most systems can accommodate multiple fee and treatment codes. This means that the computer will print the appropriate code and fee depending on what insurance company is being billed. The advantage of a computer is that information need only be entered once. For example, when a charge is entered for a particular treatment, the computer puts it on the daysheet, on the patient's ledger card, on an insurance form or patient bill, and on the accounts receivable report. Treatment and diagnosis codes and their associated descriptions and fees need only be typed into the computer one time. After a patient is treated, you need only type in the treatment code, and the description and fee come up on the screen.

Word Processing

Word processing software enables the office to turn out all typed materials much faster and more accurately than with conventional typing. Word processing is great for handling routine correspondence to patients and referring doctors as well as lengthy operative reports and patient instructions. Once a document is typed and saved on the computer, it takes only a few seconds to change pertinent information such as names and dates and then print a new copy. It allows for easy correction of mistakes without having to retype the entire page. Many word processing software packages have advanced editing features such as a spelling and grammatical checker and a thesaurus. These features allow you to quickly produce error-free documents.

Most word processing packages include mail merge capabilities. This feature takes names and addresses from a specified list and merges them with a pretyped letter. You can then print a letter that is personally addressed.

Software also exists to allow you to use your computer to assist in creating progress notes. Several products use a bar code chart and an optical scanner to quickly compile accurate treatment notes. Bar codes, similar to what you see at the grocery store, correspond to words and phrases that you commonly use when writing progress notes. At your convenience, you download the stored information from the hand-held scanner into your computer. The result is a clear, concise printout for your file.

Marketing

The computer can help in marketing the practice by enhancing communications with patients. When a patient is referred to your office, it is critical that the referring person be recognized. New patient information sheets should request information about where the patient heard about the practice. This should be put into the computer with the usual patient information to be analyzed. A computer makes it simple to track referrals over a long period of time. You can then utilize the computer's word processing capabilities to send a note to the referral source, whether it is a patient or a referring physician.

The mail merge capability of the computer can be used to send mass mailings to patients. You can use the computer to send a "welcome to the practice" letter to all new patients, send a follow-up letter to all postoperative patients, send a letter to all patients who received orthotics to remind them to come in for a follow-up visit, recall routine foot care patients with chronic foot conditions, or send birthday or holiday cards. The mail merge capability can also be used to conduct direct mail campaigns informing the public about the field of podiatry and your particular practice.

Another marketing-related use for your computer is patient education. A practice newsletter can educate patients about podiatry and keep them notified of developments in your practice. There are many publishing software packages available to choose from.

Before you can implement a successful marketing program, it is necessary to know who your patients are by detailing their address, age, sex, and place of employment. Letting your computer easily sort this information will assist you in your marketing efforts. If the computer tells you that 25% of your patients live in a certain zip code, you may want to advertise specifically in that geographic area. If 10% or your patients are employed by a nearby company, you may want to implement a promotional campaign to employees of that company.

Reports

Once stored in the computer, data can be sorted and summarized in unlimited reports. Most computer systems can churn out many different practice and financial management reports that would be very time-consuming to generate by hand. A referral report will tell you who referred your patients to the practice. An accounts receivable report tells you who owes money to the practice and how overdue it is.

Some software systems allow you to design custom reports. With these systems, you can pull information from your patient files and analyze it in a report or on a graph. You could graph how many procedures you did each month this year as compared with the same months last year. You can mix and match different information and print it in a report or on a graph.

The data included in these reports are valuable only if they are put to use. Many practices generate these reports but never use the information. These reports can assist in making practice management decisions. For example, based on productivity reports, decisions can be made regarding the accuracy of practice fees, the purchase of additional equipment, and the need for additional staff.

Appointment Scheduling

Appointment scheduling software is being used in many podiatric offices. However, if you use the computer for appointment scheduling, you must have either a multiuser computer system or a separate computer used only for appointment scheduling. The frequent need to book appointments would interrupt other computer functions. There are two primary advantages in automating your scheduling system. The first is automated appointment reminders. When making patient appointments, you can indicate whether a reminder needs to be sent. At the appropriate time, the computer can print out reminder letters or cards and in some cases, mailing labels. Another advantage to automating your patient scheduling system is instant access to appointment information. If a patient calls the office but cannot recall exactly when her appointment is, someone must take the time to go through the appointment book page by page to find the specific patient's name. With automated scheduling, you only need to type in the patient's name, and the appointment date and time will appear on the screen.

Accounts Payable

Many practices choose to computerize their accounts payable and check writing. This type of software can save time and money and provide organized financial records. They may include accounts payable, general ledger, payroll, check writing, deposit slips, and W2s.

Accounts payable software can assist with monthly financial work. It can memorize regular bills so that at the touch of a button all of the routine checks can be entered into the check register, printed, and addressed for mailing in a window envelope. All checks can be categorized, thereby giving you informative reports such as income and expenses by category. You can get detailed reports such as profit and loss statements, balance sheets, as well as reports organized and subtotaled by category, payee, and time period.

Telecommunications

The word "telecommunications" refers to a system in which the computer can communicate with other computers over conventional telephone lines. If your computer has telecommunications hardware and software, it can receive or send information over telephone lines. To have communications capabilities, your computer system must include a piece of hardware called a modem. The modem translates computer data into sound so that it can be transmitted over telephone lines. At the receiving end, another modem receives and converts the sound back into information that can be accepted by that computer.

In addition to modems, you will need software to communicate with other computers over telephone lines. The software you use depends on the type of communication taking place.

A common use for telecommunications in a doctor's office is electronic claims submission (ECS). ECS gives you "paperless claims," or the ability to send your insurance claims over telephone lines to insurance companies instead of sending in forms. By sending the claim directly to the insurance company, the office no longer needs to prepare a form, mail it, and have it received by the insurance company and manually entered into their computer. In this way, claims are paid quicker, and the possibility of error is reduced.

On-line data bases are another use of telecommunications. On-line services provide access to libraries of information. There are hundreds of online services that provide information on thousands of topics such as current information on medical research and articles and current financial information, including stock and bond prices and articles from the *Wall Street Journal.*

Many hospitals are now offering the ability to access information in their computers. It allows physicians to receive and evaluate patient changes. This provides a way to easily monitor patients without being at the hospital. In addition, a physician can send information to the hospital to order changes in the care his patient is receiving. Through the computer a physician can send directions to a screen at the nurses' stations or to the hospital pharmacy.

Two or more offices can communicate with each other by using telecommunications. In this way, information from two offices can be entered into one computer system to provide consolidated reports and centralized record keeping. Many people also access their office computers from computers in their homes. This allows for quick access to patient information at all hours.

Inventory

Inventory software helps you track product usage and costs and maintain inventory at optimal levels. This type of software can tell you when you are running low on supplies and help determine which vendor offers the best prices by keeping track of your vendors and past orders.

Clinical Information

Although computers have been in use for several years in the business office, they are only beginning to be used in the treatment rooms. One example of such a program for podiatry is computerized gait analysis.

Other programs exist such as drug interaction software. In addition, computers are being used more and more in the design of orthotics to treat biomechanical abnormalities. Software is being developed that graphically simulates various surgical procedures. Practices will be able to print the stages of a procedure and give those printouts to patients. The patient will also be able to see what the foot will look like before and after surgery.

Most offices that computerize admit that in the initial phases there is an additional work load in the learning of routine tasks. However, once the initial learning period is over, many offices have noticed an increase in their patient volume as well as an increase in their accounts receivable, simply from more efficiency in the office by using a computer. In the long run, most offices agree that the computer has saved time and saved adding additional personnel for these routine and repetitive tasks.

In today's complicated health care delivery system, an increasing amount of repetitive tasks must be performed. The computer, with the appropriate software program, can readily make these tasks easier to perform.

REFERENCES

1. Sellars D: *Computerizing Your Medical Office: A Guide for Physicians and Their Staffs.* Oradell, NJ, Medical Economics Co, 1983.

ADDITIONAL READING

Cain T, Cain NW: *Hard Disk Management for the IPB, PC, XT, AT and Compatible Systems.* New York, Prentice-Hall International Inc, 1986.

Foster DL: *The Addison-Wesley Book of IBM Software 1985*. Reading, Mass, Addison-Wesley Publishing Co, 1985.

Graham LJ, Field T: *Your IBM PC, A Guide to the IBM PC (DOS 2,0) and XT*. Berkeley, Calif, Osborne/McGraw-Hill, 1984.

Kiplinger Washington Letter Staff: *Kiplinger Forecasts: The New American Boom,* Washington, DC, Kiplinger Washington Editors Inc, 1986.

Krumm R: *Getting the Most From Utilities on the IBM PC: Perfecting the System Environment.* New York, Prentice-Hall International Inc, 1987.

Norton P: *Inside the IBM PC.* New York, Prentice-Hall International Inc, 1986.

Norton P: *PC DOS Introduction to High-Performance Computing.* New York, Prentice-Hall International Inc, 1985.

12

Third-Party Insurance: Coding, Billing, and Payment

Harry Goldsmith, D.P.M.

I. Insurance Types
  A. Indemnity Health Care Insurance (Private Insurance)
    1. Identification Cards
    2. Submission of Claims
    3. Appeals
  B. Medicare
    1. Benefits
    2. General Foot Treatment Considerations Under Medicare
      a. Routine Foot Care
      b. Treatment of Flatfoot (Pes Planus)
      c. Treatment of Chronic Subluxation of the Foot
      d. Foot Supportive Devices
      e. Nursing Home Visits
    3. Identification Cards
    4. Submission of Claims
    5. Payment Determinations
    6. Appeals
  C. Medicaid
    1. Eligibility
    2. Benefits
    3. Identification Cards
    4. Submission of Claims
    5. Appeals
  D. Medicare-Medicaid (Medi-Medi)
  E. Workmen's Compensation
    1. Fees
    2. Appeals
  F. Civilian Health and Medical Program of the Uniformed Services (CHAMPUS)
    1. Eligibility
    2. Benefits
    3. Nonbenefits
    4. CHAMPUS Identification Card
    5. Nonavailability Statement (DD Form 1251)
    6. Submission of Claims
    7. Appeals
    8. CHAMPUS and Other Insurance/Programs
II. Getting Paid for Your Services
  A. Reimbursement and Fees
  B. Relative-Value Studies and Fees
  C. Current Procedural Terminology and Coding
    1. Levels of Service
    2. Modifiers
    3. Consultations
    4. Unlisted Procedures
    5. Supply Coding
III. Diagnostic Coding of *The International Classification of Diseases.* Ninth Revision
  A. Developing a Systematic Approach to Billing
    1. Superbill
    2. The Universal Claim Form (HCFA 1500)
    3. Basic Steps for Reimbursement Management
  B. Helpful Hints for Getting Paid for Your Services
IV. Summary

Health insurance is a means of financial protection against the costs of sickness. Over the last several decades, payment and reimbursement issues, unfortunately, have moved to center stage, sharply having an impact on all concerned—the public, the health professional/institution, and the third-party payer. Changing rules and regulations coupled with preconditions and limitations of policy benefits from the insurance industry have shifted the position of the medical practitioner from patient benefactor and healer to a health care commodity. No matter how the medical profession may view itself within the economic health care system, the intrusion of a third party, i.e., the insurance industry, is having irreversible effects on medical practice.[1] As more of the population depends on some type of insurance system to protect their financial well-being from the tremendous costs associated with medical care, physicians will have to learn to adapt medical care and business practices to meet the challenges of the insurance industry. One of the first steps toward meeting this challenge is an understanding of the types of health care systems and coverage available.

INSURANCE TYPES

Indemnity Health Care Insurance (Private Insurance)

Most physician offices are familiar with indemnity-type insurance coverage. This type of coverage indemnifies, or insures, the beneficiary (the person insured to receive the benefits of the policy) against medical costs incurred due to illness, disease, or injury. Most indemnity-type plans cover only a portion of the medical expenses billed. The benefit package and limitations vary depending on the policy and the individual insurance company. The rule of thumb on indemnity plan benefits is that the greater the benefits, the higher the premium costs; conversely, the lower the premium costs, the poorer the benefit package. The insurance industry is not in business to lose money.

As a means of controlling costs and to deter unnecessary use of the beneficiary's health insurance, most indemnity plans include financial disincentives. Two of the most common are deductibles and copayments.

The deductible is that amount that must be paid by the beneficiary before the insurance benefits go into effect. Deductibles must generally be met on an annual basis. The type of deductible and amounts are dependent on the specific plan purchased. Deductibles can be individual, in which each beneficiary must meet the amount, or they can be a family type, which requires a limited number of family members to meet the deductible amounts, after which the policy requirements are satisfied for the entire family for the specific year. Some insurance policies allow for a "deductible carryover," that allows the insured to apply some or all of the deductible expenses incurred in the last 3 months of a year to deductibles of the following year.

An insurance copayment is that portion of the covered medical expense that is the responsibility of the insured. This share of cost is based on a percentage of the amount approved by the insurance company. Insurance policies are written with the expectation that payment of the copayment is the responsibility of the beneficiary.

The premium costs of an insurance policy can vary depending on the amount of deductible and the percentage of copayment. Assuming that the policy benefits remain constant, the premium dollars can be reduced by requesting a policy with a higher beneficiary deductible and/or high copayment obligations.

Over the years, private health plans have evolved three major benefit types from which they can more accurately control and limit their financial risks. These benefit plans include indemnity-type plans, service-type plans, and direct-type plans.

Indemnity type plans reimburse the subscriber for medical expenses incurred. This plan was described previously and is commonly known as a private or fee-for-service plan. Indemnity plans have the least direct or indirect involvement or control by the third-party payer because technically the submission of the claim for reimbursement is the responsibility of the beneficiary. The control of the third-party payer over the medical provider is essentially nonexistent. If the physician accepts assignment of benefits, the control or involvement of the insurer increases.

Service-type plans guarantee payment for services directly to the provider or hospital, often covering the beneficiary's bill in full. This is a preferred provider organization (PPO). The medical provider contracts with an administrating body agreeing to preaccepted rules, regulations, and reimbursement levels when seeing contracted beneficiaries. Service plans have more involvement and control by the third-party payer than the indemnity-type plan does. In the service-type plan, the medical provider receives benefits directly from the insurer as per contract agreement. The service-type plan is dependent on the provider's willingness to accept a reduced reimbursement level and increased utilization controls in return for potential increased beneficiaries and reasonably fast payment turnaround.

The PPO is a benefit-type plan that provides health care through a panel of contracted private health care providers. These providers have agreed to provide medical coverage to the subscribed beneficiaries through employers or unions at a discounted or reduced fee level. Most PPO contracts allow a dual option to the beneficiary. They may go to the medical provider of their choice (not a PPO-contracted provider), and the contract pays as an indemnity-type plan. The beneficiary has a deductible, copayment, and limitations in contract benefits. On the other hand, the beneficiaries may utilize contracted PPO providers, which minimizes the financial obligations of the beneficiary and eliminates or greatly reduces deductible and copayment requirements.[2]

Direct-type plans contract health services and coverage to the beneficiary by a medical group or organization that in return agrees to accept prepayment amounts generally on a monthly basis for each subscriber beneficiary on the plan. An example of this type plan is the health maintenance organization (HMO). This organization provides the doctors and facilities (i.e., hospitals) that administratively enroll the beneficiaries. Because the costs of medical care can be controlled by the providing organization at a much higher level of involvement than in either the indemnity- or service-type plans, the costs of the care and associated risks can be actively controlled throughout the organizational level: staffing, scheduling, specialists available, responsibility variations among the primary-care physicians, utilization controls, bonus incentives, and so forth.[1]

HMOs are divided into four subtypes: a prepaid group practice model, a staff model, an independent practice association (IPA) model, and a network HMO model.

In the prepaid group practice model, the medical providers are hired by and are part of an independent medical group, which in turn contracts with the health plan. In the staff model, the medical providers are hired directly by the health plan and paid a salary for their services.

By contrast, in the IPA model, the medical providers are not hired or paid a salary for their services, but instead they are paid fees for the services performed out of a fund created by the subscriber's premiums. These subscriber's premiums are collected by an overseeing body or organization under this prepaid health plan. Providers are under contract and generally see patients in their individual office settings. There may be risk-sharing incentives created for the providers in an IPA to keep the costs of care down.

The fourth type of HMO, the network HMO model, has two or more medical group practices contracted to provide health care services.[2]

Identification Cards

Regardless of the insurance type, each patient should be issued some type of identification card or form that may be used by the doctor's office to aid the patient in reimbursement of money for medical services rendered. A copy of the card or form (both front and back side) should be readily accessible in the patient's financial record. Verification of coverage, eligibility, and restrictions are generally imprinted on the cards along with a contact address or telephone number. If the patient does not have any identifying material from the insurance carrier that verifies coverage, the doctor's office must assume that no medical insurance coverage exists, and payment should be demanded at the time of service. Internal office policy should determine whether a refund should be issued upon presentation of an identification card at a later date.

Submission of Claims

Unfortunately, because of the broadness of policy rules and regulation variations among insurance carriers, an investigation of requirements for claims submission for each third-party payer should be done to determine whether a standard office claims submission policy applies or whether special forms, electronic billing, or report attachments are necessary or excluded. Most offices that submit claims for their patients use the universal claim form with or without superbill attachment to bill insurance carriers unless otherwise instructed.

Appeals

Anytime there is a disputed or questioned claim payment received, appeals of the decision should be considered. This is not to imply that a standard office policy to appeal all claims not meeting expected reimbursement levels should be done. It does, however, mean that if an explanation of benefits (EOB) does not accompany a questioned payment, the wording on the EOB attempts to justify a reduction in payment without any basis of fact (i.e., denial of one of two bunionectomies with the explanation that the second procedure was not paid because it was done through the same incision as the first), service procedure coding was incorrectly changed (note: be sure that the replaced code in fact does not truly and accurately reflect the service based on the information sent), and a singular bulk payment was made without coding allowance breakdowns, then an appeal should be considered.

Appeals should be initially sent to the claims supervisor in the form of a letter accompanied by copies of all necessary documentation and communication. The letter should be professional and to the point. Appeal letters may include corrected billing with explanations. Always end an appeal letter with the desire to hear from the corresponding party "in the near future," and follow up if no response is received in 3 weeks. If the "response" is another EOB without answering the questions you have raised in your appeal, another letter or telephone call should be generated to the claims supervisor. If a letter of explanation is received but it does not satisfy your concerns on how the claim was adjudicated, request peer review (podiatric consultant), and resubmit all pertinent copies of material and correspondence to the medical review department of the insurance carrier. If the responses are still unsatisfactory, you may wish to refer your complaint to your state podiatric medical society's peer review committee or the state insurance commission's office. Always keep in mind that unless you have signed a contract with the third-party payer to limit your approaching the patient for the balance of the bill, the patient is ultimately responsible for payment of this balance or for nonbenefit services.

Medicare

Medicare is a federally sponsored health insurance program that was signed into law in 1965 after years of debate. The Medicare program was established for specific categories of people. (Table 12–1).

Benefits

Medicare, run by the Health Care Financing Administration (HCFA), is actually divided into two programs, Part A and Part B.[2] Medicare Part A is the hospital benefits portion, while Medicare Part B is the supplementary medical insurance benefit, which covers usual and customary physician and outpatient services. These benefits are not automatic and require eligible persons to apply to receive the benefits of Medicare.

Part A hospital benefits include a semiprivate room and meals, nursing services, intensive care/coronary care costs, blood transfusions, medications furnished within and by the hospital, x-ray/laboratory tests, medical supplies, durable medical equipment, operating/recovery room costs, as well as physical, occupational, and speech services. Skilled nursing facility and hospice benefits are essentially the same as the hospital under Part A.

Part B benefits include medical and surgical procedures, diagnostic tests and procedures necessary for treatment, x-ray and pathology services, medical supplies, transfusions of blood and blood components, as well as speech pathology services.

Podiatric medical doctors are considered physicians under the Medicare program. The limitation to foot services is universal to any specialist treating the foot. Outpatient hospital benefits include emergency room or outpatient clinic services, laboratory tests, x-ray testing, medical supplies, drugs and biologicals that cannot be self-adminis-

TABLE 12–1.
Eligibility for Medicare

1. People 65 years or older who are retired and receiving Social Security, railroad, or civil service benefits
2. Blind individuals
3. Disabled individuals who are eligible for Social Security disability benefits and qualify by being
   - A. Disabled workers of any age
   - B. Disabled widows of workers who are fully or currently insured through federal government, civil service, Social Security Administration (SSA), supplemental security income (SSI), or the Railroad Retirement Act and whose husbands qualified for benefits under one of these programs
   - C. Adults disabled before 18 years of age whose parents are eligible for or retired on Social Security benefits
4. Children and adults with end-stage renal disease

tered, and blood transfusions furnished on an outpatient basis. In addition, Medicare will pay for outpatient physical therapy, rehabilitation, and speech pathology on a limited basis; ambulance transportation when the patient would be at risk otherwise; prosthetic services and supplies; orthopedic shoes if part of a leg brace; molded or custom shoes when a significant loss of a part of the foot necessitates a special shoe; durable medical equipment; as well as home health services on a limited basis.

Nonbenefits under Medicare include routine foot care, routine physical examinations and tests associated with those examinations, eye examinations for prescribing or fitting eyeglasses, hearing examinations for prescribing or fitting hearing aids, most immunizations, and cosmetic surgery unless needed to improve the function of a malformed part of the body or injury site.

General Foot Treatment Considerations Under Medicare

Medicare guidelines for benefits and exclusions of foot care services are nondiscriminatory of the category of physician performing the service (podiatrist, osteopath, or medical doctor). Only state licensure limits can restrict services performed such as amputation.

Coverage limitations under Medicare include routine foot care, treatment of flatfoot, treatment of chronic subluxation of the foot, foot supportive devices, and nursing home visits.

Routine Foot Care.—Routine foot care is defined by Medicare to include the cutting or removal of corns or calluses, the trimming of nails (including mycotic nails), and other hygienic and preventive maintenance care such as cleaning and soaking the feet, the use of skin creams to maintain skin tone of both ambulatory or bedfast patients, and any services performed *in the absence of localized illness, injury, or symptoms* involving the foot. Such routine care is not covered by Part B of the Medicare Program whether performed by a podiatrist, doctor of medicine, or osteopath.

The Medicare program does, however, extend coverage of certain routine foot care procedures to patients with systemic conditions that result in severe circulatory compromise or areas of desensitization of the legs or feet (Table 12–2). For coverage, the patient must be under the active care of a doctor of medicine or osteopathy for certain metabolic, neurologic, and/or peripheral vascular diseases. This coverage approval is based on medical necessity, assuming that nonprofessional care would pose a hazard to such a patient. Routine foot care is subject to frequency limitations generally determined to be every 60 days. Services considered to be routine foot care when performed within 60 days of routine treatment may be denied payment under Medicare.

TABLE 12–2.
List of Systemic Conditions Recognized by Medicare in Regard to Routine Foot Care

Diabetes mellitus
Arteriosclerosis obliterans (ASO)
Occlusive peripheral arteriosclerosis
Arteriosclerosis
Buerger's disease (thromboangiitis obliterans)
Venous insufficiency
Thrombophlebitis
Arterial embolism
Vasculitis
Diabetic neuropathy
Alcoholic neuropathy
Nutritional neuropathy
Hereditary sensory radicular neuropathy
Amyloid neuropathy
Neuropathies associated with
Malabsorption syndromes
Pernicious anemia
Carcinoma
Drugs and toxins
Multiple sclerosis
Uremia
Trauma
Leprosy and neurosyphilis
Angiokeratoma corporis diffusum
Any neuromuscular spasm–related diseases such as Parkinson's disease

To prevent denial of payment, certain billing requirements must be met for routine foot care. The "Diagnosis" section of the claim form must include the *International Classifications of Disease, ninth revision* (ICD-9) code and the name of the specific qualifying systemic disease that would warrant coverage of routine foot care (Table 12–2). Nonspecific diagnosis types that categorize a multitude of entities such as "peripheral vascular disease (PVD)" or "neuropathy" would *not* meet the criteria for qualification. The name and address of the physician who is actively treating the patient's associated systemic condition *must* be included on the claim form.

Treatment of Flatfoot (Pes Planus).—The term *flatfoot* is defined as a functional, structural, or biomechanical state. The treatment of or service rendered related to a flatfoot condition is not covered. The evaluation and treatment of *symptomatic* conditions such as inflammatory states that may be present and directly or indirectly associated with the flatfoot condition are reimbursable.

Treatment of Chronic Subluxation of the Foot.—Subluxations of the foot are defined as chronic positional partial dislocations or displacements of joint surfaces, tendons, ligaments, or muscles of the foot. Nonsurgical treatment undertaken for the sole purpose of correcting a chronic subluxated structure or condition in the foot is not covered.

Reasonable/necessary diagnosis and treatment (except by the use of noncovered orthopedic shoes and/or other supportive devices, i.e., orthotics) of symptomatic conditions such as inflammatory states, injury, or infection that result from or are associated with chronic subluxation, dislocation, or displacements of foot structures are covered services. Surgical correction of a chronic subluxated, dislocated, or displaced foot structure that is an integral part of the treatment of the foot injury or is undertaken to improve or alleviate an associated symptomatic condition is a covered service.

Foot Supportive Devices.—Medicare does not reimburse for any supportive foot device whether custom-made (orthotics) or stock premade (arch supports, inserts, heel and sole lifts or elevations, or heel wedges or pads) unless those devices are attached to and are an integral part of a leg brace. Because it is rare that such supportive devices are attached to leg braces, billing for qualified devices is "by report" only. The report should include the diagnosis, the need for a leg-braced foot support, and a brief description of the device.

Services generally associated with the evaluation, development, and fabrication of biomechanical supportive devices are also not covered under the Medicare Program. These services include range-of-motion/muscle-testing/gait studies (when related to supportive device fabrication), casting or impression molds, and appliance adjustment/accommodations of such devices.

Nursing Home Visits.—Foot care treatment of Medicare beneficiaries is a covered benefit subject to the universal Medicare restrictions and limitations described previously regardless of setting. This includes the skilled nursing home or board and care. To be reimbursable, the services must qualify under Medicare as medically necessary. Routine foot care is not a covered benefit and is denied unless documentation by the podiatrist and physician supports the patient's condition of severe circulatory compromise or areas of desensitization of the legs or feet as outlined previously.

Nonroutine foot care treatment or service should be billed under its appropriate service code and should be documented both in the medical record and on the claim form to substantiate medical necessity. Initial nursing home, board and care, or other similar facility visits should be coded under the specific and appropriate current procedural terminology (CPT) code describing the initial visit. Subsequent or established visits should be coded with the specific CPT code and the addition of either the modifier -SP (when only one patient is being seen at that facility on that date of service) or the modifier -MP (when multiple patients are seen at that facility on that date of service).

Identification Cards

A copy of the red, white, and blue Medicare identification card should always be present in the patient's files. This card contains information necessary for billing and eligibility purposes. The card lists whether the beneficiary is entitled to hospital and/or medical insurance benefits as well as the effective date for each. Beneficiaries may only be eligible for one of the two parts of the Medicare benefit; therefore the doctor's office should examine the card carefully. The identification card lists the beneficiary's Medicare number followed by a letter. This letter further defines the beneficiary status (Table 12–3).

Submission of Claims

Medicare claims are submitted by using the HCFA 1500 universal claim form. Additionally, some state Medicare carriers may be equipped to handle electronic billing. Specific information is

TABLE 12–3.
Letters Appearing on a Medicare Identification Card That Define the Beneficiary Status

A = wage earner
B = husband's number with wife 62 years or older
C = widow
D = disabled child
J, K1, or J1 = special monthly benefits
MA, A with 6 digits (A 000000), WA with 6 digits, A with 9 digits (A-000-00-0000), WA with 9 digits = railroad retirees
T = uninsured and entitled only to health insurance benefits
HDA = disabled child

required on the HCFA 1500 form and is detailed in Table 12–4.

Payment Determinations

Organizations handling claims from physicians and other suppliers of services covered under Medicare Part B are called carriers or fiscal agents. Since the policies regarding payments are different for Medicare Part A and Part B, different organizations usually process the claims for each part.

Payment determination under the Medicare program is probably the most complex and confusing of any third-party administrator. At the present time and until January 1, 1992, Medicare will be using a profile system to determine the reimbursement allowances of the medical providers who have enrolled as providers under the Medicare program. Medical providers apply for and are issued Medicare provider numbers that are used in billing for services rendered to Medicare beneficiaries. Annually, Medicare reviews the previous billing patterns and fees submitted by its medical providers and determines a value for the approved charges for each covered service, procedure, and supply allowed under the program. These approved charges are based on the lowest charge of the following:

1. Customary charge.—The charge most frequently billed by each provider for each service furnished to Medicare patients in the previous calendar year.
2. Prevailing charge.—The charge amount that is high enough to cover the customary charges in three out of every four bills submitted in the previous year for each service. These amounts are limited from year to year by an economic index formula that relates doctors' fee increases to actual increases in the cost of maintaining their practices and earning levels in general.
3. Actual charge.—The charge that is submitted on the claim by the specific provider for that service.

TABLE 12–4.
Information Required on the HCFA 1500 Form

Section 1.	Patient name as it appears on the Medicare card with last name first
Section 2.	Birth date using six digits
Section 3.	Insured person's full name
Section 4.	Patient's address
Section 5.	Sex of patient
Section 6.	Medicare number as it appears on the ID card
Section 7.	Check "self"
Section 8.	If the patient or spouse is age 65 through 69 years, employed, and covered under another health plan, check the box
Section 9.	Place information about additional health coverage
Section 10A and B	Check appropriate information
Section 12.	Patient's signatures are required on all claims other than Medi-Medi, although "signature on file" statements may be accepted by some carriers
Section 19.	Complete information for referrals
Section 20.	Complete only when service is the result of or subsequent to a related hospitalization
Section 21.	List name and address where services rendered if not in either the physician's office or the patient's home. Also this section is where the declaration of denial of use of outside services for testings and therapy is placed. A wording example is "no outside services were rendered"
Section 22.	If outside laboratory services were charged by the physician, this section must be completed
Section 23.	List relevant diagnoses by the most complete ICD-9 coding available, with the symptomatic diagnosis primary. It is recommended that a verbal description follow the ICD-9 code
Section 23B.	Enter PRO or other authorization number in this section if necessary
Section 24.	Fill in date, place of service, description of service by CPT code and verbal explanation (brief), diagnosis reference number to line item in 23, and fees per line item, and in the last column list the license number of the physician rendering the service
Section 25.	Physician's name or authorized staff person with the date
Section 26.	Assignment or nonassignment box must be checked
Section 27.	Total claim charges
Section 28.	List amount paid; if none, write "none"
Section 29.	Enter balance due
Section 30.	Enter physician's social security number
Section 31.	Complete name and address; the provider number can be placed in Section 31
Section 33.	Tax ID number should be entered if the physician is in group practice or employed by a hospital or other institution

Congress has determined that a new, more accurate system for valuing services be created. The Physician Payment Review Commission (PPRC) has accepted the Resource Based Relative Value Study (RBRVS or Harvard Study) as the basis for this new fee schedule. The old profiling determinations will be phased out when the RBRVS is scheduled for implementation in 1992.

Considerations for the development of the RBRVS were based on the need for more fairly reimbursed cognitive services (medical evaluation/diagnosis) in relation to technical service (surgical) reimbursements. The RBRVS was designed to account for specific parameters determined intrinsic to the values of medical services and procedures. Some of these factors include specialty training, practice costs, time spent, and the complexity of the service. When developed into a mathematical formula, the results confirmed suspicions that (1) cognitive services were undervalued, (2) technical services were overvalued, and (3) the relative value given to procedures and services utilizing the current Medicare fee schedule system did not relate well to the actual cost of providing those services.[3] Given the soaring costs of health care as well as the findings and enthusiasm generated by the RBRVS for potentially providing a more accurate equitable reimbursement system, the insurance industry is closely studying the RBRVS for possible adaptation into future financing methods in the private sector.

Cost containment and the ability to pay for health care led Medicare in the 1980s to develop and implement a variety of cost containment programs. To control skyrocketing hospital costs, Medicare mandated (through the Tax Equity and Fiscal Responsibility Act of 1982 [TEFRA]) reimbursement based on the final diagnosis of the hospitalized patient. With some minor variables allowed, the fees reimbursed per diagnosis were based on a national average allowance as determined by a research group. The variables included geographic location, principal and secondary diagnoses, surgical procedures, morbidity and complications, age, sex, as well as the discharge status.

In 1984, Congress developed the Medicare Participation Program. Medicare providers since that time are regularly given the option of being a participating (PAR) or nonparticipating (NON-PAR) provider. The intent of the program is to give enough incentives to participating providers to increase their numbers and thereby, reduce costs to the Medicare program. Some of the benefits for participating providers include direct payment to the provider, participating providers may increase their fees billed, claims are to be processed faster, and participating providers are listed in a directory available to Medicare beneficiaries (in theory this should increase the volume of patients seen).

Some of the disadvantages of being a participating provider include the fact that the provider must accept assignment on every Medicare patient and the provider must submit the claim forms for the patient.

The nonparticipating provider advantages include having the ability to collect the difference between the allowed amount and the maximum allowable actual charge (MAAC). The nonparticipating provider also has the choice of whether to accept or not accept assignment on a per claim basis.

The disadvantages for nonparticipating providers include the high probability that the provider will need two fee schedules—one for non-Medicare patients and one for Medicare patients—that would be consistent with MAAC limits. In cases of nonacceptance of assignment, the payment would be sent to the patient. The processing time for nonparticipating providers is higher than for participating providers, and patients must be notified officially when elective surgical charges exceed $500.00 and no assignment is taken.[3]

Medicare providers still have a choice of whether to be participating or nonparticipating providers. In the future, the nonparticipating status may be eliminated, with all providers participating under the same guidelines. As of September 1, 1990, all providers under the Medicare program whether participating or nonparticipating must submit all the claim forms generated from services rendered for the beneficiaries.

Appeals

When claim reimbursements are in dispute, the provider has a multitude of mechanisms to have the claim reviewed. Initially all information relevant to the case (copies of the claim, reports, EOB, correspondence, etc.) should be sent along with an explanation letter to the Medicare intermediary appeals department for review. Medicare does have a special form (Request for Review of Part B Medicare Claim HCFA—1964) that may be used as an option. The letter or information should be brief, to the point, and professional. Either the provider of the service or a beneficiary may request a review of the claim. If the appeal fails to satisfy the provider, the claim, whose disputed amount (may be combined with other claims) must total $100.00, may be taken to a fair hearing officer. This must be done within 6 months of the date of the appeals determination. The appeals determination letter should outline this step for you. The fair hearing officer is a neutral judge who does not specifically work for the intermediary, although he may be housed in the same facility. Complete information regarding the disputed claim should be submitted to the hearing officer so that an accurate determination may be rendered. Physicians may or may not appear in person depending on the arrangements agreed with the fair hearing officer. Once the hearing is completed, a determination will be rendered in writing from the hearing officer. If there is still dissatisfaction, the physician may request a hearing before an administrative law judge if the amount in dispute is $500.00 or more. The request for this type of hearing must be made within 60 days of the date of the fair hearing officer's determination. Additional information regarding appeals can be obtained through your Medicare intermediary.

Medicaid

The Social Security Amendments of 1965 through Title XIX established two major health assistance programs. The Medicare program, previously described, was for the elderly and disabled. The other, Medicaid (Medi-Cal in California), was for the poor. Medicaid is a welfare assistance program that is jointly administered by federal and state governments. It provides financial income and/or medical-hospital coverage for low-income families and individuals on the basis of financial needs. Medicaid is administered by each state within general guidelines set down by the federal government.[4] Coverage and benefits vary widely from state to state, with some states offering only the minimum services that are required in order to get federal funding. Other states offer expanded (in many cases substantially expanded) services that are financed by a combination of federal and state funds.

Reimbursement to doctors from the Medicaid program is generally less than the doctor's full fee. The doctor, however, has contracted when signing up for the program to agree to this fee. When a Medicaid patient is to be seen, that patient must present his valid identification card (or form) at the time of the visit. This card verifies the dates or month of eligibility. Those Medicaid patients who are unable to present a valid identification card are responsible for payment of their medical bill.

Medical providers who treat qualified and eligible Medicaid patients must accept the Medicaid allowance as payment in full. A small copayment is sometimes required from some patients. If a service is totally disallowed by Medicaid, the provider is permitted to bill the patient for that service.

Since each state designs its own Medicaid program, the benefits, procedure codes, and claim forms vary from state to state. The requirements of the various programs range from simple, itemized billing to elaborate, computerized procedures that are intended to prevent abuse of the benefits offered.[5]

Eligibility

Eligibility under the Medicaid program is restricted to the needy and low incomed. These can include the aged (64 years or older), the blind, the disabled, and members of families with dependent children who are deprived of the support of at least one parent and are financially eligible. Additionally, all cash recipients of the Aid to Families of Dependent Children (AFDC) program, certain other AFDC-related groups, most cash recipients of the Supplemental Security Income (SSI) program, and other SSI-related groups are eligible. Some states, under their general assistance programs for low-income people, have adopted a State Program of Assistance for the Medically Indigent for those who have inadequate health insurance coverage or high medical care expenses.[5]

Benefits

Although certain benefits may vary from state to state, federally mandated benefits minimally include inpatient hospital care, outpatient hospital services, laboratory and x-ray services, skilled nursing facility services, physician services (not mandated podiatric services), screening and treatment of minors under 21 years of age, immunization programs, home health care, and family planning services. State opinion services can include podiatric services, dental care, optometric services including eyeglasses and/or refractions, prescription drugs, physical therapy, prosthetic devices, psychiatric services, dermatologic services, chiropractic services, and ambulance and emergency room services.

Identification Cards

Proof of Medicaid eligibility varies from state to state. Whether a paper/plastic card or coupon book, the Medicaid identification card is usually issued monthly. Prior to receiving professional care, the current identification card must be shown to the provider. Depending on the state, a copy of the current card or a separated adhesive label must be removed from the card and attached to the submitted billing claim.

Submission of Claims

You must obtain the correct information from the patient's identification card verifying that the card is current. Medicaid claims can be submitted on the universal or HCFA 1500 form or, in states with optical scanning capability, on approved scanning forms available through the Medicaid intermediary.

Each state establishes its own time limits for the submission of claims (generally from 2 to 12 months). A claim can be rejected outright if submitted beyond the time limit, although an attempt may be made with an accompanying explanation requesting reconsideration.

Certain services may require prior authorization before a submitted claim can be considered for payment. In nonemergency situations, forms available through the state Medicaid intermediary should be submitted prior to performance of the service for authorization approval. In emergent or emergency situations, verbal authorization can be obtained *and* must be followed with submission of a written authorization request generally within 10 days of the service. Without a written authorization approval, the claim will probably be denied.

Appeals

Medicaid provides a variety of levels for appealing denied or disputed claims. A claims appeal must be filed within 90 days of the action that was the cause of the complaint (i.e., within 90 days of a receipt of payment or denial). The first level of appeals is filed with the Medicaid state intermediary. The appeal may be submitted in letter form with attached copies of the claim (corrected if necessary), an EOB from the intermediary, copies of any correspondence with the intermediary, copy of the approved treatment authorization request form, and any other relevant information that would help explain your complaint. If this appeal is not filed within 90 days of the grievous action, the appeal will probably be automatically denied.

After receipt of the first level of appeal, the fiscal intermediary will acknowledge the appeal. This generally occurs within 30 days. A determination letter supporting the appeal or denying it will follow. If the first-level appeal is not acknowledged, results are not agreed with, or the appeal is denied within 15 days of the acknowledgement, a second level of appeal can be requested from the state department that oversees the activity of the intermediary. A second level of appeal can be filed within 90 days of the date that the first-level appeal was filed. Again, all relevant material should be copied and submitted along with a clear explanation from the doctor regarding the reasons for appeal.

If the second level of appeal still does not satisfy the doctor, a third and final level of appeal may be filed with the state board of control or equivalent.

Medicare-Medicaid (Medi-Medi)

Patients who have Medicare but also qualify for Old Age Security (OAS) benefits are covered under both the Medicare program and the Medicaid program. This coverage is commonly referred to as "Medi-Medi." Under this arrangement, the Medicare benefits are considered primary, with the Medicaid program secondary. The Medicaid portion pays for denied services under Medicare, eligible services under Medicaid, as well as copayment amounts determined by Medicare. In rare circumstances when the Medicaid allowance for a service or procedure is greater than the Medicare allowance, Medicaid will pay the difference between the Medicaid allowance and the Medicare allowance. If the doctor is a contracted provider under both Medicare and Medicaid, claim assignment will automatically cross over from Medicare to Medicaid for any additional benefits. If the doctor is not a Medicaid provider or does not accept assignment, then the Medicare portion will be paid to the patient, and Medicaid will not pay its normal allowance.

Workmen's Compensation

Workmen's Compensation is a state-required insurance program that covers the medical expenses and disability benefits for workers who incur injuries or illness during the course of doing their jobs. Employers with more than a specific number of workers are required to obtain, maintain, and pay the premiums for this insurance with an authorized carrier of their own choosing. The amount of insurance required is determined by the risk involved in the employee's job. The workmen's compensation laws are state specific and vary regarding coverage, payment, reporting, and benefit waiting periods.[6]

There are five general categories of compensation benefits under workmen's compensation. They include medical treatment, temporary disability indemnity, permanent disability indemnity, rehabilitation benefits, and death benefits for survivors.

Workers may file three types of claims regarding their injuries. The first is a nondisability claim in which no work time is missed. This claim type recognizes the details of the injury and verification of medical treatment. Before an injured worker sees a doctor, his employer must authorize treatment. That can be done by telephone. Once the worker is seen and evaluated by the doctor, a report of the injury is to be completed and mailed to the insurance carrier. This claim of injury is commonly called a first report of occupational injury or illness. This "first report of injury" is generally a standard form available through medical printing and stationery companies or through workmen's compensation carriers. As the title implies, this report is filed by the doctor who is authorized to first see and treat the injured worker. Each state has a time requirement that by law must be met in filing the report. This time limit can be found out by contacting the state workmen's compensation office. If the worker after seeing the initial physician is referred to another office for a second opinion or for follow-up care, no first-report filing is necessary.

The second type of claim that a worker may file is a temporary disability claim. During the course of treatment, the worker is insured against income loss. In a temporary disability, claim is filed by the insurance adjuster who depends on the treating physician and actuarial tables to determine the amount of money that can be expected to be set aside for income loss and medical treatment. Income compensation to the injured worker is not subject to taxation. An estimate of services and procedures to be performed is generally required from the doctor and subject to approval from the insurance carrier adjuster. Even if there is no requirement, it is better to be safe and obtain the carrier's approval (get the name of the authorizing party) than to receive a denial of payment after the service was rendered. Doctors who are actively treating the injured worker have a responsibility to provide timely reports on the progress or status of the worker. These reports are initially submitted after the first 2 to 4 weeks of treatment and then on a 1- to 2-month basis as necessary. The workmen's compensation carrier/adjuster is dependent on the evaluation of the doctor to guide the payment status of the worker. Once the doctor feels that the worker's injury is stable and resolved, a final report is submitted to the carrier. A reasonable fee for each report other than the "first report" may be billed to the insurance carrier. Once the doctor releases the patient to return to work, the benefits of temporary disability end, and the adjuster can close the case.

The final type of claim is the permanent disability claim. After a significant period of time if an injured worker is unable to return to his job despite treatment under temporary disability, considerations for filing permanent disability will be undertaken. Once the treating doctor has determined that medical treatment will fail to significantly improve the medical status of the worker, a permanent and stationary (P and S) status is declared. The insurance carrier will undergo discussions and attempt a settlement with the injured worker on the basis of a permanent disability rating of the injury and losses. If it is agreed on, the settlement is called a compromise and release (C and R), with the case against the carrier closed. If the injured worker disagrees with the settlement, there are appeals processes available for the worker to improve the settlement.

Fees

Physician fee allowances for various kinds of medical care are set by the state and paid directly to the doctor by the insurance carrier. Billing codes in workmen's compensation cases are the same as generally found in the CPT manuals. Charges for services, procedures, and supplies should be itemized and clearly identified. Whenever billing for services that involve the generation of reports (i.e., x-ray films, laboratory tests, operative procedures, etc.), always attach a copy of the report with the billing. Fee schedules, claim forms, and other information can be obtained by contacting the director of workmen's compensation in the individual state.[5] Any questions regarding the care, services, or payment of claims should be directed to the assigned adjuster from the compensation insurance carrier.

Appeals

If the carrier fails to make payment of a service within a reasonable time period (45 days) following submission of the claim, the physician's office should generate a tracer letter requesting the cooperation of the carrier in reimbursement of the services unpaid. Similarly, if a payment made appears to be inconsistent with perceived reimbursement levels or the services have been denied unjustly, the doctor's office should direct a letter of appeal to the financial administrator representing the insurance carrier (they may be one entity or separate). These letters should be nonemotional and business-like and state the facts as the doctor sees them.[7]

Civilian Health and Medical Program of the Uniformed Services

Civilian Health and Medical Program of the Uniformed Services (CHAMPUS) is a government-sponsored program that provides comprehensive health care benefits for dependents of active military personnel, retired service personnel and their dependents, as well as dependents of members who died in active duty. These services are additional to health care rendered in military and Public Health Service facilities. Beneficiaries in some circumstances may go to civilian medical providers for care, with a significant share of the cost paid for by the federal government.

As with the Medicare program, there is an annual deductible that is applied before any benefits will be paid. CHAMPUS benefits may be billed either on universal claim forms or specially provided forms available through the CHAMPUS program. Patients should fill out their own forms unless there is to be an assignment of benefits.[5]

Eligibility

CHAMPUS-eligible persons must be enrolled in the Defense Enrollment Eligibility Reporting System (DEERS) computerized data base, which is used to verify beneficiary eligibility before CHAMPUS claims are paid.

Benefits

Under CHAMPUS, beneficiaries may receive medical and surgical treatment for contagious diseases and conditions as well as nervous, mental, and chronic conditions (alcoholism and certain surgeries for obesity). Prescription drugs ordered by physicians, podiatrists, or dentists and dispensed through a pharmacy are reimbursed under CHAMPUS. Ambulance service and house calls when medically necessary are additional benefits. CHAMPUS covers some organ transplants (cornea, kidney, liver, and bone marrow) with limitations. Plastic surgery is paid for in certain instances such as to restore function, correct a serious birth defect, restore a bone form after an injury, improve appearance after surgery for cancer, and breast reconstruction after a mastectomy.

Nonbenefits

Some benefits not covered under CHAMPUS include routine foot care, orthopedic shoes, and arch supports. Preventive care is also not a covered service.

CHAMPUS Identification Card

All CHAMPUS-eligible dependents 10 years and older are required to have a Uniformed Services Identification and Privilege card. Dependents under 10 years of age are not normally issued identification cards; therefore information necessary to complete their claims may be copied from either parent's card.

Non-availability Statement (DD Form 1251)

A Non-Availability Statement is required for all CHAMPUS beneficiaries who wish to receive treatment as inpatients at a civilian hospital and live within a catchment area surrounding a Uniformed Services Medical Treatment Facility (USMTF). The catchment area is defined by zip codes and is based on an area of approximately 40 miles in radius surrounding each USMTF. In order for a Non-Availability Statement to be issued, certain conditions should be present: when local conditions impose an unreasonable cost or difficulty in getting to a service medical facility, when hospitalization is required by a patient who has been receiving outpatient care from a civilian source and it is medically advisable that care continue from the civilian source for the condition, when there is no space available at the local service facility, or when the service hospital does not maintain the kind of medical facilities required.

The Non-Availability Statement should be presented to the source of care by the dependent, and this should then be attached to the claim form submitted to CHAMPUS. A Non-Availability Statement is not necessary if an emergency situation is present, if the patient lives outside the catchment area surrounding a uniformed services hospital, or if the patient is covered under another insurance plan that is the primary payer.

Submission of Claims

Always obtain the correct information from the patient's identification card. CHAMPUS claims must be billed on Form 501/HCFA 1500 (white) for professional services. A patient submitting his own claim uses Form 500 (yellow). The CHAMPUS fiscal year is from October 1 to September 30. The time limit for submitting a claim is no later than the last day of the calendar year following the year in which the services were obtained.

If the doctor agrees to accept assignment, then he agrees to accept the CHAMPUS-determined allowable or reasonable cost/charge as payment in full. Providers may choose to accept CHAMPUS assignment on a case-by-case basis. The provider then may bill the patient for his cost share (20%to 25% of these charges after the deductible has been met) and for any noncovered services or supplies but may not bill for the difference between the provider's usual charge and the allowable charge. The payment goes directly to the doctor.

If the doctor does not accept assignment, the patient completes the top portion of Form 500, attaches the doctor's itemized statement, and submits the claim himself. When the doctor does not accept assignment, the patient pays the deductible, 20% or 25% of the charges determined to be allowable, and any amount over the allowable charge.

If the patient is in an automobile accident or receives an injury that may have a third-party involvement, CHAMPUS Form 691 (Statement of Personal Injury—Possible Third-Party Liability) must be submitted with the regular claim form for cost sharing of the civilian medical care. All sections of the form should be completed by the patient.

For each claim, the claims processor issues an EOB (explanation of benefits). When the provider participates (accepts assignment), the EOB is sent to him. The patient always receives a copy of the EOB, even if the provider receives payment. The EOB details the payment of the claim. The claim identification number assigned by the claims processor should be included in any inquiry concerning payment of the claim.

Appeals

Participating providers may appeal certain decisions made by CHAMPUS. Providers who do not participate may not appeal, but CHAMPUS-eligible patients and parents or guardians of a patient under 18 years old may file appeals. Providers who do not participate may not receive any information regarding a particular claim without the signed authorization of the patient or the patient's parent or guardian. Disagreements regarding the amount allowed for a particular claim may be reviewed, upon written request, by the claims processor. Requests must be sent to the claims processor of the state in which services were provided and must be postmarked within 90 days of the date the provider receives the EOB.

An itemized statement may be attached to the CHAMPUS billing claim and should contain the following: the provider's billing letterhead (including the provider's name and address), date the services/supplies were provided, description and charge for each service/supply,[2] diagnosis or description of the condition for which treatment is being received, the number/frequency of each service, and the place of treatment. After completing the claim, send it to the fiscal intermediary in your state.

CHAMPUS and Other Insurance/Programs

By law CHAMPUS is the second payer when a beneficiary is enrolled in another health insurance program except when the other insurance is a plan administered under Title XIX of the Social Security Act (Medicaid) or coverage is specifically designed to supplement CHAMPUS benefits.[2] CHAMPUS has recently developed a pilot program known as the CHAMPUS Reform Initiative that is limited to California and Hawaii. This pilot program includes a preferred provider segment as well as an HMO. Information on this program can be received through local CHAMPUS intermediary carriers.

GETTING PAID FOR YOUR SERVICES

The development of a successful medical practice necessitates the establishment of solid control over the financial well-being of the office. Medicine can no longer be thought of as purely the art or science of healing diseases. Medicine is also a business. If this is forgotten and if the practice is not run by following basic medical office business principles, it will, at best, be inefficient or, at worst, bankrupt. Either way, the office will lose earned money. Getting paid for your services requires that a systematic approach be instituted for developing the business portion of the medical practice.

Practice reimbursement involves everyone in the office. It is essential that total agreement exist regarding the office reimbursement philosophy. The development of that philosophy begins by answering questions such as the following:

1. Will we be Medicare providers?
2. Will we be Medicaid providers?
3. Will we accept assignment on all claims? Some claims?
4. Will we be participating providers under Medicare?
5. Will we accept what insurance pays as payment in full, and is that legal in our state?
6. Will patients be required to pay their bills at time of service?
7. Will we send patients to collection for nonpayment of bills, and at what point?
8. Will we extend professional courtesy to certain patients?
9. Will we bill the insurance claims for the patient?
10. Will we participate in PPOs, IPAs, or HMOs?

Reimbursement and Fees

Reimbursement is the means by which a medical practice stays in business. Whether it is a service rendered, procedure performed, or supply dispensed, the office must develop a comprehensive listing of charges that represent the office fees for each of those services, procedures, or supplies. Those fees are unique to the practice and are developed by taking into account two general factors: overhead and profit. Guidelines that serve as examples abound. It is important to realize that individual office fees should ultimately reflect what the provider feels that his services are worth. This fee is the amount of money that is expected to be paid by the patient for the medical care that is rendered. The insurance industry is not automatically bound to accept the fees charged by providers as "reasonable." By following its own guidelines, fee allowances and reimbursement are determined. The result frequently is the reimbursement of a portion and not the entire billed amount.

There are four basic reimbursement methods used by the insurance industry. *Usual, customary, and reasonable* (UC&R) allows an insurer some latitude in determining reasonable allowances for charges submitted. The usual charge is the actual fee submitted by the provider for a procedure, service, or supply. The customary charge is an allowance for the service, procedure, or supply that is determined by the insurance company on the basis of data it may have available on similar providers in the same geographic region. The reasonable allowance is the lesser of the usual or customary charge/allowances.

Schedules of benefits are developed by the insurance carrier to list the maximum amount that plan will pay for each service, procedure, or supply. The provider's fee is not related to or affected by profiling allowances within these programs.

Maximum fee schedules are similar to schedules of benefit plans but have contracted agreements with the provider who agrees to accept the allowance as the total reimbursement. Medicaid is a good example of this type of plan.

Capitation is a reimbursement method in which the medical care is prepaid, usually on a monthly basis, to the provider who in turn provides all the contracted medical care required for the enrollees assigned to the doctor.[3]

Relative-Value Studies and Fees

In order to lend reasonable value to services and procedures represented in the various reimbursement schemes by the insurers, relative-value schedules were developed. In the early 1950s, the California Medical Association designed and published the California Relative Value Studies (CRVS), which assigned a numerical unit value for services and procedures as they related to one another. In this fashion, a brief office visit rated a lower value than a limited office visit, while an initial office visit was higher in relative value than its established office visit counterpart. Similarly in surgery, a procedure such as a permanent ingrown nail correction was given a lower unit value than a bunionectomy procedure. The assigned values were established from surveys relating existing provider fees. Over the years, the CRVS was updated and made available for purchase by providers. These relative-value studies served practitioners well as a guide to establish fees for medical care. Even though a unit value was assigned each procedure and service (which in turn was given a numeric code for identification and processing purposes), the provider ultimately was the final determinate as to the relevance of the value. When utilizing the relative-value studies, the provider would have to fix a dollar value (conversion factor) to each of the five main billing categories (medicine, anesthesia, surgery, radiology, and pathology) and then multiply that number against the assigned unit value of the code. The result is the service or procedure fee.

Many providers understood that the relative-value studies were to be used as guides, and they varied the conversion methods to suit themselves. Their fees, in essence, were individually developed. Unfortunately, the Federal Trade Commission disagreed with the idea of relative-value studies and declared them to be a variation of price fixing. Relative-value studies were ordered to discontinue assigning unit values. The Physicians' Current Procedural Terminology text, or more commonly known as the CPT, is the current offshoot of the old relative-value studies. The CPT, which is published by the American Medical Association, has no assigned unit values but acts as a universal billing guideline. It is interesting to note that relative-value studies are in fact still available in the form of state workmen's compensation schedules and in texts such as *Relative Values for Physicians* (McGraw-Hill).

Current Procedural Terminology and Coding

Without question, a need for universal coding of procedures and services was necessary to accommodate the volumes of claims processed daily by the insurance industry. Although the old relative-value studies were considered illegal, the assigned numeric coding was not. The American Medical Association, adapting the coding and descriptions available, developed the CPT in 1966. The CPT has met the challenge of providing a coding system that is both uniform and accepted by nearly every insurance company and government program. The CPT undergoes annual updating, clarification, and expansion.

Coding procedures and services when using the CPT manual is relatively simple. It is unfortunate that those providers or billers who have the greatest trouble in their billing and collections often are the same ones who have never bothered to read the CPT. While the thought of settling down to read the CPT may not be appealing, it represents what may be a pivoting factor in your business—read and understand it. It is not the intent of this chapter to duplicate the excellent material found in the CPT manual; rather the following is supplemental to the manual.

The CPT is essentially a coding manual. The service and procedure codes are listed in ascending numerical order. Like its predecessor, the CRVS, the codes within the manual are divided into five major categories: medicine, anesthesia, surgery, radiology (nuclear medicine and diagnostic ultrasound), and pathology (and laboratory). Each category is preceded by an informational guideline section. The order of coding does not necessarily correlate to ascending relative values. The importance of the coding lies in the corresponding descriptions assigned to each code. When using CPT coding, keep in mind that the single most accurate code available that pertains to the service or procedure performed is the one that is expected to be used. In surgery, this may be an operation; in medicine, an office visit or diagnostic procedure; in radiology, an x-ray film. The provider determines which codes are appropriate for all the services and procedures performed and, as needed, selects any modifiers for additional or reduced services or for extenuating circumstances. Obviously, the medical record must reflect the medical necessity for the codes and modifiers used.[3]

In a procedure-oriented section such as surgery, the code numbers represent a global fee arrangement. This is also referred to as a packaged or bundled arrangement that incorporates minor procedures found to be incidental to the major CPT-coded procedure. As an example, in the case of a hammertoe repair, code 28285, the understanding by third-party payers is that all work necessary to eliminate the hammertoe deformity falls under the 28285 code. This includes bone (such as a partial head resection or multiple ostectomies) and soft-tissue work, fixation, repair, bandaging, intraoperative injections, digital anesthesia, preoperative record preparation, *and* those services considered usual and customary for the routine follow-up care of the surgery for a period of time necessary to end treatment and discharge the patient for this problem. When using the 28285 code, third-party payers assume that the *maximum* was done to the toe to repair any deviation, contracture, or deformity. If the provider only performs the bone resection and a minimum of soft-tissue procedures (a portion of the ancillary procedures available) but is still able to correct the deformity, the 28285 coding would qualify as the coding procedure of choice. Likewise, if the provider does all the possible subprocedures available to correct the hammertoe (i.e., partial phalangeal head resection, fusion of the interphalangeal joint, metatarsal-phalangeal joint release and tenorrhaphy, and fixation), the 28285 coding would still be the only coding utilized in billing for the procedure. It is the surgeon's option to treat the deformity with whatever methods necessary. The coding definition is the "package." This package arrangement is universal and necessary to prevent the constant addition of thousands of codes, each of which would represent a modification of the original. The provider and beneficiary both profit from this system of packaging or bundling because they are reimbursed at the maximum rate even when only minimally required subprocedures to correct the deformity are performed. Unfortunately, providers tend to forget this and sometimes in their appeals feel that they were cheated when they were denied billed procedures that were in fact unbundled or fragmented from the major procedure code.

Levels of Service

The medicine section of the CPT has multiple subsections dealing with services performed in specific settings. In the office and hospital as well as skilled nursing facility settings, patient visits whether initial or established are listed in ascending order signifying increased levels of service. These levels of service (minimal, brief, limited, intermediate, extended, and comprehensive) are based on increased intensity of care, skill, effort, time, responsibility, and knowledge necessary in the treatment of the illness or condition. When billing medicine code levels, be aware that the "limited" level is the most frequently used and expected service coding level. Examination, review of history, ordering of tests as well as the adjustment of therapeutic management, discussions of findings, and basic treatment are considered to be included in the medicine coding. All other levels of service either of lower or high levels are compared with the limited level. When billing for services, it is not appropriate to use higher levels of service than the diagnosis and treatment warrant. This is an abusive practice called "upcoding." Also, the routine use of higher levels of service by the office is improper and may lead to a request for refund to the insurance company or government program. It would be better to adjust the service or procedure fee upward rather than increase the level of service coding inappropriately.

Modifiers

Recognizing that there may be exceptions to any existing code and its impact in billed fees, the CPT has a full complement of modifiers available to further clarify the billing. The more important codes are listed in Table 12–5.

Consultations

Consultations are those services rendered by the medical practitioner whose opinion is requested by another provider in further management of the patient. Consultations are generally requested in hospitals or as second opinions. The attending provider is requesting advice on the condition and care of the patient. The referral of a patient to a podiatrist's office by another physician for the treatment of a foot problem is not a consultation. Likewise, presurgical discussions with one's own patient is not a consultation as it relates to coding and billing. When treatment is rendered by the consulting doctor who then assumes the continued care of the patient for that particular problem, subsequent treatment no longer qualifies as consultation. Consultations are subject to the same definitions of levels of service as office and hospital patient visits.

TABLE 12–5.
Important Current Procedural Terminology Modifiers

-22 Unusual Services.—This modifier is used when the service performed is greater than that level usually assigned to the code. The key phrase is "greater than expected." This modifier should not be routinely used.

-51 Multiple Procedures.—This modifier identifies procedures considered secondary to the primary procedure when multiple procedures are performed at the same surgical session. This helps the insurance companies code and reimburse the primary procedure.

-52 Reduced Services.—This modifier signifies the provider's desire to demonstrate that a reduced service was performed (usually corresponding to a reduced fee). The insurer would consider the attached code number independently and not utilize the fee in any profiling scheme.

-80 Assistant Surgeon.—This modifier is added to the surgeon's billing codes to formulate a billing for the assistant surgeon's charges. The assistant surgeon then submits these modified codes to the insurer.

Unlisted Procedures

Although the CPT has over 7,000 codes and references, there are many procedures and services that may not be listed. As a consequence, "unlisted procedure" codes can be found in the CPT. These should be used only when a coding package fails to define the procedure and/or service performed. Because the unlisted code is nondescriptive, an explanation or report should accompany a billing that utilizes this code. Unlisted codes are hand reviewed and often delayed while a medical consultant determines whether there is a more appropriate alternate coding. It is recommended that providers avoid using unlisted code numbers unless absolutely necessary.

Supply Coding

The CPT essentially lists one code, 99070, to represent virtually all the supplies and materials that may be provided by the practitioner. A detailed description should accompany any billing using the 99070 coding. Medicare and some insurance carriers utilize the national HCPCS codes (Health Care Financing Administration Common Procedure Coding System) for individual supplies. These codes are not universal to all insurance companies, but they do represent a step in identifying supplies by numeric listing. This allows for ease of claims processing when dealing with supplies. HCPCS manuals may be obtained through Medicare intermediaries or purchased from private publishing houses.

The following are CPT coding hints to remember: be accurate and utilize the closest singular code that best reflects the work performed; bill the appropriate level of service performed; CPT coding within the context of the billing represents a legal entity that reflects actual services rendered and inaccurate or false coding may be considered billing fraud; never routinely use any code or modifier; the use of unlisted codes and modifiers such as -22 may delay the processing time of the claim; purchase new CPT manuals on an annual basis, and study them.

ICD-9 DIAGNOSTIC CODING

The ICD was originally published in England in the 17th century. The ninth revision is currently in use and hence the common name ICD-9. The ICD-9 is a three-volume work consisting of *Diseases Tabular List* (volume 1), *Diseases Alphabetic Index* (volume 2), and *Procedures Tabular/Alphabetic Index* (volume 3). By using the three volumes, a rapid cross-reference of information can be obtained. The ICD-9 is to diagnosis what the CPT is to procedures and services. It forms a universal language understandable by all who deal with disease identification and claims reimbursement issues.

The ICD-9 is necessarily very specific. The code numbers begin as three-digit codes that are general to the anatomic region considered. The three-digit codes are expandable with further breakdowns to a more specific four-digit subcategory and even more accurate five-digit coding. Three-digit codes should be used only when subcategories are not available.

ICD-9 coding on billing claims is required by increasing numbers of third-party payers. Medicare demands its use. Space 23 on the HCFA 1500 universal claim form is the proper location for placement of the code number. It is recommended that a brief diagnostic description be placed next to the ICD-9 code number. When listing the ICD-9 diagnoses (in cases of multiple diagnoses), keep in mind that many insurers only consider the first or possibly the first two lines of diagnosis when reimbursing services. The diagnosis that most closely represents the patient's symptomatic condition that is being treated should be on the first line, with supportive secondary diagnoses following on the list, for example,

- 726.79 Bursitis, calcaneal
- 728.71 Fasciitis, plantar
- 726.73 Calcaneal spur

The claims reviewer would consider the symptomatic diagnosis of bursitis primary and would allow injection, strapping, and physical therapy, as billed. If the calcaneal spur was primary, the claims reviewer may deny some or all the services/procedures on the basis that a calcaneal spur can be both incidental and asymptomatic.

Diagnoses that are unrelated to the medical condition being treated or related to a previous medical problem should not be listed on the billing claim. For example, it is unnecessary to list blindness, but it would be appropriate to list diabetes, which has a direct medical risk relationship to the extremities.

Remember that it is imperative that the diagnoses used in the billing be supported by the descriptions and diagnoses in the medical record.

Developing a Systematic Approach to Billing

Reimbursement management is dependent on controlling each step of the collection process from the moment the patient first enters the office until that patient's account has a zero balance. Following these steps is critical for accurate billing and proper reimbursement.[3]

Superbill

A superbill is a simple and accurate method for fee communication. The differences between a superbill and a charge slip lie in the superbill's multiple uses. While both the superbill and charge slip contain basic patient information (name, account number, date of service, etc.), the superbill has much more detail and can be considered a replacement for the attending provider's statement. It contains generated charges as they relate to the billing and diagnostic codes and doctor identification information such as name, address, social security or tax identification numbers, license number, as well as any other information that would be necessary for a third-party payer to process the claim. Most superbills are multipart forms so that one copy can be used for office accounting (ledger or computer) while the other copies can be used in insurance billing (by the office or patient) and as a receipt of service. Keep in mind that the insurance industry favors well-organized, easy-to-read superbills with sufficient data present to accurately process the claim.

The Universal Claim Form (HCFA 1500)

As third-party insurance became more commonplace during the 1950s, the need to develop a universal billing form became evident. The American Medical Association and the Health Insurance Association of America have periodically in concert and individually designed and refined various insurance claim forms. Initially, insurance carriers were reluctant to use the forms. The reason was that a single form may lack information required by the specific company. In 1975 the American Medical Association completed the development of a "universal" claim form. The government through the HCFA modified the form (called the HCFA 1500 [1-84] form). Most insurance and government programs accept the use of these universal claim forms. The uniformity of the claim design allows for ease of preparation and reviewing. Office billers should be aware that there are a small number of carriers who still insist on the provider submitting claims information on their forms.

Basic Steps for Reimbursement Management

During the initial office visit, the patient should always complete the patient information sheet and sign the assignment of benefits/release of medical record form (if it is the office policy to accept assignment). After copying the patient's insurance card and preparing the patient chart, the patient's insurance coverage should be verified by contacting the insurance company or the insured's employer. The insurance card usually has telephone numbers and coverage information printed on it to help verify the status of the policy. It is not unusual to get an occasional patient who is using an insurance card that has been terminated because the employment has ceased, premiums have not been paid, or benefits have been suspended. The timing of the verification of coverage depends on the priorities of the office and whether you are willing to chance that the coverage does not exist. The verification process is an opportunity to gain information regarding the extent of patient coverage, deductibles and copayments, exclusions, preauthorizations, second opinions, and other limitations.

Insurance coverage should be verified annually in the case of the infrequently seen patient and always prior to any scheduled surgical procedure.

After seeing and treating the patient, the provider fills out the appropriate sections of the superbill (service and/or procedure performed as well as diagnosis). The provider should also indicate the relationship of the diagnosis to service rendered so that the biller can indicate the same relationship information on the claim form. The provider should document the diagnosis and service in the medical record.

The superbill is given to the office staff responsible for collection/billing. Once all information necessary for completion of the superbill has been filled in, the patient is told the total charge for the visit as well as any balance remaining on the account. The office policy on payment is then followed (full, partial, or no payment at the time of service; acceptance of cash, check, or credit card). Once the payment is made, the patient is handed a copy of the superbill as a receipt. The patient can then use the superbill receipt in requesting reimbursement from the insurance company.

The relevant superbill information (service/procedure codes, fees, diagnosis codes, etc.) is entered into the office accounting system whether it is a ledger or computer. The biller then generates the billing claims.

Open claims and/or superbills of open claims should be filed by service date and kept in a location other than the patient medical records. This filing system allows for claims management when either the payments are received or when sorting of aged open claims is necessary.

Once payment in full is received, the open claim is removed and the payment reconciled between the claim amount and the EOB received. Payments would be posted in the ledger or on the computer. If paid in full, the account is closed. If a balance remains, the patient is billed (if there is a secondary insurance, it can be billed with a copy of the primary insurance's EOB). Partial payments are noted in the ledger/computer and on the open claims, which are then returned to the respective aging files.

If the payment received is not the amount considered by the provider to be reasonable for the service/procedure performed or if the coding submitted was altered by the third-party payer, the provider should notify the insurer by appealing the payment decision or coding alteration.

If the initial appeal is denied, a second appeal responding to the comments and conclusions of the first appeal should be submitted. This appeal should provide clarification or additional information. The second appeal should request that the information be sent to the medical review department for peer review by a consultant of the same specialty.

Remember that the patient is ultimately responsible for the account balance. The office policy may be to bill the patient when the initial EOB denial is received, thereby shifting the responsibility of the appeal process from your office. Obviously, in a contracted situation as in a PPO, HMO, or government program, the previously agreed upon regulations are to be followed regarding the appeal process, billing the patient, and benefit write-offs.

Helpful Hints for Getting Paid for Your Services

Use standard CPT coding for billing procedures and services. Avoid upcoding CPT coding, and never bill for procedures not performed.

Use the most exact ICD-9 coding available along with a brief description. List the most relevant code as primary (assume that all other codes will be ignored). Never use "rule out" to qualify the primary diagnosis on the billing claim form.

Submit neatly typed or computer-generated claims on the HCFA 1500 universal claim form (avoid handwritten claims).

When billing for surgery, tests, or laboratory work send a copy of the appropriate report with your initial billing to avoid delays or requests by the insurer for the report.

Develop a mechanism for tracking claims so that those that are 30 days postsubmission can be identified and the insurance company contacted (multiple claims for a single insurer should be batched and worked as a unit). Always note the name, telephone number called, time of the call, and comments given when contacting an insurance company.

Always verify insurance coverage during the initial visit and prior to surgery. Remember that unless the provider has contracted specifically with the PPO, HMO, or government program, the patient is ultimately the one who is responsible for the medical bill.

SUMMARY

The future holds many questions regarding the economics of health care and few answers. The influences of the health care insurance industry have altered the American way of health care delivery forever. Business survival must not be the goal of the medical office; stability through growth, efficiency, and prosperity is the target. It is essential that the medical office staff keep informed regarding the dynamic nature of third-party reimbursement. Although admittedly this is an ongoing task, the rewards are worth the effort.

REFERENCES

1. Starr P: *The Social Transformation of American Medicine.* New York, Basic Books Inc Publishers, 1982, pp 237–292.
2. Fordney MT: *Insurance Handbook for the Medical Office,* ed 3. Philadelphia, WB Saunders Co, 1989, pp 189–336.
3. Davis J: *Reimbursement Manual for the Medical Office.* Los Angeles, Practice Management Information Corp, 1990, pp 3, 43, 235–300.
4. Hogue K, Jensen C, Urban KM: *The Complete Guide*

to Health Insurance, New York, Walker & Co, 1988, p 308.
5. Farber L (ed): *Medical Economics Encyclopedia of Practice and Financial Management.* Oradell, NJ, Medical Economics Books, 1985, pp 137, 250–251.
6. American Medical Association: *Insurance Processing and Coding for the Medical Office.* Chicago, American Medical Association, 1983, p 9.
7. Hampton G: *Workers' Compensation: Mechanics of Administering Claims.* Glendale, Calif, Workers' Compensation Co, 1989.

13

Collections

Pat Burt

In any business there will be financial issues and decisions to be made. The key factor in any organization's profit will be a successful and effective collection management program or system. The lack of knowledge or general fear of not knowing the "how to" can drain the confidence of both new and experienced personnel. To help overcome this problem there are policies and systems essential to the financial success of the organization.

Work with every patient on an individual basis. Have the office and patient agree on a payment plan. Be organized at all times because this will bring the patient back to the practice for future services and may promote referrals of new patients. As an office manager concerned about escalating delinquency in the practice, you can familiarize yourself with preventive measures as well as an existing remedy action.

DELINQUENT ACCOUNTS

An account that reflects an outstanding balance with no activity (no payment credits or arrangements to pay) within 30 days is delinquent. An ineffective or incomplete patient information sheet can increase the likelihood of a delinquent account. A comprehensive and complete information sheet can be the foundation in reducing credit losses. It may be time to review and update these forms. A patient information sheet should include workmen's compensation questions (Fig 13–1), insurance information (Fig 13–2), and a promissory note. To accept an incomplete information sheet is to accept a potentially delinquent account.

Always have patients' complete home mailing addresses and telephone numbers (Fig 13–3). If they use a P.O. box, make sure that you also get a street address. Patients cannot live in their P.O. box. Be sure that the relative information is complete and different from the information listed for the patient. Request a nonrelative or friend's address and telephone number. Have a phone book available in the waiting room to assist the patient with supplying accurate information.

If you have any reason to believe that the information provided is false or inaccurate, check and verify it while the patient is waiting to be seen. This may seem time-consuming, but the time spent now will reduce effort required later.

Have the patient sign in before each visit and fill out the requested information (Fig 13–4). When scheduling new or established patients,

IF YOUR INJURY IS JOB RELATED PLEASE COMPLETE THIS SECTION/INFORMATION

Today's date ________________ WORKMAN'S COMPENSATION INJURY INFORMATION

Patient Full Name ______________________________ Home Phone (___) ________________

Date of Birth ________________ Date Of Injury ______________________________

Employer ______________________________ Work Phone (___) ________________

Employer Address ____

City ____________________ State ________________ Zip ____________________

Referred By ________________________ SS # ______________________________

Were You Treated for This Injury by Any Other Doctor? Yes ______ No ______________

If yes, Who? ________________________When? ______________________________

Describe Accident ____

____

Your Position At Work ____

ALL WORK RELATED INJURIES MUST BE AUTHORIZED BY THE EMPLOYER. WHO SHOULD WE CONTACT?

Name ______________________________ Phone (___) ________________

Company's Insurance Carrier: ____________________ Phone (___) ________________

To Whose Attention Should Bill Be Sent? ______________________________________

Supervisor's Name ____________________________ Phone (___) ________________

Date Disability Began ________________________ Where?______________________

Have You Retained An Attorney? __________ Name ______________________________

Attorney Address ____________________________ Phone (___) ________________

*********************IMPORTANT - PLEASE READ CAREFULLY *********************

If you are here for treatment due to an accident at work, be sure you have filed a report with your employer. If we are unable to verify this injury as a workman's compensation injury, you will be responsible for payment of any charges for your care.

Patient Signature ______________________________________

— —

OFFICE USE ONLY

Workman's Compensation Verified: Yes ______ No ______ By Whom? ________________

Title ____________________ Date ________________ OK To Treat ________________

Carrier ____

Carrier Address ____

File # ________________________

FIG 13–1.
Any patient with a job-related injury should complete a workman's compensation form.

MEDICAL INSURANCE INFORMATION

Medicare Number ______________ Medicaid Number ______________

Primary Insurance Co. Name ______________ Policy # ______________

Address ______________ City ________ State ______ Zip ________

Name of Person Insured ______________ Insured's SS #______________

Is This a Group Insurance Policy? ________ Group # ______________

Name of Company Insured (Employer) ______________

Secondary Insurance Co. Name ______________ Policy # ______________

Address ______________ City ________ State ______ Zip ________

Name of Person Insured ______________ Insured's SS # ______________

Is This a Group Insurance Policy? ________ Group # ______________

Name of Company Insured (Employer) ______________

CONCERNING INSURANCE

1. Patients who carry insurance should remember that professional services are rendered and charged to the patient and not to the insurance company.
2. Even though an insurance claim is filed, you will receive a statement each month if your account has a balance due. This office cannot accept responsibility for collecting your insurance claim, nor for negotiating a settlement on a disputed claim.
3. Regarding "Reasonable and Customary Charges":
   Please be aware that an insurance explanation of benefits citing "reasonable and customary charges" is a compilation of averages for a specific geographic area and does not reflect a specific fee schedule for a medical service.

I AUTHORIZE THE RELEASE OF ANY MEDICAL INFORMATION NECESSARY TO PROCESS MY INSURANCE

SIGNED ______________

I AUTHORIZE THE RELEASE OF ANY MEDICAL INFORMATION REQUESTED BY AN ATTORNEY.

SIGNED ______________

I AUTHORIZE PAYMENT DIRECTLY TO THE DOCTOR OF ANY BENEFITS DUE ME FOR SURGICAL AND/OR MEDICAL SERVICES. I UNDERSTAND THAT I AM RESPONSIBLE FOR ANY AMOUNT NOT COVERED BY INSURANCE.

SIGNED ______________

- -

IF YOU WOULD LIKE TO APPLY YOUR BALANCE TO A CHARGE ACCOUNT, PLEASE COMPLETE THE FOLLOWING:

PLEASE CHARGE THE FULL AMOUNT TO MY:

(   ) MASTERCARD   (   ) VISA   (   ) OTHER ______________

CARD NO: ______________

CARD HOLDER NAME: ______________

EXPIRATION DATE: ______________

SIGNATURE: ______________

FIG 13–2.
The medical insurance information form contains information necessary for filing claims.

Today's Date ____________________ Patient Information

Patient Full Name ________________________________ Home Phone (   ) ____________

Address ________________________________ Apt # ____________

City ____________ State ____________ Zip Code ____________

Patient Employer ________________________________ Work Phone (   ) ____________

Address ____

City ____________ State ____________ Zip Code ____________

Date of Birth ____________ Sex M F Marital Status S M D W

Social Security # ____________________

Spouse or Parent Full Name ____________________ Home Phone (   ) ____________

Address ________________________________ Apt # ____________

City ____________ State ____________ Zip Code ____________

Spouse or Parent Employer ____________________ Work Phone (   ) ____________

Address ____

City ____________ State ____________ Zip Code ____________

Emergency Contact Full Name ____________________ Relationship ____________

Address ________________________________ Apt # ____________

City ____________ State ____________ Zip Code ____________

Home Phone (   ) ________ Work Phone (   ) ____________________

Referred by (Full Name) ____________________ Phone (   ) ____________

Family Doctor ________________________________ Phone (   ) ____________

What Is Your Main Complaint ____

Date of Accident or Onset of Symptoms ________________________________

(if work-related injury please fill out workman's compensation information sheet)

PAYMENT POLICY

ALL PATIENTS ARE REQUIRED TO PAY UPON COMPLETION OF VISIT. AFTER EACH OFFICE VISIT, AN INSURANCE TICKET WILL BE GIVEN TO YOU TO FILE WITH YOUR INSURANCE COMPANY FOR REIMBURSEMENT OF YOUR FEE.

IF THE DOCTOR'S OFFICE IS FILING YOUR INSURANCE, PLEASE NOTE: AFTER 6 WEEKS IF YOUR INSURANCE COMPANY HAS NOT RESPONDED TO THE CLAIM FILED, YOU WILL BE NOTIFIED THAT THE UNPAID BALANCE IS NOW YOUR RESPONSIBILITY AND PAYABLE WITHIN 2 WEEKS OF NOTIFICATION.

I hereby acknowledge that the above information set forth is true and correct, that I have read the above payment policy, understand the contents thereof, and agree to abide by the terms set forth.

____

PATIENT or AUTHORIZED PERSON

IF SOMEONE OTHER THAN THE PATIENT IS RESPONSIBLE FOR PAYMENT PLEASE COMPLETE THIS SECTION:

Name of Responsible Party: ____________________ Relationship ____________

Address ____________________ SS # ____________

City ____________ State ____________ Zip Code ____________

OFFICE USE ONLY

Verified: Yes ______ No ______ By Whom? ____________

Date ____________ OK to treat ____________

FIG 13–3.
The patient information sheet contains essential information. Make sure that it is complete.

SIGN IN SHEET DATE: ____________________

PATIENT NAME	ADDRESS	PHONE # DAY & NIGHT	INS.,M/C, HMO

FIG 13–4.
The daily sign-in sheet should be kept on file for 1 year. It is a good tool for locating patients who move.

make sure that they are aware that payment is due at the time of service. Consumers at a department store must pay for any merchandise before leaving the building. The medical office should not expect any less. If this policy has not been required in the past, you may explain that new policies have been implemented.

Advise new patients to arrive 10 to 15 minutes before their first appointment so that information sheets can be completed. The information sheets can also be mailed to the patient prior to the appointment. This method verifies the mailing address and contributes to efficient schedule flow in the office. Established patients should be asked to update their information sheets annually.

Divorced or separated parents can present potential problems. Be aware of this situation, and be prepared to deal with it. The parent who brings a minor child in for services should be required to make payment at that time. Communicate this to the parent in advance. If she claims that the other parent is responsible for medical expenses, request a copy of this provision to have on file. Verify this information by contacting the responsible party at the time of service. Later may be too late to collect. Disputing parents can create past-due accounts that require time and attention. It is best to initially establish the responsible party and avoid any future problems.

RETURNED CHECKS

Returned check procedures are very important. The day a check is returned from the bank, the patient's account is in a delinquent state, and immediate action must be taken. Call the patient, and request that they come to the office to satisfy the returned check that day. Always request cash or a money order. The patient may prefer that the check be redeposited. There should be a nonsufficient-fund service charge added ($15.00 to $20.00). If you are not able to reach the patient, contact the nearest bank branch and inquire whether funds are available to redeposit and whether the check can be presented a second time. Remember that the patient is notified by their bank of the returned check. Therefore, they should already be aware of the situation. If the patient has failed to call about the matter, treat the account as a collection account. A sign posted in the waiting room or a paragraph included on the patient information sheet will notify patients of office policy regarding returned checks and the additional service charge that will be applied.

Have the unemployed patient sign a promissory note at the time of service (Fig 13–5). Inquire about other sources of income. Check to see whether disability or unemployment benefits are pending or available. Determine what amount can be directed toward the account on a monthly basis.

DECEASED PATIENTS

When dealing with the situation of a deceased patient, certain steps need to be taken. Determine whether there is a living spouse, and discuss what payment arrangements can be made on the ac-

PAYMENT AGREEMENT

I, ____________________________ hereby recognize that as a result of professional services rendered on ____________________ I have incurred charges in the amount of $ ____________ with
______(Doctor/Practice Name)______________________.
I hereby agree to pay the above amount. I agree to the following terms:
Monthly payments of $ ____________ by the _______ of each month. I understand that professional services are rendered and charged to the patient. Regardless of insurance coverage I may have, I am ultimately responsible for all charges to this account. I further agree that in the event of nonpayment I am responsible for any additional cost incurred for collection action, court costs, and reasonable legal fees should this be required.

Signature: ________________________ Date: ______________________________

Witness: __________________________ Date: ______________________________

Notarized: ________________________ Date: ______________________________

FIG 13–5.
A promissory note should be signed by the unemployed patient at the time of service.

count. Ask who will be handling the estate, and request the executor's name, address, and telephone number. Request that the executor provide written verification that he is aware of the existing debt and when settlement may be expected. Do not delay. You must obtain this information within 30 days because the patient's address and telephone number are of little or no practical use in your collection efforts. You may suggest that the executor sign a promissory note on behalf of the estate. Assets are not always sufficient to satisfy all outstanding obligations, and this promissory note gives the debt priority. If you are notified verbally that there is no estate, request that a family member submit a notarized statement to that effect or that an attorney handling the business affairs of the deceased submit written notification.

COLLECTION LETTERS

Patients should receive their first notice when the account reaches 30 days outstanding. Patients should receive the second notification on 60-day outstanding accounts. By now ample time has been provided for the patient to follow up with the insurance carrier and/or make arrangements on the balance. This notice should include a reminder of office policy concerning insurance filing and the patient's responsibility. Advise the patient that unpaid accounts will be forwarded to a management program for collection.

The third notification should be sent by a management service. At that time factors such as the age of the account and balance of the account would determine whether a payment schedule is advisable or payment in full is requested. This correspondence is then re-enforced with telephone contact. Updated patient information will be requested and noted at all times. If the management service determines that the outstanding account involves an insurance problem or delay, it will attempt to expedite the situation. In many instances the management service can ascertain whether there is an information error or whether additional information is required. If a practice continues to bill month after month with no patient response, have the management service handle the correspondence and telephone contact. This can be very effective. A management service places 8% of the telephone contacts in the evening hours. This is an effective collection tool available to your practice. An outside management firm allows office personnel to concentrate their efforts in other areas, which is cost and time effective.

FAIR DEBT COLLECTION PRACTICES ACT

When dealing with outstanding accounts, it is necessary to be familiar with the laws covering this area. The following information is taken from Public Law 95-109, The Fair Debt Collection Practices Act, and the Consumer Credit Protection Act.

Basic Communication With the Debtor

A debtor cannot be contacted at work if the collector knows that the debtor's employer prohibits such communication. Unless the debtor gives consent to be contacted at work or at times other than during the given time frame, a debtor may only be contacted between 8:00 A.M. and 9:00 P.M. local time at the debtor's location.

Unfair and Deceptive Practices

Interest, additional charges, or special fees cannot be added to an account and collected unless authorized by the original credit agreement or by local and state law (Section 808-1). In many cases, imposing such monetary penalties is perfectly legal. Title VIII, however, specifically forbids such practices only if they do not comply with the original credit arrangement or are not permitted by law.

Written Communications

Within 5 days of initial communication with a debtor concerning a debt, the collector must send a written notice to the debtor stating the following:

1. The amount of debt
2. The name of the creditor
3. A statement concerning the debtor's right to dispute the debt within 30 days.
4. A statement that the collector will supply account documentation to the debtor of any debts disputed within 30 days
5. A statement that upon the debtor's request, within 30 days of notification the collector will supply the name and address of the current creditor if different from the original creditor

Section 809(a)

This procedure was established to protect the right of a debtor to have a past-due account verified within a reasonable period of time. In many ways, the legislation is equally advantageous to the collector because it weeds out the accounts that may have errors.

If the initial communication with the debtor includes all of this information, a second similar notification need not be sent. If the debt has been paid within 5 days of initial contact, the written notice would be unnecessary, and there would be no legal need to provide it.

The collector must ascertain that the written correspondence has sufficient time to arrive via the mail to the debtor's location within the 5 days as required. Return mail should be checked for notices that were not delivered.

Although the debtor is given 30 days in which to question or dispute the debt, the collection process can legally continue until the account is formally disputed. If the debtor disputes the debt in writing within 30 days of written notification of the debt, the collector must forward documentation to the debtor that supports the existence and validity of the debt. All collection activity must stop until the debtor receives this written information.

Section 809(b)

The debtor's dispute could concern the entire amount or a portion of the debt. In either case, written verification of the debt containing the circumstances surrounding the debt and creditor information must be supplied to the debtor. If a legal judgement has been initiated against the debtor, copies of these documents must also be forwarded. After the collector mails this information, the collection effort may continue.

Postdated Checks

A collector will often encourage a debtor to mail a postdated check to the agency as a sign of good intentions to resolve an account. Title VIII specifically sets forth the collector's responsibilities in taking this action. If a collector accepts a check postdated by more than 5 days, the collector must notify the debtor in writing not more than 10 days nor less than 3 days prior to the date on which the check will be deposited (Section 808-2). This notification is intended to serve as a reminder to the debtor that funds must be available in the checking account to cover the postdated check.

MEDICAL DELINQUENCY MANAGEMENT PROGRAM

A medical delinquency management program is a service that provides medical practices and health professionals with complete analysis and evaluation of the accounts receivable status. The management company provides a comprehensive report on a monthly basis. The management program initiates telephone contact with a patient who has a delinquent account, establishes communication, and attempts to salvage the account by providing personalized attention. Successful management programs promote effective delinquent account programs and offer a tremendous benefit potential for the medical professional.

INSURANCE

To reduce insurance-related paperwork as much as possible, request that the patient complete his own insurance forms. Patient follow-up and cooperation may be necessary to help resolve problems or delays involving the insurance carrier. If the patient does not understand the provisions and limitations of his policy and coverage, encourage him to contact his employer or carrier for clarification.

Verify, in advance, any provisions, limitations, and requirements of the insurance coverage. In the case of surgery or second opinions, you may request a 20% prepayment to secure the patient's portion of responsibility.

Handle workmen's compensation claims as you would personal insurance coverage. Verify all pertinent information, and document the party that provides the information/authorization.

COMPUTER OR LEDGER CARD SYSTEMS

Both computer systems and ledger card systems can work in collections. Become familiar and compare what a computer system can do for the practice. It can offer much more than billing alone. Many systems offer functions and programs that can greatly enhance office efficiency and improve the work load. Computer systems print a complete accounts receivable report; a delinquency report; and Medicare, Medicaid, workmen's compensation, and HMO reports on a regular basis. It is also very important to stay current and informed regarding Medicare and Medicaid provisions and procedures, which are subject to change.

Ledger cards can work like a "mini"-computer. Devise a color code system to code the ledger cards. The coding tells you at a glance the status of any particular item. Follow-up is important. Do not let office assets "sit" on ledger cards. Always manage the accounts receivable as if they are money owed to you personally. If the practice falters financially, it affects you as an employee.

These guidelines and strategies are designed to work with your office to increase productivity, lower delinquent accounts receivable, and ensure financial health for the practice.

BIBLIOGRAPHY

Consumer Credit Protection Act Amendments and Public Law 95-109, 1986.

Fair Debt Collection Practices Act, United States Code, 1987.

14

Medical Terminology

Peggy Kane, P.M.A.C.

Medical terminology is an essential part of the podiatric medical assistant's knowledge. In order to have a working knowledge of the terminology it is important to first learn the prefixes and the suffixes.

PREFIXES AND SUFFIXES IN MEDICAL TERMINOLOGY

Prefixes	Examples
a = without	*a*chroma = without color
acro = an extremity	*acro*dermatitis = dermatitis of the extremities
an = without	*an*algesic = drug used to alleviate pain
antero = in front of	*antero*inferior = situated in front and below
bi = two	*bi*lateral = two sided or both extremities
chlor = green	*chlor*oma = a disease marked by multiple greenish growths on the periosteum of the bones of the skull
cutis = skin	sub*cutaneous* = situated or occurring beneath the skin
cryo = cold	*cryo*genic = producing low temperature
cyto = cell	*cyto*genesis = development of cells
deci = ten	*deci*gram = one tenth of a gram
derma = skin	*derma*titis = inflammation of the skin
endo (en) = within	*en*chondroma = hyperplastic growth of cartilage tissue remaining in the anterior or substance of a bone
equi = equal	*equi*librium = a state of balance between opposing forces or influences
erythro = red	*erythro*cyte = a red blood corpuscle
extra = outside	*extra*capsular = outside a capsule
fibro = fiber	*fibro*sitis = inflammation of fibrous tissue
hepta = seven	*hepta*chromic = possessing vision of all seven colors of the spectrum
hetero = different	*hetero*graft = a bone graft obtained from another person's body
hydro = water	*hydro*kinetic = relating to movement of water or other fluid, as in a whirlpool bath
hyper = more, too many	*hyper*ostosis = excessive growth of bony tissue
hypo = deficiency	*hypo*myotonia = deficient muscle tonicity
im = not	*im*mune = not susceptible to a particular disease
in = not	*in*activate = destroy activity or effects of an agent or substance.
inter = between	*inter*metatarsal space = a space between the metatarsal bones

(Continued.)

Prefixes	Examples
juxta = adjoining or situated	*juxta*-articular = situated near a joint or in a region of a joint
latero = on the side of	*latero*version = abnormal turning to one side
leuco (leuko) = white	*leuko*cyte = a colorless, ameboid cell mass such as a white blood corpuscle
macro = abnormally large	*macro*dactyly = abnormal largeness of toes or fingers
media = in the middle of	*media*stinum = septum between two parts of an organ or cavity.
melan = black	*melan*oma = a tumor or malignant growth characterized by black pigmentation
micro = small	*micro*organisms = a microscopic animal or plant, usually referring to bacteria
multi = many	*multi*articular = pertaining to many joints
myco = fungus	*myco*sis = any disease caused by fungus
narco = numbness	*narco*tic = a drug that produces sleep or stupor
neo = new	*neo*plasm = any new abnormal growth, specifically a new growth of tissue in which the growth is uncontrolled and progressive
non = not	*non*union = absence of healing of a fracture
octo = eight	*oct*ad = an element having a valency of eight
pan(t) = all	*pan*talgia = pain over the entire body
poly = many	*poly*neuritis = inflammation of many nerves
post = after	*post*operative = after surgery
postero = posterior	*postero*lateral = behind and to the outer side.
pre = before	*pre*operative = before surgery
purpur = purple	*purpur*a = a disease characterized by the formation of purple patches on the skin and the mucous membranes
pseudo = false	*pseudo*edema = a puffy state resembling edema
pyo = pus	*py*orrhea = a discharge of pus
quadri = four	*quadri*plegia = paralysis of all limbs
quint = five	*quint*uplet = one of five offspring produced at a single birth
re = again	*re*currence = the return of symptoms after a temporary absence
retro = backwards	*retro*version = the state of turning back or the tipping backward of an entire organ
sclero = hard	*sclero*derma = edematous hardening of the skin
scolio = curved	*scoli*osis = an appreciable lateral deviation in the normally straight vertical line of the spine
semi = half	*semi*flexion = the position of the limb midway between flexion and extension
sex = six	*sex*digitate = six toes
sub = below	*sub*tarsal = below the tarsus
super = more or too many	*super*numerary sesamoid = an extra sesamoid bone
supra = above or over	*supra*malleolar = situated above the malleolar
syn = union or associated	*syn*drome = a series of symptoms associated with a disease
teno (tendo) = relating to tendon	*tend*onitis = inflammation of the tendon
thrombo = clot	*thromb*osis = the formation, development, or presence of a clot within a blood vessel
trans = across	*trans*verse plane = a horizontal flat plane dividing the body into upper and lower sections
tri = three or thrice	*tri*plegia = paralysis of three extremities
uni = one	*uni*lateral = single, one-sided
vaso = vessel	*vaso*dilator = causing dilation of blood vessels
veni = vein	*veni*puncture = puncture of a vein for collection of blood specimens

(Continued.)

Suffixes	Examples
al = related to or pertaining to	dors*al* = pertaining to the back
ago = disease	lumb*ago* = an ache in the lower part of the back
algia = pain	neur*algia* = a condition of pain along the course of a nerve
blast = immature cell	fibro*blast* = any cell element from which fibers are developed
cele = hernia	arthro*cele* = a joint swelling
cide = an agent that kills	germi*cide* = an agent that destroys pathogenic microorganisms
coccus = a spherical bacteria	strepto*coccus* = a genus of microorganisms consisting of spherical or ovoid cells occurring in pairs or in short or long chains
cule = miniature	mole*cule* = a very small mass of matter
dynia = pain	osteo*dynia* = pain in the bone
emia = of the blood	ur*emia* = accumulation in the blood of substances ordinarily eliminated in the urine
er = one who performs	practition*er* = one engaged in some profession, particularly law or medicine
ectomy = cut out, excise	bunion*ectomy* = excision of a bunion
esthesia = sensation	an*esthesia* = loss of feeling or sensation
genesis = creation	chondro*genesis* = the formation of cartilage
genic = origin	neuro*genic* = occurring because of a nervous system disorder
gram = tracing a picture	radio*gram* = a picture of internal structures of the body produced by the action of x-rays
ible = able, capable of	vi*able* = alive or capable of living
ic = related to, pertaining to	necrot*ic* = pertaining to or characterized by necrosis
id = condition	rheumato*id* = condition resembling rheumatoid arthritis
igo = disease	vert*igo* = dizziness, a sensation of rotation or movement of one's self
ism = condition	alcohol*ism* = condition or state due to too much alcohol
ist = agent or person concerned	podiatr*ist* = a specialist in foot care
itis = an inflammation	burs*itis* = inflammation of a bursa
malacia = softening	osteo*malacia* = softening of the bones
ology = science, study of	path*ology* = the sum of what is known regarding diseases
oma = tumor	neur*oma* = a tumor or new growth largely made up of nerve cells and nerve fibers; a tumor growing from a nerve
osis = condition	arthr*osis* = disease or abnormal condition of a joint
ous = related to	odorifer*ous* = fragrant, emitting an order
pathy = disease	desmo*pathy* = disease of the ligaments
plegia = paralysis	hemipara*plegia* = paralysis of the lower half of one side of the body
rrhagia = excessive flow	osteo*rrhagia* = hemorrhage from bone
rrhea = profuse flow	py*orrhea* = discharge of pus
rrhexis = rupture	onycho*rrhexis* = breakage of nails
tion = condition	dysfunc*tion* = unable to function

BIOMECHANICAL OR POSITIONAL TERMINOLOGY

Abduction = away from the midline of the body (Fig 14–1) (hallux abductus = angulation of the great toe away from the midline of the body, or toward the other toes)

Adduction = toward the midline of the body (Fig 14–1) (hallux adductus = angulation of the great toe toward the midline of the body, or away from the other toes)

Adductus = drawing toward the sagittal (medial) plane or, in the digits, toward the midline of the body

Anterior = front

Distal = farthest from any point of reference

Dorsal = back or top

Dorsiflexion = sagittal plane movement of the toes or foot upward toward the front of the leg or tibia (Fig 14–2)

Everted = tilting of the foot in a frontal plane so that the plantar surface faces away from the midline of the body

Extension = straightening

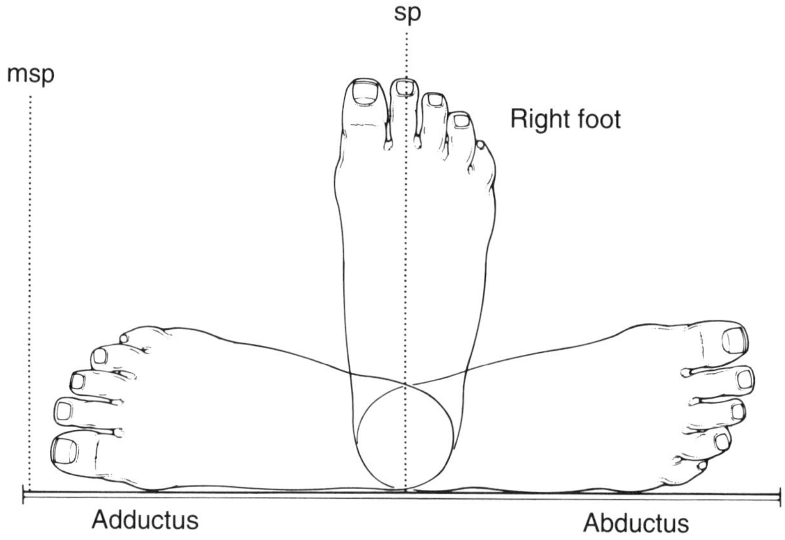

FIG 14–1.
Adductus is a structural position of a part of the foot involving movement of the part in the transverse plane only. The distal aspect of the part is angulated toward the midline of the body and away from the sagittal plane and passes through the proximal aspect of the part (*msp* = medial sagittal plane; *sp* = sagittal plane). Abductus is a structural position of a part of the foot involving movement of the part in the transverse plane only. The distal aspect of the part is deviated away from the midline of the body and away from the sagittal plane and passes through the proximal aspect of the part or away from some other specified reference point.

Flexion = bending
Frontal plane = a vertical plane passing through the body from the left side to the right side so that it is divided into front and back segments (Fig 14–3)
Genu valgum = knock-kneed due to narrow angulation at the hips
Genu varum = bowlegged due to wide angulation at the hips
Inferior = below
Inverted = tilting of the foot in the frontal plane so that the plantar surface faces toward the midline of the body
Lateral = part farther from the midline

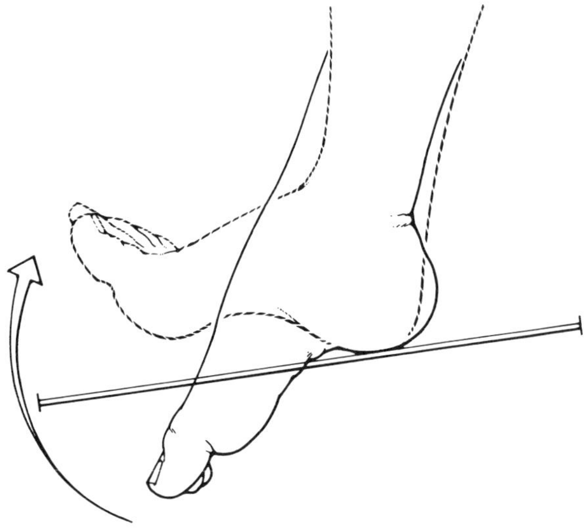

FIG 14–2.
A foot or any part of a foot is in a dorsiflexion position when the distal aspect of the foot or part is angulated in a sagittal plane toward the tibia.

Medial = part closer to the midline
Pes cavus = highly arched foot
Pes planus = flatfoot
Plantar = bottom surface of the foot
Plantar flexion = sagittal plane movement of the toes or foot downward and away from the leg or tibia (Fig 14–4)
Posterior = back
Pronation = a triplane motion consisting of simultaneous movement of the foot in the direction of abduction, eversion, and dorsiflexion
Proximal = nearest or closest to any point of reference
Sagittal plane = a vertical plane passing through the body from front to back that divides the body into right and left portions or segments. The midsagittal or median plane divides the body into equal right and left halves (Fig 14–5)
Supination = triplane motion consisting of simultaneous movement of the foot in the direction of adduction, inversion, and plantar flexion
Superior = above
Transverse plane = a horizontal flat plane dividing the body into upper (superior) and lower (inferior) segments (Fig 14–6)
Valgus = an eversion or turning out of the plantar aspect of the toes or foot
Varus = an inversion or turning in of the toes or foot

NAIL TERMINOLOGY

Anonychia = complete absence of one or more nails

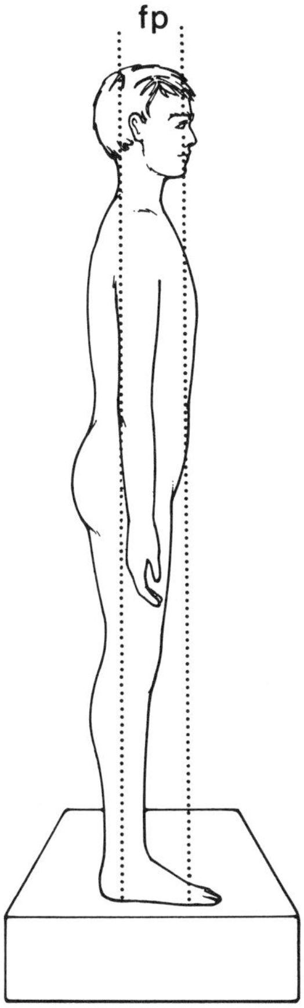

FIG 14–3.
Frontal plane *(fp)* is a flat plane passing through the body, while in the anatomic position, that divides the body into anterior and posterior segments.

Leukonychia = a condition of white or white spots on the nail plate
Matrix = root of a nail
Mycotic = fungal (onychomycosis)
Onychauxis (club nail) = overgrowth of nails: thick, elongated, raised, irregular, grooved, and plantarly incurvated nails
Onychia (also called onychitis) = a condition in which the nail matrix and the very superficial soft tissue of the toenails are tender and inflamed
Onycho = nail
Onychocryptosis (ingrown nail) = a condition in which a free edge plate penetrates the soft tissue of the nail fold
Onychogryphosis = deformity of the nail accompanied by a hypertrophy that begins at the matrix and extends either laterally, medially, forward, or downward over the end of the toe.
Onychoheterotopia = eutrophic or abnormal position of the nails

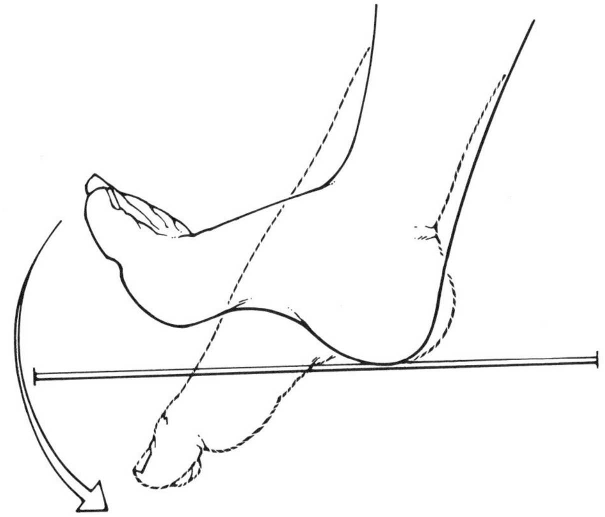

FIG 14–4.
A foot or any part of a foot is in a plantar-flexed position when the distal aspect of the foot is angulated in a sagittal plane farther away from the tibia.

Onycholysis = a condition in which the nail plate is separated from the nail bed at its distal and lateral attachments
Onychomadesis = a condition in which the separation of the nail plate from its nail bed begins at the proximal aspect of the nail plate and progress distally until the entire nail is shed
Onychomalacia = softness of nails
Onychomycosis = any fungal nail infection
Onychophagia = nail biting
Onychophosis = formation of a callus in the nail groove
Onychoschizia = fragile nail resulting in the distal splitting of the nail plate
Onychorrhexis = a splitting of the nail free edge due to abnormal brittleness
Paronychia = an infection of skin folds surrounding the nail

PODIATRIC ABBREVIATIONS

Abn	Abnormal
AC	Before meals
AK	Above the knee
Anes	Anesthesia
AP	Anterioposterior
APC	Aspirin, phenacetin, caffeine

(Continued.)

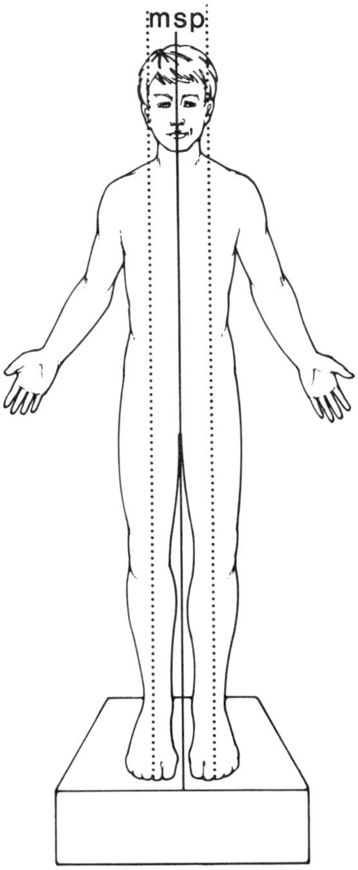

FIG 14-5.
Medial sagittal plane *(msp)* is a flat sagittal plane that divides the body into equal right and left segments and touches the floor at a position midway between the parallel feet when the body is in the anatomic position.

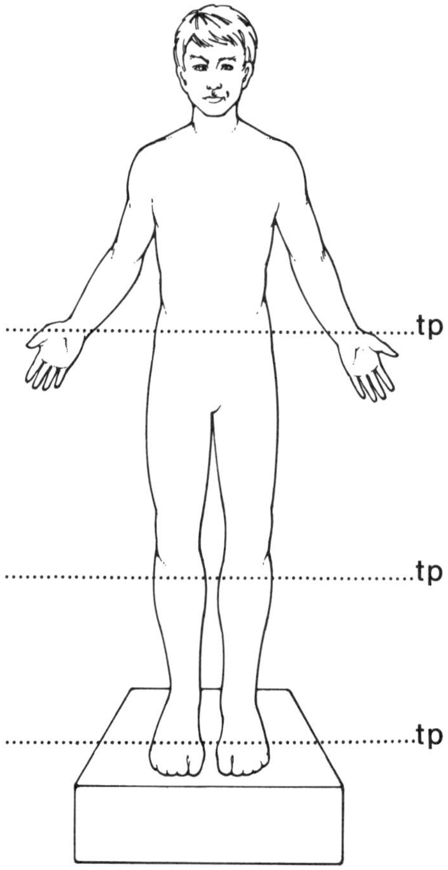

FIG 14–6.
Transverse plane *(tp)* is a flat horizontal plane that lies parallel to the horizon, passes through the body while in the anatomic position, and divides the body into superior and inferior parts.

Asst	Assistant
B/L	Bilateral
BID	Twice a day
BK	Below the knee
BP	Blood pressure
BS	Blood sugar
Bun	Bunion
Bx	Biopsy
C	Callus, corn
Cap	Capsule
Cg	Cartilage
CBC	Complete blood count
CC	Chief complaint
cm	centimeter
CO_2	Carbon dioxide
CPR	Cardiopulmonary resuscitation
CVA	Cardiovascular accident
DFX/DF	Dorsiflex, dorsiflexion
DIPJ	Distal interphalangeal joint
DJD	Degenerative joint disease
DM	Diabetes mellitus
DOB	Date of birth
DP	Dorsoplantar
DSD	Dry sterile dressing
DTR	Deep tendon reflex
Ex	Exercise
Exc	Excision
Exten	Extension
F	Female
Ft	Foot
FF	Flatfoot
FH	Family history
Flex	Flexion
Fx	Fracture
FWB	Full weight bearing
g	Gram
gt	Drop *(gutta)*
HAV	Hallux abducto valgus
HBP	High blood pressure
HD	Heloma durum
HL	Hallux limitus
HM	Heloma molle
H&P	History and physical
HR	Hallux ridigus
HS	Heel spur
HT	Hammertoe
HV	Hallux valgus
Hy	Hydrotherapy or whirlpool

(Continued.)

Hx	History
I&D	Incision and drainage
Inf	Inferior
Inj	Injection
IPJ	Interphalangeal joint
IPK	Intractable plantar keratosis
IV	Intravenous
J	Joint
Lat	Lateral
LE	Lower extremity
LF	Left foot
Lig	Ligament
LLE	Left lower extremity
LO	Lateral oblique x-ray view
LROM	Limitation of range of motion
L-R	Left to right
M	Muscle
Man	Manipulation
MC	Metatarsocuneiform
mg	Milligram
MO	Medial oblique x-ray view
MPJ	Metatarsophalangeal joint
MT	Metatarsal
MTJ	Midtarsal joint
N/A	Not applicable
N/C	No complaints/no charge
Neg	Negative
NM	Neuromuscular
NP	New patient
NWB	Non weight bearing
O	Oblique
OA	Osteoarthritis
Obl	Oblique
Occ	Occasional
OR	Operating room
Orth	Orthotics
PB	Paraffin bath
PH	Past history
PI	Present illness
PIPJ	Proximal interphalangeal joint
PO	Posterior, postoperative
PP	Proximal phalanx
Prep	Sterile preparation
Prox	Proximal
Pt	Patient
PVD	Peripheral vascular disease
q4h	Every 4 hours
q6h	Every 6 hours
qid	Four times daily
R	Right
R/F	Right foot
ROM	Range of motion
SH	Social history
STJ	Subtalar joint
stat	Immediately
Sub	Inferior, beneath
Sup	Superior, superficial
Sx	Surgery
T	Temperature
T&C	Tenotomy and capsulotomy
tid	Three times a day
TPR	Temperature, pulse, and respiration rate
UA	Uric acid, urinalysis
Ung	Ointment
WB	Weight bearing
WNL	Within normal limits
Wt	Weight
X	X-ray
X&D	Examination and diagnosis
YO	Year old

BIBLIOGRAPHY

Blauvelt CT, Nelson FR: *A Manual of Orthopedic Terminology,* ed 3. St Louis, CV Mosby Co, 1985.

Jablonski S: *Dictionary of Medical Acronyms & Abbreviations.* St Louis, CV Mosby Co, 1987.

Kane P, D'Agostino G: *Dictionary for the Podiatric Medical Assistant.* Tucker, Ga, Finco Co, 1990.

SECTION III

Back Office Procedures

15

Principles of Anatomy

James E. Zelichowski, D.P.M.

Anatomy is the study of structure. To accurately describe the structure of the human body with consistency, anatomists have described a certain anatomic position of reference and certain terms of description. The anatomic position is the position in which the body is in the erect standing posture, with the head and feet directed anteriorly, or forward.

With the patient in the anatomic position, certain imaginary body planes oriented in the vertical and horizontal directions can be used to further describe the relationships of body parts. These planes are the three cardinal body planes that lie at right angles to each other. The coronal plane is a vertical plane that passes from one side of the body to the other and divides it into anterior (front) and posterior (back) parts. The sagittal plane is also a vertical plane, but it passes from anterior to posterior and divides the body into right and left parts. The horizontal, or transverse, plane divides the body into an upper or superior part and a lower, or inferior part (Figs 15–1 and 15–2). Additional terminology used to define position include the term *medial*, which is a relative term and means closer to the midline, while the term *lateral* refers to positions away from the midline. For example, the fifth toe is lateral to the fourth toe, and the tibia is medial to the fibula. Anterior refers to the front, while posterior refers to the back. Structures that lie near the front of the body are said to be anterior, while those structures near the back of the body are considered posterior.

In the foot, the term *plantar* refers to the inferior or bottom of the foot, while the term *dorsal* refers to the top of the foot. Structures further away from the limb are said to be distal, while those structures closer are said to be proximal. For example, the great toe is distal to the heel.

The lower extremity can be divided into several anatomic regions that include the hip (or gluteal region); the thigh (or femoral region); the knee (or genu); the leg (or crus); the ankle (or talus); and the foot (or pes region). Each of these regions contains bones, muscles, joints, ligaments, nerves, and vessels, all of which can further be divided into compartments within a certain region. We shall concentrate in this text on the regions and compartments of the leg and the foot.

THE SKELETAL SYSTEM

Bones of the Leg

The leg is made up of two bones, the tibia and fibula. The tibia is a strong and massive bone on the medial side of the leg. It alone receives weight transmitted to it by the femur located in the thigh, and it conveys that weight to the foot. The anterior portion of the tibia (the shin) can be palpated from knee to ankle.

The tibial tuberosity, a bony prominence, may

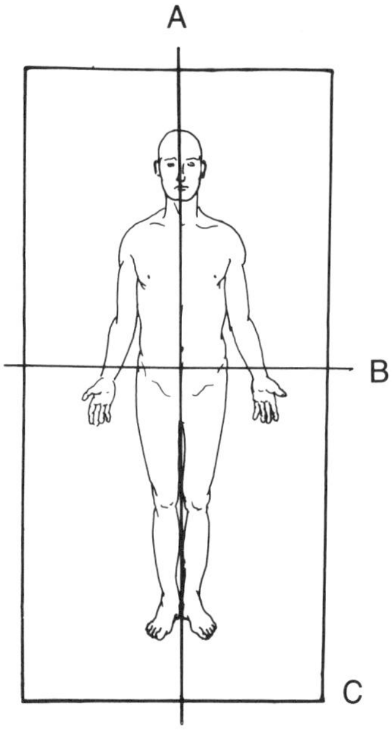

FIG 15–1.
The anatomic position with the three cardinal body planes: **A,** the sagittal or vertical plane; **B,** the transverse or horizontal plane; **C,** the coronal or frontal plane.

be palpated just below the knee. It is the site where the strong patellar tendon inserts from above. Above the tibial tuberosity, the bone expands into two large condyles, or platforms, that articulate with the femur. The sharp edge of the anterior surface of the tibia can be traced in the midline of the leg down to its lower end where it swings medially to end as the front edge of the medial malleolus. This bony projection borders the ankle joint medially and also acts as a pulley for several tendons. The inferior surface of the tibia is made up of a large articular facet. Together with the lateral malleolus, the inferior surface of the tibia forms a mortise that provides stability of the ankle joint (Fig 15–3).

The lateral bone of the leg, the fibula, is shaped like a long thin stick. Its shaft is twisted and molded by the origins of numerous muscles that arise from it. The fibula's upper end, or head, articulates with the lateral part of the tibial condyle. The shaft of the fibula is united with the tibia by a strong interosseous membrane. The lower end is pointed and projects downward beyond the tibia and is known as the lateral or fibular malleolus. On its medial aspect is the triangular articular area that completes the ankle joint mortise.

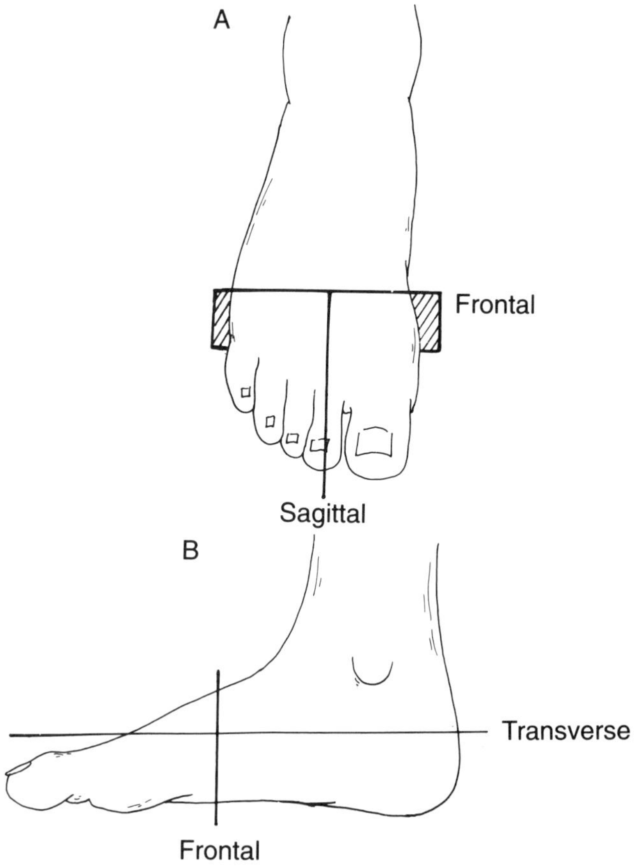

FIG 15–2.
The three body planes and relative position of body parts as they relate to the foot: **A,** frontal and sagittal planes; **B,** transverse and frontal planes.

Bones of the Foot

The skeleton of the body consists of over 200 bones. The foot itself is usually composed of 26 bones. These 26 bones are arranged in three different sets, the bones of the rearfoot (hindfoot), the midfoot, and the forefoot (Fig 15–4).

The tarsal bones are the largest bones in the foot and consist of the talus, calcaneus, cuboid, navicular, and the medial, intermediate, and lateral cuneiforms. The talus and calcaneus are the largest tarsal bones and receive the weight from the body above.

The talus rests on the superior surface of the calcaneus (heel bone) and occupies the mortise of the ankle joint (Fig 15–5). It is a short bone consisting of a head, neck, and body. The body rests on the articular surface occupying the middle third of the upper surface of the calcaneus. The head and neck of the talus are divided medially at

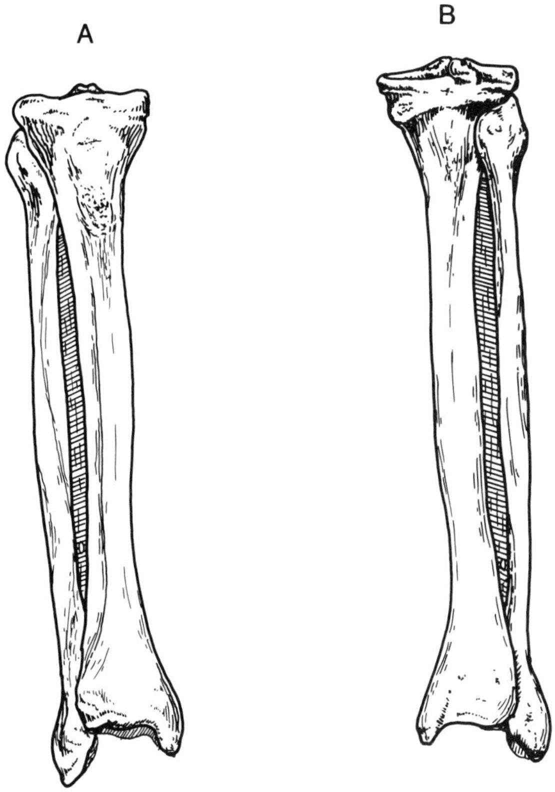

FIG 15–3.
A, anterior, or front, view of the right tibia and fibula. **B,** posterior, or behind, view of the right tibia and fibula.

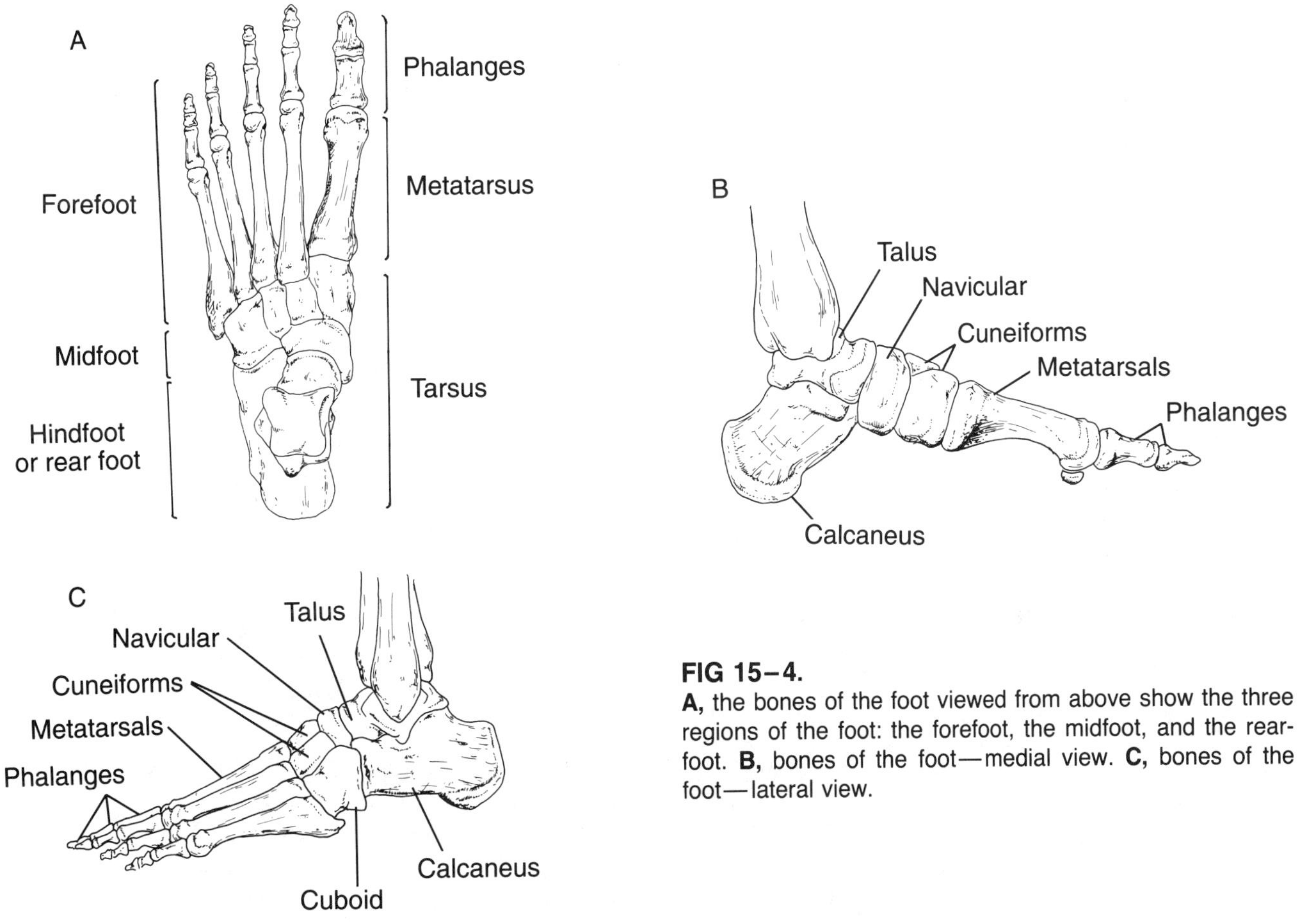

FIG 15–4.
A, the bones of the foot viewed from above show the three regions of the foot: the forefoot, the midfoot, and the rearfoot. **B,** bones of the foot—medial view. **C,** bones of the foot—lateral view.

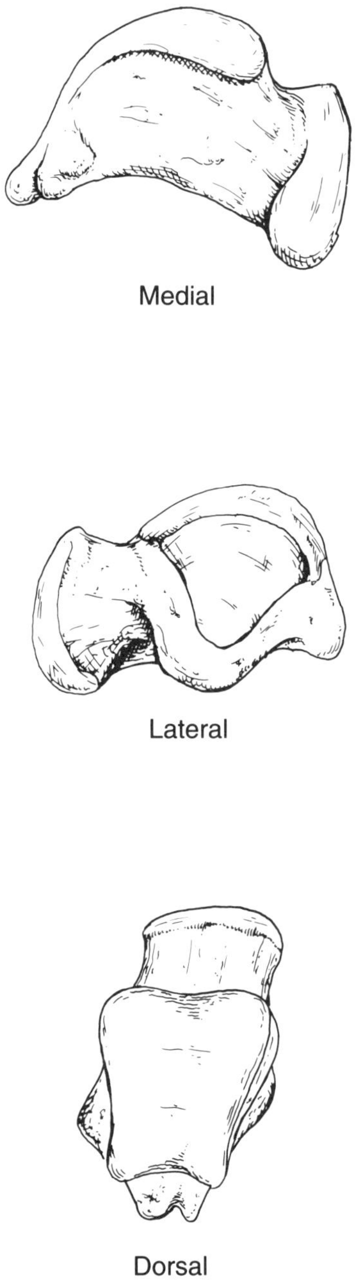

FIG 15–5.
Medial, lateral, and dorsal views of the talus.

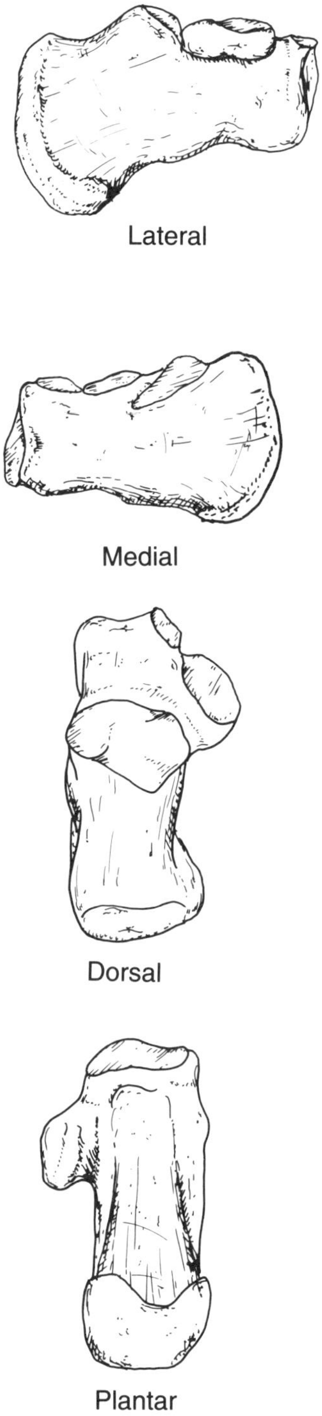

FIG 15–6.
Lateral, medial, dorsal, and plantar views of the calcaneus. Note the three articular surfaces on the dorsal surface that articulate with the talus.

the distal third of the calcaneus. Several ligaments attach to the talus and help bind it to the calcaneus, navicular, tibia, and fibula. There are no muscular attachments to the talus.

The calcaneus is the largest of the tarsal bones (Fig 15–6). It is rectangular in shape and has six surfaces. The anterior surface articulates with the cuboid bone. The dorsal or superior surface articulates with the talus. The medial surface contains a ledge of bone called the sustentaculum tali that supports the head and neck of the talus. The lateral, plantar, and posterior surfaces serve for the attachment of muscles, ligaments, and tendons.

The dorsal surface contains three articular areas on which the talus rests. Between these articular surfaces of the calcaneus is a nonarticular area occupied by an interosseous ligament. This ligament binds the talus to the calcaneus. The central third of the posterior surface serves for attachment of the Achilles tendon to the powerful calf muscle, which can extend the ankle and raise the body on tiptoes.

The plantar surface is rough posteriorly and forms a major weight-bearing area of the calcaneus. This area is referred to as the calcaneal tuberosity.

On the medial surface is a large shelflike projection, the sustentaculum tali, that has a groove for the tendon of the flexor hallucis longus on its inferior surface. The anterior and posterior surfaces of the sustentaculum tali are sites for the attachment of ligaments. The medial surface is the main attachment for the strong medial collateral ligaments of the ankle joint.

The bones of the midfoot, the navicular, cuboid, and three cuneiforms give additional flexibility to the foot. The navicular is concave proximally and convex distally, which gives it a boatlike shape. The medial surface of the navicular is rough and projects inferiorly as the navicular tuberosity. This serves as the major insertion for the tibialis posterior tendon.

The cuboid articulates with the calcaneus proximally and the fourth and fifth metatarsals distally. The cuboid has dorsal, plantar, medial, lateral, posterior, and anterior surfaces.

The dorsal surface is rough due to the attachments of several ligaments. On the plantar surface is an oblique-shaped ridge of bone, the peroneal ridge. Just distal to the peroneal ridge lies the peroneal groove and sulcus, along which the peroneus longus tendon passes on route to the medial cuneiform.

The anterior and posterior surfaces are covered by articular facets. Anteriorly, the surface of the cuboid is covered by one large facet for the bases of the fourth and fifth metatarsal bones. The posterior surface has a saddle-shaped articular facet that rests against the calcaneus.

There are three cuneiform bones, the first, or medial; the second, or intermediate; and the third, or lateral cuneiform. These three bones form the most distal row of the tarsus, and all articulate proximally with the navicular bone. Distally, the medial cuneiform articulates with the base of the first metatarsal. The intermediate cuneiform articulates with the base of the second metatarsal, and the lateral cuneiform articulates with the base of the third metatarsal.

Cuneiform, Latin for the word "wedge," refers to the shape of each cuneiform bone. The shape and arrangement of the bones contribute to the transverse arch of the foot.

The five metatarsal bones compose the metatarsus and are numbered from one to five. Each metatarsal has a head distally, a shaft, and a base proximally. The base of each metatarsal articulates proximally with the tarsal bones, while the head of each metatarsal articulates distally with the base of the proximal phalanx of each digit. Distally, the metatarsals are bound together near the heads by a strong ligament, the deep transverse metatarsal ligament.

The shafts are long and slender, with the first metatarsal being the thickest, shortest, and heaviest of the metatarsals. Its head is covered with articular cartilage for articulation with the base of the proximal phalanx. This articular surface extends downward to be continuous with the articular surface for the tibial and fibular sesamoid bones.

The medial, or tibial, sesamoid bone and the lateral, or fibular, sesamoid bone of the first metatarsophalangeal joint lie within the tendons of the flexor hallucis brevis muscle. Each sesamoid is oval in shape and articulates with the plantar surface of the first metatarsal.

The phalanges form the most distal portion of the pedal skeleton. There are usually 14 phalanges in each foot: 2 in the hallux and 3 in the lesser digits. Phalanges are considered to be miniature long bones and have a head, a shaft, and a base. The phalanges are arranged as distal, intermediate (middle), and proximal.

THE ARTICULAR SYSTEM

Ankle or Talocrural Joint

The ankle joint is the articulation between the talus of the foot and the fibula and tibia of the leg. The ankle, or talocrural joint, is commonly classified as a hinge joint. Its movements are dorsiflexion and plantar flexion.

The ankle joint is surrounded by a fibrous capsule and is reinforced by collateral ligaments. The lateral and medial collateral ligaments are the major stabilizing structures of the ankle joint (Fig 15–7). Of the two ligaments the sheetlike medial, or deltoid ligament is the strongest and widest. From its attachment at the tip of the medial malleolus, the ligament fans out to its attachments on the navicular, calcaneus, and talus. The lateral collateral ligament of the ankle joint is made up of

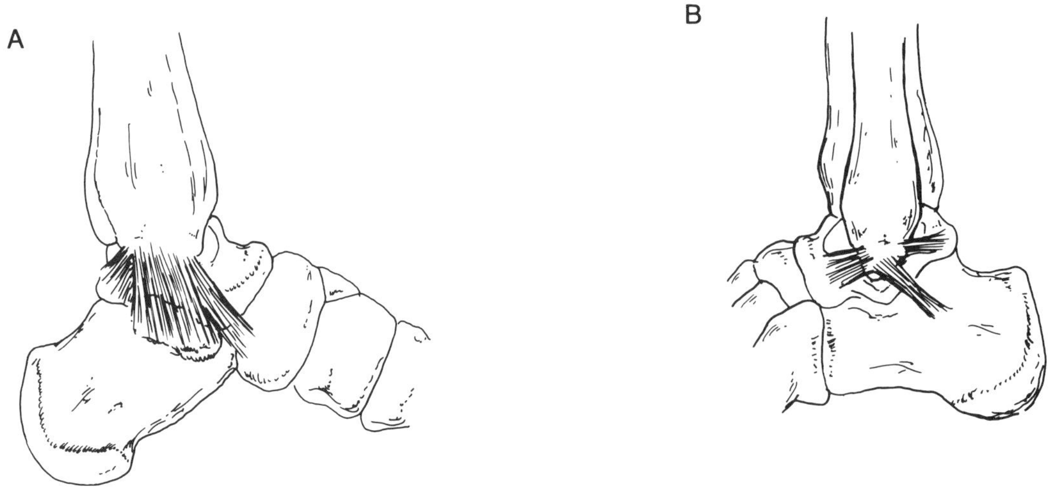

FIG 15–7.
A, the medial collateral, or deltoid ligament of the ankle joint. **B,** the lateral collateral ligaments of the ankle joint.

three separate ligaments: the anterior talofibular ligament, the calcaneofibular ligament, and the posterior talofibular ligament.

Joints of the Foot

The subtalar, or talocalcaneal, joint is located just below the ankle joint. The surfaces of this multiaxial joint work together to produce triplane movements of pronation and supination.

The midtarsal, or transverse tarsal, joint, which lies just distal to the subtalar joint, is made up of articulations of the talonavicular joint and the calcaneocuboid joint. Gliding and rotational movements occur at these joints and add to major movements of pronation and supination (Fig 15–8). Articulations between the distal row of the tarsus and the base of the five metatarsals make up the tarsometatarsal, or Lisfranc's, joint. Movement at these joints allows gliding of the metatarsals upon the distal row of tarsal bones.

The metatarsophalangeal joints are made up of

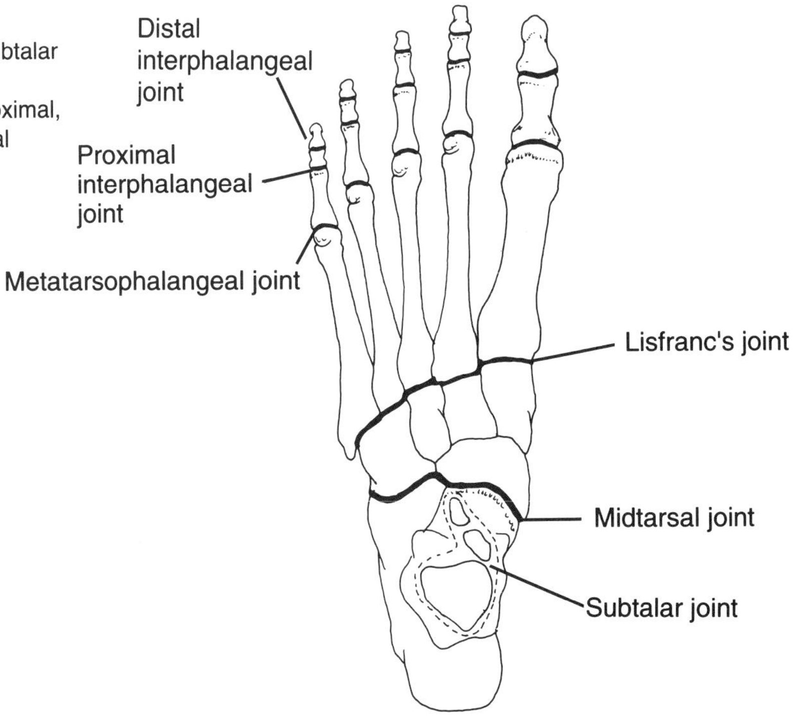

FIG 15–8.
The functional joints of the foot: the subtalar joint, midtarsal joint, Lisfranc's joint, metatarsophalangeal joint, and the proximal, intermediate, and distal interphalangeal joints.

articulations between the heads of the five metatarsals and the bases of the five proximal phalanges. Each has a joint capsule and is re-enforced by collateral ligaments medially and laterally. Movement of the metatarsophalangeal joints provide dorsiflexion and plantar flexion. The interphalangeal joints are made up of articulations of the proximal and middle and the middle and distal phalanges of the lesser toes. All interphalangeal joints provide movement of plantar flexion and dorsiflexion, or flexion and extension, of the toes.

THE MUSCULAR SYSTEM

Muscles of the Leg

The muscles of the leg are divided into three compartments by intermuscular septa that are a continuation from the deep fascia that surrounds the leg. The anterior compartment of the leg contains four muscles that dorsiflex the ankle joint. The lateral compartment of the leg contains two muscles that evert and help plantar-flex the foot. The posterior compartment of the leg contains flexor muscles that primarily plantar-flex the foot.

The anterior compartment contains four muscles. Medially to laterally, these are the tibialis anterior (Fig 15–9), extensor hallucis longus (Fig 15–10), extensor digitorum longus (Fig 15–11), and the peroneus tertius (Fig 15–10). These muscles all originate from the lower portion of the leg and insert into bones of the forefoot. Their primary action is dorsiflexion of the foot on the ankle. The tibialis anterior is also a strong supinator of the foot. The extensor hallucis longus and ex-

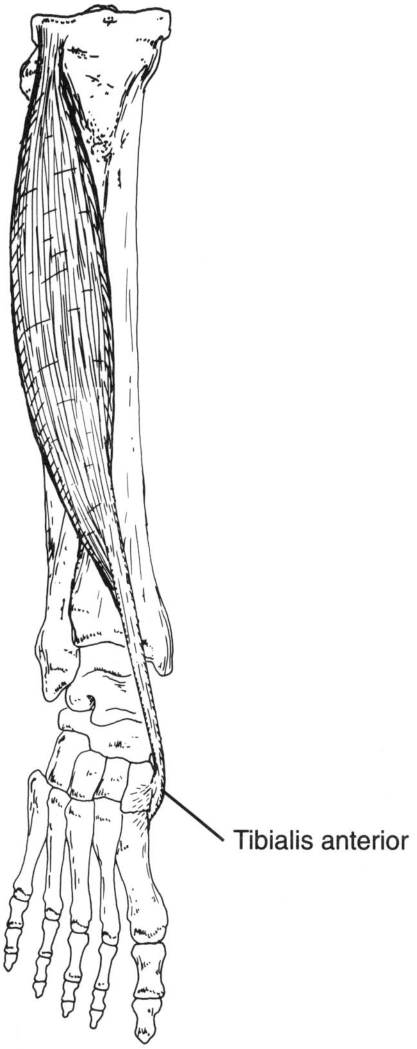

FIG 15–9.
The tibialis anterior muscle.

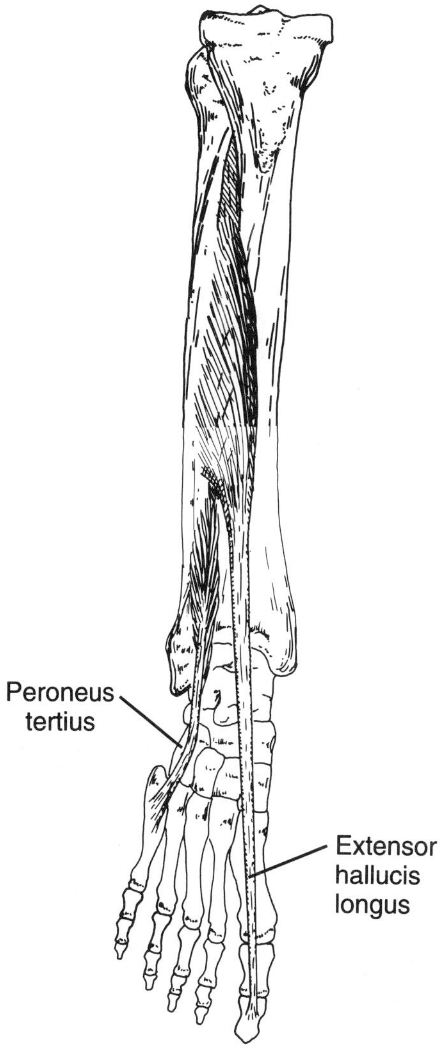

FIG 15–10.
The extensor hallucis longus and peroneus tertius muscles.

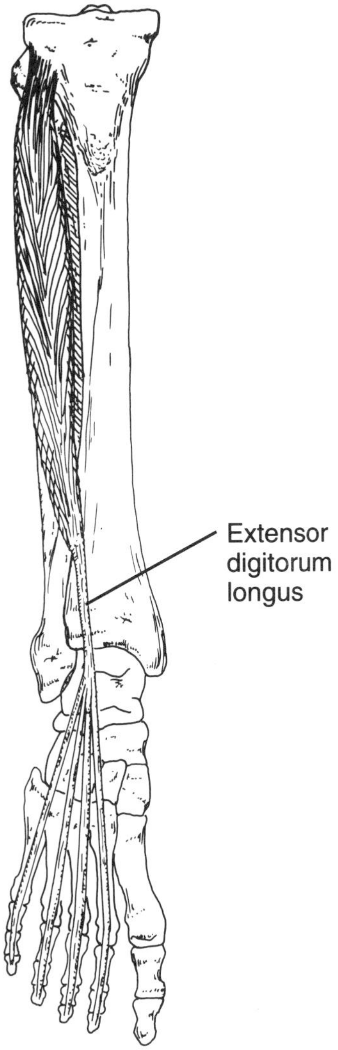

FIG 15–11.
The extensor digitorum longus muscle.

tensor digitorum longus dorsiflex, or extend, the hallux and lesser toes, respectively.

The lateral compartment contains the peroneus longus and the peroneus brevis muscles (Fig 15–12). These arise from the lateral surface of the fibula and pass behind the lateral malleolus, with the peroneus brevis lying anterior to the peroneus longus. The peroneus longus crosses along the plantar aspect of the foot in the peroneal groove of the cuboid bone and inserts into the first metatarsal and medial cuneiform. The peroneus brevis inserts at the fifth metatarsal base. Both muscles act to evert the foot and assist in plantar flexion of the ankle.

The posterior compartment of the leg can be divided into superficial and deep compartments. Both compartments contain muscles that act as plantar flexors of the toes and ankle.

The superficial layer of the posterior compartment contains the gastrocnemius (Fig 15–13), soleus (Fig 15–14), and plantaris muscles. The medial and lateral heads of the gastrocnemius muscle unite with the underlying soleus muscle to form the Achilles tendon, which inserts into the posterior aspect of the calcaneus. This is the most powerful plantar flexor of the ankle joint. The plantaris muscle forms a small tendon located medial to the Achilles tendon.

The deep layer of the posterior compartment contains the popliteus, flexor digitorum longus

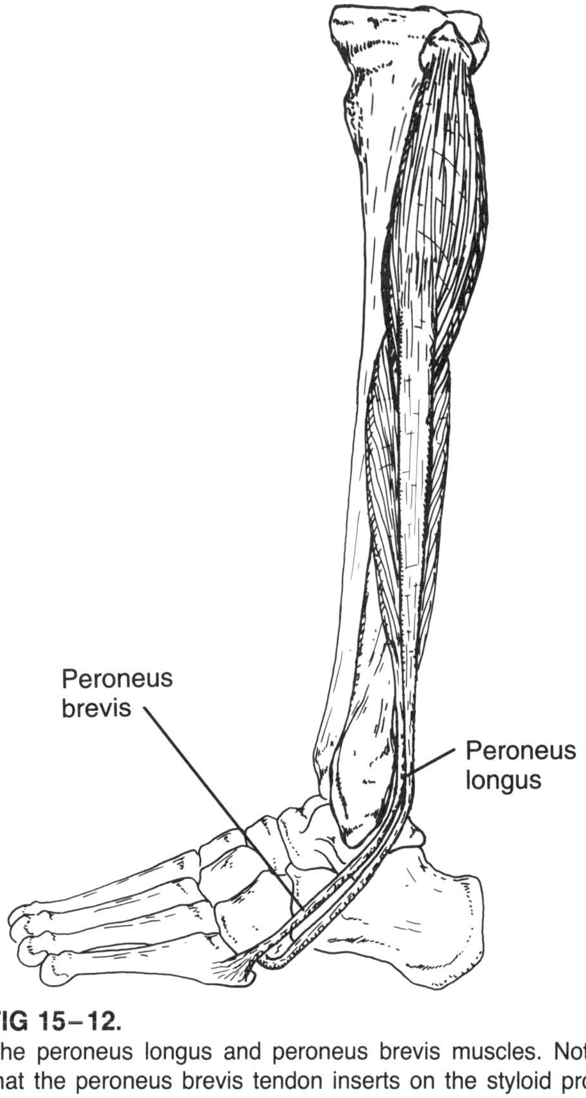

FIG 15–12.
The peroneus longus and peroneus brevis muscles. Note that the peroneus brevis tendon inserts on the styloid process of the fifth metatarsal while the tendon of the peroneus longus enters the plantar aspect of the foot under the cuboid to insert on the base of the first metatarsal and the medial cuneiform bone.

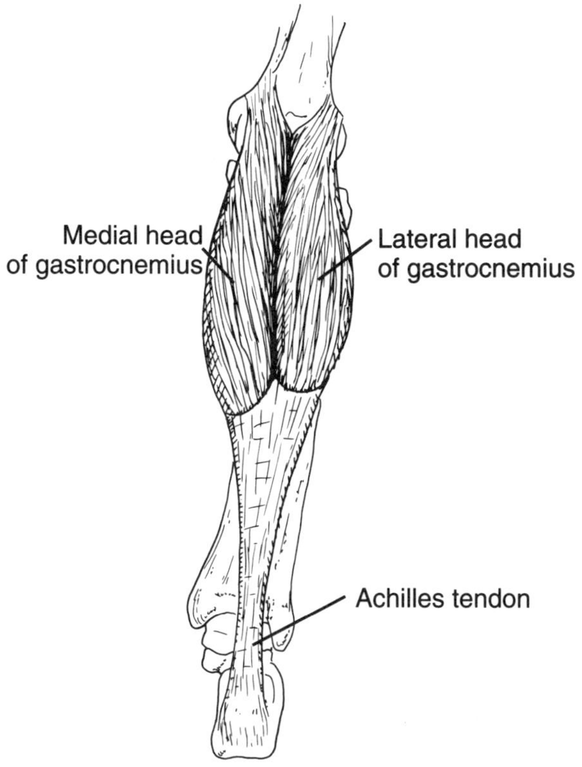

FIG 15–13.
The gastrocnemius muscle and the tendo Achillis.

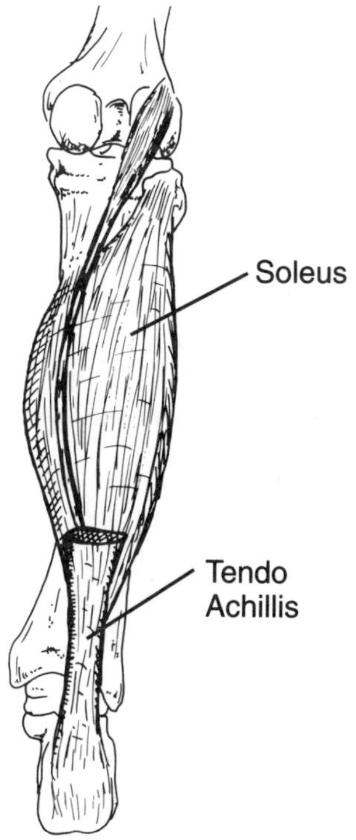

FIG 15–14.
The soleus muscle, which lies deep to the gastrocnemius muscle, helps to form the tendo Achillis.

(Fig 15–15), tibialis posterior (Fig 15–16), and flexor hallucis longus (Fig 15–17) muscles. The popliteus muscle flexes the leg on the thigh as it arises more proximally from the lateral surface of the femur. The remaining muscles arise from the posterior aspect of the tibia and/or fibula and course distally. The flexor hallucis longus and flexor digitorum longus insert into the hallux and lesser toes, respectively, and produce flexion of the digits. The tibialis posterior tendon inserts into the navicular with expansion to many other midfoot bones. It is the strongest invertor of the foot.

Muscles of the Foot

There are four layers of muscles and tendons in the sole of the foot. All essentially take origin from one of two locations in the foot. The first is the calcaneal tuberosity; the other is near the bases and along the shafts of the metatarsals.

The muscles of the first layer are the most superficial. These include (medially to laterally) the abductor hallucis, the flexor digitorum brevis, and the abductor digiti minimi (Fig 15–18). All three muscles along with the ligament of the sole of the foot help to flex the toes and maintain the arches of the foot during ambulation.

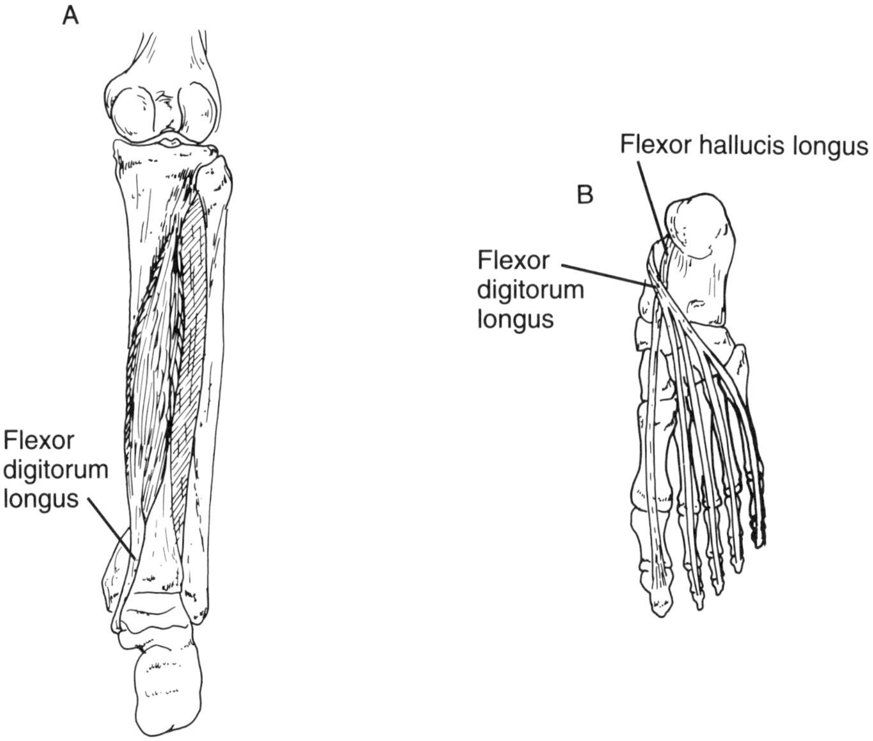

FIG 15–15.
A, the flexor digitorum longus muscle viewed from behind. **B,** note that the tendon of the flexor digitorum longus divides into four slips in the sole of the foot.

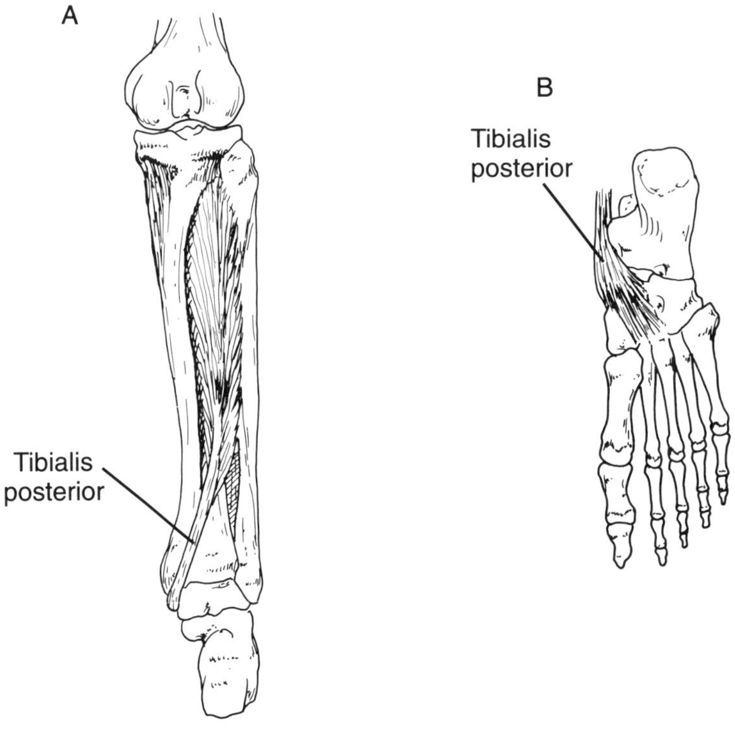

FIG 15–16.
The tibialis posterior muscle **(A)** and its multiple insertions in the plantar aspect of the foot **(B).**

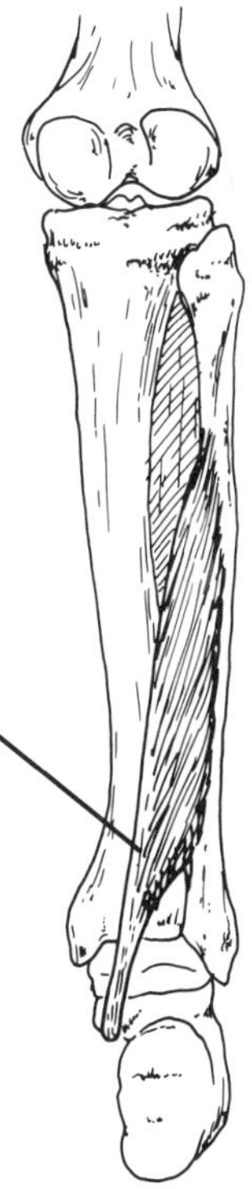

FIG 15–17.
The flexor hallucis longus muscle and tendon.

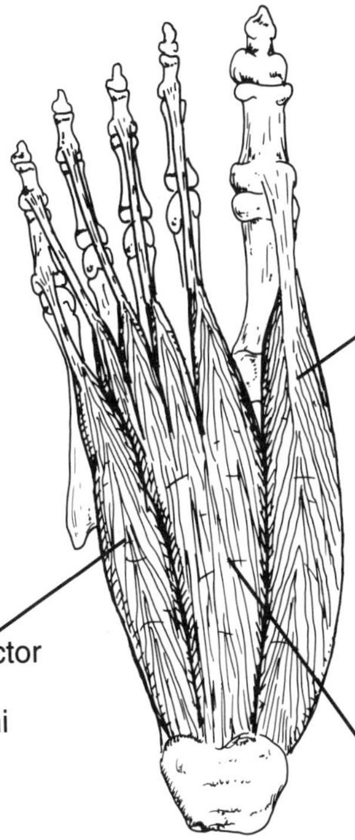

FIG 15–18.
The muscles of the first layer of the plantar aspect of the foot.

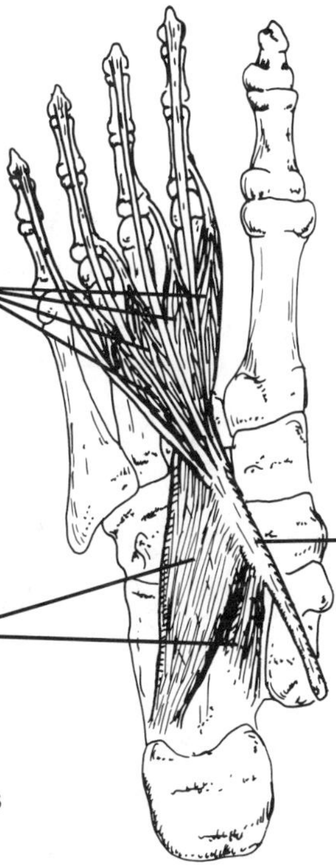

FIG 15–19.
The muscles of the second layer of the plantar aspect of the foot.

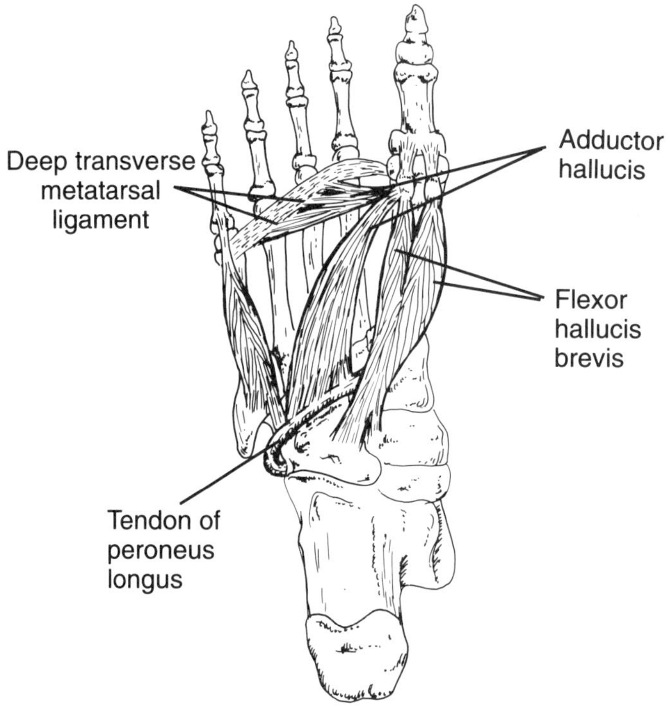

FIG 15–20.
The muscles of the third layer of the plantar aspect of the foot.

There are two muscles in the second layer that lie deep to the first layer. These are the quadratus plantae and the four lumbrical muscles (Fig 15–19). These muscles assist the flexor digitorum longus and extensor digitorum longus muscles.

There are three muscles in the third layer. These include the flexor hallucis brevis, the adductor hallucis, and the flexor digiti minimi (Fig 15–20). These muscles assist plantar flexion of the involved digit.

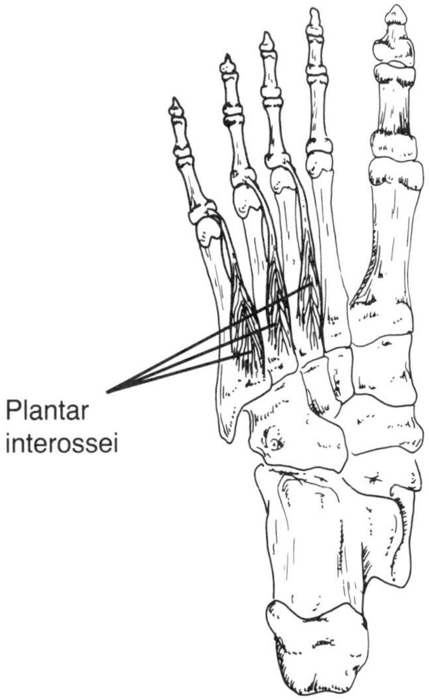

FIG 15–21.
The three plantar interossei muscles help make up part of the fourth layer of the muscle of the plantar aspect of the foot.

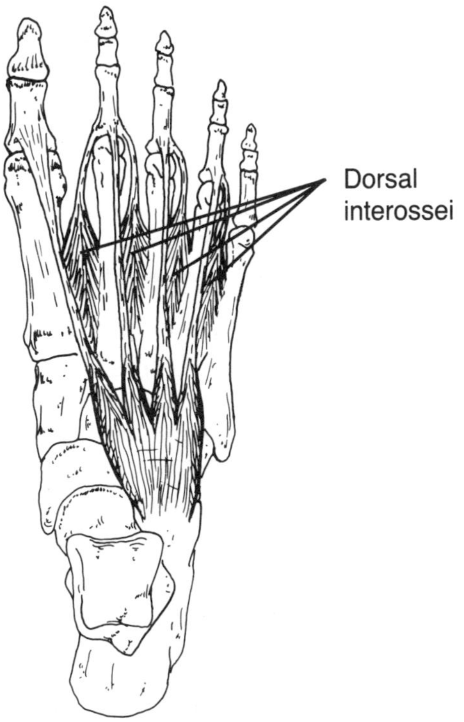

FIG 15–22.
View from above. The four dorsal interossei muscles complete the fourth layer of the muscles of the plantar aspect of the foot. The extensor digitorum brevis is the only intrinsic muscle of the dorsum of the foot. Note that the medial muscle belly of the extensor digitorum brevis is well defined and is referred to as the extensor hallucis brevis.

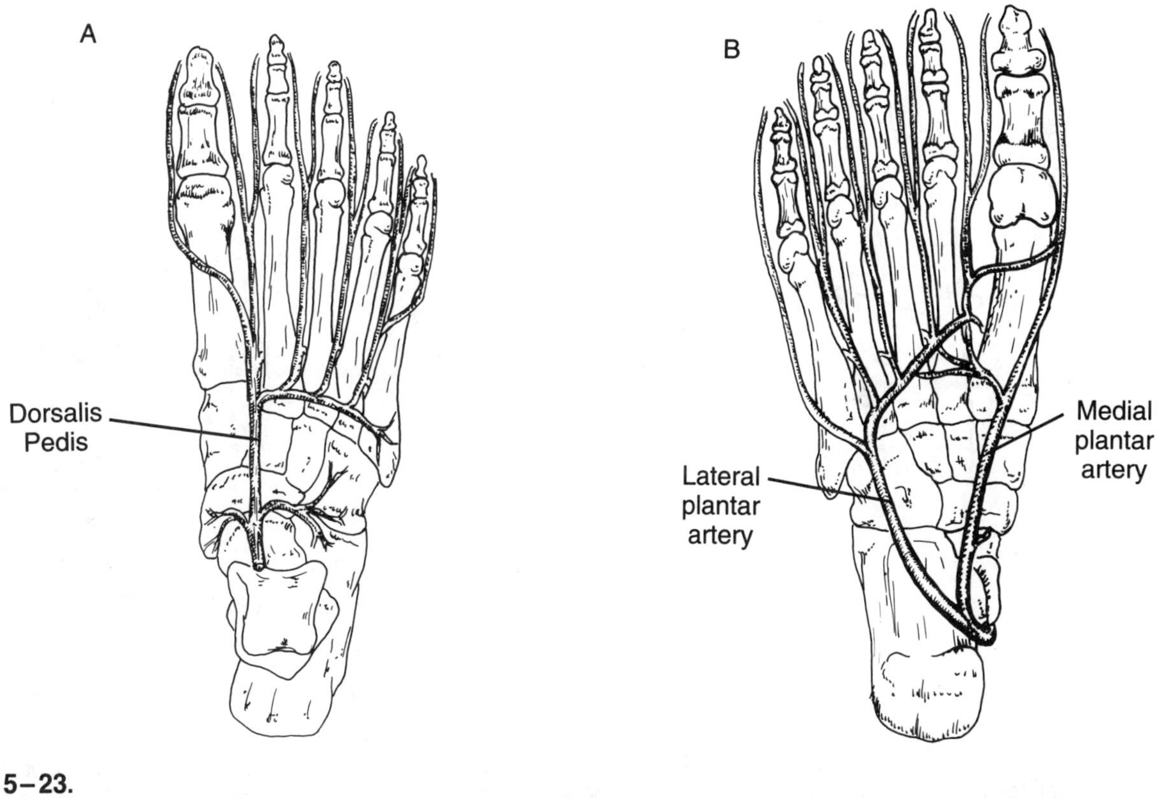

FIG 15–23.
A, arterial supply to the dorsal aspect of the foot. **B,** the medial and lateral plantar arteries help supply the plantar aspect of the foot.

The interossei muscles make up the fourth layer of muscles of the plantar aspect of the foot. There are three plantar interossei (Fig 15–21) and four dorsal interossei muscles (Fig 15–22). Their primary action is to abduct or adduct the digits and stabilize them during ambulation.

The extensor digitorum brevis muscle (Fig 15–22) is the only intrinsic muscle on the dorsal aspect of the foot. It arises from the dorsal surface of the calcaneus and inserts via tendon slips into the hallux, second, third, and fourth digits. Its action is to dorsiflex, or extend, the phalanges.

THE CIRCULATORY SYSTEM

Arteries of the Leg and Foot

The popliteal artery is the continuation of the femoral artery of the thigh. As the popliteal artery descends into the leg, it gives off two terminal branches, the larger posterior tibial artery and the smaller anterior tibial artery. The posterior tibial artery descends the back of the leg deep to the gastrocnemius and soleus muscles.

A large branch of the posterior tibial artery, the peroneal, or fibular, artery supplies the posterior and lateral portions of the leg. As the posterior tibial artery descends, many branches radiate to muscles in the leg before it enters the foot behind the medial malleolus. Here it divides into the medial and lateral plantar arteries, which supply structures in the sole of the foot. The anterior tibial artery passes down the leg just anterior to the interosseous membrane. It gives off many branches to muscles in the leg before entering the dorsum of the foot as the dorsalis pedis artery, which supplies the dorsal aspect of the foot.

The plantar arteries are the principal vessels of the foot. The medial plantar artery supplies muscles of the great toe, while the lateral plantar artery supplies the remainder of the plantar aspect of the foot (Fig 15–23).

Veins of the Leg and Foot

All veins in the foot and leg contain a series of valves that allow the blood to flow toward the heart. Veins of the leg and foot can be separated into two categories, superficial and deep. The deeper veins of the lower portion of the limb cor-

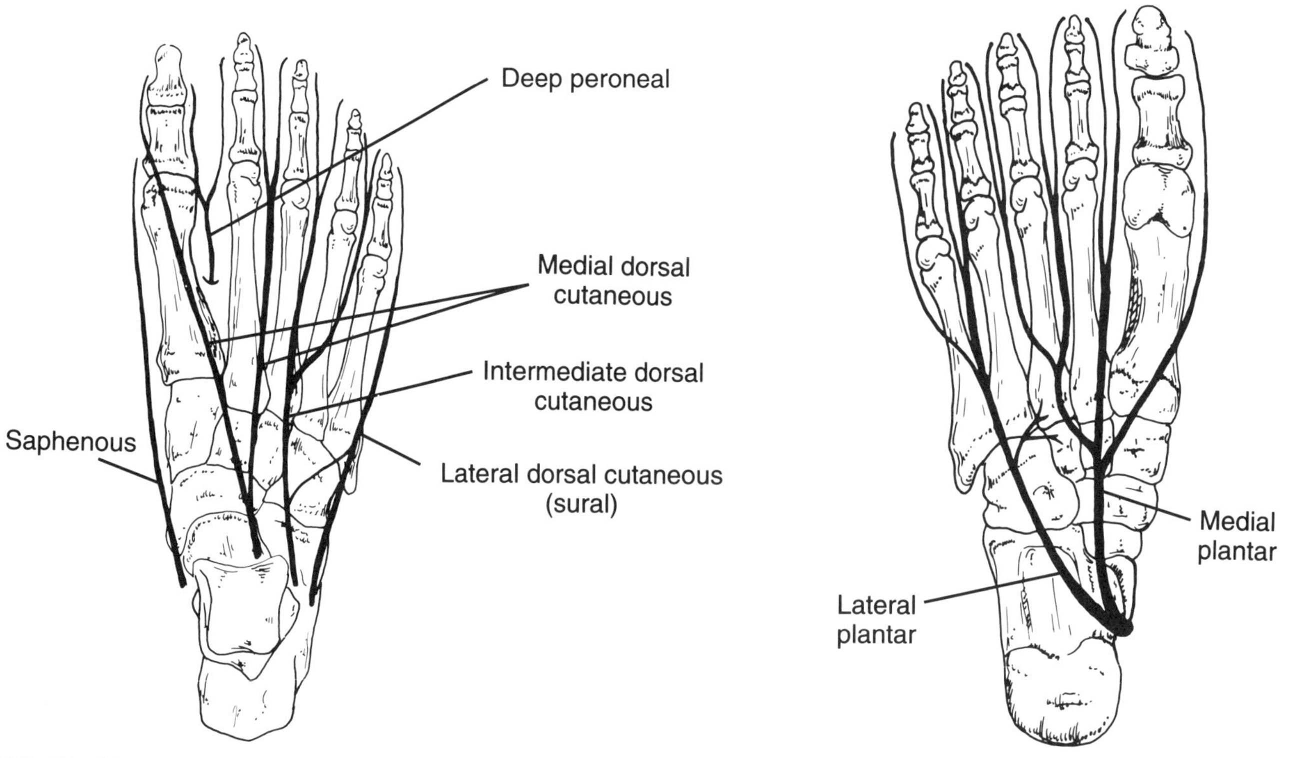

FIG 15–24.
A, nerves of the dorsal aspect of the foot. From medial to lateral are the saphenous nerve, the medial dorsal cutaneous nerve, the deep peroneal nerve, the intermediate dorsal cutaneous nerve, and the lateral cutaneous (sural) nerve. **B,** the medial and lateral plantar nerves branch out to innervate muscles and skin of the plantar aspect of the foot.

respond and run along side the adjacent arteries. There are two main superficial veins in the lower part of the limb that begin in the foot. The small, or lesser, saphenous vein courses along the lateral side of the foot behind the lateral malleolus and runs up the posterior lateral side of the calf to enter the popliteal vein. The larger, or greater, saphenous vein courses along the medial side of the foot anterior to the medial malleolus and up the posteromedial side of the calf and thigh.

THE NERVOUS SYSTEM

Nerves of the lower part of the limb, like veins, are named and run with their corresponding arteries. The leg receives innervation from the sciatic nerve of the thigh, which divides behind the knee into two branches, the tibial nerve and the common peroneal nerve. The common peroneal nerve quickly divides into a superficial and a deep peroneal nerve around the head of the fibula. The superficial peroneal nerve courses down and supplies the lateral side of the leg and the skin over the dorsal aspect of the foot. The deep peroneal nerve supplies the anterior muscles of the leg and foot. The tibial nerve is the continuation of the sciatic nerve, which courses through the back of the leg. It gives off many branches to muscles to supply the posterior portion of the leg before entering the foot. The tibial nerve divides behind the medial malleolus into the medial and lateral plantar nerves. These supply the intrinsic muscles as well as the skin of the sole of the foot (Fig 15–24).

16

Common Podiatric Procedures

Thomas J. Chang, D.P.M.
Luke D. Cicchinelli, D.P.M.

I. Hallux Valgus (Bunions)
    A. Etiology
    B. Procedures
II. Hammertoes
    A. Etiology
    B. Procedures
III. Heel Pain
    A. Etiology
IV. Warts
    A. Etiology
    B. Procedures
V. Neuroma
    A. Etiology
    B. Treatment
VI. Nail Pathology

Podiatrists see an array of pathology in clinical practice. This discussion will highlight certain commonly seen diseases and symptom complexes.

HALLUX VALGUS (BUNIONS)

The deformity of hallux valgus, or hallux abducto valgus (bunion), is one of the most common deformities treated by podiatrists (Fig 16–1). Its severity and etiology are varied. Concomitant forefoot derangements are frequently encountered. Successful relief of symptoms from this aggravating condition depends upon a complete understanding of the factors contributing to its cause, the overall health and functional capacity of the patient, and an appreciation for the patient's expectations of the outcome.

Etiology

Certain factors predispose a patient to develop hallux abducto valgus. Generally, biomechanical considerations including the hypermobile foot, pronated foot, or flatfoot are the most common. Other causes include arthritic, neuromuscular, and traumatic conditions. The rheumatoid arthritic patient often has a severe hallux abducto valgus deformity. Patients with cerebral palsy can also demonstrate the deformity, although not as severely. These abnormal pedal forces in the foot result in deviation of the hallux laterally, often with a valgus or outward twist as the first metatarsal splays into adduction and increases the intermetatarsal angle. The medial aspect of the first metatarsal head is prominent, and the first metatarsophalangeal joint can potentially become arthritic. Soft-tissue contractures develop laterally and encompass the fibular sesamoid. This helps maintain the deformity and limits dorsiflexion of the hallux on the first metatarsal head. Several different procedures are utilized to address this condition. The severity of the deformity will dictate the choice of procedure.

Procedures

Conservative therapy consists of modifications of shoe wear, splinting, and local palliative care such as debridement of hyperkeratotic lesions or injections. If these therapies fail to provide adequate relief, surgery is indicated. Surgery is by far the more lasting and effective option when per-

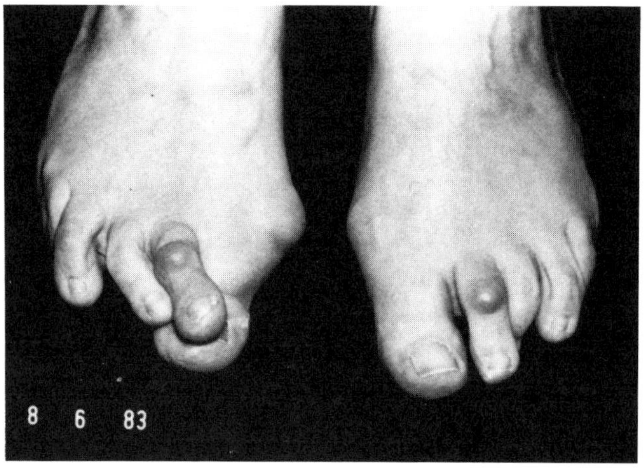

FIG 16–1.
Severe bunion deformity with digital deviations as seen in rheumatoid arthritis.

formed correctly. The choice of procedure depends on the quality of the first metatarsophalangeal joint range of motion and the size of the intermetatarsal angle. An elderly patient with a severely arthritic first metatarsophalangeal joint and low functional expectations may be a candidate for an arthroplasty or joint remodeling procedure such as the Keller (Fig 16–2,A). The base of the proximal phalanx is removed, thereby increasing available motion. The dorsal medial prominence of the first metatarsal head is resected simultaneously. When the joint quality is adequate and the intermetatarsal angle is normal or low, the Silver bunionectomy or modified McBride procedure is frequently utilized. The dorsal medial eminence is removed in the Silver procedure (Fig 16–2,B). The modified McBride procedure consists of release of the lateral soft-tissue contractures in

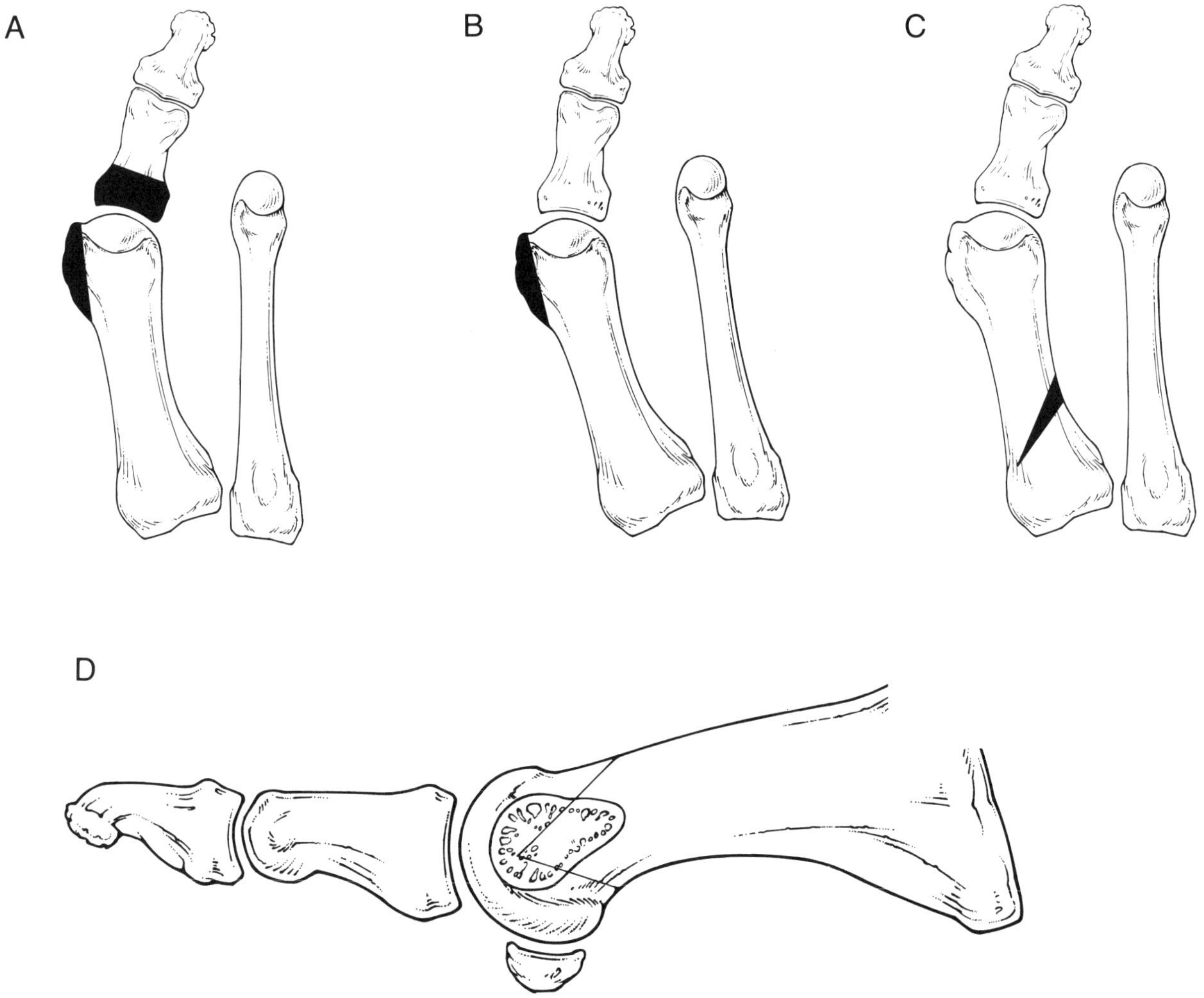

FIG 16–2.
A, the Keller procedure; **B,** the Silver procedure; **C,** the base wedge procedure; **D,** the Austin procedure.

addition to bony resection. As the intermetatarsal angle increases, osteotomy is needed for realignment of bone. Proximal osteotomies are cuts at the base of the first metatarsal and reduce large intermetatarsal angles effectively. This is because of the larger lever arm for rotation (Fig 16–2,C). Distal or capital osteotomies allow a change in position solely at the first metatarsal head and reduce mild to moderate intermetatarsal angles. The classic distal or capital osteotomy is the Austin (V-shaped) procedure (Fig 16–2,D), which allows the metatarsal head to shift laterally. This reduces the medial prominence and effectively realigns the joint. The postoperative dressing is important in assisting the maintenance of surgical correction while the soft tissues and bone heal appropriately. The rehabilitative time and weight-bearing status of the postoperative patient is often physician specific, with a general guideline of 6 to 8 weeks required for complete and stable osseous healing.

HAMMERTOES

Hammertoes (Fig 16–3) are as common as bunions in the podiatric practice. The same abnormal biomechanical forces contribute to the etiology of both conditions. The general term of hammertoe can be segregated more specifically into mallet toes, clawtoes, or the classic hammertoes. A mallet toe is a flexion deformity of the distal phalanx on the middle phalanx without involvement of the proximal interphalangeal joints. A clawtoe exists where the distal and middle phalanx are flexed on a dorsiflexed proximal phalanx. The classic hammertoe exists when the proximal phalanx is dorsiflexed and the middle phalanx is plantar-flexed. Focal hyperkeratoses over the now-prominent interphalangeal joints, or knuckles, and the tips of the toes are due to shoe wear friction and increased ground contact.

Etiology

Digital deformities are often the result of abnormal pronatory forces on the feet as well. As joint relationships change with abnormal biomechanics, certain muscle groups lose or gain mechanical advantage over others. Frequently the intrinsic muscles (those arising and inserting within the foot) are overpowered by the extrinsics (those arising in the leg and inserting in the foot), and this creates instability and subsequent contractures. Improper shoe wear and abnormal length patterns of the digits can contribute and compound the deformities (Fig 16–4).

Procedures

Accommodative padding and palliative debridement of hyperkeratotic lesions (corns) once again have a role in the treatment of hammertoes,

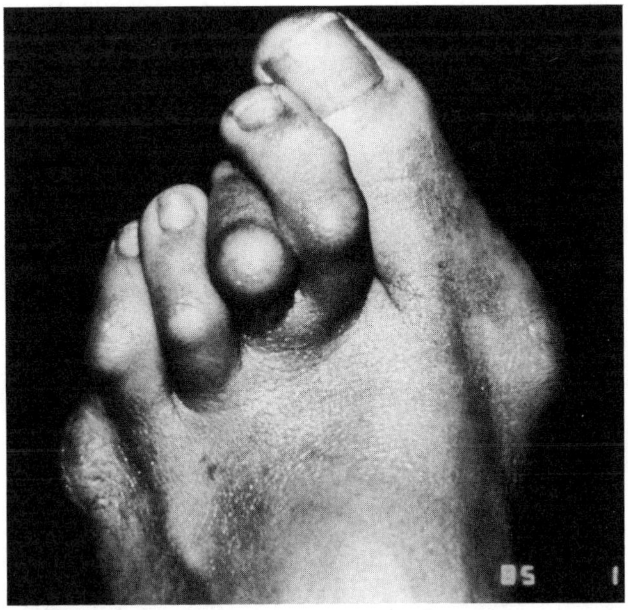

FIG 16–3.
Bunion (hallux abducto valgus) deformity with severe hammertoes. Note the hyperkeratotic lesions on the digits

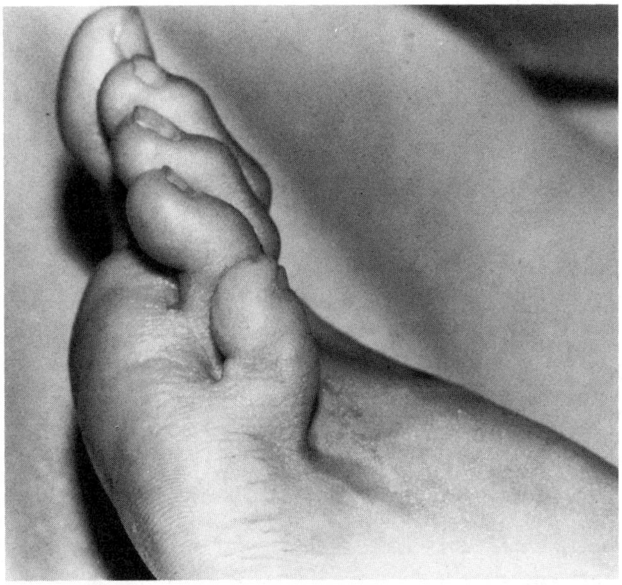

FIG 16–4.
Lateral view of digital contractures (hammertoes).

but surgical procedures remain the definitive solution. The treatment options are arthroplasty, or remodeling of a joint, and arthrodesis, or fusion of a joint. Digital arthroplasty almost exclusively consists of removal of the head of a phalanx (Fig 16–5,A). This is indicated more for flexible to semirigid deformities and allows for relaxation of the soft tissues or tension of deforming forces as the osseous content in the toes is shortened.

Arthrodesis is indicated where stability is lacking within the metatarsophalangeal joint segment as well as the digit and where intrinsic muscle function has been significantly compromised. Arthrodesis options include the peg-in-hole arthrodesis or the end-to-end arthrodesis. The peg-in-hole procedure whereby a peg is made from the head of the proximal phalanx and a hole is formed in the base of the middle phalanx affords increased stability of the joints in addition to shortening (Fig 16–5,B). End-to-end arthrodesis consists of removing the cartilage from the head of the proximal portion of the bone and the base of the distal third of the bone followed by apposition (Fig 16–5,C). This procedure results in less stability than the peg-in-hole technique, and length is maintained. A rigid lever is created of the toe, which helps to stabilize the metatarsophalangeal joint as well as the digit itself. Kirschner wires (K-wires) are used for 4 to 6 weeks to hold alignment and thereby assist healing in the corrected position.

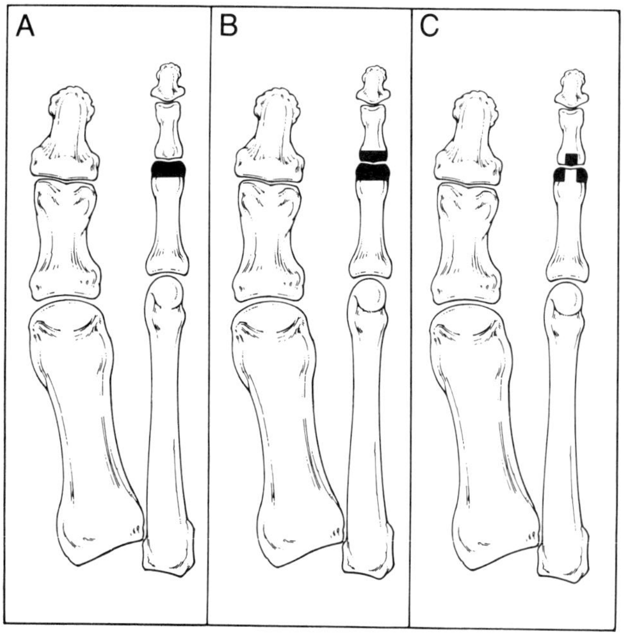

FIG 16–5.
A, digital arthroplasty **B,** the end-to-end arthrodesis. **C,** the peg-in-hole arthrodesis.

The overlapping second digit (Fig 16–6) presents an interesting combination of the previous two deformities. This condition is a hammertoe that exists in conjunction with hallux abducto valgus. Chronic inflammation of the second metatarsophalangeal joint weakens the soft-tissue structures and diminishes stability. While the hallux moves laterally or abducts, the second digit rides dorsally and may sublux medially. Treatment usually includes release of contracture at the second metatarsophalangeal joint and fusion of the second digit. Fusion is normally chosen over arthroplasty with the overlapping toe because arthrodesis adds stability laterally (also known as the buttressing effect). A Kirschner wire crosses the metatarsophalangeal joint until clinical healing and good position is evident. Correction of the hallux abducto valgus deformity at the same time is virtually mandatory to allow relocation of the second digit.

HEEL PAIN

Heel pain presents with a variety of etiologies, severity of symptoms, and patient populations. The predominant cause is biomechanic; however, metabolic, traumatic, and rheumatologic etiologies are also seen. Commonly referred to as heel spur syndrome or plantar fasciitis, osseous proliferation at the plantar tubercle of the calcaneus is the radiographic finding (Fig 16–7). However, a true spur need not be present to make the diagno-

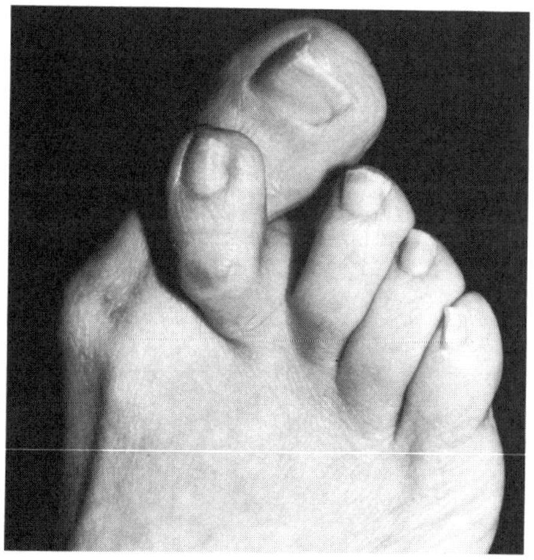

FIG 16–6.
The overlapping toe in conjunction with hallux abducto valgus deformity.

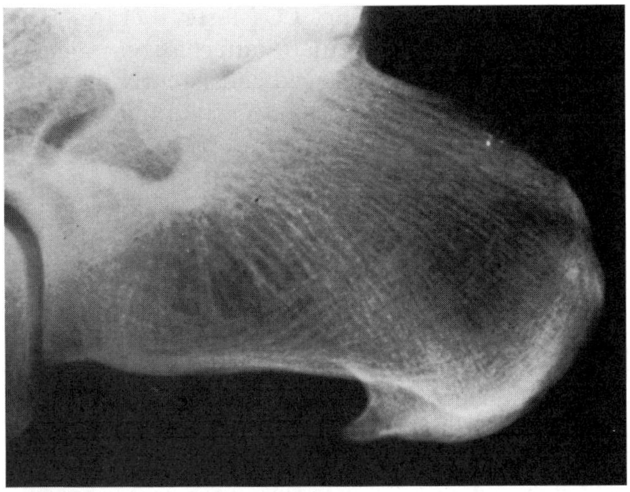

FIG 16–7.
Radiograph of a prominent heel spur.

sis. Similarly, heel spurs can be present and yet be asymptomatic.

Etiology

Biomechanically, tension of the plantar fascia along the longitudinal arch of the foot creates the heel spur syndrome (Fig 16–8). Chronic inflammation and irritation secondary to tension can lead to calcification and spur formation at its origin at the tuberosity of the calcaneus. An asymptomatic spur may be traumatized and eventuate in a symptom complex that can be very disabling.

Treatment is predominantly conservative therapy, but recalcitrant cases make surgery a viable option. Procedures include partial fasciectomy (removal of a small piece of fascia to prevent reattachment), fasciotomy, and resection of the spur itself. An incision is usually made plantar-medially, and the plantar fascial attachment to the calcaneus is identified. The proximity of muscles during the dissection may necessitate the use of a postoperative drain. The patient's postoperative course usually consists of a period of non–weight-bearing with gradual ambulation in a surgical shoe to the patient's tolerance.

WARTS

A wart (verruca) is a benign, highly vascular lesion[1] (Fig 16–9). Although not aggressively invasive in nature, warts can be very painful and debilitating, and it is common to encounter patients who have dealt with and tolerated these lesions for several months.

Warts are commonly seen in children and young adults, with a predisposition in young married women and anxious individuals.[2] The plantar wart is the most commonly treated type. In 25 A.D., Celcius coined the term "myrmecia," which means anthill, for plantar warts.[3] Our understanding of this viral infection is progressing tremendously, yet in accordance with a viral etiology, definitive treatment options are not fully established.

Etiology

The wart is caused by a human virus, the papillomavirus. The virus appears to directly penetrate

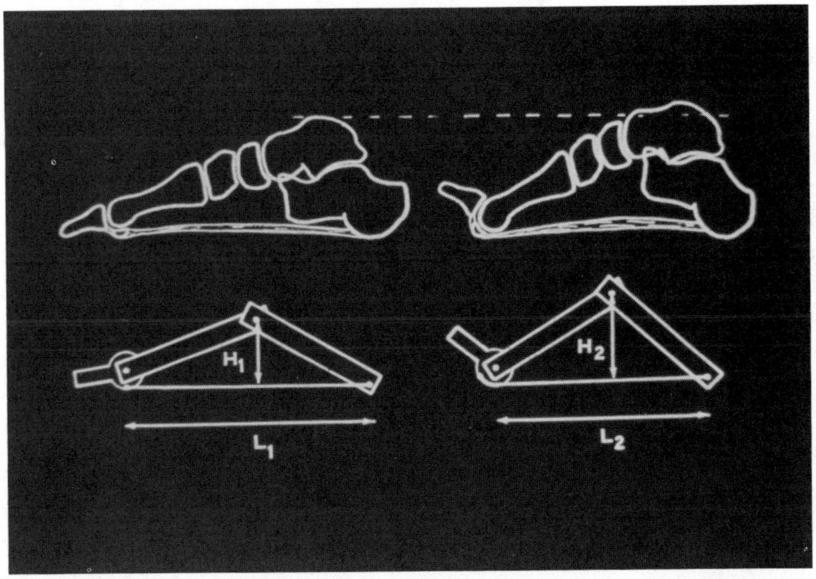

FIG 16–8.
The pulley-like tension complex created by the plantar fascia is illustrated by anatomic and mechanical modes.

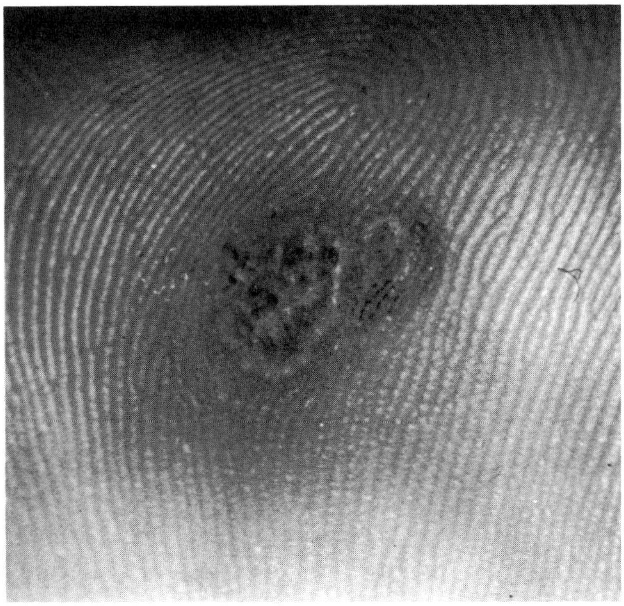

FIG 16–9.
A plantar wart with the classic signs of widened skin lines and black puncta.

the skin in areas especially susceptible to trauma and more often the direct weight-bearing regions.[3] Epidermal changes characteristic of the disease develop after the inoculation. The virus is considered "ectotrophic," i.e., it will only invade cells of epithelial origin, thus affecting the skin and mucous membranes.

There are 15 types of human papillomaviruses isolated. Of these strains, type 1 is shown to result in solitary plantar and occasionally palmar warts. Type 2 commonly results in mosaic plantar warts.[3]

Although plantar warts can mimic other hyperkeratotic lesions routinely seen, warts have certain characteristics that can aid in their differentiation. Close inspection of the lesion will reveal a discontinuity of normal skin lines. The warty lesion will actually push the skin lines apart during its outward growth. Warts will also appear to be studded with black puncta that will reveal pinpoint hemorrhages upon debridement. These are the capillary buds that grow into this vascular lesion. Palpation of this lesion is usually more tender upon lateral and medial (sideways) pressure, whereas a normal corn elicits more tenderness upon direct palpation.

Procedures

There are a variety of treatment options for plantar warts that range from ancient medicinal rituals to state-of-the-art CO_2 laser therapy. The great number of treatment alternatives suggest that no modality has proved consistently effective in eradicating this process. Biopsy studies of the lesion are not recommended unless there is suspicion of a carcinoma. Specific treatment of the etiologic viral infection has not been developed.

Lookingbill and Marks[2] state that 35% to 65% of warty lesions will self-resolve in a period of 2 years. Since the lesion is confined to the epidermis, it can be removed with little if any scarring.[4] The goal of treatment is destruction of the keratinocytes infected with the virus. This is attempted by either physical or chemotherapeutic means.

The common treatments with the highest success rates are divided into two categories, physical and chemical. A physical treatment of liquid nitrogen has long been employed for the treatment of warts. The application is generally painless and consists of dipping a cotton-tipped applicator in liquid nitrogen and holding it against the pared plantar wart for 30 to 90 seconds. However, the inflammatory reaction that occurs shortly after treatment results in intense edema and vesicle formation, which is a source of discomfort. The lesion is seen in 5 to 7 days and scooped out with a curette. Often two to three consecutive treatments are necessary for a complete cure.

Surgical intervention is usually the definitive treatment for these plantar lesions. A local anesthetic is infiltrated around the perioperative site followed by a superficial incision to demarcate the wart from the normal surrounding tissue. A blunt instrument is then utilized to effectively "shell out" the entire lesion without violating the epidermal-dermal interface. The cavity is then curetted cleanly and a sterile dressing applied (Fig 16–10). CO_2 laser therapy is another physical treatment that has been utilized for several years. The monochromatic light accurately vaporizes the tissues upon contact and has produced favorable results.[5]

Chemical treatment includes acid therapy. This therapy is utilized to irritate tissues and induce inflammatory processes with eventual necrosis of the wart. Compounds commonly include monochloroacetic and trichloroacetic acids and salicylic acids of various concentrations.[5] Care must be taken to avoid application of the caustic materials to normal tissue. This is best achieved by an aperture pad in the form of ¼- or ⅜-in. felt. This pad also serves to remove weight-bearing forces off of the painful lesion. The lesion is first debrided to the level of pinpoint bleeding, and then the aperture pad can be applied followed by the

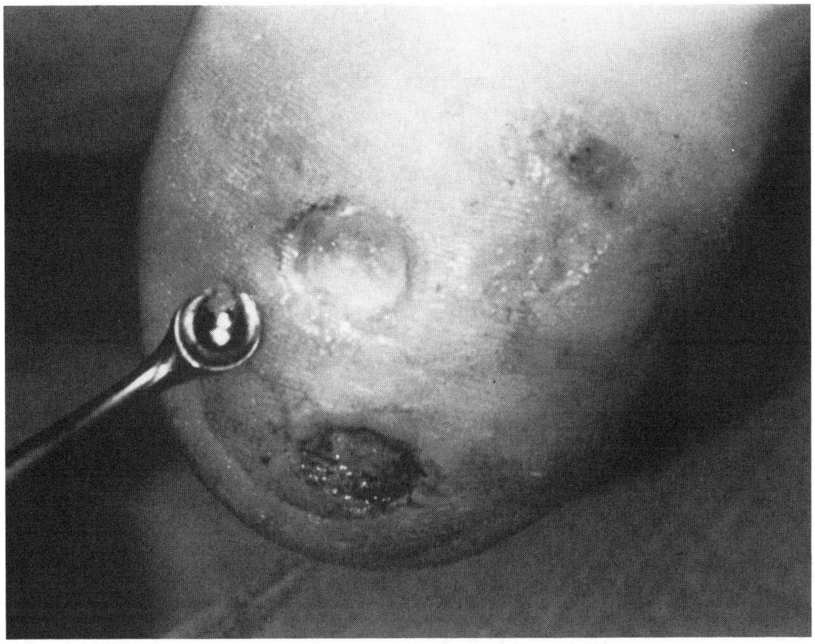

FIG 16–10.
A curette used for debridement of a warty lesion.

acid therapy. The aperture pad is then covered by a piece of moleskin. The lesion should be checked weekly. Usually, several applications are necessary for favorable results.

NEUROMA

A neuroma is a benign enlargement of a nerve. Most commonly this is found in the third intermetatarsal space, which is referred to as "Morton's neuroma."[6] The second interspace is the next most common location of a digital neuroma, with first and fourth interspace neuromas occurring rarely. Neuromas are more frequently found in women at ages ranging from 18 to 60 years.[7] The enlargement makes the nerve more susceptible to irritation from adjacent structures, most commonly the metatarsal heads, phalangeal bases, and plantar ligaments. The patient's complaints vary from a dull aching pain to a sharp shooting sensation, often with distal and proximal tingling and numbness. Digital hyperesthesia is also a noted common symptom.

Etiology

Anatomically, the third common digital nerve receives contributions from the medial plantar nerve and a communicating branch from its lateral plantar counterpart. The nerve is thicker as a result of these contributions and then courses distally around the metatarsal heads toward the digits (Fig 16–11). Trauma and/or irritation of the nerve in this region can initiate an inflammatory process that results in acute and chronic symptomatology. Microtrauma due to restricting shoe gear, soft-tissue compression, and biomechanical forces are common etiologies for neuroma formation.

If suspected, a neuroma can be assessed clini-

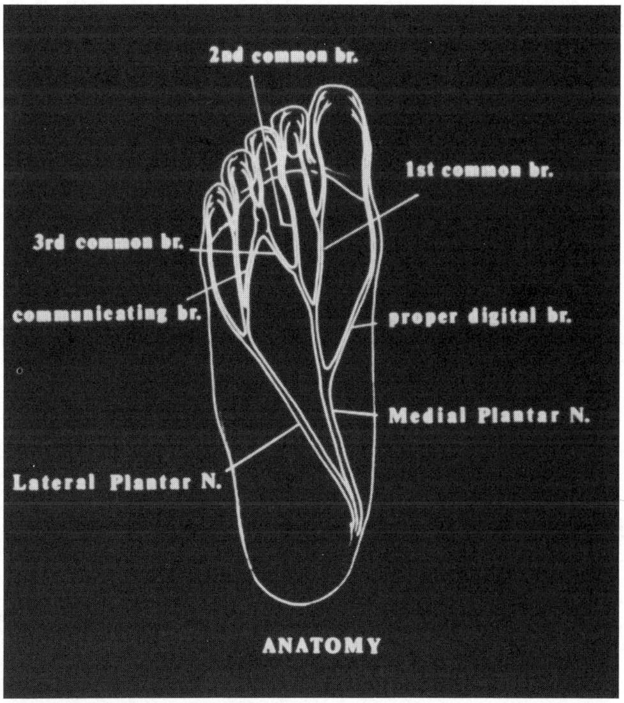

FIG 16–11.
Morton's neuroma formed from the third common digital nerve and a communicating branch.

cally by several methods. Classically, a "Mulder's click" can be elicited to help substantiate the diagnosis. This is described as a silent, palpable, and sometimes painful "click" in the affected intermetatarsal space when the metatarsal heads are compressed upon each other.[8] Direct palpation is also helpful starting plantar-distally at the distal metatarsal head and directed proximal-dorsally. This will usually elicit a response if applied correctly.

Treatment

Initial conservative treatment consists of padding. An attempt should be directed at balancing or spreading the metatarsal heads and relieving pressure off of the nerve. A metatarsal pad of felt can be beveled at its anterior aspect and placed just proximal to the plantar condyles of metatarsal 3 and 4. Low Dye strapping can also prove beneficial in controlling pronatory/hypermobile forces, and this can improve neuroma symptoms.[7, 9]

Injection therapy can also be utilized. The intermetatarsal space is infiltrated with a mixture of a long-acting local anesthetic and steroid. The local will act to anesthetize the traumatized nerve branch, and the steroid will calm the inflammatory reaction within the nerve. For example, 0.75 cc of bupivacaine (Marcaine) mixed with 0.25 cc of Celestone Soluspan is injected just proximal and distal to the metatarsal heads. The effect found is variable and usually lasts from several days to several months. This regimen can be repeated, but generally it should not exceed three to four doses due to the negative effects of chronic local steroid deposition within tissues.[10]

If these conservative measures prove unsuccessful, surgical excision of the neuroma is the definitive treatment of choice. Several incisional approaches have been described and include dorsal and plantar longitudinal, web splitting, and transverse plantar incisions. Although the plantar approaches afford the best visualization and exposure to the nerve, the nature of the surgical incision leaves the patient non–weight-bearing for several weeks. A plantar incision is preferred for recurrent neuromas requiring a second surgery because tissue fibrosis and adhesions make the advantage of better exposure extremely beneficial. The web-splitting incision can result in postoperative maceration and irritation within the interspace. The greatest advantage to the dorsal approach is the immediate weight-bearing capacity of the patient. Healing is also more rapid on the dorsal skin vs. the plantar skin[11] (Fig 16–12).

The metatarsal heads are first palpated, and a dorsal incision is made starting 1 cm distal to the metatarsal heads and extending 3 cm proximally. Care is taken to avoid any vascular structures as dissection is carried down to the level of the deep transverse intermetatarsal ligament. Once this ligament is found and transected, the neuroma can be found immediately deep to this structure. Care is taken to isolate and identify all branches coursing distally to the digits, and these are resected distally as far as possible (Fig 16–13). The neuroma is then traced proximally and resected cleanly. The incision is closed with an effort to maintain anatomic layers, and a sterile dressing is applied. The patient can ambulate with a surgical shoe.

NAIL PATHOLOGY

Nail pathology is frequently encountered, and a working knowledge of not only conservative treat-

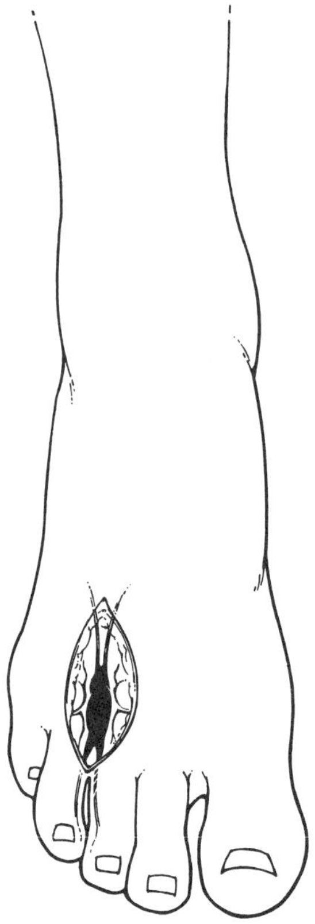

FIG 16–12.
The common dorsal incision with immediate weight-bearing postoperatively.

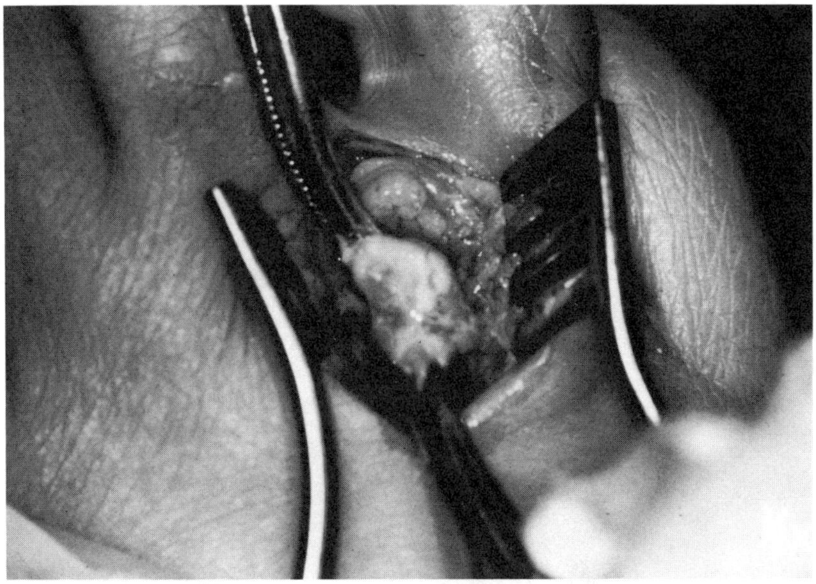

FIG 16–13.
Intraoperative neuroma. It is important to identify its proximal and distal branches.

ment for these problems but also proper surgical treatment is necessary. Common presentations of onychocryptosis (ingrown nail) (Fig 16–14) and onychomycosis (fungus nail) are at times best treated with surgical approaches consisting of partial and/or total nail avulsion. Nail tissue is derived from the matrix cells located underneath the eponychium. The matrix cells are often left untouched during initial avulsion procedures. As an option, the matrix can be addressed during these procedures in an effort to obtain permanent correction. Matrix cells can be removed either by chemical cauterization with phenol or with surgical excision. These methods are discussed below.

Proper anesthesia must be obtained prior to any surgical treatment. This is best obtained by a simple "H" block at the level of the base of the proximal phalanx.[12] There are four main nerve branches innervating each digit and these must be addressed. Usually 3 to 5 cc of 1% lidocaine (Xylocaine) without epinephrine should be adequate to achieve anesthesia in the hallux. Less is required for a lesser digit. A 27-gauge needle is preferred to minimize trauma to the patient. Palpate the dorsomedial aspect of the phalangeal base, and swab the area with alcohol. With the use of a skin refrigerant (ethyl chloride), spray the region, and quickly penetrate the skin with the needle. Infiltrate a ½ cc wheal in this region, and then slowly proceed plantarly by injecting slowly as you go. At the level of the plantar-medial base, infiltrate another ½ cc wheal. You should be able to observe this wheal being infiltrated if you are at the proper level. The identical procedure should be followed for the lateral aspect of the hallux/digit. Some physicians choose to inject across the dorsal and plantar aspects of the digit. This is good practice to ensure a complete anesthetic ring. The digit is then prepared and draped in the usual sterile manner.

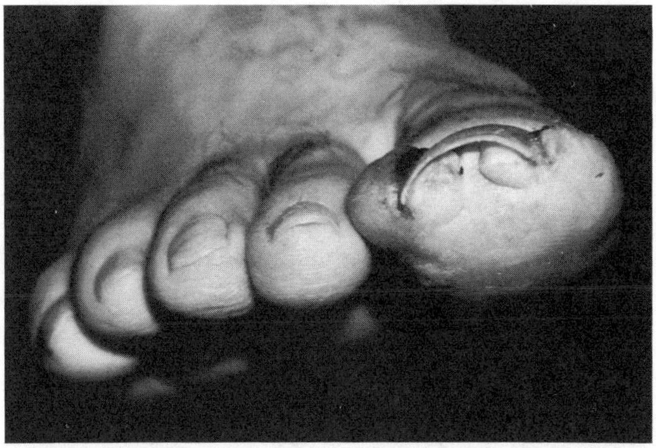

FIG 16–14.
Onychocryptosis (ingrown nail) of the medial and lateral hallux borders. Note the proud flesh laterally.

The three most common partial nail procedures include simple excision, Winograd matrixectomy, and Frost matrixectomy. In a simple excision, an English anvil nail splitter is used to score the nail longitudinally at the region of deformity. This is carried proximally to the level of the eponychium. A no. 81 blade is then used to continue this cut beneath the eponychium to the level of the extensor ridge, which will be felt by the blade. The nail fragment is clamped securely with hemostats and

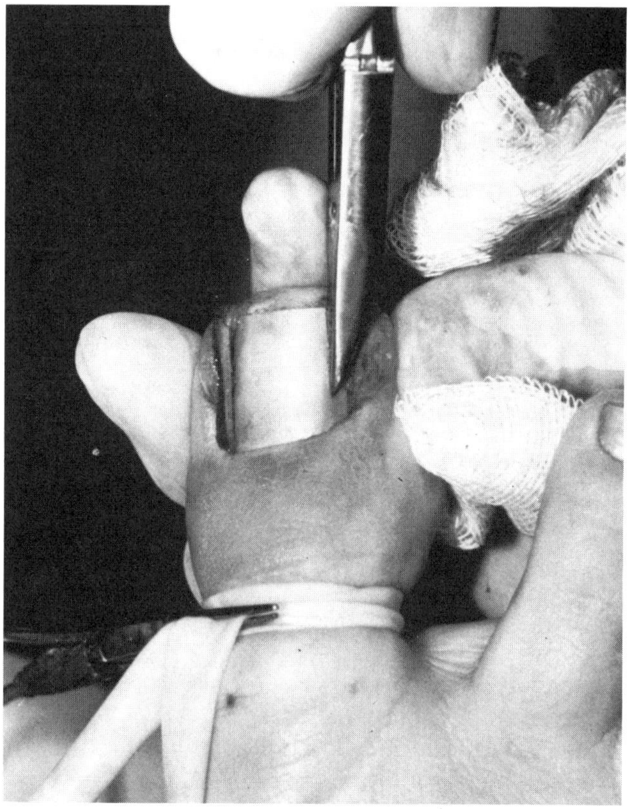

FIG 16–15.
Nail nipper utilized to score the nail longitudinally. This is carried to the extensor ridge.

removed by rotation toward the midline of the nail (Fig 16–15). A curette is then used to remove any further debris from the nail groove and eponychial region.

The Winograd matrixectomy[13] procedure provides removal of the offending nail portion as well as the soft-tissue growth (proud flesh) occasionally found within the nail groove. The midline incision is extended a little proximal to the eponychium to excise the matrix cells along with the nail. Both incisions are made down to the bone, and the wedge is cleanly excised. Absorbable suture is used to reapproximate the skin to the nail. The suture is brought downward through the nail to avoid raising the nail off its bed and is best tied with simple interrupted stitches.

The Frost matrixectomy[14] procedure provides clear exposure to the matrix without the destruction seen in the Winograd procedure. A longitudinal incision is made along the nail and extended proximal to the eponychium in a "J" configuration. This flap will expose the underlying nail and matrix region. The matrix is then cleanly excised. A simple interrupted stitch is used to bring the edges together.

All these wounds should be irrigated with normal saline and dressed with sterile materials. It is recommended that antibiotic cream be applied within the nail bed and groove and the region be covered with a piece of Adaptic prior to the dressing (Fig 16–16).

At times it is preferable to remove the nail in its entirety.[12] A nail elevator is used to free the nail

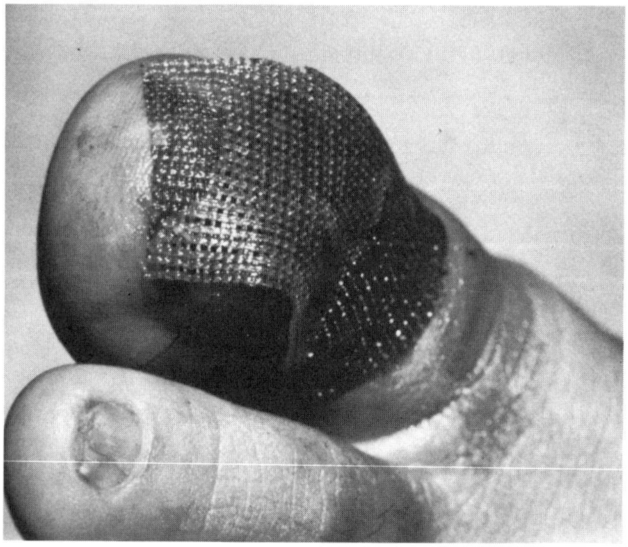

FIG 16–16.
Povidone-iodine (Betadine)-soaked Adaptic applied to the surgical wound.

plate from the underlying nail bed as well as the eponychium. Rotating a hemostat clamped medially and laterally will free the nail. Cauterization is similar to that used on a partial nail. The matrix is effectively destroyed with the application of 88% pure liquified phenol to this region after nail avulsion. The standard phenol and alcohol procedure[15] is a common office practice. A local anesthetic block is administered as described above and the region prepared and draped. A Penrose drain is placed at the proximal aspect of the hallux to serve as a tourniquet during the procedure. A nail elevator is used to free the nail from its bed. Place the elevator distally and slowly work the instrument proximally up to the extensor ridge. Pressure should be applied superiorly to avoid laceration of the nail bed. When the nail is free from the bed, a hemostat is used to pry the nail free from its proximal attachments in two steps. Grasp the medial portion of the nail and rotate the hemostat toward the midline to free the medial soft-tissue attachments. Repeat this with the lateral side. Curette medially and laterally beneath the eponychium to remove any debris left in the area.

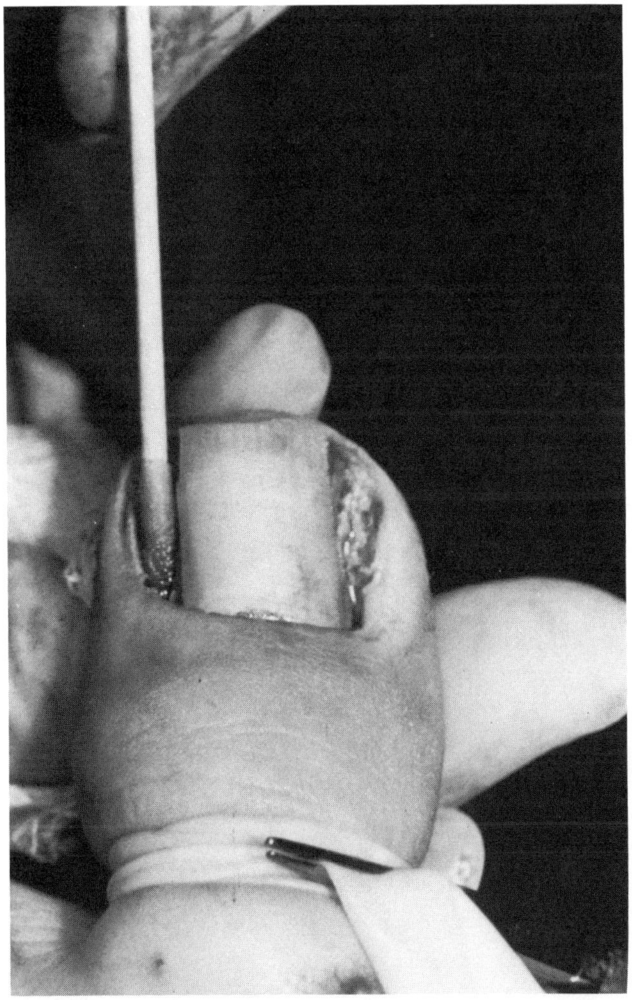

FIG 16–17.
Phenol application to the lateral hallux nail border. Note the Penrose drain utilized for hemostasis.

Phenol is now applied to the matrix and nail bed regions. Three cotton-tipped applicators are needed. A clear ointment should be used to protect the skin from phenol exposure. Spread this ointment over the eponychial and hyponychial regions. Apply the phenol to the matrix in three applications of 30 to 45 seconds each (Fig 16–17). The applicators are placed under the eponychium and rotated along the extensor ridge while making sure that the matrix is entirely exposed.[15] Briefly cover the nail bed with the third application. Alcohol is applied with a cotton-tipped applicator to neutralize the remaining phenol. In actuality, removal of the tourniquet at this time will allow tissue bleeding, which effectively serves to flush the phenol from the wound.

Antibiotic ointment and a piece of Adaptic are placed on the wound. A firm compressive dressing is applied. After the first 48 to 72 hours, the patient is instructed to soak the foot twice a day in warm water with Epsom salts and redress the hallux. Drainage will occur up to 2 to 3 weeks, and the wound should be monitored carefully during this time.

The treatments of common podiatric deformities are as varied as their causes. All can resolve a patient's symptomatology when used in the appropriate clinical situation.

REFERENCES

1. Yale JF: *Podiatric Medicine*. Baltimore, Williams & Wilkins, 1987, pp 168–178.
2. Lookingbill DP, Marks JG: *Principles of Dermatology*. Philadelphia, WB Saunders Co, 1986, pp 56–59.
3. Glover MG: Plantar warts—Foot fellows review. *Foot Ankle* 1990; 11:172–178.
4. Habif TP: *Clinical Dermatology*. St Louis, CV Mosby Co, 1990, pp 269–276.
5. Bartolomei FJ, McCarthy DJ: Cutaneous manifestation of viral diseases, in McCarthy DJ (ed): *Podiatric Dermatology*. Baltimore, Williams & Wilkins, 1986, pp 146–154.
6. Morton TG: A peculiar and painful affection of the fourth metatarsophalangeal articulation. *Am J Med Sci* 1976; 71:35.
7. Miller SJ: Morton's neuroma—A syndrome, in McGlamry ED (ed): *Comprehensive Textbook of Foot*

Surgery. Baltimore, Williams & Wilkins, 1987, pp 38–56.
8. Mulder JD: The causative mechanism in Morton's metatarsalgia. *J Bone Joint Surg [Br]* 1951; 33:94–99.
9. Schreiber LJ: Method of padding for Morton's neuralgia. *J Am Podiatr Assoc* 1939; 29:5–10.
10. Wright EW: Injection therapy in Morton's neuralgia. *J Am Podiatr Assoc* 1955; 45:566–567.
11. Kitting RW, McGlamry ED: Removal of an intermetatarsal neuroma. *J Am Podiatr Assoc* 1973; 63:274.
12. Dockery GL: Nails: Fundamental conditions and procedures, in McGlamry ED (ed): *Comprehensive Textbook of Foot Surgery*. Baltimore, Williams & Wilkins, 1987, pp 3–37.
13. Winograd AM: A modification in the technic of operation for ingrown toenail. *JAMA* 1929; 91:229–230.
14. Frost LA: Surgical resection for the incurvated nail. *Curr Medical Dig* 1962; 29:119–121.
15. Nyman SP: The phenol-alcohol technique for toenail excision. *J N J Chirop Soc* 1956; 5:2–4.

ADDITIONAL READING

Austin DW, Leventon EO: A new osteotomy for hallux valgus. *Clin Orthop* 1981; 157:25–30.

Keller WL: The surgical treatment of bunions and hallux valgus. *N Y State J Med* 1904; 80:741–742, 1904.

McBride ED: A conservative operation for bunions. *J Bone Joint Surg* 1928; 10:735–739.

Miller SJ: Surgical technique for resection of Morton's neuroma. *J Am Podiatr Assoc* 1981; 71:181–188.

Silver D: The operative treatment of hallux valgus. *J Bone Joint Surg* 1923; 5:225–231.

17

Office Supplies and Storage

Caroline Welch, P.M.A.C.

I. Padding and Strapping
II. Instrumentation and Supplies
III. Major Equipment
IV. Sterile Dressing Materials
V. Casting Materials
VI. Storage and Supply Area

A well-stocked treatment room is very important. It is necessary to check all treatment rooms and areas daily to ensure that all materials are available for proper patient care. Be certain that all supplies are accessible to the podiatrist and the assistant. Time is lost if the doctor or assistant must stop to retrieve materials in the middle of a procedure.

PADDING AND STRAPPING

Padding materials are ordered from manufacturers or medical supply houses. Individual offices may fabricate special pads designed to meet their specific needs. Moleskin (1/32-in.) and 1/16- and 1/8-in. adhesive-backed felt pads are most commonly used. Holes may be punched in the center of the pad to form an aperture or cutout pad. The size of the hole should be larger than the lesion or sensitive area it is protecting. When the pad is applied to a digit, various types of tape such as ½ to 1-in. self-adhering gauze tape (Fabco, First Aid Bandage Co, Leominster, Mass) or elastic adhesive bandage (Elastoplast, Beiersdorf, Inc, Norwalk, Conn) may be used to secure the pad. Moleskin is used to secure plantar pads for lesions on the bottom of the foot.

Tubular foam and foam toe separators are valuable in treating toe pathology. Digital traction devices or buttress pads are used for deformities of the lesser toes. These can be fabricated from other office materials or purchased premade by various manufacturers.

Strapping is utilized in the treatment of sprains, plantar fasciitis and heel spur syndrome, minor fractures, and tendonitis. Plantar rest straps, Low Dye strappings, and heel locks are used every day by a podiatrist. Adhesive and nonadhesive felts and foams are used in combination with various adhesive tapes or elastic tapes. Coban (3M, St Paul, Minn), elastic bandages, and 1- to 3-in. tape should be available. Webril (The Kendall Co, Boston) or Kerlix (Johnson & Johnson Products, New Brunswick, NJ) are helpful in adding padding or compression. Tubular gauze may be used as a covering to protect strappings.

INSTRUMENTATION AND SUPPLIES

Table 17–1 provides a list of miscellaneous necessities that should be present in every treatment room. Items used less frequently may be placed in the specific room where they are most often needed. For example, sterile water and sterile scrub brushes should be kept in the surgery room along with sterile gloves and other surgical supplies. If a specific room is set aside for casting, then casting materials can be kept there; otherwise, they are stored in a central store room. Bulky items such as surgical shoes and cast boots are stored in cabinets or on shelves in a storage room.

Commonly used stainless steel instruments are stored in cold sterilization containers placed on the table top. This tray will often contain a nail nipper, tissue nipper, palliative blade handle, curette, nail elevator, hemostat, pickup, suture removal scissors, and nail burrs. Alcohol, acetone,

TABLE 17–1.
Treatment Room Supplies

Scissors, straight and curved
Hemostat kept in cold sterilization
Cotton balls and cotton-tipped applicators
2 × 2-in. and 4 × 4-in. gauze pads, 2- and 3-in. Kling (Johnson & Johnson Products, New Brunswick, NJ)
Spot sized, ¾-in., 1-in., and extra-large Band-Aids (Johnson & Johnson Products)
Plastic-backed towels
Thermometer
Blades for surgical and palliative care
Creams and ointments
Local anesthetics and injectable steroids
Syringes (1–10 cc)
Needles (½- to 1½-in. inch length; 18–27 gauge)
Biomedical disposable waste containers
Nonsterile disposable gloves
Tractograph or protractor
Prescription pads, pens, instructional materials
Paper shoes

povidone-iodine solution, skin adherent, tincture of benzoin, sterile water, and saline may be stored in properly labeled containers on the table top.

Various prepackaged minor surgical packs should be available. These include a nail surgery pack, wart surgery pack, and a suturing or laceration pack.

MAJOR EQUIPMENT

Each treatment room needs a treatment chair or table that is in good, safe working condition. Be certain that all armrests are secure to prevent injury to the patient. A side chair is recommended for visitors who accompany the patient.

A podiatric drill is used in palliative care of the toenails and hyperkeratotic lesions. Drills may be hand operated from the countertop or may be anchored to the wall or cabinet. A foot rheostat is preferable.

Adequate lighting, whether it be incandescent or fluorescent light, is a must for any treatment room. Typically, a surgical light is also needed for close-up work. A flashlight should be readily available in the event of a power failure. View boxes are utilized to review x-ray films. Special bulbs are needed for the view box and surgical lights. Spare bulbs should be kept on hand in a central location.

A trash container is a very essential piece of equipment. All bloody materials as well as syringes and needles should be disposed of in a proper biowaste container.

STERILE DRESSING MATERIALS

Sterile dressing changes can be performed in a designated room or in any treatment room. The materials needed may be stored in each treatment room, or they can be made available in a kit and stored in a transportable basket (Table 17–2).

CASTING MATERIALS

Casting materials may be maintained in a specific cast room. However, many offices store the materials on a portable cart and move it to the room where it is needed. When not in use, the cart may be stored in the laboratory or in a central storage room. Table 17–3 contains a list of materials for the casting cart.

STORAGE AND SUPPLY AREA

Supplies that are used on a daily basis should be stored in each individual treatment room. Any additional supplies should be kept in a well-organized storage room (Table 17–4) that is easily accessible to all the treatment rooms. Supplies can

TABLE 17–2.
Sterile Dressing Kit

2 × 2-in. and 4 × 4-in. gauze
Sterile 2- and 3-in. Kling
Kerlix and Webril
Adaptic (Johnson & Johnson Products, New Brunswick, NJ)
Steri-Strips (3M, St. Paul, Minn)
Nu-Gauze (plain and iodoform) (Johnson & Johnson Products)
Tubular gauze
Tape (hypoallergenic, adhesive and elastic)
Povidone-iodine, chlorhexedine gluconate, hydrogen peroxide

TABLE 17–3.
Casting Cart Supplies

2-, 3-, and 4-in. synthetic and/or plaster casting material
Synthetic and/or plaster splints including 5 × 30-in. extrafast-setting plaster splints
3- and 4-in. Webril
2-, 3-, and 4-in. stockinettes
Tongue blades
3-, 4-, and 6-in. elastic bandages
Cast Padding (Johnson & Johnson Products, New Brunswick, NJ)
Water pan
Scissors
Nonsterile disposable gloves
Drape sheets or plastic-backed towels
Cast stand (optional)

TABLE 17–4.
Storage Room Supplies

Cast boots and surgical shoes
Padding and strapping supplies
Elastic bandages, Unna boot dressings, ankle supports,
Sterile drapes, gowns, caps, masks, shoe covers, gloves, and other operating room necessities
Sterile dressing supplies
Sterile instrument packs
Casting supplies including a cast cutter and separator
Wheelchair, walker, and crutches
Autoclaving supplies
Overstock of all treatment room supplies
Medications including injectables and topicals
Drug samples
Emergency kit, oxygen tank, fire extinguisher
Laboratory supplies including culturettes and specimen bottles
X-ray supplies including film, folders, chemicals, etc. (These may also be stored in the x-ray room if space is available.)

also be stored in work stations if adequate cabinet space is provided.

General inventory control is very important for any office. A notebook should be kept with an alphabetic listing of all the supplies and suppliers. List the suppliers, their representatives, and any pertinent information so that this information is readily accessible.

18

Patient Mobility

Heidi Stapp, P.M.A.C.

I. Assisting With Ambulation
II. Patient Placement
III. Placing the Patient Into the Treatment Chair
IV. Preparing the Patient for the Doctor
V. Preparing the Patient to Leave

ASSISTING WITH AMBULATION

The routine ambulatory patient seen in the office needs little assistance. Guidance from the reception area to the treatment room is usually all that is necessary. The postoperative patient, injured patient, or wheelchair patient, however, need varying degrees of special assistance.

The patient making the first postoperative visit may appear unstable on his feet. Make sure that a wheelchair is available for use. If possible, the driver of the patient should come into the office first and ask for assistance. Frequently, the patient can be wheeled directly from the car into the desired treatment room. The speed at which each patient recovers from surgery is dependent upon the type of surgery, the extent of surgery, and any complications that may have arisen. The podiatric assistant must be able to recognize these recovery variables and be prepared to provide the proper type of ambulation assistance required for the postoperative patient.

A wheelchair should be available for the injured patient because this patient may be unable to place any weight on the affected foot or leg. Crutches may also be used by this patient.

The patient permanently confined to a wheelchair and the non–weight-bearing postoperative patient temporarily confined to a wheelchair may need assistance. Doorways in the office should be wide enough to accommodate the wheelchair. In small offices, maneuvering alone may be quite difficult. Make sure that the pathway is clear as these patients enter the halls, and be available to provide assistance in maneuvering.

When assisting a patient in a wheelchair, make sure that both footrests are used because the patient's feet may get tangled under the chair when in motion. Some footrests also raise to the level of the wheelchair seat to support the postoperative patient requiring limb elevation. Be cautious not to bump into any door frames or furniture when moving the wheelchair.

Patients who ambulate with the use of a walker, cane, or crutches may simply need direction to the treatment room with the assistant at their side for additional support if needed.

Each podiatry office should have ambulatory aids available. A wheelchair, adjustable walker, adjustable canes, and youth- and adult-sized crutches should be accessible specifically for in-office use. Each podiatry assistant should be able to instruct the patient in the proper use of each of these aids.

To fit a patient for a cane, measure the distance from the greater trochanter of the femur to the floor with the patient wearing shoes. A cane is used only for balance, not bearing weight. The cane should be carried in the hand opposite the affected limb and brought forward with the affected limb.

A patient is fitted for a walker in the same manner as for a cane. Measure the distance from the greater trochanter of the femur to the floor with the patient wearing shoes. The walker is used for balance and occasionally for weight bearing. Many elderly patients prefer the security of a walker vs. a cane; however a walker predisposes the patient to forward trunk flexion.

Axillary crutches should be measured from a point approximately 3 in. below the axilla to a point 6 in. lateral and anterior to the shoe. Handgrip placement should be set with 20 to 25 degrees of flexion at the elbow so that the hands, not the axillae, bear the weight. Caution the patient that placing the weight on the axilla can cause undue pressure and nerve damage. Crutch tips are the most important part of the crutch. If the tips are cracked, worn, or wet, they will decrease the ability to support any weight and put the patient at risk for possible falls.

When the patient begins walking with the crutches, the tripod position or three-point gait should be used to allow for maintenance of a non–weight-bearing status of the affected limb. Weight will only be placed on the unaffected limb and the crutches. The four-point gait is used when the patient is able to become partial or full weight bearing.[1]

If crutches are unavailable, assistance should be provided by one or two podiatry assistants. Before assisting a patient with walking, the assistant should do the following:

1. Assess the patient's ability to balance, the patient's strength, the presence of pain, and the activity tolerance.
2. Advise the patient of the distance he is expected to walk and who will be assisting him.
3. Inform the patient that he can stop and rest at any point.
4. Clear an unobstructed pathway so the patient will not expend extra energy walking around obstacles.
5. Determine that the environment is safe, with no loose floor tiles or carpeting. Handrails should be utilized if they are available.[1]

Support should be provided by the assistant by placing both hands at the patient's waist. Patients should be told not to lean from side to side because this can cause distortion of balance and an increased risk of falls.

When using the two-assistant method, one assistant should be positioned on each side of the patient. Each assistant's near arm is around the patient's waist, and the assistant's other arm is around the inferior aspect of the patient's arm. This allows for support of the axillae.[1]

PATIENT PLACEMENT

Before assisting each patient into the treatment room, be aware of the proposed treatment modality. Many offices have rooms designed for casting or strappings, radiography, physical therapy, and minor or major surgery. Placing the patient initially in the proper treatment room will save time and prevent unnecessary shifting from room to room.

Patients with hemiplegia (one-sided paralysis) or hemiparesis (one-sided weakness) will need consideration in the choice of treatment chairs. These patients must be placed in a treatment chair with a normal side of entry corresponding to their unaffected side.

The office may have special treatment rooms designed to accommodate children. If using a podopediatric chair, be cautious because these chairs do not have sidearms. The parent should sit in the treatment chair and hold an infant or toddler. Young children are inquisitive and will not sit still for long periods of time, whereas school-age children are more apt to sit in the chair unassisted. Regardless of age, no child should ever be left unattended because they may topple off the side of the chair.

The elderly patient is generally unstable and is at a greater risk for falls and injuries. The assistant should assist the elderly patient into the chair and place the sidearm in the proper position immediately.

PLACING THE PATIENT INTO THE TREATMENT CHAIR

The patient using a walker requires assistance into the chair. If the patient is entering the chair from the front, he should place the back of the strong legs of the walker (usually the set of legs without wheels) against the chair before sitting down. The patient places one of his legs against the chair and the opposite hand on the armrest. The patient then places his free hand on the other arm rest, leans forward, and gently lowers himself into the chair.

The patient using a cane places the unaffected limb against the chair and then proceeds in the same manner as a patient with a walker. If either of these types of patients are entering the chair from the side, assistance will be needed in swinging the legs around to the front.[2]

The patient with crutches who is entering from

the front of the chair should approach the chair and place the stronger leg close to it. With both crutches under the opposite arm, the patient places a hand on the side of the chair. Set the crutches aside. The patient should then pivot around on the stronger leg. By grasping the arms with both hands, the patient can slowly lower himself into the chair. Again, assistance may be necessary to swing the patient's legs around if entering from the side of the chair.[2]

When transferring a wheelchair patient with some lower extremity muscle strength and function into the treatment chair, place the wheelchair parallel to the treatment chair. It is important to make sure that both wheels are in the locked position. As the patient stands near the treatment chair, the wheelchair may be used as something stable to hold onto. Once the patient has stabilized, pull the wheelchair away, and assist the patient into the chair.

For the non–weight-bearing postoperative patient, again position the wheelchair parallel to the treatment chair, and lock the wheels. Lower the arm on the treatment chair, remove the sidearm of the wheelchair, and place it next to the chair. Two assistants lift the patient into the treatment chair, one assistant at the patient's feet and the other at the patient's shoulders. Gently lift the legs and the underarms of the patient and transfer him to the treatment chair. Remove the wheelchair, and place the sidearm of the treatment chair into position.

PREPARING THE PATIENT FOR THE DOCTOR

Offer elderly, injured, or postoperative patients assistance in removing their shoes and stockings. Bear in mind that a child may want to be treated as a grown-up and therefore refuse assistance.

Reassure the patient, and make him feel as comfortable as possible. Raise the footrests and armrests, and adjust the back of the treatment chair once the patient is seated.

In some offices the podiatrist may require certain patients to receive a whirlpool before being seen. Knowledge of which procedures and treatments require whirlpools allows the assistant to anticipate the therapy, escort the patient to the proper room, and begin treatment. If the assistant knows the office protocol for specific procedures, reads past progress notes, and becomes familiar with the doctor's method of practice, the flow and efficiency of the office will be greatly enhanced.

It is good practice to recline the back of the patient's chair before removing any dressings. Many patients do not wish to see their wound site, and reclining the chair will alleviate some of their anxiety. Talking to the patient as you work also relieves many unnecessary fears.[1]

Before you leave the patient, make sure that he is seated comfortably. It is a good idea to keep plenty of updated magazines in the treatment rooms for the patient's use while waiting.

PREPARING THE PATIENT TO LEAVE

As the patient's treatment ends, prepare him to leave the office. The assistant should offer help in putting on shoes and stockings.

The podiatrist will explain the types of discomfort the patient may experience. The assistant can assess whether the patient is experiencing discomfort by observing the facial expression, vocalizations, and body movements of the patient. Let the patient remain until he feels somewhat relieved of the pain and is ready to leave.

When helping the patient out of the chair, have him swing his legs over the side and rest for a few seconds before standing up. The patient should stand slowly, again pausing for a few seconds. When the patient stands too quickly, his blood pressure may drop and cause orthostatic hypotension manifested as dizziness and light-headedness. Should this occur, the chair is directly behind him for easy access.

The assistant should provide support around the patient's waist so that he has a steady center of gravity. If the patient needs a walker, cane, or crutches, fit them accordingly, instruct the patient on their use, and assist the patient out of the office as discussed previously.

The podiatric assistant should be concerned with assisting the patient in every aspect. Knowing how to assist patients during ambulation will help to establish an excellent office-patient relationship.

REFERENCES

1. Perry AG, Potter PA: Body mechanics, in Perry AG, Potter PA (eds): *Fundamentals of Nursing,* ed 2. St Louis, CV Mosby Co, 1989, pp 1221–1225.
2. Freed MM, Hofkosh J, Kaplan LI, et al: Using ambulatory aids. *Patient Care* 1987; 10:36–39.

19

History and Physical Examination

Gary Fields, D.P.M.

Each journey, no matter how long or difficult, begins with a first step. In an analogous situation, the first step in the diagnosis and treatment of a patient begins with the history and physical examination. This initial examination is the most important contact with the patient because it sets the stage for all future interactions.

THE CHIEF COMPLAINT

In order to identify the chief complaint, the patient should be questioned in a logical sequence. Questions should have a specific purpose and not be haphazard. There are three standard questions that patients are asked. The first and most obvious question is "What brings you into the office?" The second question is "When did it first begin?" or "How long have you had this problem?" The third question is "Did anything happen that may have caused the problem (i.e., exercise, trauma)?" Additional questions are asked depending upon the nature and scope of the problem such as "Does it itch, hurt, bleed, or tingle?" The patient should also be asked whether any treatment had been prescribed by any other physician for the same or similar condition. If the patient had been seen by another physician, a wealth of information can be gleaned from the patient's response. What was the other physician's diagnosis and course of treatment? Did it work? If it did work, why didn't the patient go back? If it didn't work, was it because of an incorrect diagnosis or an inadequate treatment plan? Did the patient follow the other physician's orders correctly? This information can be useful in determining the appropriate diagnosis and treatment plan for the patient.

Questions should not be phrased to "lead" the patient's answers. "Describe the kind of pain you're having" is better than "Are you having pain?" Patients have a desire to help the doctor and the assistant. In their desire to be agreeable, they may admit to symptoms they do not really have. Whenever possible, the interpretation should be organized to yield narrow-range responses. "Does rest relieve or aggravate your symptoms?" "Is it worse in the beginning of the day, or does it become worse as the day progresses?" Depending upon the response, the examiner can narrow or broaden the questions if necessary.

It is important to ask the patient what makes the condition feel better and what makes it feel worse. The patient may already have begun a treatment plan that has had some degree of success. Even if a diagnosis is not made at this initial visit, this information will be useful in helping the patient get symptomatic relief until an appropriate treatment regimen is decided upon.

As one becomes more familiar with the various clinical presentations in a podiatric office, many of the questions will become narrow and specific to the chief complaint. When a patient indicates that a painful heel has been making life miserable for the past 3 months, the examiner may only need to know: whether it hurts on the bottom or the back of the heel, whether it hurts more after periods of inactivity, or whether it has been treated before by someone else. A tentative diagnosis of heel spur syndrome can be made depending upon the answers to these questions.

A common pitfall that should be avoided is questioning the patient during the physical examination. Do not base the questions solely on what is being examined because it may not be the chief complaint. For example, a patient with a severe bunion deformity may be complaining of painful joints in both feet. Fixating on the bunion deformity may prompt questions concerning this deformity, not the joint pains. Do not ignore the bunion deformity. However, address it appropriately within the discussion of the treatment plan, or correlate it with the chief complaint.

MEDICAL AND SURGICAL HISTORY

After the discussion of the chief complaint, questions should turn to a more generalized nature. These questions help accumulate additional information about the patient.

A thorough history begins with obtaining information about childhood diseases. The younger the patient, the more detailed the questioning should be. It is more important to list milestone events such as when the child first began to stand or walk for a young patient with a gait abnormality than for a senior citizen with a hammertoe. When appropriate, a listing of childhood diseases should be charted, especially if rheumatic fever is mentioned. This disease commonly damages the valves of the heart and makes the heart susceptible to bacterial infiltration from other anatomic locations, even the foot. For this reason, preventive antibiotics are given prior to any surgical procedure for a patient with a history of rheumatic heart disease.

All past and present medical diseases should be listed. It is imperative that the patient be asked whether he is suffering from a specific disease or an abnormality in an organ system rather than asking him whether he is suffering from any medical problems in general. All too often a patient will tell you he is healthy even though he is taking medication for blood pressure or diabetes.

Start in an organized manner, and question the patient about the head down to the lower extremities. Keep questions simple, and use layman's terms whenever possible. The term hypertension may not be recognized as easily as high blood pressure. Begin by asking the patient if she has ever had or is having problems with her head, ears, eyes, nose, or throat (HEENT); heart or lungs (cardiorespiratory system); stomach, liver, or intestines (gastrointestinal system); kidneys or bladder (genitourinary system); nerves (nervous system); skin, hair, or nails (dermatologic system); and circulation, varicose veins, or swelling (vascular system). Positive responses are recorded including the diagnosis, date of onset, and treatment, for example, diabetes mellitus, diagnosed October 1984 and treated with insulin, 30 units of NPH 100.

Depending upon the nature of the chief complaint and the responses given, questions about symptoms within each organ system are appropriate. As in the previous example, the diabetic patient, may be asked whether she is having any burning or numbness in her feet or legs. It is equally important to indicate a negative response as well as a positive one. Over a period of time, it is possible to see a development of symptoms that were denied at the initial office visit. Medical records are entering into the legal arena for close scrutiny both for and against the physician and medical staff. Questions not asked sometimes take on more significance than those asked. The past surgical history is recorded as to the surgical procedure, the dates performed, any complications or residual problems, and when necessary, the doctor and hospital performing the surgery. Medication, both prescription and nonprescription, should be recorded including the dosage, number, and duration prescribed. The indications for the medication should also be recorded. This not only confirms the responses given in previous categories but also acts as a filter for any forgotten ailments. A patient may deny having heart disease but will admit to taking propranolol (Inderal) for "heart palpitations."

Traumatic events such as fractures, dislocations, severe chronic sprains, and accidents requiring hospitalization should be recorded along with the date of their occurrence and treatment and any complications.

Personal habits including the use of tobacco, alcohol, and caffeine should be recorded. It should also be noted whether the patient is taking vitamins or tonics or is on a special diet.

Some offices use a printed questionnaire to gather historical information. When used to facilitate the retrieval of medical information in an organized fashion, it can be a very useful tool during the initial examination. However, it should never be used instead of direct questioning of the patient.

PHYSICAL EXAMINATION

The physical examination usually begins as soon as you meet the patient. Develop your sense of observation, and use it when in contact with the patient. Observe whether the patient is limping, in overt pain, or nervous. Note whether there is any paralysis or abnormality of the extremity, any signs of arthritis (joint enlargement) in the hands, or tremors during rest or movement. The patient's vital signs are taken and recorded. Refer to the chapter on vital signs for a more detailed explanation.

The podiatrists will now start the physical examination of the patient. Shoes and stockings are removed from both extremities, and a quick visual inspection is made for obvious abnormalities.

Vascular Examination

The examination of the vascular system begins with an assessment of the dorsalis pedis and posterior tibial pulses bilaterally and simultaneously. The first and second fingers are used to palpate the pulses. Both dorsalis pedis pulses are elicited together and then both posterior tibial pulses together. This allows the examiner to determine whether one pulse is greater than the other. Each pulse is graded on a scale ranging from 0 to 4, with 0 being absent and 4 being bounding. One can easily determine whether an arrythmia is present provided that palpitation of the pulse is held for at least 7 to 10 seconds.

Skin temperature and the temperature gradient are determined by feeling the toes, feet, ankles, and legs bilaterally. Normally the temperature of the extremity should get warmer the more proximal you go. The degree of temperature change is also important. If the toes are ice-cold but the ankle is warm, this could indicate vascular compromise. If the ankle is inflamed due to arthritis, it may be warmer than the leg and much warmer than the toes. Both sides are checked simultaneously with the back of the hands for greater sensitivity.

Capillary filling time or capillary return is determined by applying pressure for 1 to 2 seconds against the skin of the tip of the toe or nail bed and counting the seconds for the color to return. A normal response is up to 3 seconds. A delay in filling the capillary bed is an indication of arterial spasm or disease. The color of the skin and nail beds is noted and listed as pink (normal), blanched (mild-to-moderate arterial disease or spasm), or cyanotic (severe arterial disease or spasm).

Venous filling time is determined by identifying a prominent vein on the foot or ankle. Elevate the leg for 30 to 45 seconds to drain the blood from that vein, and then return the leg to a vertical dependent position. The time it takes for the return of blood into that vein is the venous filling time. Normal filling is under 30 seconds. Delay indicates arterial insufficiency. Other determinants of vascular disease are the presence or absence of hair on the digits, the presence or absence of shiny atrophic skin, and signs of previous ulcerations or amputations. Diseases of the arterial system are significant. Each artery supplies blood bringing vital nutrients and oxygen to the tissues. Our ability to fight infection is compromised if arterial supply is diminished. Because the lower extremities are a primary site for signs and symptoms of vascular disease, a comprehensive and thorough evaluation should be performed at the initial visit and prior to any surgical procedure. Documentation of these findings is a necessity. Many offices are now equipped with noninvasive vascular analyzers that produce a printed tracing or analysis of the patient's circulation. The venous system should be visually assessed by noting whether and where varicose veins are present and the extent of involvement. If the venous insufficiency is extensive and chronic, pigment deposition and induration will be present along the lower third of the leg, usually along the medial portion. Inadequate venous drainage causes congestion of blood flow from the limbs. This can lead to edema (swelling) of the feet, ankles, and legs. If chronic and severe enough, skin ulcerations of the leg will ensue. Blood pooling in the extremities also predisposes the patient to thrombophlebitis.

Examination of the Nervous System

The nervous system of the lower extremities is divided into two basic functions. The motor part sends information from the brain and spinal cord to the muscles to affect movement. The sensory part brings information from the feet and legs back to the brain for conscious and subconscious evaluation. The sensory portion is responsible for the perception of pain, temperature, and touch and for position sense of the toes, feet, and legs.

Evaluation of the nervous system begins with testing the motor portion. This is done by eliciting a reflex action in the Achilles and patella tendons. The stretch that occurs by quickly tapping the tendon sends an impulse through the tendon and muscle, then along the nerve to the spinal cord, and then back to the muscle; this causes a slight contraction of that muscle, hence causing the reflex. Diseases of the brain or upper motor neurons will allow for a greater contraction than usual. Diseases of the nerves, spinal cord, or lower motor neurons will cause no contraction or reflex to occur. In order for an appropriate response to occur, the muscle involved must be under slight tension and without any interference of movement. The response is graded on a scale of 0 to 4, with 0 being no movement, 2 being normal, and 4 being hyperactive.

The presence of abnormal or pathologic reflexes are checked by stroking the plantar aspect (sole) of the foot with a blunt object. The normal response is flexion of the toes. An abnormal response of Babinski is extension of the hallux and fanning of the lesser toes. The presence of the Babinski response is an indication of an upper motor neuron disease. Pain perception is tested by asking the patient to close his eyes and then lightly touching various locations on both feet and legs with a pointed and dull object. The patient is asked to respond after each touch whether it was the sharp or dull end of the instrument used.

Muscle strength is also tested. The patient resists the examiner's attempts to move various anatomic parts. Muscle size, suppleness, and circumference should be visually checked, and if necessary, a tape measurement of the circumference of the calf and thigh is performed.

Vibratory sensation is tested by the use of a 128-cps tuning fork. The tuning fork is struck and placed on a bony prominence such as the first metatarsophalangeal joint. The patient is asked whether he feels the vibrations and, if so, when they stop. The patient and the examiner should feel the vibrations stop almost simultaneously. If the patient loses the sensation much sooner than the examiner, pathology is indicated. If the vibration is not felt at the forefoot, then the ankle bone is used as the test location.

The Romberg test is used to assess the position sense of the patient. The patient stands with arms outstretched in front of the examiner. The patient is then asked to close his eyes. Loss of balance or excessive swaying is noted.

The skin of the toes, feet, and legs are checked thoroughly for signs of scaliness, rashes, hypertrophy, atrophy, tumors, pigmentations, hygiene, sweating, dryness, odor, scratches, infections, or ulcerations. Nail pathology is also noted.

Skeletal Examination

All biomechanical abnormalities are noted. These abnormalities include the presence of bunions, hammertoes, corns, calluses, and high- or low-arched feet. The range of motion of all joints of the foot and ankle are evaluated in a systematic fashion. The patient should be examined while weight bearing. If pertinent, a gait evaluation can also be performed.

The foot is a complex structure. A thorough history and examination are essential to the appropriate diagnosis and treatment of injuries and diseases of the foot.

20

Vital Signs: Barometers of Life

Thomas F. Smith, D.P.M., F.A.C.F.S.
Lynn M. Smith, M.S.

I. Temperature
   A. Equipment
   B. Method
II. Pulse
   A. Equipment
   B. Method
III. Respiration
   A. Equipment
   B. Method
IV. Blood Pressure
   A. Equipment
   B. Technique
V. Conclusion

The ability to accurately and consistently determine the vital signs of a patient should be understood by all podiatric assistants. An emergency office situation is not a time to practice these techniques. Vital signs should be an integral part of the patient record from the initial office visit. Taking vital signs on a regular basis provides the podiatric assistant with an opportunity to practice the techniques as well as perform the function in a routine and consistent manner. Obtaining vital signs on the initial office visit also helps to establish a baseline value for each patient in the practice. If an emergency situation arises, the interpretation of the vital signs can be more meaningful.

Normal values for each vital sign vary depending on the particular age, activity level, and health status of the patient. Various methods and techniques can be utilized to establish vital signs in patients with physical or emotional impairments. All methods for establishing vital signs should be well understood to aid the assistant in performing this function.

The four basic vital signs that will be reviewed include temperature, pulse, respirations, and blood pressure. The basic equipment and methods needed for determining these signs will be discussed.

TEMPERATURE

Body temperature is a reflection of the metabolic state of the patient. Body temperature is measured in degrees Fahrenheit (°F) or degrees centigrade (°C). Most practices use degrees Fahrenheit; however, tables are available for conversion to centigrade (Table 20–1).

The oral, axillary, or rectal temperature determination represents the core temperature of the entire body. Local temperature, or calor, indicates the increased temperature of a particular part of the body. Increased temperature of a particular part can be noted in the case of infection. This may not necessarily indicate an increased temperature for the entire body.

The accurate determination of body temperature is very important to the podiatrist in understanding the overall health status of the patient. The body temperature reflects its ability to both produce and dissipate heat to the atmosphere. *Fever* is the term for an increase in body temperature, and *hypothermia* is the term for a reduction in body temperature. Slight variations in body temperature in a normal patient can be expected.

TABLE 20–1.
Fahrenheit and Centigrade Conversion Formulas

To convert Fahrenheit to centigrade: Subtract 32 and multiply by 5/9
To convert centigrade to Fahrenheit: Multiply by 9/5 and add 32

Such variation is commonly noted during the menstrual cycle of women. The body temperature may increase by 1 to 2 degrees at the time of ovulation. This determination is a common method of birth control and fertility management.

Equipment

The thermometer is used to determine body temperature. A thermometer is an enclosed glass tube with a bulb at one end filled with mercury or an alcohol solution. The fluid will expand or contract based upon the temperature of the environment. This fluid movement is calibrated and read in degrees as temperature. Two types of thermometers, oral and rectal, are used. The oral thermometer has a less bulbous appearance than the rectal version.

The thermometer should be cleansed daily and maintained in an antiseptic fluid. Careful inspection of the thermometer for defects or cracks is of great importance. The column of fluid within the thermometer should also be regularly inspected. Any break or bubbles within the fluid represent a defect in the thermometer, and it should be immediately discarded and replaced.

Electronic thermometers provide a fast determination of body temperature. Temperature determination by the electronic method is neither more nor less accurate than by traditional thermometers. Electronic thermometers are considered to be more sanitary since the probe is covered with a disposable sheath. All manufacturers have a suggested maintenance and care routine that should be consistently followed.

Disposable temperature tapes and strips are also available. These strips determine body temperature within a range of degrees, not to a specific and accurate degree, and therefore are not generally used in the office setting. These strips are used primarily for constant monitoring of body temperature in the anesthetized patient in the operating room.

Method

There are several methods of obtaining body temperature. The podiatric assistant should be familiar with each technique. Conditions such as paralysis, flu, colds, head congestion, and oral pathology may dictate the need for a specific method. The age of the patient and the ability to maintain an oral thermometer in place should also be taken into account when determining the most appropriate method.

The oral method of determining body temperature is the most common. The patient should be questioned to determine whether he has recently smoked or drank hot or cold liquids. Either of these factors will negate the effectiveness of the oral thermometer, and a 30-minute delay is necessary before an accurate oral temperature can be taken.

Check and cleanse the thermometer. The fluid column should be well below the normal body temperature value. If the column is not, immerse the thermometer bulb in cold running water. Place the thermometer beneath the patient's tongue (Fig 20–1). The patient should close his lips tightly around the thermometer to maintain it in place (Fig 20–2). Tight lips also help to ensure the most accurate determination of the body temperature. The patient is instructed to breath through his nose. The thermometer is then left in place for approximately 4 to 5 minutes.

Following the appropriate waiting time, the thermometer is removed and the temperature read and charted. Normal oral body temperature values range from 97.7°F to 99.5°F. Do not hold the bulb end while reading the thermometer. The warmth of the hand can raise the temperature reading. Cleanse the thermometer, and return it to the storage container.

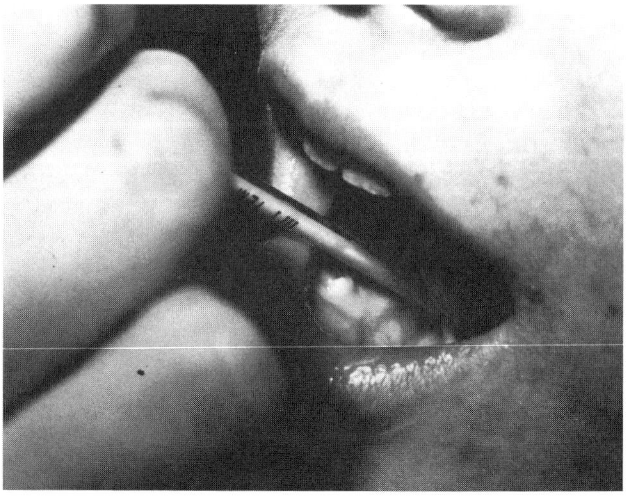

FIG 20–1.
An oral thermometer is placed under the tongue.

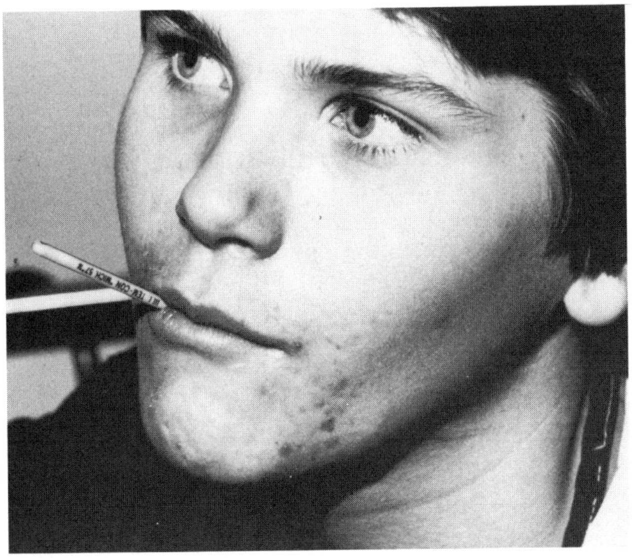

FIG 20–2.
The lips are tightly sealed around the thermometer.

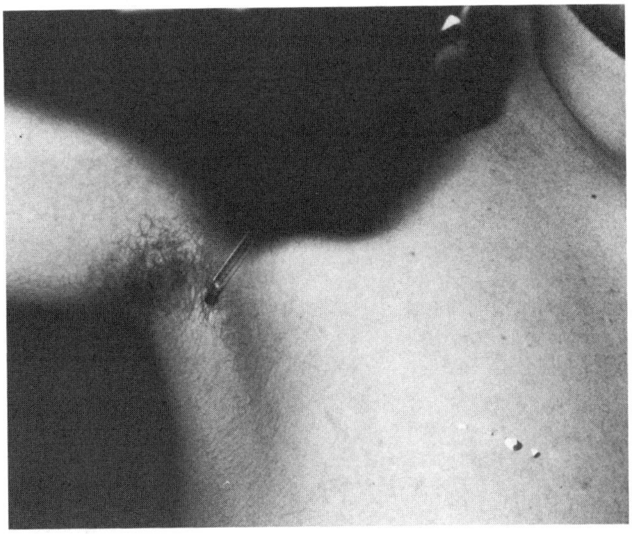

FIG 20–3.
The axilla, or armpit, is dried, and the oral thermometer bulb is centrally placed.

An alternative means of determining body temperature is the axillary method. The thermometer is placed within the axillary fold, or armpit, to determine body temperature. This method can be very helpful in patients who cannot maintain a thermometer within the mouth due to oral pathology or colds, flu, or congestion. This method is also useful in children and infants.

The oral thermometer is utilized for this determination. The thermometer is removed from the storage container, checked, and cleansed. Reduce the column of fluid below the normal temperature value. Dry the armpit, or axilla, and place the thermometer well within the central cavity of the axilla (Fig 20–3). Bring the arm down over the thermometer (Fig 20–4), and have the patient grasp his opposite shoulder to help maintain its position. The thermometer should remain in place for 7 minutes. The assistant may ask a parent to assist in this process or may remain with the patient to ensure proper placement of the thermometer.

After 7 minutes, the thermometer is removed and read, and the value is charted. The normal axillary temperature value is 1 degree less than the oral value, with the range being from 96.7°F. to 98.5°F.

The third determination of body temperature is the rectal method. This method is the most accurate reflection of body temperature and is utilized for patients who can not maintain an oral or axillary positioning of a thermometer.

The thermometer is checked and cleansed prior to insertion. The bulbous rectal thermometer must be used for this type of determination. The adult patient is generally positioned on their side, while an infant is placed supine. The thermometer bulb is bathed in a lubricant and placed approximately 1 to 1½ in. within the anal opening. The patient and thermometer should be constantly monitored by the assistant. The assistant should keep a hand on the buttocks and the thermometer to maintain correct placement and to ensure against breakage.

The thermometer is left in place for 2 minutes. The assistant should constantly reassure the patient and make every effort to maintain the modesty and privacy of the patient. After 2 minutes, the thermometer is read, cleansed, and replaced in

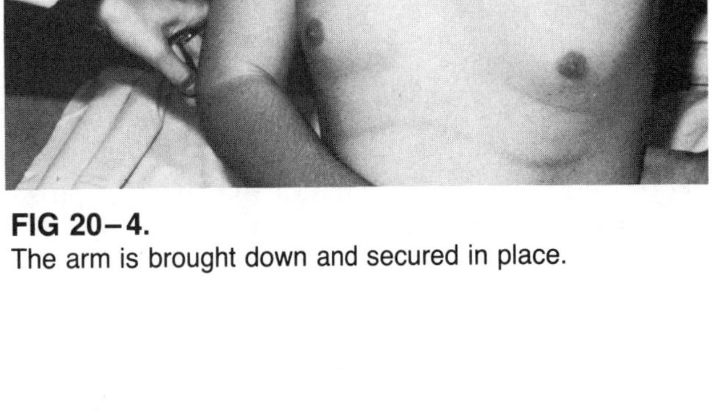

FIG 20–4.
The arm is brought down and secured in place.

the storage container. The temperature value and method of determination is then charted. The normal temperature value for rectal determination is 1°F. higher than the oral temperature and ranges from 98.7°F to 100.5°F.

Because of the differences in normal value ranges, it is important to note whether the oral, axillary, or rectal method was used. A review of a chart for a patient might indicate an elevation in temperature when in fact the elevation might be attributed to the method of determination used.

PULSE

The pulse is an extremely important determination in assessing the cardiovascular status of a patient. The resting pulse of a patient can vary over a significant range during the course of a particular day.

Each particular pulse definition is termed by the artery from which the pulse is taken. A pulse taken at the arm or wrist is termed the radial pulse. Pedal pulses are termed the dorsalis pedis and posterior tibial.

The pulse represents the flow or force generated by the heart in pumping the blood. The wave of force is followed from the heart through the entire arterial system to the fingertips of the examiner. The arteries represent a flexible system of tubing that carries this wave of force from the heart to the extremities. Any disruption of the tubing such as calcification or hardening may create difficulty in determining the person's pulse rate. Adequate pulsations from the heart may be present but may not be palpated due to disruptions in the physical makeup of the arterial tree.

When determining the pulse of a patient it is important not only to count the rate but also to note the volume and rhythm. The volume of the pulse is determined by how easily the pulse is found. If the pulse is bounding, easily found, or visualized, this may indicate an abnormality with the heart or an increased level of blood pressure. A pulse that is thready or difficult to establish may represent low blood pressure or a problem with the cardiovascular system such as hardening or calcification (Fig 20–5).

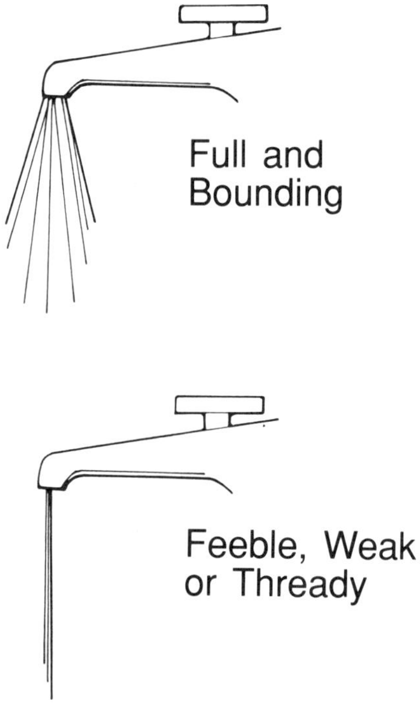

FIG 20–5.
Diagrammatic representation of the volume of pulse.

The rhythm of the pulse is probably one of the more important factors in determining the vital signs of a patient. The rhythm of the pulse is directly related to the rhythm of the heart. A pulse, whether fast or slow, should have a consistent rhythm or beat. Discrepancies in the rhythm of the heart (arrhythmias) may represent life-threatening situations to the elderly patient. An inconsistent rhythm or beat should be noted immediately for referral to an internist for further evaluation.

The rate of the pulse is recorded on the chart. Tachycardia is an increased heart rate, and bradycardia is a reduced heart rate. The heart rate is counted for a period of time and then determined as a rate per minute. Remember, it is important not only to note the rate but also to monitor the rhythm and volume of pulsations when measuring a pulse.

Many individual variations in pulse are evident. An extremely young child has a very high pulse rate, while an elderly or athletic patient may have a reduced pulse rate. Anxious or nervous patients may demonstrate wide variations in pulse rates.

Equipment

The only equipment that is needed to establish a pulse is a watch with an accurate sweep second hand. The examiner's fingers must be adept at palpating a pulse and maintaining that position to count the pulsations. Doppler ultrasound can be utilized to assess the pulse in a patient where palpation is difficult. The Doppler stethoscope provides a method of listening to the pulsations through an artery that cannot be palpated.

Method

The radial pulse at the wrist level is the most common pulse taken. This artery is very close to the surface and overlies a bony structure, which makes palpation very easy (Fig 20–6, A and B). To find the radial pulse the examiner's fingers are placed first at the hypothenar eminence (the bulbous area of the thumb) at its most lateral projection. The fingers are then slid proximally to the wrist bone and next to the thumb. This bone is the radius. The fingers are then directed to the underside of the wrist. The pulse is felt on the undersurface of the radial bone.

The patient should be seated with the arm in an extended and relaxed position. The pulse is palpated a short period of time to evaluate the rhythm and volume. Once a satisfactory rhythm and volume have been ascertained, count the number of pulsations. Gentle pressure of the fingers on the artery will help in maintaining the palpation of the pulse. The number of pulsations can be counted for a period of 60 seconds. It is also possible to count the pulsations over a 30-second period and then multiply that value times two. A 15-second determination multiplied by four is not recommended because the slight variations over a 15-second period may not adequately represent the true pulse value. Normal pulse rates are noted in Table 20–2.

TABLE 20–2.
Normal Pulse Rates for Different Age Groups

Age Group	Pulse Rate (Per Minute)
Before birth	140–150
At birth	130–140
First year of life	115–130
Childhood years	80–115
Adult years	72–80
Later years	60–80

The dorsalis pedis pulse is a common area to check pulsations within the foot. The first intermetatarsal space, or the space between the first and second metatarsal bones, is palpated. The fingers are then worked proximally to the midtarsal region. The dorsalis pedis pulse can be palpated in the midtarsal region just proximal to the first intermetatarsal space. The pulse rate is measured in the same manner as the radial pulse. The posterior tibial pulse is palpated posterior and inferior to the medial malleolus. Pulsation on the medial side of the ankle is the most easily found because it is the largest artery entering into the foot and ankle. Pulses may also be taken at the knee, hip, elbow, and many other locations where arteries approach the body surface.

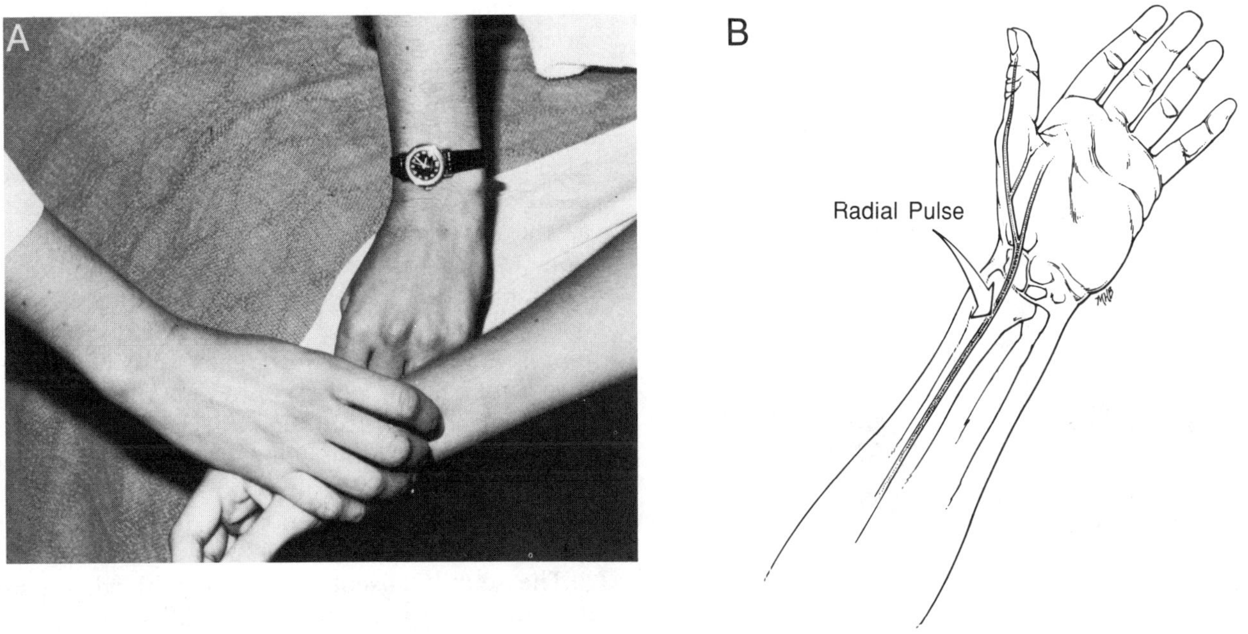

FIG 20–6.
A, clinical representation of a radial pulse determination. **B,** diagrammatic representation of a radial pulse.

RESPIRATION

Respiration represents the normal inhalation and exhalation of a patient. There is a voluntary control of respirations as well as an automatic control system of respiration management. Therefore, respiration must be counted in a subtle fashion so as not to alert the patient (Fig 20–7). If the patient is aware that respiration is being monitored, alterations in the rate may occur.

The character of the respirations as well as the rate should be noted. Observe whether the patient is relaxed or laboring. Try to detect the degree of muscular or voluntary effort being exerted by the patient. Labored respirations may represent a difficulty with the breathing tubes forcing the air in and out of the lungs, or they can be noted in patients who are febrile or extremely ill. Patients who are septic and febrile may have labored breathing called stridor. In this instance, the patient can actually be observed to be working at breathing. As the person inhales and exhales, the examiner should also be listening for certain sounds representing fluid, buildup of mucus, or spasms within the respiratory tree.

The rate of respirations is determined for a particular patient. Bradypnea is a reduced respiratory rate, and tachypnea is an increased respiratory rate.

Equipment

A watch with a sweep second hand is needed to determine the rate of respiration. A very subtle and crafty examiner must take note of the respirations undetected to prevent changes by the patient in the normal rate of respirations. After the pulse determination has been completed, the examiner should continue to give the impression that the pulse rate is being evaluated. Observe the mouth or chest, and count the respirations.

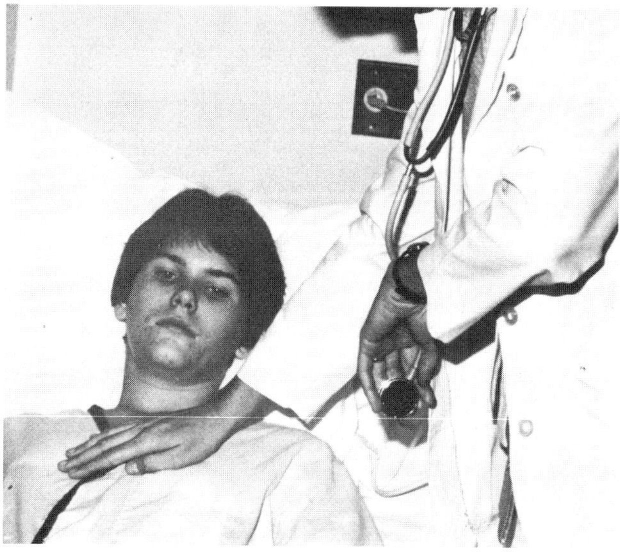

FIG 20–7.
Inappropriate method of determining respirations. The patient is alerted by the hand placement of the evaluator.

Method

The patient should be comfortably seated. Subtly monitor the rate for a 30-second interval. Multiply this factor by two to get the respiration rate. If desired, the rate can also be monitored for 60 seconds. The quality and quantity of respirations being observed are then noted and charted. The normal respiratory rate is 16 to 20 respirations per minute.

BLOOD PRESSURE

Blood pressure represents the pressure within the arterial system at any given time and is accentuated by the beat or contracture of the heart. The heart increases and decreases the blood pressure over the cycle of the heartbeat. The pressure within the arterial system can become a pathologic process greatly affecting the health status of a patient.

Blood pressure is designated and charted by two values, systole and diastole. Systole is the greatest pressure the heart creates within the arterial system at the moment of contracture. This value is represented as the numerator in a fractional display. The diastole represents the resting blood pressure within the system at the lowest point of heart force contraction. It is represented as the lower number, or denominator, in a fraction. In a blood pressure of 120/80, the number 120 represents the systolic pressure, and the number 80 represents the diastolic pressure. Systole represents the moment of greatest pressure within the system, and diastole represents the moment of lowest pressure within the system.

Hypertension is an increase in the amount of pressure within the arterial system. Hypotension indicates a lower-than-normal level of pressure within the arterial system.

The sounds auscultated during blood pressure determination are called Korotkoff sounds. These are the sounds of the valves closing in and about the heart at the moments of pressure variations. The valves within the heart help regulate the flow of blood in a consistent direction.

Blood pressure is noted by millimeters of mercury. Millimeters of mercury is a determination of pressure similar to what would be noted in a barometric reading for weather. The pressure system within the heart and arterial system is what is being assessed in a blood pressure determination. The value of 120/80 actually demonstrates 120 mmHg/80 mmHg.

Equipment

A stethoscope and a sphygmomanometer are needed to determine blood pressure. The earpieces of the stethoscope are inserted into the ear canals and used to listen for the heart sounds. The earpieces should angle toward the stethoscope. If you are having difficulty in hearing through a stethoscope, adjust the angle of the earpieces. Tubing connects the earpieces to the diaphragm or bell unit of the stethoscope. The bell unit picks up the pulsations and transfers them to the earpieces. The diaphragm head is much larger than the bell unit head and must be manipulated over the artery for an accurate determination of arterial sounds (Fig 20–8).

The arm of the patient should be relaxed to make the inner portion of the elbow as soft as possible. This greatly aids in stethoscope placement and auscultation of heart sounds.

The sphygmomanometer is used to occlude arterial flow and measure blood pressure. The sphygmomanometer acts as a tourniquet occluding blood flow into the extremity. Once the blood flow has been completely stopped, the pressure within the sphygmomanometer is slowly released. As the pressure is released by the thumb valve, the blood pressure in the arm overcomes the cuff pressure and passes into the extremity. At that point the blood pressure is determined.

Two types of blood pressure equipment are available, the mercury system and the aneroid system. The mercury system uses a column of mercury to determine the blood pressure. The falling column of mercury is observed by the examiner (Fig 20–9). The aneroid system uses a dial system where the sweep of a dial over a set of numbers is used to determine the blood pressure (Fig 20–10). Both systems are acceptable; however, the mercury column is considered to be more accurate.

The sphygmomanometer is made up of several parts. The cuff envelops the arm as the tourniquet. The size of the cuff is important and should fit securely about the arm. Certain sizes of cuffs are available for pediatric, adult, and obese patients.

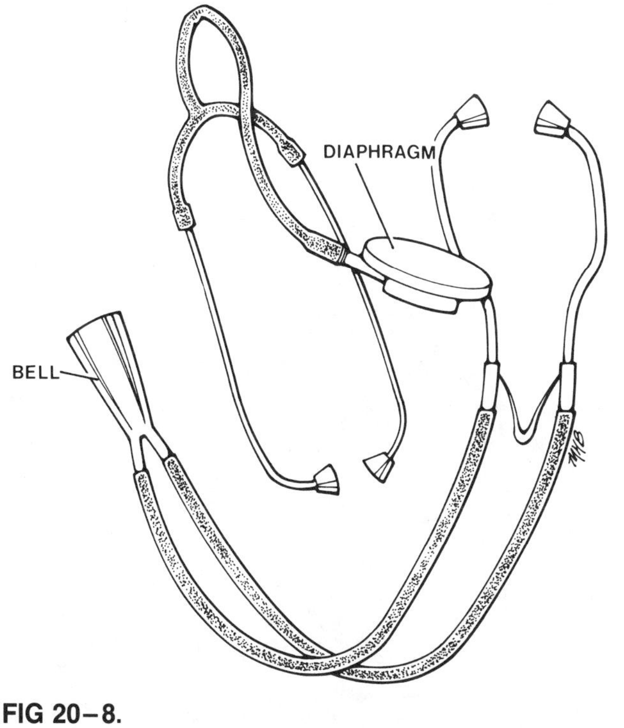

FIG 20–8.
The bell- and diaphragm-type stethoscopes. Note the earpieces, tubing, and bell or diaphragm components of the devices.

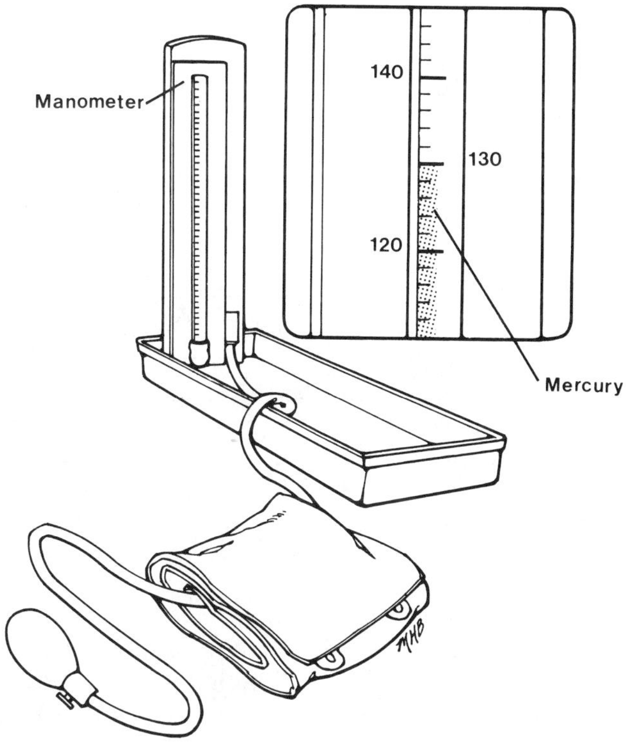

FIG 20–9.
Mercury column sphygmomanometer.

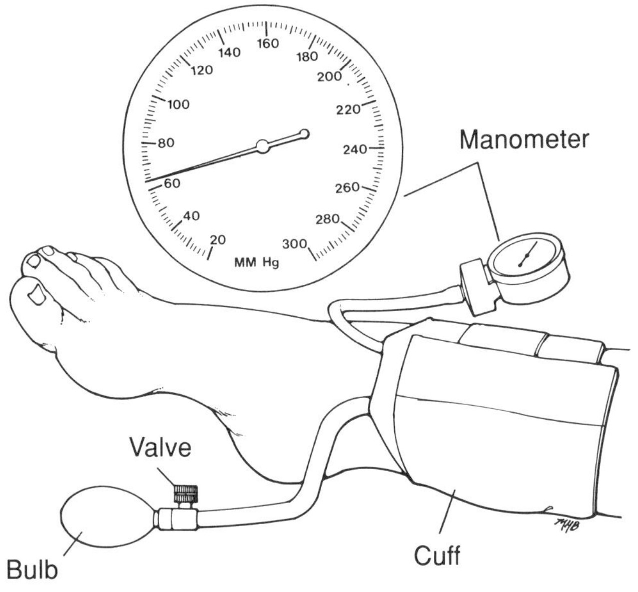

FIG 20–10.
Aneroid sphygmomanometer.

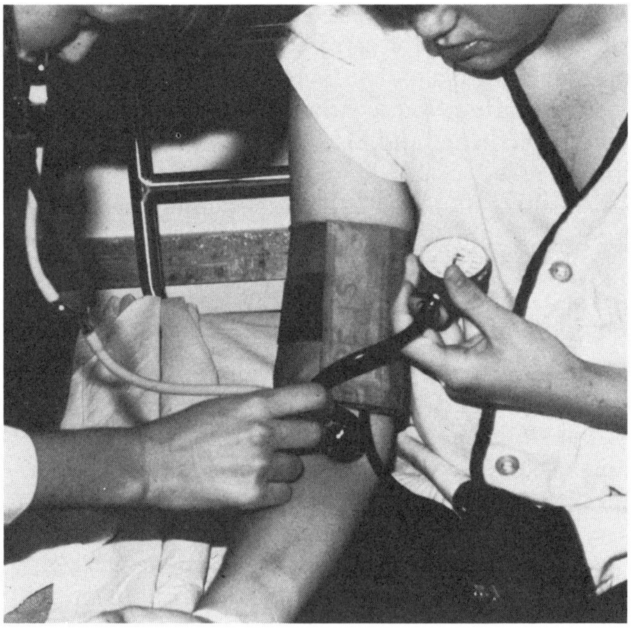

FIG 20–11.
Accurate placement of the cuff, tubing, and stethoscope in determining brachial blood pressure in the arm.

Within the cuff is a bulb that occludes blood flow to the artery. Accurate placement of the cuff and bulb with respect to the artery is needed for consistent determination of blood pressure.

A tubing system connects the cuff, thumb valve, and pump bulb. The pump bulb represents a controlled exhaust system to regulate the pressure of the tourniquet. The valve can be closed and the pump bulb compressed to increase the pressure within the system. As the thumb valve is released, the pressure is released within the system. The amount of pressure within the system is registered on the manometer, aneroid dial, or mercury column.

Technique

The readily accessible brachial artery in the arm is commonly used to record blood pressure. Prior to placing the cuff on the arm, question the patient to determine that no injury is present on the intended arm. Also determine whether the patient has a kidney hemodialysis shunt or fistula. If such a device has been placed in the arm or shoulder, do not use it for blood pressure determination.

The patient should be seated and relaxed with the arm at heart level. The arm is flexed at the elbow and positioned with the elbow down. Shirt sleeves should be loosened and rolled up to the shoulder so as not to impede circulation. The tubing exiting the cuff should be placed directly over the inner aspect of the elbow just above where the stethoscope will be placed to listen for the pulse. The cuff should be empty of air pressure and the valve open. The cuff is then applied snugly on the completely bare upper arm (Fig 20–11).

A pulse may be palpated in the wrist as you inflate the cuff. When the pulse disappears, the cuff

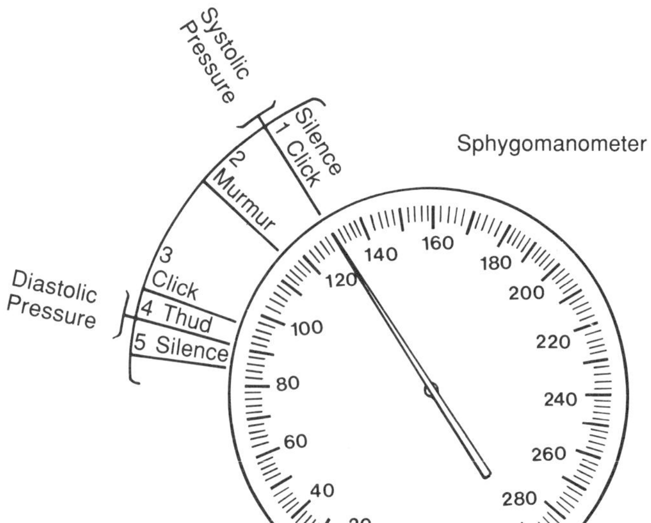

FIG 20–12.
Korotkoff sounds noted in taking arterial blood pressure.

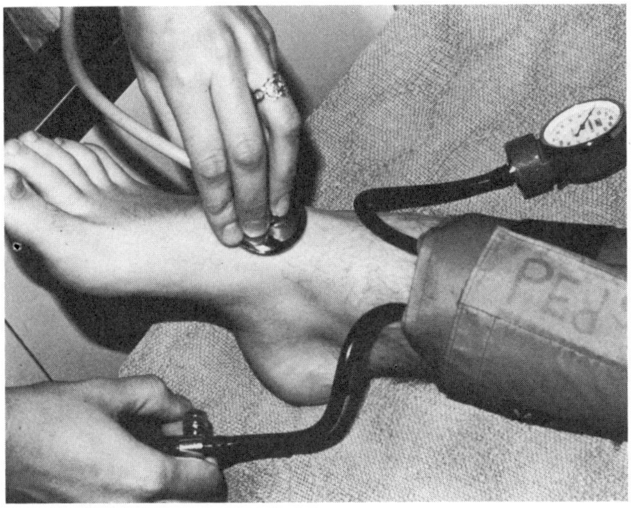

FIG 20–13.
Accurate placement of the cuff, tubing, and stethoscope in determining dorsalis pedis blood pressure in the foot.

has been inflated adequately. The cuff should be inflated to well above the resting blood pressure. If heart sounds are noted prior to releasing the blood pressure cuff, inflation is inadequate.

The first auscultation should be silence, which signifies that all blood entering the arm has been occluded. The pressure is then slowly released from the cuff. The first sound to be heard will be the systolic reading of blood pressure. This is the pressure that first overcomes the pressure in the cuff and signifies the highest blood pressure present at any given time within the circulatory system. This sound will continue to be heard as pressure is slowly released from the cuff. At a given point all heart sounds will cease or significantly change. This point is the resting, or diastolic, blood pressure within the system (Fig 20–12).

If a reading must be retaken, wait at least 5 minutes with the cuff deflated completely to ensure an adequate return and stabilization of circulation within the arm.

Blood pressure can be taken in the foot (Fig 20–13). The blood pressure taken in the arm vs. that of the foot is termed the ischemic, or ankle-arm, index. The ischemic index is utilized as a predictor for healing in patients with poor circulation.

CONCLUSION

Accurate determination of vital signs is critical to the podiatric office. Baseline values should be a part of every patient's chart and are easily established during the initial office visit. By consistently taking vital signs in the office on a daily basis, the technique becomes familiar to the podiatric assistant and more consistent and reliable to the interpreter.

21

Medical Office Safety

Bradley D. Castellano, D.P.M.

One of the most important responsibilities of the podiatric assistant is the safety of patients and others in the medical office. A safe office environment must be maintained on a daily basis to protect everyone using the medical office. Accidents will happen despite the most careful attention to office safety. Therefore, a specific plan for management of any injury that occurs in the medical office environment should be well understood by everyone employed. Equipment for obtaining vital signs—stethoscope, blood pressure cuff, thermometer—should be kept in a known location. The phone numbers for the local fire department, ambulance service, and poison control should be kept on or near the telephone in case of emergency.

Patients visiting a medical office must be treated as special people. Besides the fact that most will be preoccupied with their own illness, persons visiting the doctor's office are in an environment that is very foreign to them. Hydraulic chairs, instruments, x-ray machines, and other equipment commonly found in the medical office are easily taken for granted by office personnel. To the patient, however, these devices can be dangerous if handled improperly.

Supervision is the key to preventing most problems. Leaving patients unattended is probably one of the most frequent causes of accidents in the medical office. Careful monitoring and a healthy respect for the potentially harmful conditions that exist in the medical office are the best preventive measures (Fig 21–1)

CREATING A SAFE OFFICE

Everyone employed by the medical practice has a responsibility for the safety of the patients and visitors of that office. However, the employees must also take responsibility for their own safety. Generally, both of these goals are achieved by creating a safe office environment. Patients are kept from harm by regulating their access to potentially harmful areas and equipment. Employees are protected through education and by providing safe equipment for their use.

Reception Room

Analyzing the traffic flow through your medical office is the first step in providing patient safety. The reception area is usually the first exposure of the patient to the office. It should be well lighted, and equipped with comfortable, sturdy furniture. Seating should be easily accessible and elevated to allow less agile and otherwise handicapped patients ease in rising from the seated position.

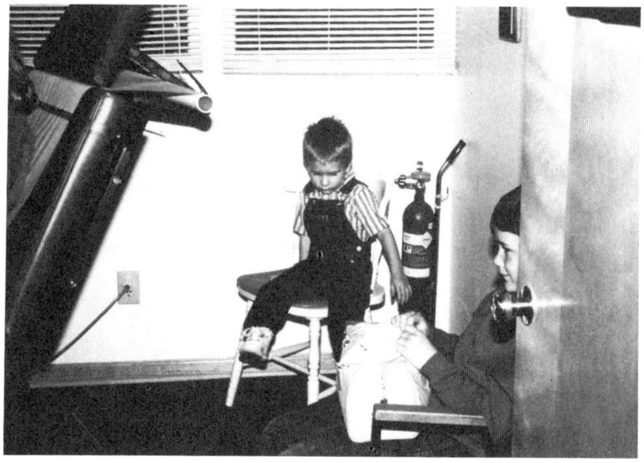

FIG 21–1.
Recognizing potentially harmful situations is the first step toward preventing injuries.

Restrooms

Most states have very specific regulations for the equipment and access to public restrooms. Doorways should be wide, and handrails should be installed to allow all patients access to the facilities. Door locks must be easily released from the outside and inside in case of emergency.

Treatment Rooms

Patients should be escorted into the examination room and helped into the treatment chair. This serves two purposes: first it helps prevent accidental falls while maneuvering into the chair itself, and second it prevents the patient from handling objects and instruments that have been placed out of their reach. Once in the treatment chair instruct the patient not to lean over or reach for objects placed on the floor such as purses, shoes, or hosiery.

Most treatment chairs have controls for elevating the chair or changing its position. These should be out of reach of the patient to prevent inadvertent "dumping" of the patient. (Fig 21–2). Children who accompany an adult patient should similarly be kept away from the chair's controls.

If patients must be left unsupervised for a short period of time, the chair should be left in its lowest position with the patient seated comfortably. Armrests should be in the up position. Unconscious or heavily sedated patients should not be left unattended.

Care should be taken to prevent crush injuries of the fingers when lowering the chair. Armrests should not overhang other furniture or equipment (Fig 21–3).

Once the treatment is completed, patients should be assisted out of the treatment chair. The patient should not be allowed to reach for shoes or hosiery while seated in the treatment chair. Replacing a patient's socks and shoes for them is a courtesy many will appreciate, and this action may prevent a serious fall.

Operating Rooms

Patients undergoing surgical procedures in the office setting will require careful monitoring. Many times sedatives are administered, and these drugs may have various untoward effects on the

FIG 21–2.
Treatment chairs provide the potential for falls and other injuries and can be positioned to cause "dumping" of a patient.

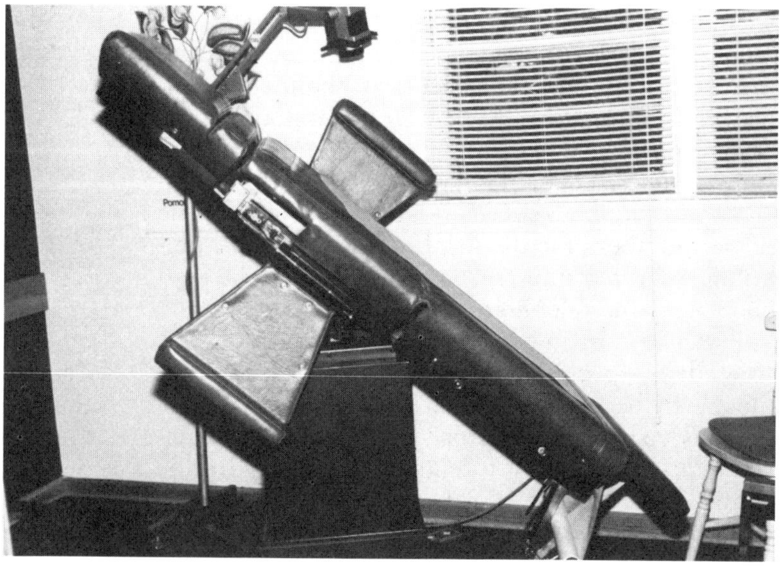

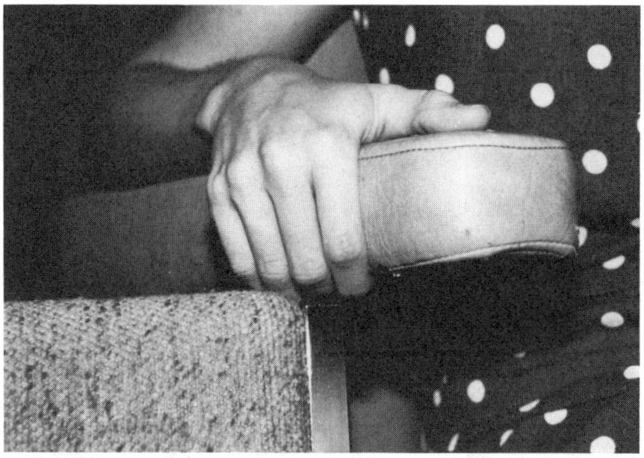

FIG 21–3.
Lowering of the treatment chair onto furniture or other equipment can cause a crush injury or tipping of the chair when it is lowered.

patient. Rarely, a patient may be rendered unconscious with the use of parenteral medications such as narcotics, benzodiazapines, or even antihistamines. Therefore, the equipment for maintenance of the airway and respiration must be readily on hand in the event of apnea or severe respiratory depression. Pulse oximetry is an excellent method of monitoring patients under the influence of medications that may result in respiratory depression. If oximetry devices are not available, the patient should be constantly observed by a trained assistant who is not directly involved in the surgical procedure.

Whirlpools

Whirlpool baths are helpful modalities used by many practitioners. Supervision of the patient and easy access to the on/off switch will provide relatively safe use of this device. Wet floors are potentially hazardous, and careful drying should be performed to prevent falls.

Chemicals and Medicines

Naturally, all medicines and chemicals used in the podiatry office are kept out of reach of patients. Many of the substances are poison, caustic, or flammable. Therefore, all chemicals and medicines should be kept in labeled containers (Fig 21–4). A list of antidotes and neutralizing agents should also be kept available at all times. Disposable containers should not be reused or filled with other substances for which they were not originally intended.

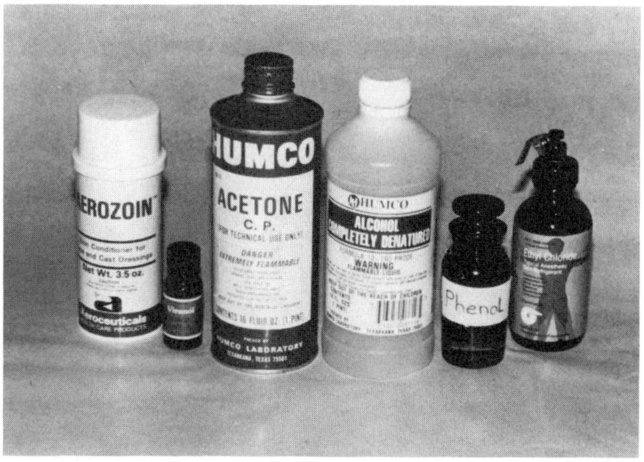

FIG 21–4.
Many chemicals and medicines utilized in the podiatry office are caustic or flammable.

OCCUPATIONAL EXPOSURE TO INFECTIOUS MATERIALS

The transmission of infection in the health care setting is an important issue in the medical community. Epidemics of acquired immunodeficiency syndrome (AIDS) and hepatitis have necessitated the implementation of special precautions to prevent accidental exposure of the health care worker to body fluids.

Hand Instruments

Instrumentation utilized in most podiatric practices include cutting devices of different types. Razor blades, nail nippers, and other tools should be handled with healthy respect (Fig 21–5). All such devices should be stored out of reach of the patients. Gloves should be used anytime sharp instruments are handled.

Replacing blades on scalpel and chisel handles should not be performed with unprotected fingers. In most cases, a hemostat or needle holder can be employed to safely perform this task.

Toenail debridement with hand instruments should be performed with eye protection to prevent projectile injury. In addition to this, eye protection is utilized anytime splattering of blood or body fluids is possible.

Syringes and Needles

Accidental needle punctures are common in all settings that utilize these devices. Most of these injuries occur during "recapping" of the needle after its use (Fig 21–6). For this reason a "no-recap"

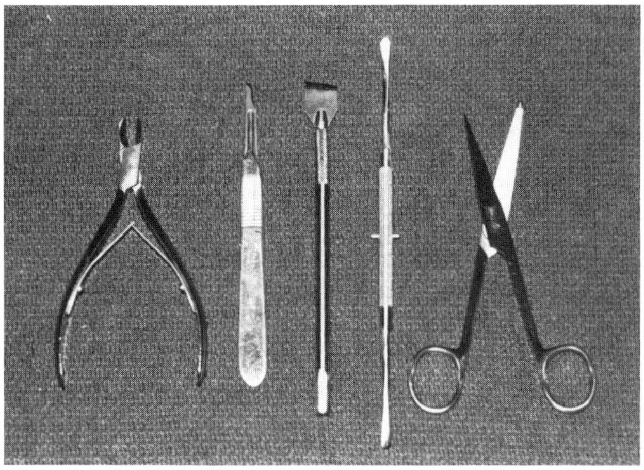

FIG 21–5.
Accidental puncture or lacerations result when these sharp instruments are handled improperly.

policy should be adopted by all medical facilities. Methods for safe disposal of syringes and needles are regulated in most states. All employees who handle needles should be instructed in the use of the disposal devices (Fig 21–7). If a needle must be recapped, it should be done by scooping the cap from a table without holding the cap itself until the needle is safely covered.

The management of occupational exposures to potentially infectious body fluids has been described by many sources.[1,2] The first step in the management of any occupational exposure is first aid for the injury. The wound or mucous membrane should be rinsed thoroughly with water.

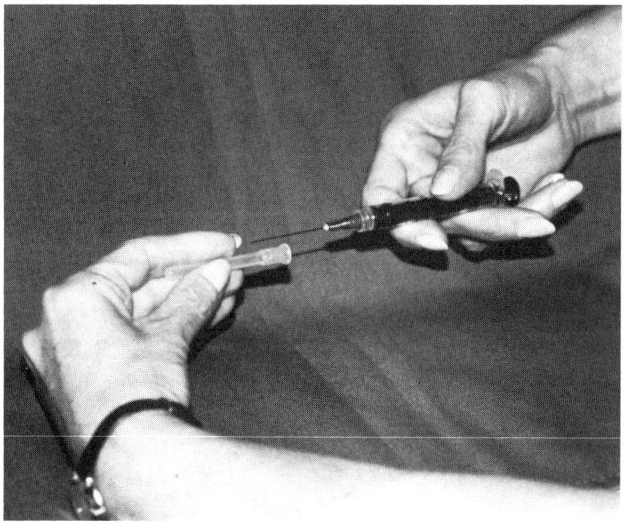

FIG 21–6.
Most accidental needle sticks are the result of attempted recapping of the utilized syringe needle.

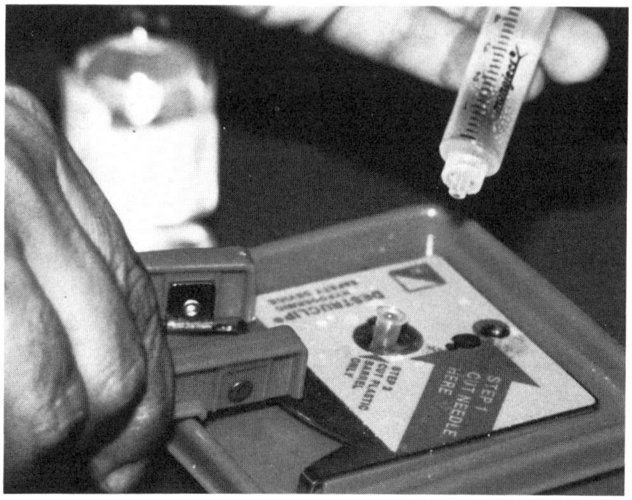

FIG 21–7.
Many types of devices and containers are available for the safe disposal of hazardous materials utilized in the medical office.

Punctures and lacerations are cleansed with disinfecting solution such as dilute bleach. In addition to local treatment the exposure should be reported to the supervisor. A policy for serologic testing of the "donor" patient and the "recipient" health care worker for human immunodeficiency virus type 1 (HIV-1) and hepatitis should be formulated and followed.

Power Equipment

The hazards of power equipment utilized in the podiatric office are for the most part minimal. However, some devices do present the potential for injury.

Cast cutters are an electrically powered tool with an oscillating saw blade. These devices are safe when properly utilized. Only trained personnel should operate the saw. Generally, these devices do not cut freely movable skin if lightly contacted. However, skin may be broken if excessive pressure is used or if the skin over a boney prominence is contacted. Excessive heat can also result if the saw blade remains in constant contact with the hardened cast. This is especially true with fiberglass and other synthetic cast materials. Therefore, care must be taken not to burn the patient's skin.

Sanders and grinders are sometimes used in the podiatric practice. These machines have high-velocity rotating surfaces that can easily cause injury if used improperly. Eye protection should always be instituted when utilizing these instru-

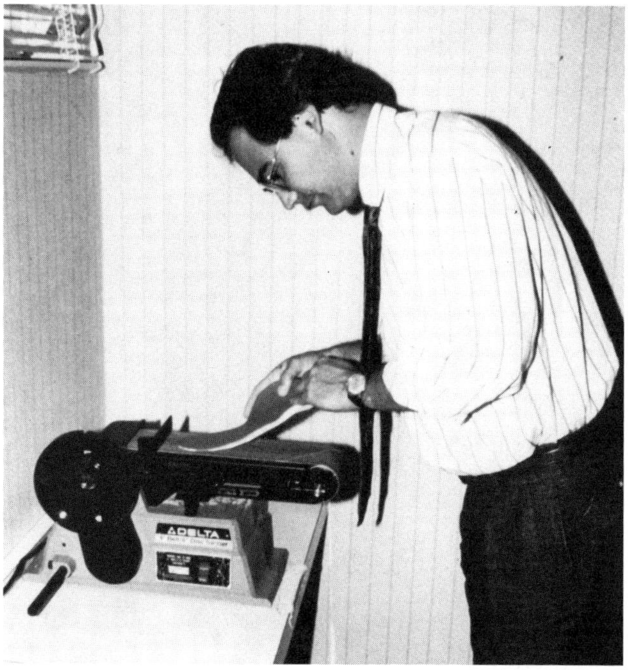

FIG 21–8.
Loose hair and garments must be protected from potential entanglement in the power equipment.

ments. Loose clothing and hair can easily become entangled in the rotating devices and cause serious injury (Fig 21–8) Therefore, precautions to prevent this may include the wearing of hats, aprons, etc.

ACCIDENT AND INCIDENT REPORTS

If an injury to a patient or health care worker occurs, an account of the accident should be written and filed. Specific measures describing the injury and the treatment rendered should be recorded for the protection of the victim and the medical practice.

The prevention of accidental injuries in the medical office is important for health, economic, and medicolegal reasons. Health care workers and physicians must take responsibility for the patients' and their own safety in the office and hospital setting. Preventive measures should include employee education and maintenance of medical equipment. Specific rules and guidelines should be established for the management of any accident or injury that may occur in the medical office.

REFERENCES

1. Centers for Disease Control: Recommendations for prevention of HIV transmission in health-care settings. *MMWR* 1987; 36(suppl):1–19.
2. Kuhls TL, Cherry JD: The management of health-care workers' accidental parenteral exposures to biological specimens of HIV seropositive individuals. *Infect Control* 1987; 8:211–218.

22

Palliative Care

A.R. Pitts, Jr., D.P.M.
T.E. Pitts, D.P.M.

I. Debridement of Dystrophic or Mycotic Toenails
II. Debridement of Corns and Calluses

The profession of podiatry initially consisted of palliative care and conservative procedures. Today, podiatrists obtain highly advanced and specialized training and have developed sophisticated surgical procedures of the foot and ankle.

The average life span continues to increase. Therefore, the podiatrist as well as the assistant must be equipped and motivated to provide palliative care to the elderly and to the patient unable to undergo surgical correction.

The objective of palliative treatment is to provide temporary relief from painful corns, calluses, and/or nails. Palliative treatment is only a temporary solution. The underlying cause of the problem must be treated in order to provide permanent relief. In some cases, the severity of the symptomatology, the extent of the deformity, and the complexity of the overall pedal status rule out continued conservative or palliative treatment. In these situations, surgery may be required.

Patients who suffer from diabetes mellitus, peripheral vascular disease, rheumatoid arthritis, and other systemic diseases are at a greater risk for developing complications from routine palliative debridement. Knowledge of the special needs of these patients is important to the podiatric assistant.

Many podiatric assistants have been trained to debride nails, corns, and calluses. It is important that the podiatrist ascertain that the assistant is performing the procedure correctly. The final result should be checked prior to the application of any pads or dressings.

DEBRIDEMENT OF DYSTROPHIC OR MYCOTIC TOENAILS

Nail disorders are commonly encountered by the podiatrist. It is important to remember that many cutaneous as well as systemic diseases show signs of nail involvement. Some of these disorders include psoriasis, eczema, diabetes mellitus, syphilis, peripheral vascular disease, tuberculosis, and arthritis.

"Onychomycosis," or fungal nail, is one of the more frequent nail manifestations treated by podiatrists. Fungal nails are often dry, thick, and yellow/brown in color. *Trichophyton rubrum* is the most common causative organism and may involve only a small portion of the nail plate or the entire nail plate. The abnormal shapes associated with these nails are due to fungal involvement of the nail matrix, which produces the nail.

Both oral and topical medications are available to treat mycotic nails; however, these preparations are often ineffective in penetrating the nail plate in a sufficient concentration. Therefore, conservative palliative debridement of the nails is the mainstay of treatment. If the nail is painful, it can be surgically removed. Instruments commonly used in the debridement of nails include nail nipper, tissue nipper, spatula and nail packer, curette, and power burr (Fig 22–1).

When debriding nails (Fig 22–2,A and B), the physician or assistant should begin at one corner

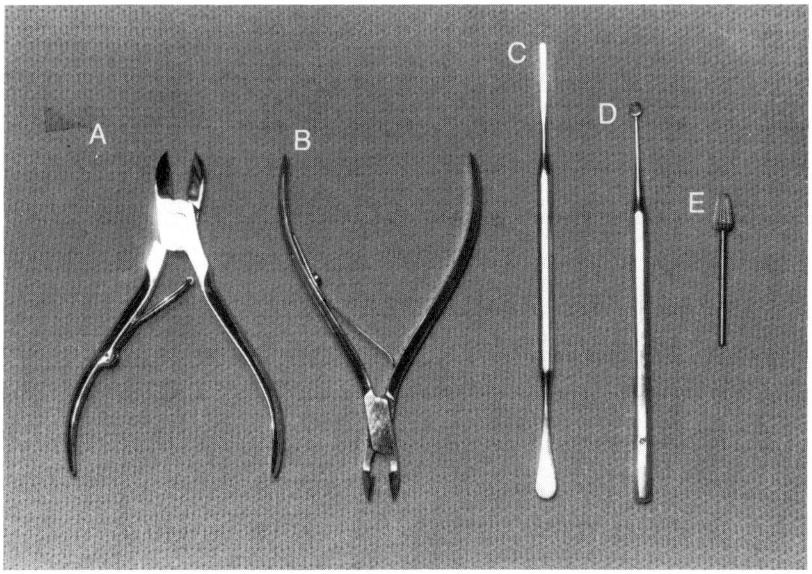

FIG 22–1.
Nail debridement instruments: **A,** nail nipper; **B,** tissue nipper; **C,** spatula and nail packer; **D,** curette; **E,** power burr bit.

of the tip of the nail and cut straight across the nail by using small bites with the nail nipper (Fig 22–2,C and D). Never take large bites of the nail with the nail nipper (Fig 22–2,E). This may result in cracking the proximal portion of the nail or even lacerating the nail bed. Once the tip of the nail is reduced to the proper length (Fig. 22–2,F), the medial and lateral nail border as well as the distal tip of the nail is curetted (Fig 22–2,G). When debriding with the nail nipper or curette, care must be taken to avoid laceration of the distal pulp of tissue (Fig 22–2,H). The power burr may then be used to reduce the thickness of the nail and smooth any rough edges (Fig 22–2,I and J).

DEBRIDEMENT OF CORNS AND CALLUSES

Calluses are discretely thickened areas of skin with yellow or grey coloration commonly found on the feet. Calluses, also called "hyperkeratosis" or "tylomas," are usually located in areas subject to constant friction or pressure such as the ball of the foot. While calluses are often caused by shoes that constantly rub against the skin, tylomas can also be produced by biomechanical abnormalities, bony prominences, malfunctioning sweat glands, or certain hereditary diseases.

Corns, or "helomas," are small, hard calluses that usually occur on the digits in an area overlying a bony prominence. Corns may be separated into a variety of subtypes including the ordinary hard corn (heloma durum), soft corns (heloma molle), seed corn (heloma milliare), and neurovascular corns (heloma neurofibrosum).

A hard corn typically presents as a small callous lesion with a hard central core. It occurs more frequently on the dorsum of the digits. Soft corns are usually located in the web spaces where moisture often accumulates, and they cause maceration. Neurovascular corns, although less common, are extremely painful lesions that often bleed actively upon debridement. Seed corns are small pinpoint lesions that occur in both weight-bearing and non–weight-bearing areas of the feet.

Sometimes a nucleus, or hard core, is found following superficial debridement of a callus. These lesions, referred to as intractable plantar keratosis (IPK), are often found on the skin beneath the metatarsal heads. When debriding these lesions, the deep nucleus within the callus must be excised or enucleated to relieve the painful sensation of stepping on a pebble.

Initial treatment of corns and calluses consists of debridement or shaving the lesions with a sharp blade. There are many different models and manufacturers of scalpel handles and blades. It is important to stabilize the area being debrided by placing tension on both sides of the lesion with the thumb and index finger of the opposite hand. Debridement should continue until the underlying normal pinkish skin appears; however, the debridement should not be too aggressive since mild hyperkeratoses have a protective function.

The two most preferred methods for holding the chisel handle or scalpel for debriding corns and

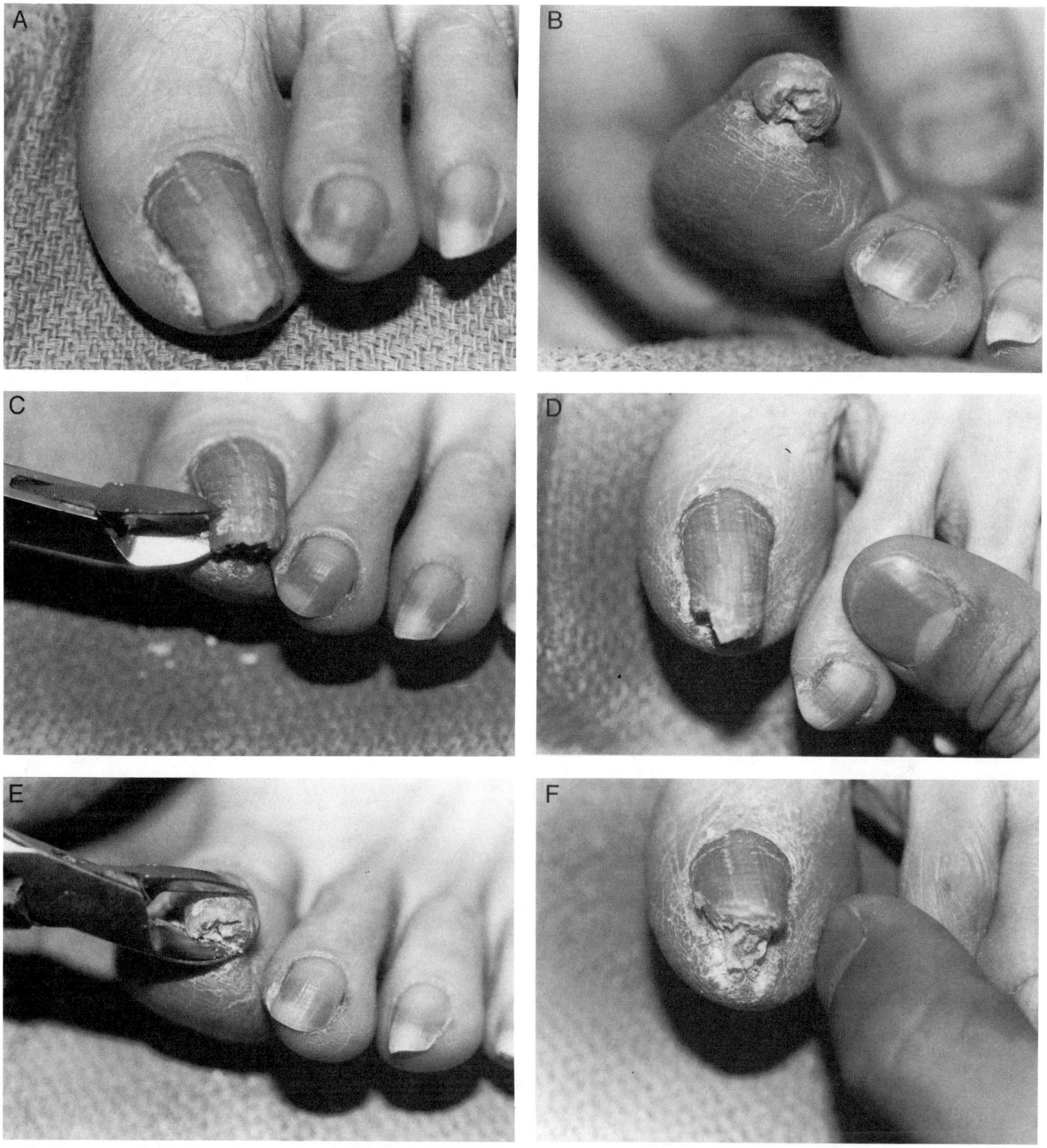

FIG 22–2.
A, mycotic nail. **B,** frontal plane view of a mycotic nail. **C** and **D,** using small bites and cutting the nail straight across. **E,** improper technique is depicted. Do not take large bites out of the nail with the nipper. **F,** proper nail length.

(Continued.)

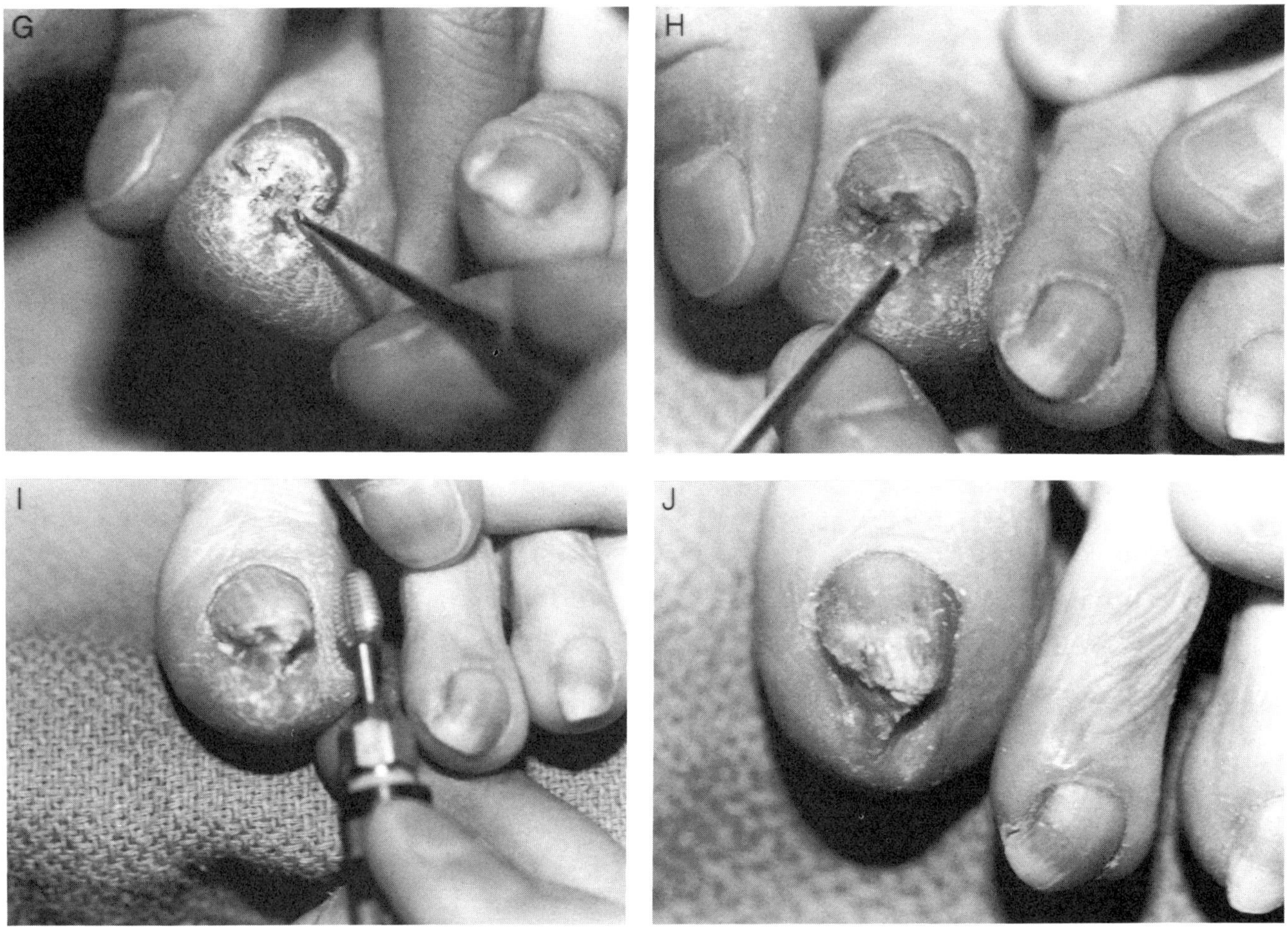

FIG 22-2 (cont.).
G, curetting nail margins. **H,** distal pulp of tissue **I,** burring rough edges of the nail. **J,** appearance of nail after debridement.

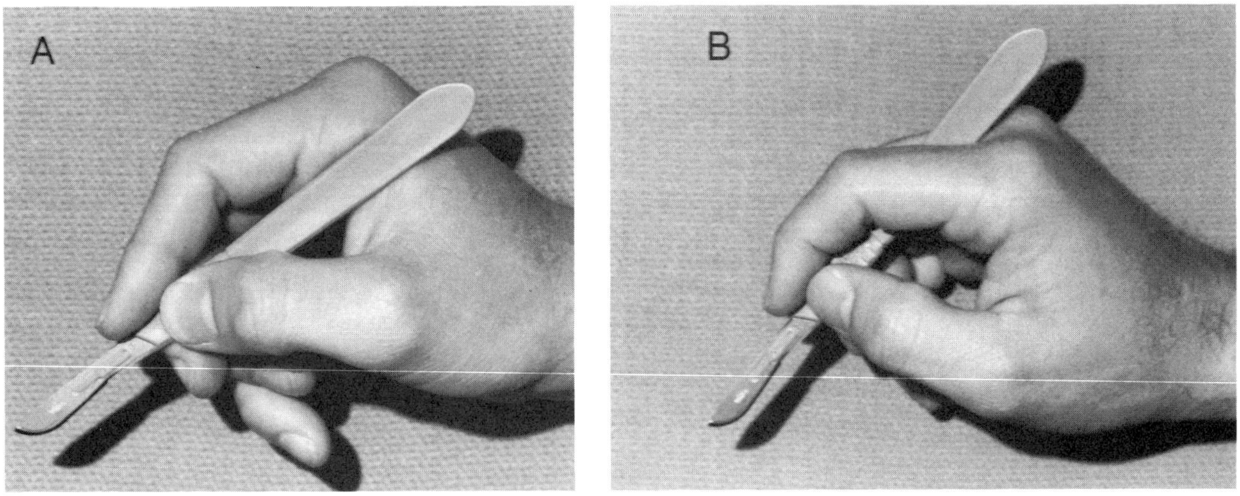

FIG 22–3.
A, pencil-grip method of holding the scalpel or chisel. **B,** alternative method of holding the scalpel or chisel.

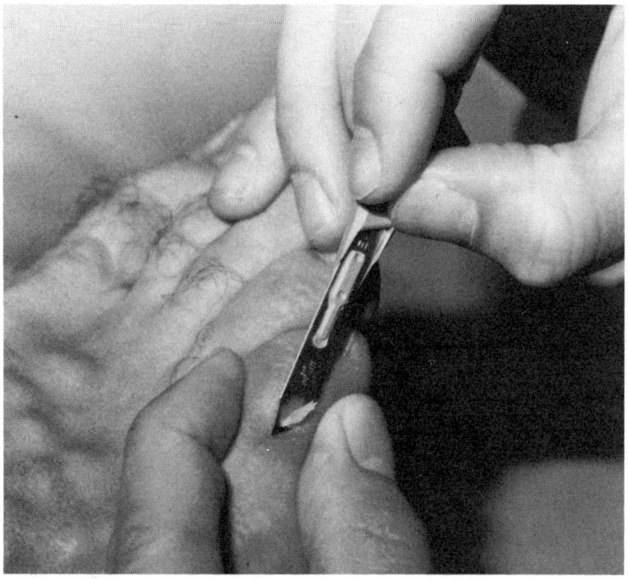

FIG 22–4.
Debriding a corn. The digit is stabilized with one hand while the corn is debrided with the opposite hand. The lesion is shaved with the blade held at an angle of approximately 15 degrees to the skin.

calluses are demonstrated in Figure 22–3. The blade should be held approximately at a 15-degree angle to the skin while shaving the lesion. The cutting motion should be in a distal-to-proximal diagonal direction (Fig 22–4).

While initial treatment consists of routine debridement of the corns or calluses, the underlying cause must be assessed and treated by the podiatrist in order to alleviate or lessen the problem. For example, corns resulting from hammertoes may benefit from padding, silicone moldable devices, changes in shoe gear, or even surgical correction.

Palliative care is an important skill for the podiatric assistant to acquire. Continued practice and careful attention to technique will help the assistant achieve proficiency.

23

Principles of Aseptic Technique, Scrubbing, Preparation, and Draping

A. Louis Jimenez, D.P.M.

I. Historical Review
II. Surgical Conscience
III. Sources of Infection
IV. Barriers
V. Operating Room Attire
VI. Scrubbing
  A. Surgical Hand Scrub
  B. Length of Scrub
VII. Gowning and Gloving
VIII. Foot Preparation
IX. Draping

With changes in the health care delivery system, third-party providers are encouraging more outpatient surgery, and therefore, more and more podiatrists are doing surgery in the office. In order to prevent and minimize perioperative complications, a detailed knowledge of aseptic technique is mandatory. The following chapter discusses aseptic techniques, preparation, scrubbing, gowning, and gloving.

HISTORICAL REVIEW

Early concepts of infection and the crude methods used to combat it seem strange by today's standards. In ancient times, demons and evil spirits were thought to cause pestilence and infection. Weird methods were often used, most of which were futile. However, purification by fire had more viability than was thought of at the time. Hippocrates (460 B.C.) foreshadowed asepsis when he advocated wine or boiled water for irrigating wounds. Galen (131–200 A.D.) gave evidence of having boiled instruments used for wounded gladiators. Francastorius (1546) presented the theory of contagion. This theory proposed the idea of contamination by air or fomites. His workings opened the door for the modern concept of infection.

As the 17th century approached, scientific theory was emerging, and the fever of superstitious beliefs was being shaken. Spallanzoni, a follower of Leeuwenhoek (inventor of the microscope), identified microbes and proved that many lived without air.

During the 19th century, surgical techniques markedly advanced from the day when surgeons operated in Prince Albert coats and used the same blood- and pus-absorbing sponges for every patient. It was common for a surgeon to hold the scalpel between his teeth to protect it. He wound sutures from a nonsterile spool and hung them from a buttonhole of his Prince Albert coat. A household pin cushion was kept for needles, and his ivory or bone carved instrument handles were filled with bacteria, dirt, and filth.

Semmelweis (1818–1865) established the theory of puerperal fever (childbed fever) and required all doctors and students to wash their hands in chlorinated lime solution before examining patients. He decreased the mortality rate by 1/12 in his maternity ward. Pasteur gave validity to the germ theory when he proved that bacteria came from other bacteria. He laid the foundation for bacteriology as a science and taught the role of bacteria as a cause of infection. Koch advocated the use of bichloride of mercury as an antiseptic and was the forerunner of interest in antisepsis.

Lister (1865), thinking that bacteria were airborne, started using carbolic spray in the operating room. Later, he used the spray in the wound and on the operating teams' hands and soaked sutures in it. It was not until 1879 that Lister's antiseptic principle of surgery was finally accepted by the medical profession. Gustav Neuber advocated scrubbing furniture with disinfectant solution, required gowns and caps to be worn, and sterilized everything in contact with the wound. Sterilization by boiling was introduced in the mid-1880s. Everything used during an operation, including linens, dressings, and gowns, were boiled. In 1876, heat-resistent bacteria, usually spore formers, were demonstrated. Ernst Von Bergmann, et al. (1886) introduced the steam sterilizer. Steam in itself is not enough to kill heat-resistant spore-forming microorganisms. Steam must be under pressure to increase the temperature in order to kill spore-forming organisms.

As sterilization developed, other factors in antiseptic techniques evolved, including the use of a controlled environment, modern operating room attire, and precise housekeeping methods. Surgeons learned that all items that came in contact with the wound should be free of microorganisms.

SURGICAL CONSCIENCE

Optimal patient care requires an inherent surgical conscience, self-discipline, and the application of the principles of asepsis and sterile technique. This is referred to as "thinking sterile." This conscience gives the person the instinct to know when a "break" is present. An inherent surgical conscience dictates to that person, whether in a group or alone, that absolute aseptic technique must be followed. This person admits to breaks in technique and knows that this is the way to learn. No one who "breaks" should be castigated since part of learning is making mistakes.

SOURCES OF INFECTION

Sources of infection include hair, skin, nasopharynx, fomites, and air. Fomites are particles present on inanimate objects (furniture, walls, floors, equipment, supplies, etc.), which can also be sources of contamination. The skin of the average person sheds 4,000 to 10,000 squamae per minute. These sheddings can become part of a contaminant in a surgical wound. Contaminants spread through the nasal pharynx are produced by talking, coughing, and sneezing. Air may be a source of contamination, especially when doors into the operating room are left open or excessive movement is created by allowing the door to swing multiple times. This movement creates eddy currents causing contaminants present on the floor and in the air to move and possibly land on the open wound.

BARRIERS

Barriers are established to isolate the operative site from infectious contaminants. Barriers to the skin, nasopharyngeal flora and hair, fomites, and airborne contamination retard or prevent the transfer of microorganisms (Table 23–1).

Adherence to the strict principles of aseptic technique is mandatory for safety of the patient. The following principles should be followed at all times:

1. Only sterile items are kept on a sterile field.
2. Gowns are sterile only in front from the waist to the shoulder including the the sleeves.
3. Tables are sterile only at table level.
4. Persons who are sterile touch only sterile items or areas; persons who are not sterile touch only nonsterile items or areas.

TABLE 23–1.
Barriers to Prevent the Transfer of Microorganisms

Barriers of skin
Preoperative skin preparation
Special operating room attire
Sterile drapes
Barriers to nasopharyngeal flora and hair
Masks and hoods
Removal of hair from operative site
Exclusion of operating room personnel with acute infections or skin lesions
Use of an anesthesia screen to separate the anesthesia area from the operative area.
Barriers to fomites
Proper packaging of supplies and sterilization procedures
Dust covers for storage items
Disinfection of operating room surfaces
Clean preoperative bed linens
Barriers to airborne contamination
Conventional air-conditioning systems when properly designed, installed, and maintained provide fresh air that removes airborne bacteria by removing dust and aerosol particles. Air filters limit dust and lint contaminants in the air
Air should be recirculated at a rate of not less than 25 air exchanges per hour

5. Nonsterile persons should avoid reaching over a sterile field; sterile persons should avoid leaning over an unsterile field.

6. The edges of anything that enclose sterile contents are considered sterile.

7. A sterile field is created as close as possible to the time of use.

8. Sterile areas are continuously kept in view.

9. Sterile persons keep well within the sterile area.

10. Sterile persons should keep contact with sterile areas to a minimum. For example, the instrument nurse should not lean on sterile tables or draped patients.

11. Unsterile persons avoid sterile areas.

12. Destruction of the integrity of microbial barriers results in contamination.

13. Microorganisms should be kept to an irreducible minimum.

OPERATING ROOM ATTIRE

The purpose of operating room attire is to provide effective barriers that prevent the spread of microorganisms to and from the patient. These barriers diminish contamination of the operative wound and sterile field by direct body contact. Operating room attire has been shown to reduce the particle count of shedding from over 10,000 particles per minute to 3,000 particles per minute, or 50,000 microorganisms per cubic foot to 500 microorganisms per cubic foot. Standard operating room attire consists of a mask covering the nose and mouth, a head cover, shoe covers, and snug-fitting pants and shirt (Fig 23–1,A–C).

Halsted (1896) popularized the use of gloves. Prior to 1958, gloves were made mostly of rubber and had to be resterilized and repaired. Disposable latex gloves became popular after 1958. Masks today contain efficient fiberglass or polypropylene filters. These masks are disposable, and proper protocol calls for mask changes between every case. Sterile gowns have also been added as standard attire.

Operating room attire should not be worn outside the operating room suite. This practice protects the operating room environment from microorganisms that are inherent in other areas of the office or hospital. Eyeglasses should be wiped with

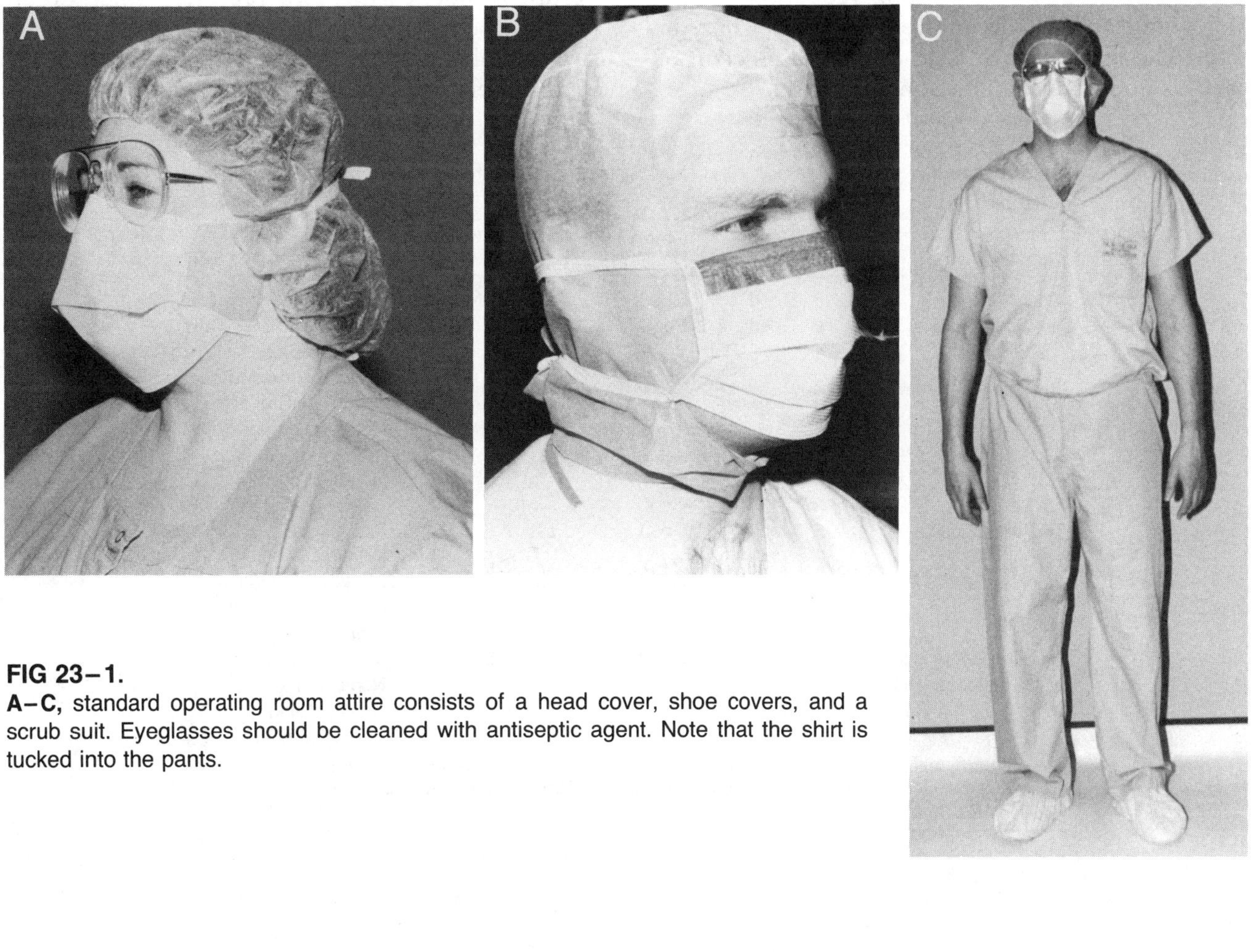

FIG 23–1.
A–C, standard operating room attire consists of a head cover, shoe covers, and a scrub suit. Eyeglasses should be cleaned with antiseptic agent. Note that the shirt is tucked into the pants.

a tissue containing antiseptic solution before each operation to avoid cross-contamination.

Impeccable hygiene is a must. Personnel with acute infections, breaks in their skin, or contagious conditions should not be permitted in the operating room suite. Personnel with burns, cuts, or skin abrasions should not handle or scrub sterile equipment because serum, a bacterial medium, may seep from the eroded area.

Adequate scrubbing and hand washing facilities should be provided for all operating room team members. Scrub sinks should be deep enough to avoid splashing on surgical attire because this will result in contamination of the gown by a "strike-through" of moisture. Scrub sinks should be used only for scrubbing or hand washing. They should not be used to clean or rinse contaminated instruments or equipment.

SCRUBBING

Scrubbing solutions are antiseptics (Table 23–2). These are products with antimicrobial activity that are designed for use on skin or superficial tissue. They function to dilute inoculum via mechanical scrubbing, prolong reduction of skin flora, and defat and remove secretions from the skin. The products are fast acting and efficient as well as nonirritating and nonsensitizing.

Once an area is painted, a film remains that serves as a barrier. The most common antiseptics are povidone-iodine (Betadine), cholorhexidene gluconate, 4% (Hibiclens), and hexachlorophene. Betadine and Hibiclens are active against gram-positive and gram-negative bacteria. Hexachlorophene, however, is not active against gram-negative bacteria.

SURGICAL HAND SCRUB

The surgical scrub is a procedure to remove as many microorganisms as possible from the hands and arms by mechanical washing and chemical antiseptic agents.

The skin is inhabited by two types of microorganisms, resident and transient. Transient organisms are loosely held to the skin and are acquired by direct contact. These organisms are usually totally removed by normal washing with soap, detergent, and water. Resident organisms reside below the skin surface in hair follicles and sebaceous and sweat glands and are more difficult to remove since they are more adherent. Their growth is inhibited by the chemical stage of the surgical scrub. Resident skin flora represent microorganisms present in the hospital environment. Many are coagulase-positive staphylococci (Fig 23–2).

In order to free the skin of as many organisms

TABLE 23–2.
Antiseptics*

Agent	Gram Positive	Gram Negative	Speed of Killing Bacteria	Comments
Alcohol	Good	Good	Fast	Drying
Hexachlorophene, 3% aqueous	Good	Poor	Slow	Cumulative activity after repeated use. Toxic absorbed through skin. CNS effects. Not good preparation agent No effect on *Pseudomonas*
Tincture of iodine	Good	Good	Fast	Skin burns Irritating
Iodophores	Good	Good	Fast	Somewhat irritating Persistent effect if not rinsed off
Chlorhexidine gluconate, 4% aqueous (Hibiclens)	Good	Good	Intermediate	Nonirritating Nontoxic Nonsterilizing Persistent effect

*From Fields L: Principles of sterile technique, in Jimenez AL (ed): *Doctors Hospital Podiatric Education and Research Institute Second Annual Assistants Surgical Seminar.* Tucker, Ga, Podiatry Institute Publishing Co, 1985, pp 2–3. Used by permission.

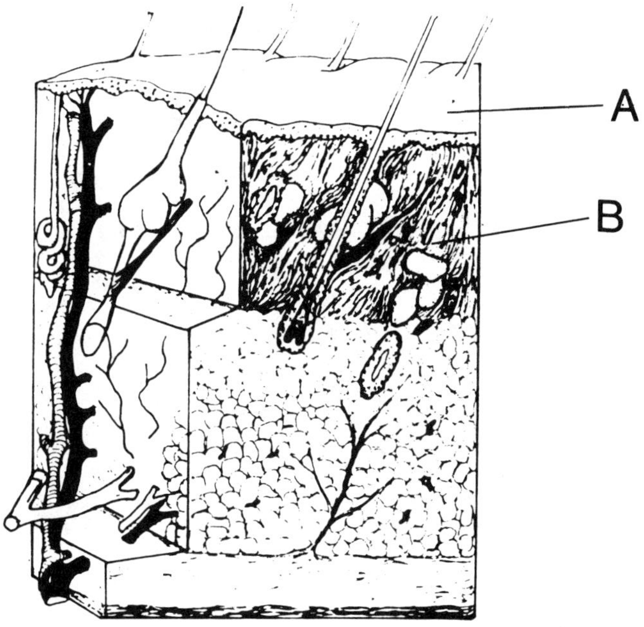

FIG 23–2.
A, transient bacteria inhabit the superficial layer of skin. **B,** resident bacteria reside in deeper layers of skin where hair follicles and sebaceous and sweat glands are present.

as possible, two processes, mechanical and chemical, are used. The mechanical method removes soil and transient organisms with friction. The chemical method reduces resident flora and inactivates microorganisms with a microbicidal or antiseptic agent.

The purpose of the surgical scrub is to remove soil, debris, natural skin oils, hand lotions, and microorganisms from the hands and forearms of sterile team members. More specifically, you scrub to decrease the number of microorganisms on skin to an irreducible minimum, keep the population of microorganisms minimal during the operative procedures by suppression of growth, and reduce the hazard of microbial contamination of the operative wound by skin flora.

Brushes used for scrubbing can be either resterilizable or disposable (Fig 23–3). They should not be of such a harsh quality as to cause skin abrasions.

To avoid glove puncturing, fingernails should be cut so that they do not reach past the fingertip. Cuticles should remain uncut. Remove any nail polish. Lacquer may chip and create crevices that can harbor microorganisms. Chips of lacquer also act as irritants. Jewelry should be removed, and all hair should be covered. Adjust the disposable mask and any eyeglasses to fit comfortably. Then

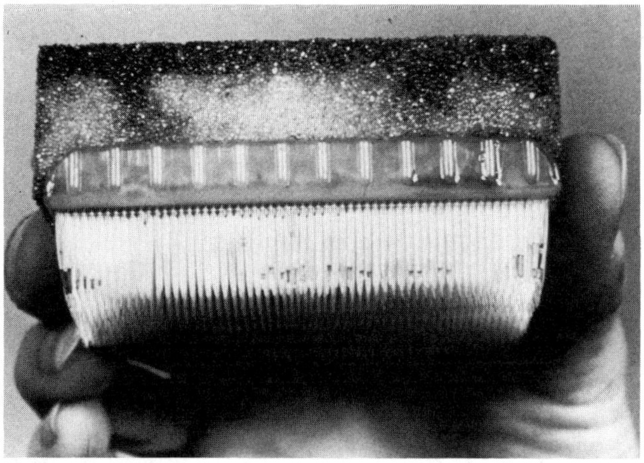

FIG 23–3.
This scrub brush has a foamy soft section containing antimicrobial detergent and bristles to assist in the scrub.

set the water temperature to a comfortable level. You are now ready to begin the scrub.

LENGTH OF SCRUB

The length of the scrub varies from office to office, with the currently accepted time for the first and subsequent scrubs to be 5 minutes. The procedure for the scrub varies from office to office as well. However, the idea is to use appropriate principles of aseptic techniques. There are two methods of scrubbing, the time method and the brushstroke method. Both methods expose all aspects of the hands and arms to mechanical and chemical antisepsis and are based on an anatomic pattern of scrubbing.

The scrub process begins by removing transient microorganisms by using an antiseptic detergent to wash the hands and arms (Fig 23–4,A). Fingernails are cleaned with a plastic or metal nail cleaner (Fig 23–4,B). The nails are then scrubbed for 30 seconds on each side with a brush containing an antimicrobial detergent. Think of the fingers, hands, and arms as each having four sides. Start with the lateral aspect of the little finger. Move from one finger to the next on the palmar side, and then scrub the thumb. Continue over the dorsum (top) of the fingers and hands. Next, scrub the palmar surface of the hand to the wrist, scrub up the arm in thirds, and end 5 cm above the elbow (Fig 23–5,A–F). The scrub procedure may be started on the index finger and progress laterally and then proximally to the elbow.

Rinse off the detergent by starting at the hands

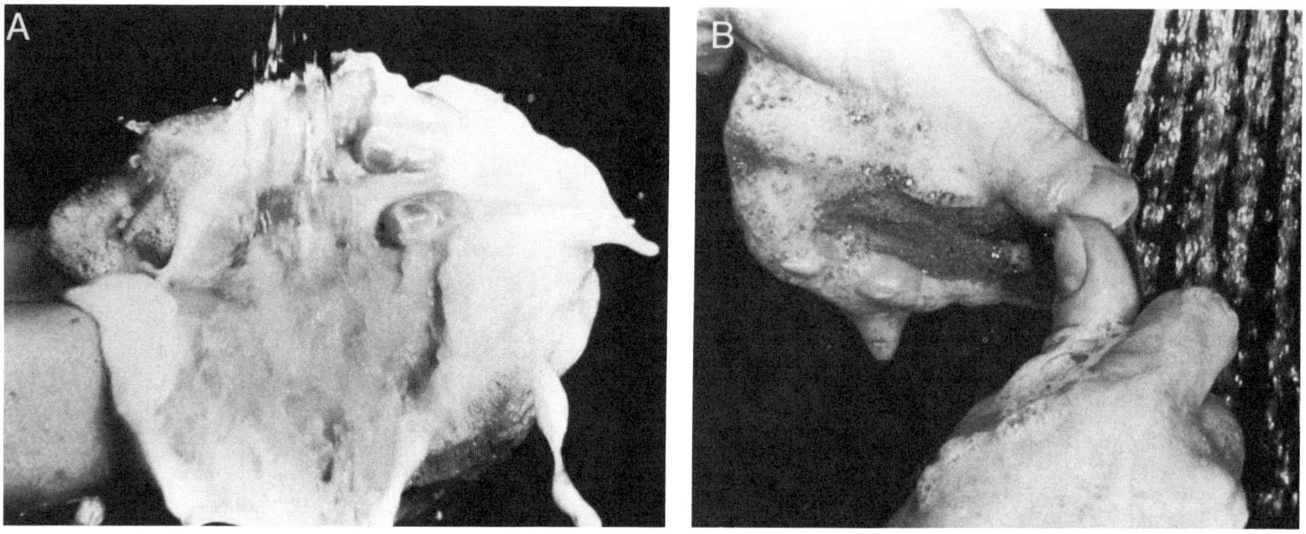

FIG 23–4.
A, washing hands with a detergent and rinsing prior to scrubbing removes transient bacteria. **B,** debris under fingernails is removed with a pick.

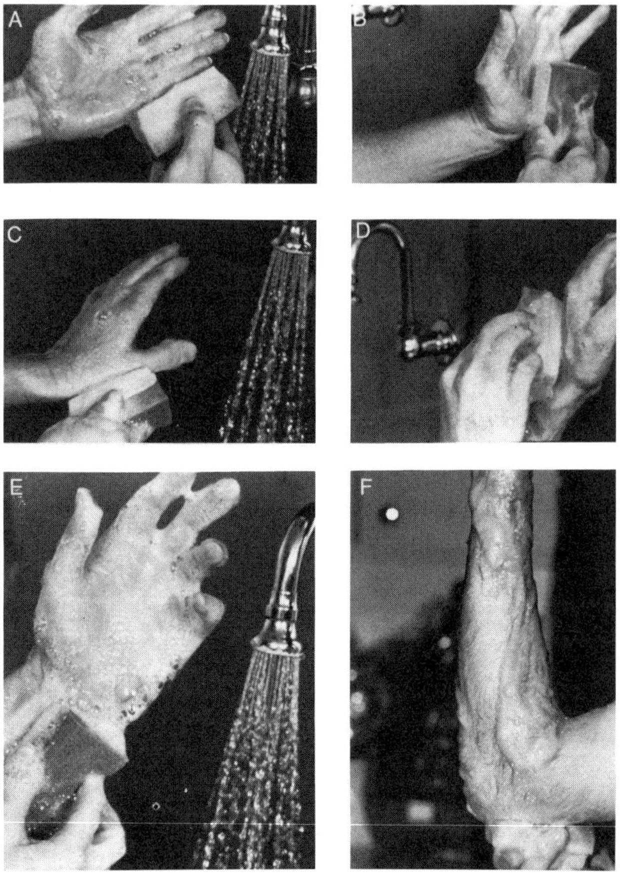

FIG 23–5.
A–D, the scrub procedure has been started at the index finger and progressed laterally to the fifth digit and then to the palm, followed by the thumb and dorsum of the hand. **E** and **F,** the scrub now progresses until the elbow is reached.

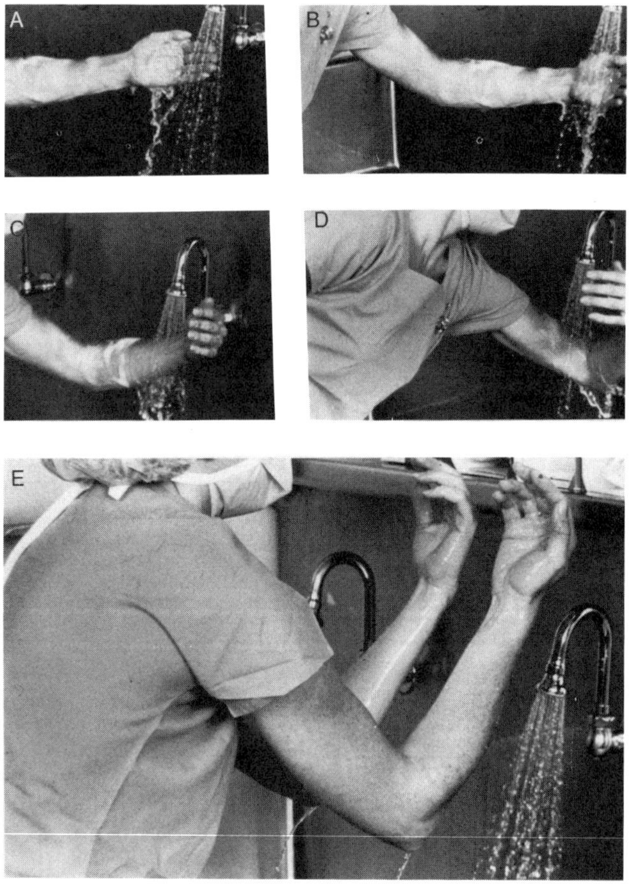

FIG 23–6.
A–D, the antiseptic agent is rinsed off the hands and arms. As the hand passes through the stream of water, it is held higher than the elbow to allow the water to flow toward the elbow. **E,** excess water is allowed to drip from the elbows.

(Fig 23–6,A–D). When rinsing, make sure to keep the hands higher than the elbows (Fig 23–6,E) to allow the water to run to the level of the elbow into the sink. Do not drop the hands lower than the elbow because as water can run back from the elbow down the arm toward the hand. This will contaminate the area that was previously scrubbed.

The brush-stroke method employs scrubbing nails 50 strokes, each side of the fingers 40 strokes, the backs and palms of the hands 10 strokes, and the arms 40 strokes for each third of the arm.

Drying of the hands starts by grasping the towel from the top of an opened gown package and opening it full length by holding one end. Bend forward slightly at the waist so as to keep the towel away from scrub attire. Dry each hand thoroughly and independently. To dry one arm, hold the towel in the opposite hand, and use an oscillating motion of the arm as you draw the towel up to the elbow (Fig 23–7,A and B). Reverse the towel, and dry the opposite arm with the unused (upper) end of the towel (Fig 23–7,C and D).

GOWNING AND GLOVING

Immediately after the hands are dry, put on the sterile gown (Fig 23–8), followed by the sterile gloves. Sterile gloves and gowns are worn to prevent the skin from serving as a contaminating source and to create a barrier between sterile and unsterile areas. After the arms are placed through the gown, either the closed-glove technique (Fig

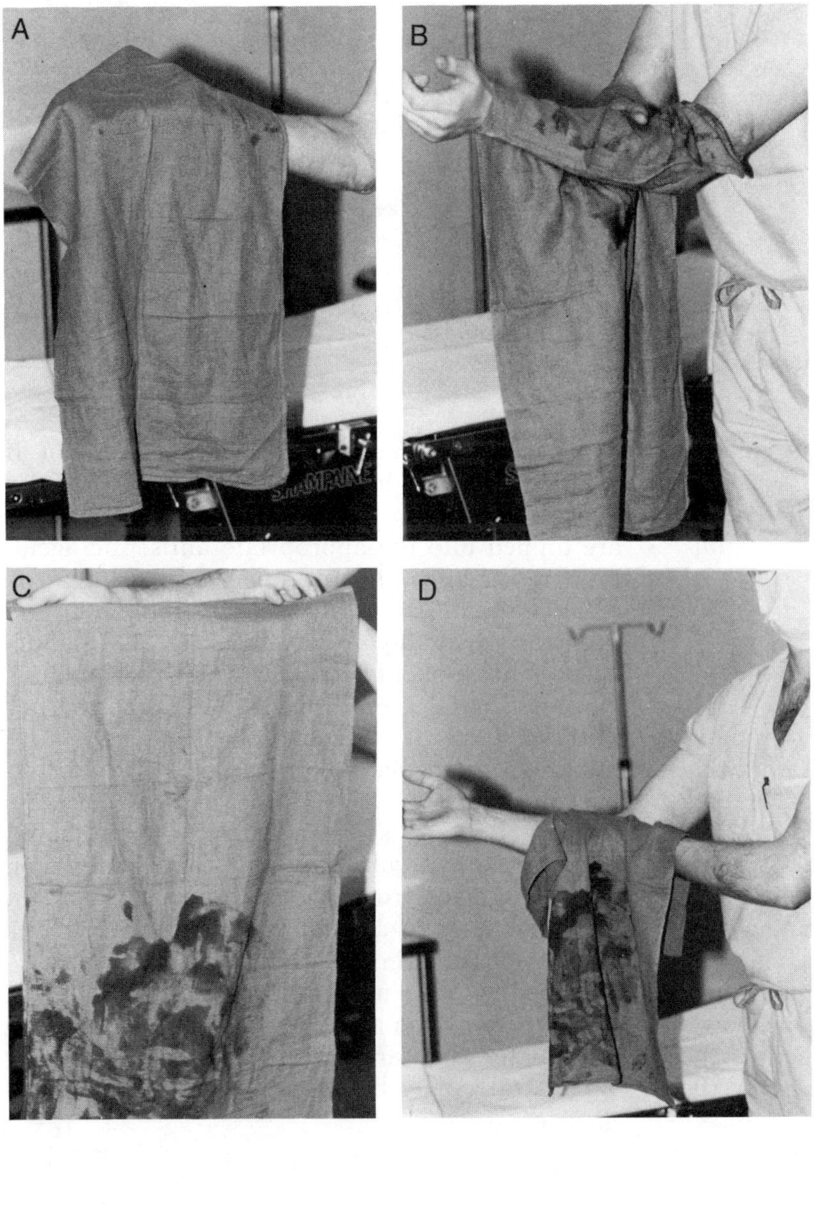

FIG 23–7.
A and **B,** each hand is dried distally to proximally ending at the elbow. **C** and **D,** one end of the towel is used for each hand and arm.

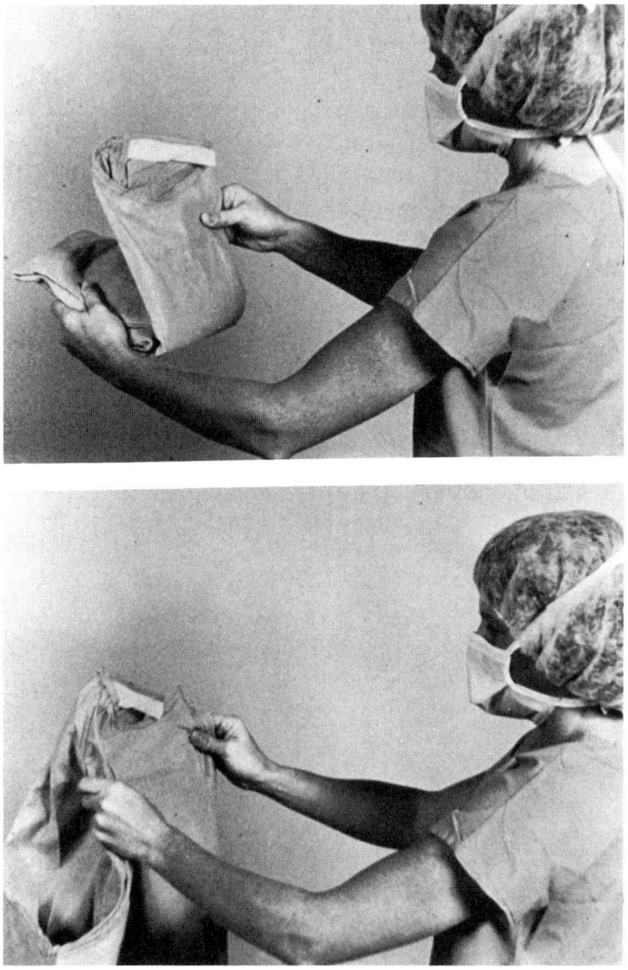

FIG 23–8.
A sterile gown is picked up by the inside part and allowed to unfold.

23–9,A–I) or the open-glove technique can be used (Fig 23–10,A–E).

The closed-glove technique is much more difficult, but continued practice gives one the confidence to employ this technique.

FOOT PREPARATION

The first step in foot preparation is to remove the hair, either by shaving or by a depilatory (Fig 23–11,A and B). Hair removal should be done in a waiting area outside of the operating room. Hair carries a large number of bacteria, and the shaving process will remove a large number of skin sheddings, both of which will contaminate a sterile area.

The nurse performing the scrub should wash her hands and don sterile gloves. All scrub bowls and brushes (Fig 23–12) should be opened by the circulator. Barrier drapes are used to cover the nonsurgical foot and to isolate the surgical foot. If the procedure is bilateral, the barrier drape is placed under both feet. Sterile 4 × 4-in. sponges are dipped into the appropriate antiseptic agent. Prepare the area with the sponges by using a circular motion. Begin distally at the toes, and progress proximally to the ankle (Fig 23–13). Special attention should be paid to all nail margins and interdigital areas because these areas harbor more bacteria. The scrub procedure lasts 5 to 7 minutes. The sponges are discarded after completing the ankle.

If an area is missed, the same sponges should not be used to scrub that area. This would bring microorganisms from the ankles, which contain more bacteria, to an area that contains a lower number of bacteria. The area that was missed is scrubbed with the next group of sponges.

A paper or cloth towel is placed over the foot to absorb the preparatory solution (Fig 23–14). Warm water may be poured over the foot to re-

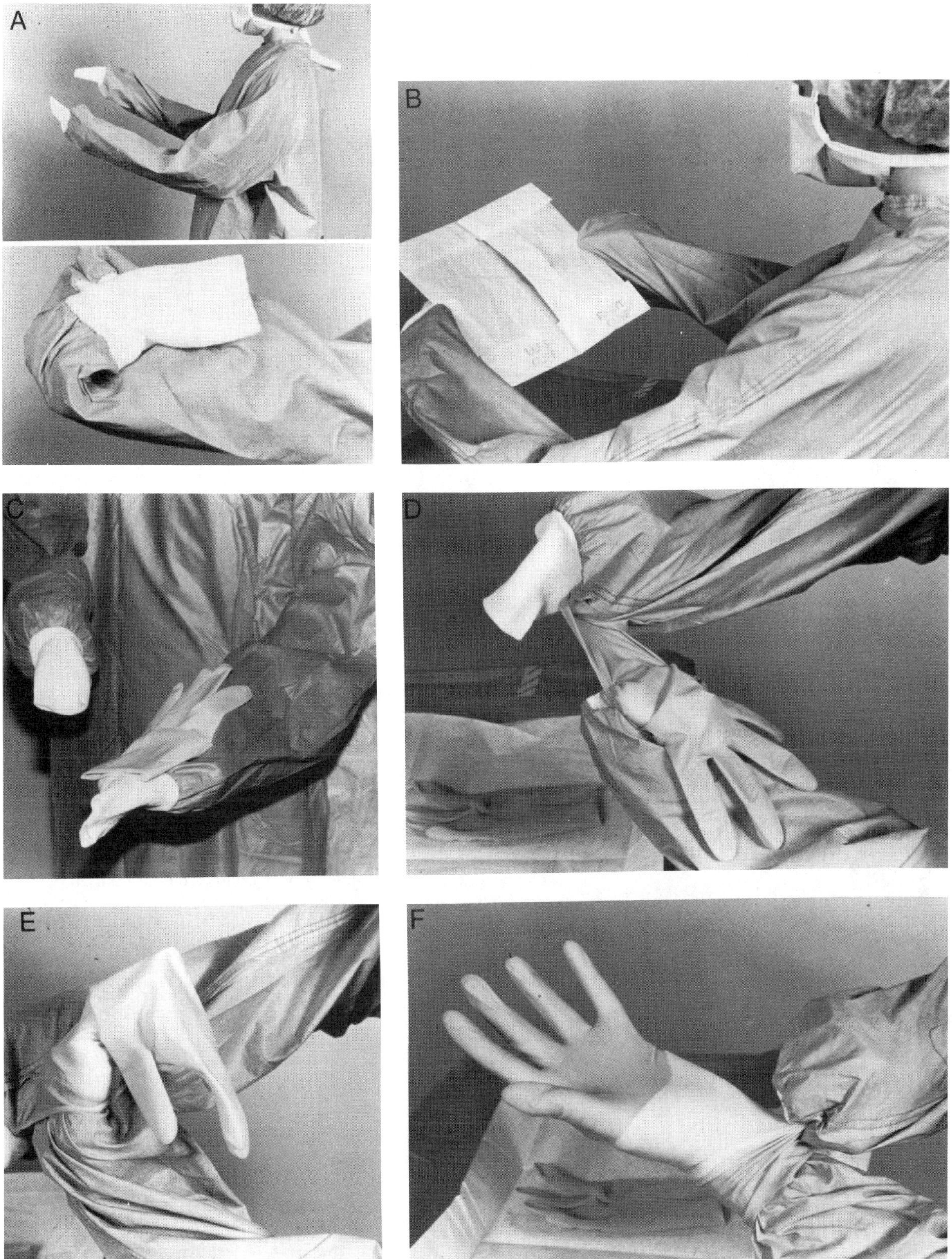

FIG 23–9.
For legend, see page 170.

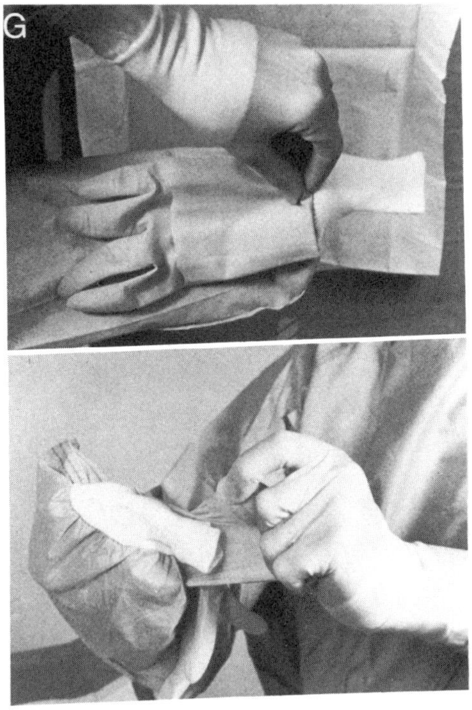

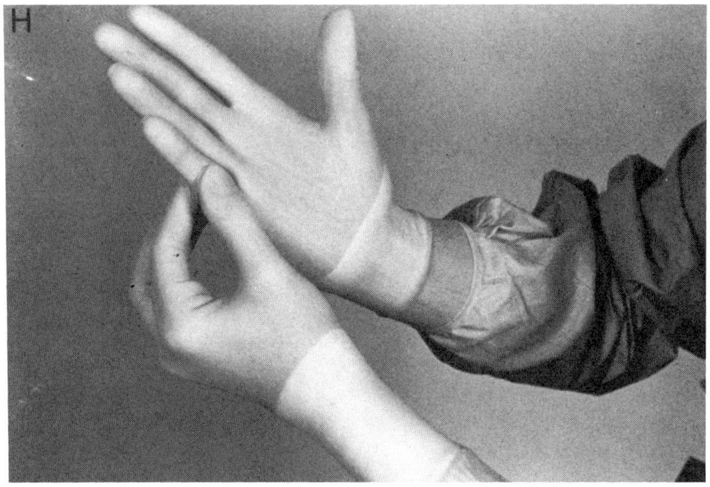

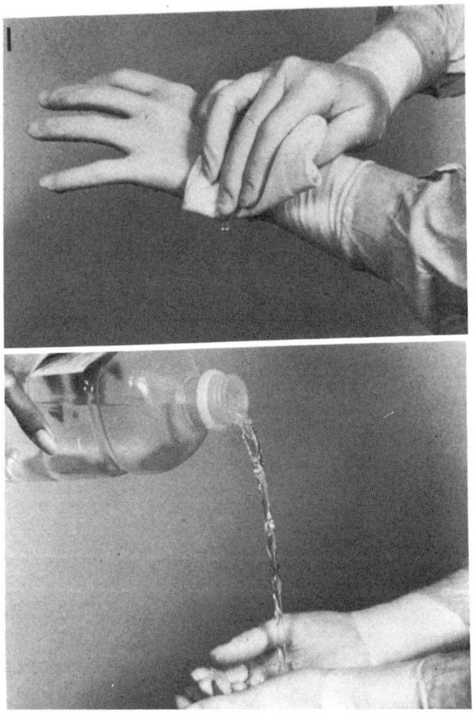

FIG 23–9.
A, the hands stop where the cuffs join the sleeve. **B,** without the hands exiting the cuff, the gloves are opened and laid on a flat surface. **C,** the label of the glove is placed against the outstretched palm within the sleeve so that the fingers point toward the elbow. **D,** the thumb and fingers within the sleeve grasp the glove at the level of the cuff. **E,** the right hand holds the glove and pulls it onto the left hand. **F,** once the fingers of the left hand are within the glove, the right hand grasps the gown cuff and glove simultaneously to allow the entire hand to slip into the glove. **G,** the same procedure is performed with the opposite hand. **H,** once both gloves are on, the fingers of the gloves are pulled proximally and circumferentially positioned to create comfort. **I,** cornstarch on the gloves is rinsed off. This helps prevent foreign reactions within tissue.

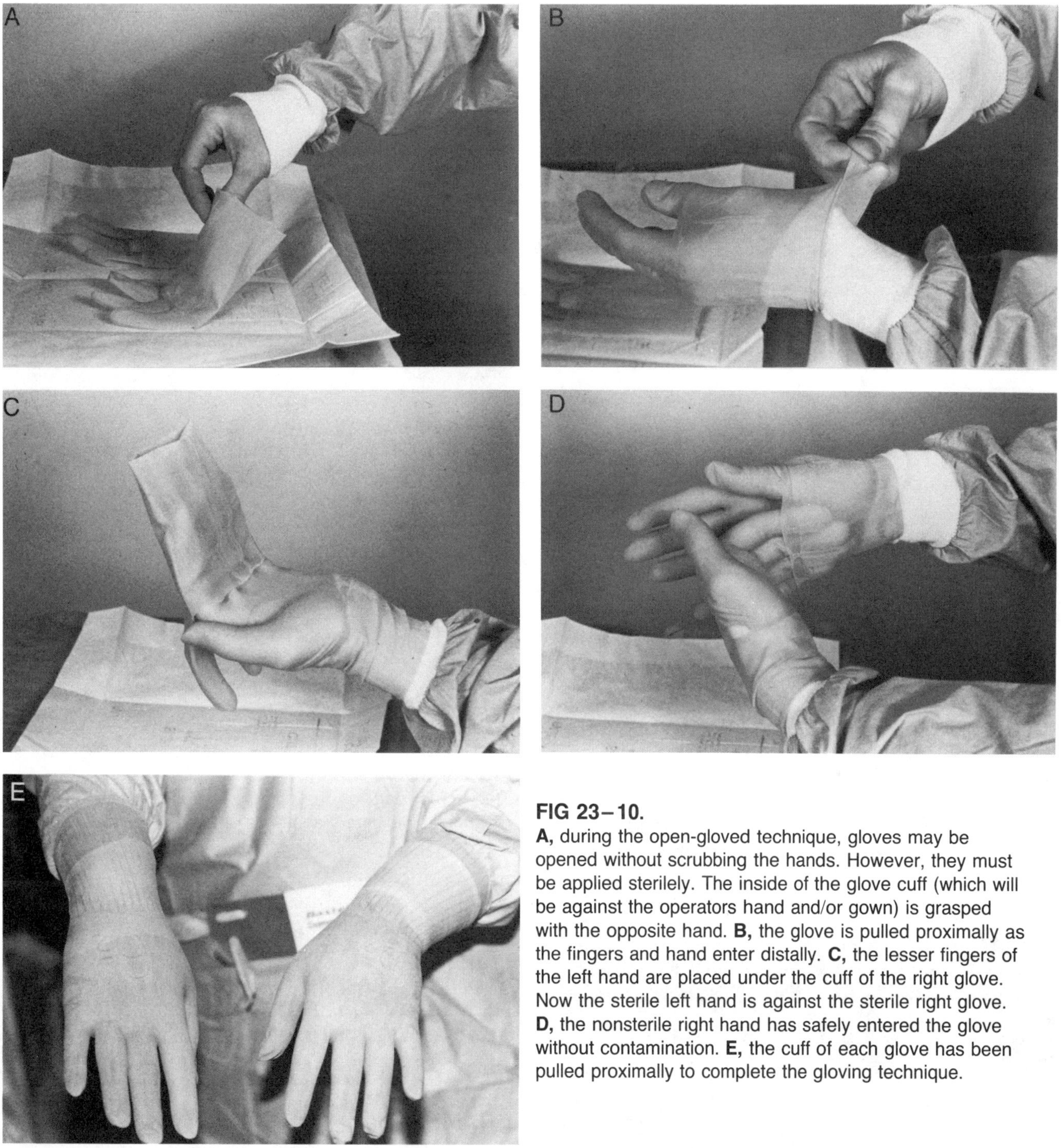

FIG 23–10.
A, during the open-gloved technique, gloves may be opened without scrubbing the hands. However, they must be applied sterilely. The inside of the glove cuff (which will be against the operators hand and/or gown) is grasped with the opposite hand. **B,** the glove is pulled proximally as the fingers and hand enter distally. **C,** the lesser fingers of the left hand are placed under the cuff of the right glove. Now the sterile left hand is against the sterile right glove. **D,** the nonsterile right hand has safely entered the glove without contamination. **E,** the cuff of each glove has been pulled proximally to complete the gloving technique.

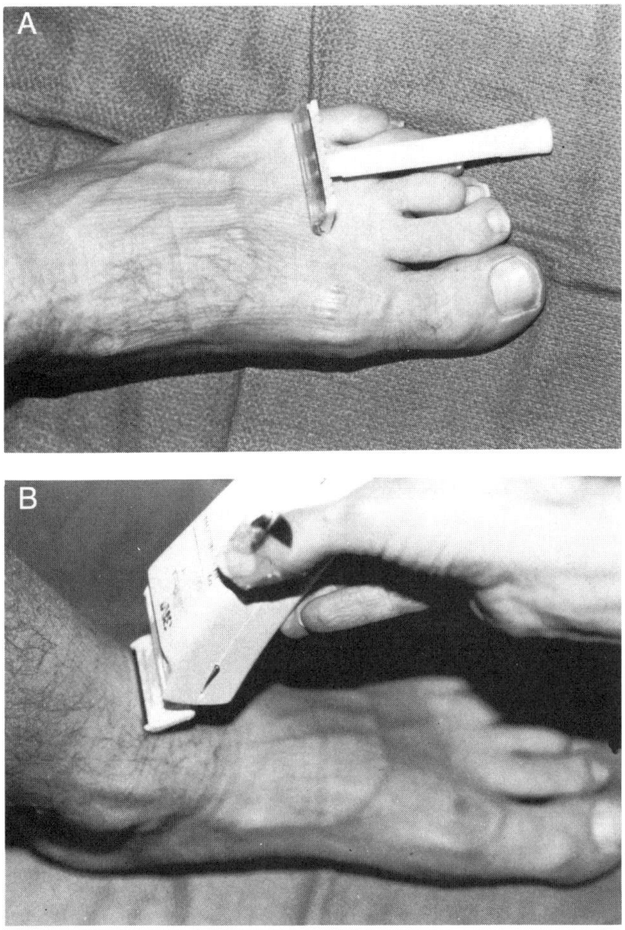

FIG 23–11.
A, a razor can be used to shave hair from the surgical foot. Care should be taken not to nick the skin because this can result in infection. **B,** a battery-powered shaver is not as abrasive to skin as a razor.

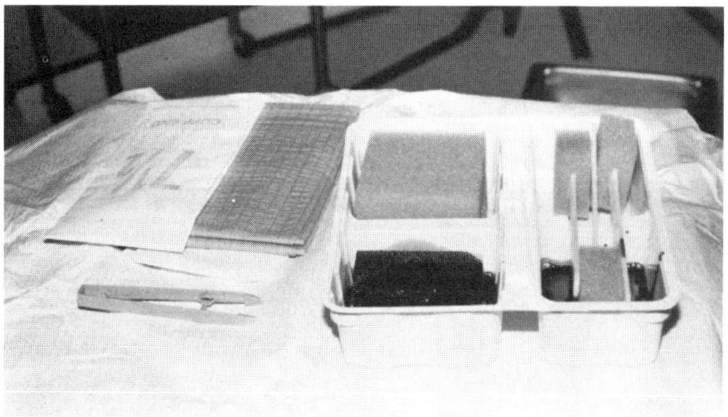

FIG 23–12.
Many different disposable "prep setups" are commercially available. They generally consist of sterile towels, gloves, sponges, and brushes to which an antiseptic agent is added.

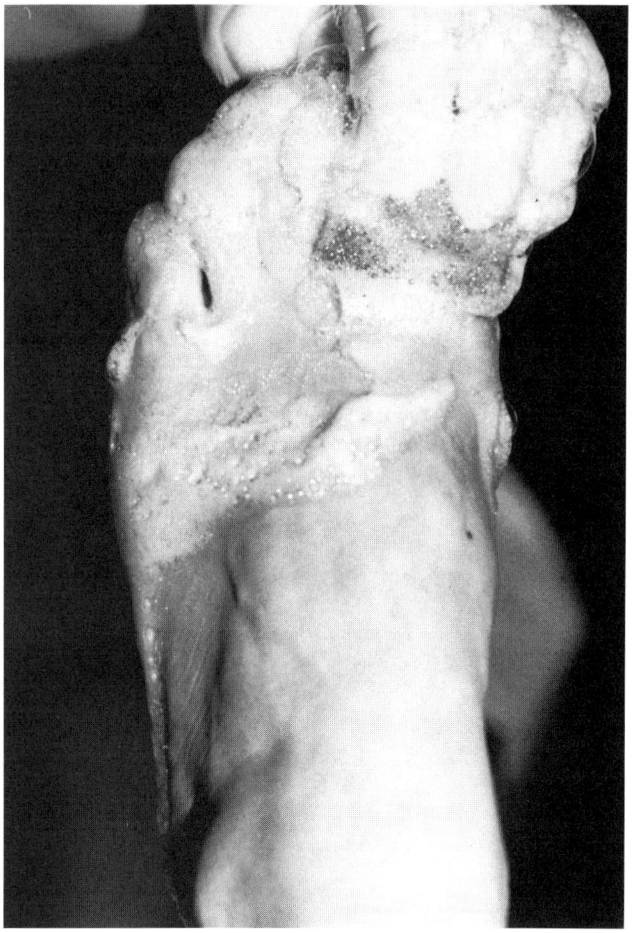

FIG 23–13.
The scrub part of the foot preparation starts distally, progresses proximally and ends at the ankle.

move the antiseptic agent. The table is put into a slight Trendelenburg position (foot higher than the head) so that the water runs away from the toes and toward the ankle. Large absorbent towels or pans are used to catch the excess water. New sterile gloves are then put on, and the foot is painted with the appropriate antiseptic (Fig 23–15,A–C).

DRAPING

Elevate the legs approximately 12 in. above the table level. Place a nonporous drape over the nonsurgical foot and under the sterile foot. Standard technique dictates that two bottom drapes be used. If a puncture occurs in the top drape, sterility will still be maintained (Fig 23–16,A and B). A protective towel is then wrapped about the ankle (Fig 23–16,C and D). Some surgeons prefer to use

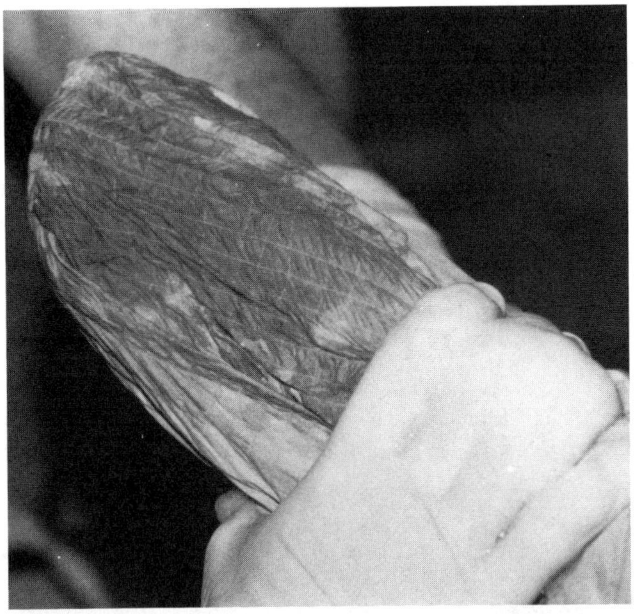

FIG 23–14.
An absorbent towel is used to remove the antiseptic scrub agent from the foot and ankle.

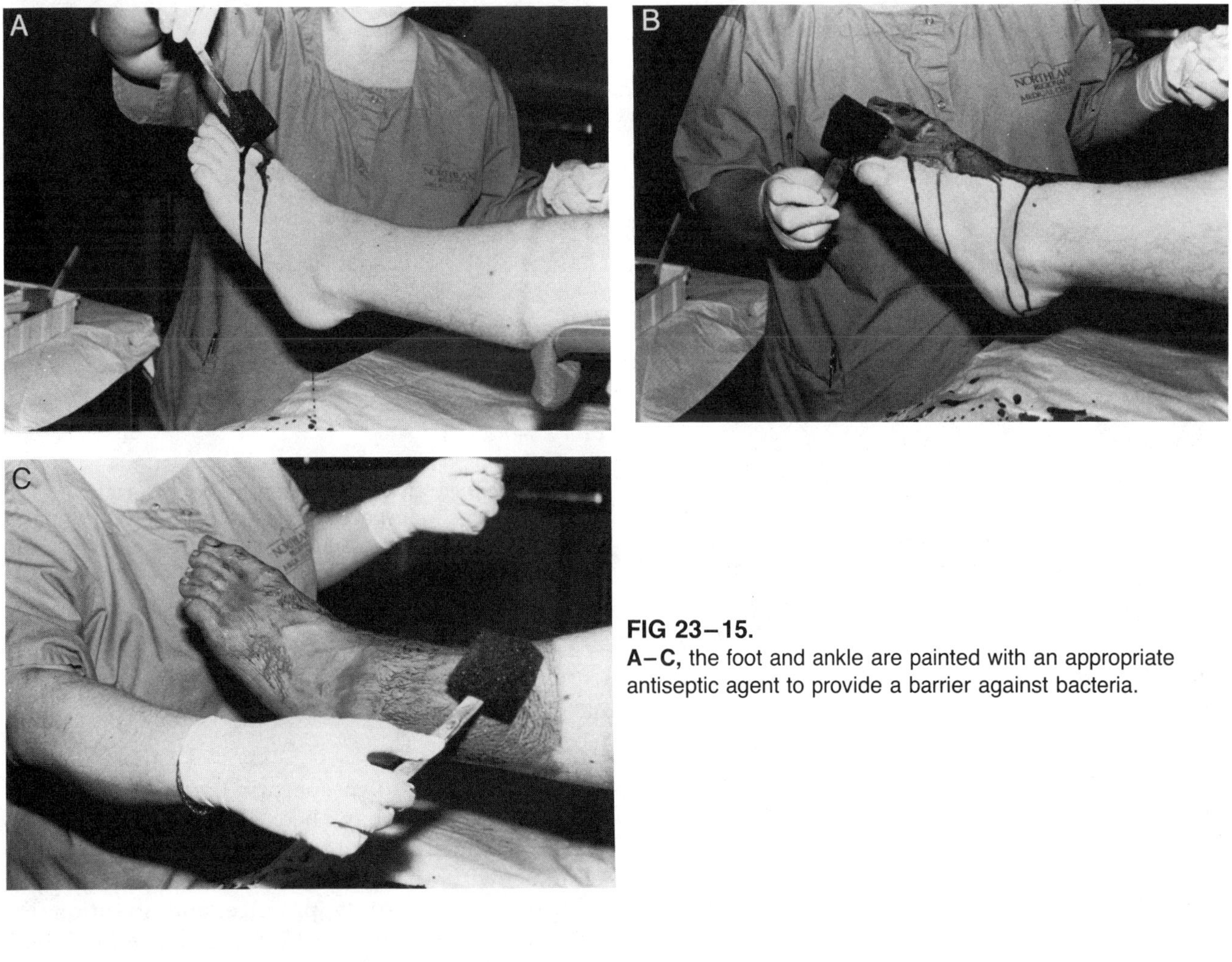

FIG 23–15.
A–C, the foot and ankle are painted with an appropriate antiseptic agent to provide a barrier against bacteria.

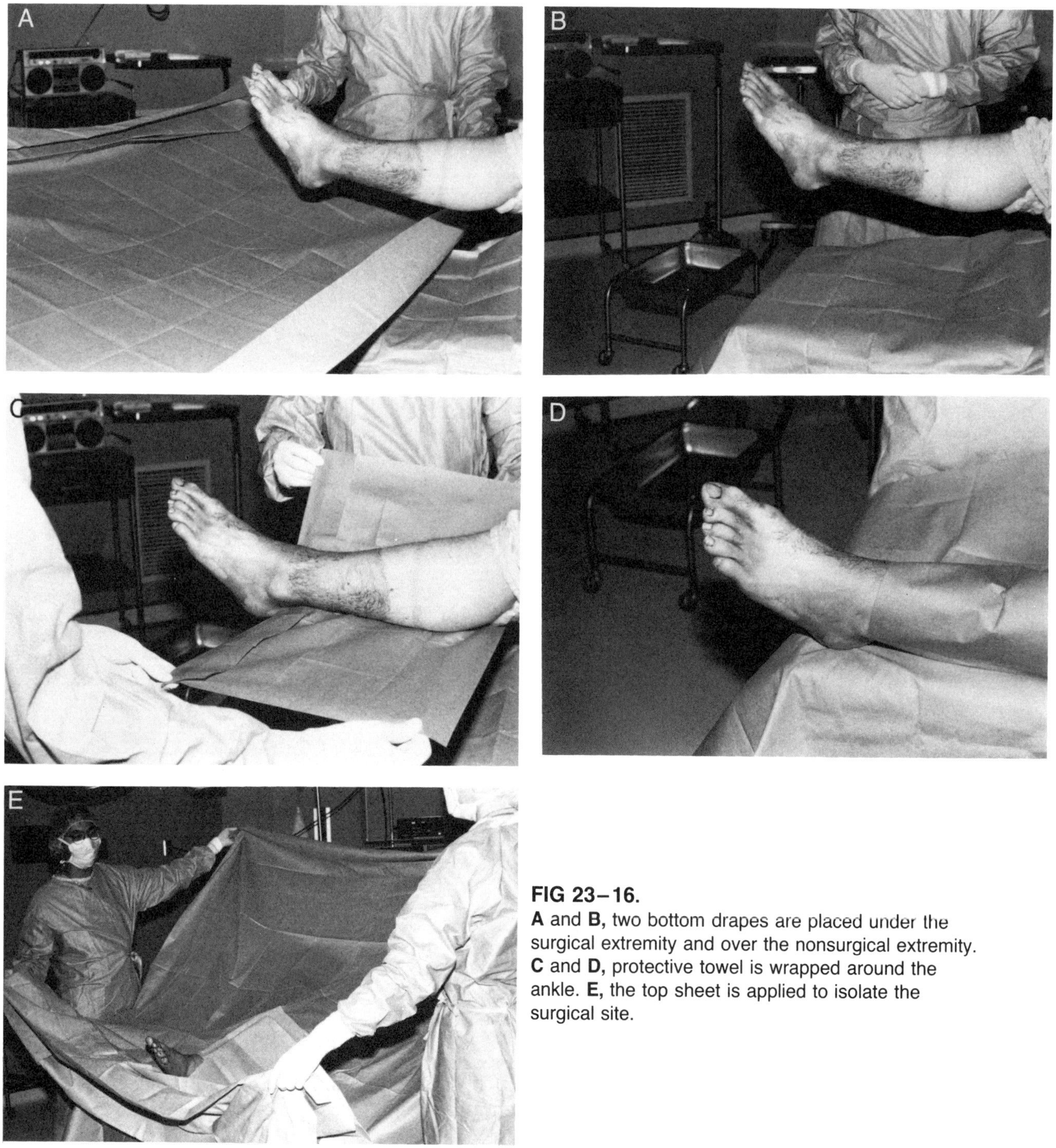

FIG 23–16.
A and **B,** two bottom drapes are placed under the surgical extremity and over the nonsurgical extremity. **C** and **D,** protective towel is wrapped around the ankle. **E,** the top sheet is applied to isolate the surgical site.

a stockinette over the foot and ankle in an attempt to provide a protective sterile atmosphere. A top drape is used to cover the area from the ankle proximally, thereby completely isolating the foot from other areas of possible contamination (Fig 23–16,E). Surgery can now be performed.

The methods of preparation, scrubbing, gowning, and gloving have been discussed. Each podiatric medical assistant should be completely familiar with the principles of aseptic technique. With continued study, practice, and attention, the podiatric medical assistant can learn to "think sterile" and help keep contamination and infection to a minimum.

BIBLIOGRAPHY

1. Atkinson LJ, Kohn ML: *Operating Room Techniques,* ed 5. New York, McGraw-Hill International Book Co, 1978.
2. Jimenez AL: *Doctors Hospital Podiatric Education and Research Institute Second Annual Podiatric Assistant Surgical Seminar.* Tucker Ga, Podiatry Institute Publishing Company, 1985.

24

The Surgical Assistant

Dennis E. Martin, D.P.M.

When the podiatric assistant chooses to become part of the surgical team, she has entered an area of the profession that carries with it tremendous excitement and responsibility. Aside from actual participation in the surgical procedure, the assistant will also be responsible for the preoperative preparation and immediate postoperative management of the surgical patient. Therefore, a better title for this professional may be the *perioperative assistant* because of the multiple roles played in the preoperative, intraoperative, and postoperative periods of surgery. The terms surgical assistant and perioperative assistant will be used interchangeably throughout this chapter.

Looking at the surgical procedure as a "perioperative" experience helps to ensure a smooth course for the patient before, during, and after surgery. To add a sense of continuity to the discussion, the various duties and responsibilities of the surgical assistant will be described chronologically as they occur in the perioperative period.

PREOPERATIVE PREPARATION

The assistant's job in the preoperative period entails preparation of the operating room and preparation of the surgical patient.

Patient Preparation

Preparation of the surgical patient actually begins prior to the day of surgery. A phone call should be placed to the patient 1 to 2 days prior to the date of the surgery to confirm vital information. This includes the date, time, and location of the surgery as well as the surgeon, diagnosis, and nature of the procedure to be performed. This is a time to encourage the patient to ask or express any last-minute questions or concerns so that they may be answered by you and/or the surgeon.

The patient's chart is reviewed prior to the day of surgery. It is important to appreciate any significant medical history. Certain disease states, for example, diabetes or rheumatoid arthritis, merit special consideration in the surgical patient. Also note any current medications or allergies identified in the chart. This will help alleviate any drug interactions with any of the various medications used during surgery.

The final portion of the patient's chart that should be examined is the preoperative laboratory studies. Certain baseline laboratory studies should be performed on all patients. These studies include the red blood cell (RBC) count, the white blood cell (WBC) count, hematocrit (Hct), and hemoglobin (Hb), collectively known as a complete blood count (CBC).

Red blood cells, also called erythrocytes, are responsible for carrying oxygen to all the tissues throughout the body. The red blood cell count is

TABLE 24–1.
Types of Anemia

Iron deficiency anemia
Thalassemia
Anemia of chronic disease—infection, renal disease, endocrine disease, chronic inflammation
Blood loss
Bone marrow failure
Hemolysis
Folate deficiency
Vitamin B_{12} deficiency (pernicious anemia)
Liver disease
Medications—anticonvulsants

an estimate of the number of red blood cells circulating in the body. There are normally between 4 and 6 million red cells per milliliter in the adult. However, the number of red cells as well as their size, shape, and color will vary with different disease states.

Hemoglobin is the primary constituent of the red blood cell that carries the oxygen throughout the body. It is the hemoglobin that is responsible for the bright red color of blood when it is combined with oxygen. The concentration of hemoglobin is reported in grams per 100 ml. The normal value for an adult male patient is 13.5 to 18.0 g/100 mL, and for an adult female it is 12.0 to 16.0 g/100 mL. The most common disorder associated with hemoglobin is anemia, a deficiency of red blood cells. This deficiency can result from a rapid loss or a slow production of red cells. There are several types of anemia representing a variety of disease states (Table 24–1). Anemia means that there is decreased oxygen transport to the tissues, with a resultant increased work load on the heart.

The hematocrit is another value used to assess the amount of red blood cells in the body. More specifically, it is the volume of packed red blood cells found in 100 mL of blood. The hematocrit is expressed as a percentage. For example, a hematocrit value of 46% implies that there are 46 mL of red blood cells in 100 mL of blood. The normal hematocrit in an adult male is 40% to 50%, and in the female it is 38% to 47%.[1]

The WBC count is an expression of the number of WBCs in 1 μL of blood. There are five different types of white cells, also called leukocytes: basophils, neutrophils, eosinophils, lymphocytes, and monocytes. As a group, the leukocytes fight infections, allergies, poisons, and other foreign invaders. However, individually, the five types of cells play very different roles in the overall fighting process. Table 24–2 gives a breakdown of the various types of white cells, including their primary function and normal percentages, The normal WBC count is usually between 4,500 and 11,000. However this total number of white cells gives only partial information. It is the *differential white cell count* (the breakdown of the five types) that allows a more specific diagnosis to be made.

In the preoperative patient, an increased white cell count (leukocytosis) or a decreased white cell count (leukopenia) can be significant. Leukocytosis can suggest an infectious state taking place somewhere in the body. This can put the proposed surgical site at risk of becoming secondarily contaminated. A leukopenia, or decreased number of white cells, may impair the body's ability to heal after the surgical procedure and lead to postoperative wound complications.

In addition to the CBC, a urinalysis is ordered in the majority of preoperative patients. This simple test can give very valuable information regard-

TABLE 24–2.
Differential White Blood Cell Count

Type	Primary Function	Normal Percentage of Total Count
Neutrophils	To destroy microorganisms and other foreign substances increased with bacterial infections	40–70
Lymphocytes	Will be increased in viral infections and chronic infectious processes	24–44
Monocytes	Also involved in the infection fighting process. An increase in this subset of cells can be seen with protozoa infections, malaria, and tuberculosis	3–8
Eosinophils	Will be elevated in allergies and allergic reactions as well as in parasitic infections	1–3
Basophils	Principal source of histamine in the bloodstream and they contain heparin	0–1

ing certain disease states such as diabetes or kidney disease. A clean-catch (midstream) specimen should be collected to avoid contamination from contact with the external parts of the genitourinary tract. The specimen should be read as soon as possible after collection to avoid the changes in pH, multiplication of bacteria, and disintegration of white cells that occur with time. The standard urinalysis consists of a macroscopic and microscopic examination (Table 24–3).

The urinalysis can also be used as a preliminary screening test for pregnancy. Any female of childbearing age (menses through menopause) undergoing general anesthesia or intravenous sedation should have a preoperative pregnancy test. The potentially devastating effects these medications can have on a fetus make this simple test a mandatory part of the preoperative workup. Any patient who has had a previous tubal ligation or hysterectomy is obviously exempted.

The CBC and urinalysis are usually the only two preoperative tests required in a healthy patient. If the patient relates a positive medical history, then a variety of other preoperative tests can be ordered to assess the current state of the existing disease. Any abnormalities in the results of these preoperative screening tests should be brought to the attention of the attending podiatrist.

Because a large number of diabetic patients present with foot problems, it is important to briefly review the preoperative glucose assessment. Glucose is the end product of carbohydrate metabolism in the human body. The utilization of glucose by the body's cells is intimately related to the level of available insulin, which is typically decreased in the diabetic patient. Therefore, a glucose test is used to assess the body's ability to utilize the available blood sugar. When this ability is impaired and the level of blood glucose is elevated (hyperglycemia), the risk of surgical complications and general medical complications is greatly increased. Thus, it is important to get a measurement of the glucose level preoperatively. Because the level will vary greatly depending on when the last meal was consumed, the most representative measurement would be a *fasting blood sugar.* This is taken 8 to 10 hours after the last meal or drink. The fasting blood sugar determination can be ordered as part of the preoperative blood work or can be performed by the assistant in the office with a finger stick maneuver (Fig 24–1,A–F). Normal values for a healthy patient should fall between 60 to 100 mg/dL glucose, varying slightly with different laboratories.

TABLE 24–3.
Urinalysis

Examination	Normal Values
Macroscopic	
Color	Pale yellow to deep amber
pH	4.6–8
Specific gravity	1.001–1.035
Glucose	Negative
Ketones	Negative
Protein	Negative
Bilirubin	Negative
Microscopic	
Red blood cells	0–3 per hpf
White blood cells	0–4 per hpf
Bacteria	None
Casts	None
Crystals	None

The preoperative x-ray films should be evaluated to make sure that they correlate with the patient and the proposed procedure. If it has been several months or longer since x-ray films were taken, current radiographs may be needed.

The final phase of the preoperative patient preparation occurs on the day of surgery. The patient is greeted and escorted to the appropriate examination room for final preparations. Relevant medical history is reviewed and relayed to the physician before any surgical or anesthetic procedure is performed. Vital signs (pulse, respiration, blood pressure, and temperature) are taken and documented on the chart. The consent form is explained to the patient by the physician, and then the patient's signature is witnessed. The proposed surgical site is examined for any breaks in skin or other potential complications.

The patient's overall status is relayed to the physician. If all considerations are normal and meet with the physician's approval, the patient is then ready for the preoperative sedation and/or anesthetic.

Before discussing the intraoperative responsibilities of the assistant, the preoperative preparation of the operating room will be reviewed.

Operating Room Preparation

The operating suite must be cleaned and prepared prior to any surgical procedure. This preparation includes the physical cleaning of the room as well as making sure that all the required instruments are sterile and ready for use.

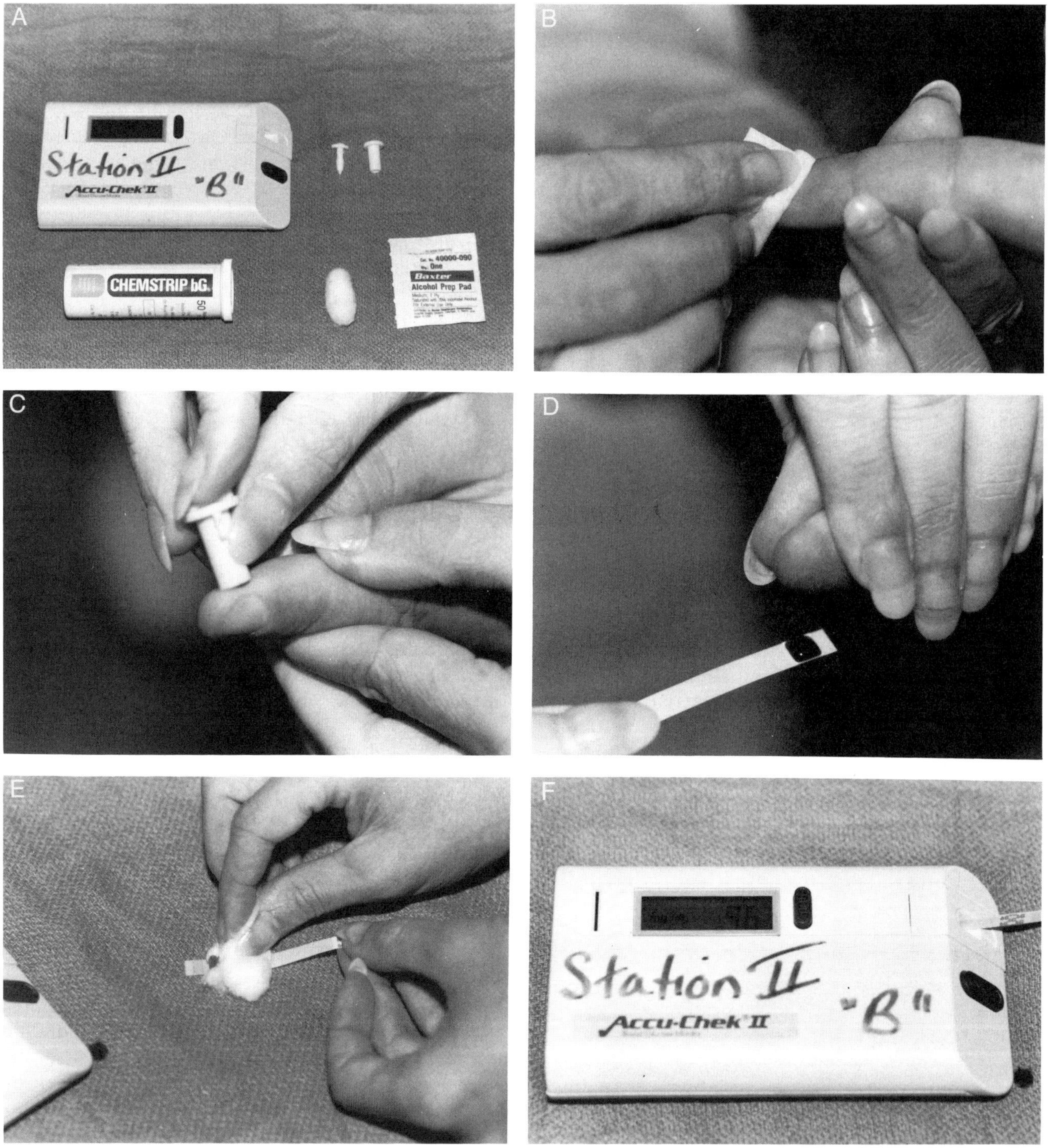

FIG 24–1.
Finger stick glucose analysis **A,** essential supplies, including an Accu-Chek scanner, lancet, Chemstrips, cotton ball, and alcohol wipe. **B,** preparation of the finger with an alcohol wipe. **C,** finger stick with the lancet. **D,** apply one drop of blood to the Chemstrip and wait 60 seconds. **E,** excess blood is wiped from strip with a cotton ball. **F,** Chemstrip entered into the machine where the blood glucose will be read automatically.

There are a variety of factors that can predispose a wound to contamination. One of these factors is inadequate disinfection of the room. Therefore, by properly cleaning the room preoperatively the risk of postoperative patient infection is minimized.

The room should be cleaned each morning, between each case, and at the end of the day. The Association of Operating Room Nurses (AORN) has set forth the following outline of recommended practices for operating room sanitation.[1]

Recommended Practices

1. Prior to the first scheduled procedure of the day, horizontal surfaces should be damp-dusted. These horizontal (flat) surfaces include floors, tables, equipment, overhead lamps, and other ceiling- and wall-mounted equipment. Dusting should be done with a clean cloth moistened with an appropriate agent.
2. During the surgical procedure, efforts should be directed at confining contamination. This is done to minimize the risk of transmitting contamination from the operating room to other areas of the office or hospital. These efforts include the use of gloves and/or instruments by personnel when cleaning and discarding contaminated supplies from the surgery.
3. All items that have come in contact with the patient and/or sterile field should be considered contaminated, and their disposition should reflect appropriate control measures. This refers to the disposing of gowns, gloves, drapes, etc., used in surgery. This also includes the between-case disinfecting of horizontal surfaces. Floors should be cleaned by the wet vacuuming method or by using a clean mop head and solution. Shoe covers should also be changed between cases.
4. At the completion of the day's schedule, the operating room, scrub/utility area, and corridors should be cleaned. At the completion of this cleaning regimen, the cleaning equipment should be disassembled, cleaned, and dried before storage.
5. Designated areas of the surgical suite should be cleaned according to an established routine. This refers to periodic cleaning of areas outside the operating room itself such as cabinet shelves, offices, lounges, etc.
6. Policies and procedures on operating room sanitation should be written, reviewed annually, and readily available within the institution.

The second step in the preoperative preparation of the operating suite is to make sure that all instruments and required equipment are sterile and ready for use. This includes not only the actual surgical instruments but also any ancillary equipment in the room (gas tanks/cylinders, tourniquets, power tools, or fixation devices).

The gas cylinders most often used in an operating room setting are oxygen, nitrous oxide, and nitrogen. To help identify them, they are color coded green (oxygen), navy blue (nitrous oxide), and gray (nitrogen). The assistant should be able to identify the cylinders and be able to turn the valves on and off. The amount of gas in the tanks should be checked before each case.

There are two basic types of lower extremity tourniquets used in podiatric surgery, rubber bandage tourniquets and pneumatic cuffs (Fig 24–2). The rubber tourniquets include the Penrose drain, typically used in digital procedures, and the Martin's or Esmark bandage, typically secured around the ankle. These tourniquets have the advantage of being able to drain the blood from the segment as they are applied (Fig 24–3).

Pneumatic cuffs, also called "Kidde cuffs," are automatic, compressed-gas inflating devices that are applied around the thigh or ankle in a manner similar to a blood pressure cuff (Fig 24–4). These types of tourniquets can result in permanent nerve and blood supply damage if left on for too long or if inflated at too great a pressure. Proper tourniquet inflation pressure is determined from the pa-

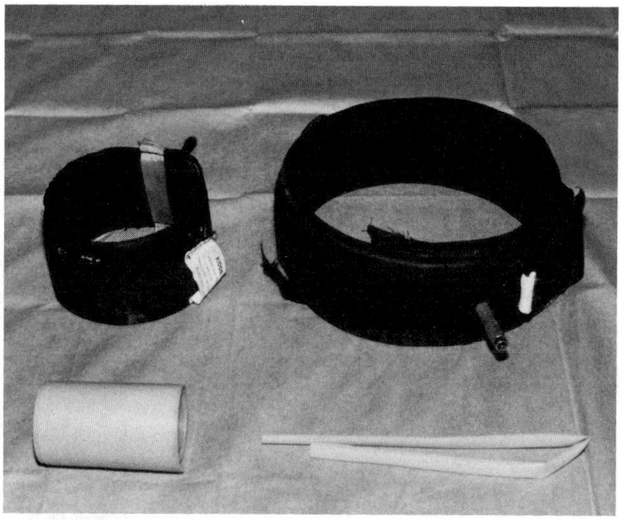

FIG 24–2.
Tourniquets: pneumatic ankle and thigh cuffs *(top)* and rubber bandage tourniquets *(bottom)*.

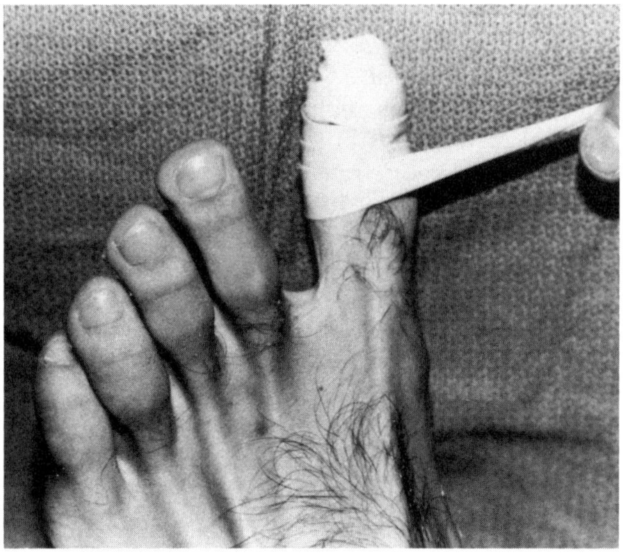

FIG 24–3.
Blood is expelled from the digit as the tourniquet is applied.

tient's preoperative blood pressure (systolic), the area of placement, and the patient's size. Most authorities feel that an inflation pressure of 100 mm Hg above the preoperative systolic blood pressure is acceptable. The average adequate tourniquet pressure at the thigh is 300 to 350 mm Hg, with pressures over 500 mm Hg considered to be unsafe. The maximum ankle pressure should not exceed 250 mm Hg in an adult and 150 mm Hg in a child.

Regardless of the area of placement, no tourniquet should be left inflated for more than 2 to 3 hours because irreversible damage can occur to the extremity. If the procedure is lengthy and extends beyond the 2-hour time limit, the tourniquet is deflated for a period of time. This downtime, also called "breathing time," is necessary to allow the tissues to be perfused and nourished with blood. Therefore, to avoid unnecessary damage the assistant should be aware of how long the tourniquet has been inflated and inform the surgeon of the elapsed time every 15 to 30 minutes.

Tourniquet injury can also result from incorrect application of the cuff. Tourniquets should be applied to areas of maximal circumference and as high as possible on the limb to avoid any direct damage to the underlying nerves and vessels.

The tourniquet should be routinely checked and calibrated with a mercury manometer or other measuring device. This will ensure that the pressure reading on the gauge of the tourniquet is a true indication of the pressure being applied against the extremity. The assistant should be aware of certain disease states that are absolute contraindications to the use of any type of tourniquet. These include sickle cell disease, peripheral vascular disease, and deep venous thrombosis. Other disease states considered to be relative contraindications to tourniquet use include sickle cell trait, diabetes, rheumatoid arthritis, and other conditions that are associated with vasculitis and blood vessel disorders.

The power instrumentation and fixation equip-

FIG 24–4.
Pneumatic ankle cuff in place prior to foot scrub.

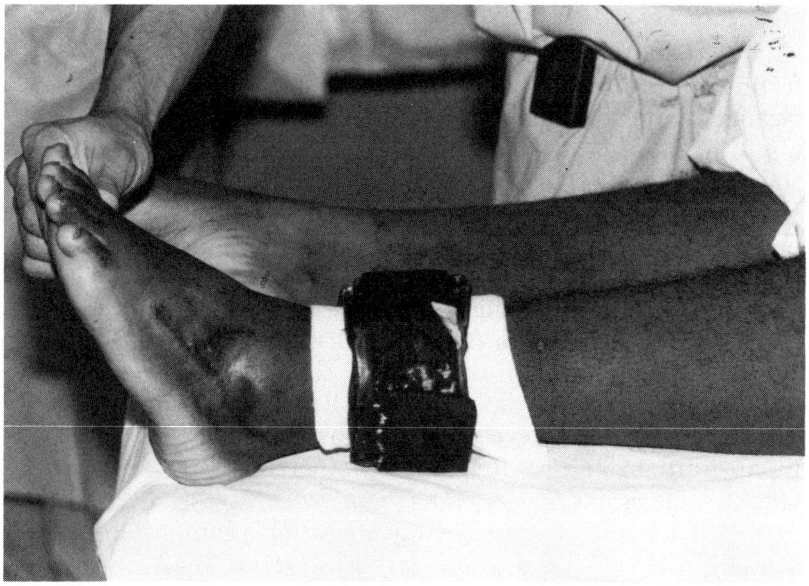

ment should be examined prior to each case to avoid any unnecessary delays during the procedure. Each instrument should be sterile and functioning properly. If the surgeon will be using internal fixation equipment, the boxes should be checked to be sure that they contain the necessary drills, screws, or K-wires. Because different podiatric procedures require a variety of screw sizes, it is important to replace the screws used after each case.

The final part of preparing the operating room for the surgery is to inspect the supply cabinet in the room. All materials that may be used in the case should be readily accessible including injectables, sutures, implant materials, and dressing supplies.

INTRAOPERATIVE RESPONSIBILITIES

The surgical assistant is an integral member of the surgical team. The surgical team is composed of both scrubbed and circulating persons. Scrubbed members include those who scrub their hands and arms and don sterile gowns and gloves. The circulating personnel supply the needs of the scrubbed members, coordinate room activities, and attend to the needs of the patient. The assistant should be familiar with all duties and responsibilities associated with both facets of the surgical team.

The assistant should have a firm understanding of surgical sepsis (infection) and asepsis (prevention of infection). If all members of the surgical team are aware of the factors that may predispose a wound to infection, appropriate steps can be taken to avoid these factors and minimize the risk of complication.

Wound Infection and Sources of Contamination

Wound infection is a very serious postoperative complication associated with significant patient morbidity and in more severe cases possibly mortality. As the bacteria invade the wound, the patient's wound healing becomes delayed and possibly completely destroyed. This not only results in a breakdown of the wound but also allows the bacteria to spread and possibly enter the general circulation and cause infectious processes throughout the body.

Although modern aseptic techniques have dramatically lowered the incidence of postoperative infections, they still occur. Therefore, it is important to identify all sources of contamination and those factors that predispose a wound to infection.

Bacteria are found in the air as well as on the floors, walls, and clothing of all personnel in the operating room, including the patient. It is these airborne bacteria that are most difficult to deal with and responsible for a significant number of postoperative infections. There are some measures that can be used to limit the number of airborne bacteria, including reducing the traffic in and out of the room, proper cleaning between cases, and the use of proper ventilation and filtering in the room. The other source of airborne contamination is via bacteria exhaled from the respiratory tracts of the operating room personnel. This can be kept to a minimum by having all personnel involved in the case wear snug-fitting caps and masks. Other steps should include keeping conversation to a minimum and restricting any personnel currently suffering from a respiratory infection from participating in the surgery

The skin is another site of normal bacteria habitation, with *Staphylococcus* being the most common organism. Therefore, to minimize the risk of contamination from this source, the skin around the operative site must be adequately prepared and isolated preoperatively. A complete description of gowning, gloving, scrubbing, and preparation and draping techniques is presented in Chapter 23.

Aside from bacterial contamination, there are several other factors that can predispose a surgical wound to infection. These factors can be divided into intrinsic factors (related to the patient) and extrinsic factors (related to the environment). Intrinsic factors refer to the patient's medical status. For example, certain disease states like diabetes, anemia, leukopenia (decreased white cells), rheumatoid arthritis, alcoholism, and vitamin deficiency can impair wound healing and make the patient susceptible to infection.

Extrinsic factors include factors such as a poor preoperative foot preparation, or inadequate hand scrubbing technique by the sterile team members. Other examples are poor surgical technique including prolonged wound exposure, rough handling of the tissues, and poor control of hemostasis (bleeding) during the case.

Extrinsic factors can also be directly related to the patient. An uncooperative patient may not follow postoperative instructions or may begin weight bearing too soon. Both of these scenarios can greatly increase the risk of wound complications. Contamination of the sterile postoperative dressings is another predisposing factor to infection.

Principles of Sterile Technique

The basic principles and practices described are to be used as a guide in establishing and maintaining a sterile surgical field. These principles are based on the recommendations of the AORN (1).

- Recommended practice 1.—Scrubbed persons should wear sterile gowns and gloves.
- Recommended practice 2.—Sterile drapes should be used to establish a sterile field.

  The sterile drapes should be placed on the patient and on all furniture and equipment that is to be part of the sterile field. In the draping process, the material should be held above waist level, in a compact position, and draped from the operative site to the periphery. To avoid contamination in the draping process, the gloved hands should be protected by cuffing draping material over the hands (Fig 24–5). Once the sterile drapes have been placed in position, they should be moved as little as possible. Any draping material that falls below table level must be considered unsterile.
- Recommended practice 3.—All items used within a sterile field should be sterile.

  Before dispensing any item to the sterile field, the nonscrubbed person handing the item should check package integrity, the chemical process indicator for sterility, and the expiration date.
- Recommended practice 4.—All items introduced into a sterile field should be dispensed by methods that maintain sterility of the item and integrity of the sterile field.

  A sterile package should be opened from the far side first and the near side last (Fig 24–6,A–E). This avoids contamination by the unsterile arm passing over the sterile item. Likewise, all wrapper tails should be secured when supplies are presented to the sterile field (Fig. 24–7). This helps to avoid accidental contact with the sterile scrubbed person by the unsterile package edges. When presenting the sterile items, they should be directly handed to the scrubbed person or placed securely on the sterile field. Items should not be thrown onto the field because they may roll off the edge, become contaminated, or possibly cause other items to be displaced.

  When presenting or dispensing solutions to the sterile field, the entire contents should be poured or the remainder discarded. This is done because sterility cannot be guaranteed if the cap is replaced and the bottle reused at a later time. When solutions are being poured, the receptacle should be placed near the edge of the table or directly held by the scrubbed person (Fig 24–8,A and B). Pouring should be done to avoid any splashing onto the surgical field.

  All cables, tubing, etc., for equipment should be secured with a nonperforating device. Any nonsterile equipment brought into the surgical field (laser, x-ray device) should be draped with a sterile material (Fig 24–9). Any item of questionable sterility should be considered contaminated and appropriately discarded.

  Also included in this recommendation is the covering of all operative areas with sterile dressings prior to removing the drapes. This minimizes the risk of contamination to the incision sites as the unsterile portions of the drapes come in contact with the foot.

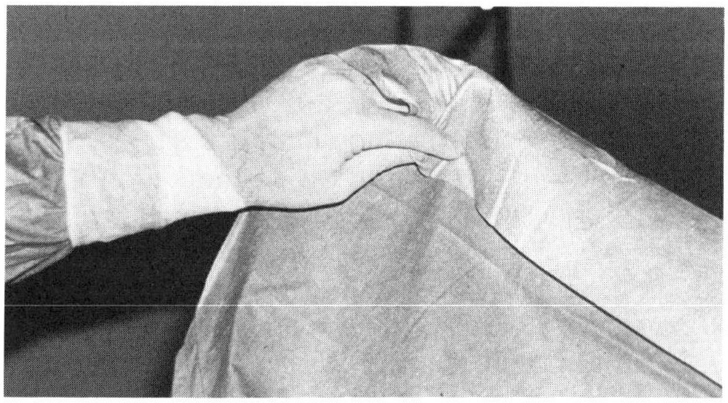

FIG 24–5.
Sterile gloves protected by a cuffed drape.

Now that the basic principles of sterile technique have been presented and the importance of maintaining an aseptic wound environment appreciated, the specific intraoperative responsibilities of the podiatric surgical assistant can be described. These intraoperative duties can be broken into five categories: (1) patient preparation, (2) assistant and instrument preparation, (3) sterile team preparation, (4) patient draping, and (5) operative assisting. If adequate personnel are avail-

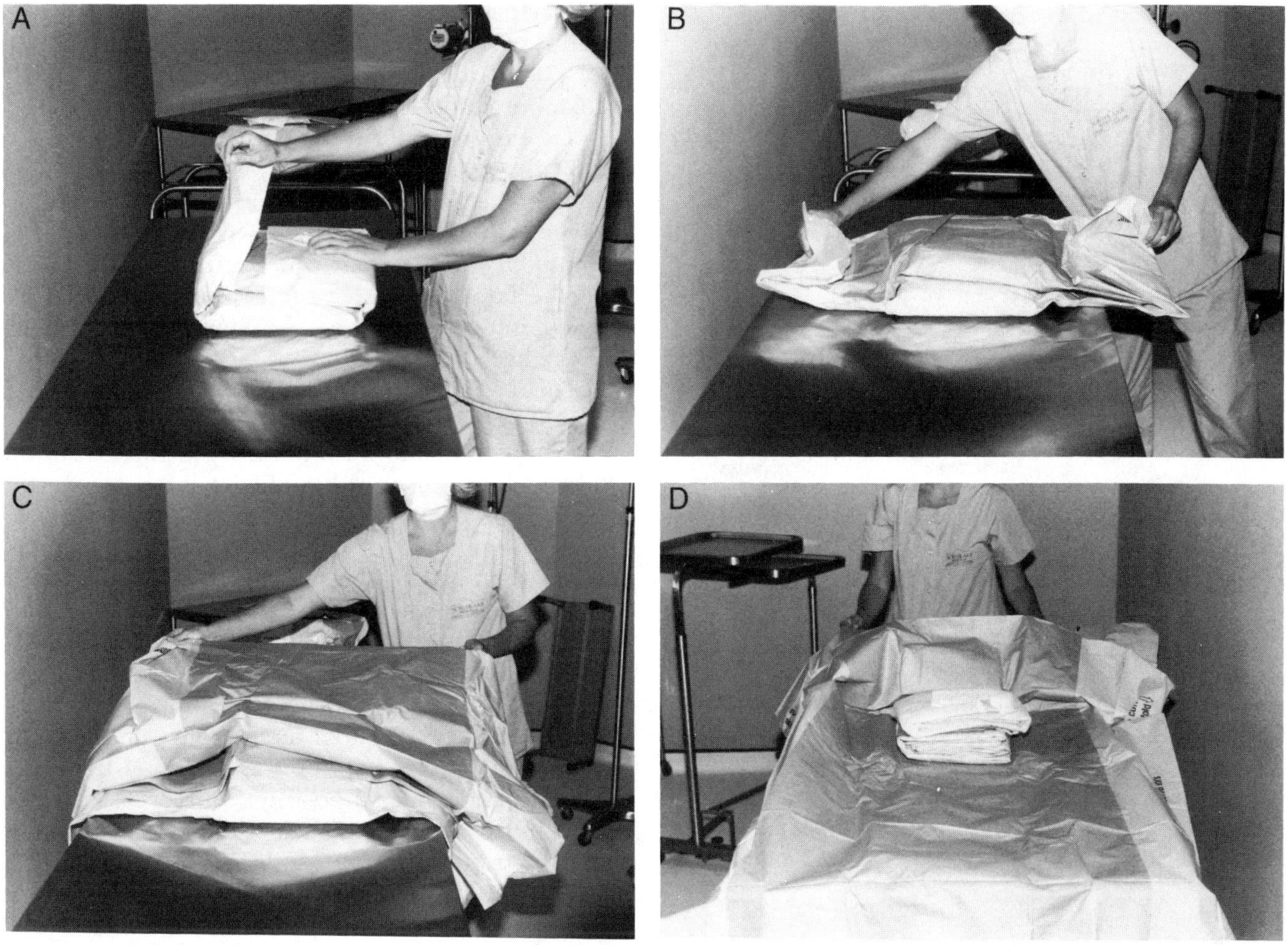

FIG 24–6.
A–E, proper method of opening a sterile pack.

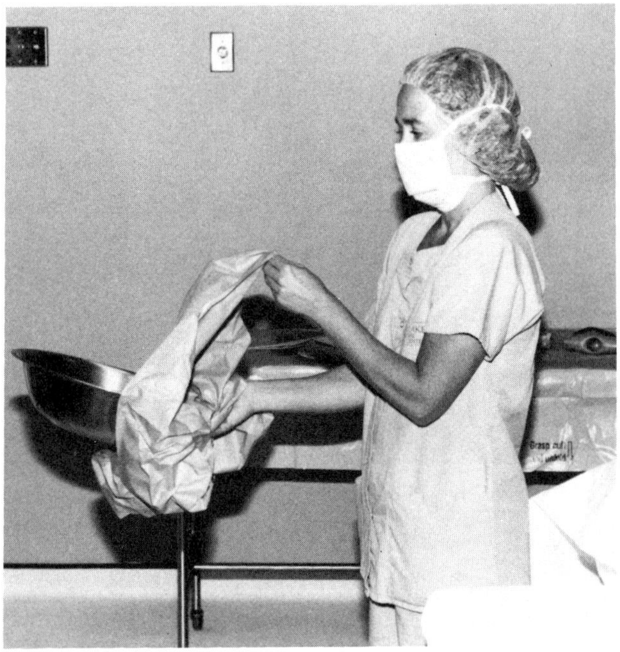

FIG 24–7.
Securing of all wrapper tails to avoid accidental contamination.

able, these responsibilities can be divided between a sterile surgical assistant and a nonsterile circulating assistant.

Patient Preparation

The preparation of the patient begins with bringing the patient into the room and properly positioning him on the operating table. The proper patient position will depend on the procedure to be performed. Typical positions required for podiatric surgery include supine, prone, Trendelenburg, and lateral (Fig 24–10).

The supine position is the attitude the patient typically assumes while the anesthesia is being induced. This is also the position used for the majority of podiatric procedures. The prone position is commonly used when procedures are performed on the back of the leg or foot such as heel cord lengthening or excision of a Haglund's deformity of the heel.

The Trendelenburg position places the head of the table lower than the foot. This position allows the surgeon to stand comfortably at the foot of the table while the anesthesiologist is seated at the head. This position also allows the blood to flow away from the foot. The reverse Trendelenburg raises the head of the table higher than the foot. Often, the anesthesiologist will tilt the table to aid the patient's breathing.

The lateral patient position is used when exposure is required for structures along the outside portion of the leg or foot (i.e., reconstruction of ankle ligaments or osteotomy of the heel bone). To maintain this lateral position, support is required both in front of and in back of the patient throughout the procedure (Fig 24–11,A and B).

If a thigh tourniquet is to be used during the case, it should be applied prior to the surgical scrubbing of the foot. Several layers of protective padding should be applied before placing the tourniquet on the limb (Fig 24–12,A and B). Ankle tourniquets can be applied either before or after

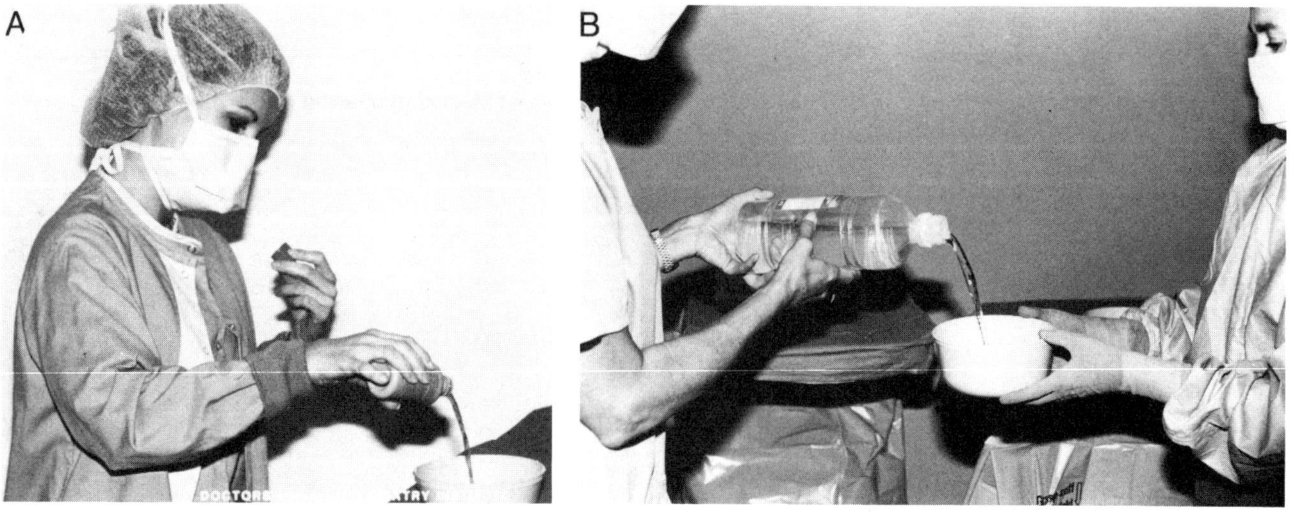

FIG 24–8.
Pouring of solutions directly into the receptacle **(A)** or into a sterile bowl as the assistant holds it away from sterile field **(B).**

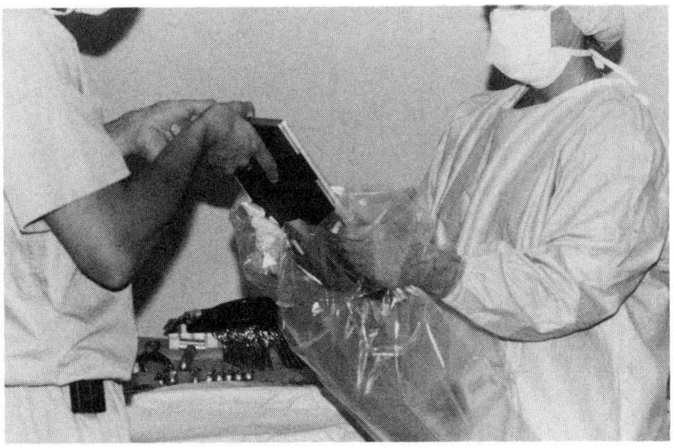

FIG 24–9.
Unsterile x-ray cassette placed into a sterile wrapper.

the preparation of the surgical foot. If applied after the preparation, measures must be taken to maintain the sterility of the limb.

Attention can now be directed to the surgical foot for the preoperative skin preparation. This can be divided into two parts, the removal of hair from the surgical site, and scrubbing the surgical site with an appropriate antimicrobial agent. The purpose of these two exercises is to remove dirt and transient microbes from the skin. This is essential in the prevention of postoperative infection.

Once the foot is fully prepared, it is maintained in this sterile, supported position until the surgical team is prepared to drape the extremity.

Assistant Preparation

While the circulating nurse is positioning the patient and scrubbing the surgical limb, the surgical assistant can prepare the instrument stand as well as gown and glove the surgeon. Before doing these latter duties, the surgical assistant must first perform an acceptable surgical scrubbing of both hands and forearms with an appropriate antimicrobial agent. This is done in order to minimize the number of microorganisms on the skin in these areas.

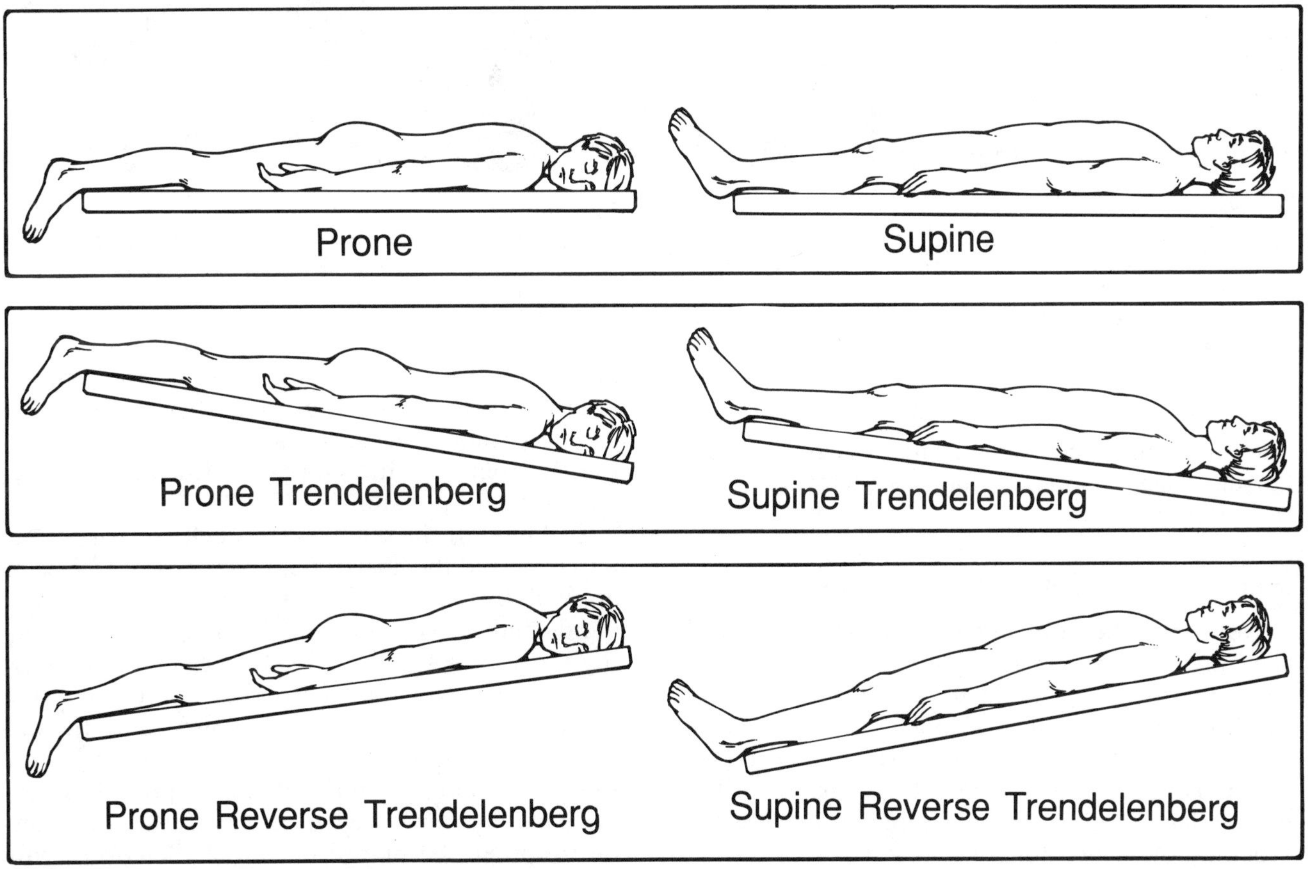

FIG 24–10.
Common patient positions used in podiatric surgery.

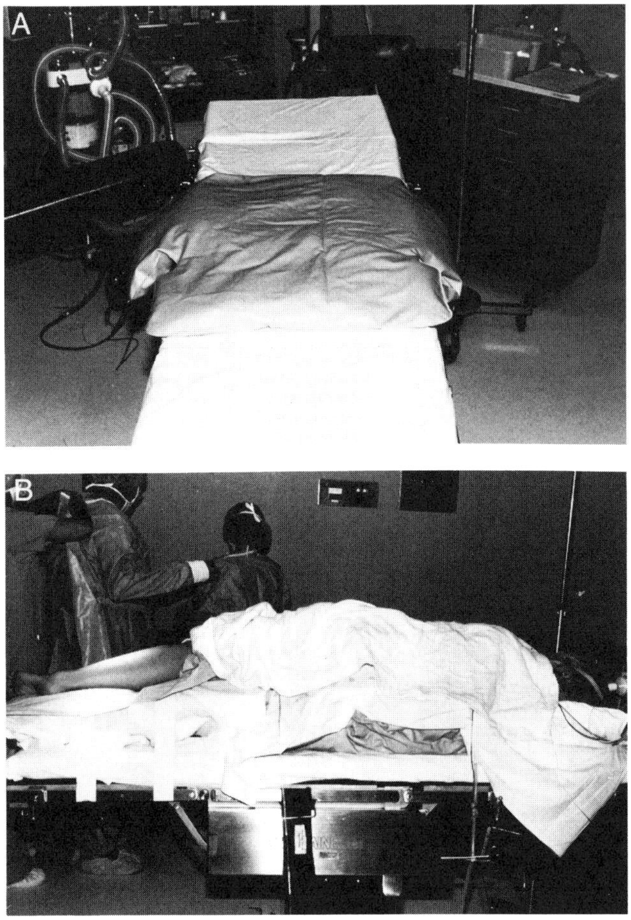

FIG 24–11.
A, support pack prior to patient positioning and vacuum suctioning. **B,** patient in the lateral position with a support pack molded in front and in back of the patient. By applying suction to the pack, a vacuum is created that allows the pack to harden and maintain the desired position.

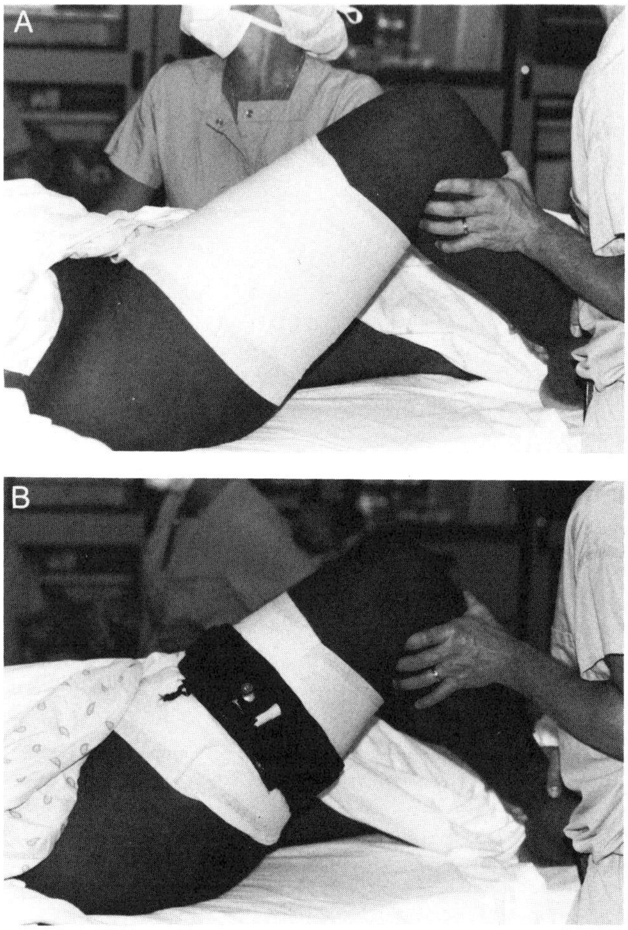

FIG 24–12.
A, protective padding applied prior to tourniquet placement. **B,** tourniquet in place over the protective padding.

Because she is the first member of the surgical team to scrub, the assistant must gown and glove herself. (See Chapter 23 for a description of the technique.)

Instrument and Back Table Preparation

Now that the assistant is gowned and gloved, she can prepare the back table and instrument stand for surgery. The linen packs on the back table were opened by the nonsterile circulating nurse prior to the scrubbed assistant entering the room. This is done by contacting only the edges and undersurface of the back table drape. Without reaching over the table, the four flaps are opened by pulling them toward oneself. This is acceptable because the areas that are touched will be dropped below table level (an unsterile area). The assistant can now arrange the table to accommodate the instruments and other sterile items. The assistant should arrange the back table in a fashion that will facilitate easy identification and retrieval of desired supplies (Fig 24–13).

Included in the pack on the back table is a sterile cover for the instrument Mayo stand. This is applied by the sterile assistant by placing her hands and arms in the cuff of the cover and placing it over the stand while being sure not to allow any part of cover top to drop below the waist (Fig 24–14). Once it is securely over the stand, the circulating assistant can pull it from below to allow the cover to sit flat on the stand. To provide an extra barrier against instrument perforation, a sterile towel can be placed on top of the cover. Only the instruments that will be used in the surgery should be placed on the Mayo stand. They should

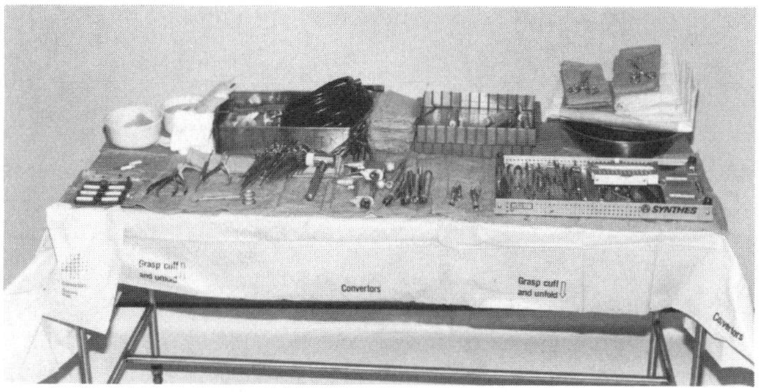

FIG 24–13.
Organized "back table."

be arranged in an orderly fashion, with the more frequently used instruments placed nearest the operating table.

If additional supplies are needed, it is the circulating assistant's responsibility to retrieve these items. When sterile instrument packs are desired (i.e., power instruments, internal fixation trays), the circulator must transfer them to the scrubbed assistant in a sterile fashion. These packs are always double-wrapped, with the outer layer considered to be unsterile and the inner wrap sterile. Therefore to maintain sterility, the circulator must hold the pack in one hand while unwrapping with the other. The sterile inner contents are then handed directly to the scrubbed assistant. Larger packs can be set down on a stand and opened in a fashion similar to that described for opening the back table pack. Smaller items (knife blades, suture packs, individual instruments) are packaged in peel-back containers. These are handed by grasping one flap with the thumb edge while stabilizing the package in the other hand. The flaps are then peeled back with both hands expressing the contents from within to be grabbed by the scrubbed assistant (Fig 24–15).

Surgeon Preparation

Once the patient has been prepared and the instrument tables organized, the surgeon and other members of the sterile surgical team can scrub their hands and prepare for surgery. Since the first assistant is already fully gowned and gloved, she can assist the others in getting dressed. After scrubbing, the surgeon is presented a surgical gown by the assistant. Since the assistant is sterile, she will hold the gown on the outside at the level of the shoulders and guide the inside of the sleeves over the outstretched hands of the surgeon (Fig 24–16). When placing the gown over the shoulders of the surgeon, care is taken to not allow the gloves to contact any unsterile area. The circulator will then tie the gown in the back.

The surgeon is then gloved by using a second form of "open gloving." This form, in contrast to the one described in Chapter 23, involves two people. The sterile assistant holds the glove with the palm facing the surgeon. This position puts the glove's thumb directly opposite the surgeon's thumb. With the fingers buried under the gloves edges, the assistant will pull from side to side to open the entrance into the glove (Fig 24–17,A and B). As the surgeon's hand enters the glove, the assistant exerts mild upward pressure and brings the glove completely over the stockinette cuff on the gown. This is then repeated for the second

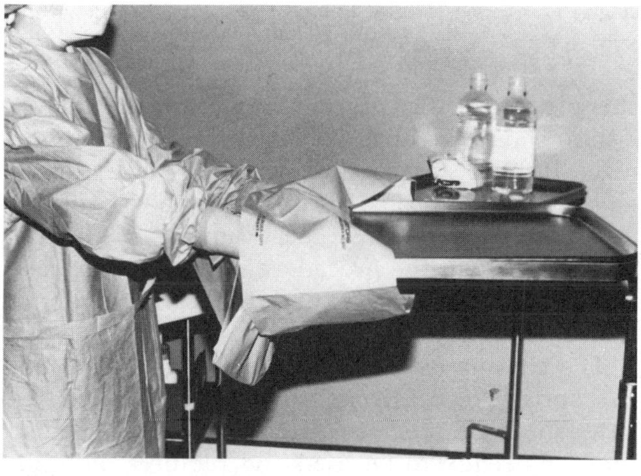

FIG 24–14.
Assistant draping the Mayo stand in a sterile fashion. Note the protected position of the hands inside the drape sleeve.

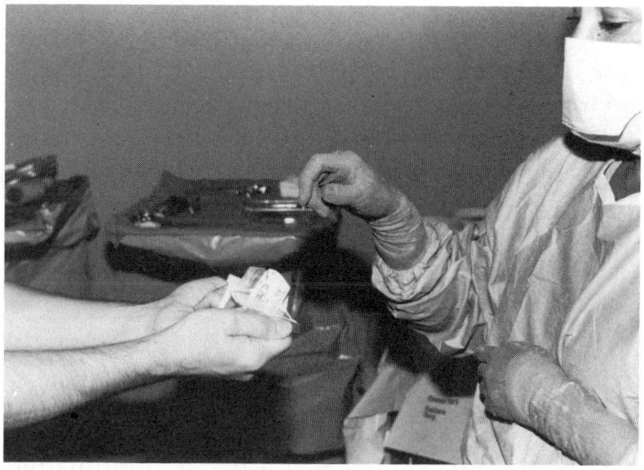

FIG 24–15.
Unsterile circulating nurse handing a sterile suture to the scrubbed assistant.

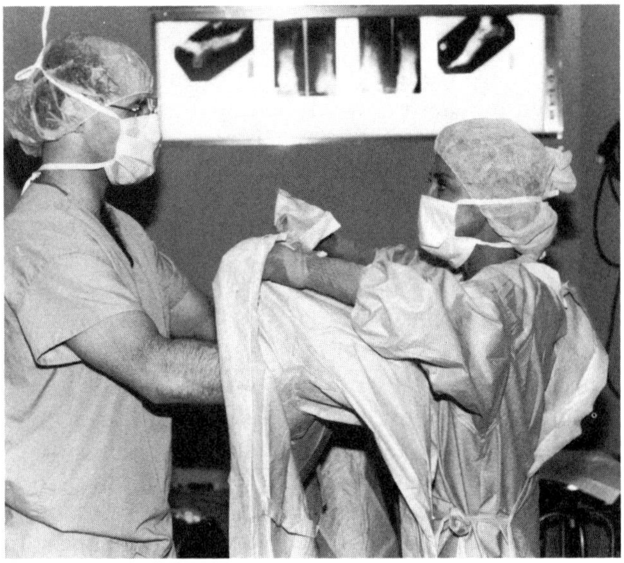

FIG 24–16.
Sterile assistant guiding the gown over the outstretched hands of the surgeon. Note the protected position of the assistant's hands.

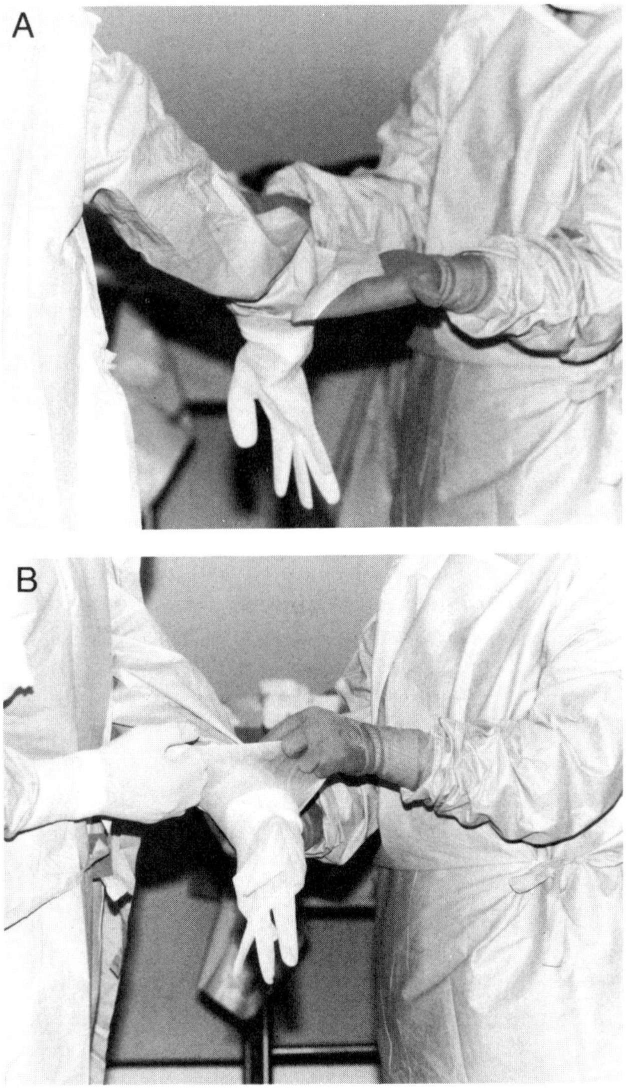

FIG 24–17.
A and **B,** second form of "open gloving" used to glove the surgeon.

glove, with the surgeon assisting with the already gloved hand.

Patient Draping

The surgeon and assistant are now prepared to drape the surgical limb. This is done in order to create a sterile field around the operative site. Draping techniques will vary from institution to institution depending on the surgeon's preference.

Surgical Assisting

In addition to making sure that the procedure goes as smoothly as possible, the surgical assistant is also responsible for maintaining a safe, sterile environment for the patient as well as all members of the surgical team. These duties will demand a thorough understanding of the principles of aseptic technique, a knowledge of the procedures being performed and instrumentation used, as well as an all-important sense of anticipation. The well-prepared surgical assistant can make a significant contribution in executing a successful and time-efficient surgery.

As alluded to above, the assistant will be responsible for the surgical instrumentation used during the procedure. To ensure a prompt and safe transferal of instruments to the surgeon, the assistant must know exactly where each of the instruments sits on the Mayo stand. To facilitate this process, at the beginning of each case the assistant should arrange the instruments in an organized fashion so that they may be readily identified when needed (Fig 24–18). The table should be arranged the same way every time and kept this way throughout the procedure so that with repetition the assistant can account for each instrument with little effort.

The passing of surgical instruments should not be haphazard. Each instrument should be passed in a deliberate and specific fashion and oriented so that it is ready to be used and requires no additional handling by the surgeon. For example, when a knife (no. 10 or 15 blade) is passed, it should be placed carefully but firmly in the sur-

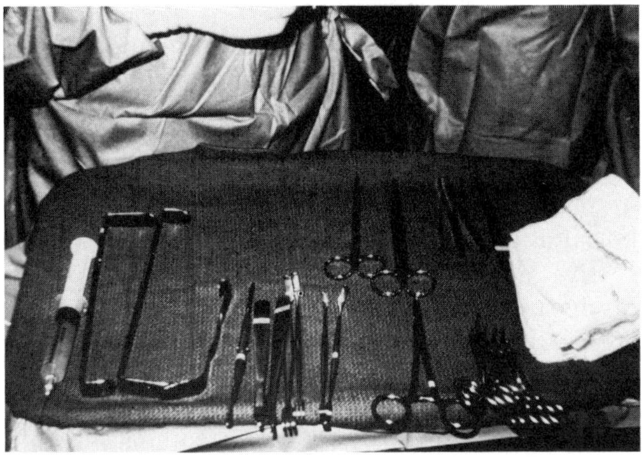

FIG 24-18.
Organized Mayo stand with the most commonly and frequently used instruments.

geon's outstretched hand with the blade facing away (Fig 24-19). In this position, the blade is ready to use, and unwanted, wasted movement is avoided. When passing hemostats or scissors, the instrument should be held at the hinge and passed firmly with the handle facing the surgeon (Fig 24-20). Needle holders are passed in a similar fashion, but care is taken to load the needle so that it is in the position that it will be used and the point is directed away from both the assistant and surgeon. This position will vary according to whether the surgeon is right- or left-handed (Fig 24-21).

Because many of the surgical procedures will be performed with the patient receiving local anesthesia, it is important to keep conversation to a minimum. The simplest way to limit the amount

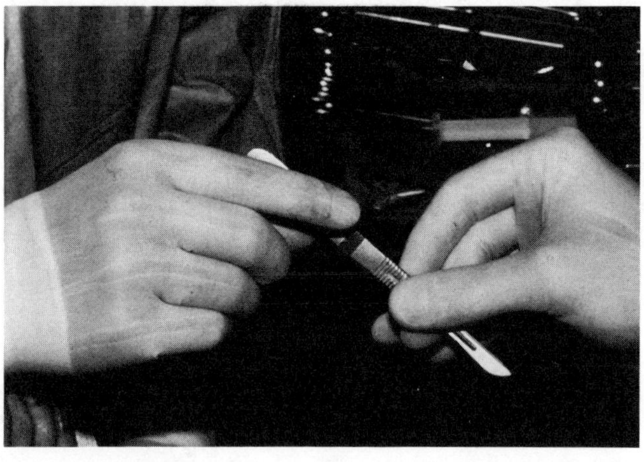

FIG 24-19.
Accurate exchange of a no. 10 blade from the assistant to the surgeon's hand.

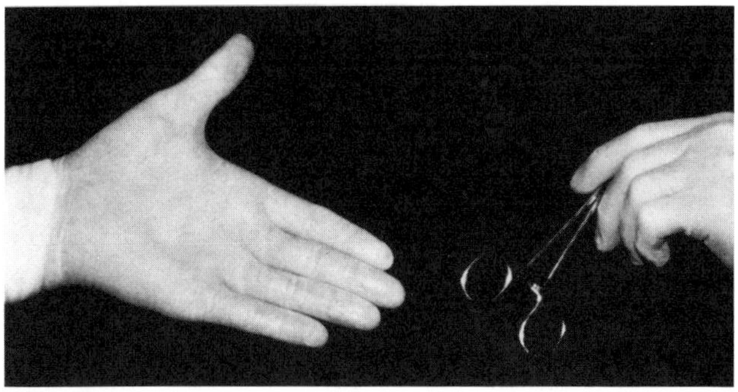

FIG 24-20.
Hemostats are passed by holding them at their hinge and firmly snapping them into the surgeon's outstretched hand.

of discussion between the assistant and surgeon is through the use of hand signals. Again this requires a knowledgeable and attentive assistant since many of the hand signals can be used for several different instruments. For example the surgeon may signal for scissors, but only a well-informed assistant will know what type of scissors are needed at that point in the procedure (Mayo, Metzenbaum, etc.).

The final step in becoming a good surgical assistant is developing a strong sense of anticipation. This quality goes hand in hand with the assistant becoming familiar with the types of procedures being performed and the instrumentation that is required. With hard work and practice, the assistant will know which instrument the surgeon will need next and have it ready to pass before he asks for it. This teamwork approach allows the surgeon to concentrate only on his actions without worrying about those of the assistant. Once this sense of anticipation is established, surgical time will be dramatically reduced.

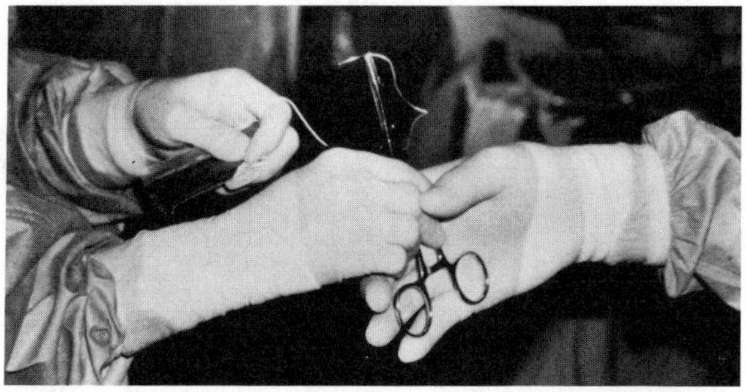

FIG 24-21.
Accurate loading of the needle and placement of the needle holder into the surgeon's right hand. In this position, the needle is ready to be used. The needle would be loaded in the opposite direction for a left-handed surgeon.

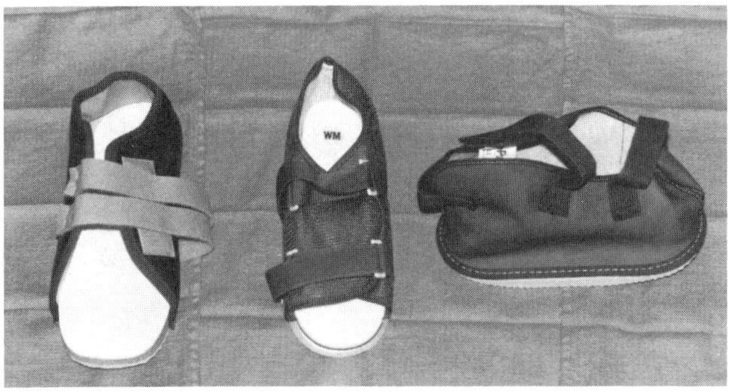

FIG 24–22.
Postoperative surgical shoes and cast boot.

Once the procedure has been completed, the surgical foot is cleaned and a sterile dressing applied. For a complete discussion on dressing and bandaging techniques, please refer to Chapter 28. Any specimens are now put in the proper container and sent to the appropriate laboratory (microbiology, pathology, etc.).

Before the patient is removed from the surgical suite, a final set of vital signs are taken and recorded. The patient is then sent to a recovery area for further monitoring.

POSTOPERATIVE RESPONSIBILITIES

When the patient has fully recovered from the anesthesia, final discharge preparations can be made. Depending upon the procedure performed and the type of dressing applied, the appropriate postoperative shoe (surgical shoe or cast shoe) should be dispensed and applied to the surgical foot (Fig 24–22). If crutches or a walker is needed postoperatively, the patient should demonstrate proficiency in the correct usage before being allowed to leave the office or hospital. Final postoperative radiographs should also be obtained before discharge.

Specific postoperative instructions should be given to the patient in both verbal and written forms. Instructions will vary depending on the procedure performed and the attending surgeon. It is imperative that the patient understand the importance of following the instructions to ensure optimal recovery. Prescriptions are also dispensed at this time. Typical postoperative prescriptions include analgesics for pain control, anti-inflammatory medications, and antibiotics. The allergy history should be reviewed once again to avoid any drug interactions or complications.

Confirm the patient's transportation arrangements, and obtain a phone number where he can be reached. This will allow the surgeon or the assistant to contact the patient that evening to check on his progress, and address any concerns the patient may have.

The final postoperative responsibility of the assistant is to clean the surgical suite and prepare for the next case. Any disposable sharp instru-

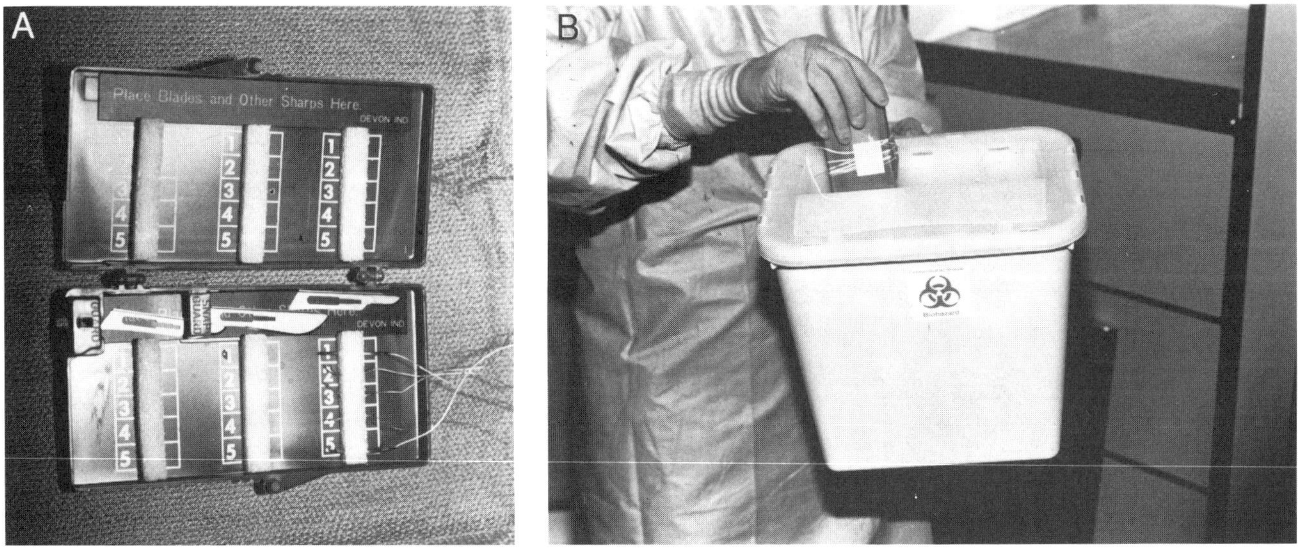

FIG 24–23.
A, needles and blades placed in a protective container. This not only helps to avoid accidental injury but also serves as a method of needle counting. **B,** once all sharp objects are in the container, it is placed in an appropriate receptacle.

ments (blades, needles) should be discarded in appropriate containers to avoid any accidental injury (Fig 24–23,A and B). The room is then cleaned and disinfected. The instruments will initially be hand cleaned in "soapy water" and, then dried, packaged, and sterilized for later use.

REFERENCE

1. Association of Operation Room Nurses: *Recommended Practices for OR Sanitation, AORN Standards and Recommended Practices for Perioperative Nursing,* part III. Denver, Association of Operation Room Nurses, 1988, pp 1–8.

25

Instrumentation

Dennis E. Martin, D.P.M.
T.E. Pitts, D.P.M.

I. Cutting Instruments
II. Grasping Instruments
III. Retracting Instruments
IV. Surgical Instrument Packs

This chapter will introduce the podiatric assistant to the various types of instruments used in podiatric surgery. An effective surgical assistant must have a working knowledge of the basic instrumentation and an ability to anticipate when each of the instruments are needed. Instruments may be divided into three categories: cutting, grasping, and retracting instruments.

CUTTING INSTRUMENTS

The scalpel (Fig 25–1) is used for tissue dissection. It consists of a handle and either a disposable or nondisposable blade. The no. 3 handle is the most frequently used handle for podiatric surgery; however, a number of different sized handles are available. Some scalpels have a metric scale engraved on one side for measuring tissue.

The blade portion of the scalpel is also available in a variety of shapes and sizes. The initial skin incision is usually made with a broad no. 10 blade, and then a smaller no. 15 blade is preferable for incising deeper tissues. Some surgeons also prefer a no. 15 blade for the initial skin incision of the digits or when precise work is required. Because of its sharp point, the no. 11 blade is useful for incising abscesses or other fluid collections. Beaver blades are often used for palliative care and are also occasionally utilized during digital procedures. The blades numbered 62 to 69 are used on a no. 3 minihandle, while the larger blades numbered 81 to 88 are used on a no. 4 handle.

In addition to surgical blades, scissors (Fig 25–2) are also commonly used for tissue dissection. Examples of scissors routinely used in podiatric surgery include Mayo, Metzenbaum, collar-and-crown (Sistrunk), iris, and suture scissors.

Mayo scissors are heavy and blunt and are used for cutting tough structures such as heavy fascia, tendons, or ligaments. These scissors are available with either straight or curved blades. Straight blades are generally used superficially, while curved blades are preferred when dissecting deeper structures.

Metzenbaum scissors are lightweight, blunt-tipped, narrow, and slightly curved for dissection of lighter structures such as fascia or capsule. Collar-and-crown, or Sistrunk, scissors are especially useful for dissection of sesamoids, while iris scissors are commonly used for precise dissection. Remember that tissue scissors are delicate instruments and should never be used as general-purpose scissors. Suture scissors, or general-purpose scissors, are specifically designed for cutting sutures, gauze, drains, and other materials and should never be used for cutting tissue.

All scissors should be grasped in the right hand since they are specifically designed for right-handed use. Scissors are held in the finger rings

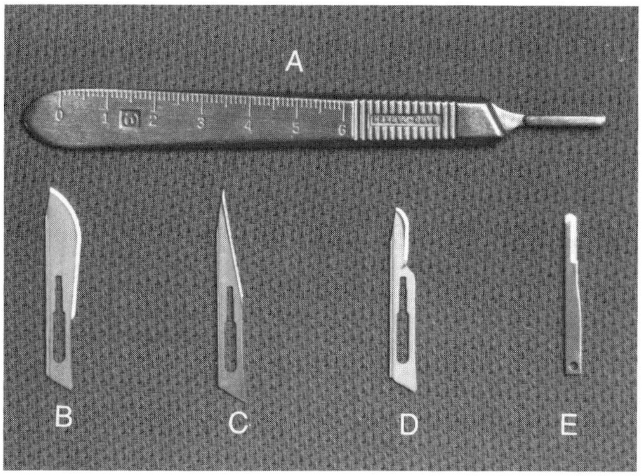

FIG 25–1.
Surgical handle and blades: no. 3 handle **(A)**, no. 10 blade **(B)**, no. 11 blade **(C)**, no. 15 blade **(D)**, and beaver blade **(E)**.

with the thumb and fourth digit and with the index finger on the hinge portion of the scissors (Fig 25–3). The tips of the scissors should be used when cutting to prevent accidental trauma to surrounding tissue. If the assistant or surgeon cuts with the blades near the hinge portion of the scissors, then he may damage surrounding tissue with the unseen tips of the scissors. Proper shearing by the scissors is obtained by applying mild outward pressure with the thumb and inward pressure with the fourth digit. Sutures should be cut with

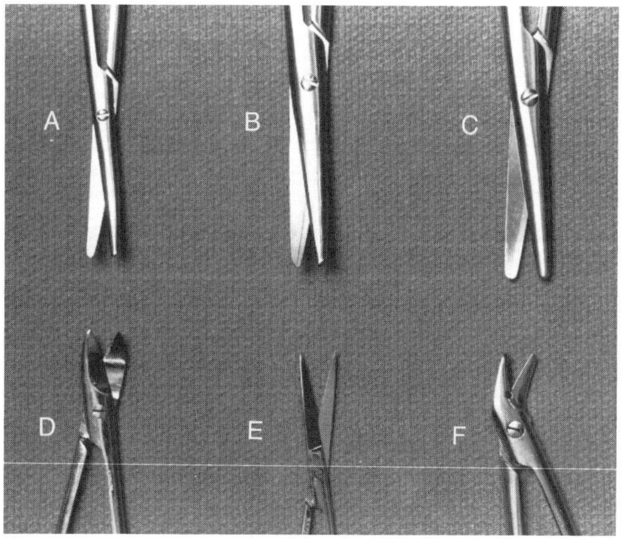

FIG 25–2.
Scissors: Metzenbaum **(A)**, Mayo **(B)**, utility or suture **(C)**, crown and collar (Sistrunk) **(D)**, iris **(E)**, and wire cutting **(F)**.

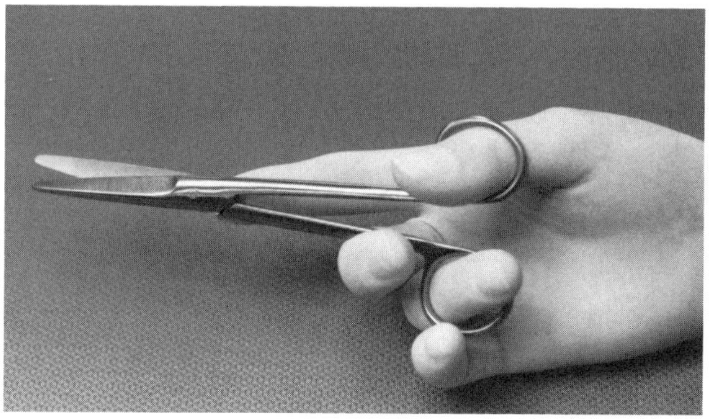

FIG 25–3.
Scissors grasping technique.

the tips of the scissors slightly above the suture knot and angled slightly at approximately 25 degrees.

Many instruments have been developed for the purpose of cutting and resecting bone and cartilage. Bone-cutting forceps, rongeurs, osteotomes, chisels, gouges, periosteal elevators, curettes, trephines, and rasps are all examples of bone- or cartilage-cutting or -removing instruments.

Bone-cutting forceps and rongeurs (Fig 25–4) may be single- or double-hinged instruments. Double-hinged instruments require less effort due to the increased mechanical advantage. Both of these instruments are used for removing bony overgrowth such as exostoses or spurs.

Osteotomes, chisels, and gouges (Fig 25–5) are also used to reduce bony prominences. The differences in these instruments lie in their cutting edge. Both edges of the osteotome (Lambotte) have cutting surfaces, but only one edge of the

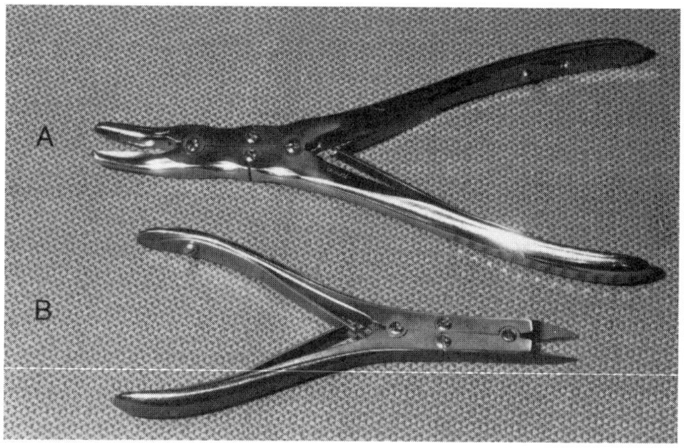

FIG 25–4.
Double-action rongeur **(A)** and double-action bone-cutting forceps. **(B)**.

FIG 25–5.
Chisel **(A)**, osteotome **(B)**, and gouge **(C)**.

chisel has a cutting surface. The gouge, like the chisel, has only one cutting edge; however, the edge of the gouge is curved. Each of these instruments are driven with a mallet in a manner similar to a nail being driven with a hammer.

Periosteal elevators (Fig 25–6) have smooth, broad blades that are used to separate the periosteum (tissue layer surrounding the bone) from the underlying bone. The Freer and Sayer elevators are often used during forefoot dissection, while the

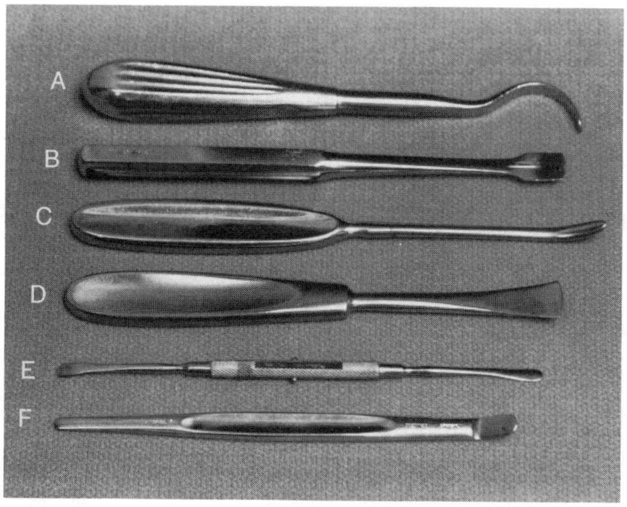

FIG 25–6.
Periosteal elevators: curved Crego **(A)**, Key **(B)**, narrow Langenbeck **(C)**, wide Langenbeck **(D)**, Freer **(E)**, and Sayre **(F)**.

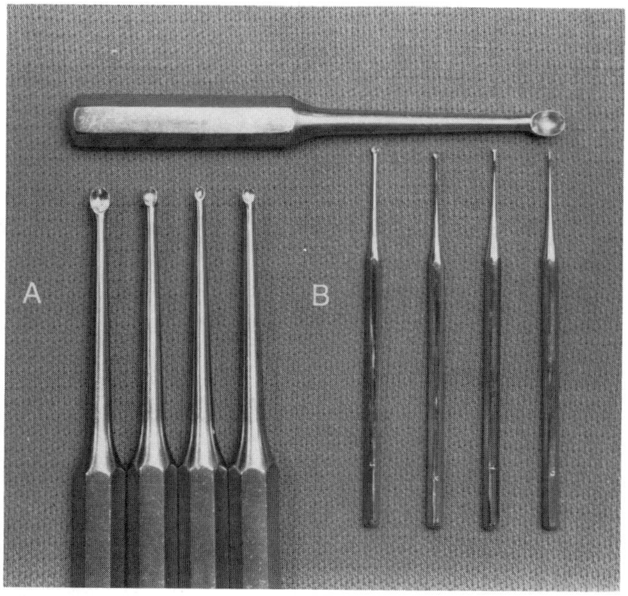

FIG 25–7.
Bone (large) curettes **(A)** and dermal (small) curettes **(B)**.

Key, Langenbeck, and Crego elevators are primarily used in rearfoot and ankle surgery.

Curettes (Fig 25–7) are useful for reducing or debriding both bone and soft tissue by means of a scooplike blade attached to a handle. The large, heavy set of curettes is designed for bone, while the small, light set is designed for soft tissue.

Trephines (Fig 25–8) are T-shaped instruments consisting of a hollow tube with a circular cutting edge at the tip of the tube. Trephines and their corresponding obturators or plungers are useful for the removal of plugs of bone for a bone biopsy or bone graft.

Rasps (Fig 25–9) are used to provide a smooth contour to uneven or roughened bony surfaces.

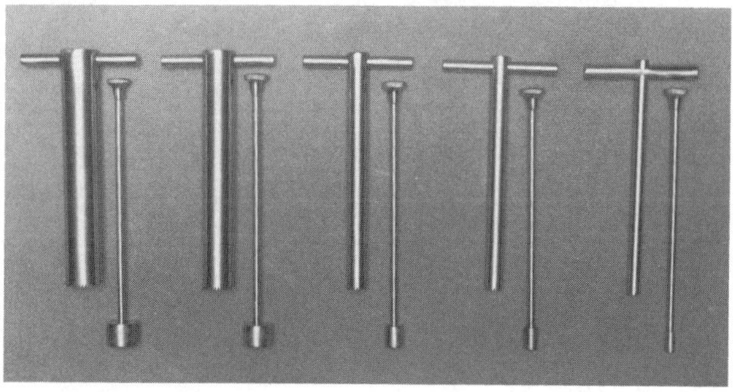

FIG 25–8.
Set of trephines with corresponding obturators.

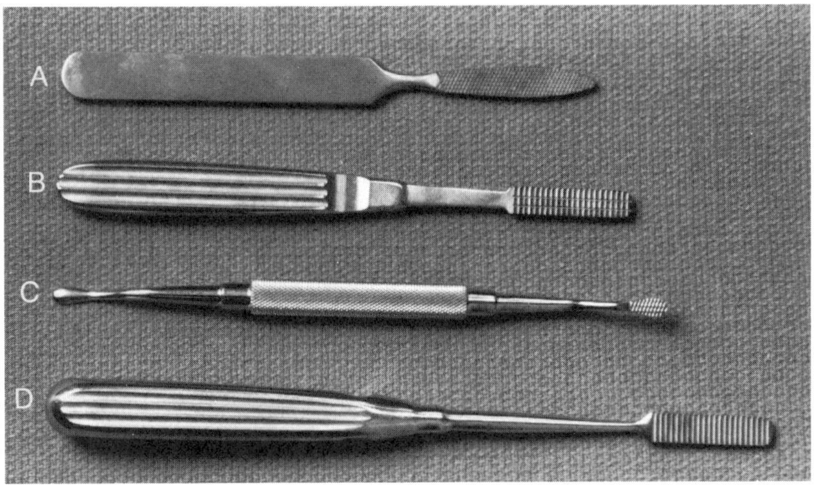

FIG 25–9.
Rasping instruments: Joseph's nasal or beaver-tail rasp **(A)**, Maltz rasp **(B)**, Bell rasp **(C)**, and Parkes rasp **(D)**.

They are usually utilized after a bony prominence has been resected with power or hand instruments. The Maltz and Parkes rasps have rough surfaces and are used to reduce moderate bony prominences. The Bell and Joseph's (also called beaver-tail) rasps have fine cutting surfaces that are ideal for smoothing uneven or roughened bony surfaces.

While some surgeons prefer hand-held bone-cutting and -remodeling instruments, many others prefer power instrumentation. Both pneumatic and electrical power equipment are commercially available, and the selection is based on the surgeon's preference. The Zimmer, Hall, and Stryker power instruments are commonly used for podiatric surgery; however, a variety of other systems are available. Most systems include a sagittal saw, reciprocating saw, oscillating saw, drill, wire driver and various blades, burrs, and rasps (Fig 25–10).

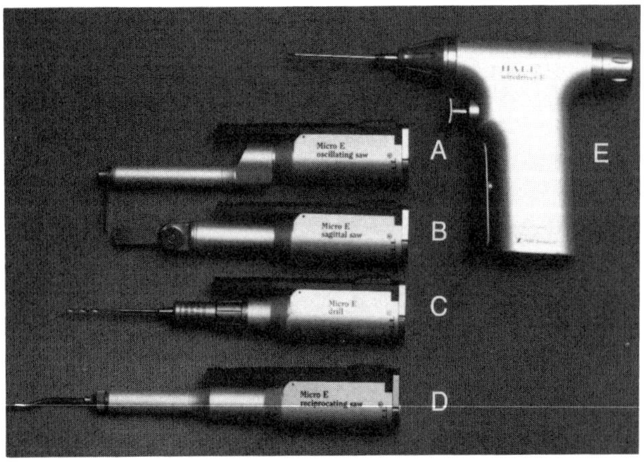

FIG 25–10.
Hall electric power system; oscillating saw **(A)**, sagittal saw **(B)**, drill **(C)**, reciprocating saw **(D)**, and wire driver **(E)**.

GRASPING INSTRUMENTS

Grasping instruments may be divided into five categories, including thumb forceps, hemostatic forceps, traction forceps, bone reduction forceps, and needle holders. Thumb forceps (Fig 25–11) are designed to grasp and hold tissue during dissection. The tips of the many different types of forceps vary in size from sharp teeth to fine serrations. Brown-Adson forceps are fine-toothed forceps commonly used for skin closure. The rat-tooth or one-two pickup is a sharp-toothed pickup used for grasping denser tissues. Atraumatic or smooth forceps have fine serrations at the tips and are particularly useful for skin closure, grasping delicate tissues that might otherwise be perforated, or grasping gauze and other surgical dressings.

A type of forceps designed specifically for the control of bleeding is called a hemostatic forceps (Fig 25–12). It is used when the surgeon requires clamping of an active bleeding vessel. Hemostatic forceps commonly used in podiatric surgery include the basic hemostat (also called a stat or snap), and the mosquito, Crile, and Kelly hemostats. All of these instruments have box ratchet locks that allow the surgeon or assistant to apply a controlled force on the vessel. The mosquito is a smaller, more delicate hemostat, while the Crile and Kelly are heavier and larger in design. The he-

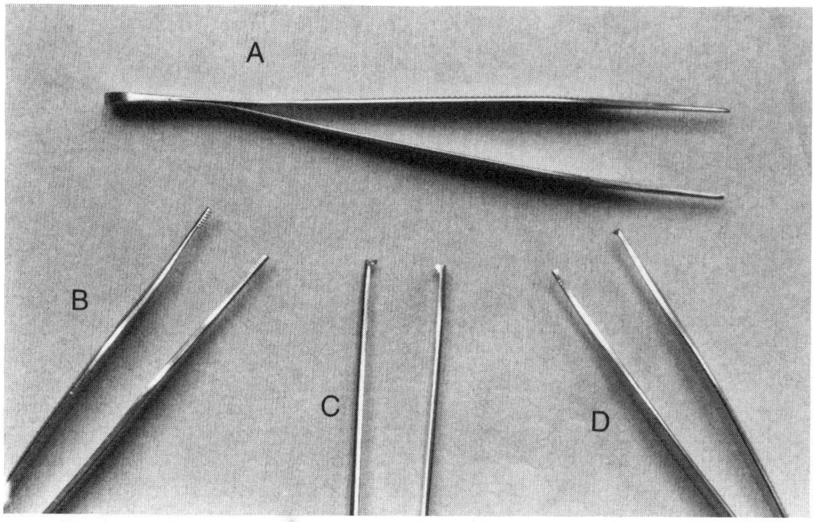

FIG 25–11.
Thumb forceps: atraumatic **(A)**, Brown-Adson **(B)**, one-two or rat-tooth **(C)**, and small one-two **(D)**.

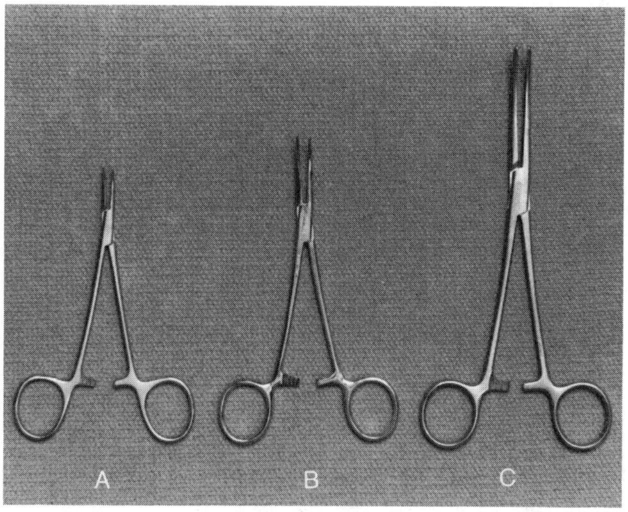

FIG 25–12.
Hemostats: mosquito **(A)**, Crile **(B)**, and Kelly **(C)**.

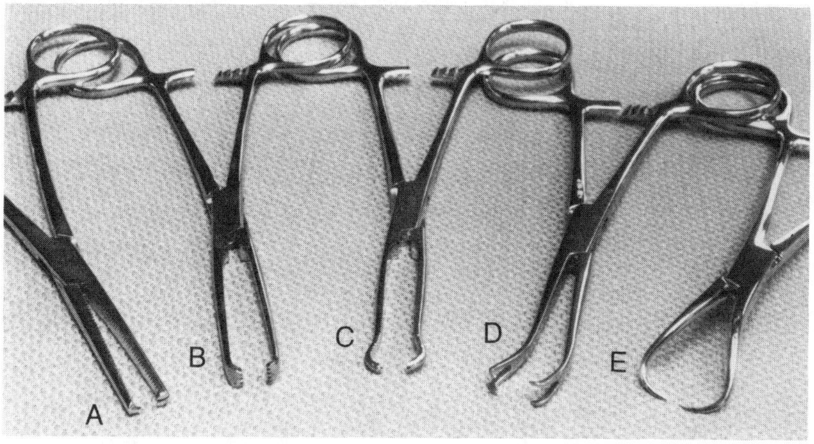

FIG 25–13.
Traction forceps: Kocher **(A)**, Allis **(B)**, phalangeal **(C)**, sesamoid **(D)**, and towel clamp **(E)**.

mostats are available with curved or straight jaws.

Grasping or traction forceps are designed to firmly hold or immobilize dense tissues to facilitate dissection (Fig 25–13). The instruments have box ratchet locks similar to hemostats but are heavier in design and have more powerful jaws. The jaw portion of the forceps may have sharp teeth or single pointed ends.

Towel clamps are used for draping the operative area, but because of their sharp, pointed ends, they are sometimes used for grasping bone. Small ossicles or bony fragments may be grasped by utilizing a phalangeal clamp or sesamoid clamp. The Allis and Kocher clamps are typically used when strong retraction of deep fascia is necessary. Examples of bone reduction forceps or clamps used for grasping or holding small and medium-sized bone fragments include the alligator bone clamp, small plate-holding forceps, double-sharp forceps, and small self-centering forceps (Fig 25–14,A). Instruments used for holding large fragments of bone include the Ver-

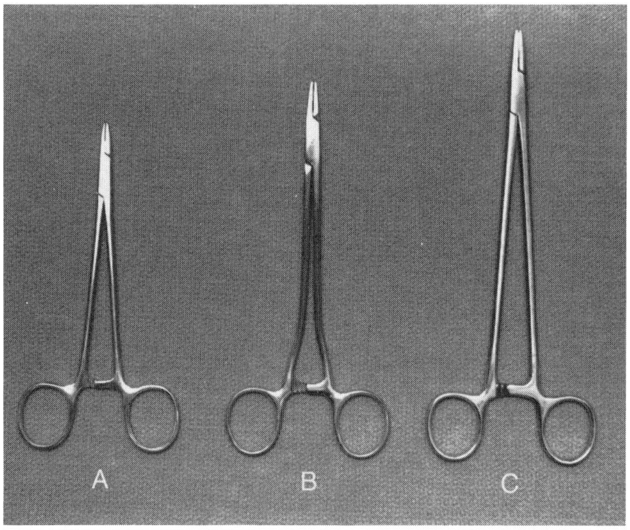

FIG 25–15.
Needle holders: Ryder or vascular **(A),** Sarot **(B),** and large Mayo-Hegar **(C).**

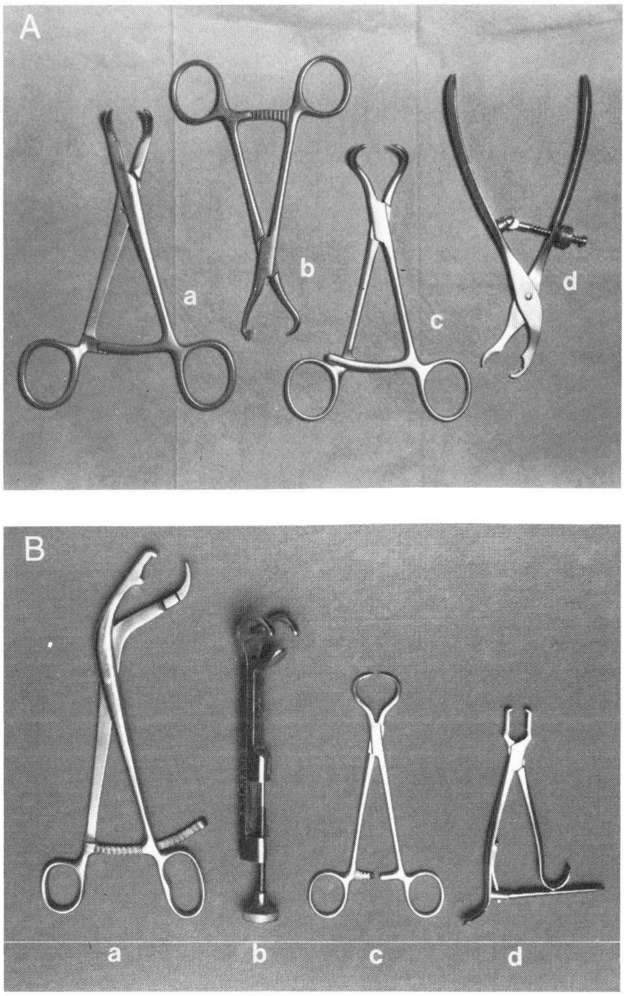

FIG 25–14.
A, alligator bone clamp *(a),* small plate-holding forceps *(b),* double-sharp forceps *(c),* and small self-centering forceps *(d).* **B,** Verbrugge *(a)* Lowman *(b),* Lewin *(c),* and "baby" Lane *(d).*

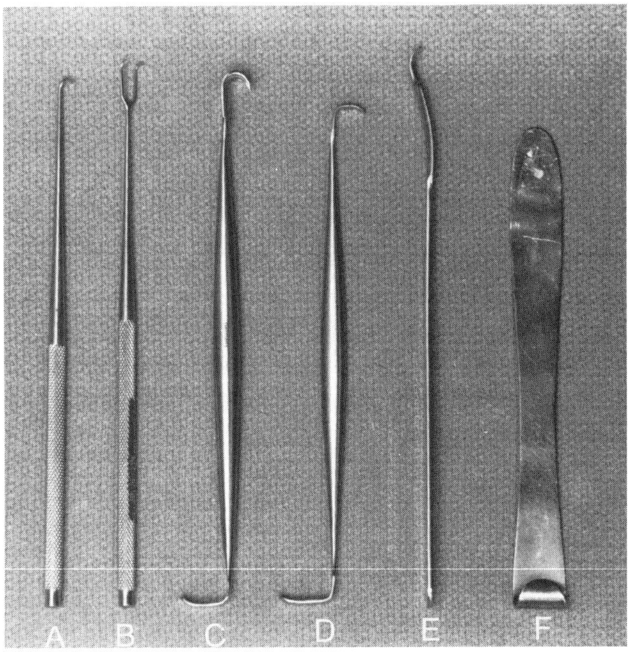

FIG 25–16.
Hand-held retractors: single-prong skin hook **(A),** double-prong skin hook **(B),** Senn **(C),** Ragnell **(D),** mini-Hohmann **(E),** and Seeburger **(F).**

brugge, Lowman, "baby" Lane, and Lewin (Fig 25–14,B)

A needle holder may also be considered to be a specialized form of traction forceps. In general, short-handled needle holders are designed for reapproximating superficial tissue layers, whereas long-handled needle holders are used to close deeper layers. The most commonly used needle holders include the Ryder or vascular, Mayo-Hegar, Halsey, and Sarot designs (Fig 25–15).

RETRACTING INSTRUMENTS

Retractors are instruments used to provide adequate exposure of the wound by holding tissue aside. Retractors also serve to protect vital structures such as the superficial and deep neurovascular bundles. The commonly used hand held retractors include the single- or double-pronged skin hooks and Senn, Ragnell, mini-Hohmann, and Seeburger retractors (Fig 25–16).

Examples of larger retractors used in rearfoot and ankle surgery when a wide exposure is needed include the Volkmann (rake), large malleable ribbon, and Army-Navy (Fig 25–17). All of these manual retractors allow the assistant to control the traction placed on the tissue. The assistant must also remember to release the traction periodically to avoid extensive tissue damage.

Self-retaining retractors are also commonly used. The blades of the retractors are applied to the opposing wound edges and then spread apart and locked in place at the appropriate tension. This frees the surgeon and assistant to perform other tasks. The Weitlaner and digital (Holzheimer) retractors are used in forefoot procedures, while lamina spreaders are utilized in rearfoot procedures where a larger area of exposure is needed (Fig 25–18). As with hand-held retractors, the self-retaining retractors must be released periodically to release tension on the wound edges and prevent excessive tissue damage.

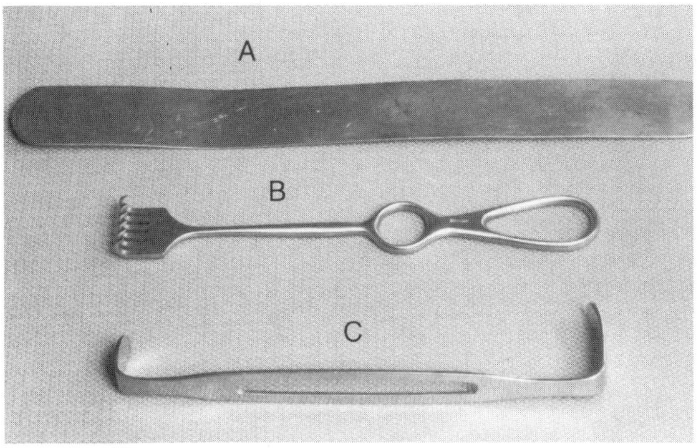

FIG 25–17.
Large hand-held retractors: Large malleable ribbon **(A)**, large rake **(B)**, and Army-Navy or right-angle retractor **(C)**.

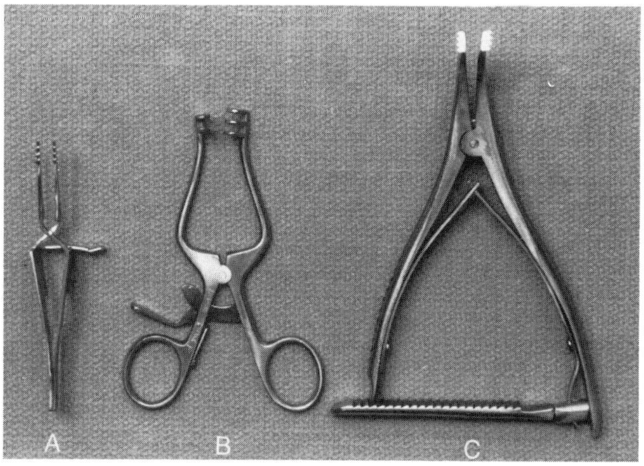

FIG 25–18.
Large self-retaining retractors: Digital retractor **(A)**, Weitlaner **(B)**, and lamina spreader **(C)**.

SURGICAL INSTRUMENT PACKS

Podiatric surgical instruments are often divided into various instrument packs to allow for efficient sterilization and storage. The contents of the

TABLE 25–1.
Forefoot Pack

Blade handles
Thumb forceps (atraumatic, Rat-tooth or one-two pickup, Brown-Adson, large toothed)
Hemostatic forceps (curved and straight mosquito, Kelly, Crile)
Traction forceps (Kocher, Allis, towel clamp, sponge clamp, sesamoid clamp, phalangeal clamp)
Needle holders (plastic, Sarot)
Retractors (single- and double-prong skin locks, Senn, Ragnell, Army-Navy, Seeburger, mini-Hohmann, Weitlaner 3–2 and 4–3 prong, digital self-retaining)
Scissors (Metzenbaum, Mayo, suture, collar and crown, iris, monofilament wire cutter)
Periosteal elevators (Freer, Sayre, broad and narrow Langenbeck)
Bone cutting instruments (double-action rongeur, double-action bone-cutting forceps, needle nose rongeur, curved osteotome, Lambotte osteotomes, chisel)
Bone reduction forceps (Lewin, double sharp, alligator)
Rasps (Joseph's nasal or beaver tail, Bell, Parkes, Maltz)
Miscellaneous (wire bender, wire cutter, needle nose pliers, ruler, medium mallet, wire brush rasp cleaner)

TABLE 25–2.
Rearfoot Packs

Retractors
Lamina spreader (self-retaining)
Large rakes
Large ribbon
Cutting instruments
Key and Crego periosteal elevators
Large osteotomes
Gouges
Trephines
Curettes
Kerrison rongeur
Large double-action rongeur
Large double-action bone-cutting forceps
Miscellaneous
Large pin cutter
Blount staple holder, driver, remover
Assortment of Blount staples

packs will vary according to the individual needs of the podiatric surgeon. Examples of the more commonly used surgical packs include a forefoot pack (Table 25–1), rearfoot pack (Table 25–2), and a nail surgical pack (Table 25–3). For rearfoot cases, the forefoot pack should be opened in addition to the rearfoot pack since the forefoot pack contains many of the basic instruments needed for most podiatric surgical cases.

TABLE 25–3.
Nail Surgical Pack

Blade handles (no. 3 scalpel blade and beaver blade handles)
Thumb forceps (Brown-Adson)
Hemostatic forceps (straight mosquito and Crile)
Needle holder (small)
Scissors and nippers (iris and suture scissors, English anvil nail nipper, large and small nail nippers)
Elevators and curettes (Freer elevator, small and large nail plate elevators, dermal curettes)
Miscellaneous (cotton-tipped applicators, medicine cup, bandage material)

BIBLIOGRAPHY

1. Brooks SM: *Instrumentation for the Operating Room.* Chicago, CV Mosby Co, 1989, pp 1–50.
2. Donick II: *Podiatry for the Assistant,* ed 2. Baltimore, Williams & Wilkins, 1989, pp 91–106.
3. Malay DS: Instrumentation, in McGlamry ED (ed) *Fundamentals of Foot Surgery.* Baltimore, Williams & Wilkins, 1987, pp 234–245.

26

Strapping, Padding, and Shielding

E. Dalton McGlamry, D.P.M.

Paddings, strappings, and shieldings are among the oldest modalities used in the treatment of the foot. There is an almost endless variety of pads, shields, and strappings, but the principles of application are much the same for all of them.

PADDING PRINCIPLES

Padding is applied to an area to absorb friction or to relieve pressure from the area or from an adjacent area. Padding that covers an area directly and is quite thin is usually designed to absorb friction from that area. Thicker padding that surrounds the painful area, usually with a cutout for the painful area, is designed to absorb or disperse pressure over a wider area, thus relieving pain. Balance pads constitute still another type of therapeutic padding. Thicker padding materials are generally used and are applied to areas adjacent to the point of complaint. The balance pad simply shifts weight bearing from a point of excess concentration to an adjacent and more desirable point.

ADHESIVE OR REMOVABLE

Pads and shields may be adherent or removable. Those that are adherent may be bonded to the foot either by using adhesive-backed materials (moleskin or adhesive felt or foam) or by applying skin adherent to the foot. In the latter case, plain felt can be held in place by the skin adherent and subsequently covered with appropriate strapping.

Removable pads and shields take many forms but have in common the capacity to be removed for bathing and for sleep. Removable pads may be quite simple and only intended for use for a week or two, or the pads may be latexed to provide for a greatly increased life span.

TYPES OF PADS

Moleskin Pads

Moleskin is a flannel-backed adhesive tape. It is somewhat thicker than normal adhesive tape and is very smooth on its top flannel surface. It is usually applied over an area in which one wishes to reduce friction. Moleskin is also used to prepare cutout pads, also referred to as donut pads.

Moleskin has the advantage of being rather thin, thus taking up little space inside the shoe. This can be an important consideration if the patient requires padding or shielding of a toe but will be wearing a dress pump or other shoe with minimal extra space available.

Donut or Cutout Pads

A donut pad is one in which a section of the pad is cut out to provide a protective pocket for a painful area or a boney prominence. The padding material may be thin, as with moleskin, or may be any thickness of felt. The pad may be adherent or removable.

Fifth-Toe and Tailor's Bunion Pads

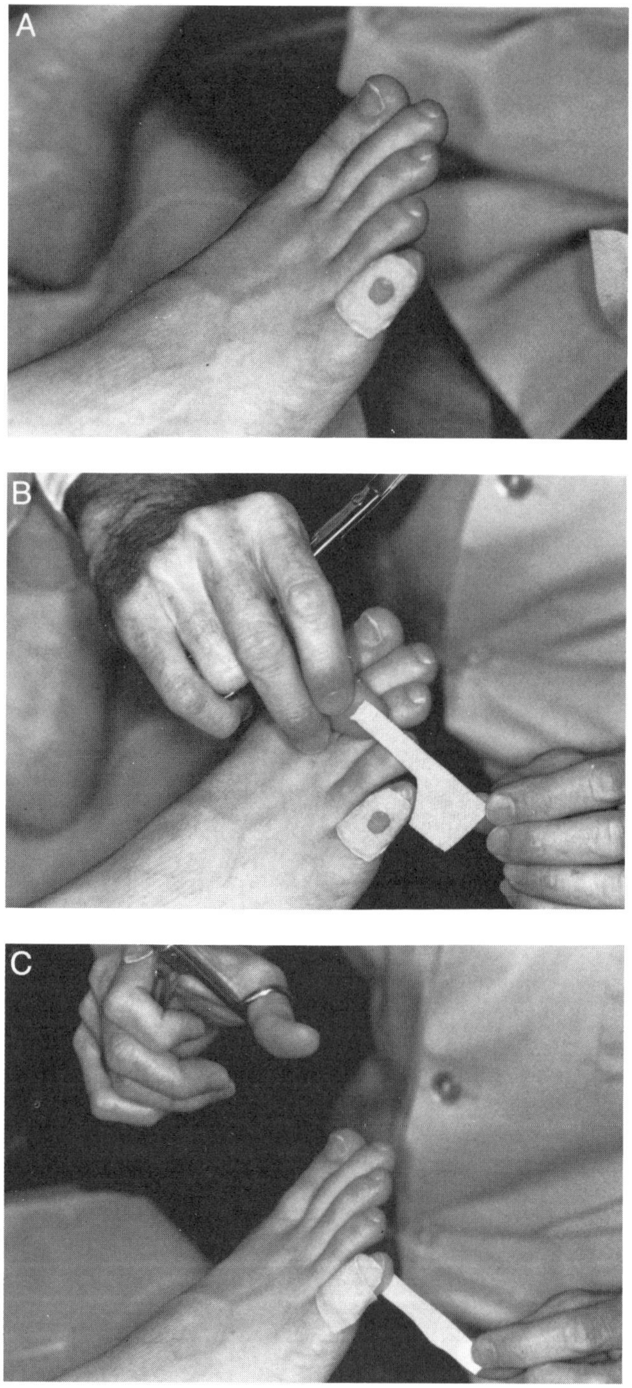

FIG 26–1.

A, felt cutout or donut pad for the fifth toe. The pad here is made from 1/16-in. adhesive felt. The pad could be made equally well from nonadhesive tape by using skin adherent to hold the pad in place.

B, to cover the pad use 1-in. wide Elastoplast tape with a scoop-out of tape that leaves a tail to tie down the distal end. Always cut the tape with the sticky side turned up. This tends to make the tape fall away from the scissors and makes cutting much easier.

C, Elastoplast covering is applied in the direction of derotation. For the right fifth toe, it is applied clockwise as one faces the foot. On the left foot, the direction is counterclockwise.

FIG 26–1 (cont.).
D, completed padding with bandaging.

E, fifth-toe cutout pad with a tailor's bunion pad. The padding here is moleskin. Oftentimes an appropriate ointment may be placed in the aperture of the pad along with a small amount of cotton before bandaging in place.

F, adhesive tape may cover the proximal pad or may cover both pads. In this case tape covers the tailor's bunion pad.

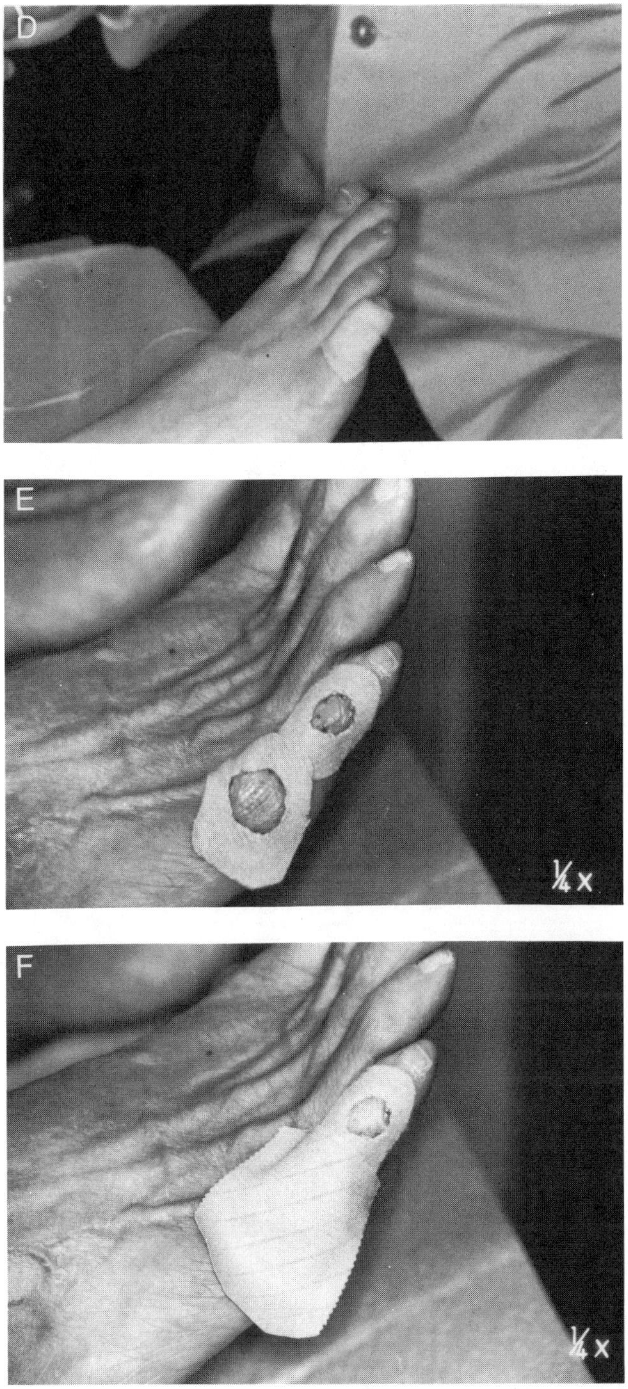

FIG 26–1 (cont.).
G, covering of the fifth-toe pad and distal tie-down is provided by an appropriately shaped strip of 1-in. Elastoplast tape.

H, completed padding and bandaging of the tailor's bunion and fifth toe. Note the importance of the distal tie-down of the bandage. This is to prevent rolling up of the taping as stockings are pulled on over the toes.

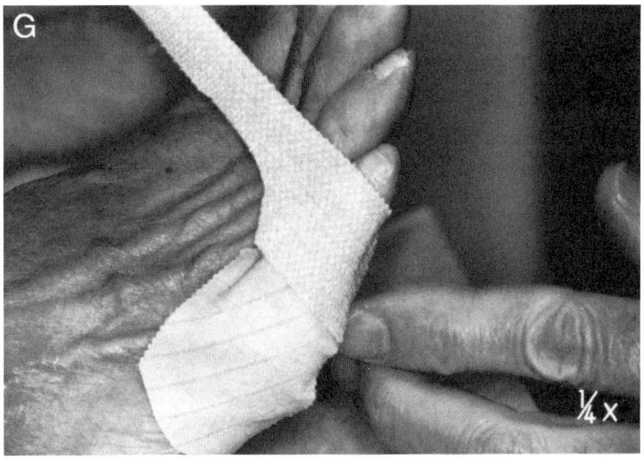

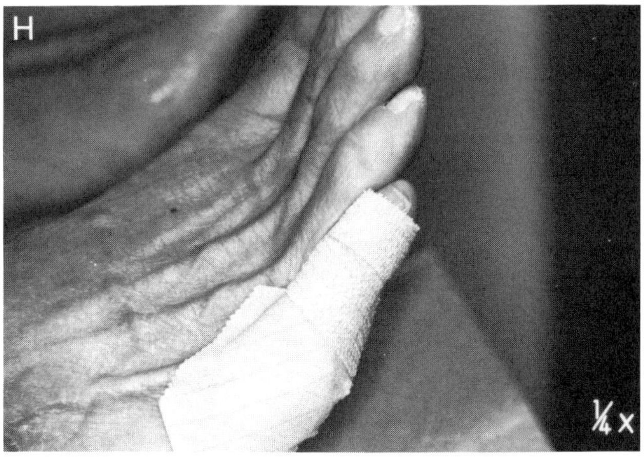

COHESIVE GAUZE BANDAGING OF PADS AND SHIELDS

Cohesive gauze is a bandaging material often used to cover pads and shields. It consists of a special-weave gauze that has been impregnated with latex. This latex makes it stick to itself, but it will not stick to the skin or to the socks or stockings. It is quite thin and thus takes up little space in the shoe. There are two common forms of cohesive gauze. One has an open weave to the edges and is available as Fabco bandage. It is thinner and, because of the open weave of the edges, will not easily cut into the skin. A closed-weave cohesive bandage is available as Gauzetex. It is somewhat thicker and requires a little more experience to apply well. Because of its closed weave to the edge it is more likely to cut into the skin if not applied evenly.

Fifth-Toe Shield With Fabco Cohesive Bandage

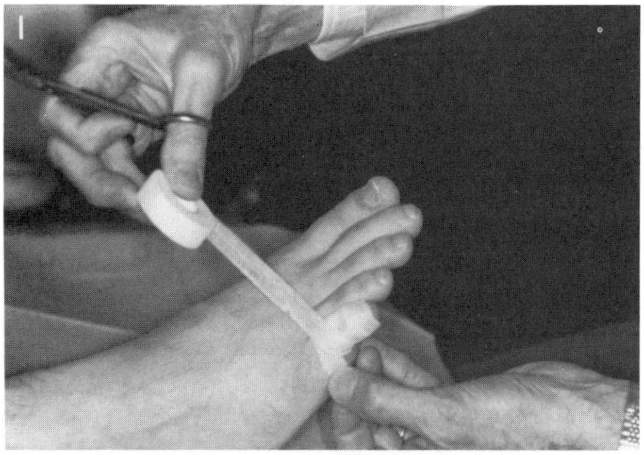

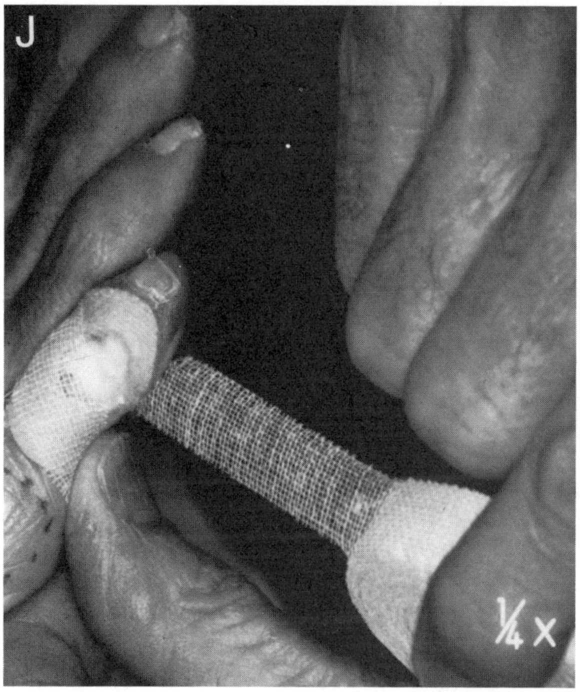

FIG 26–1 (cont.).
I, a Fabco cohesive gauze bandage is applied over the fifth-toe cutout padding.

J, ointment and cotton have been applied to the aperture before the application of bandaging. Often a small square of tape covers the pad before applying cohesive gauze. This will prevent leaking through of the ointment onto the stockings.

Cutout Pad for a Pinch Callus, Great Toe

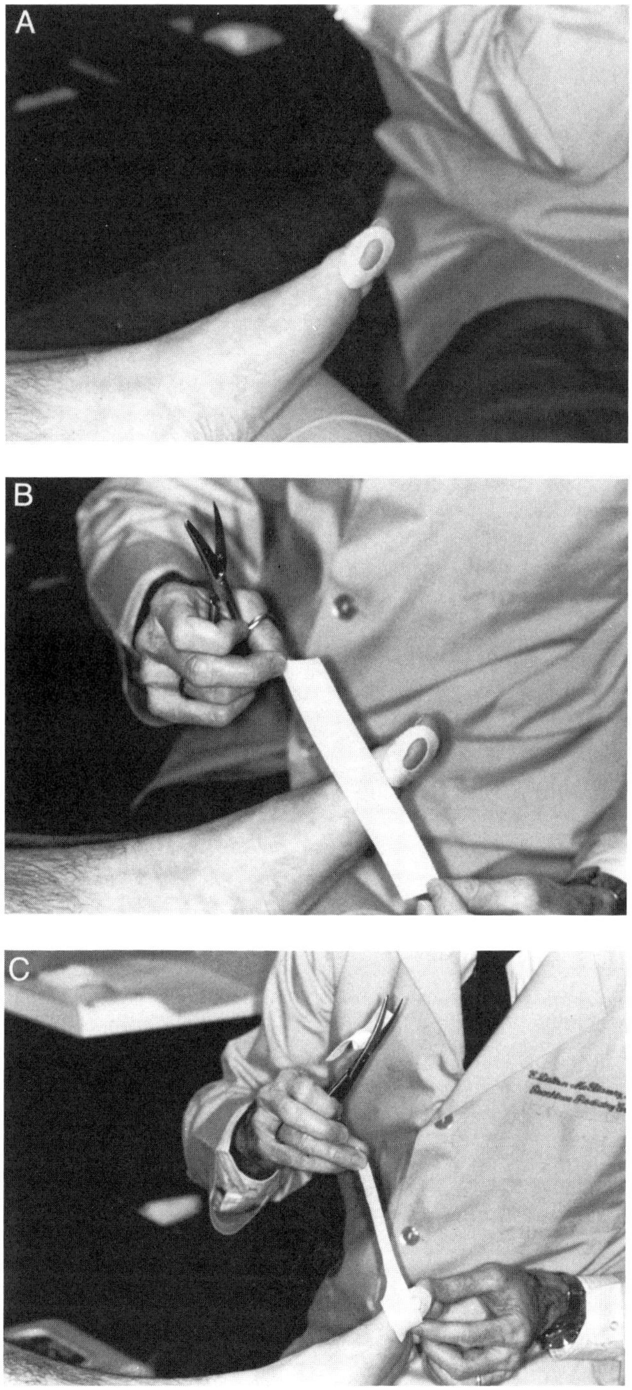

FIG 26–2.

A, a nonadhesive felt cutout pad is held in place by skin adherent no. 2 (podiatry supply companies).

B, Elastoplast adhesive tape is selected as covering for the pad.

C, a scoop-out of tape provides an effective tail for a distal tie-down of cutout pad.

Distal Cutout or Donut Pad for a Lesser Toe

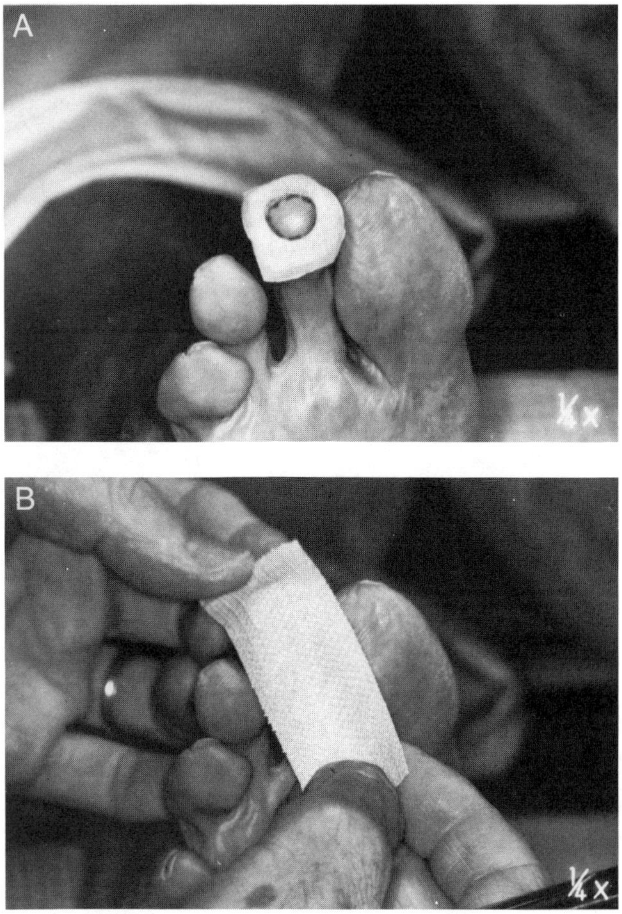

FIG 26–3.
A, distal cutout or donut pad of ⅛-in. adhesive felt.

B, Elastoplast tape covering is applied over the end of the toe and extends dorsally and plantarly. The tape is applied with little or no stretch.

FIG 26–3 (cont.).
C, corners are pinched together and then cut away with scissors. This allows the cover to mold in place well. Tape is applied with little or no stretch to prevent it from popping loose. The tips of the tape should especially be laid down and patted into adherence.

D, completed bandaging lies in place well and is not disturbed when stockings are pulled over it.

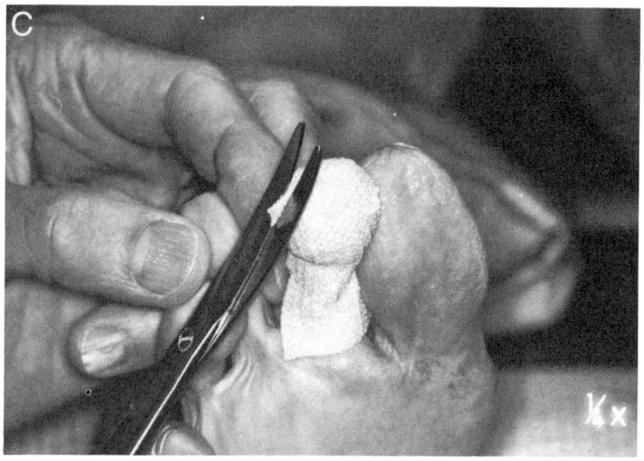

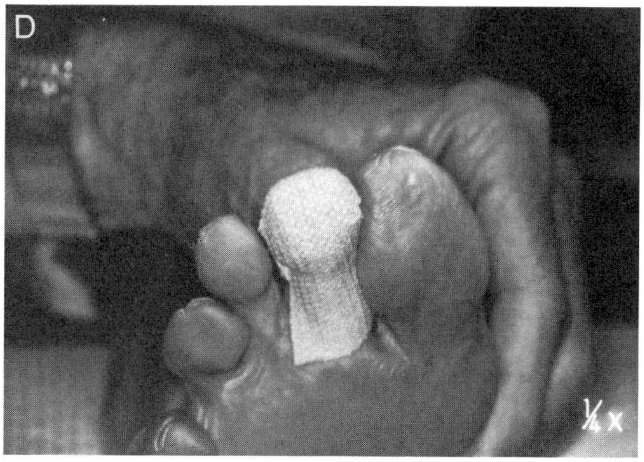

Interdigital Pads for Heloma Molle

Interdigital padding is sometimes a donut configuration. But often a pressure lesion may be too far proximal to permit a cutout pad to be used. In such instances a felt or foam rubber pad may be used distal to the lesion and up to the end of the toe. This effectively removes the pressure from the boney prominence that causes the heloma molle. An appropriate ointment and cotton can be used directly over the lesion and bandaging carried out with tape or cohesive gauze.

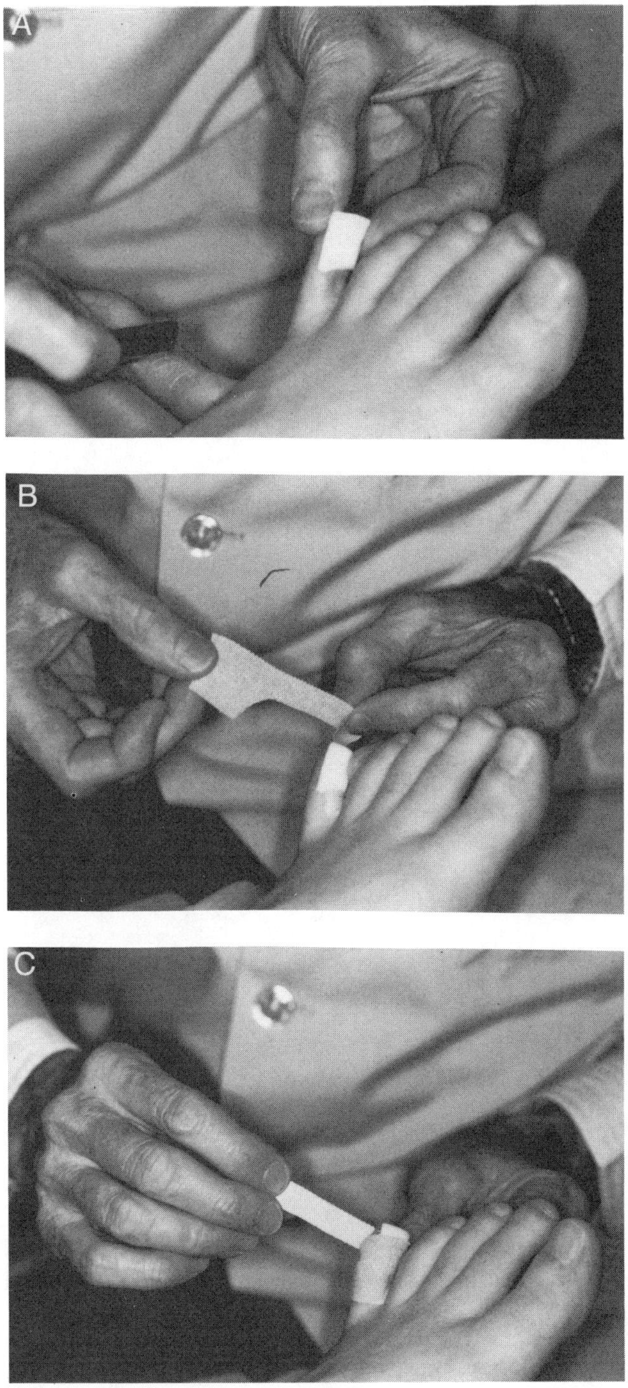

FIG 26–4.
A, adhesive felt $\frac{1}{16}$ in. thick is applied distal to the heloma molle.

B, Elastoplast tape with a scoop-out tail is used for covering.

C, covering in place over the felt pad.

Interdigital Foam Wedges

Interdigital foam wedges can be prepared from polyurethane or from foam rubber. Polyurethane foam is easier to sculpt. Once an interdigital lesion has been relieved, a patient may prevent rapid recurrence by wearing such a wedge on a daily basis.

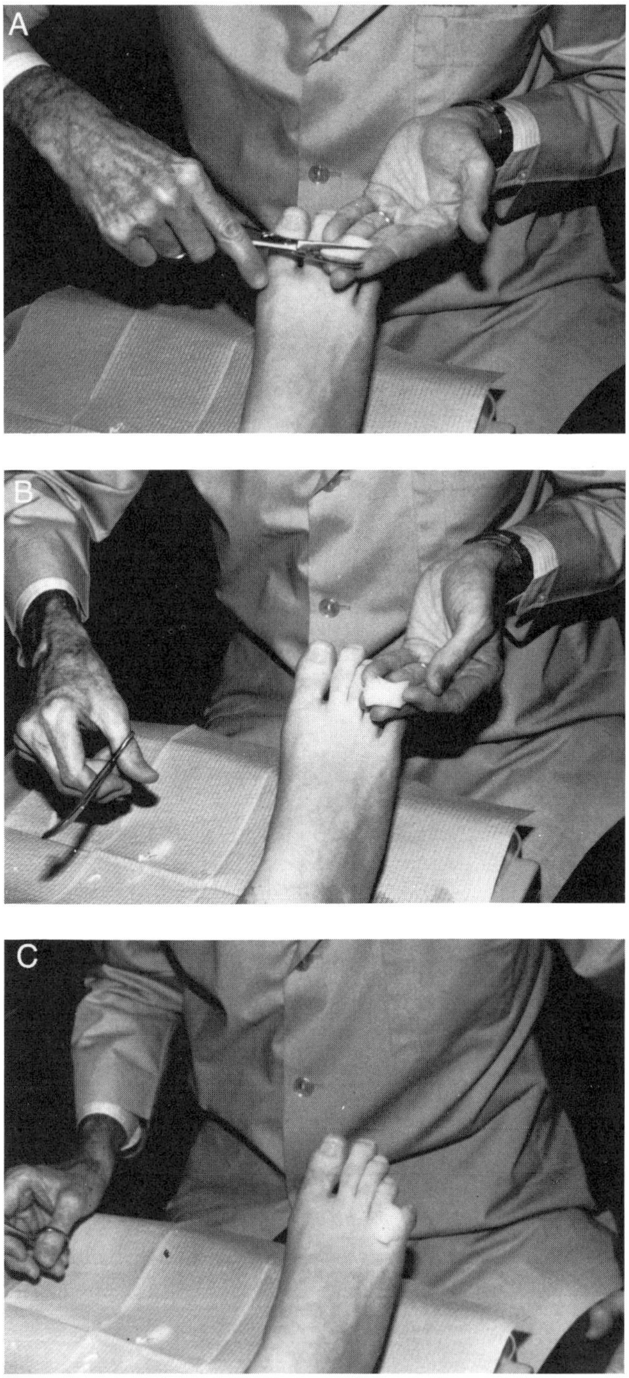

FIG 26–5.
A, a small block of foam is bent backward over one finger and held in place by pinching with the two adjacent fingers. Scissors are used to scoop out along the central finger.

B, when the foam is released, the scooped-out side is concave along its entire scooped-out side. This provides a fitted side to the toe and prevents the wedge from slipping out.

C, foam wedge in place between the toes.

BUNION AND TAILOR'S BUNION PADS AND SHIELDS

Bunion pads and shields may be adherent to the foot and appropriately bandaged or taped in place, or they may be made so as to be removable. Removable pads may be quite temporary, or they may be latexed and made quite durable.

Tube Gauze and Adhesive Felt Bunion Shield

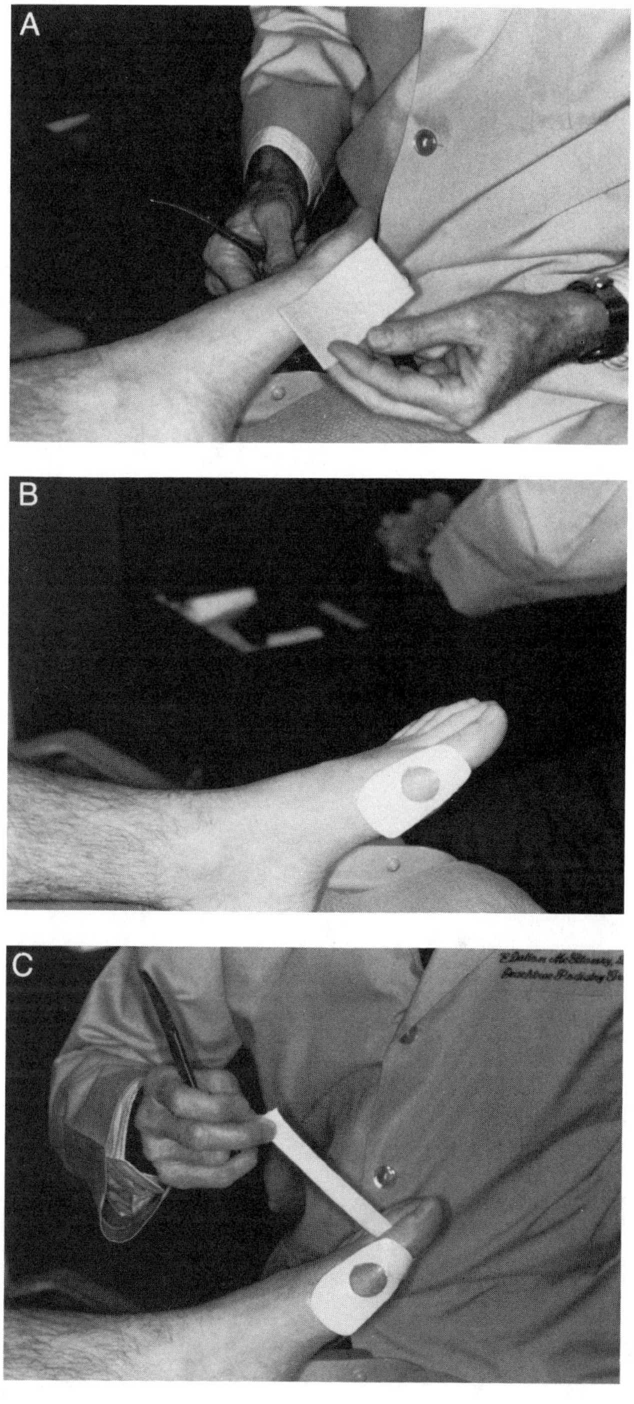

FIG 26–6.

A, the skin around the area of the bunion has been painted with skin adherent no. 2. A rectangular piece of ⅛-in.-thick adhesive felt is cut.

B, an aperture is cut just the size to accommodate the bunion enlargement. The backing is peeled off the adhesive. The bunion pad is placed on the foot *adhesive side outward, away from the skin.* The skin adherent holds the pad in place.

C, a piece of no. 1 tube gauze is used as a strap. One end is placed against the sticky adhesive outside of the pad.

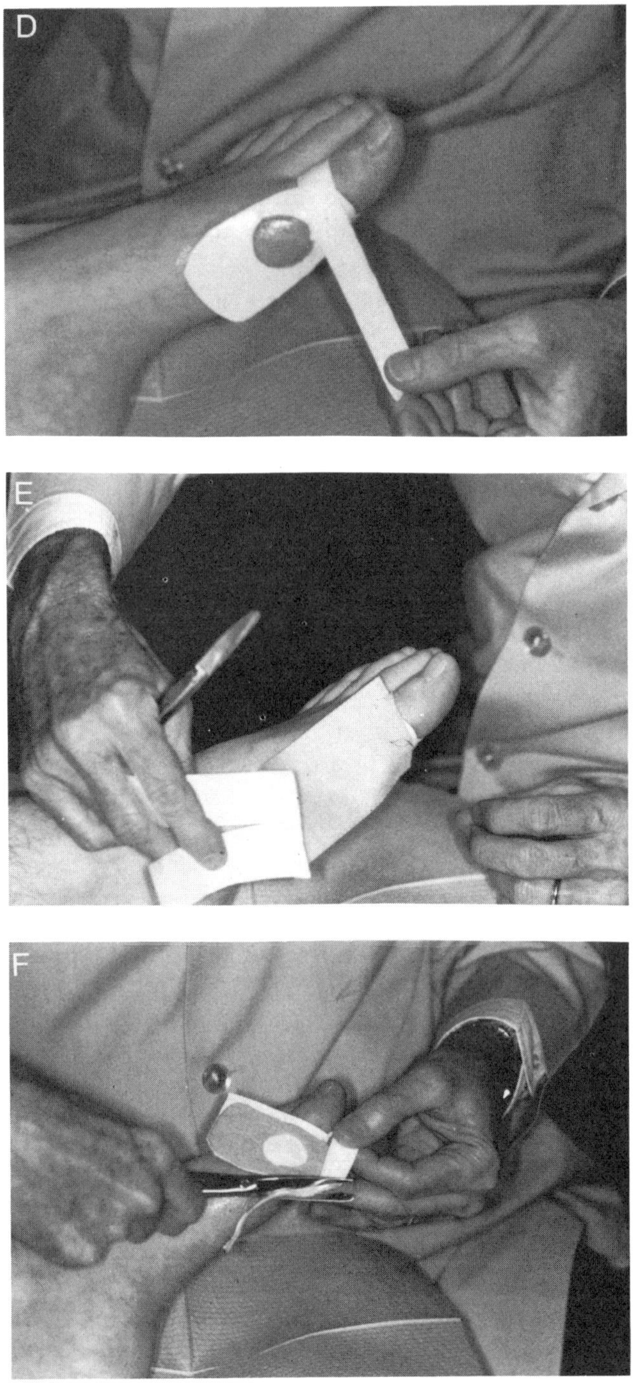

FIG 26–6 (cont.).
D, the other end of the no. 1 tube gauze is wrapped firmly around the base of the toe and pressed onto the sticky adhesive side of the felt bunion pad. It is now ready for covering.

E, moleskin is used to cover the outer side of the bunion shield. The moleskin also helps to lock the no. 1 tube gauze into place against the outer adhesive side of the felt shield.

F, the pad is peeled free from the foot and removed for trimming of the moleskin cover. The aperture of the pad is again cut out to leave an opening.

FIG 26–6 (cont.).
G, the completed temporary bunion shield is now removable and can be used easily for a week or two. The skin adherent will help to hold the pad in place for the first day until it is thoroughly molded to the contour of the joint.

H, liquid, ammonia-based latex is painted on the shield with a cotton-tipped applicator that has been enlarged by adding additional cotton. The latex is painted over the entire surface of the shield and the strap.

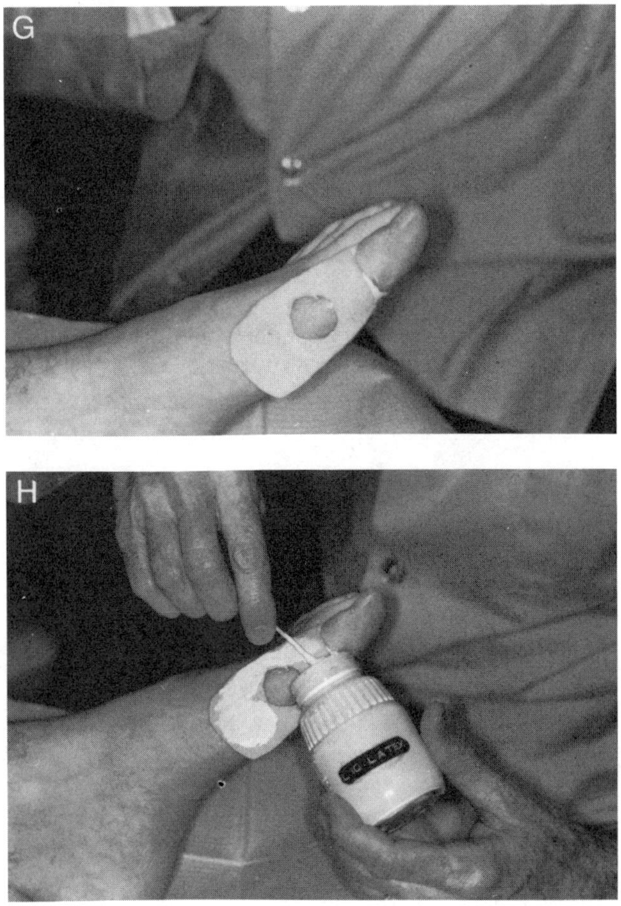

FIG 26–6 (cont.).
I, the latex is instantly set by spraying with a catalyst. The catalyst consists of *equal parts of water and white vinegar.* The catalyst is kept in any spray bottle for easy application to the latexed surface. After spraying the surface with catalyst, it is patted gently with the fingertips. Allow it to dry for 2 minutes, and then blot it and apply talcum. Any latex that is on the skin will easily peel off and is normally not irritating to skin.

J, the finished removable latexed bunion shield is quite durable and can be worn for weeks or months. If greater durability is needed, a second or third layer of latex is added as described above.

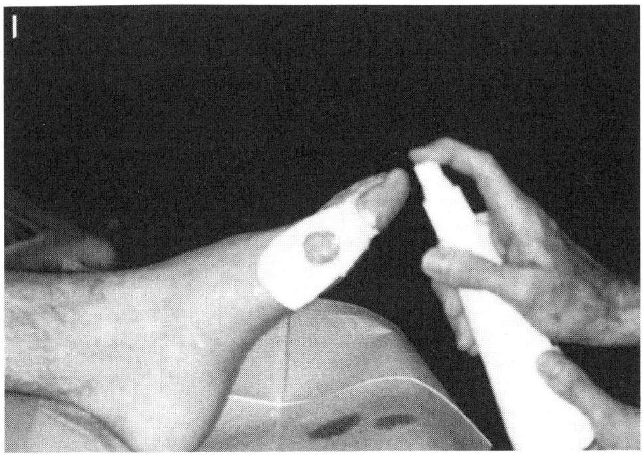

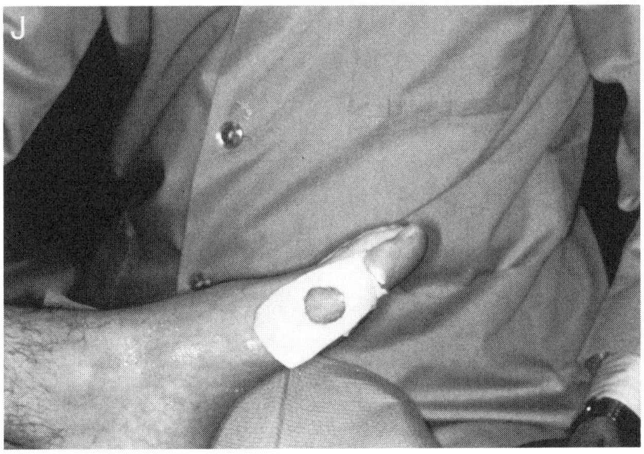

Tube Gauze and Adhesive Felt Tailor's Bunion Shield

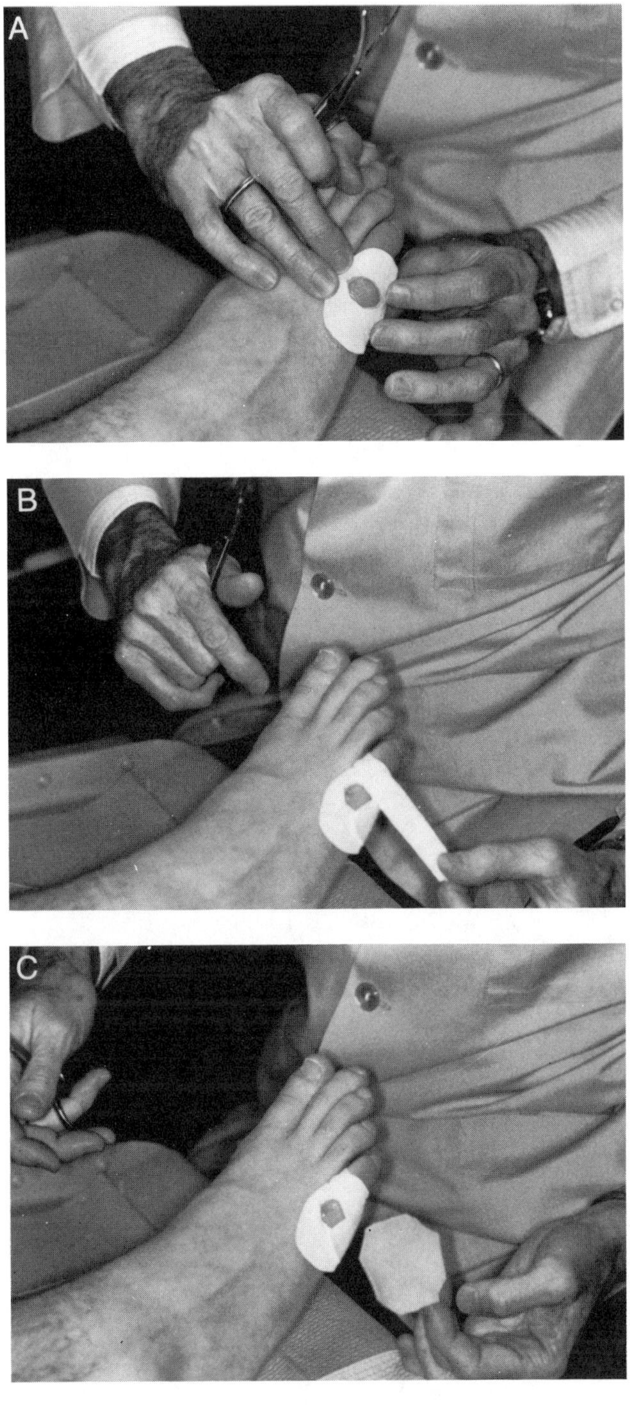

FIG 26–7.
A, a rectangular piece of ⅛-in. adhesive felt is cut to shield the tailor's bunion. The skin is painted with skin adherent no. 2. The backing is peeled off the felt shield. The shield, adhesive side out away from patient, is pressed against the foot.

B, no. 1 tube gauze is used as a strap around the fifth toe and the tips of the tube gauze pressed against the adhesive surface of the felt.

C, moleskin is used to cover the tailor's bunion shield. The shield is then removed and trimmed and the aperture again cut out.

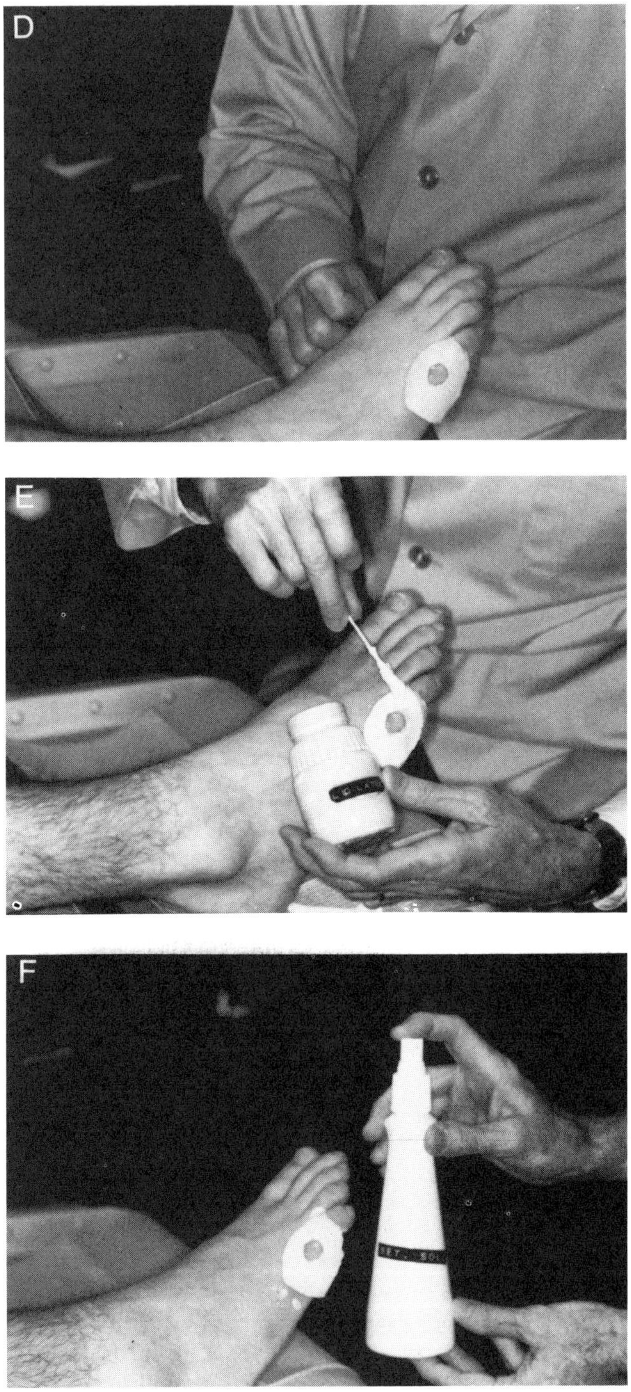

FIG 26–7 (cont.).
D, completed shield in place on the foot.

E, ammonia-based latex rubber is painted onto shield with an enhanced cotton-tipped applicator. The entire shield and strap is thoroughly impregnated.

F, catalyst (equal parts of white vinegar and water) is sprayed onto the entire latexed surface. The surface is patted lightly with the fingertip. Setting of the latex occurs in less than 2 minutes. The shield is powdered, and the patient is instructed to remove it at bedtime. By that time it is well molded to the foot and can usually be worn for weeks or months. A second or third coat of latex can be added if greater durability is needed.

Nonadhesive Felt and Latex Bunion Shield

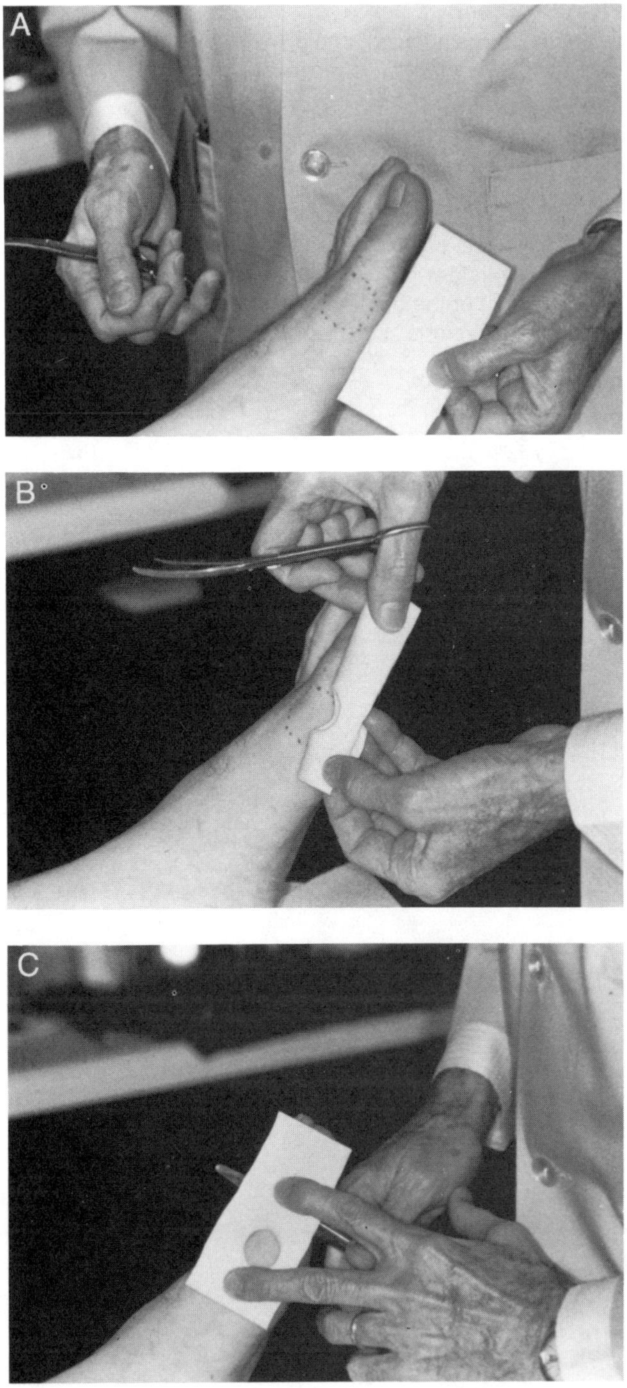

FIG 26–8.

A, felt bunion shields are easily constructed from $\frac{1}{8}$- to $\frac{3}{16}$-in. thick nonadhesive felt. The skin is first painted with skin adherent no. 2 around the area of the bunion. A block of felt is selected.

B, felt is folded and a half circle cut at the appropriate level in the doubled felt.

C, the felt is opened and the aperture placed around the bunion enlargement. Scissors are placed tightly in the web between the toes and the level of the web noted with a finger on the felt.

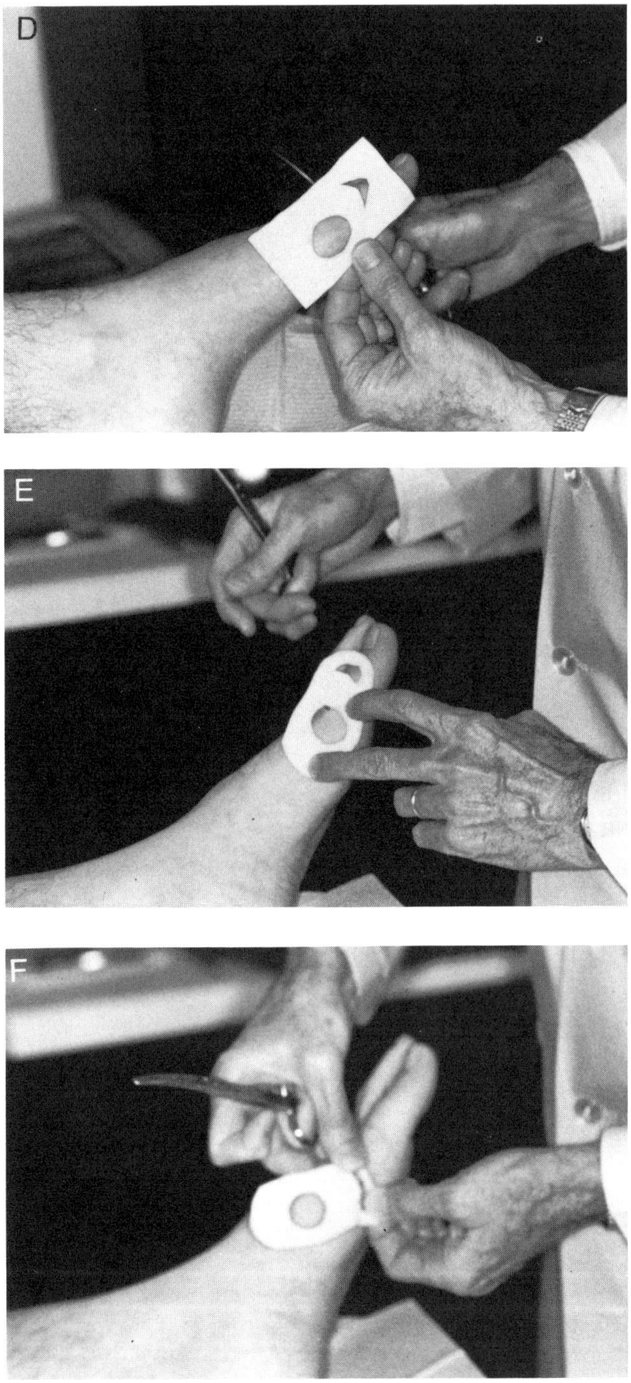

FIG 26–8 (cont.).
D, the felt is again folded, and a "V" is cut at the point of the web level. When the felt is reopened, a smilelike aperture is present for the great toe.

E, excess felt is trimmed away.

F, the loop of felt that will encircle the great toe is manipulated for several seconds to remove the sizing from the felt and to make it less bulky. If the opening is still too small for easy passage of the great toe, then the loop is manipulated again until it stretches sufficiently.

FIG 26–8 (cont.).
G, the shield is replaced on the foot and pressed against the skin adherent. It is then painted with one to two coats of ammonia-based latex.

H, each coat of ammonia-based latex is followed by spraying with catalyst (equal parts of white vinegar and water). The surface is patted with a finger after a 1- to 2-minute wait and is then powdered and worn in place until bedtime. The shield is now removable and washable and can be worn for months. If the surface becomes soiled from oxidation of the latex, it can be cleaned with vinegar.

I, the finished shield should be examined on the next visit and any rough edges trimmed with scissors.

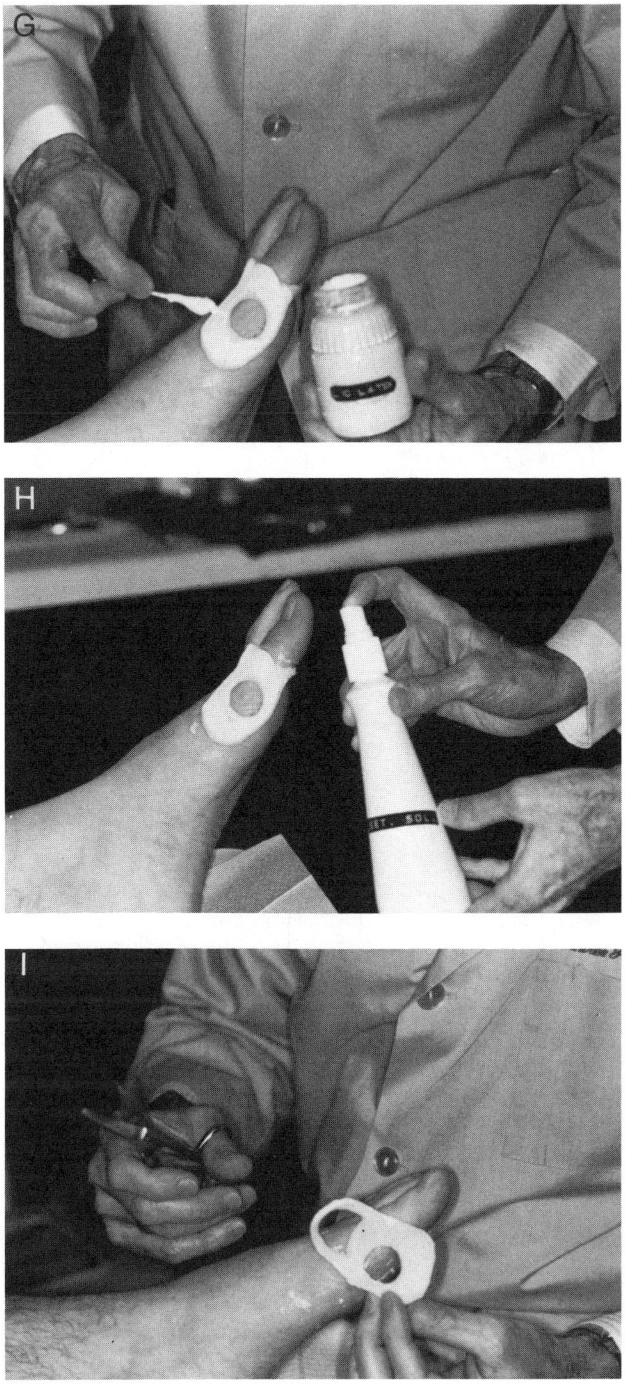

BALANCE PADDING

First-Metatarsal Balance Pad

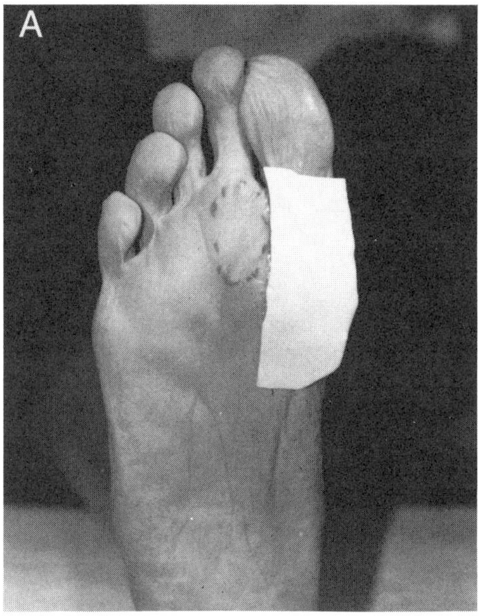

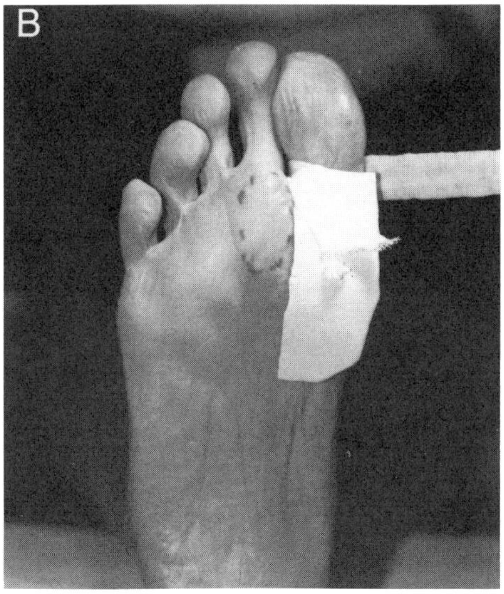

FIG 26–9.

A, A first metatarsal, or M-1, balance pad is used to relieve pressure under the second and third metatarsals and to force the first metatarsal to carry more weight. A block of ⅛- to $^{3}/_{16}$-in.–thick adhesive felt is cut the width of the first metatarsal. It is placed adhesive side outward. The proximal part of the pad is curved inward at the point where a sock lining typically curves inward.

B, the area to be padded is painted with skin adherent no. 2. The backing is peeled from the adhesive pad and the pad pressed in place against the foot with the adhesive side away from the patient. A strip of no. 1 tube gauze is cut and one end pressed against the sticky outer side of the felt.

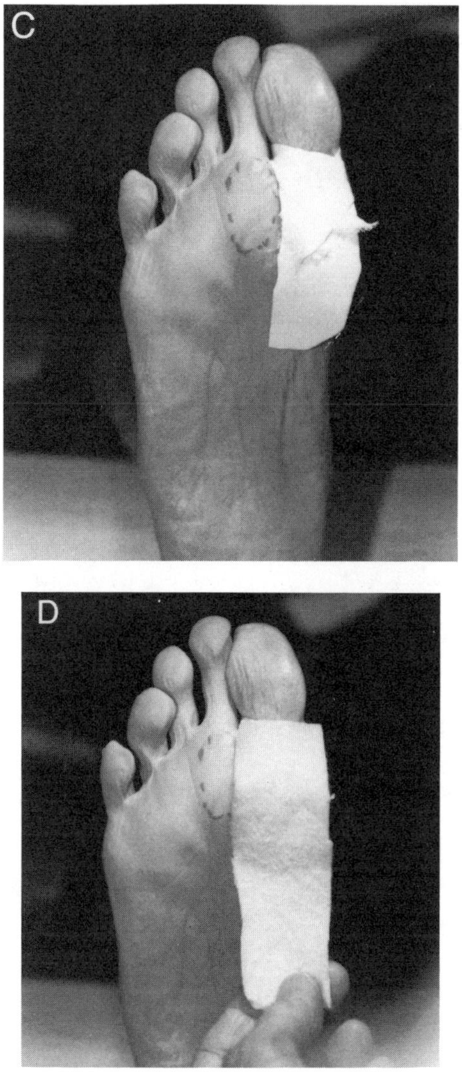

FIG 26–9 (cont.).
C, the tube gauze is looped around the great toe and the other end pressed against the adhesive felt.

D, the outer surface is covered with moleskin.

FIG 26–9 (cont.).
E, the pad is removed from the foot and the cover trimmed to fit.

F, the completed pad after trimming.

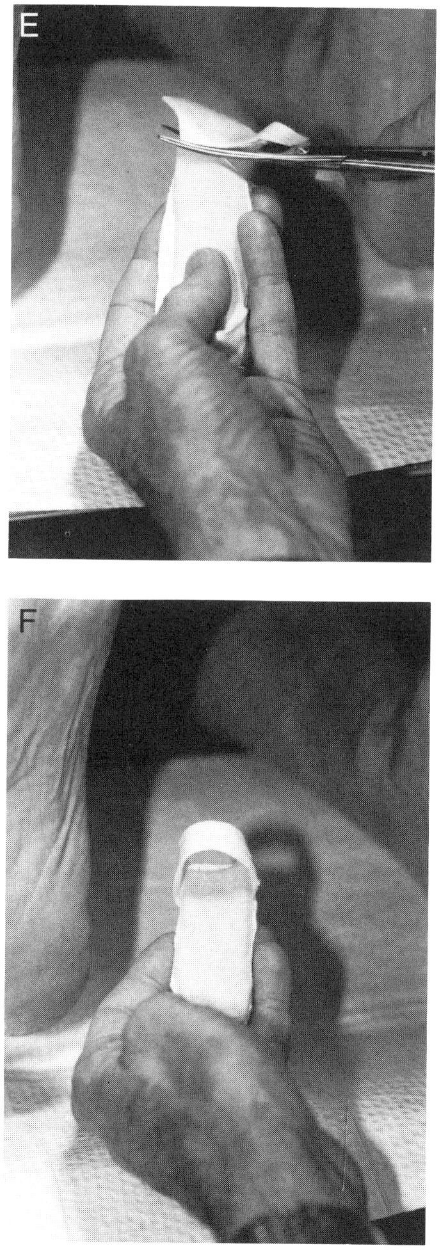

FIG 26–9 (cont.).
G, the M-1 sling pad is replaced on the foot. Ammonia-based latex is applied to the tube gauze loop and to the entire outer surface of the pad.

H, the pad is sprayed with catalyst (equal parts white vinegar and water) and allowed to set for 1 to 2 minutes. It is then blotted dry and powdered before the patient dons stockings and shoes. The pad can be removed at bedtime and reapplied each morning. It is washable and can usually be worn for months.

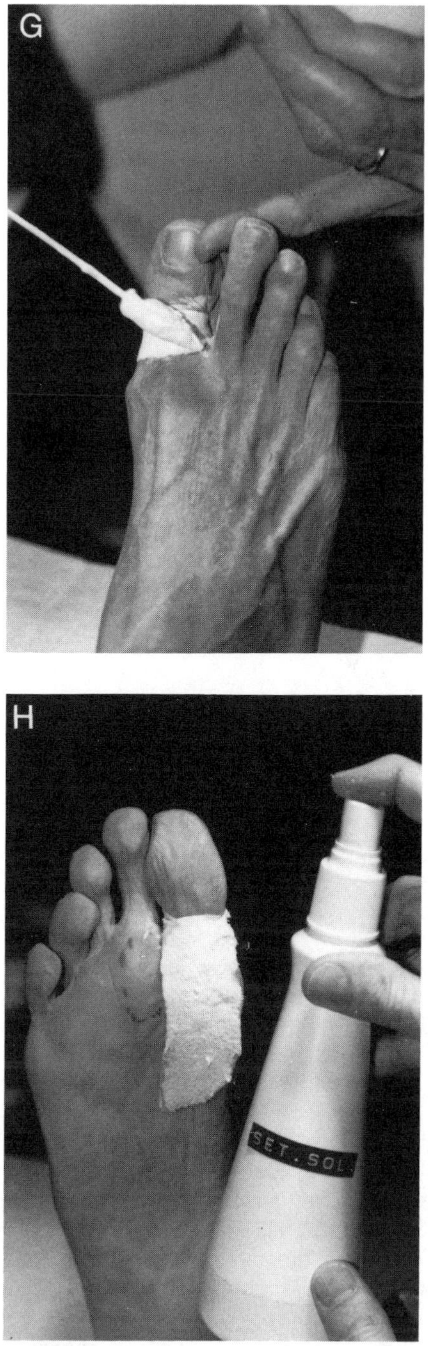

Metatarsal 2, 3, 4 Sling Pad

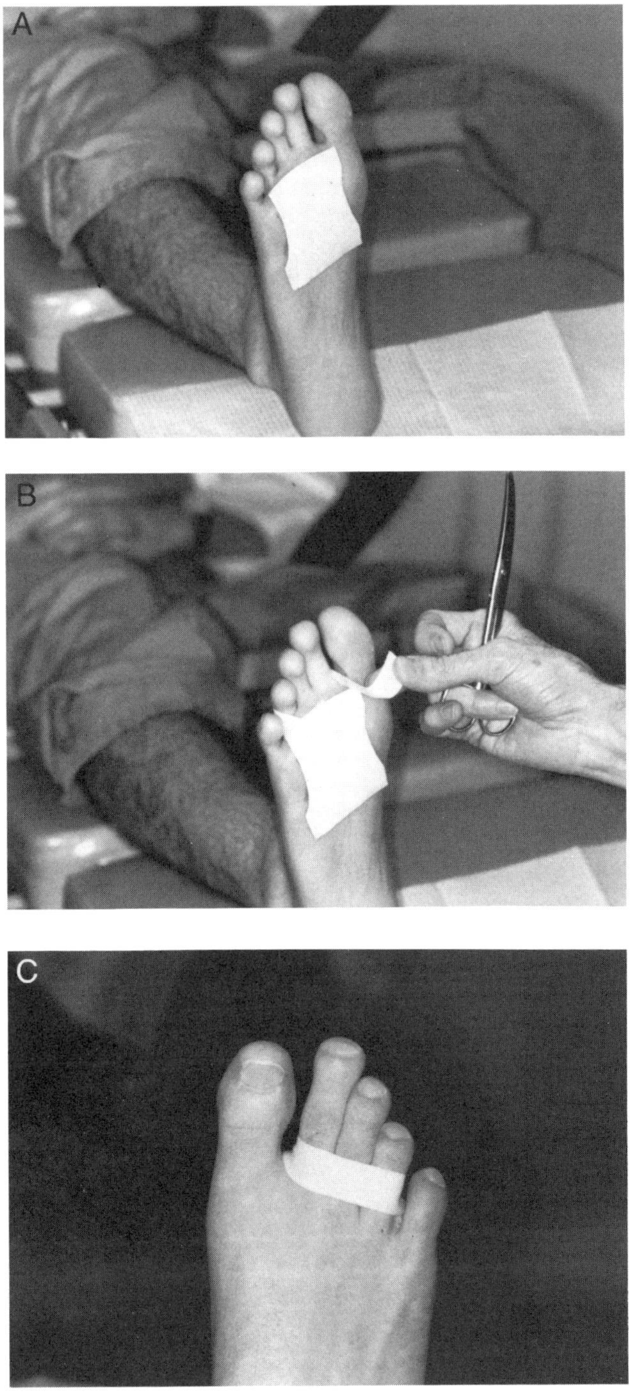

FIG 26–10.

A, a metatarsal 2, 3, 4 (M-2,3,4) balance pad, also called a dancer's pad, is cut from $1/8$ to $3/16$-in. felt. The skin of the area to be supported is painted with skin adherent no. 2. The pad is trimmed and placed against the foot with adhesive side away from the foot.

B, a length of no. 1 tube gauze is cut and one end pressed against the adhesive side of the felt under the fourth metatarsal head. The tube gauze is looped around the three middle toes as far proximally as possible and the other end brought down underneath the second metatarsal and pressed into place against the adhesive side of the felt.

C, a dorsal view shows the tube gauze looped around the three middle toes.

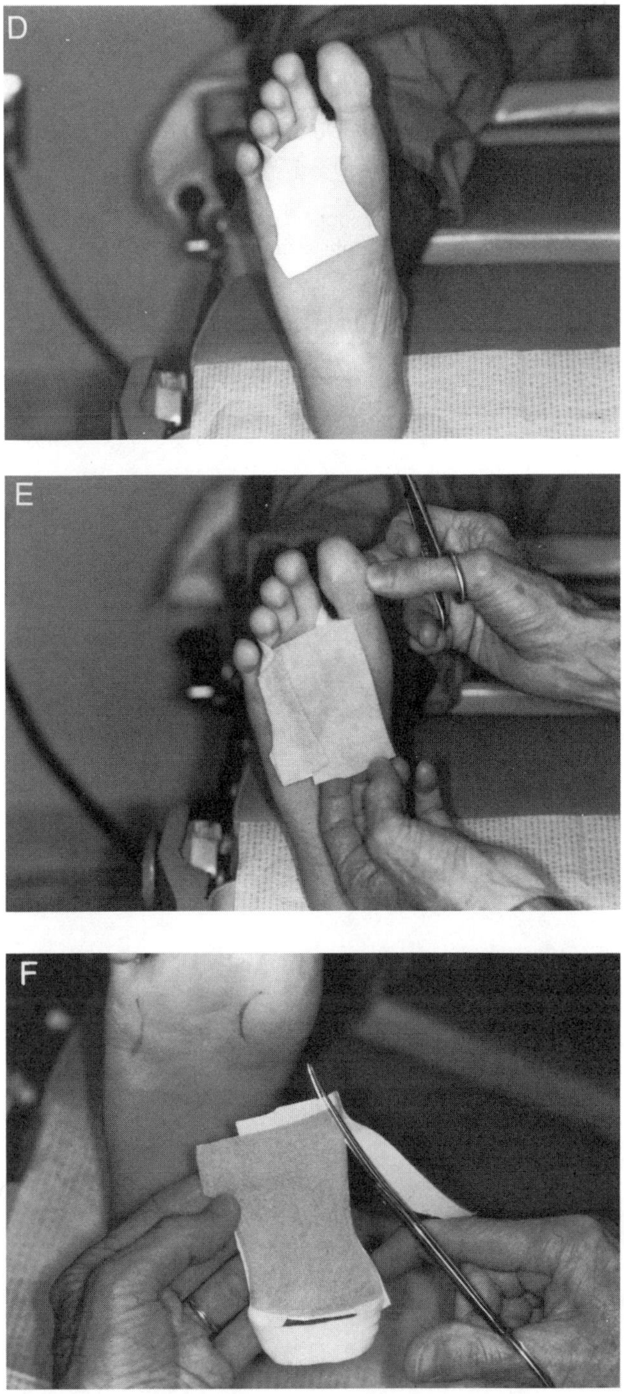

FIG 26–10 (cont.).
D, sling pad in position ready for covering.

E, the pad is covered with moleskin to provide a smooth outer surface and lock the tube gauze loop into position.

F, the pad is removed, and the moleskin covering is trimmed.

FIG 26–10 (cont.).
G, the finished pad is replaced and pressed against skin on the surface of the foot.

H, the pad is now removable but should be worn until bedtime to allow it to mold to the foot well.

I, the pad shown after applying two coats of ammonia-based latex rubber and setting with catalyst.

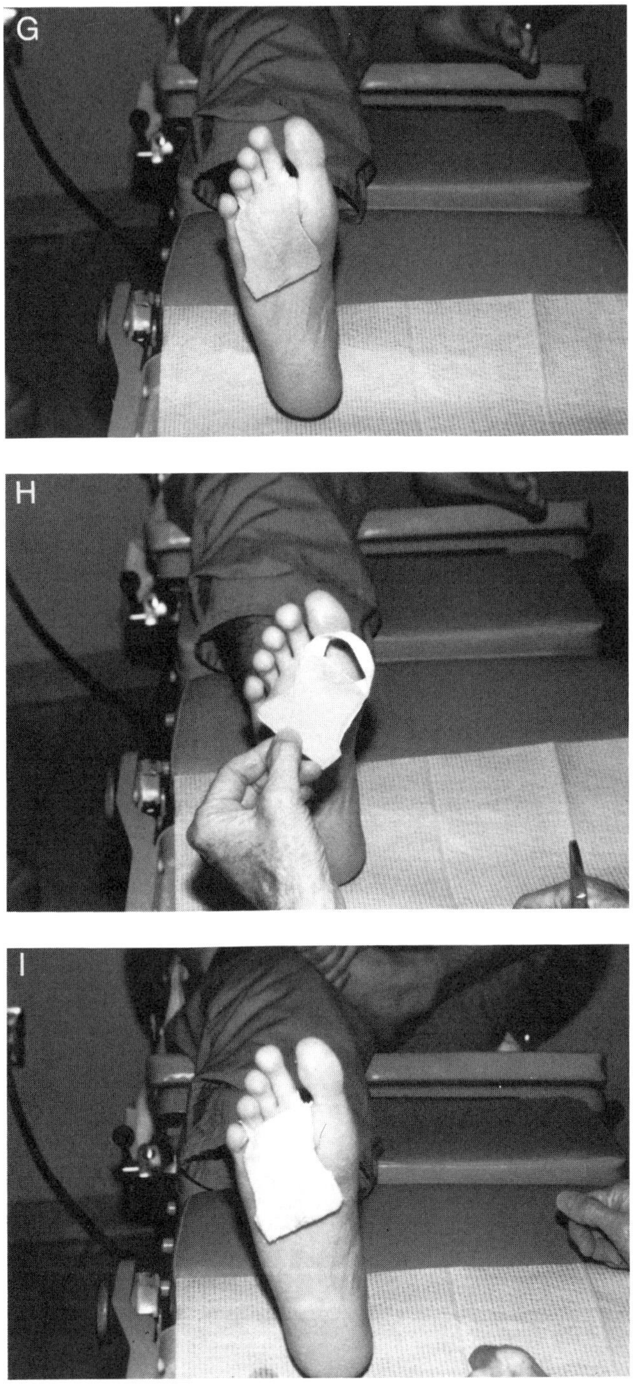

Metatarsal 1 and 4, 5 Sling Pad

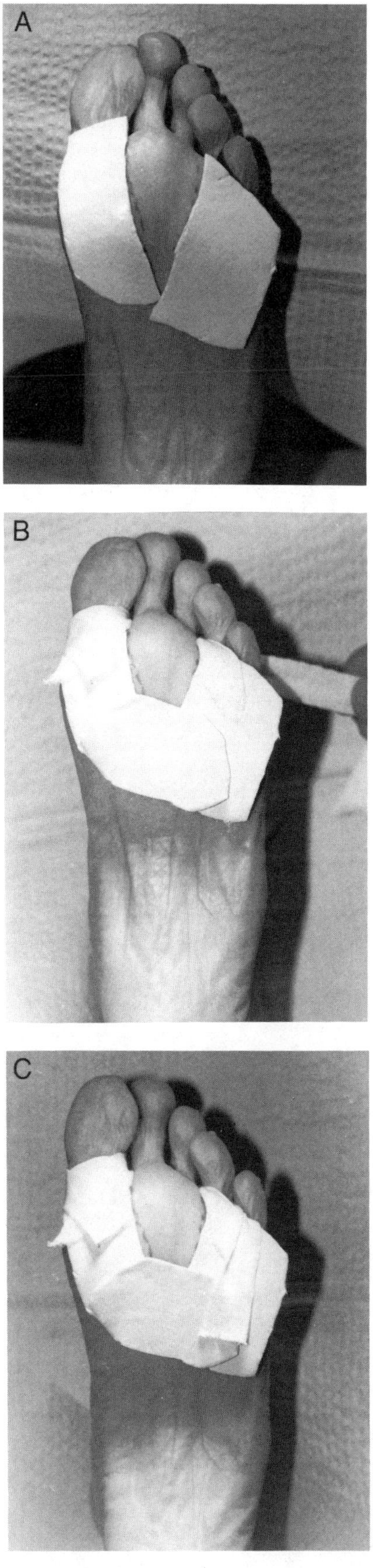

FIG 26–11.
A, metatarsal balance pads under metatarsals 1, 4, and 5 are designed to transfer excess pressure from the second and third metatarsals to the first, fourth, and fifth metatarsals. The skin has been painted with skin adherent no. 2 in the areas to be padded. Adhesive felt pads have been cut to fit the areas to be supported. Pads are pressed against the foot with the adhesive side away from the foot.

B, the pads here are connected with a metatarsal pad or metatarsal bar of adhesive felt with the adhesive side away from patient.

C, no. 1 tube gauze is used to make a loop around the hallux and a second loop around the fourth toe. The tips of the tube gauze are pressed against the exposed adhesive side of the felt. The pad is now ready to be covered on its outer surface.

FIG 26–11 (cont.).
D, plantar view of the pad in place after covering and trimming.

E, dorsal view of the pad after completing. The pad may or may not be covered with latex rubber depending on the length of time the patient is expected to wear the device.

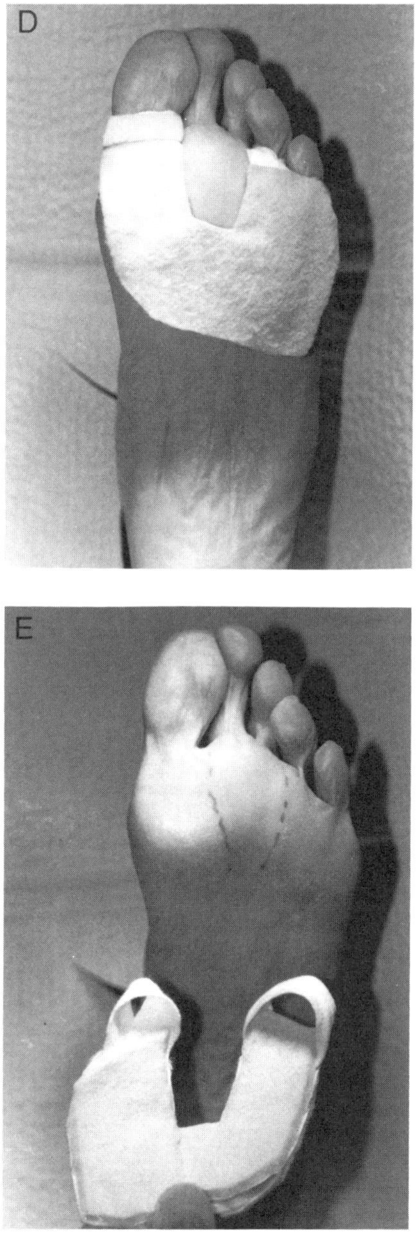

TAPING TECHNIQUE

Proper Use of Adhesive Tape

One may use adhesive tape for years and never become efficient in its use. There are a number of fundamental principles that if learned early will make the use of tape easier and more effective.

Preparation for Taping

Skin should be thoroughly cleansed before taping. Hair should either be removed or a barrier layer of covering interposed. Skin to be taped should be painted with skin adherent prior to application of the strapping. If a barrier layer such as tube gauze is to be applied prior to taping, then the skin adherent should be applied first.

Positioning for Taping

When the foot and ankle are to be taped, it is most important that the foot be dorsiflexed to a right angle with the leg. Often the patient can hold this position. If needed, a stirrup of tape or tube gauze can be looped around the forefoot and the patient asked to hold the other end. Position is important to the success of the taping.

Cutting of Tape

Tape can either be cut or torn. Tearing of tape is an art and is awkward for many people. It is much quicker once the art is acquired. Cutting of tape should always be done with the adhesive side facing upward. When cut this way the tape tends to fall away from the cutting edge of the scissors rather than getting caught in it. Scissor blades should be cleaned with acetone daily, and a lightweight oil or petroleum jelly rubbed across the blades. This facilitates cutting the tape.

Application of Tape to Foot

Tape is applied firmly, although never tightly. The tip of the tape should be laid in position and patted against the skin. If the tip of the tape is applied under tension, it will tend to spring loose.

Finishing strips of tape

When finishing strips are being applied, the foot is allowed to drop into a relaxed attitude. The finishing strips are laid in place, never stretched. They are patted into position to encourage adhesion.

Barrier Layer

If a strapping is going to be used for considerable support or compression or if the strapping is to be in place for more than 4 days, the use of a barrier layer is encouraged. The barrier layer should be highly absorbent. We prefer to paint the foot and ankle with skin adherent no. 2 and then apply tube gauze as a barrier coat from the base of the toes to well above the ankle. If the skin has been prepared well with skin adherent, the tube gauze will adhere easily and will not pull free under taping.

Types of Strappings

There are many types and variations of strappings. One can generally classify strappings into two categories: foot strappings and ankle strappings. Those described herein are but a few of many that are widely used.

Low-Dye Strapping

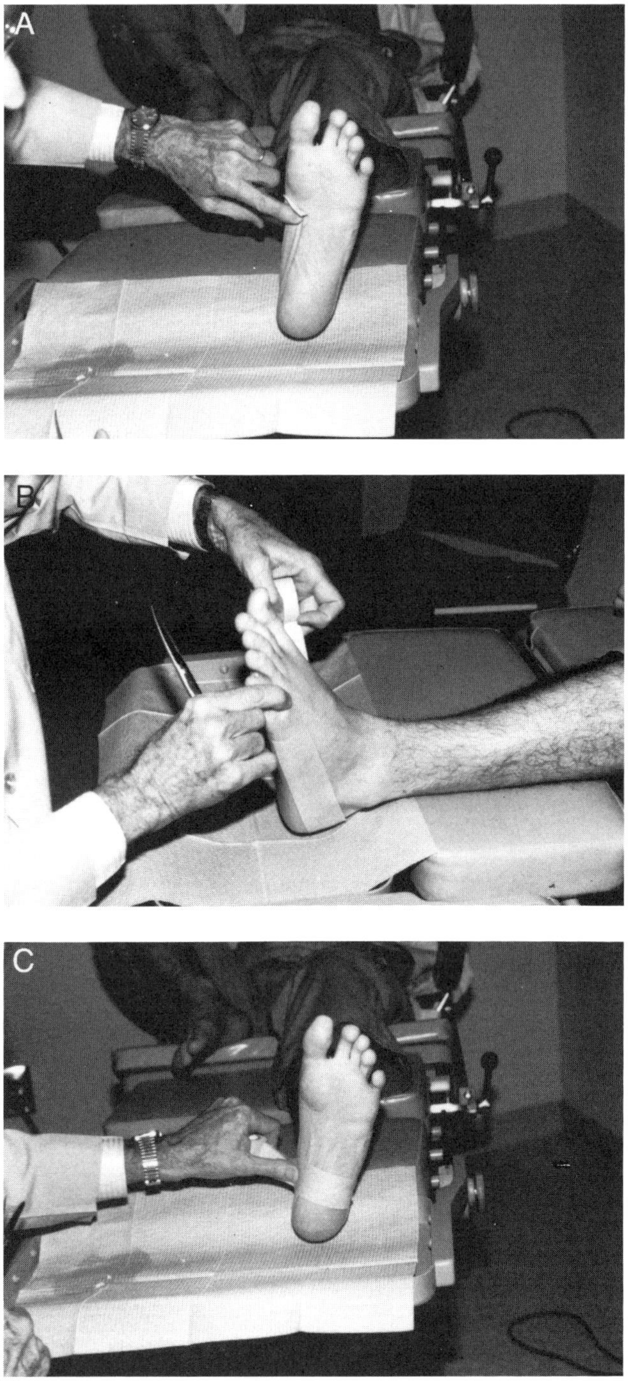

FIG 26–12.

A, skin adherent is first applied to the area to be taped. The first two strips of a Low Dye strapping are longitudinal. One or 1½-in. tape is used. It extends from the fifth metatarsal head along the lateral side of the foot, circles around the back of the heel, and then runs forward along the medial side of the foot to the neck of the first metatarsal.

B, the second strip is essentially the same but may end a bit more plantar to the first metatarsal. These two strips are applied with the ankle at or near a right angle.

C, transverse tape strips are next applied plantarly. Each strip begins laterally and attaches to the original longitudinal strips. The transverse strips are applied with mild tension laterally to medially, except for the tips of the tape, which are laid down and pressed into place.

FIG 26–12 (cont.).
D, successive transverse strips overlap each other by half their width all the way forward to the level of the metatarsal necks.

E, a final finishing strap is applied by following the course of the first strap and overlapping the rough ends of all the transverse strips. The finishing strap is applied without tension and is pressed into place to bind down all the underlying tape ends.

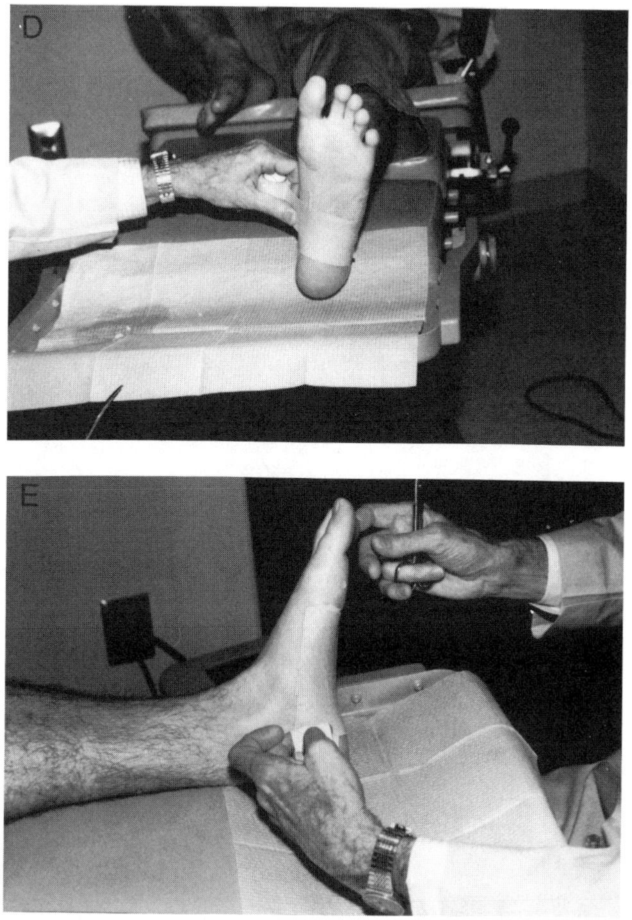

FIG 26–12 (cont.).
F, medial view of a finished Low Dye strapping.

G, Plantar view of a Low Dye strapping.

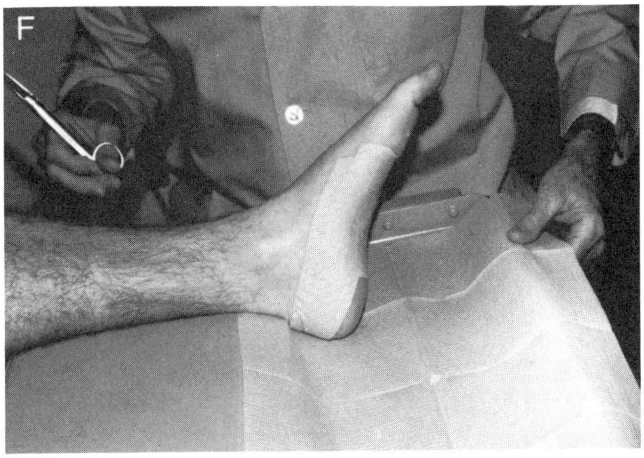

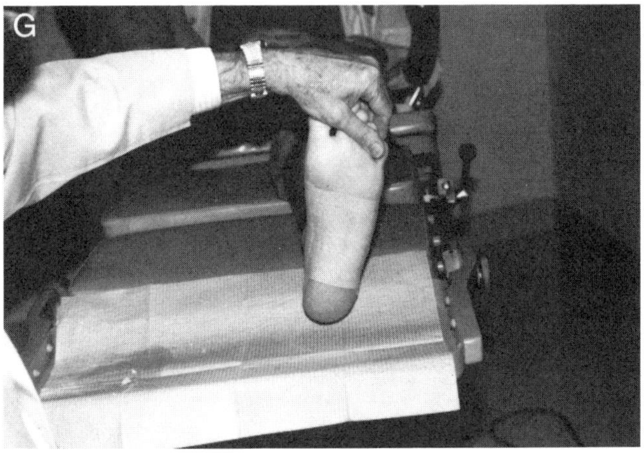

Flexible Cast Ankle/Foot Strapping

The flexible cast ankle/foot strapping employs a combination of two very effective strappings. One is an elastoplast figure-of-8 bandage that is most effective in reducing edema and speeding recovery from ankle injury but is not as supportive of ligaments as many other strappings. The second component of the flexible ankle/foot cast is a Gibney boot strapping, also called a basket weave. Application is made with the foot at a right angle to the leg. The position of the ankle joint is most important.

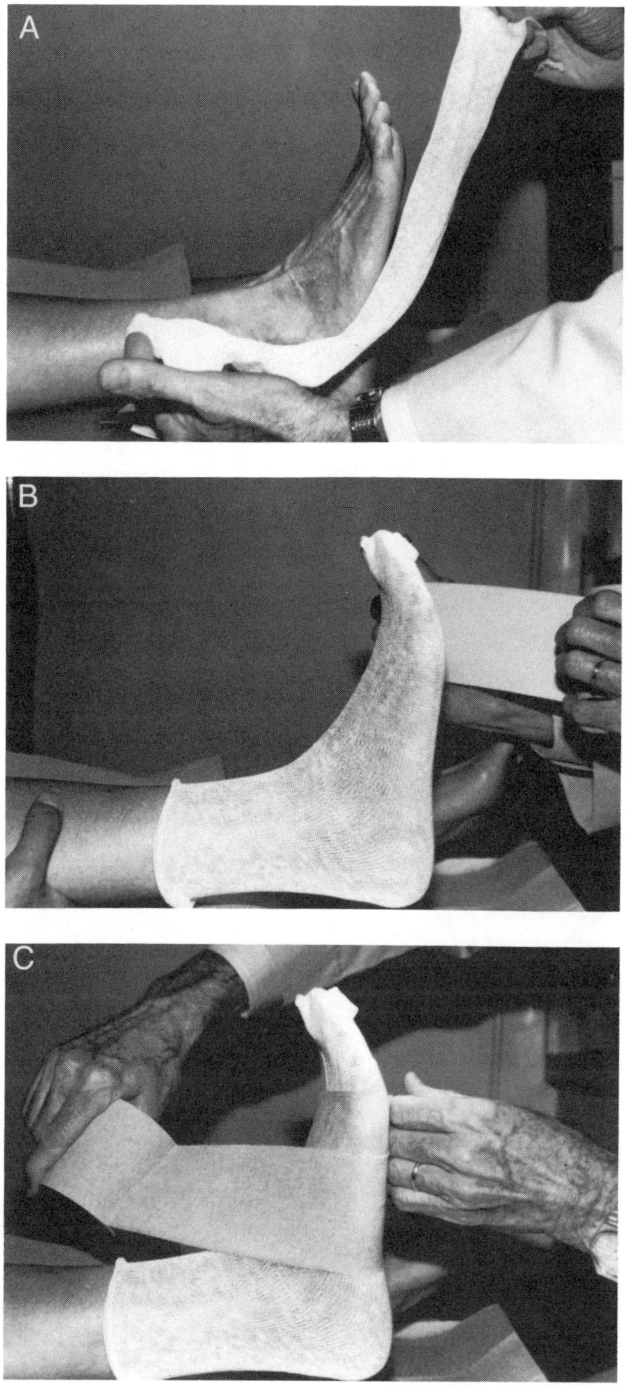

FIG 26–13.

A, the foot and ankle are first painted with skin adherent. A length of single thickness tube gauze is then applied, smoothed, and rubbed into place while the foot is held with the ankle at a right angle.

B, 2- or 3-in. Elastoplast (2-in. is recommended until you are quite experienced in its application) is wrapped from the base of the toes to well above the ankle.

C, Once the ankle is approached, a figure-of-8 configuration is used. The bandage encircles the ankle and then doubles back around the rearfoot.

FIG 26–13 (cont.).
D, the bandage again encircles the ankle.

E, the bandage doubles back around the rearfoot to encircle most of the plantar surface of the heel and then back to above the ankle.

F, the bandage ends well above the ankle. It is applied without tension but is applied with just enough stretch to encourage fit.

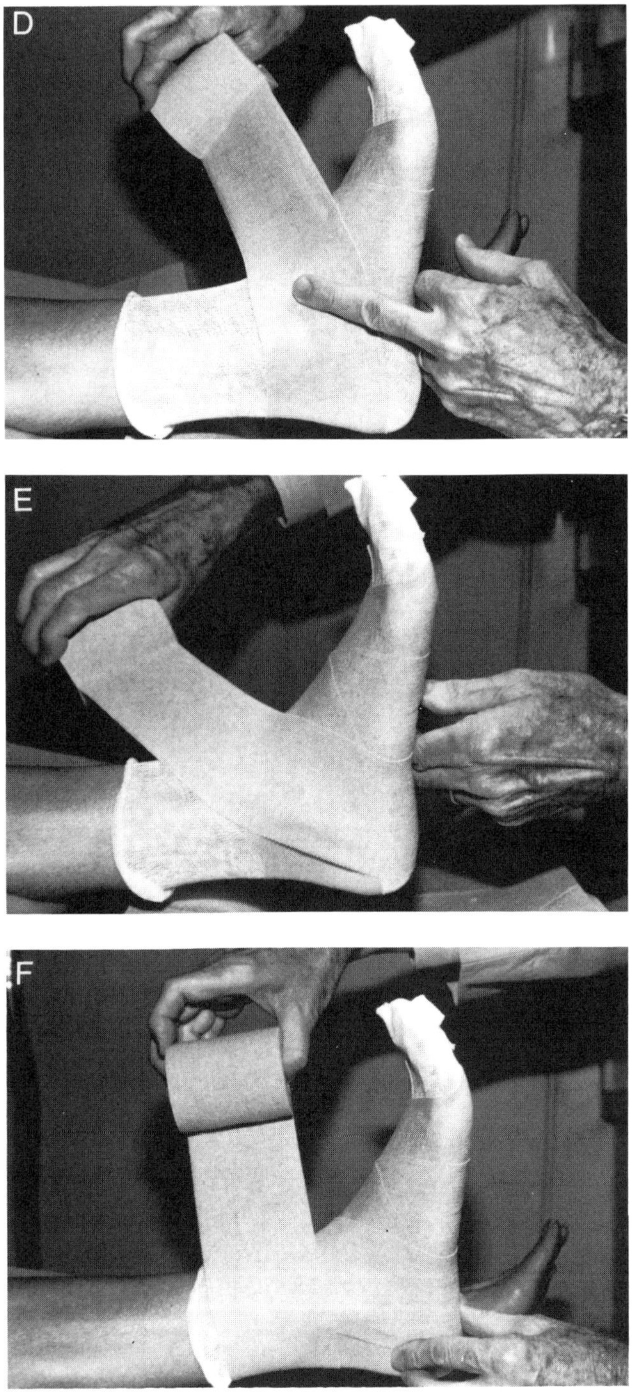

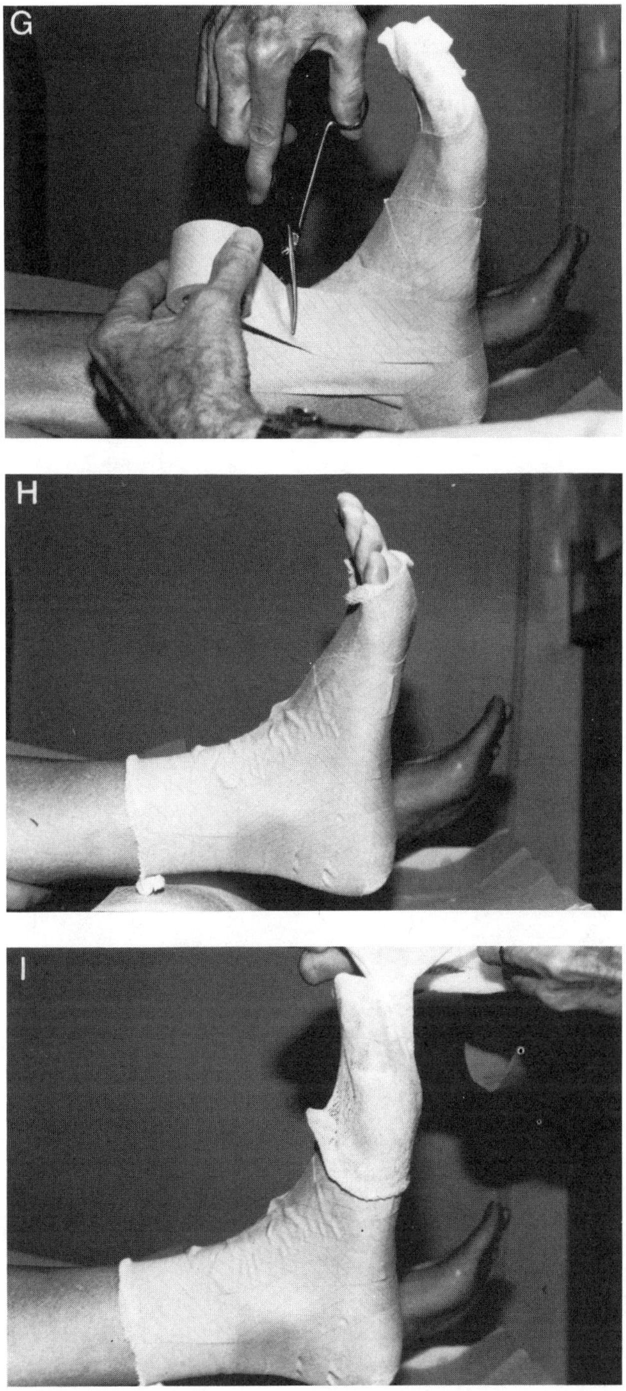

FIG 26–13 (cont.).

G, the second portion of the bandaging is a basket weave strapping directly over the Elastoplast. The straps are applied by first alternating a longitudinal strip from the fifth metatarsal along the lateral side of the foot, behind the heel, and then forward along the medial side of the foot to the head of the first metatarsal. The second and alternating strap runs from the lateral side of the ankle across the plantar aspect of the foot and then up the medial side of the ankle. Strips continue to alternate in that fashion, one longitudinal and then one vertical, until the strapping extends forward to the metatarsal necks. The straps do not cross the front of the ankle or the top of the foot. A 1-in. section down the front of the ankle and top of the foot allows for expansion. A finishing strip is added to tie down the tape ends along the medial and lateral margins of the strapping.

H, finished strapping provides both strong compression and very strong ligamentous support.

I, a second section of tube gauze is applied to cover the forefoot and then twisted at the toe and doubled back.

FIG 26–13 (cont.).
J, tube gauze covering the entire bandage.

K, the upper edge of the tube gauze is taped in place. The tube gauze covering ensures that the bandage will stay in place for as long as needed without rolling up or being pulled loose by stockings or bed covers. The bandage will be removed a week later just as neat and secure as when originally applied.

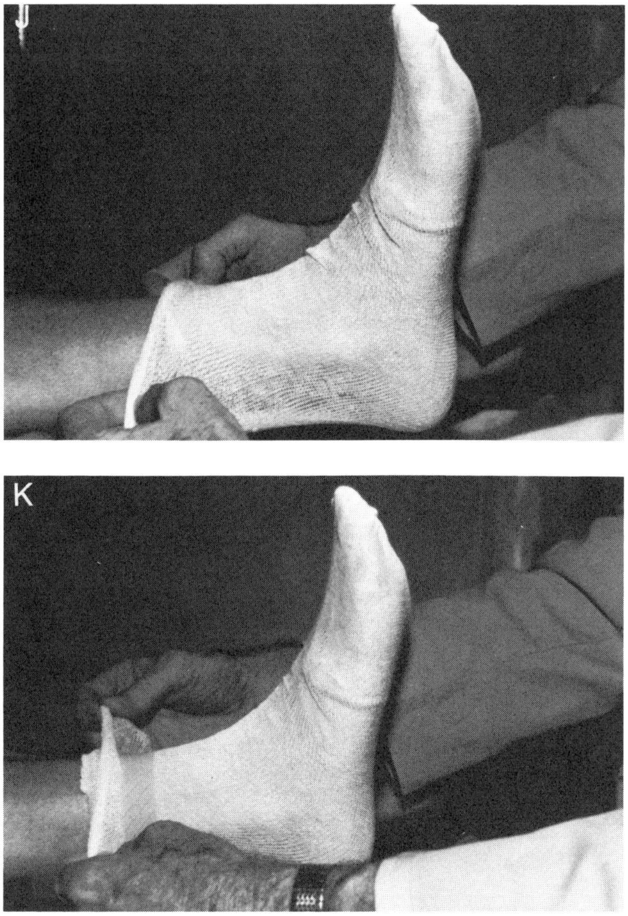

27

Retainers

E. Dalton McGlamry, D.P.M.

In a strict sense, a retainer is a device that is used to retain or to maintain alignment of a toe, a metatarsal, a foot, or an ankle. In a broad sense, retainers have taken on far wider functions.

Retainers are used to maintain or to improve alignment, especially of the metatarsophalangeal joints and the toes. They are used to improve alignment while providing a protective function to help relieve tenderness and disperse pressure over wider areas.

Retainers, properly sculptured, can do much to relieve edema and to improve motion. Reduction of scar thickening or hypertrophy is a special and little known function of retainers. This can be especially important in the patient with a known history of hypertrophic scars or keloid formation.

MATERIALS

Materials for preparing retainers are as varied as the retainers themselves. Most commonly they include common podiatric materials such as wool felt, tube gauze, moleskin, adhesive felt, and ammonia-based latex rubber. Increasingly used are silicone rubber molding compound, polyurethane foam, and Vultex liquid rubber.

WEDGE RETAINERS

Wedge retainers are simple and rapidly prepared retainers (Fig 27–1, A–F).

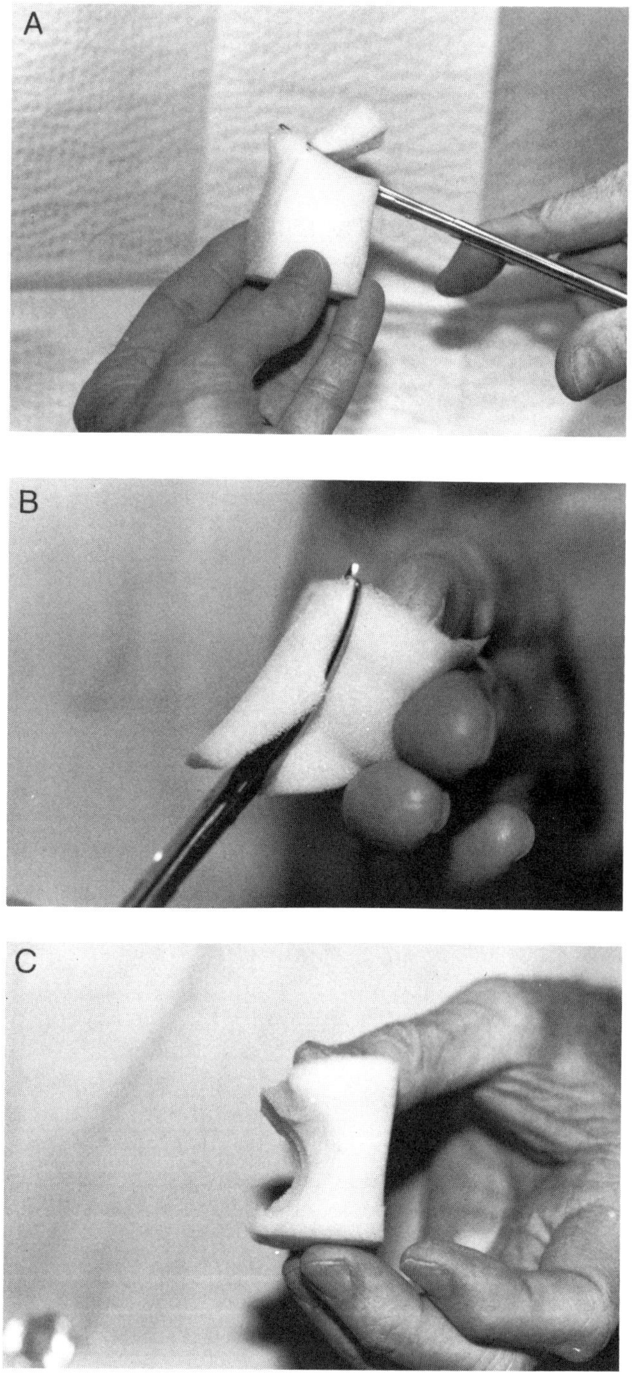

FIG 27–1.
A, a wedge of polyurethane foam is shaped to fit the sloped incline of the toe web.

B, the wedge is folded lengthwise over one finger and is pinched between the two adjacent fingers to bend it backward. Scissors are used to make multiple transverse scoops across the stretched portion of the foam.

C, when released, the foam springs back to its original shape, and the transverse scoops now provide a concave surface to fit well against the hallux.

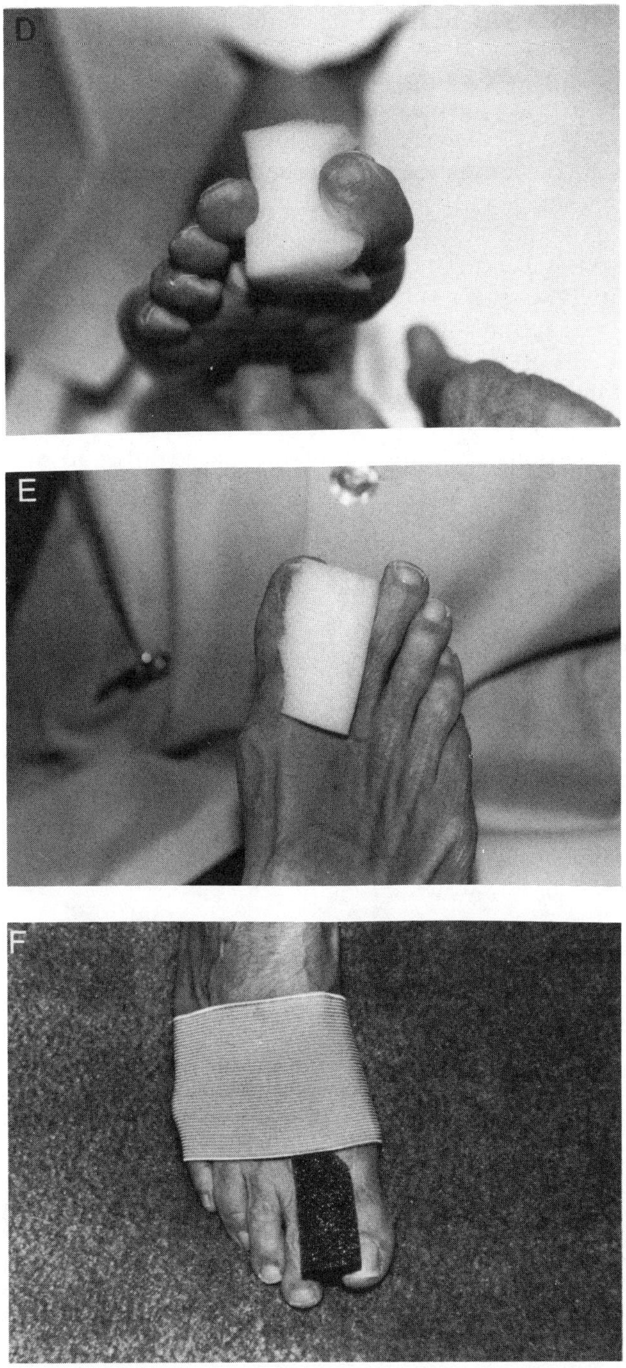

FIG 27–1 (cont.).
D, urethane wedge in place. Such wedges help to maintain alignment after effective correction of bunion deformity.

E, dorsal view of a urethane wedge hallux retainer.

F, urethane wedge of tinted urethane combined with an elastic metatarsal strap used to prevent splaying of the metatarsal while retaining alignment of the hallux.

TRACTION SLINGS

Traction slings may be preprepared for general nonspecific use by inserting a length of dental roll cotton in a length of no. 1 tube gauze. Such slings can be completed in less than a minute when the patient is in the office. They are helpful in encouraging toe and metatarsal function and are often quite useful in providing symptomatic relief of metatarsalgia and neuroma pain.

Traction slings that are custom prepared are far more useful and have a much more specific action. Once the traction sling is completed, it may be worn as is, or it may be coated with one or two applications of liquid ammonia based latex to add durability (Fig 27–2, A–J).

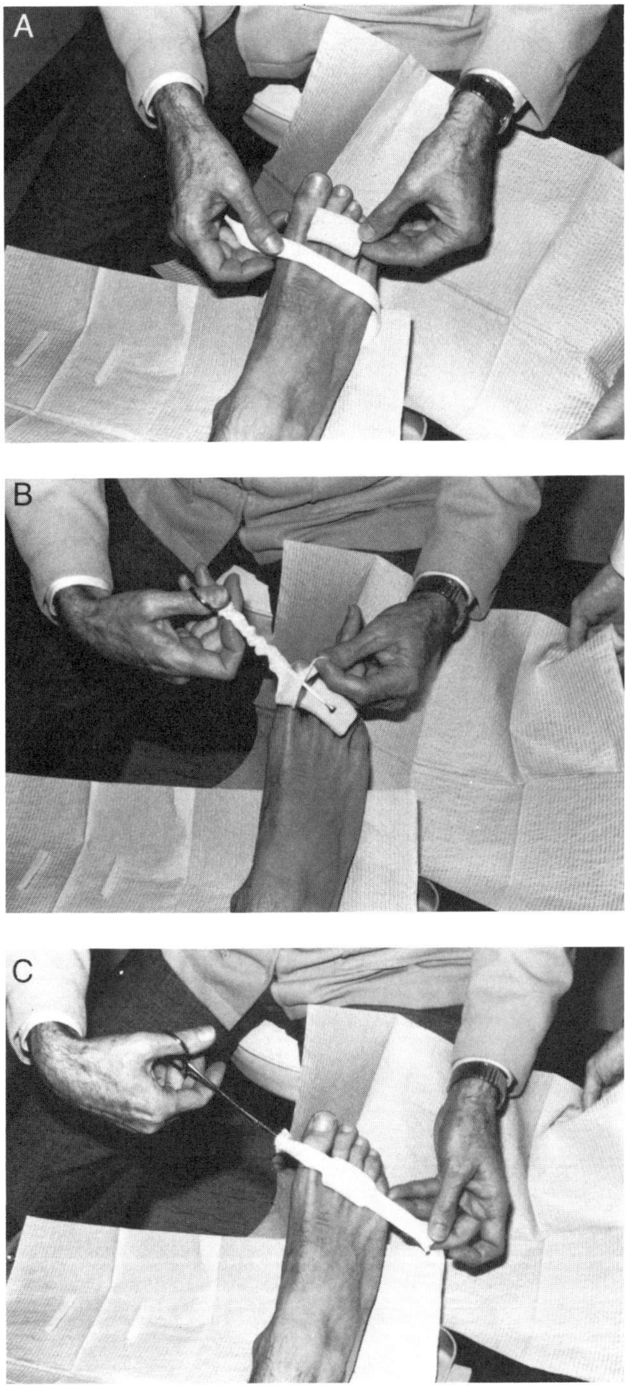

FIG 27–2.

A, a length of no. 1 tube gauze is cut, as is a block of felt (preferably 75% wool, 25% cotton Polikoff-type felt). The felt should usually be 3/16-in. thick. It should extend from the medial side of the second toe to the lateral side of the fourth toe, from the first to the fourth interdigital space. The strip of felt should be wide enough to fill the sulcus beneath the toes from the pulp of the toe back to the web space.

B, a hemostat or other clamp type instrument is passed through the length of tube gauze. The strip of now beveled felt is grasped and pulled within the center of the tube gauze.

C, the tube gauze is stretched with the felt centered within.

FIG 27–2 (cont.).
D, the felt plantar ram is positioned within the sulcus. It should fill the sulcus from the ball of the foot to the pulp of the toes.

E, a square of moleskin is laid adhesive side up over the base of the second, third, and fourth toes. The ends of the straps are pulled across the moleskin (being certain that they are kept well proximal to the joints of the toes).

F, if dorsal force is needed, a dorsal ram of adhesive felt can be added dorsally. If a retainer for the hallux is needed, the dorsal ram is extended between the first and second toes.

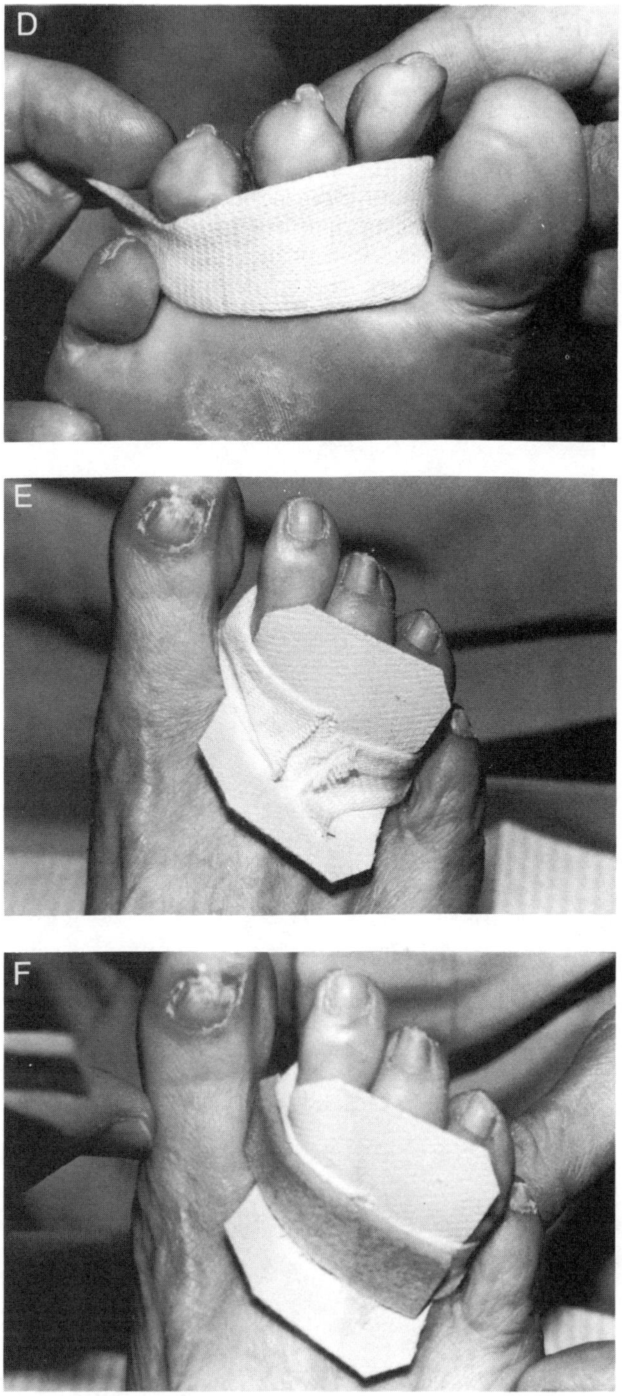

FIG 27–2 (cont.).
G, the proximal edge of moleskin is folded forward. It is important that the distal edge of the moleskin be folded in last. This prevents the stocking from rolling up the edge of the moleskin as it is pulled onto the foot.

H, a completed retainer in place includes a plantar ram that fills the sulcus; a dorsal ram across the second, third, and fourth toes; and a hallux ram to support the hallux position. The retainer can be worn as is but does not hold its shape as well as when latex is applied.

I, liquid ammonia-based latex is painted on the entire outer surface of the retainer. Usually two coats of latex are desirable.

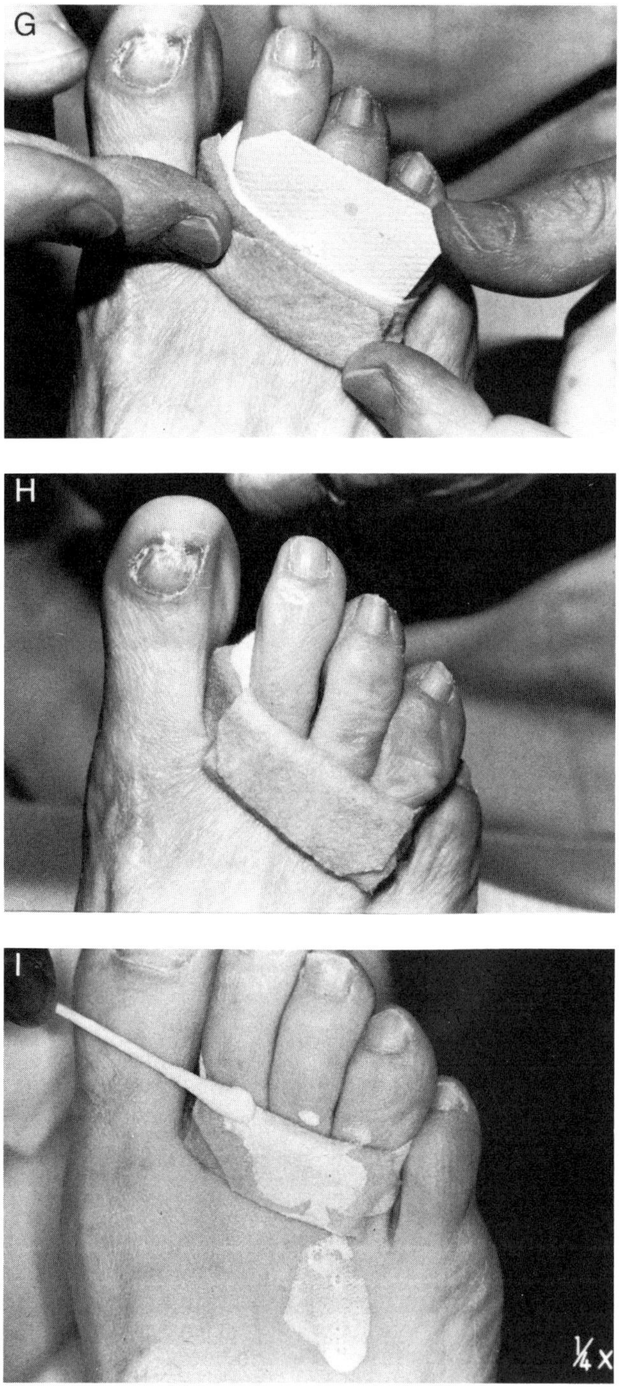

Traction slings are among the most useful of removable forefoot retainers. They are useful in maintaining the alignment of the lesser toes following surgical correction. Traction slings are also useful in a prophylactic sense to relieve heloma molle between the great toe and second toe. They are useful in relieving dorsal and distal heloma and are especially helpful in relieving metatarsalgia beneath the central three metatarsals.

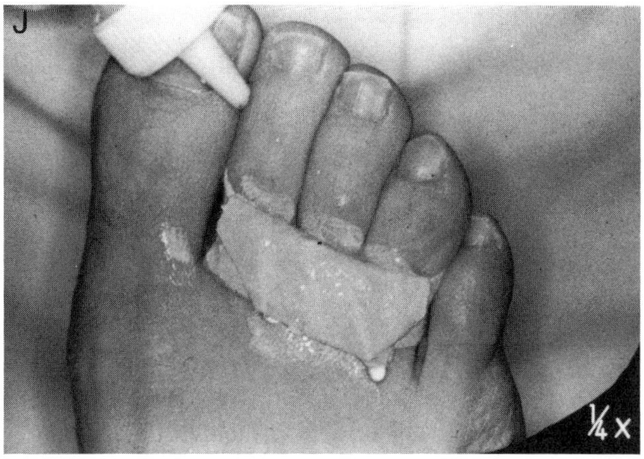

FIG 27–2 (cont.).
J, after each coat of latex, a catalyst (equal parts white vinegar and water) is sprayed or sprinkled on the latex to cause instant curing. Any latex that contacts the skin can simply be peeled away once hardened.

POLYURETHANE RETAINERS

Polyurethane molds are custom-molded retainers for the forefoot. They are easily and quickly made provided that one has an established kit containing all the necessary materials for preparing the molds. A number of supplies and materials are needed. Having them readily available greatly facilitates the preparation of polyurethane molds. Supplies needed are listed in Fig 27–3.

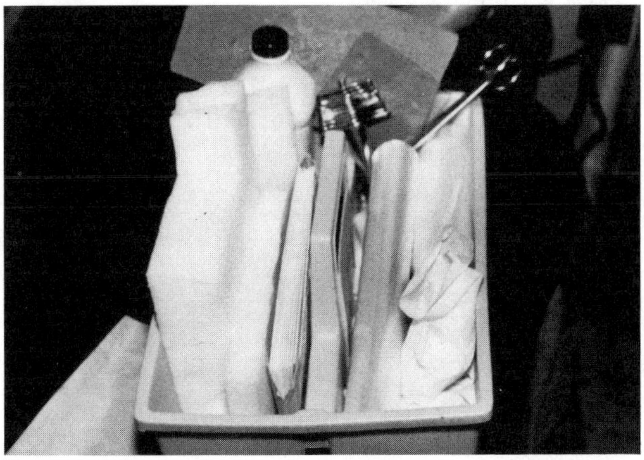

FIG 27–3.
Supplies for polyurethane molds are listed below:
- One-inch polyurethane
- Two-inch polyurethane
- Set of quality punches
- Compression template
- Punch board
- Pair of long-blade straight scissors (serrated)
- Liquid Vultex solution
- Plastic-backed paper towels
- Plastic disposable gloves
- Small-size plastic bags
- Medium-size plastic bags
- Large-size plastic bags
- Plastic clear tape, 1 in.
- Shoe horn
- Instruction sheets

Slit-Crest Retainer

The slit-crest retainer is so named because it uses an aperture for the second toe and one for the fourth toe with a slit connecting the two. It is probably the easiest to prepare and the easiest to wear (Fig 27–4, A–E).

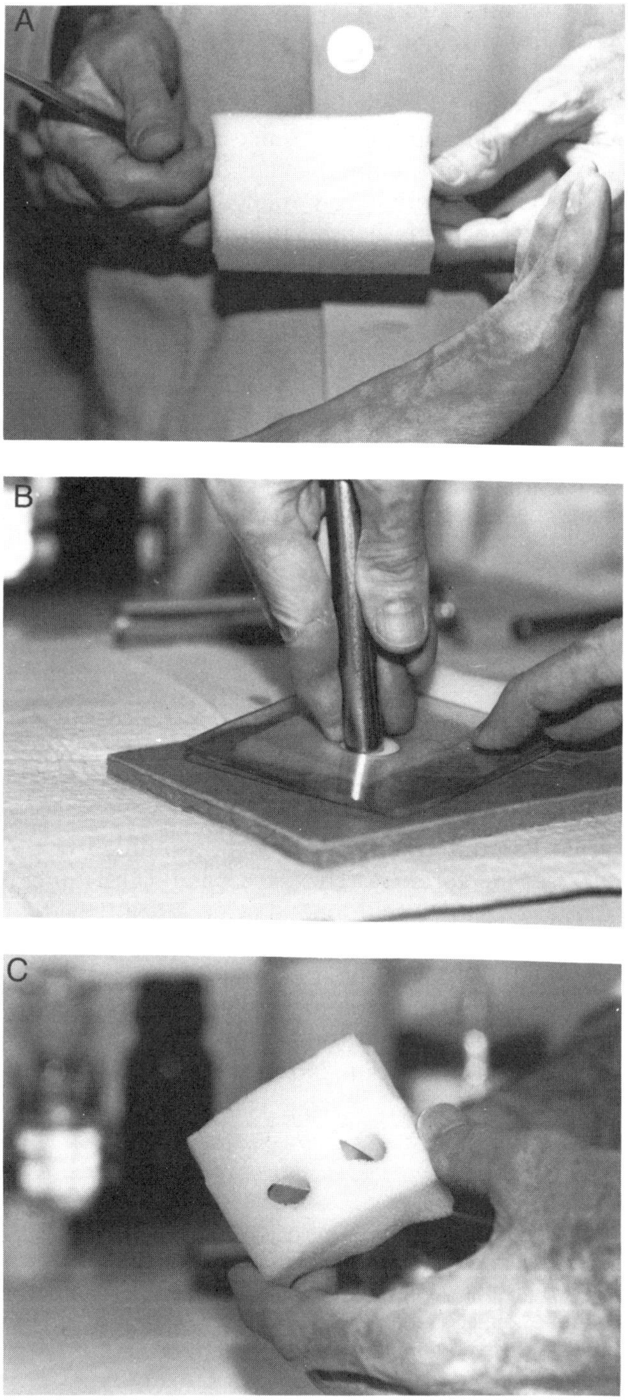

FIG 27–4.
A, a block of urethane is selected. A 2-in. thickness is used if one wishes to mold out to the end of the toes. One inch is adequate if the mold is to occupy minimum space in the shoe.

B, a polyurethane block is placed on the punch board and compressed with an acrylic template with a central aperture. The template allows compression of the urethane to make it easier to cut with the punches.

C, holes are punched for the second and fourth toes, just slightly closer together than the toes measure. Long, straight-blade scissors are used to slit the urethane between the two apertures.

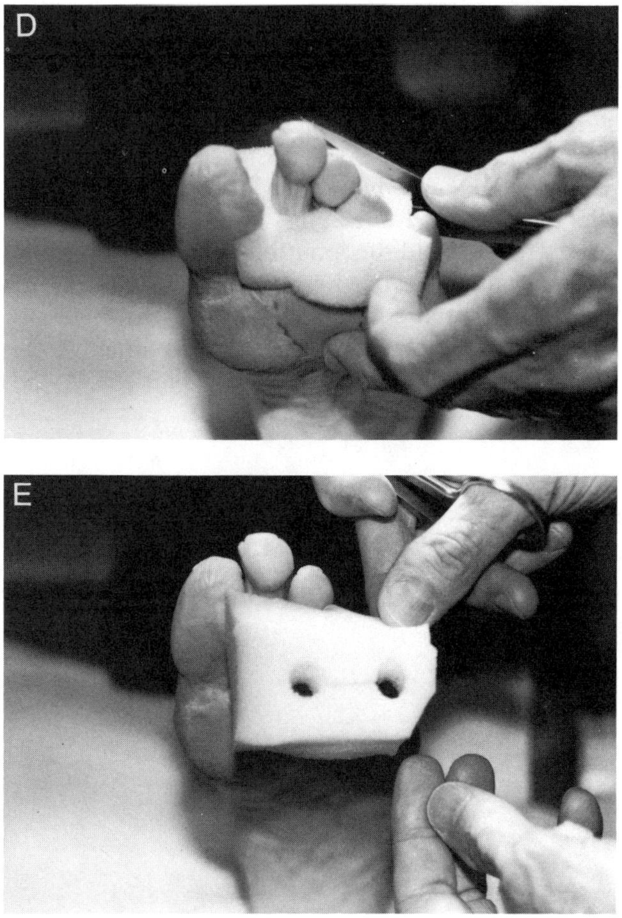

FIG 27–4 (cont.).
D, the slit-crest retainer is slipped around the three middle toes and sculptured with the straight scissors. It is usually wise to thin the urethane under the fourth toe to avoid excess pressure.

E, the sculptured slit-crest retainer is now ready to impregnate with Vultex.

Hallux-Dorsal-Plantar Flap Retainer

The hallux mold with dorsal or plantar or dorsal and plantar flaps is useful in relieving chronic synovitis or sesamoiditis at the first metatarsophalangeal joint. It is even more useful for dissipating edema. We have seen nothing to equal its effectiveness in speeding the elimination of edema. It should be pointed out that urethane molds cannot be used until the patient has returned to closed shoes since the entire process is dependent on pressure to mold the retainer to the foot and to the shape of the shoe (Fig 27–5, A–H).

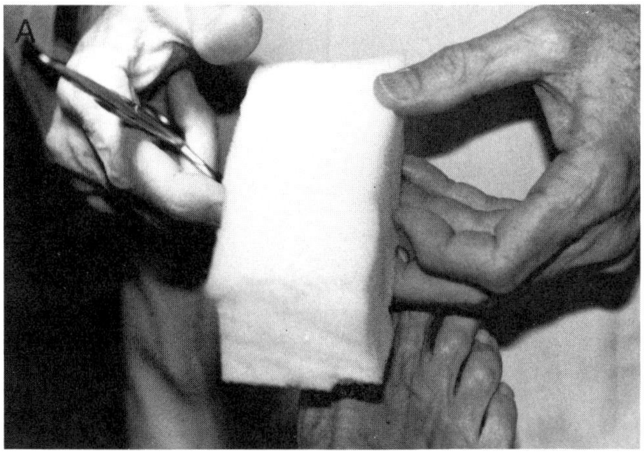

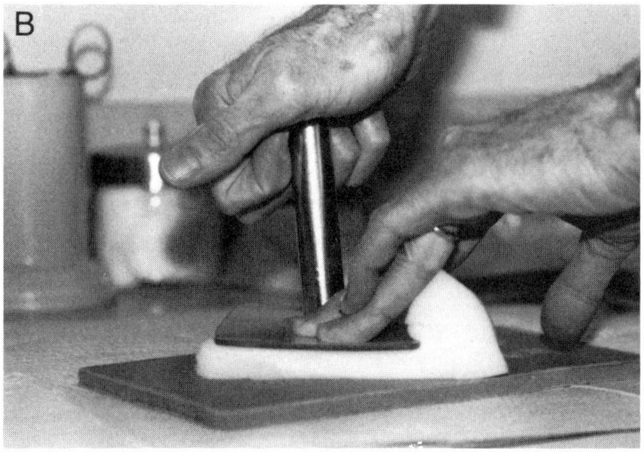

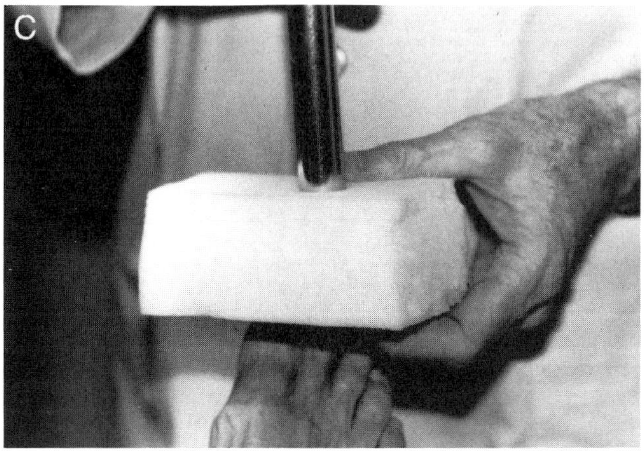

FIG 27–5.
A, a block of 2-in. polyurethane foam is selected.

B, the foam is compressed against the punch board while an aperture is punched for the hallux. Often the largest punch may be smaller than the hallux. In such cases a second overlapping or eccentric hole is punched to slightly enlarge the aperture.

C, the punch is left in place here simply to demonstrate the relationship of the aperture to the foam block.

FIG 27–5 (cont.).
D, flaps are constructed by cutting slits parallel to the aperture that will be occupied by the great toe. Two such slits are made, one to initiate the plantar flap and one for the dorsal flap.

E, two additional cuts are made to intersect with the first cuts. This results in thinning the dorsal and plantar flaps, usually to a ½-in. thickness. Excessively thick flaps are a mistake and serve no useful purpose.

F, roughly shaped hallux retainer with dorsal and plantar flaps.

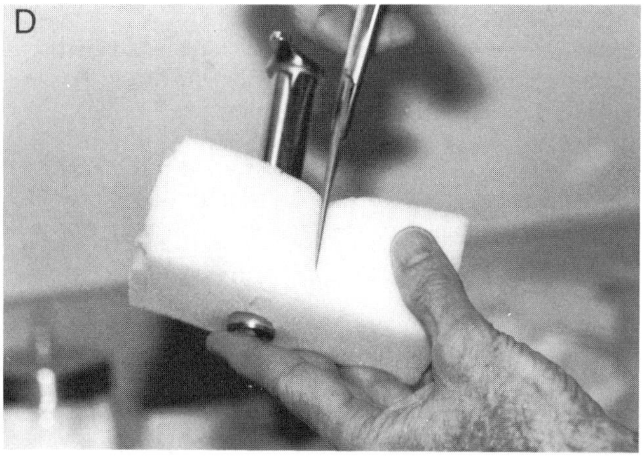

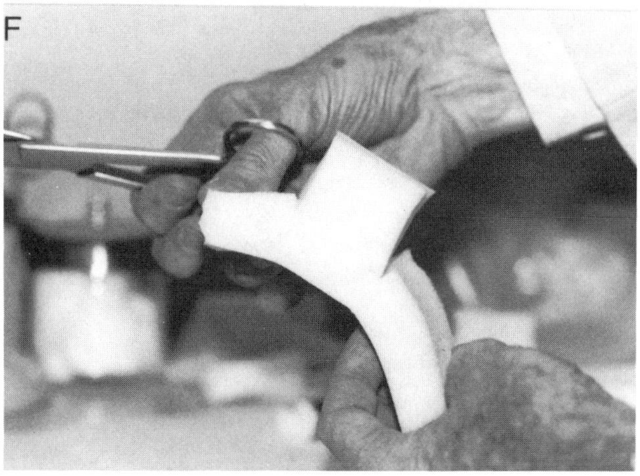

FIG 27–5 (cont.).
G, the retainer is further sculptured and flaps shaped and thinned as desired. The side of the mold that abuts the second toe is scooped out to contour to the toe.

H, the retainer is slipped on the toe, and the dorsal and plantar flaps are held in place against the foot while final sculpturing is completed. The retainer is now ready for Vultex impregnation and molding.

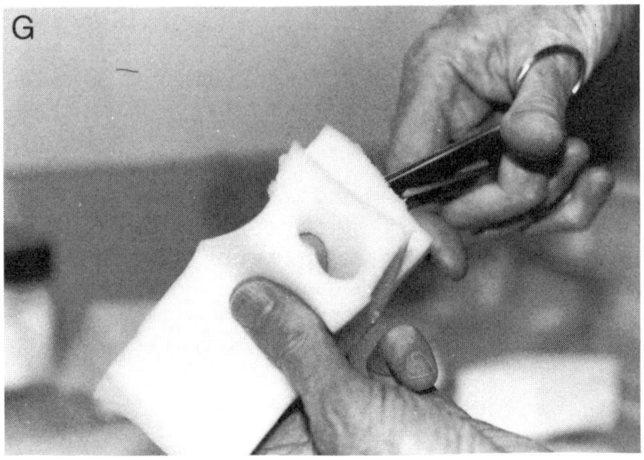

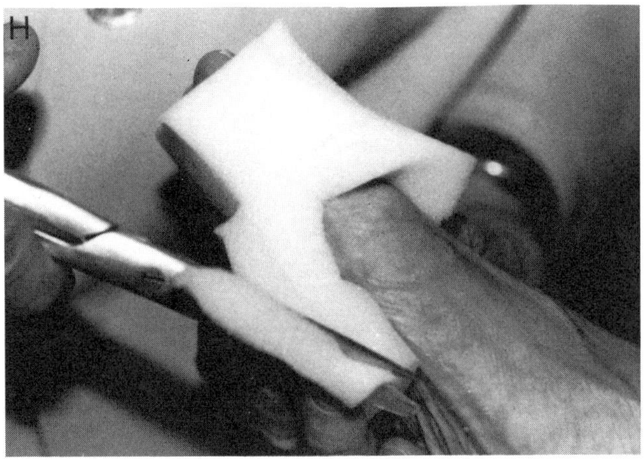

Molding of the Retainer

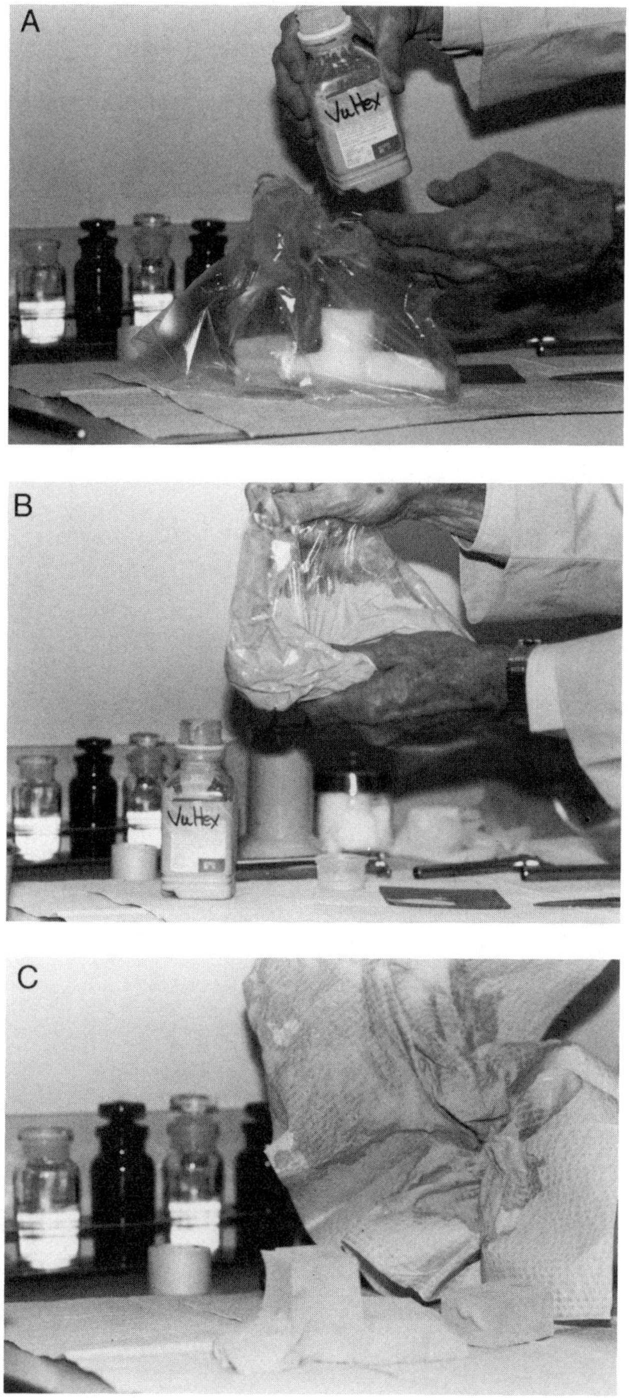

FIG 27–6.
A, the sculptured retainers are placed in a large plastic baggie and a liberal amount of Vultex poured into the bag.

B, the top of the baggie is held closed, and the liquid is massaged into the polyurethane by repeatedly compressing the retainer. It must be worked in thoroughly so that every cell in the urethane is soaked with Vultex.

C, the impregnated retainers are poured out onto a bed of paper toweling and blotted well. The more Vultex that is blotted out of the retainer, the softer it will be. The less Vultex blotted out, the firmer the retainer.

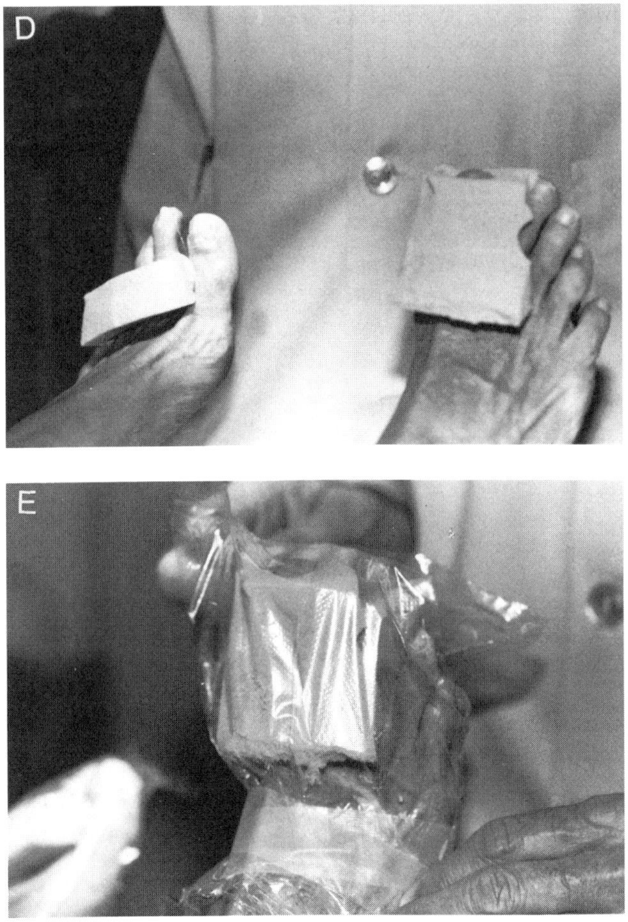

FIG 27–6 (cont.).
D, the retainers are slipped in place on the toes.

E, a small plastic bag is slipped over the forefoot and taped in place. It must not be tight over the ends of the toes. All air should be expressed from the plastic bag slowly. A larger plastic bag is applied to cover the entire foot and ankle. This latter plastic bag is essential in case of rupture of the first. There is no known solvent to remove Vultex from shoe linings or stockings.

FIG 27–6 (cont.).
F, a stocking is applied over the second plastic bag.

G, a shoe horn is used to assist sliding the foot into the shoe. If the shoe is snug, put a third plastic bag over the sock and the foot will easily slide into the shoe. This third plastic bag can be removed after 30 minutes when the mold will have reduced by half to two-thirds in size.

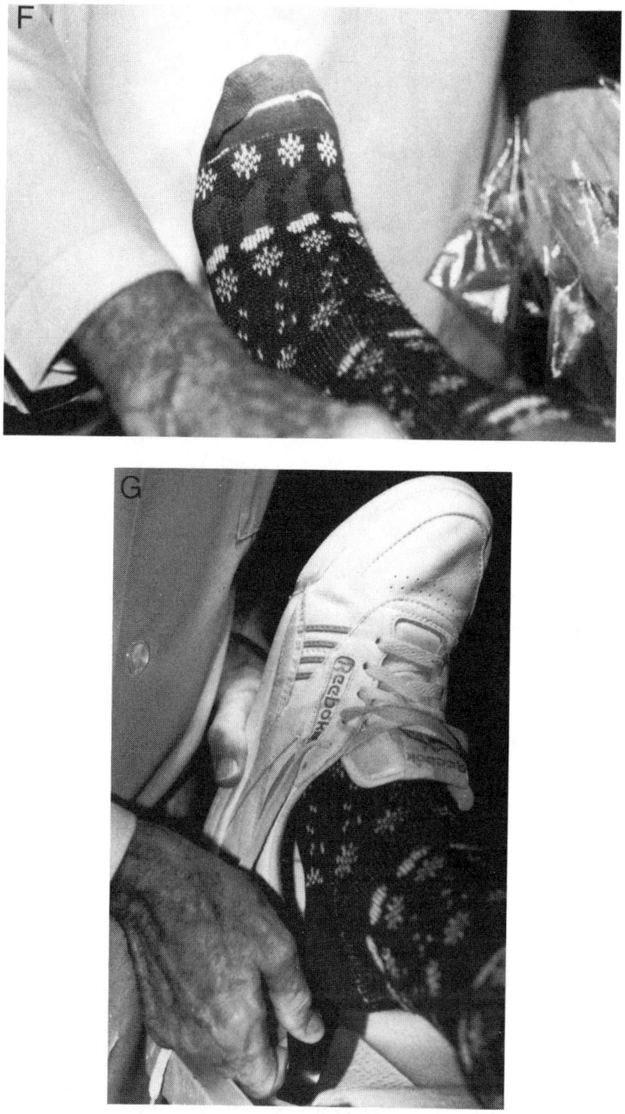

Finishing the Retainer

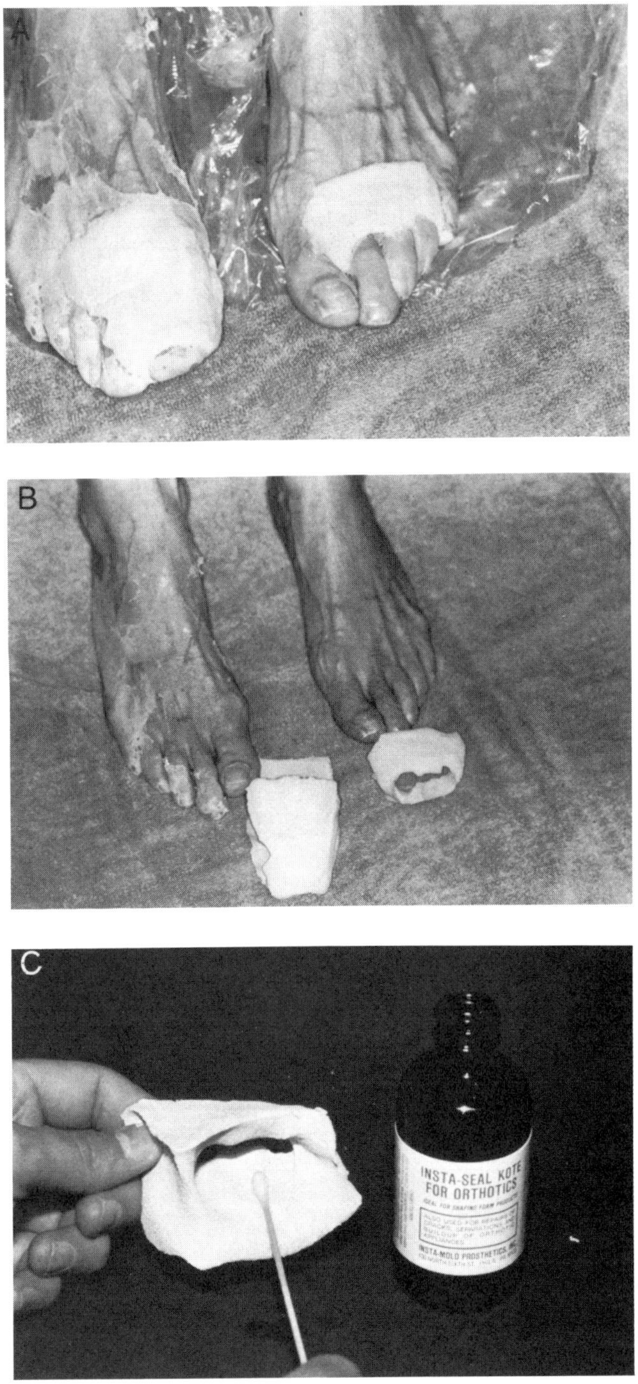

FIG 27–7.
A, retainers are worn until bedtime or a minimum of 6 hours. By that time the molding is secure. The plastic bags are removed, and excess Vultex can be peeled from the skin.

B, the patient returns to the office a day or two later, and the retainers are trimmed of any rough edges.

C, the retainer is sealed with a silicone liquid suspension. Two or three coats are needed to protect, strengthen, and add to the hygienic qualities.

Sculpturing of the retainer is an art in itself. For example, one may make a slit crest thicker on top if toes need to be held downward, or one may make the plantar crest wider or thicker if more metatarsal support is needed. The retainer can be made thicker at the first digital interspace if support is needed for the hallux. A little thought in the design of the retainer can make a world of difference in how it functions.

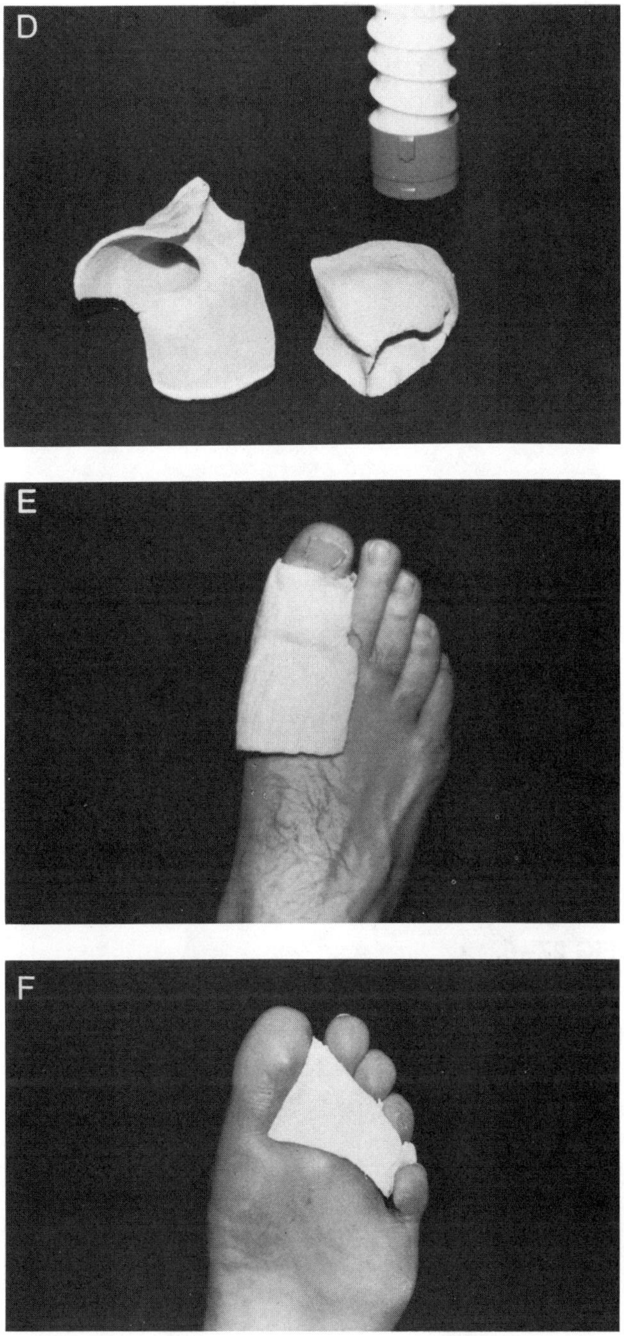

FIG 27–7 (cont.).
D, silicone sealant can be dried quickly under an air blower. If a blower is not available, it will require an hour or more to dry.

E, completed hallux-dorsal-plantar flap retainer.

F, completed slit crest.

OTHER SPECIAL RETAINERS

Dozens of variations are possible for digital and forefoot retainers. Basic materials plus a good imagination make possible almost unlimited variations. An example is seen in the 2+ plantar flap.

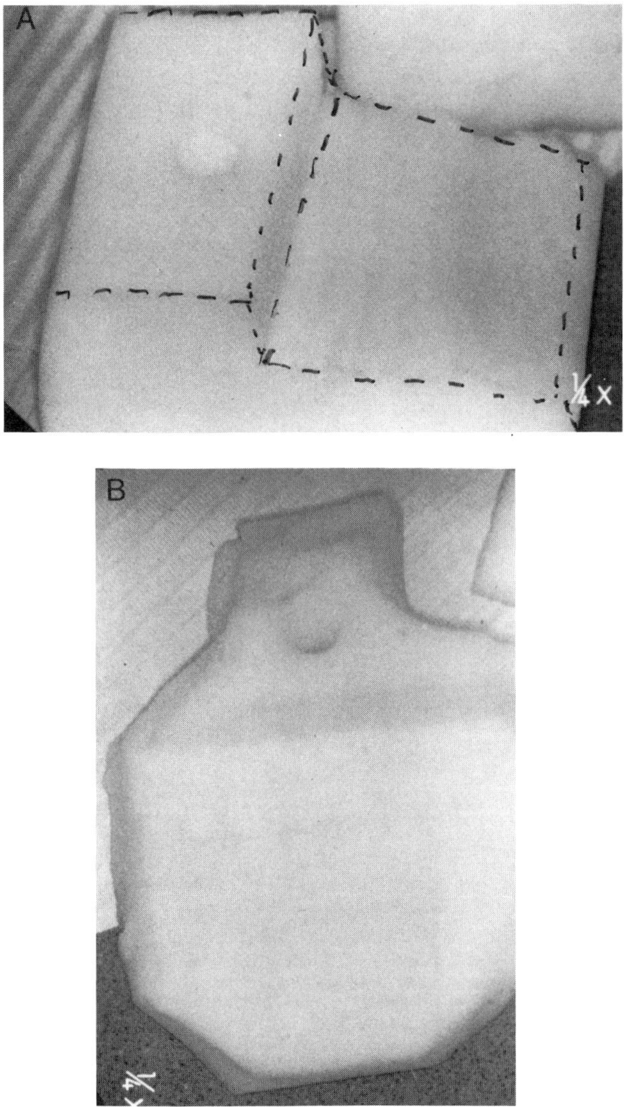

FIG 27–8.
A, a block of 2-in. polyurethane is selected, an aperture cut for the second toe, and a plantar flap designed.

B, the retainer is sculptured to eliminate excess bulk between toes and plantar to the toe.

FIG 27–8 (cont.).
C, the retainer is impregnated with Vultex, blotted, and placed on the second toe.

D, dorsal view of the retainer after it is molded.

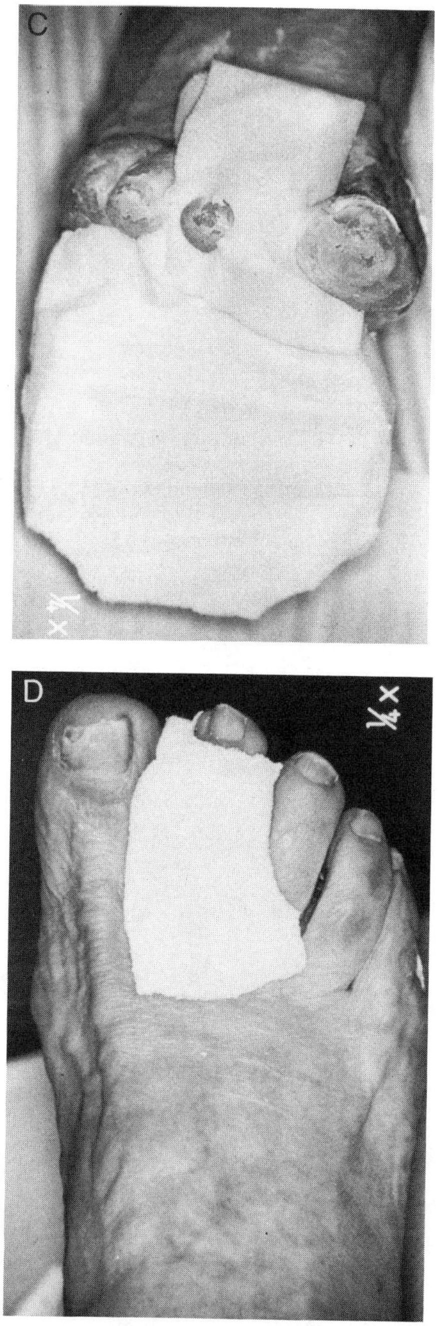

The polyurethane retainer is a highly versatile device. Special appreciation is herewith expressed to Dr. Alan Whitney, the originator of the urethane mold.

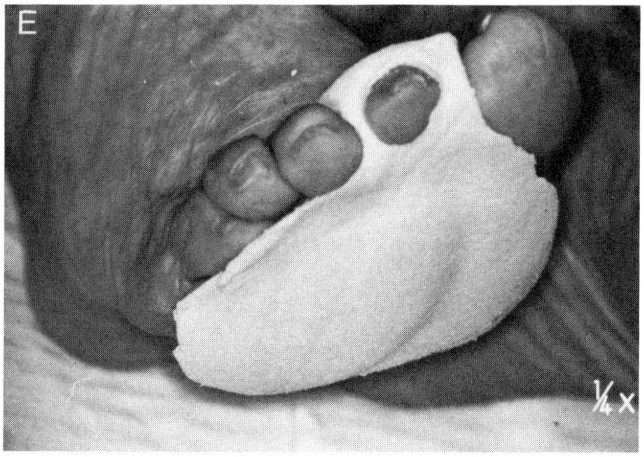

FIG 27–8 (cont.).
E, plantar view of the retainer after it is molded.

28

Postoperative Bandaging

E. Dalton McGlamry, D.P.M.

I. Specific Types of Postoperative Bandages
   A. Bandaging After Nail Surgery
   B. Bandaging After Fifth-Toe Arthroplasty
   C. Fifth-Toe Edema Cast
   D. Bandaging Following Hallux Valgus Surgery
   E. Bandaging Following Hallux Valgus and Multiple Toe Surgeries
II. Control of Edema
   A. The Elastic Bandage
   B. Venous Heart
   C. Tubular Elastic
III. Summary

Postoperative bandaging serves many specific functions. Its most important functions include protection of the surgical area, maintenance of alignment, control of edema, and control of hemorrhage.

While it is important to learn how to properly apply bandages, it is often just as important to learn how to position the body part for bandaging. For example, most bandages that incorporate the ankle are applied with the ankle at a 90-degree angle. If the ankle is not maintained in this position when bandaging, one will often find that the bandage will bind at the front of the ankle when weight bearing begins.

Most postoperative bandages are applied on top of an appropriate dressing. The dressing may be gauze squares or other appropriate material. Adequate dressing should be in place to softly pad the wound before beginning application of the bandage.

In this chapter, some of the more commonly used bandages will be reviewed. If one becomes thoroughly familiar with these bandaging techniques, the many other types of bandages that are used should be easily understood and used.

SPECIFIC TYPES OF POSTOPERATIVE BANDAGES

Bandaging After Nail Surgery

This is a simple and compact bandage that can be used following nail surgery. It can fit easily into a closed shoe and uses tube gauze to bandage or hold 2 × 2-in. gauze to the surgical area (Fig 28–1, A–E).

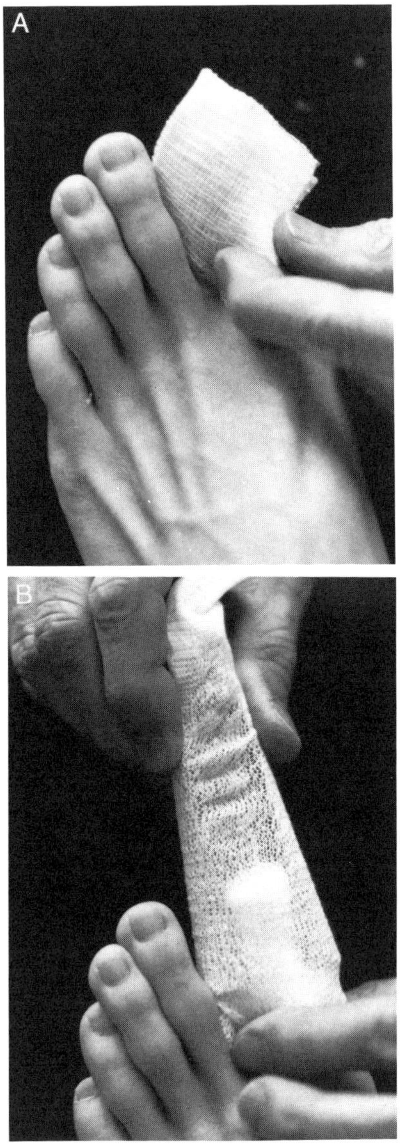

FIG 28–1.
A, 2 × 2-in. gauze pads cover the surgical area.

B, no. 2 tube gauze is loaded onto a digital applicator and applied over the 2 × 2-in. pads. The tip of the tube gauze is grasped by the fingertips.

FIG 28–1 (cont.).
C, the applicator is stretched distally, and a half twist is made in the gauze.

D, the tube gauze is folded back upon itself. A section of 1-in.-wide tape is scooped in the center to fit into the web area.

E, tape is laid lightly around the base of the bandage to adhere to both bandage and skin in order to provide a firm anchor.

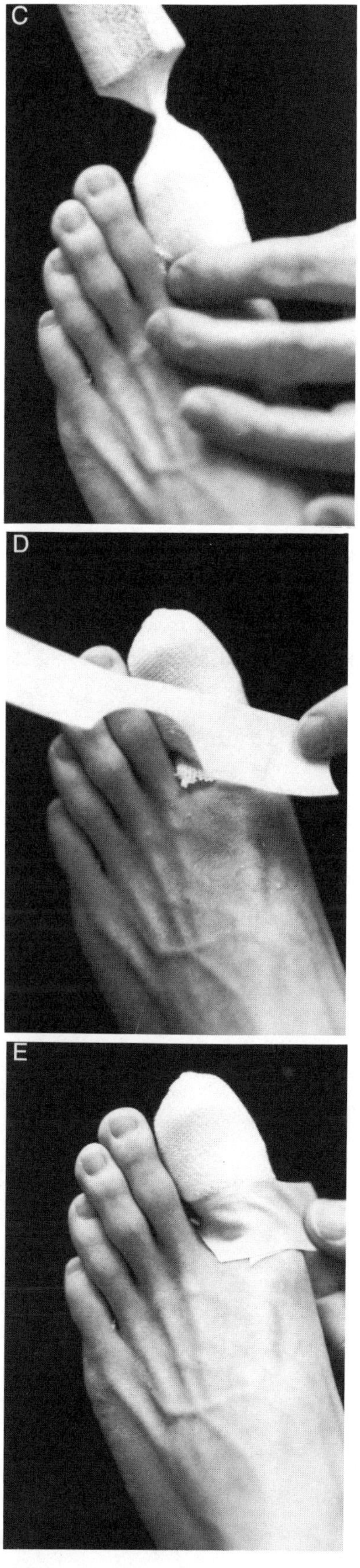

Bandaging After Fifth-Toe Arthroplasty

Following fifth-toe arthroplasty the toe requires good padding, moderate compression, and secure splinting. All are easily accomplished with appropriate dressing and bandaging (Fig 28–2, A–D).

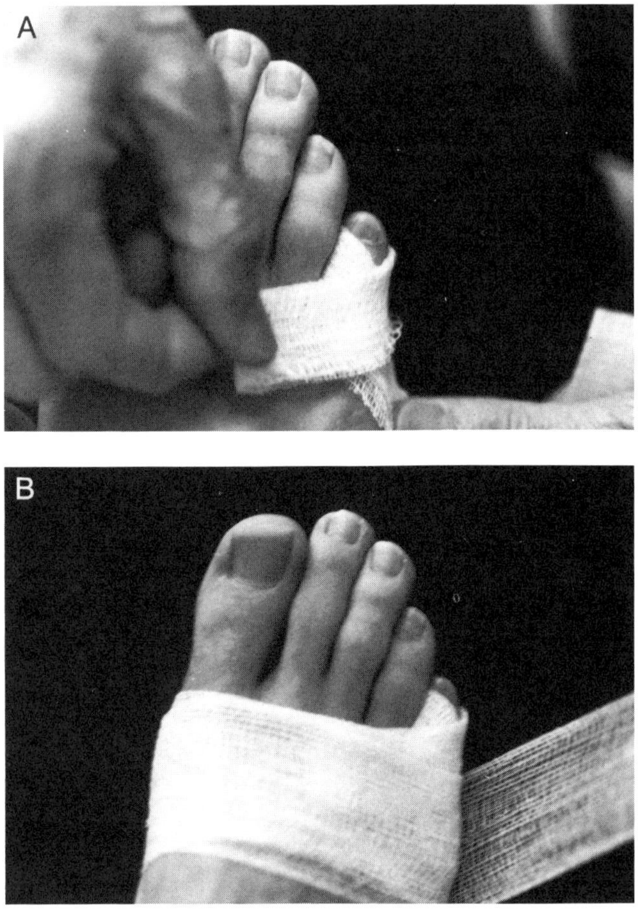

FIG 28–2.

A, a 2 × 2-in. gauze pad has been opened to 2 × 6-in., folded longitudinally, and looped around the fifth toe and crossed over the top.

B, a 2-in. elasticized gauze (Kling) bandage wraps the forefoot and anchors the dressing in place. Additional layers of 2 × 2-in. pads may be added over the toe to provide additional padding as the bandage progresses.

FIG 28–2 (cont.).
C, the Kling bandage continues in a figure-of-8 configuration. Here the fifth toe is secured to the fourth toe to provide additional splinting.

D, the second and third toes are subsequently incorporated in the bandage to provide additional stability to the fifth toe. The added padding and bandaging on the fifth toe helps to minimize swelling and provide added comfort.

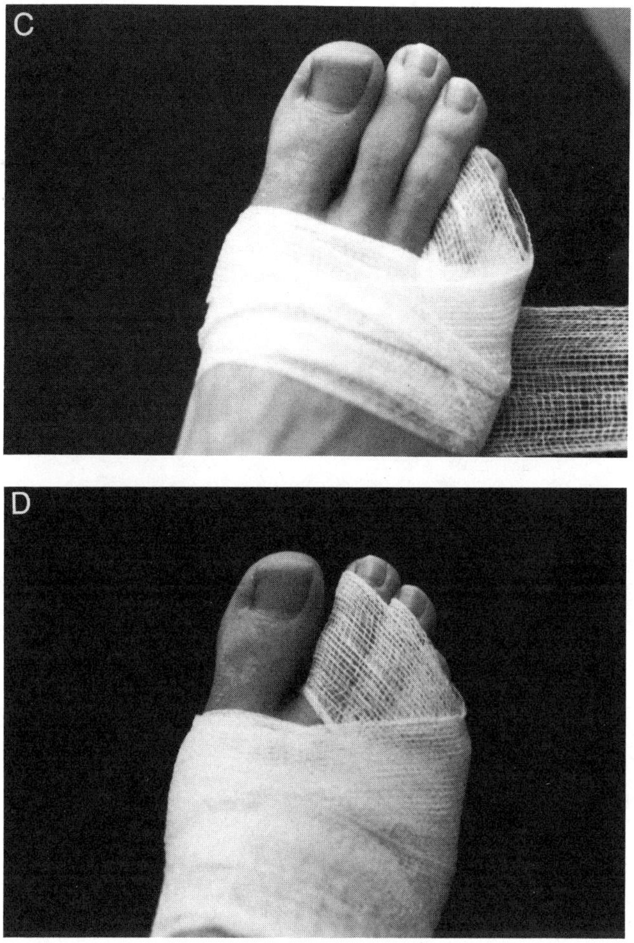

Fifth-Toe Edema Cast

Following fifth-toe surgery, residual edema is often a source of continued discomfort to the patient. A simple solution to the problem is the application of an Elastoplast digital cast (Fig 28–3, A–C).

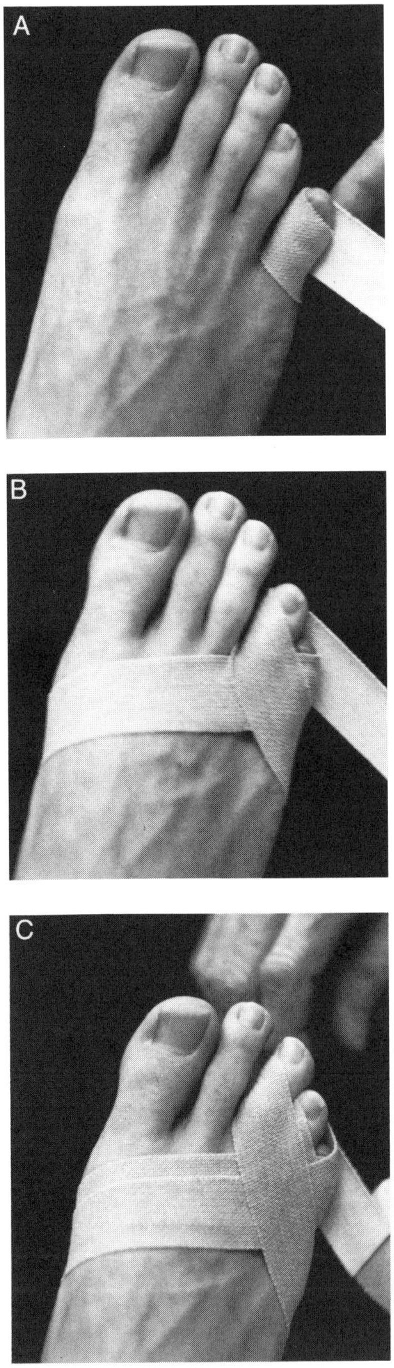

FIG 28–3.
A, 1-in. Elastoplast tape is applied around the fifth toe just snugly enough to fit well. It does not need to be tight.

B, the Elastoplast strip continues around the forefoot and then around the fourth toe in a figure-of-8 configuration.

C, finally the third toe is incorporated in the bandage. The patient should wear a sock or stocking over the bandage day and night to prevent rolling. The bandage can be changed weekly for a period of 2 or 3 weeks until the edema dissipates.

Bandaging Following Hallux Valgus Surgery

Bandaging following hallux valgus surgery must provide sufficient padding and compression to control edema and minimize hemorrhage. It must splint the position of the toe so as to support the corrected alignment. It must be flexible enough to allow early range-of-motion exercises (Fig 28–4, A–G).

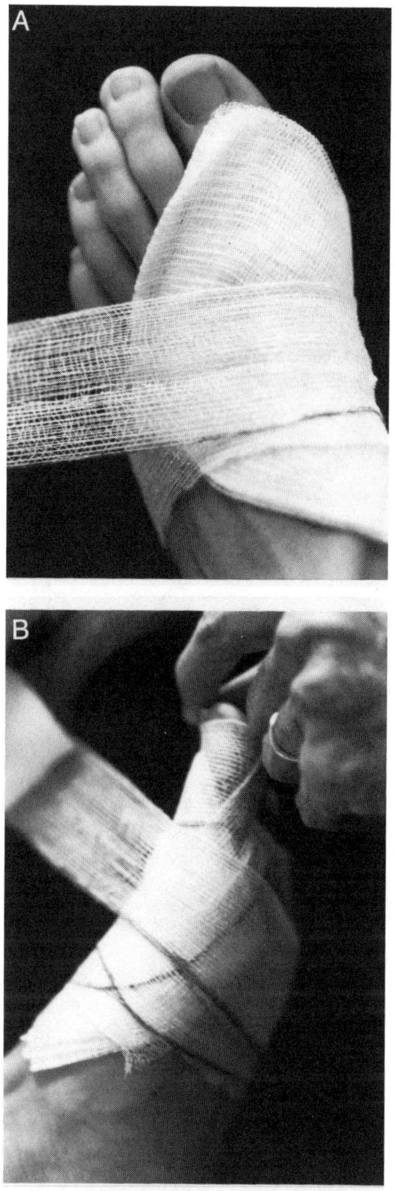

FIG 28–4.
A, 4 × 4-in gauze pads anchored by 2-in. Kling bandaging.

B, a figure-of-8 configuration with a Kling bandage encircles the forefoot.

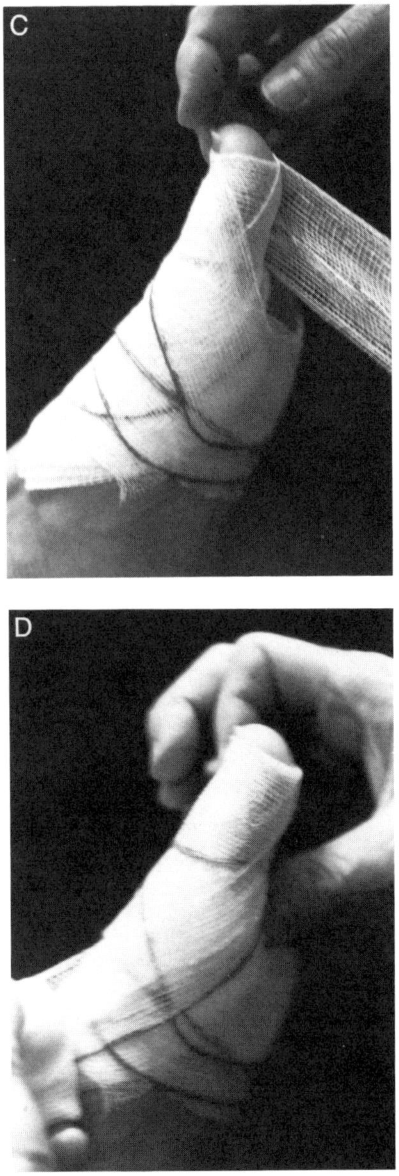

FIG 28–4 (cont.).
C, the toe is then circled twice with Kling bandage before again circling the forefoot. All bandage is applied while the ankle is held dorsiflexed and the first metatarsal bone is supported.

D, bringing the bandage plantarly under the metatarsal head prevents the toe from being pulled upward by the bandage.

FIG 28–4 (cont.).
E, completed figure-of-8 hallux valgus bandage.

F, tube gauze covers the forefoot, and a half twist is applied distal to the toes.

G, tube gauze folded to cover the foot and ankle and tape strip anchors above the ankle. Tube gauze will prevent the bandage from becoming frayed or rolled for several weeks.

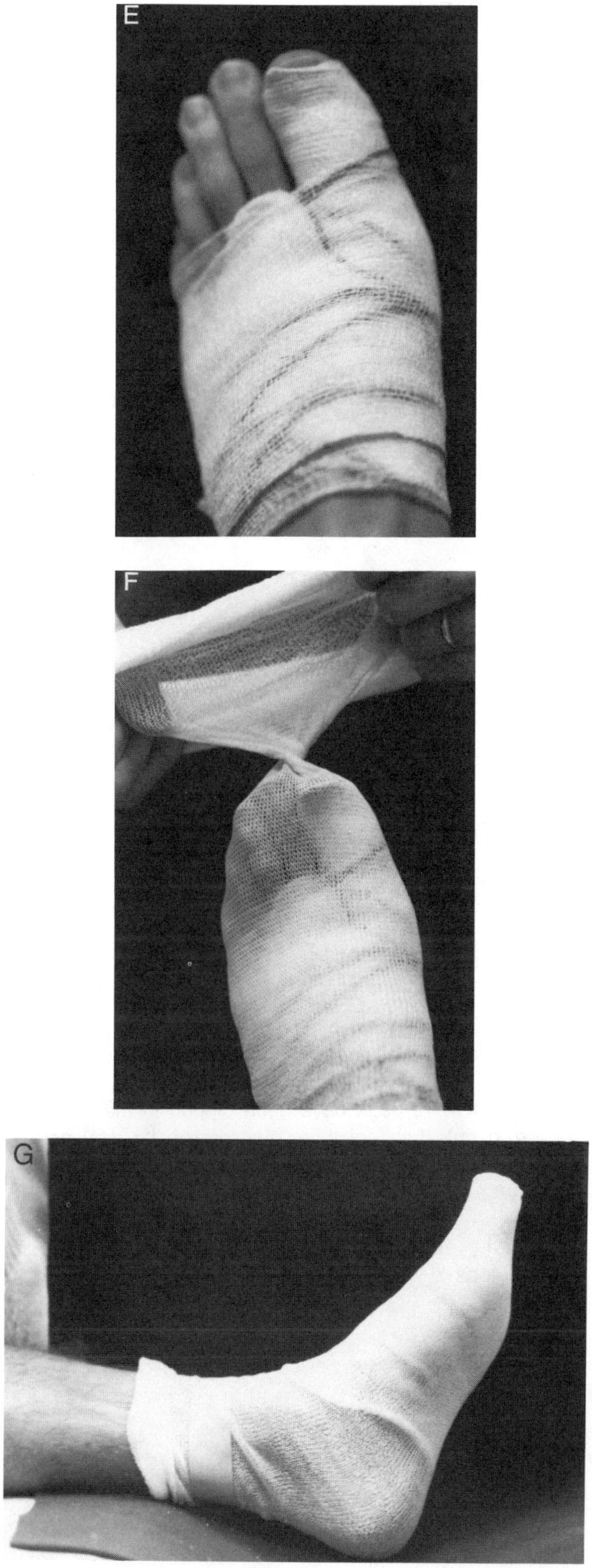

Bandaging Following Hallux Valgus and Multiple Toe Surgeries

Bandaging of the forefoot following surgery on multiple toes can be difficult. Bandaging can be accomplished rapidly by having the dressing and bandaging materials ready and having a plan for their rapid application. The foot should be supported and the ankle dorsiflexed to nearly a right angle (Fig 28–5, A–H).

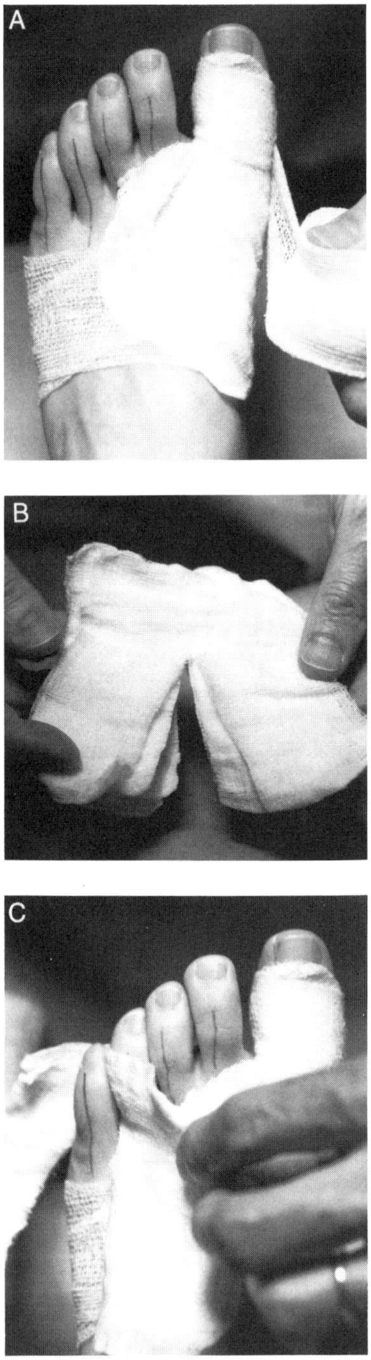

FIG 28–5.
A, hallux valgus dressing and bandaging in place.

B, four 4 × 4-in. pads have been dipped in sterile saline, squeezed out, then cut three quarters of the way across. These will be used to make a sandwich of each of the four lesser toes.

C, a slit 4 × 4-in. gauze pad is slipped between the fourth and fifth toes.

FIG 28–5 (cont.).
D, the gauze pad is folded top and bottom around the fifth toe. An assistant holds the pad in place.

E, a second gauze pad is slipped between the third and fourth toes and folded over top and bottom as with first 4 × 4-in. pad.

F, additional slit 4 × 4-in. gauze pads are placed between the second and third toes and between the first and second toes.

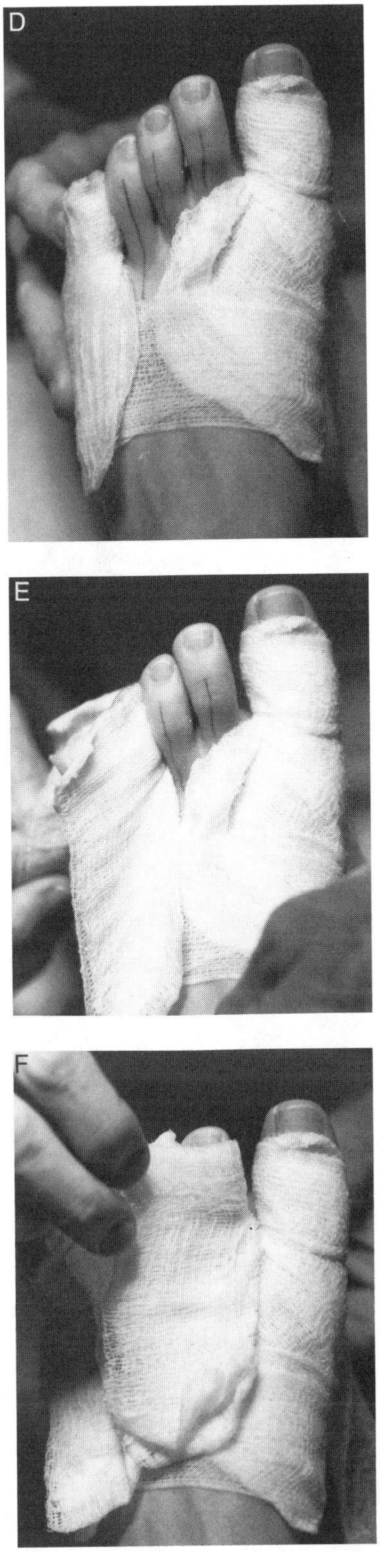

FIG 28–5 (cont.).
G, a Kling bandage anchors the four slit 4 × 4-in. pads in position.

H, completed bandage.

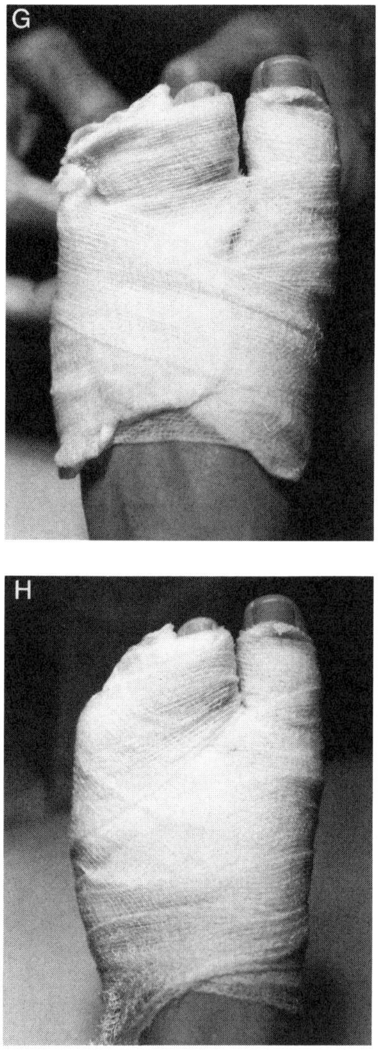

CONTROL OF EDEMA

Control of swelling is desirable following all types of surgery on the extremities. When multiple procedures are performed, control of edema is especially vital to a rapid and comfortable recovery. The surgical bandage can be applied with sufficient support to control swelling. But when the surgical bandage is removed, swelling often increases unless some support is provided during an early return to activities.

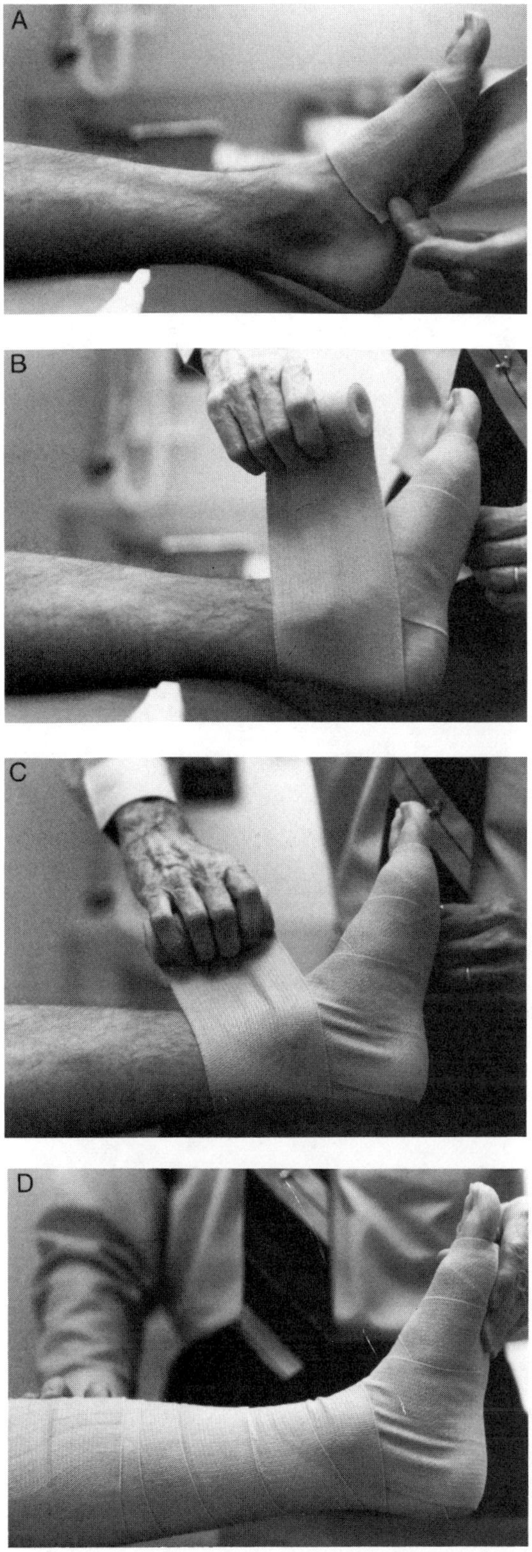

The Elastic Bandage

FIG 28–6.
A, elastic wrap may be begun with an anchor turn at the arch level.

B, the second and third turns may encircle the forefoot and metatarsophalangeal joint area to control forefoot edema. The bandage then encircles the heel and returns to the arch and rearfoot area. This provides a figure-of-8 configuration and is always applied with the ankle dorsiflexed to nearly a right angle.

C, after enclosing the heel, the bandage continues up the leg to the desired level. The bandage should be slightly more snug on the foot and looser as it progresses up the leg.

D, the completed bandage should be covered with a sock, stocking, or tube gauze to prevent slippage.

Venous Heart

Concentrated compression is often needed within a bandage. The use of a block of soft polyurethane foam can provide that concentrated pressure. Such pressure can often prevent thick scars or can serve to remove heavy swelling from a surgical site. The same technique is used in treating leg ulcers that are due to stasis (Fig 28–7, A–C).

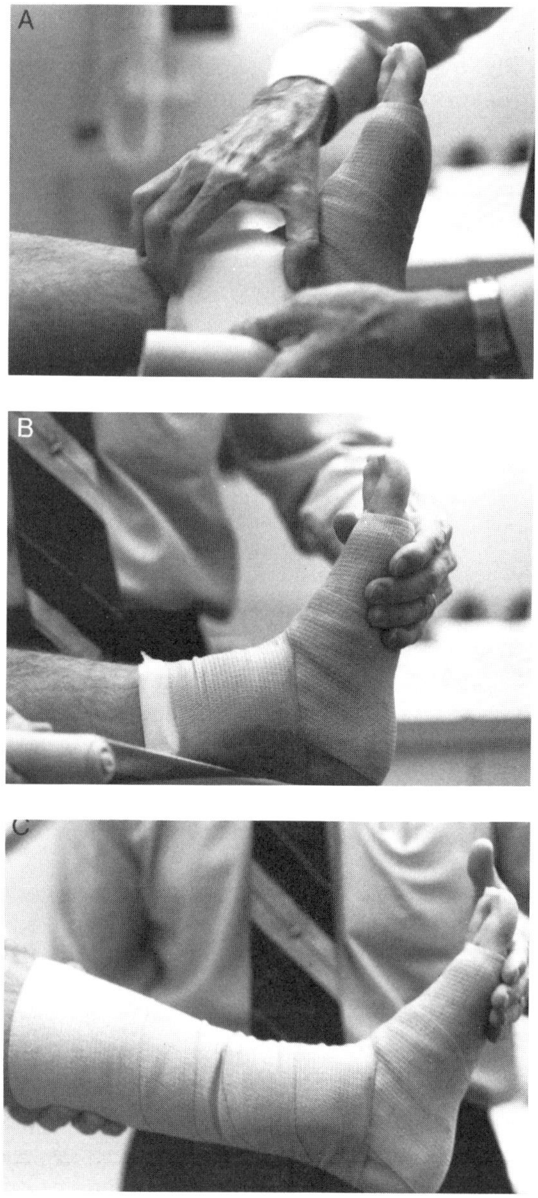

FIG 28–7.
A, the bandage is anchored well and appropriate gauze padding applied. This provides a very concentrated pressure to the site.

B, a venous heart is incorporated with progressive turns of the bandage.

C, completed bandage in place.

Tubular Elastic

Elastic supportive sleeve material is available in various sizes. While it is easy and convenient to use, one needs to be aware of its shortcomings. For example, the bandage is the same size from one end to the other, yet the foot's largest circumference is at the level of the heel and ankle. Such a bandage is therefore tightest at the ankle. This can result in a significant increase in swelling of the forefoot. To offset this problem one uses two thicknesses on the forefoot and only one thickness at the heel and ankle level (Fig 28–8, A and B).

SUMMARY

Appropriate bandaging can contribute greatly to the successful outcome of surgery. Such bandages are important in maintaining alignment, protecting the sterile environment, controlling hemorrhage, and preventing or controlling swelling. A thorough understanding of bandaging and of positioning of the part for bandaging is an important part of the knowledge of all who treat the foot.

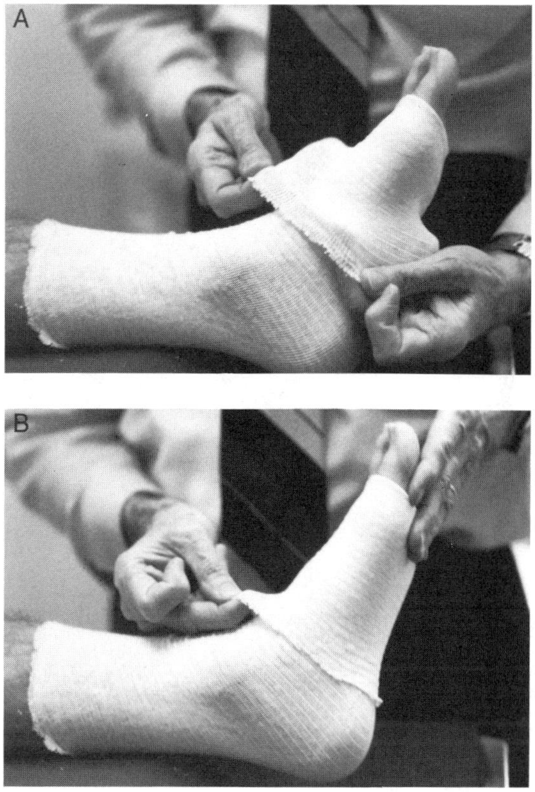

FIG 28–8.
A, Tubigrip applied to the foot and ankle. The forefoot is covered with a second fold.

B, Tubigrip trimmed to be certain that a double thickness does not cover the heel or ankle.

29

Neutral Position Casting

Stuart J. Ruch, D.P.M.

While a good laboratory is very important, the negative cast coming into the laboratory is *the most* important part of a functional orthotic device. The most complete and extensive biomechanical examination is of little or no value to the patient if the findings of this examination are not reflected in the models of the patient's feet. For example, if the doctor's examination of the patient's foot reveals a 5-degree varus relationship of the forefoot to the rearfoot on the frontal plane and the model of the patient's foot reflects a 5-degree valgus relationship of these two components of the foot, then an orthotic device fabricated over the model would not be effective in the treatment of this individual. It is therefore obvious that an exact reproduction or model of a patient's foot is mandatory for positive results in biomechanical therapy.

FUNCTION OF ORTHOSES

Orthotic devices are used to treat almost everything seen in the practice of podiatry. They are used to treat frontal-, sagittal-, and transverse-plane problems, metatarsal and heel pain, and sports-related problems and injuries. In many cases, the podiatrist can control the symptoms associated with these conditions with the use of an orthotic device. However, correction of a deformity is not to be expected with orthotic use alone.

Control of abnormal pronation is probably the one entity for which an orthotic device is used most often. Redirection of gravitational forces through the foot to promote normal development is another primary use of orthotics. The most frequent abuse of orthotic devices is improper control as a result of poor casting technique.

Root and associates[1] have devised a method of neutral position casting that produces good results if the suggested steps are observed and followed during the procedure. A neutral position cast is one in which the anatomic relationship of the forefoot relative to the rearfoot is captured accurately by elimination of altering forces. Eliminating altering forces means that the subtalar joint is in its neutral position and the midtarsal joint is in its locked position. The subtalar joint is in its neutral position when it is neither pronated nor supinated. The midtarsal joint is in its locked position when a dorsiflexory force is applied against the fourth and fifth metatarsals so that only the forefoot is fully pronated at the midtarsal joint. There are four important steps in properly preparing the patient for a neutral position cast. The first two should be accomplished before applying the plaster.

TECHNIQUE FOR NEUTRAL POSITION CASTING

Placement of the Patient

Different authorities profess that the patient be in a prone, supine, or sitting position for casting. It is imperative that the patient completely relax during the casting procedure. Any muscle activity can alter the negative cast. Horizontal placement allows the patient to completely relax. Although the patient can totally relax in a prone position, it is impossible to observe and eliminate movements of the leg. Therefore, it is recommended that the patient be placed in a supine attitude for casting.

Placement of the Leg

The knee joint should be extended, and the doctor or assistant must push against the plantar surface of the forefoot while observing the patella. The kneecap should not move medially or laterally. If there is medial movement or internal rotation while dorsiflexing the foot, the subtalar joint pronates. If there is lateral movement of the kneecap or external rotation, the subtalar joint supinates. When either of these motions occur, the leg should be repositioned and the process repeated until there is no movement in the frontal plane of the patella. The leg must be in such a position that by dorsiflexing the foot at the ankle no movement of the patella is observed. Plaster is then applied to the foot.

Extra-fast–setting splints are recommended. Two 5 × 30-in. splints are required for one foot. Occasionally three splints may be needed for an extra large foot. To cast a pair of average-sized adult feet, you will need four 5 × 30-in. splints, a pan of cool water, and disposable rubber or plastic gloves. Cool water is preferred because it allows the plaster to set up a little slower and the finished casts are stronger.

The plaster is applied to the bare skin of the patient's foot. Powder or cream is not needed as a separating medium. The first splint is folded upon itself to make a double thickness splint of plaster measuring 5 × 15-in. This is then immersed into the pan of cool water until it is thoroughly soaked.

The surplus water is squeezed from the plaster splint until no more water drips from it. It is then opened to its 5 × 15-in. size once again. The top half inch is then folded or doubled over on itself. This results in a splint that is 4½ × 15 in. with a half-inch strip having four layers of plaster at the top and two layers elsewhere. This half-inch strip provides additional reinforcement around the top of the cast.

This splint is then applied to the foot, with the half-inch strip four layers thick being dorsal. The center of the splint is placed against the posterior of the heel. The ends are then positioned against the lateral and medial borders of the foot (Fig 29–1). The top of the cast should be just inferior to the malleoli. The lateral portion of the splint is then folded under the plantar surface of the foot and massaged into place until it sticks to the skin without falling away (Fig 29–2). The medial portion of the splint is folded under the medial aspect of the foot. It should overlap the lateral portion. Again, massage the splint until the two portions of plaster blend into one. Massage until the plaster is smooth and all folds are eliminated.

A tuck of splint now remains unblended into the casting (Fig 29–3,A). Fold this excess up the posterior of the heel (Fig 29–3,B). This will provide a nice, smooth, natural contour overlying the plantar aspect of the entire foot.

The second splint is the more difficult of the two splints to apply. The contours of the anterior portion of the foot are not conducive to the application of the splint from side to side. They are more conducive to application from top to bottom. Nevertheless, for the best impression, they should be applied from side to side.

The second splint is soaked in water and squeezed dry. The full 5 × 15-in. splint is used

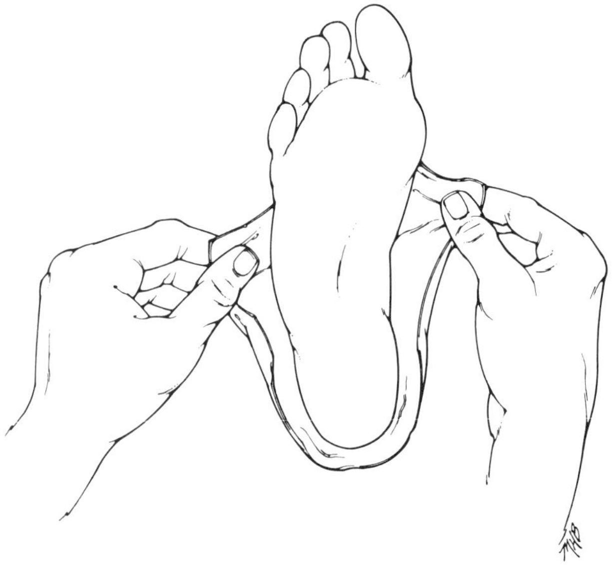

FIG 29–1.
The first splint is applied to the foot.

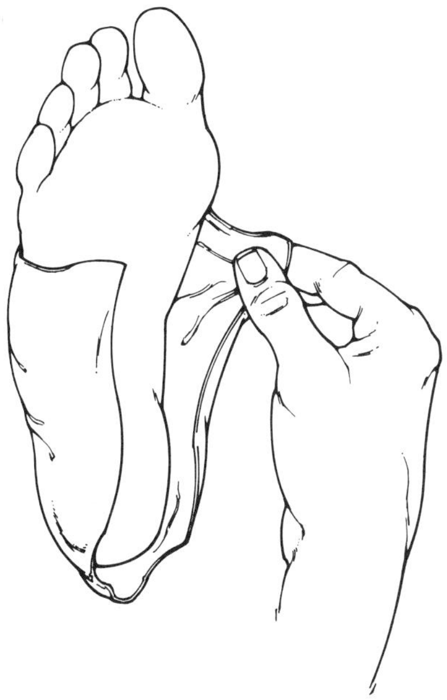

FIG 29–2.
The lateral portion of the splint is folded under the plantar aspect of the foot and massaged into place.

without the half-inch reinforcement fold on the top. The total width of the plaster is required to cover the plantar aspect of the forefoot. The lateral aspect is covered with the splint first by overlapping the lateral anterior portion of the first splint. It is now folded under the plantar surface of the foot. Massage it into place until it adheres to the skin and blends with the plaster of the first splint.

The plaster is then applied around the forefoot and applied posteriorly along the medial aspect of the foot. As the splint is placed into position around the toes, it is lifted away to create a loose distal tuck in the splint that allows for extension as the foot is held in the neutral position.

The medial portion of the splint is then folded under the medial aspect of the foot. Overlap the distal portion of the first splint by covering the medial aspect of the foot and overlapping the lateral portion of both splints. Again massage the splints until all ends of the plaster splints blend into one. Massage until all folds are eliminated and the plaster is smooth.

All excess plaster is moved to the sulcus of the toes. Any unevenness from plaster underlying the metatarsals could produce an incorrect evaluation of the negative cast.

Once both strips of plaster have been applied to the foot and smoothed, you must place the foot into neutral position and maintain this position until the plaster sets.

Placement of the Foot

The subtalar joint must be in its neutral position, and the midtarsal joint must be in its pronated position. Locating the neutral position of

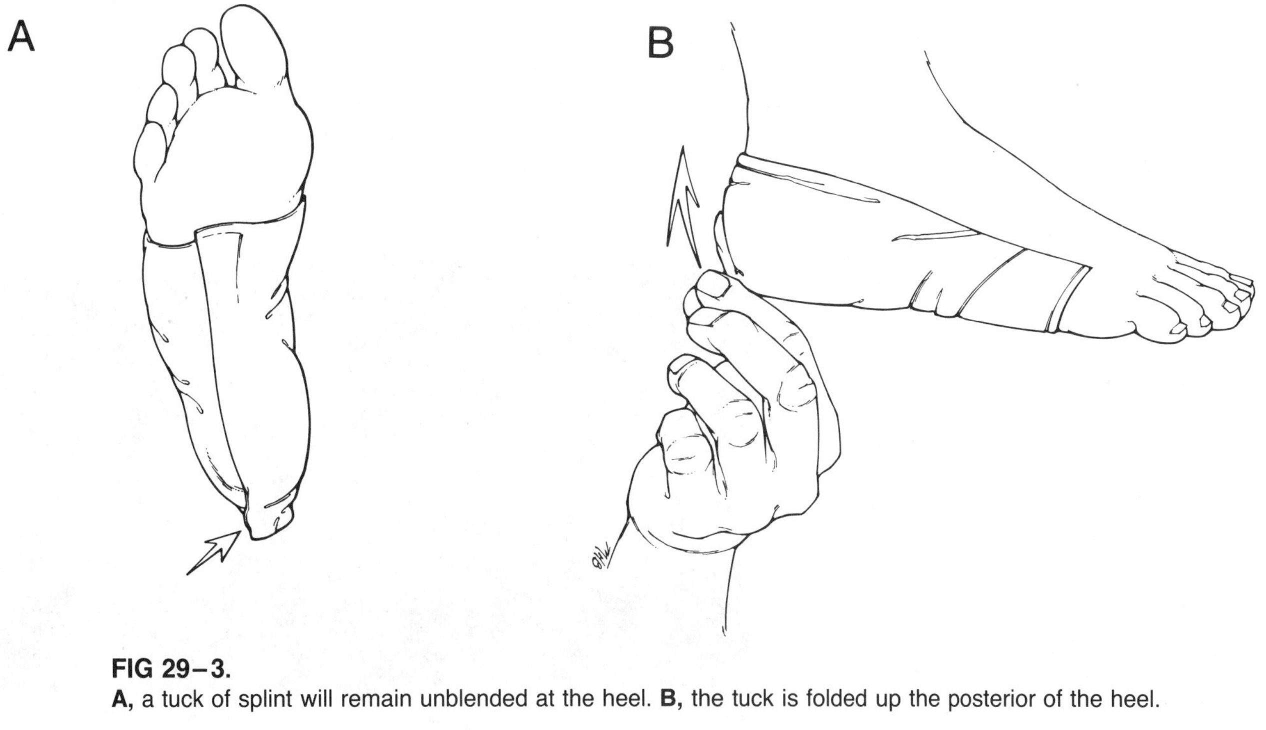

FIG 29–3.
A, a tuck of splint will remain unblended at the heel. **B,** the tuck is folded up the posterior of the heel.

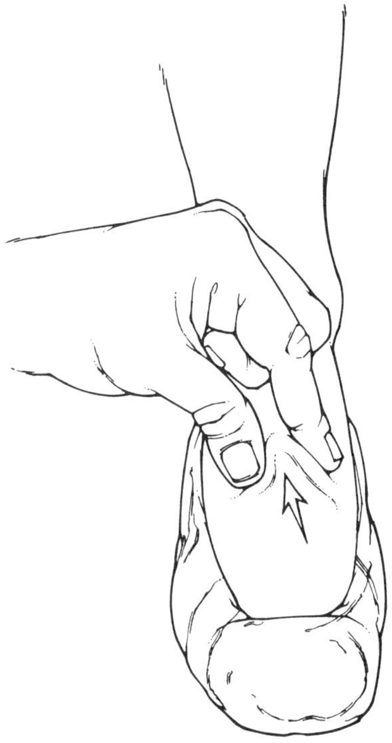

FIG 29–4.
When removing the cast, first pull the skin away from the top surface of the cast.

the subtalar joint is accomplished by both observation and palpation.

Perception of the foot when the full range of motion of the subtalar joint is accomplished will provide a fully pronated point in space and a fully supinated point in space. Move the joint to its fully pronated point, and then move toward supination to a point one third of the distance from pronation between the two points in space. Check this neutral position by palpation of the medial and lateral sides of the subtalar joint. The medial and lateral sides of the talus and calcaneus will feel regular and smooth in their linkage with each other.

Pronating the midtarsal joint is accomplished by lifting the foot, everting the forefoot, and abducting the forefoot. The foot is lifted by the toes. This mechanically dorsiflexes the ankle to resistance. It is not necessary to force dorsiflexion or to lift the limb from the surface upon which it is resting. Forcing this dorsiflexion will cause pronation in the subtalar joint.

With proper positioning of the patient's toes during the lifting of the foot, eversion of the forefoot will automatically take place. Palpation of the medial and lateral sides of the subtalar joint while lifting the foot and everting the forefoot will be a check and balance against subtalar pronation as

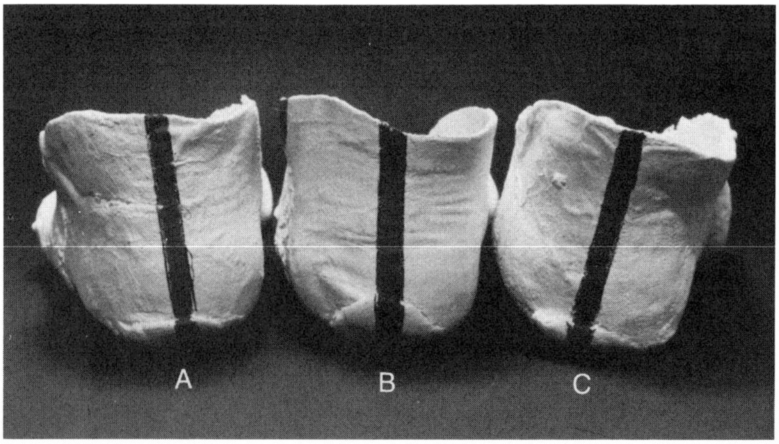

FIG 29–5.
Three casts of the same foot. **A,** a valgus forefoot-to-rearfoot relationship. **B,** a neutral forefoot-to-rearfoot relationship. **C,** a varus forefoot to rearfoot relationship. Compare the negative cast with the foot. They should match.

the forefoot is very gently and very minutely abducted.

Placement of the Toes

The ulnar surface of the thumb is positioned into the sulcus of the fourth and fifth toes. The thumb should embrace the *bases of the proximal phalanges.* By applying a force against the base with the thumb, the fourth and fifth toes will dorsiflex at the metatarsophalangeal joints.

The palmar aspect of the base of the index finger is now placed on the dorsum of the fourth and fifth toes at the level of the *proximal phalangeal heads.* Rotate the wrist and hand as a single unit away from the dorsum of the foot. This motion plantar-flexes the fourth and fifth toes on the fourth and fifth metatarsals, and dorsiflexion of the fourth and fifth metatarsals will occur, thereby everting the forefoot.

The hand should not compress the lateral aspect of the foot during this step. If compression occurs, you will observe a flattening of the soft tissue overlying the fifth metatarsal head that disrupts the natural contour in this area.

Dr. Root and colleagues[1] have outlined the following seven steps in casting the foot in a neutral position:

FIG 29–6.
Check the lateral aspect of the cast to be sure that the plaster has been applied high enough to cover the lower portion of the lateral malleolus.

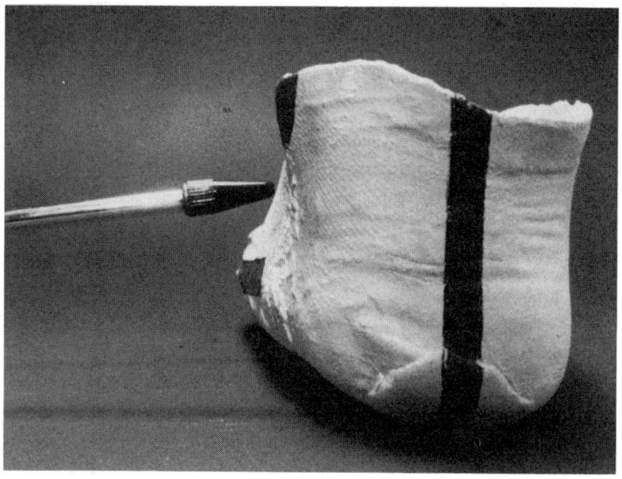

FIG 29–7.
Bisection of the heel of the cast depends upon the "C" shape inferior to the lateral malleolus.

1. Check for leg rotation.
2. Relax the patient completely.
3. Be gentle.
4. Be sure that the subtalar joint is in the neutral position.
5. Grasp the toes.
6. Lift the foot to resistance.
7. Abduct the forefoot.

Removing the Cast From the Foot

The cast is removed when the plaster has set. The skin is freed from the top edges of the cast by moving the skin under the plaster (Fig 29–4). Gently shake the foot with one hand while holding the

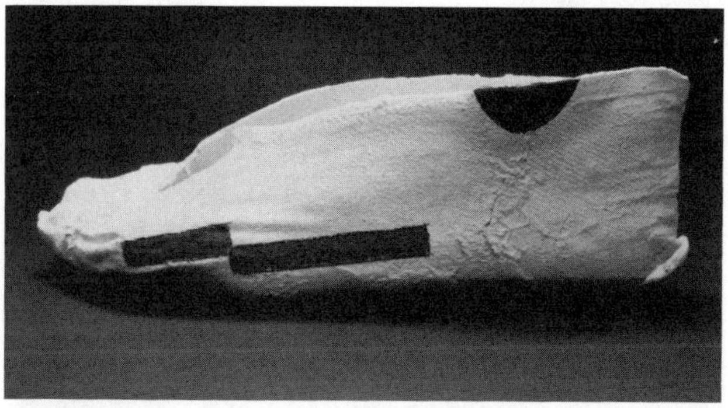

FIG 29–8.
By drawing a line overlying the lateral aspect of the fifth metatarsal and fifth toe, you will be able to determine by their positions whether or not the midtarsal joint is pronated or in its "locked" position. If the lines are parallel or plantarflexed relative to each other, you will have achieved this most important step in the casting procedure.

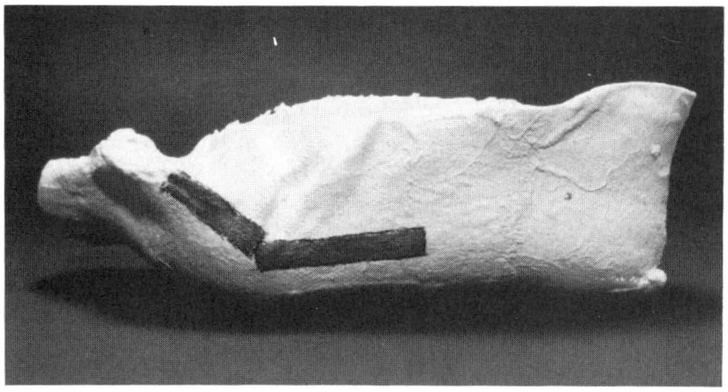

FIG 29–9.
If you have a dorsiflexed position of the lines relative to each other, you will have produced a false impression of the forefoot-to-rearfoot relationship.

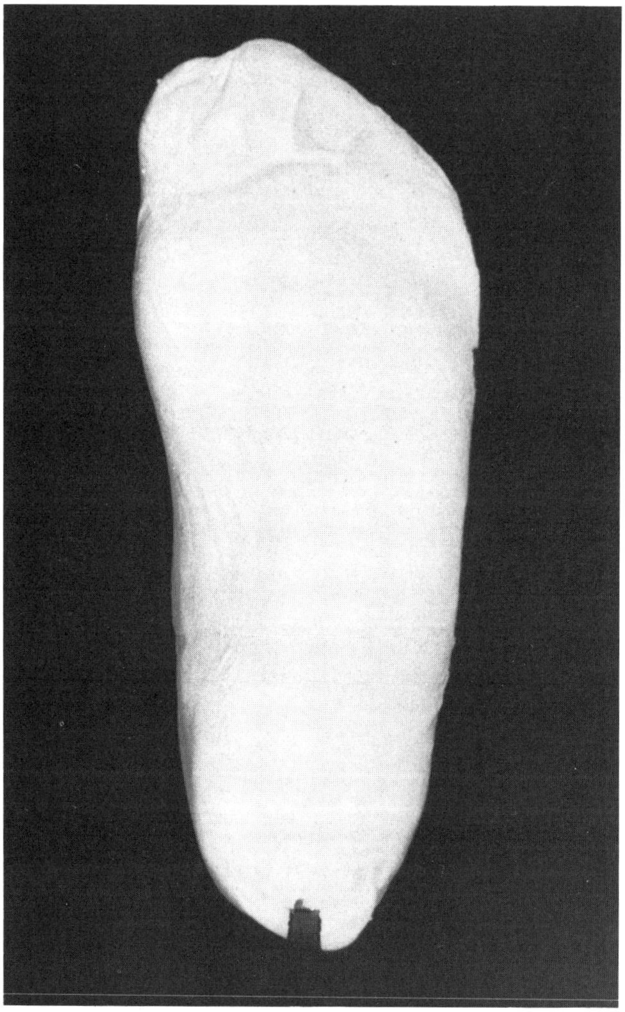

FIG 29–10.
Viewing the cast from the dorsum should reveal the exact shape of the foot from the dorsum. Viewing from the plantar aspect should also reveal an exact duplicate of the foot. The plaster should be smooth and represent the natural contour of the foot.

toes of the cast. Pull distally after the heel of the cast is pulled plantarly off the heel of the foot. Do not exert any force against the heel of the cast. Continue to shake the foot out of the cast.

EVALUATING THE CAST RELATIVE TO THE FOOT

Check the Frontal Plane

With the patient in the prone position, compare the negative cast with the foot. Be sure that they match (Fig 29–5). Check the lateral aspect of the heel of the cast to be sure that the plaster splint has been applied high enough to cover the inferior aspect of the lateral malleolus (Fig 29–6). The lab-

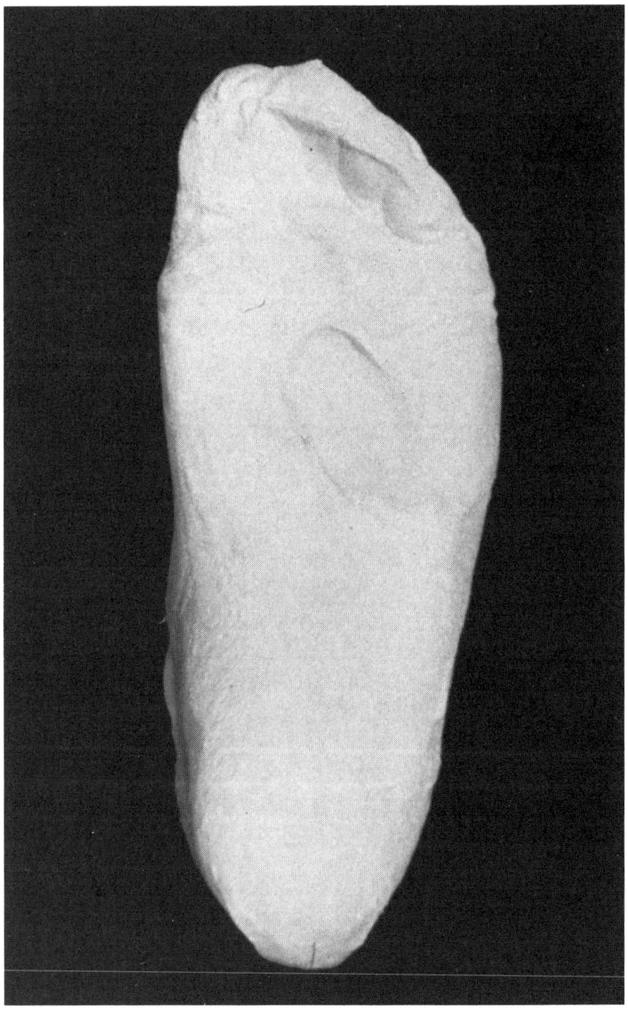

FIG 29–11.
Depressions in the natural contour of the plantar aspect of the plaster cast should be avoided. These can be the cause of changes in the forefoot-to-rearfoot relationship during the casting procedure.

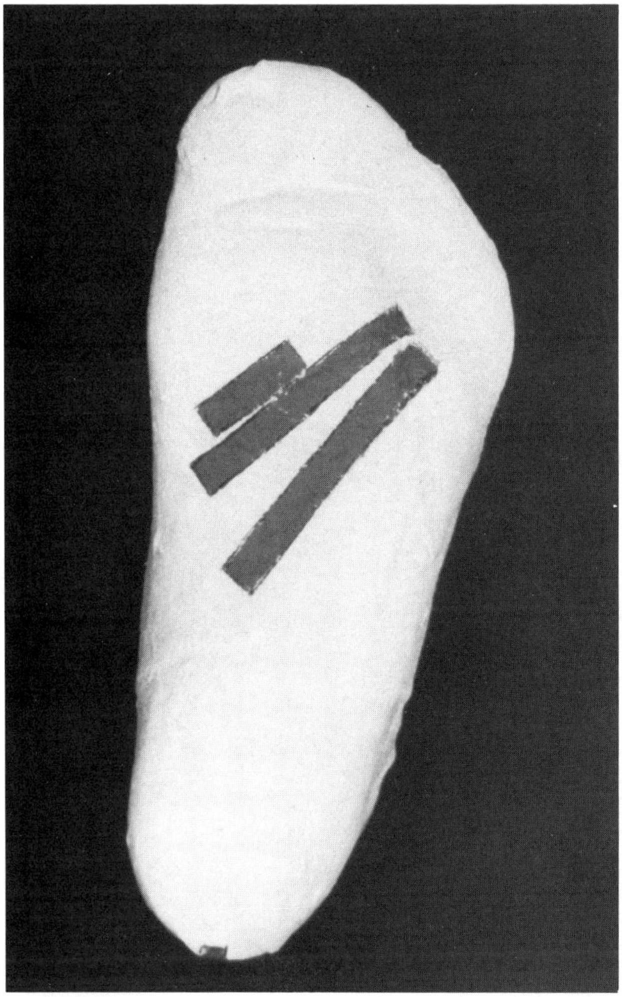

FIG 29–12.
A "stretch mark" represented by the lines of the plantar aspect of this cast would indicate a possible change in the forefoot-to-rearfoot relationship during the casting procedure.

oratory relies on the "C" shape inferior to the lateral malleolus to bisect the heel of the cast (Fig 29–7).

Check the Sagittal Plane

Draw a line overlying the lateral aspect of the fifth metatarsal shaft, and draw a line over the lateral aspect of the fifth toe. There should be a parallel or plantar-flexed relationship. If you observe this, you know that you have locked the midtarsal joint (Fig 29–8). If the lines are dorsiflexed relative to each other, a false varus relationship of the forefoot to the rearfoot has been created in the cast (Fig 20–9).

Check the Transverse Plane

When compared with the foot the cast should be similar in shape from the dorsum. Observation of the plantar surface of the cast should reveal that all excess plaster has moved into the sulcus under the toes. The plantar aspect of the cast should be smooth and represent the natural contour of the foot (Figs 29–10 and 29–11).

In order to get an excellently functioning orthotic device, the neutral cast must be taken with the subtalar joint in the neutral position, the midtarsal joint locked, and the plantar surface contour of the foot captured without wrinkles (Fig 29–12).

REFERENCE

1. Root ML, Orien WP, Weed JH: *Neutral Position Casting Techniques.* Los Angeles, Clinical Biomechanics, 1971, pp 18–28.

30

Below-Knee Casting

Michael S. Downey, D.P.M., F.A.C.F.S.

> But if thou make thine apparatus with lime and white of egg it will be much handsomer and still more useful; in fact, it will become as hard as stone and will not need to be removed until the healing is complete. . .—Rhazes, 860 A.D.

The value of immobilization in the healing of damaged living tissues has long been understood. Since Hippocrates first wrote of the use of splinting and immobilization in 350 B.C., the techniques of casting have matured into a distinct medical art form. Today, physicians treating the lower extremity routinely utilize cast materials for numerous applications including orthotic construction casts, slipper casts, below-knee casts, and above-knee casts. The techniques of below-knee cast application and removal will be discussed in detail in this chapter.

INDICATIONS

Prerequisite to proper casting techniques is a thorough understanding of the indications for the application of a below-knee cast. The methods used in constructing a below-knee cast will vary depending upon the desired objective. Below-knee casts are applied for four basic reasons: immobilization, compression, protection, and/or correction.[1]

The most common reason for application of a below-knee cast is to immobilize a specific area of the foot, ankle, or lower part of the leg. Bones, joints, and soft tissues can be prevented from moving with a cast. As a general rule, if a bone is to be effectively immobilized, at least one joint proximal (above) and one joint distal (below) the involved bone must be immobilized as well. For example, if the first metatarsal bone is to be immobilized, the first metatarsophalangeal joint (distal joint, or joint below) and first metatarsocuneiform joint (proximal joint, or joint above) must be prevented from moving. Since the first metatarsal bone is a component of each of these joints, if either of these joints were allowed to move, the first metatarsal bone would move as the joint motion occurred, and immobilization would fail. A below-knee cast might be necessary following a surgical first metatarsal osteotomy, which is commonly performed when correcting a bunion deformity. A joint is immobilized by restricting all the bones that form and move with the joint. For example, immobilizing the ankle joint necessitates restricting the motion of the tibia, fibula, and talus. Treatment of an inflamed joint may also involve cast immobilization. Finally, soft-tissue structures such as tendons, ligaments, and nerves are immobilized in various ways to keep tension off the structure(s) to be immobilized. For example, in an Achilles tendon rupture, the ankle must be immobilized during the healing process to eliminate tension and motion of the tendon. Thus, common applications of a below-knee cast for immobilization include the closed or open reduction of fractures, surgical osteotomies, tendon or ligament injury and/or repair, and inflamed soft tissues and joints (Figs 30–1,A and B, and 30–2).

Below-knee casts can also be utilized to create compression. The purpose of the cast in this situation would be to control and reduce edema. The compression cast usually involves multiple layers of padding to allow for some regulated swelling within the cast. If these extra layers of padding were not utilized, the hard outer layer of cast material would limit any swelling, and the patient would complain of pressure pain. Because of the extra layers of soft material in a compression cast, less correction and immobilization is provided. Therefore, once the edema is controlled or predictable, a more tightly conformed cast with less padding can be applied. Compression casts such as the Jones' compression dressing are typically applied after acute trauma or in the immediate postoperative phase.

Casts may be applied to provide protection of a part. Below-knee casts are used for protection in patients who are noncompliant. A protective below-knee cast can also be used to shield an area in a mentally handicapped or immature patient. A common example is the pediatric patient where the child might cause further damage to a therapeutic measure or dressing if his lower extremity is not protected with a cast. Additionally, a pro-

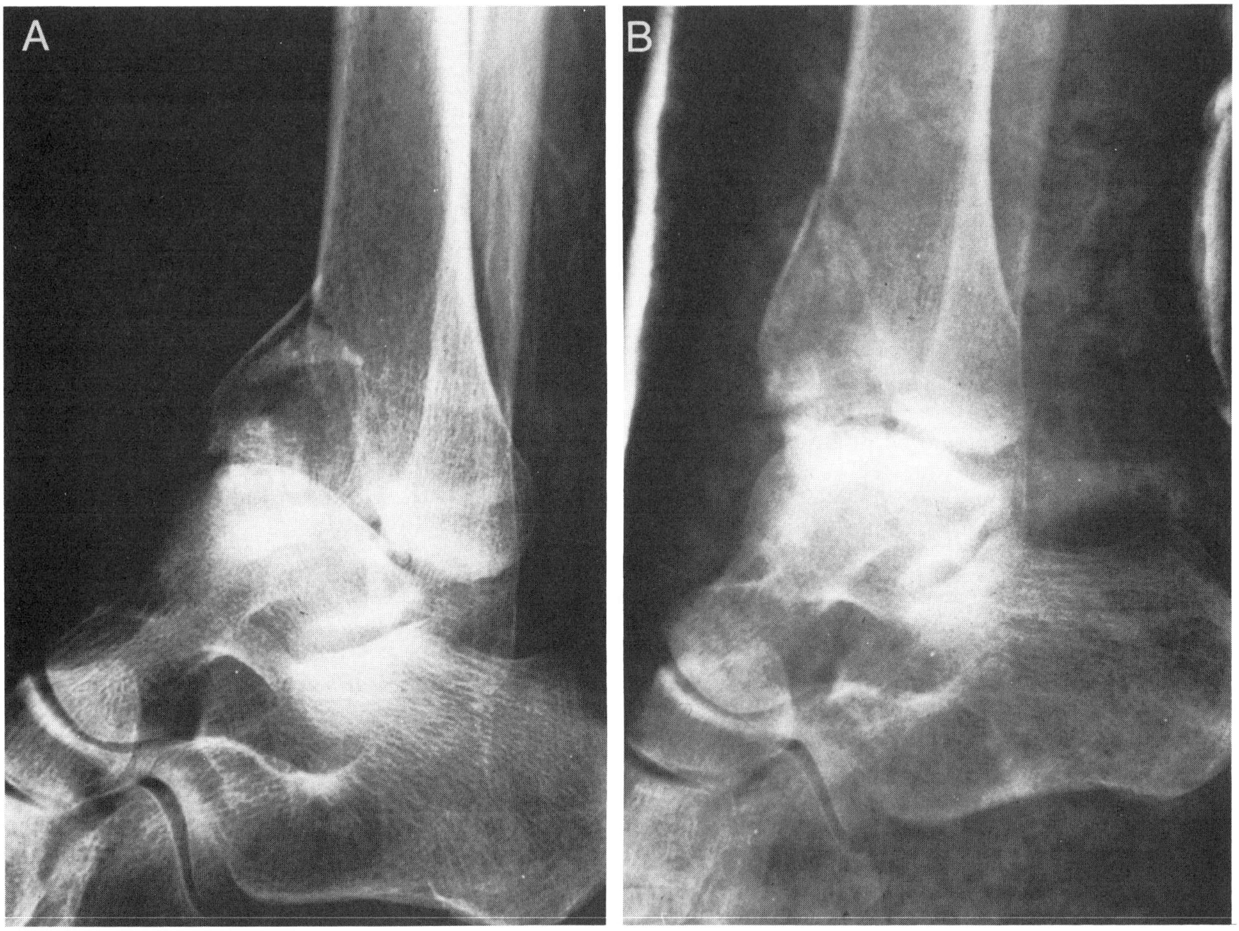

FIG 30–1.
Use of a below-knee cast to immobilize the ankle joint following a fracture of the distal end of the tibia. **A,** note the fracture of the distal anterior portion of the tibia with displacement of the talus anteriorly and proximally. **B,** same injury after closed reduction and application of a below-knee plaster cast for immobilization. Note the improved alignment of the fracture and position of the talus. After closed reduction, the cast is needed to immobilize the ankle to prevent recurrent displacement of the fracture.

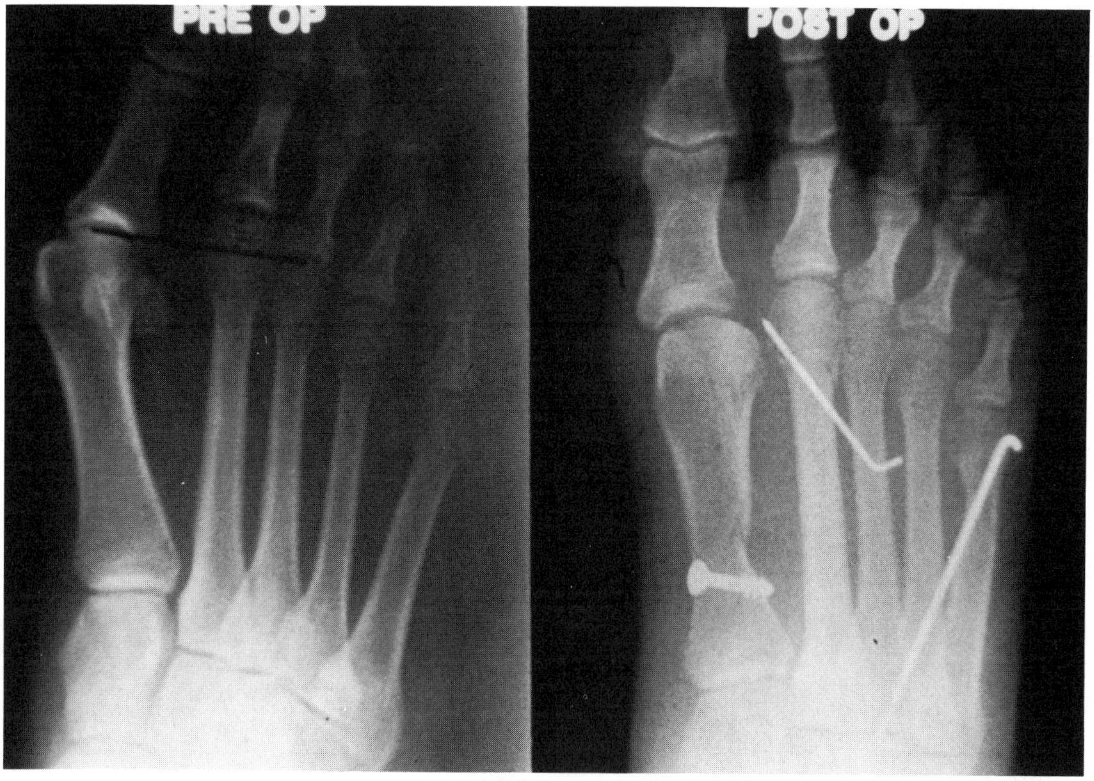

FIG 30–2.
Preoperative and postoperative radiographs of a patient. Note that multiple surgical osteotomies were performed, including a closing base wedge osteotomy of the first metatarsal with screw fixation, a dorsiflexory osteotomy of the second metatarsal with Kirschner wire fixation, and a distal wedge osteotomy of the fifth metatarsal with Kirschner wire fixation. A below-knee cast was utilized postoperatively to immobilize the foot, thus giving additional support to the fixation devices and minimizing motion of the bone cuts.

tective "total-contact cast" can be used in a patient with an insensitive foot, as is seen in a diabetic patient with neuropathy, to protect an ulcer or other area from weight bearing. When a person has lost sensation in his foot, there is no internal mechanism left that can warn him of the dangers of continuing to walk on the injured or problematic area. A total-contact cast protects this area by dispersing the pressure of weight bearing to other uninjured areas of the foot and by protecting the injured area from shearing forces.[2–4]

Finally, the below-knee cast can be used to effect correction. Many pediatric deformities are amenable to conservative cast manipulation if performed early and aggressively. As Ganley stated, "Proper management requires early, specific, gentle, persistent force held long enough for full correction."[5] Correctable deformities, if treated early, include calcaneovalgus, metatarsus adductus, equinovarus, ankle equinus, and tibial torsion deformities (Figs 30–3 and 30–4). Corrective casts require specific techniques that should

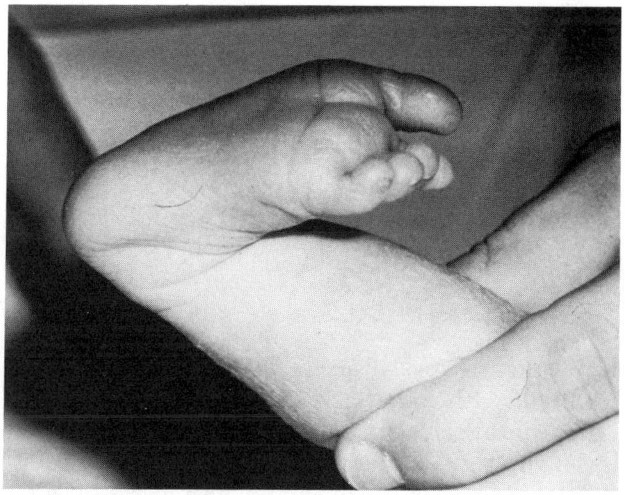

FIG 30–3.
Talipes calcaneovalgus (reverse clubfoot) deformity in a 1-month-old child.

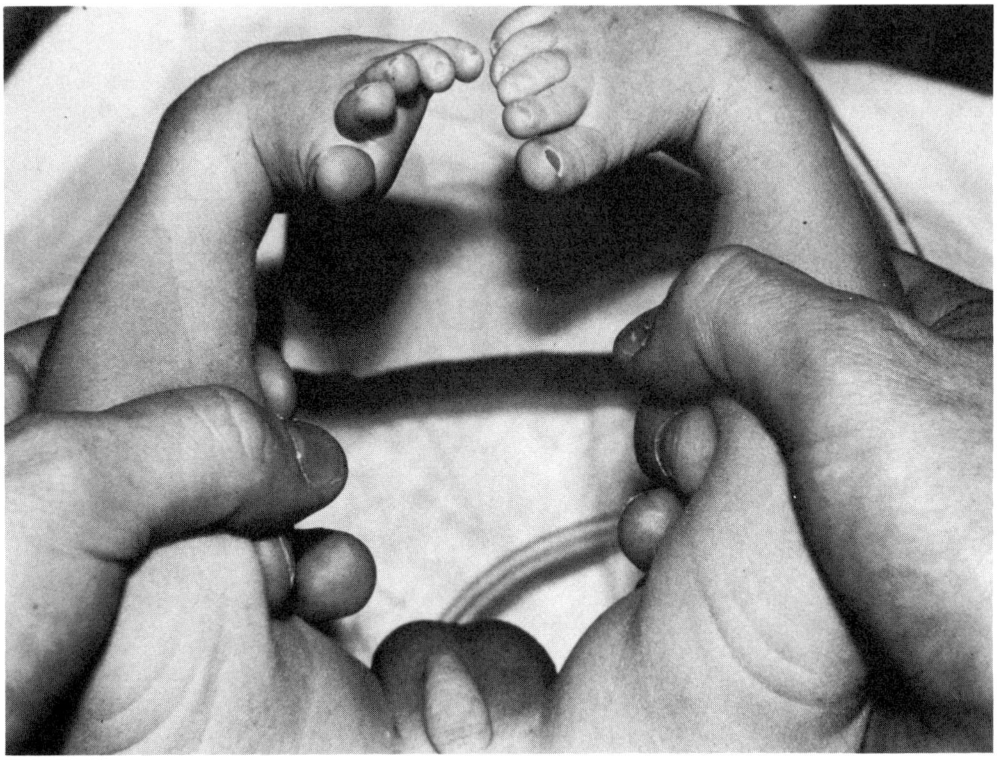

FIG 30–4.
Bilateral talipes equinovarus (clubfoot) in a newborn.

be studied prior to their application. Generally, a well-molded and -conformed cast is needed to achieve maximum correction. Plaster is easily molded and conforms better than synthetic materials. Additionally, plaster can be soaked off in a bathtub or basin of water. This can be of significant advantage when regular removal of serial casts is needed in the pediatric patient because the parents can remove the cast at home prior to returning to the office for application of another cast (Fig 30–5).

CASTING MATERIALS

A Dutch Army surgeon, Antonius Mathijsen, is credited with popularizing plaster of paris in 1852. Mathijsen's innovation provided a decrease in setting time from more than a day for existing plasters to less than 2 hours for his plaster-of-paris bandage. Even today, setting time is an important consideration in the selection of a casting material. Although plaster of paris is still utilized, a plethora of synthetic cast materials are now available. Thus, in selecting a cast material several factors must be weighed.

The "ideal" cast material would have the following properties: easy application/removal, moldability, durability, light weight, fast setting, good porosity, radiolucency, long shelf life, low cost, and aesthetic appearance. Unfortunately, neither plaster of paris nor any of the synthetic cast materials have all of these advantages.

Plaster of paris affords many of these advantages, including ease of application and removal, moldability, long shelf life, and low cost. However, plaster has poor durability and is fairly heavy, slow setting, and nonporous. Its radiodensity makes it difficult to see through when performing an x-ray study. Due to its ease of application and removal, low cost, and especially its moldability, plaster casts are routinely used for corrective casting in infants. Further, temporary casts, posterior splints, and the outer layer of compression dressings are frequently made with plaster, again primarily because of its lower cost. Today, moldability and cost are the primary reasons plaster is still used. If a well-molded, tight cast is mandated for correction or immobilization, plaster of paris is still the material of choice.

In contrast, synthetic materials are generally durable, lightweight, fast setting, porous, and

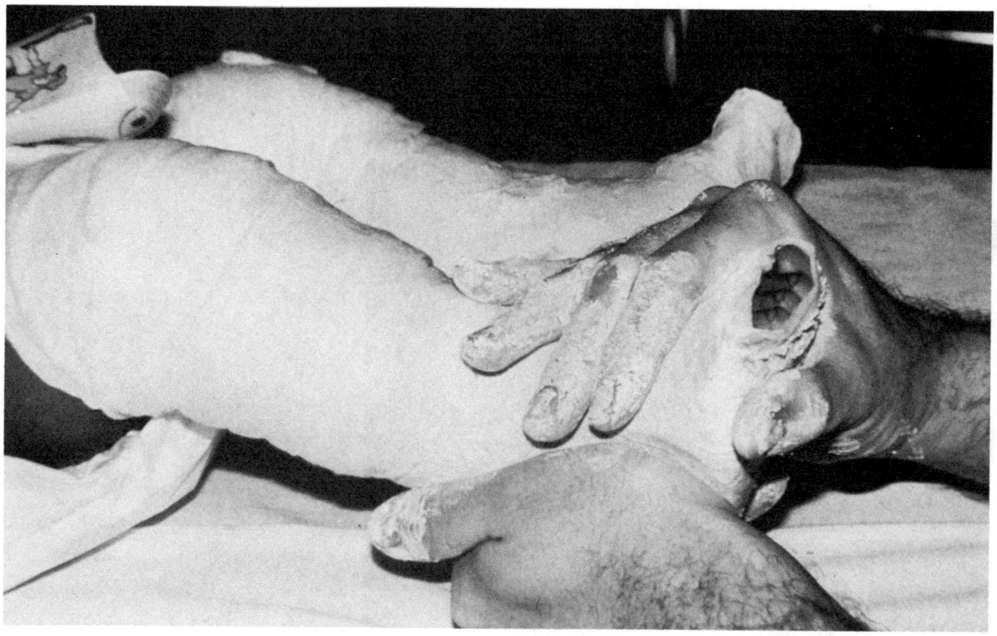

FIG 30–5.
Plaster of paris casts are preferred for corrective casting because they conform and mold well and are easily removed.

more aesthetic in appearance. Disadvantages of synthetic materials include difficulty in removal because they must be cut off, poor moldability, short shelf life, and increased cost. Additionally, synthetic materials vary markedly in their radiolucency. Some are fairly radiolucent, while some are as radiodense as plaster. If radiolucency is desired for easier radiographic evaluation, then a synthetic material with improved radiolucency should be chosen. Synthetic casts are used in virtually all situations where moldability and the added cost of the cast material are not of primary concern. Today, synthetic cast materials are available in a multitude of colors, and the final cast appearance is sleek and handsome.

A variation in material options would be the use of a combined plaster-synthetic cast. This cast, as described by Hice et al.,[6] consists of a plaster inner shell and a synthetic outer shell. The plaster of paris is used for the inner layer due to its superior moldability. The synthetic material is used for the outer layers to provide increased durability, less weight, and an improved cosmetic appearance. However, there is a lack of porosity and poor radiolucency due to the plaster. Additionally, there is difficulty with removal and a higher cost due to the synthetic outer layer. This marriage of these casting materials will be beneficial when the aforementioned advantages are of primary importance.

PATIENT PREPARATION AND POSITIONING

Prior to the application of a below-knee cast, the patient must be prepared and positioned for the casting procedure. The goals of this preparation are to maximize the patient's mental and physical comfort during the cast application process and to allow application of the cast in the quickest and most technically correct manner. Cast application may be a new experience for patients, and any fears they may have should be discussed and allayed. Reassurance that they will experience minimal discomfort will make patients more relaxed and cooperative. Additionally, all the necessary supplies (stockinette, cast padding, elastic bandages, tongue depressors, cast material, water, gloves, etc.) should be close at hand and readily available. Once the casting procedure has started, there is little time to search or wait for absent items.

Similarly, the positioning of patients and their extremity is crucial to the proper application of a below-knee cast. Below-knee casts are applied with the ankle joint in its neutral position and the foot at 90 degrees, or perpendicular, to the leg. Except in rare instances, the foot should not be pronated or supinated (Fig 30–6,A–C). The cast may be applied with the patient in one of three positions: supine, prone, or sitting.

In the supine position, the patient is reclined

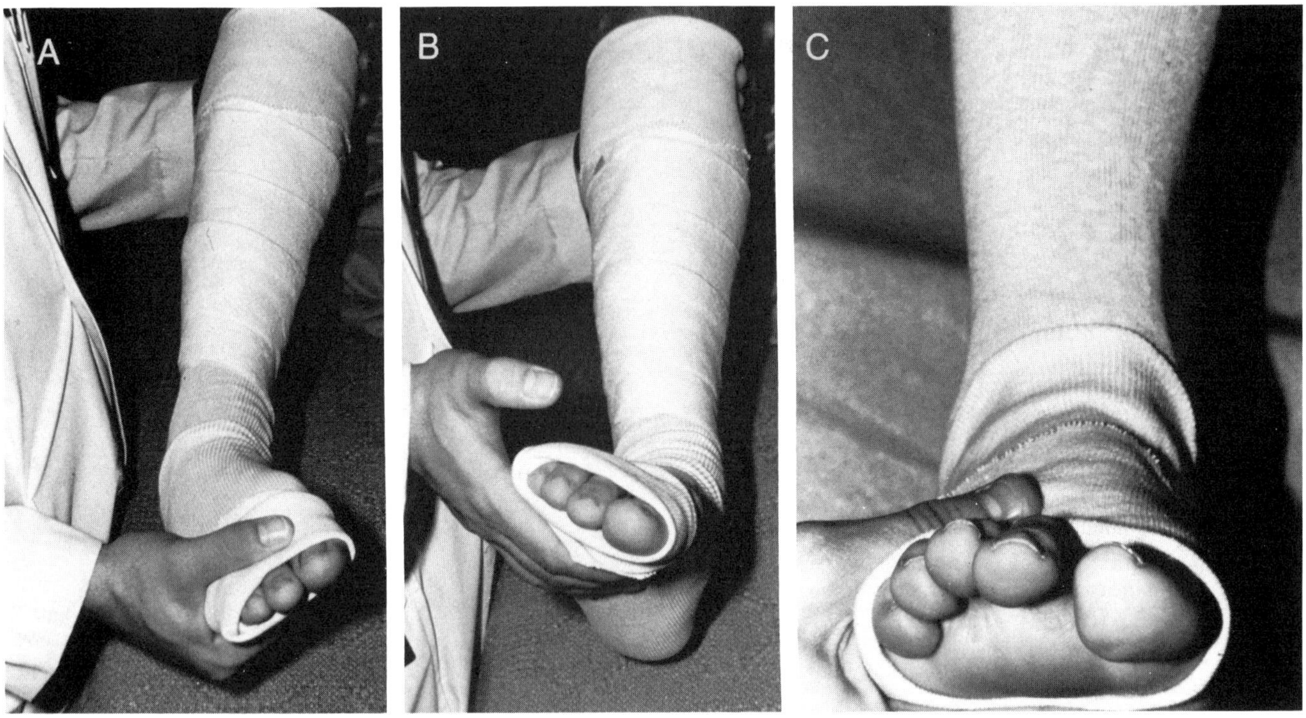

FIG 30–6.
Improper positioning of the lower extremity during casting can hinder proper healing and necessitate additional physical therapy and rehabilitative measures after cast removal. **A,** improper, supinated foot position. **B,** improper, pronated foot position. **C,** correct neutral foot position for application of a synthetic below-knee cast.

with the hip and knee flexed. An assistant holds the leg while the cast is applied by supporting the knee and the plantar aspect of the foot. The holder should always stand on the lateral side of the leg to be cast. One hand of the holder goes under the posterior fold of the knee with the thumb wrapping around the lateral aspect of the lower portion of the leg in the region of the fibular head. The other hand is then held with the fingers fully extended and is used to support the forefoot. The holder gently but firmly positions the limb by elevating it off the table, flexing the hip and knee, and placing the ankle joint in its neutral position (Fig 30–7). The holder must encourage the patient to relax his entire limb to allow the holder to properly hold and position the extremity. The patient will only relax and relinquish the full weight of his limb if he has been mentally prepared and has complete confidence in the holder. Once properly positioned, the holder must constantly maintain the proper limb position until the cast has sufficiently cured or hardened.

In the prone position, the patient is laying face downward or on his stomach with his knee flexed. The assistant applies dorsiflexory pressure to the ankle joint from the plantar aspect of the foot. This is accomplished by placing a hand with the fingers fully extended on the forefoot and applying pressure downward (Fig 30–8).

In the sitting position, the patient sits up and the lower part of the leg is allowed to dangle over the end of the casting table or chair. An assistant or "L"-shaped casting bar is used to maintain proper position of the foot and ankle (Fig 30–9,A and B).

Regardless of the casting position, constant evaluation of lower extremity alignment during the casting process is imperative. Maintenance of proper alignment during the casting procedure will prevent improper cast position and cast irritation and reduce the need for removal and reapplication. Proper lower extremity position must be maintained until the cast has begun to harden and the ankle joint cannot move.

CAST APPLICATION

The application of a good below-knee cast is as much an art as is the practice of surgery. A well-

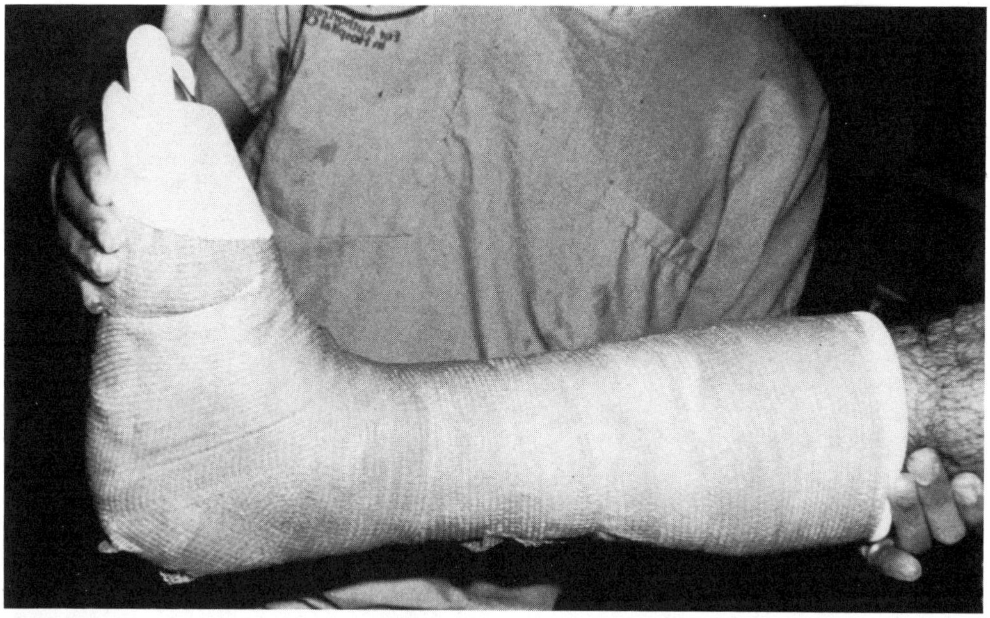

FIG 30–7.
Patient positioning for a supine below-knee cast.

applied cast will achieve its intended goals and objectives while minimizing patient discomfort. The key to a comfortable cast is the avoidance of cast pressure, which occurs when a cast irritates certain anatomic structures or is too constricting.

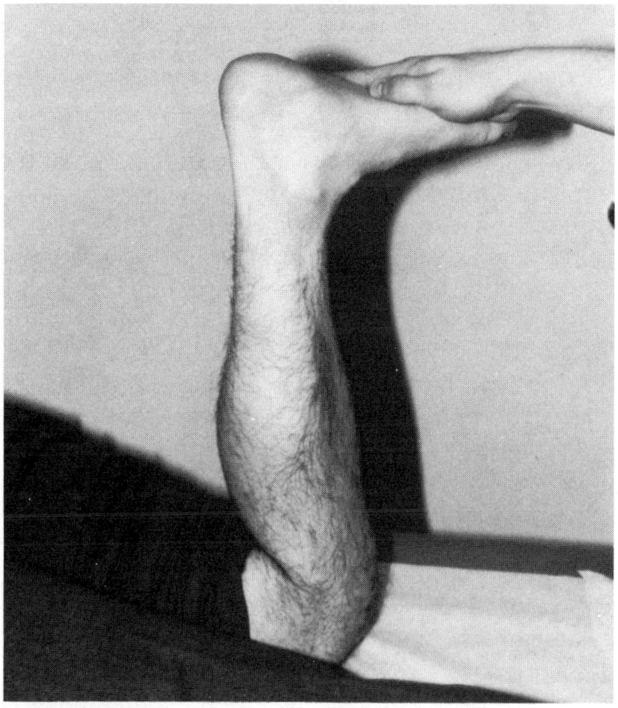

FIG 30–8.
Patient positioning for a prone below-knee cast.

A properly applied cast avoids pressure areas and reinforces stress areas.[1] Common anatomic areas irritated by a poorly applied below-knee cast include the fibular head and neck; the anterior tibial crest, or shin; the medial and lateral malleoli; the heel area; the anterior fold of the ankle; the first and fifth metatarsal heads; and the base of the fifth metatarsal (Fig 30–10,A and B). Avoidance of these pressure points is critical. Pressure irritation is not only painful but can also lead to nerve damage, vascular compromise, or ulceration (Fig 30–11,A–C). Stress areas include all joints or areas where a cast might break down. The heel and ankle joint area are the most important stress areas and must be appropriately reinforced.

Depending upon the amount of edema present or anticipated, a compression cast or below-knee cast may be applied. A compression cast, as mentioned earlier, is used to control and/or reduce edema. A below-knee cast is more confining and is used when edema has been curbed and/or minimal additional edema is anticipated.

Compression Cast

The compression cast, or Jones' compression dressing, was described by Sir Robert Jones. The cast consists of multiple layers of cast padding and elastic bandages with an outer splint or hard

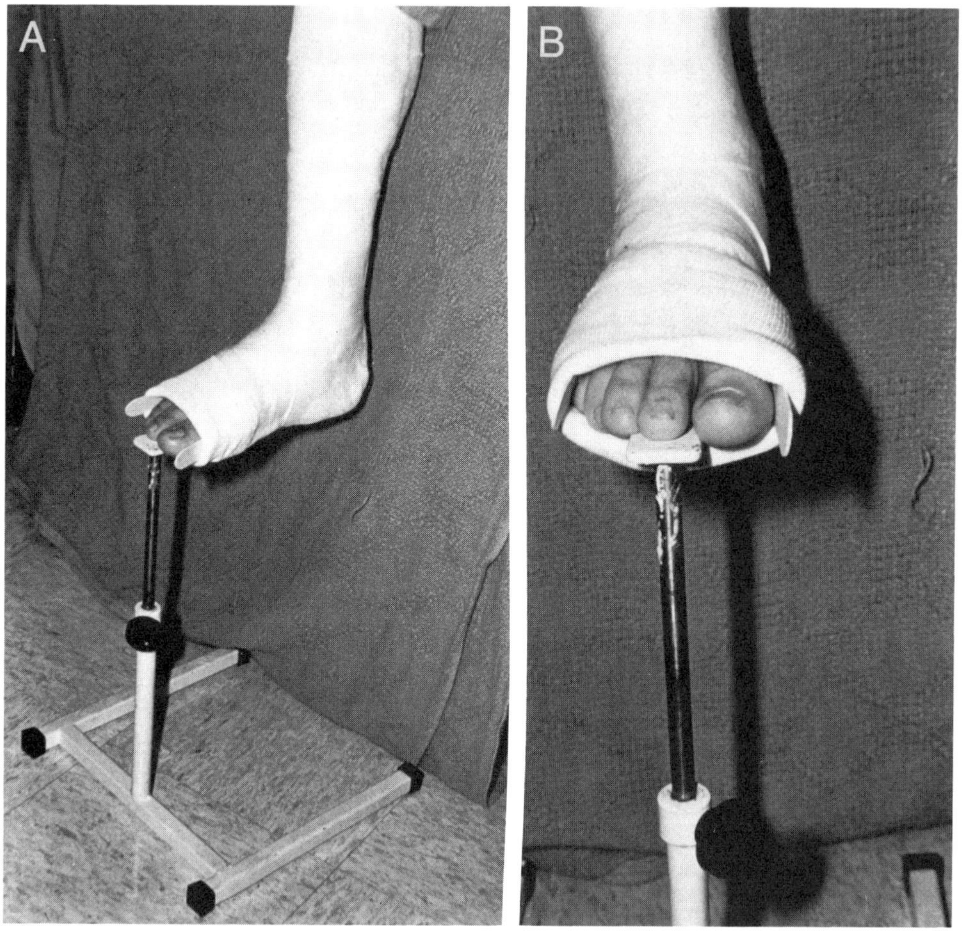

FIG 30–9.
A and **B,** patient positioning for a sitting below-knee cast using an L-shaped casting bar. Note that the leg is dangling over the end of the table.

shell to provide some support and immobilization. The soft materials will give mild compression while allowing some limited swelling to occur. A rigid cast does not allow for swelling and may need to be removed if the patient feels pressure pain or if the circulation to the toes appears to be cut off by cast pressure. The disadvantage of the compression cast is that strict immobilization is lost. Thus, the thinner the padding, the more confining the cast and the greater the immobilization. The thicker the padding, the less confining the cast and the more limited the immobilization.

There are three distinct materials used in a compression cast: cast padding, elastic wraps or compression bandages, and rigid cast material. The cast is applied in several layers with the patient positioned properly as mentioned earlier. The cast consists of alternating layers of the cast padding and elastic wraps. The outer layer is then a splint or shell of rigid material. There are many individualized variations and modifications to the typical compression cast. The following is one possible manner of application.

The first layer is the cast padding. Several types and widths of cast padding are marketed (Fig 30–12). For a compression cast, soft, pliable, 4-in. cast padding with some elasticity is preferable. If the patient has a surgical dressing applied, the cast padding is applied over the surgical dressing (Fig 30–13,A). If no dressing is present, the cast padding is applied directly to the skin. The cast padding molds well to the contour of the lower extremity (Fig 30–13,B). The second layer is an elastic wrap applied distally to proximally (Fig 30–13,C). The elastic bandage creates a pressure gradient that applies more pressure distally and less pressure proximally. The third layer is another layer of cast padding, and the fourth layer is another elastic wrap (Fig 30–13,D and E). Each layer of cast padding or elastic bandage should be

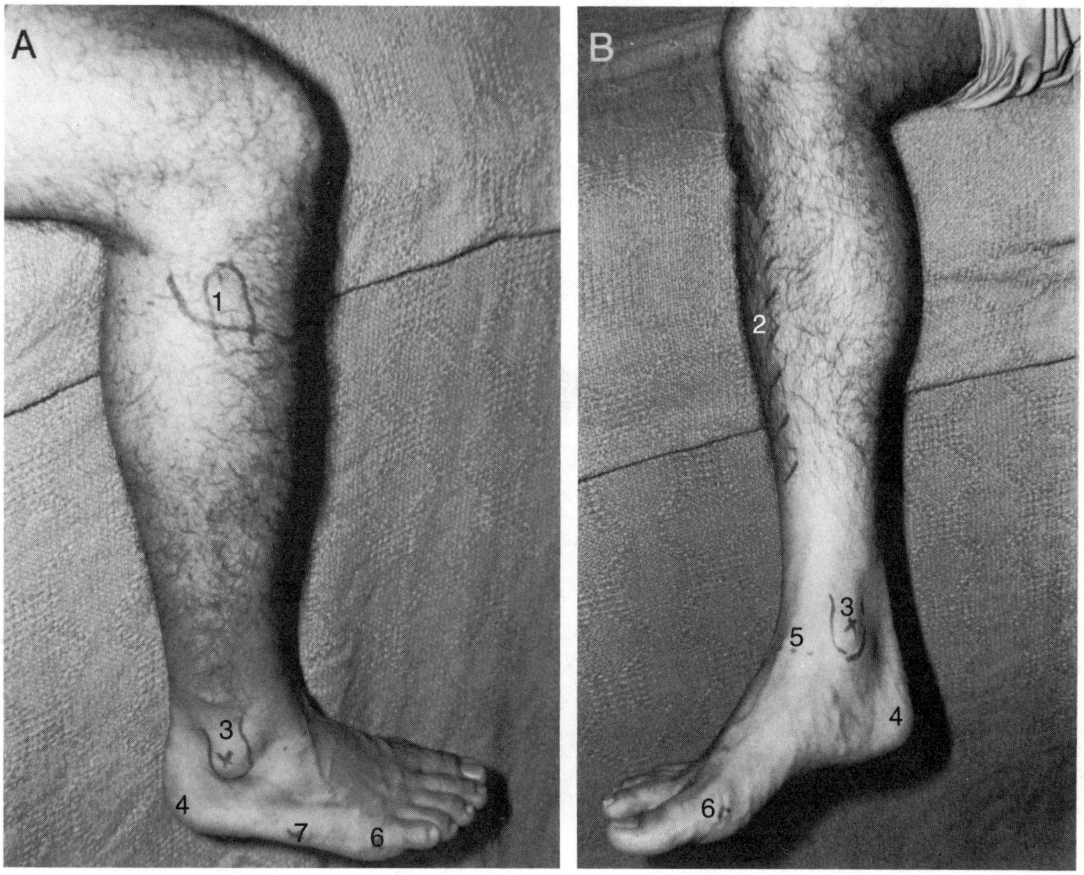

FIG 30–10.
A and **B,** common anatomic pressure areas when applying a below-knee cast: (1) the fibular head and neck; (2) the anterior tibial crest, or shin; (3) the medial and lateral malleoli; (4) the heel area; (5) the anterior fold of the ankle; (6) the first and fifth metatarsal heads; and (7) the base of the fifth metatarsal.

applied more snugly and under greater tension than the preceding layer of the same material. If desired, a fifth layer consisting of cast padding is applied. This layer provides a small amount of additional compression and separates the second elastic wrap from the rigid cast material. Finally, either a plaster or synthetic outer layer is applied (Fig 30–13,F). This may be applied in a splint fashion or as a circumferential cast. If the cast is to be removed and reapplied in serial fashion, the splint may be preferable because it can be easily removed without a cast cutter. If a splint is utilized, a final elastic wrap will be needed to hold the splint in place.

Below-Knee Cast

A standard below-knee cast consists of three components: stockinette, cast padding, and cast material. The amount of padding material varies depending upon the desired cast fit. If a very tightly fitting and conforming cast is desired, the stockinette may be eliminated and the cast padding minimized. A cast applied over an area where swelling is expected necessitates more cast padding. If considerable edema is anticipated, a compression cast should be chosen. The following is one possible manner of cast application.

The first layer of the below-knee cast is a stockinette. This stockinette comes in several diameters, with either the 3- or 4-in. stockinette typically being used in the adolescent or adult patient. The stockinette provides a barrier between the cast padding and the underlying surgical dressing and/or skin and acts as a uniform, nonslip surface for application of the cast padding. Additionally, the stockinette will add to the aesthetic value of the cast. If a surgical dressing is present, the stockinette is applied over the dress-

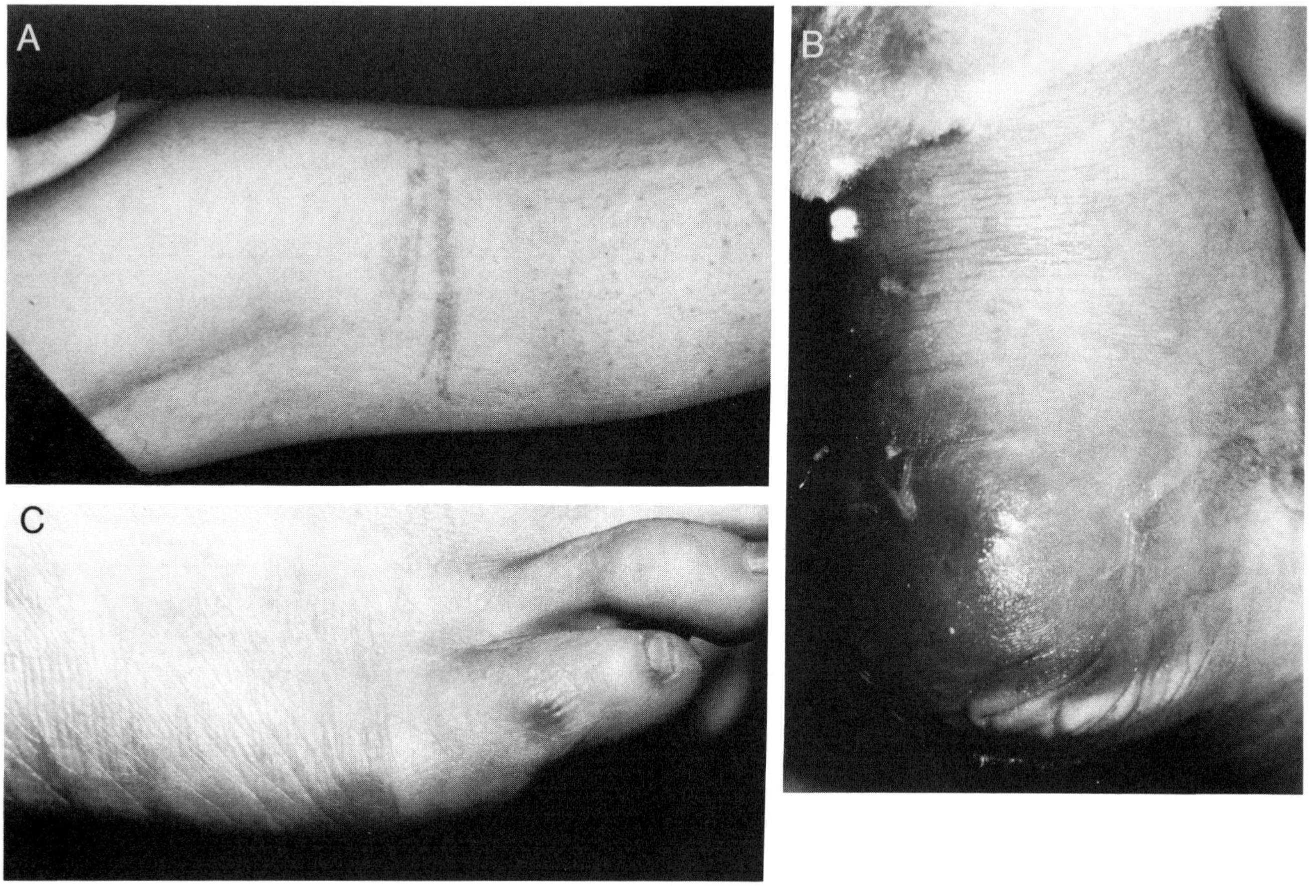

FIG 30–11.
Examples of pressure irritation caused by poorly applied below-knee casts. **A,** irritation to the common peroneal nerve at the fibular head and neck. The patient had dropfoot neurapraxia (temporary paralysis of anterior leg muscles) after cast removal. **B,** preulcerative irritation and maceration to the posterior heel area. Additional padding of the heel prevents this problem. **C,** preulcerative irritation to the fifth metatarsal head area and fifth toe. The use of tongue blades during cast application can prevent this sequela.

FIG 30–12.
Examples of some currently available cast padding.

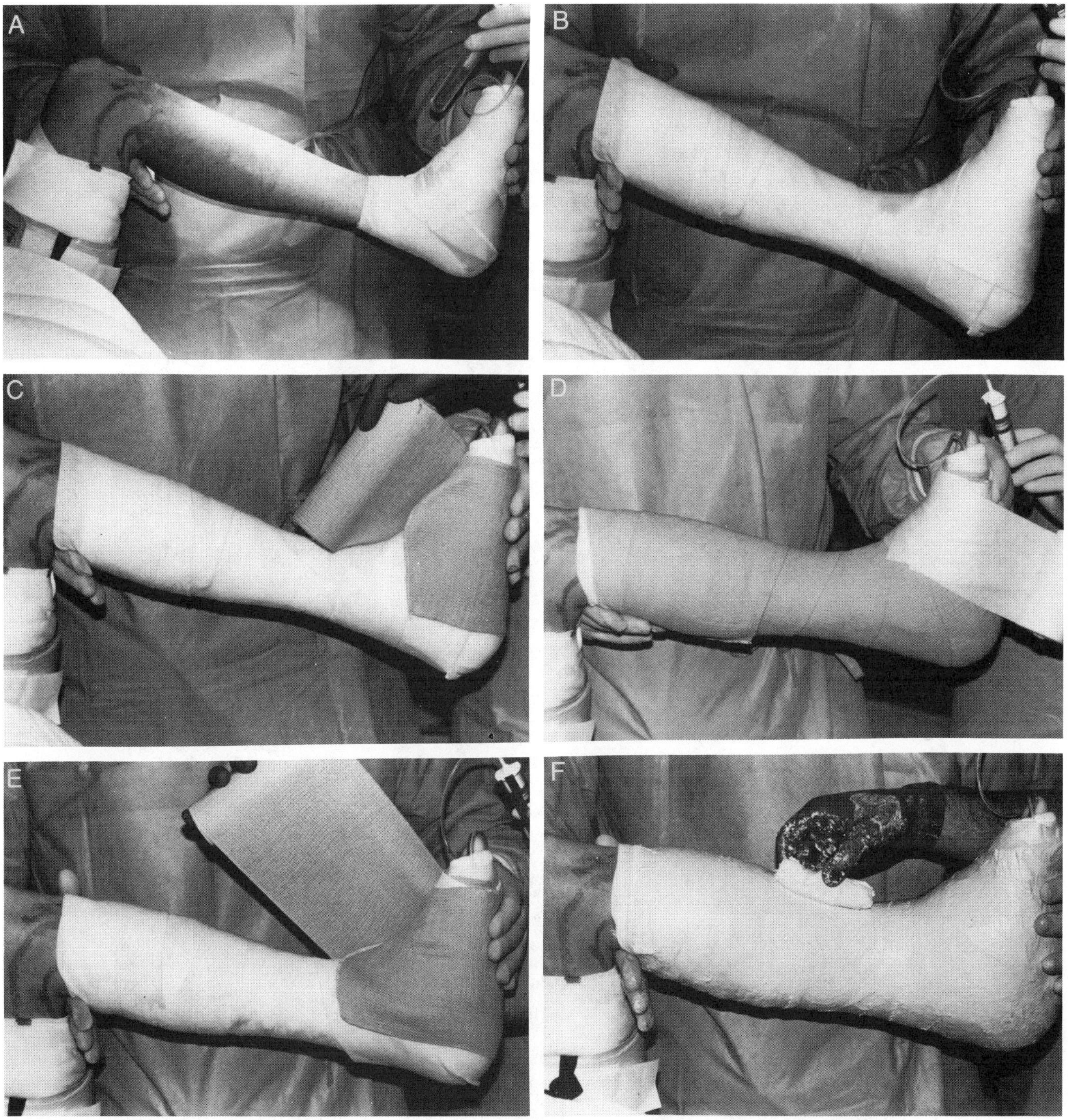

FIG 30–13.
Demonstration of the application of a compression cast. **A,** proper positioning of the lower extremity for the supine application of a compression cast. Postoperative surgical dressing has been applied. **B,** first layer of cast padding applied directly to the surgical dressing and skin. **C,** second layer—an elastic bandage applied distally to proximally to create a pressure gradient. **D,** the third layer is another layer of cast padding. **E,** the fourth layer is another elastic wrap. In this fashion, alternating layers of cast padding and elastic wraps may be continued if desired. **F,** the final layer is rigid material. In this case, plaster of paris is applied in a cylindrical shell fashion.

ing. If no dressing is present, the stockinette is applied directly over the skin. The stockinette should not have any wrinkles in it after application. A natural fold in the stockinette occurs over the anterior crease of the ankle joint. This fold may either be cut out or left neatly in place (Fig 30–14,A and B).

The second layer of the cast is cast padding. As with stockinette material, numerous types and widths of cast padding are available (Fig 30–12).

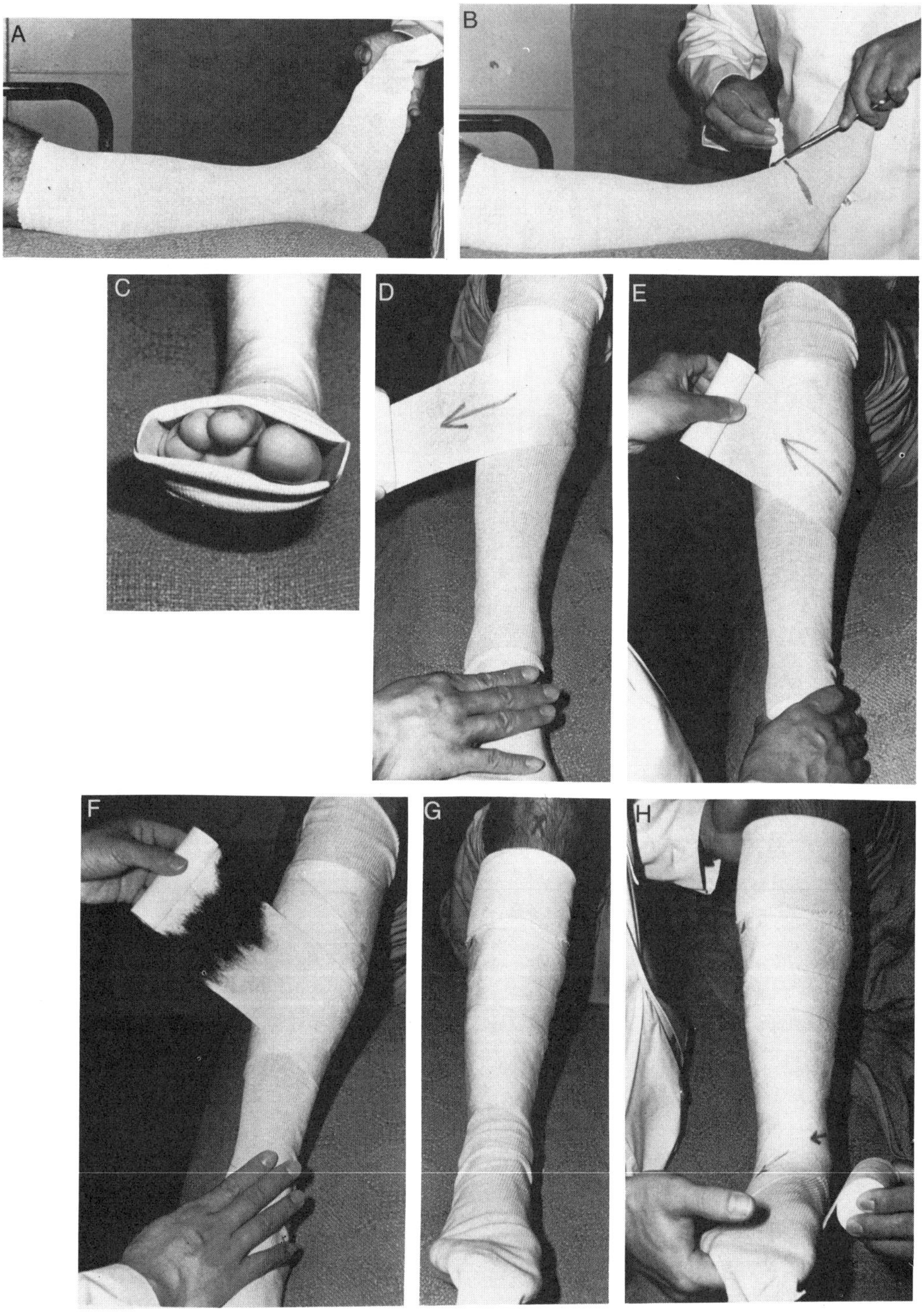

FIG 30–14.
A–R, Demonstration of the application of a below-knee cast.

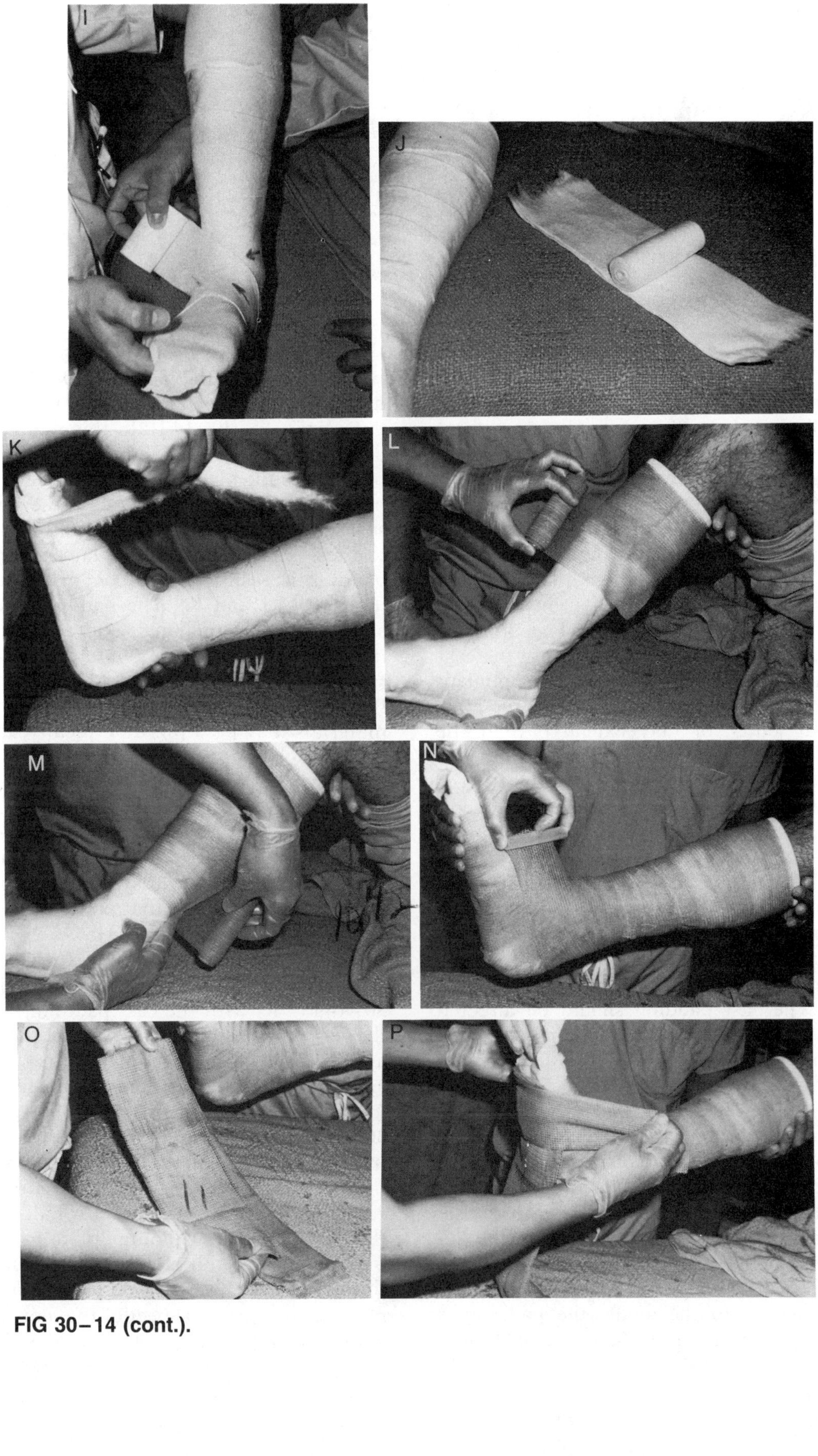

FIG 30–14 (cont.).

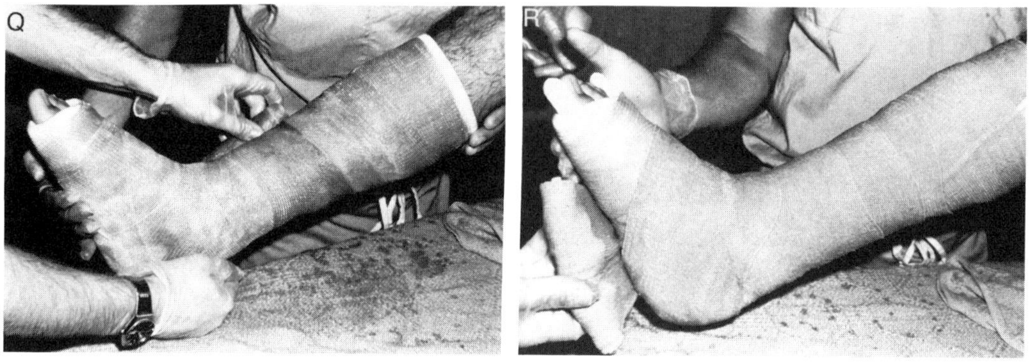

FIG 30–14 (cont.).

Typically, 3- or 4-in.-wide cast padding is utilized in the application of a below-knee cast. The padding is applied to protect prominent areas and pressure points and is placed over all areas where cast material will be applied. A half-inch additional margin at both ends of the cast, where no cast material will be applied, will prevent the more rigid cast material from irritating the skin. The padding is applied so that the upper margin of the cast will be two finger breadths below the fibular head and neck. This will prevent irritation to the common peroneal nerve (see Figs 30–10,A and 30–11,A). The lower, or distal, end of the cast may stop just proximal to the metatarsophalangeal joints, may extend just distal to the metatarsophalangeal joints, or may extend beyond the tips of the toes. Pressure to the first and fifth metatarsal heads and digits can be avoided with the temporary insertion of tongue blades placed medially and laterally beneath the stockinette (Fig 30–14,C).

Cast padding is applied by using a truncated weave. Application starts proximally and proceeds distally. Since the girth of the leg is greater proximally around the calf than it is distally around the ankle, the padding is angulated or truncated as it is applied. The cast padding should be directed slightly distally over the anterior tibial crest, circle posteriorly around the leg, and return directed slightly proximally (Fig 30–14,D and E). The cast padding is then pulled snug and torn. This provides two layers of padding over the anterior tibial crest for every one layer of padding over the muscular calf (Fig 30–14,F). This process is continued distally down the leg, with each subsequent layer overlapping the previous layer by approximately half its width (Fig 30–14,G). The ankle is then padded in a figure-of-8 fashion. Starting proximal to the ankle, the padding is brought over the anterior crease of the ankle in a slightly distal direction and brought around the plantar aspect of the foot (Fig 30–14,H). The padding is then returned proximally to cross its previous origin (Fig 30–14,I). In this manner, the padding is continued to the end of the foot. Additional padding to the plantar aspect of the foot, heel, and posterior portion of the leg is achieved by taking several layers of cast padding and applying them to these areas in one long plate. This additional padding is easily torn to conform to these areas (Fig 30–14,J and K). The padding over the foot and leg is then palpated, and any prominent or lightly padded areas are reinforced.

The final layer of the cast is the cast material. Plaster, synthetic material, or a combination of materials may be utilized. Typically, three to five rolls of 3- or 4-in. cast material are utilized in an adult below-knee cast. The cast material is applied proximally to distally. The first roll of material starts about a half inch below the upper edge of the cast padding and proceeds distally (Fig 30–14,L). Today, most synthetic cast materials have enough elasticity that no folds are created as one proceeds down the leg. However, if necessary, folds can be made in the materials, but they should be neat and kept to a minimum (Fig 30–14,M). As with the cast padding, each turn of the cast material should overlap the previously applied cast tape by about half its width. At the ankle, a figure-of-8 pattern is once again employed to lock the ankle joint in its proper position (Fig 30–14,N). The cast material is then continued cylindrically to the predetermined distal extent of the cast. Care is again taken to ensure that the cast padding protrudes about a half inch beyond the cast material. A plantar plate can be created by unraveling a roll of cast material into a single thick platform (Fig 30–14,O). This can then be applied to the plantar aspect of the foot with continuation to the posterior portion of the ankle and leg

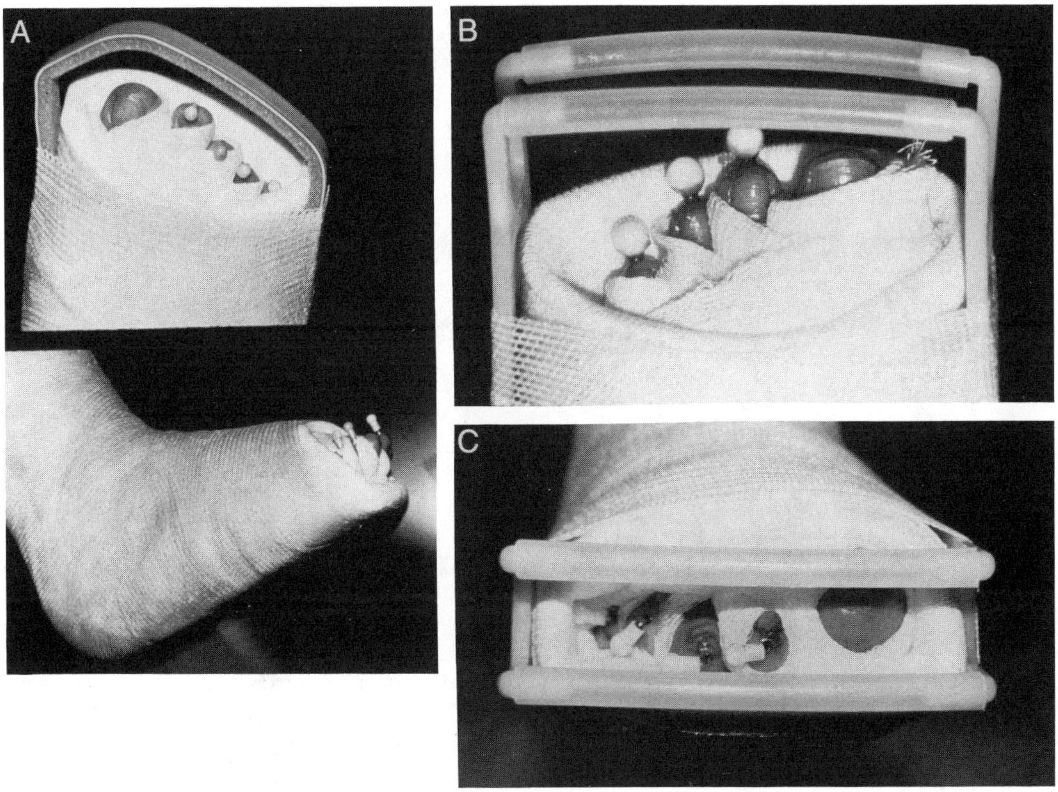

FIG 30–15.
Examples of toe protection that may be incorporated into the cast during application. **A,** aluminum moldable splint similar to material commonly used for finger injuries. **B** and **C,** adjustable plastic splint designed specifically for toe protection.

(Fig 30–14,P). At this point, the stockinette, extending proximally and distally from underneath the cast padding and cast material, can be folded back and incorporated into the final layers of the cast material. Utilizing the stockinette in this manner will allow protection of the cast padding and a more aesthetic cast appearance. Once the final roll is applied and the cast has begun to harden, the tongue blades may be removed (Fig 30–14,Q). The cast cures or hardens via an exothermic process, and the patient should be forewarned to expect some warmth. A cool elastic bandage may be used, if desired, to dissipate the temperature change and to help laminate the layers of cast material (Fig 30–14,R). After several minutes, the elastic bandage is removed, and the casting procedure is complete.

SPECIAL CONSIDERATIONS AND CAST MODIFICATIONS

Several modifications can be applied to the below-knee cast. These include toe guards to protect the digits and/or fixation materials extending from them (Fig 30–15,A–C) and walking heels that may be applied to the plantar aspect of the cast (Fig 30–16).

Several devices are available to make the patient with a below-knee cast safer and more comfortable. If the patient is to be weight bearing on

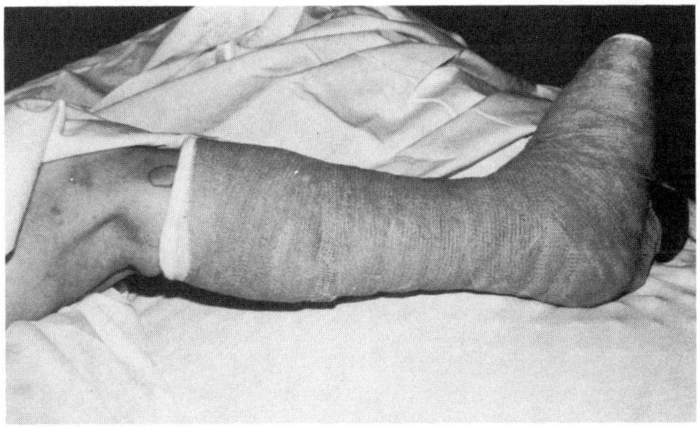

FIG 30–16.
Below-knee cast with a rubber plantar walking heel. The majority of direct pressure during cast weight bearing will be through this walking heel.

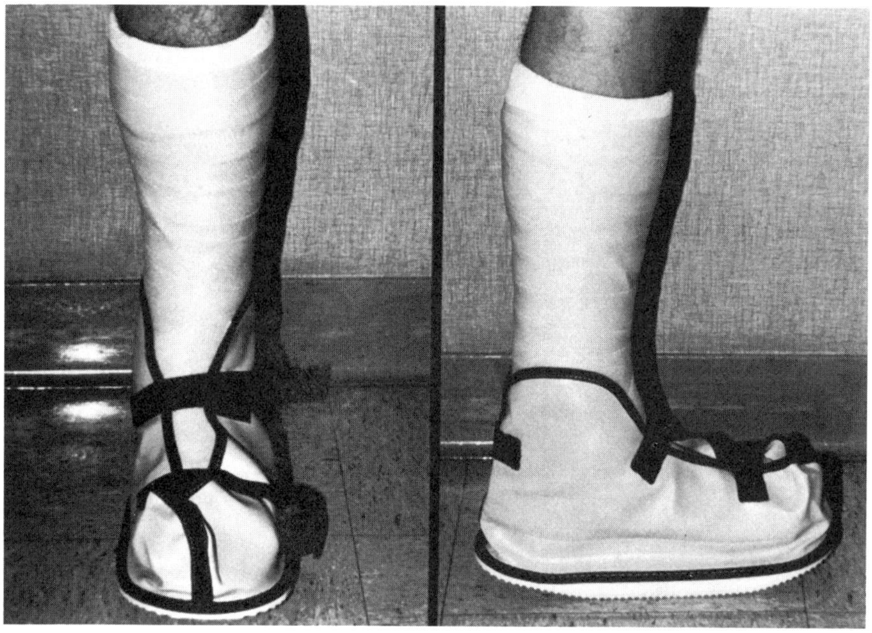

FIG 30–17.
Example of a cast boot that will give increased protection and traction to a patient in a weight-bearing below-knee cast.

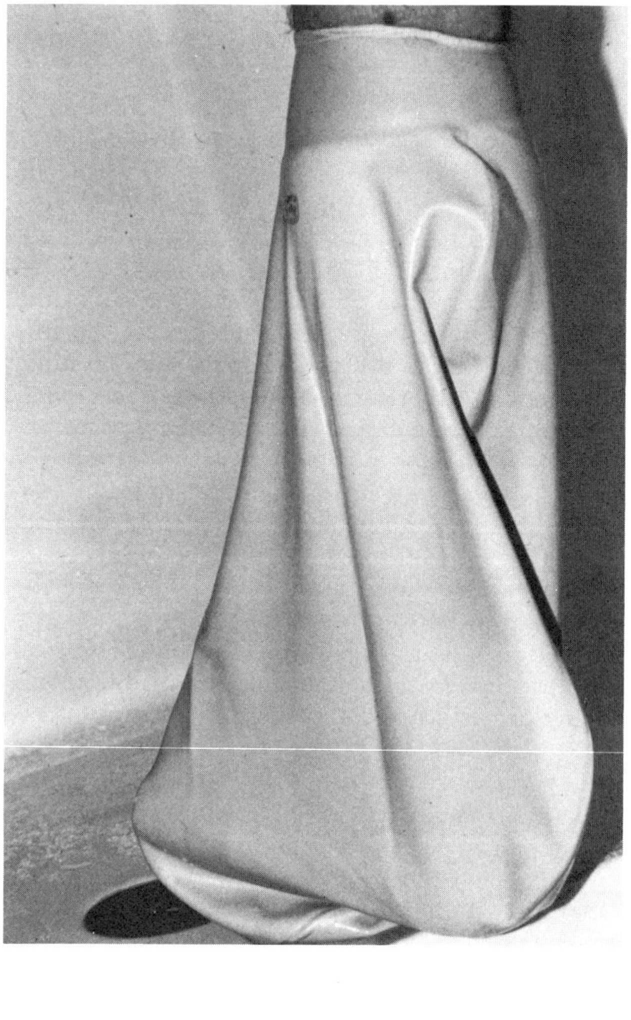

FIG 30–18.
Example of a rubber cast protector. These devices are convenient to the patient but are not infallibly waterproof.

the cast extremity, a rubber walking heel or a cast shoe may be used (Fig 30–17). It should be remembered that cast padding materials are not waterproof, and the patient should be instructed on how to properly protect the cast when bathing. If the patient is to wear the cast for a prolonged period of time, several cast protectors are available for bathing (Fig 30–18).

When early mobilization of joints and structures is desired to prevent atrophy, weakness, and stiffness associated with cast disease, a split or bivalved cast should be considered. A below-knee cast may be split or bivalved to allow easy removal by the patient for active and passive exercises. The cast can then be reapplied with elastic bandages when the patient is not exercising. To split or bivalve a below-knee cast, the cast is cut along its medial and lateral sides to create anterior and posterior halves. The stockinette and cast padding are then taped into place with moleskin, elastic tape, or any other suitable material (Fig 30–19,A and B). The bivalved cast is becoming more common to accelerate aftercare and rehabilitation and to diminish the disability associated with prolonged casting.

CAST REMOVAL

Below-knee casts are removed in a simple process with a cast saw. However, many patients, particularly children and the mentally handicapped, have an extreme fear of being cut. Forewarning, explanation, and reassurance make the removal of a cast a tolerable experience in most cases. The cast cutter works by vibrating the cast material apart, not by a rotating, cutting blade. Injury to the patient during cast removal is very rare, but even the most educated and confident patient can be apprehensive.

Casts are removed by splitting them down both sides. At the proximal and distal ends of the cast, a finger can be inserted to lift the cast away from the patient's skin. This allows one to start the cast-

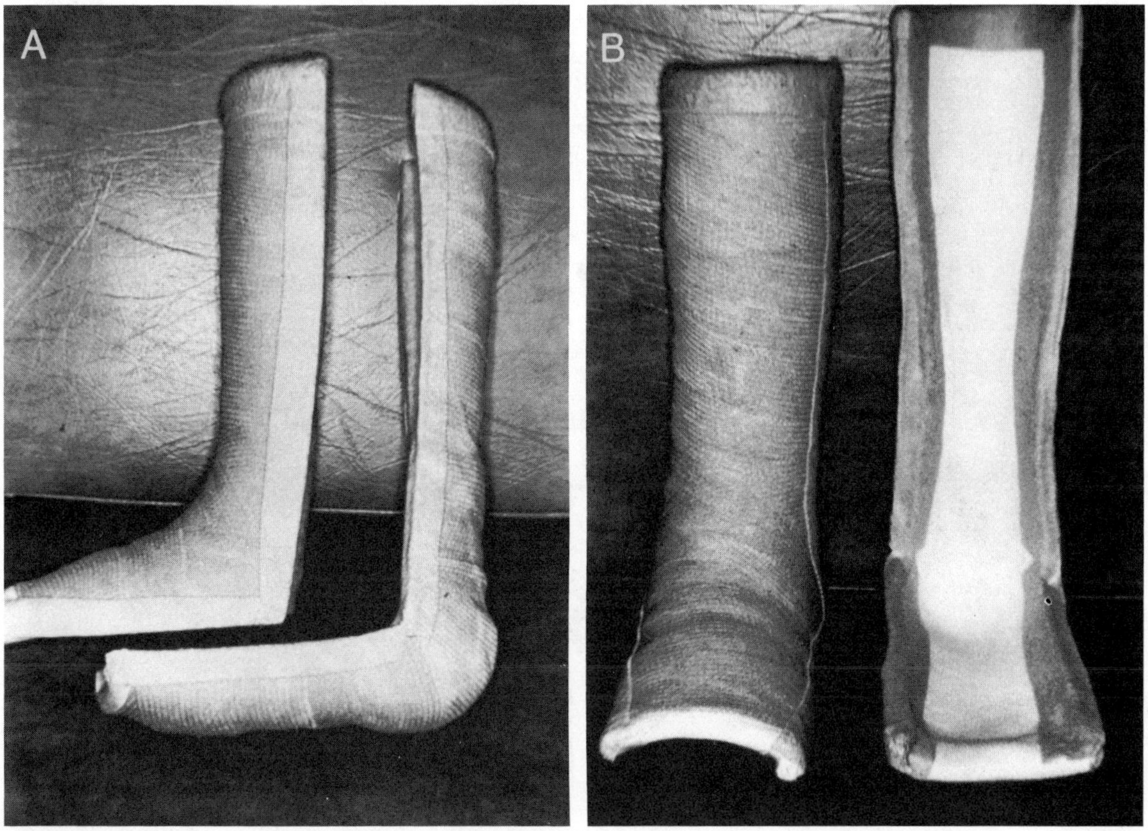

FIG 30–19.
A, and **B,** example of a bivalved below-knee cast. Note that the cast padding and stockinette have been reinforced along the edges with elastic tape.

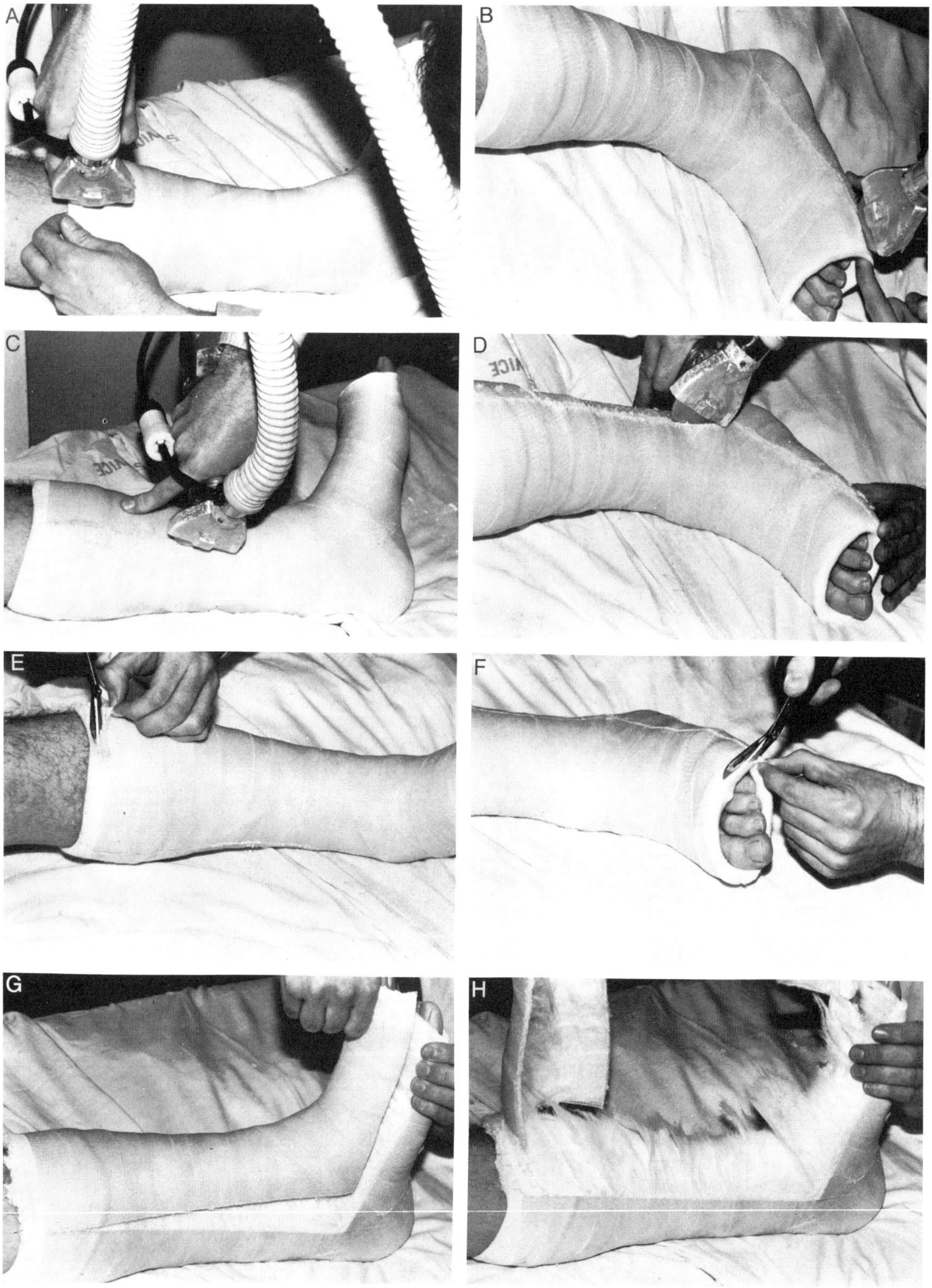

FIG 30–20.
A–K, demonstration of the removal of a below-knee cast.

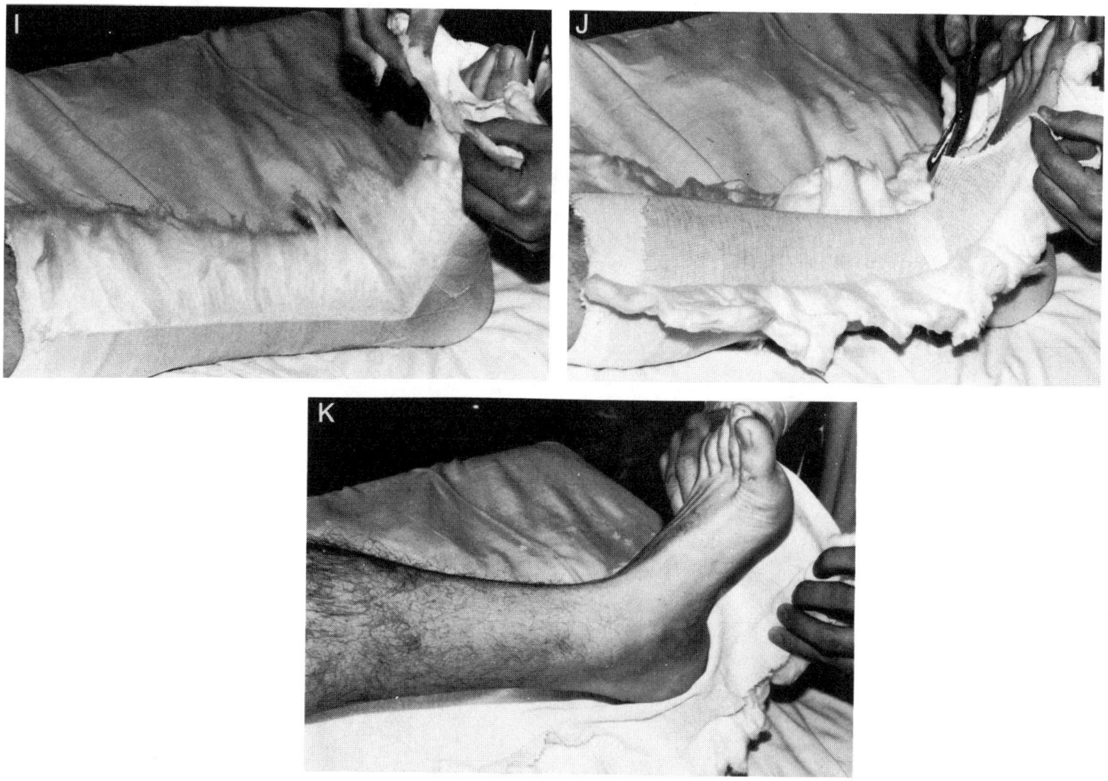

FIG 30–20 (cont.).

removing cut without any risk of touching the patient with the saw blade (Fig 30–20,A and B). The cast saw is always stabilized against the cast so that the blade moves along with the patient's leg (Fig 30–20,C). In this manner, if the patient should move suddenly or jump, the cast cutter will not go deeper and possibly frighten, burn, or cut the patient. A rhythmic, controlled up-and-down motion is used as the cast saw blade is advanced along both the medial and lateral sides of the cast (Fig 30–20,D). The cast padding should protect the patient from the cast blade. After the medial and lateral cuts are made, additional cuts may be effected over the malleoli or tender areas to make cast removal easier and more comfortable. A cast splitter or separator will help spread the cast apart. Once the cast cuts are completed, scissors are used to cut the stockinette both proximally and distally along the anterior half of the cast (Fig 30–20,E and F). The anterior half of the cast can then be easily removed (Fig 30–20,G and H). The underlying cast padding is then ripped apart manually or cut with scissors (Fig 30–20,I and J). The cast can then be easily removed by lifting the foot and leg out of the posterior half of the cast (Fig 30–20,K).

SUMMARY

Proper cast application is a distinct medical art form. The more one understands the concepts about their indications, application, and removal, the better prepared one will be for the practice of this art. Once prepared, the skill of casting is only achieved through practical application.

> "Skill in plastercraft is not to be learned from books but only by continuous repetition. . . . One who regards the application of plasters as a menial task is advised to transfer his attention to another specialty."—John Charnley (1950)

REFERENCES

1. Downey MS: Casting techniques: Below knee cast, in Jimenez AL (ed): *Third Annual Podiatric Medical Assistant's Surgical Seminar Syllabus.* Tucker, Ga, Podiatry Institute Publishing Co, 1986, pp 114–118.
2. Coleman WC, Brand PW, Birke JA: The total contact cast: A therapy for plantar ulceration on insensitive feet. *J Am Podiatr Assoc* 1984; 74:548–552.
3. Hollander MR, Holton K, Mader D: Total contact povidone-iodine perfusion cast for the treatment of

neuropathic ulcers. *J Foot Surg* 1986; 25:484–488.
4. Burnett O: Total contact cast. *Clin Podiatr Med Surg* 1987; 4:471–479.
5. Ganley JV: Corrective casting in infants. *Clin Podiatr* 1984; 1:501–516.
6. Hice GA, Solomon W, Faschada P: The plaster-synthetic cast. *J Am Podiatr Assoc* 1983; 73:427–431.

ADDITIONAL REFERENCES

Charnley J: *The Closed Treatment of Common Fractures*, ed 3. New York, Churchill Livingstone Inc, 1961.
Miller SJ: Postoperative management, in McGlamry ED (ed): *Fundamentals of Foot Surgery*. Baltimore, Williams & Wilkins, 1987, pp 294–314.
Wu KK: *Techniques in Surgical Casting and Splinting*. Philadelphia, Lea & Febiger, 1987.

31

Wound Healing: Redressing and Suture and Fixation Removal

Thomas J. Merrill, D.P.M.

I. Inflammation Phase
II. Fibroplasia Phase
III. Maturation Phase
IV. Dressing Changes
V. Suture Removal
VI. Skin Staple Removal
VII. Fixation Removal

The decisions concerning surgical dressing changes, suture removal, and fixation removal are based on an understanding of wound healing. The evaluation of the healing process will determine the type of dressing used, the amount of immobilization needed, the recognition of complications, and the timing of suture or fixation removal.

The body responds immediately to the trauma of surgery. During surgery, chemicals that control the process of wound healing are being released by the body. This response process is divided into three phases: inflammation, fibroplasia, and maturation. Each phase identifies a specific contribution to the healing process.

INFLAMMATION PHASE

During surgery, the body responds to the attack with vascular constriction. This initial vasoconstriction controls blood loss. After the bleeding has stopped by coagulation, the vessels dilate and allow increased circulation to the area. White blood cells are signaled to migrate to the area. This is called the inflammatory reaction. These cells look for bacteria and digest necrotic tissue. Within 12 hours after the incision is made, an inflammatory fibrin mesh fills the wound and seals it from the environment. This seal forms along the incision and at the entrance sites of sutures and fixation pins. Epithelial cells, small capillary buds, and nutritional proteins migrate across this delicate fibrin bridge. The external support and immobilization of Steri-Strip tape, a bandage, a surgical shoe, or a cast helps to preserve this seal and enhance the healing of the wound. Ice, elevation, and compression help to decrease the pain and swelling. Because of this cellular infiltration, the inflammation phase is also called the productive, substrate, or lag phase of wound healing. This initial response to trauma continues for 3 to 6 days and is followed by the fibroplasia phase.

FIBROPLASIA PHASE

The cellular components of our bodies are held together by collagen fibers (Fig 31–1). Collagen fibers are arranged in specific directions to support the body structures. Fibroblasts are the cells that produce collagen. They are stimulated to synthesize collagen during this phase of wound healing. The new collagen lacks organization and direction (Fig 31–2). As remodeling occurs, the tensile strength gradually increases. Because of the in-

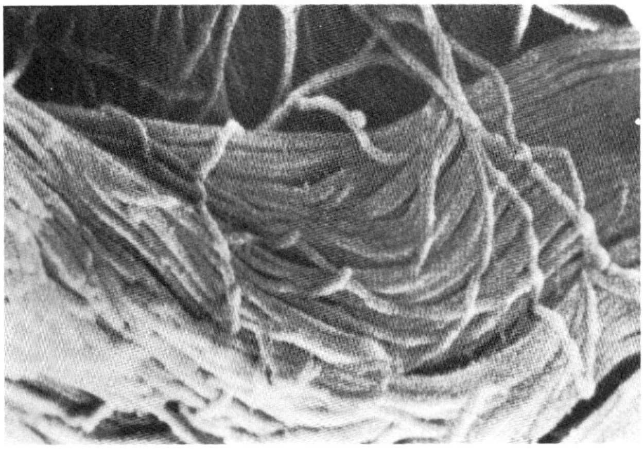

FIG 31–1.
A magnification of normal collagen fibers. Note the organization and direction of the fibers. (Original magnification ×1,000.)

creased production of collagen, this phase is also called the collagen phase of wound healing. This increased production normally continues until 17 to 21 days after surgery and then subsides (Fig 31–3). An overproduction of collagen can produce an unsightly or painful scar. These scars are called hypertrophic scars or keloids. A hypertrophic scar develops immediately after surgery, remains within the area of the initial trauma, and usually improves over time (Fig 31–4). A keloid is a scar that is an inherited tendency, develops over a period of time, expands beyond the boundaries of the initial incision, and will increase over time (Fig 31–5). A hypertrophic scar will usually respond to conservative treatments, whereas a keloid often requires skin plastic reconstruction of the area.

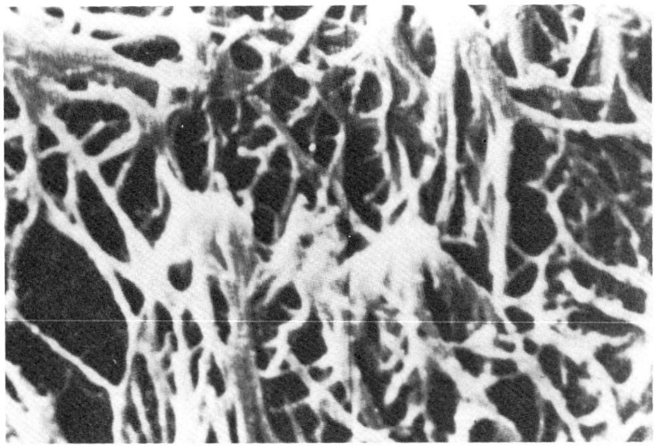

FIG 31–2.
A magnification of collagen fibers immediately after surgery. The fibers are disoriented and offer little tissue support. (Original magnification ×1,000.)

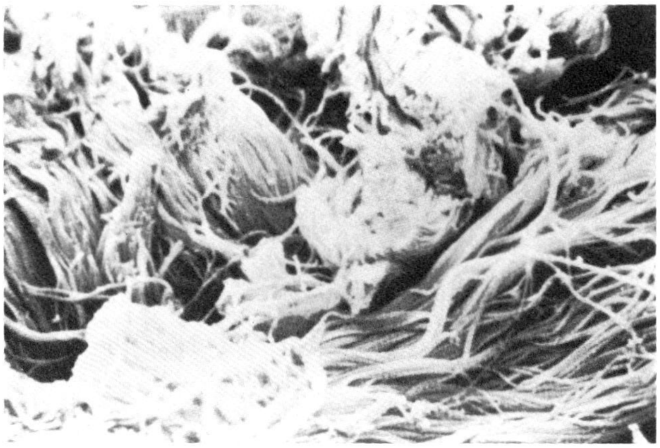

FIG 31–3.
A magnification of collagen fibers 21 days after surgery. The fibers are more dense and are beginning to remodel. (Original magnification ×1,000.)

MATURATION PHASE

The remodeling of the collagen is the maturation phase. The cellular activity of the area gradually decreases. Cellular components leave the area, and the vascular channels are obliterated. As the initial swelling, pain, and inflammation of the surgery subsides, the body continues to reorganize the collagen fibers. They are broken down and redirected. The collagen becomes more dense, and the incision contracts. At 21 days after surgery, the wound has 15% of its ultimate tensile strength. This is enough strength to support normal activity. Depending upon the surgical site, this phase may be complete 42 days after surgery. The collagen will continue to remodel and strengthen over the next 2 years, although the wound will never be as strong as normal tissue.

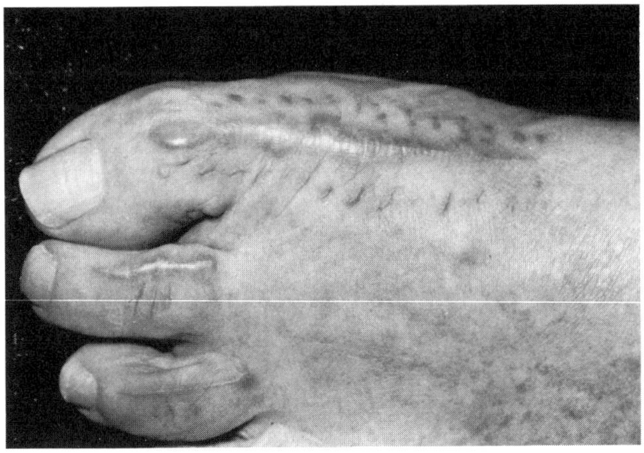

FIG 31–4.
A hypertrophic scar does not extend beyond the area of trauma and will gradually improve over time.

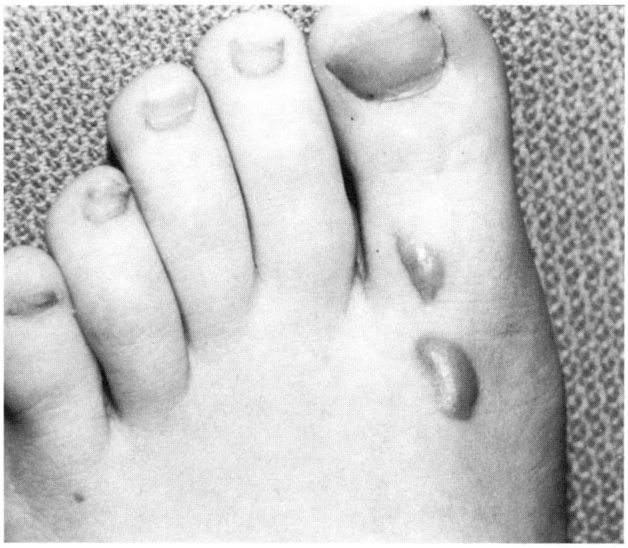

FIG 31–5.
A keloid will expand beyond the boundaries of the trauma and will increase over time. These keloids formed at the location of two insect bites and have increased in size during the course of 1 year.

DRESSING CHANGES

Sterile surgical dressings should be kept dry and undisturbed for at least 3 days. Elevation and inactivity are the best analgesics available. The mild compression of the dressing will support the skin during the inflammation stage of wound healing and help to control swelling. If the dressing becomes tight, the inflammation can cause skin ulceration, decreased circulation, and even severe necrosis. The signs of a tight dressing include localized pain that is in an area away from the surgical site or pain that is totally unresponsive to pain medication. The dressing should be kept dry because moisture on the skin can carry bacteria down the suture tract and penetrate the body.

The patient should undergo the initial dressing change 3 to 7 days after surgery to inspect the wound and provide a fresh, comfortable, sterile dressing. The patient may be anxious about having the protective bandage removed and may have fears about how the incision will look. Reassure the patient that there will be only mild discomfort and that the stiff, uncomfortable dressing will be replaced with a new, clean, comfortable, soft dressing. The patient should be in a reclined position, and the armrests should be in place in case the patient feels faint.

The initial dressing change is very important to assess the possibility of infection, wound dehiscence, suture reaction, or hematoma formation. The dressing should be carefully removed to prevent disturbance of the delicate epithelial cells that have sealed the wound. Surgical pins should not be moved or turned during the dressing change to preserve the epithelial cells that have sealed the pin entrance. Povidone iodine solution (Betadine), chlorhexidine gluconate (Hibiclens), sterile water, or sterile hydrogen peroxide can be used if there is a large amount of dried hemorrhage (Fig 31–6). The incision is inspected for edema. Tight sutures may result and strangulate tissue (Fig 31–7,A and B). The sutures should be removed and the site repaired with Steri-Strips. Sutures must also be removed from an infected incision. The suture material itself will protect bacteria from the body's immune system and any antibiotics in the circulation. A Gram's stain and culture should be taken if there is drainage.

SUTURE REMOVAL

The suture tract provides an opening in the skin and an entrance for bacteria. Sterile technique consisting of hand washing, sterile gloves, and sterile instruments should be used. The configura-

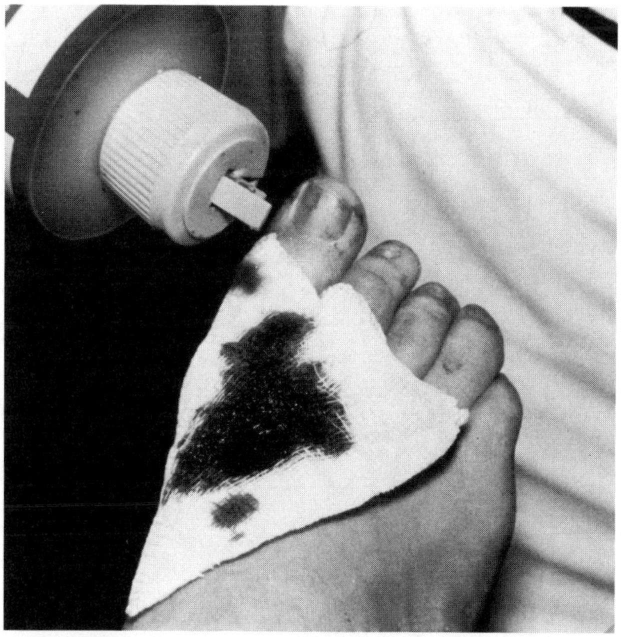

FIG 31–6.
Antiseptic antibiotic skin cleansers such as povidone-iodine solution or chlorhexidine gluconate solution can be used to soften dried hemorrhage on a dressing. Water or hydrogen peroxide can also be used if they are sterile.

FIG 31–7.
A, a suture cannot expand to allow for swelling and must be removed if it is strangulating the tissue within. **B,** the postoperative swelling has made these sutures tight. The tight sutures must be removed and can be replaced with Steri-Strips.

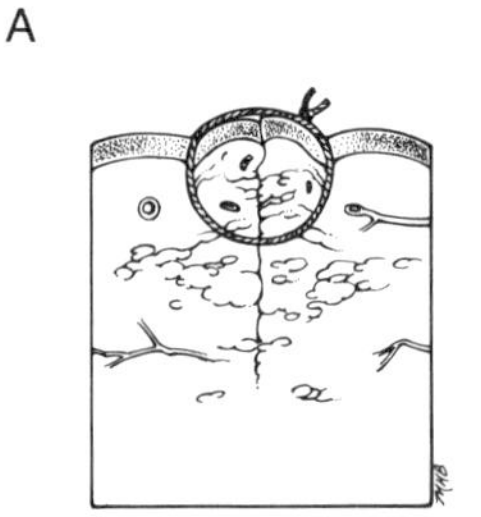

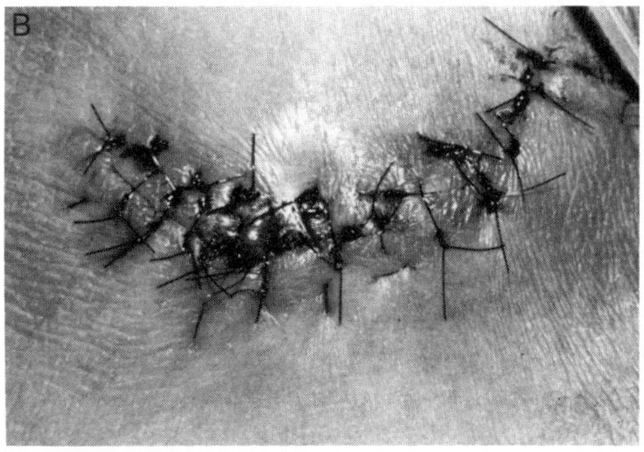

tion of the suture is visualized (Fig 31–8), and the knot is located. The knot is lifted away from the skin and the suture is cut close to the skin (Fig 31–9 and 31–10). When this method is used, the long, contaminated suture tail will not be pulled down into the fresh, healing wound. Care must be taken not to abandon a piece of the suture under the skin. The sutures are not removed from one end to the other; rather, alternating sutures are removed. If the security of the incision is in doubt, one or two sutures can be removed to see whether the skin edges are sufficiently adherent, (Fig 31–11). Every other suture may be removed at one visit and the remaining sutures removed a week later.

Once the healing process can support the incision, the sutures should be removed. The immature scar should be supported with Steri-Strips for 3 weeks to prevent wound dehiscence (separation). The external support will decrease the collagen response of the body and decrease the chance of a hypertrophic scar or keloid. If the sutures are not removed, epithelial cells will continue to migrate down the suture tracts and produce unsightly "railroad track" scars (Fig 31–12). In certain

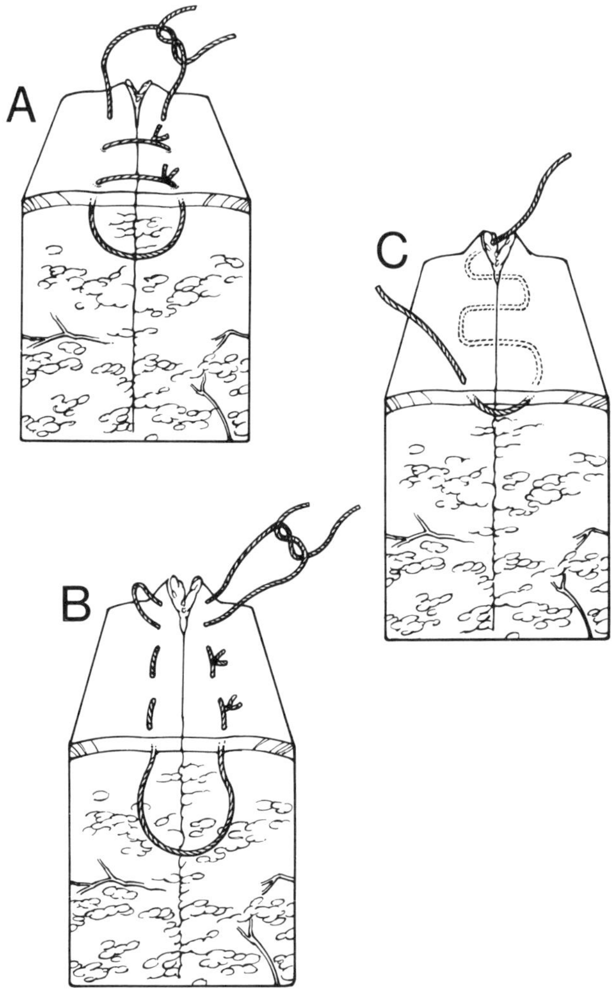

FIG 31–8.
There are many suture configurations: **A,** simple interrupted suture; **B,** horizontal mattress suture; **C,** continuous running subcuticular suture.

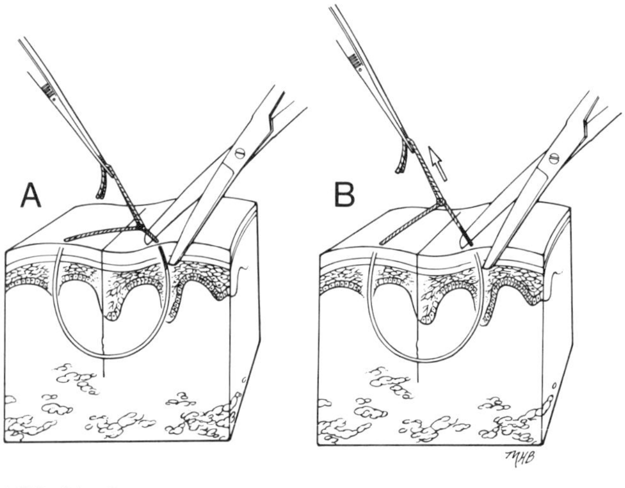

FIG 31–9.
A, the suture knot is lifted from the skin, **B,** the seal is broken, and the sterile section of the suture is cut to prevent the exposed and contaminated suture tail from being pulled through the wound.

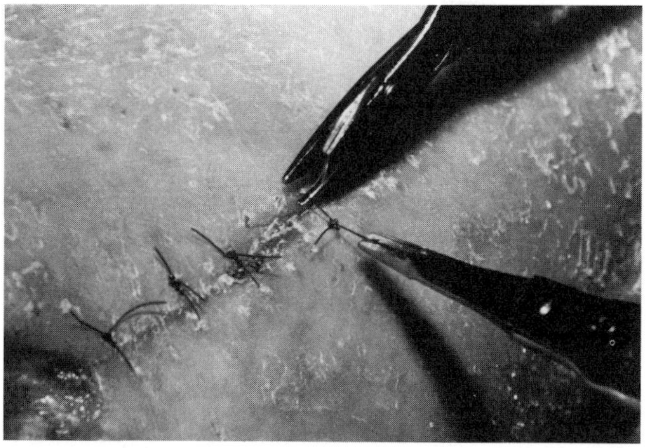

FIG 31–10.
The fibrin seal is broken, and a section of the suture that was below the skin is cut. Note that the skin is dry from being in a bandage.

cases, an absorbable suture can be used to close the skin. These sutures do not have to be removed and are broken down by the body (Fig 31–13). The irregular, raised, purplish appearance of the immature scar tissue can be of great concern to the patient. The patient should be reassured that the scar will decrease and lighten in color as it matures and remodels over the next several months. The deep red color of the incision is an indication that the deeper structures are also continuing to heal.

The incision line is painted with povidone-iodine (Betadine), chlorhexidine gluconate (Hibiclens), or alcohol to decrease bacteria on the skin, and the foot is redressed in a dry sterile dressing. The patient should wait a day for the suture tract to seal before getting the area wet. Bandaging dries out the skin, and a moisturizing lotion should be used when bathing is begun. Reassure

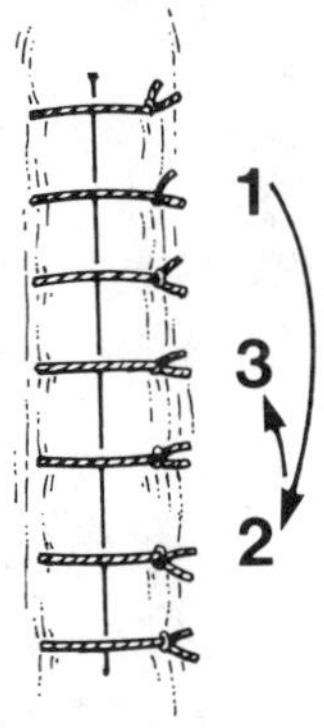

FIG 31–11.
The order of suture removal is every other suture so that the strength of the wound can be evaluated.

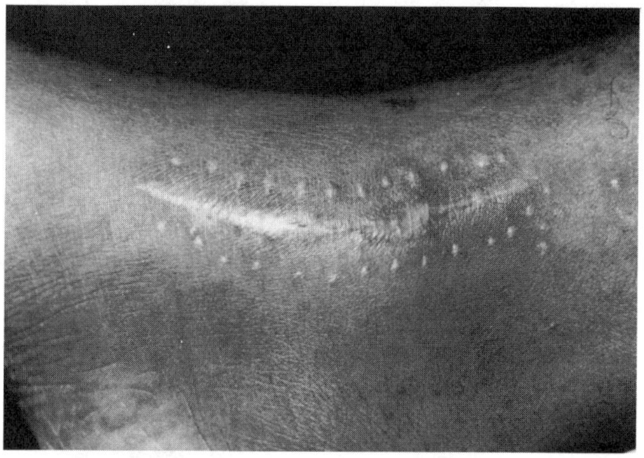

FIG 31–12.
A "railroad track" scar.

the patient that the scar will continue to remodel and improve in appearance over the next 2 years.

SKIN STAPLE REMOVAL

Skin staples should be removed at the same time and in the same sequence as sutures. As with sutures, skin staples are also removed if they become tight or if infection is identified. A staple remover is used to bend the metal staple and release the skin below (Fig 31–14,A–C).

FIXATION REMOVAL

Surgical pins are used to hold bone cuts together or to immobilize tendons or joint capsules.

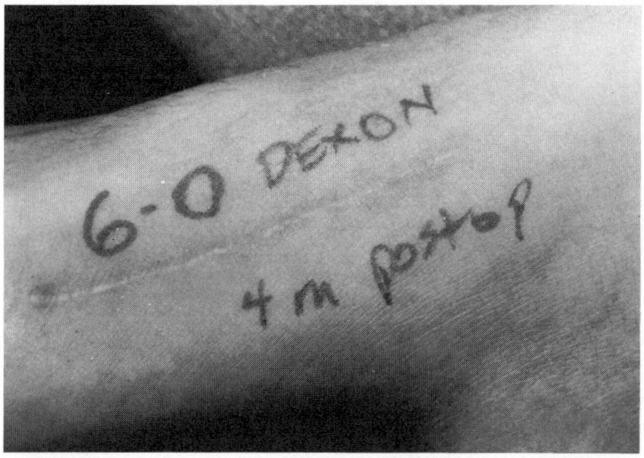

FIG 31–13.
A running subcuticular configuration was used with an absorbable suture to produce a very nice scar 4 months postoperatively.

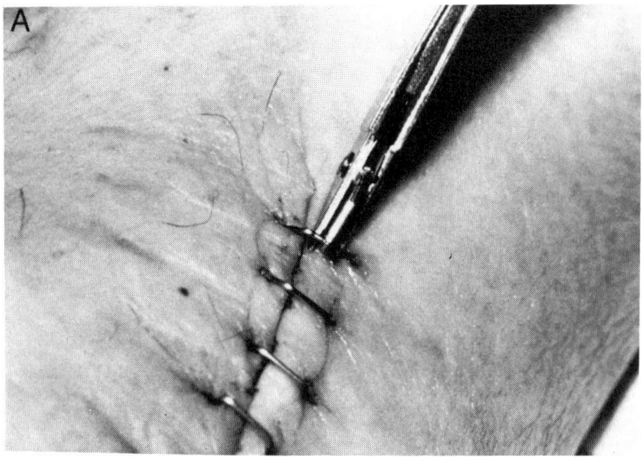

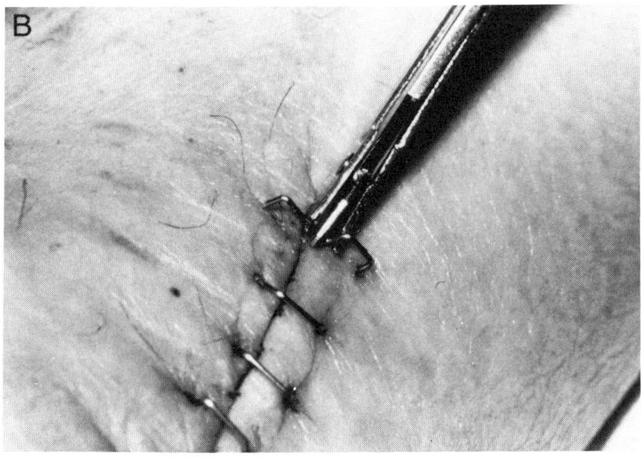

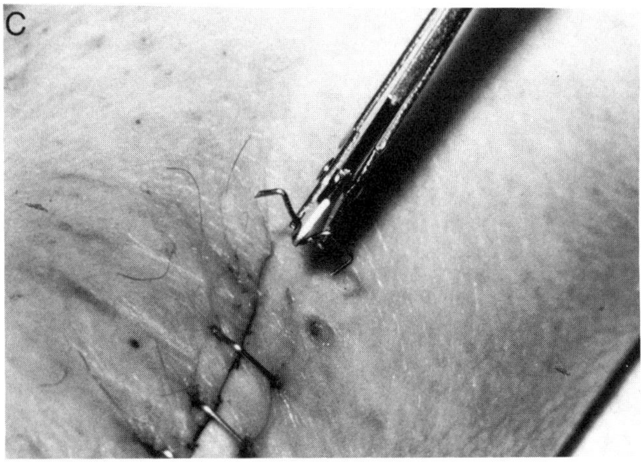

FIG 31–14.
A, a staple remover has three teeth that attach to the skin staple. **B,** as the jaws of the instrument are compressed, the skin staple is bent. **C,** this releases the skin that the staple had been supporting.

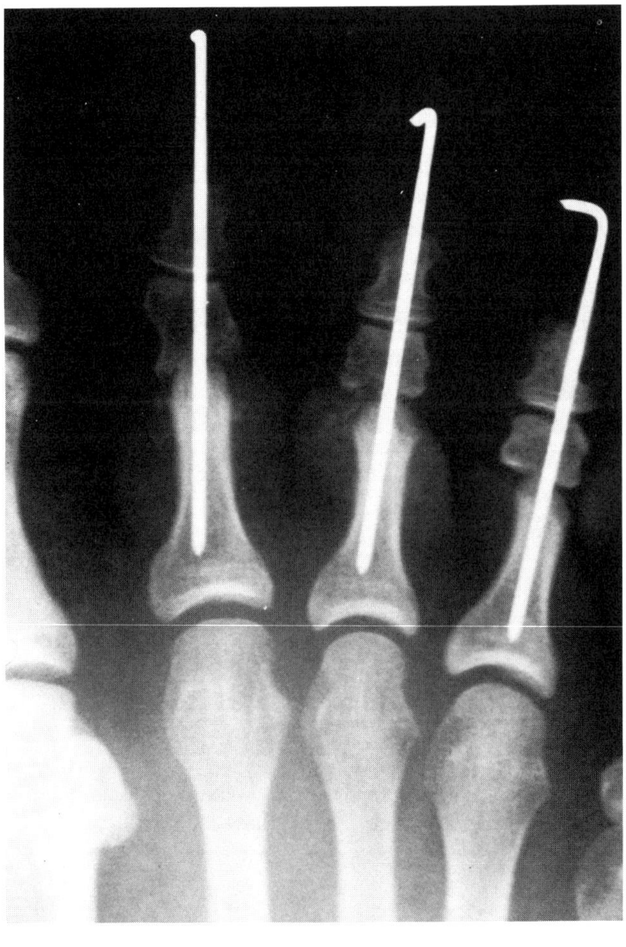

FIG 31–15.
Radiographs are used to follow the progress of the bone healing and check the position of the fixation.

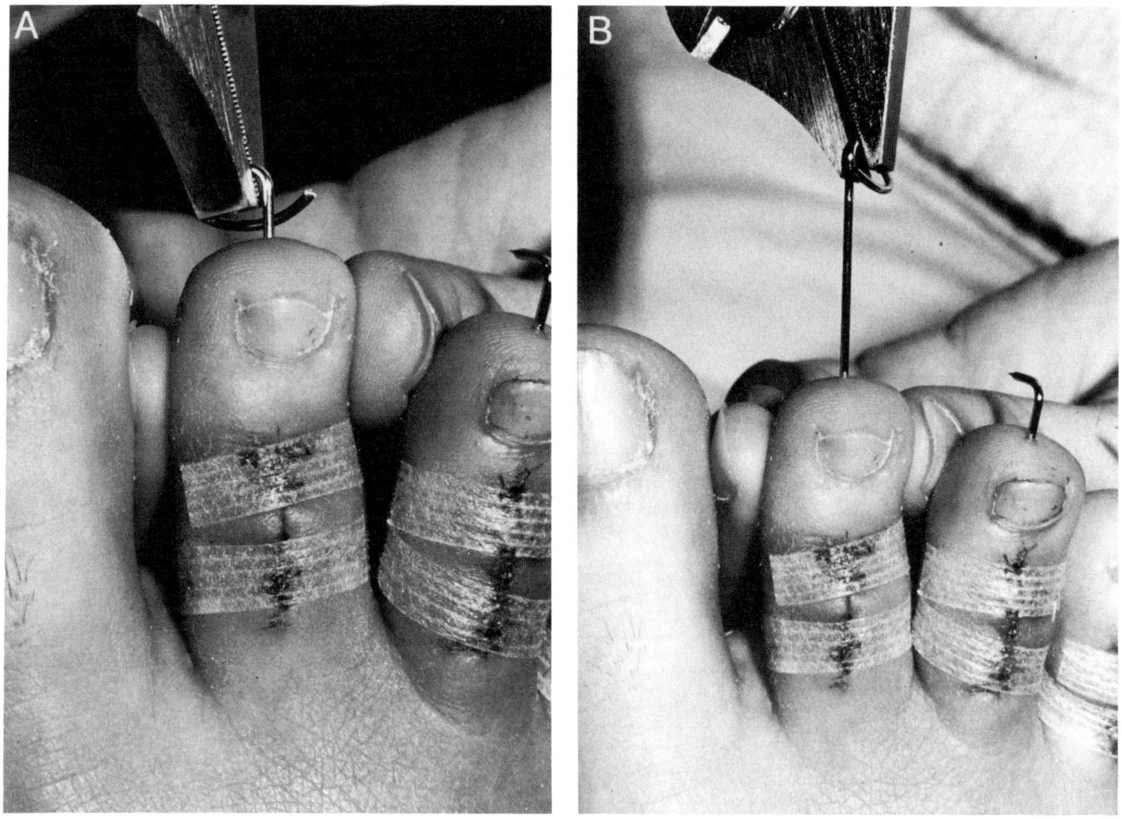

FIG 31–16.
A, the toe is stabilized, and the fixation pin is grasped firmly with a pair of pliers. **B,** the pin is rotated to break the epithelial seal that has formed. A steady, smooth, linear pull is used to extract the pin.

The pins should remain in place until there is satisfactory bone or soft-tissue support from the wound healing. Bone, tendon, and capsule take about 6 weeks to heal. The pins can be removed earlier, depending on the location of the surgery and the external immobilization available. As with sutures, if the pins are constricting circulation, especially in a toe, or if infection is present, the pins should be removed.

Kirschner wire pins are available in four sizes (pin diameter measured in inches), 0.028, 0.035, 0.045, and 0.062. Usually a lesser toe is fixated with a 0.035- or 0.045-in. wire, and a first metatarsal osteotomy is fixated with a 0.062-in. wire. As with sutures, a delicate fibrin clot forms to seal the wire against the skin. Motion between the wire and the skin will break this seal and allow bacteria to invade the body. This is the cause of most "pin tract" infections. External immobilization with a bandage, rigid surgical shoe, or cast will decrease this motion and protect the seal.

A radiograph at the time of pin removal will show any healing or alignment problems (Fig 31–15). A bent pin is much more difficult to remove, and a local anesthetic block may be needed. The patient may be anxious about having the pin removed. Reassure the patient that the body does not heal directly to the pin but rather the body seals itself from the pin. It is advisable to recline the patient and possibly obstruct the patient's view of the area to reduce apprehension. The foot or toe must be held firm during the pin removal. The wire is turned to break the epithelial seal that has formed, and a smooth, linear motion is used (Fig 31–16,A and B). A radiograph should be taken to document removal of the fixation. Antibiotic solution or cream and a small bandage are applied to the pin sites. The patient should keep the area dry for at least 3 days.

A knowledge of the wound healing process will help to determine the necessity and the timing of suture or fixation removal. Careful attention to the healing process, protection of the incision, and adequate skin care will produce the best scar possible.

32

Injections

Alfred J. Phillips, D.P.M.

Administering injections is a common practice in the podiatric office. Injections are performed for a variety of reasons. Local anesthesia is used for the majority of podiatric surgical procedures, including office procedures, the treatment of warts, and infected or ingrown toenails. Corticosteroid injections are used for the relief of acute inflammatory pain such as that associated with heel spur syndrome or neuromas. Synovial cysts, or ganglions, are extravasations of joint capsule or a tendon sheath. These cysts are filled with synovial fluid and are at times inflamed and enlarged. When they are symptomatic, the fluid must be aspirated.

It is important for the podiatric assistant to learn the proper preparation of the injectable material as well as the proper way to perform injections. The correct placement of the injectable material and the performance of the injection as painlessly as possible are critical in injection therapy.

NEEDLES AND SYRINGES

Needles come in various lengths and diameters. The most common lengths used in podiatry are ½, 1, 1¼, and 1½ in. A particular length is chosen with respect to the distance from the skin to the furthest site where the injectable material is to be placed. A short needle is used to raise a wheal when removing a wart, while a longer needle would be used to place a corticosteroid deep into the medial aspect of the heel.

The gauge of the needle describes its relative diameter. In podiatric procedures, commonly used needles vary from 18 to 27 gauge. The lower the gauge, the greater the diameter of the needle. A low gauge needle (19 to 23) is used when drawing up an injectable material from the vial or when aspirating a cyst. A higher gauge needle (25 to 27) is used for giving injections.

The syringes commonly used in podiatric practice vary from 3 to 20 cc. The smaller the syringe, the less pressure that is placed on the injectable and the less pain during the injection technique. It is not a good practice to use a 10-cc syringe to inject a digit or a 3-cc syringe with multiple refills to perform a block on a forefoot. The amount of anesthetic needed should determine the syringe to be used.

PREPARATION OF INJECTABLES

Before drawing up any injectable, double check the label. Serious complications can occur if the wrong injectable is used. Also check the expiration date of the vial, and discard the vial if the expiration date has passed (Fig 32–1).

Maintaining sterility is important when drawing up an injectable. When using a new vial both the rubber underneath the cap and the contents are sterile. If the vial has been previously opened,

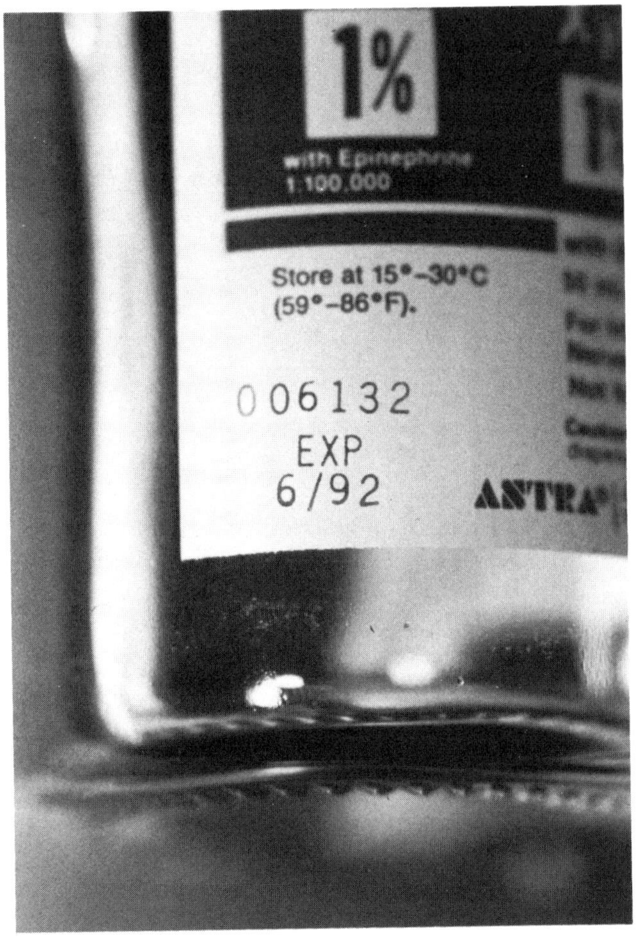

FIG 32–1.
Always check the expiration date on the vial before administering the injection.

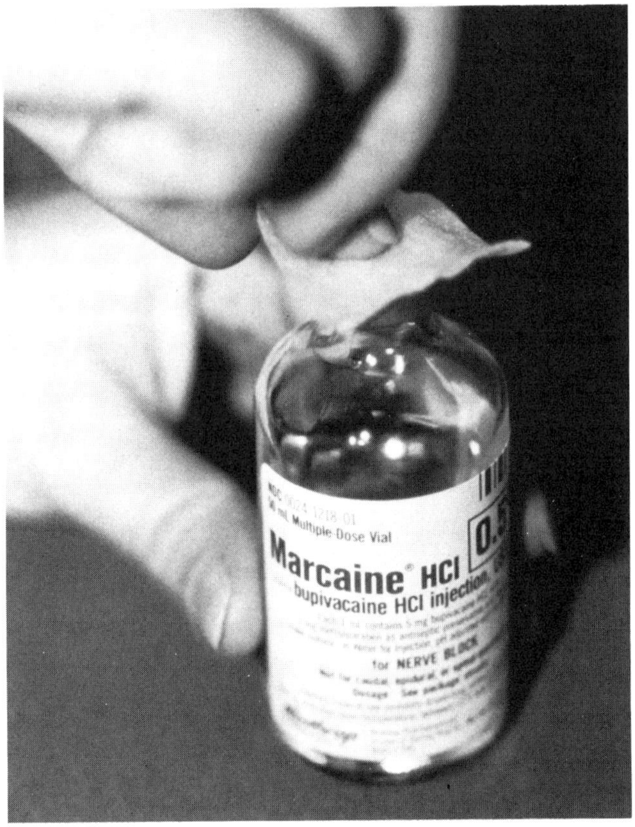

FIG 32–2.
Wipe the top of the vial with an alcohol pad.

an alcohol pad should be wiped on the top of the vial to maintain sterility (Fig 32–2).

Inject air into the vial before drawing up the injectable to prevent a vacuum within the vial. If 1½ cc of injectable is to be drawn up, then 1½ cc of air should first be injected into the vial.

COMMON INJECTIONS

Anesthetic blocks

Local anesthetics affect the electrical impulse of the nerve and block transmission of pain receptors. To be effective, local anesthetics must be placed on or near the nerve.

There are two varieties of local anesthetics, short acting and long acting. Short-acting local anesthetics have a quick onset but last for a relatively short time. Long-acting local anesthetics take longer to take effect but last for a relatively longer period of time. Frequently, the podiatrist needs local anesthesia that begins acting quickly but lasts for an extended period of time. In this case, a short-acting anesthetic is mixed with a long-acting anesthetic to produce the desired effect. The most frequently used short-acting local anesthetic is lidocaine (Xylocaine, Astra Pharma ceuticals, Westboro, Mass). Bupivacaine (Marcaine, Winthrop Pharmaceuticals, New York) is the most commonly used long-acting anesthetic. Xylocaine and Marcaine are marketed in different concentrations. The higher the number, the greater the concentration. Xylocaine is available in 0.5%, 1%, and 2% concentrations. Marcaine is available in 0.25% and 0.5% concentrations.

Some local anesthetics have epinephrine added. Epinephrine constricts capillaries and is used to help control bleeding during a procedure such as the excochleation of a wart, which has a tendency to bleed profusely. Epinephrine also extends the effects of the local anesthetic for a longer period of time. The effects of a short-acting anesthetic with epinephrine will be longer than that of the short-acting anesthetic alone. Local anesthetics with epinephrine are contraindicated in patients with certain conditions such as peripheral vascular disease. Epinephrine would further decrease circulation to an already compromised foot. Always check the patient history and the vial itself before administering local anesthetics. Local anesthetics that contain epinephrine have a red label.

Delivering an Anesthetic Block

The patient should be in a reclined position with the head propped up on a pillow. Try to get the patient to relax as much as possible. It is helpful if the assistant can distract the patient's attention by talking to him. Spirits of ammonia should be available in order to revive the patient if he faints.

Prepare the skin with alcohol. Tighten the hub of the needle. This can be done with the needle cap or a hemostat. Remove any air within the syringe by tapping an index finger on the side of the syringe. This will force any air bubbles that have formed on the sides to the top of the syringe. The plunger of the syringe is then depressed until a few drops of the injectable squirt from the needle.

Ethyl chloride and Fluro-Ethyl are coolants that are sprayed on the skin at the injection site. The spray freezes the superficial layer of the skin and makes the initial injection less painful. The coolant should be sprayed from a minimum of a foot away from the injection site. Stop spraying as soon as a white frosting of the skin is visible (Fig 32–3). Freezing the skin for a prolonged period of time can cause severe burning.

The patient is told that he will feel a small pinch, and the tip of the needle is placed into the injection site through the top layer of skin. A small amount of anesthetic is injected to form a small bump known as a wheal underneath the skin. Once this wheal is formed, the needle is advanced in the direction needed to perform the block.

Care should be taken not to inject the local anesthetic into a blood vessel. When injecting anesthetics into deeper tissue or near blood vessels the plunger of the syringe should be drawn back in an attempt to aspirate any blood. This should be done before injecting any anesthetics. If blood is aspirated, the needle should be moved before injecting. This will prevent rapid toxicity caused by the local anesthetic.

Anesthetic injections can be performed relatively painlessly if they are performed slowly. Let the patient tell you when he feels discomfort. Stop injecting, but keep the needle under the skin.

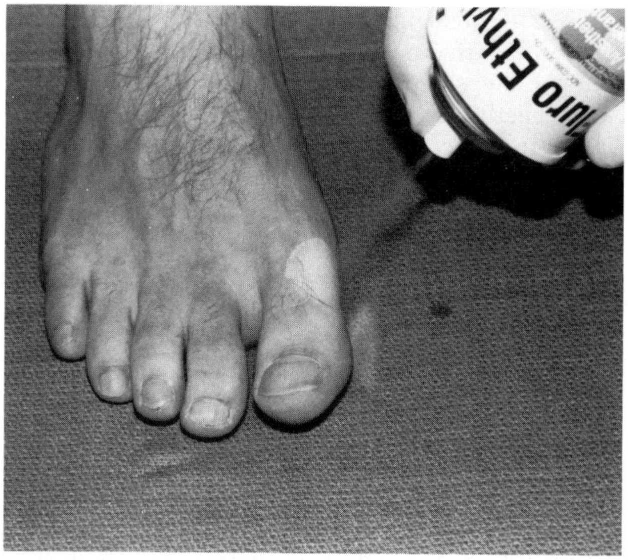

FIG 32–3.
Ethyl chloride and Fluro-Ethyl are coolants that are sprayed on the injection site to freeze the superficial layer of skin.

When the pain subsides, continue the injection. This will reduce the psychologic trauma of the injection.

There are many specific types of anesthetic blocks for the foot. A block of a specific nerve is performed to anesthetize that particular nerve's distribution. The posterior tibial nerve innervates the plantar aspect of the foot. The nerve is located just behind the posterior tibial artery where a pulse can be felt (Fig 32–4). After palpating the

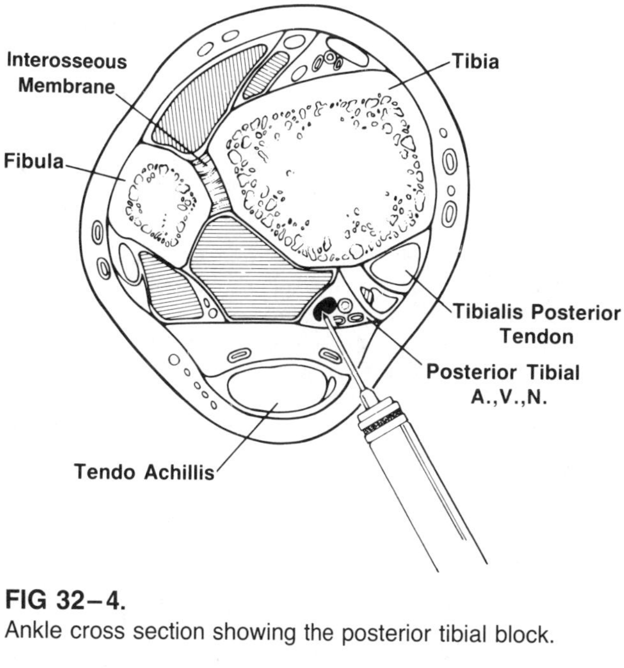

FIG 32–4.
Ankle cross section showing the posterior tibial block.

pulse and creating a wheal on the inner aspect of the ankle, the needle is placed posterior to the pulse. The syringe is aspirated before injecting any anesthetic. This is a relatively difficult block and must be carefully performed.

Frequently, in the office the lesser digits and the hallux are anesthetized to perform certain procedures. Each digit contains four nerves located on each corner of the digit.[1] An effective anesthetic block will have to anesthetize each nerve. A "V" block is frequently utilized to anesthetize the lesser digits. A wheal is made on the dorsal aspect of the digit. The needle is then extended superficially down both sides of the digit and the anesthetic released (Fig 32–5). The advantage of performing the block in this manner is that it requires only one needle stick. Another technique described by Mercado is performed by two needle sticks, one on either side of the digit.[2]

A hallux block is frequently used when performing an ingrown nail procedure. Because the hallux is wider than the lesser toes, it is difficult to perform a "V" block. A three-point block provides profound anesthesia. The technique is described in Figure 32–6.

Corticosteroid Injections

Injections of corticosteroids reduce acute inflammatory reactions. They can be very valuable in reducing pain associated with heel spur syndrome, neuroma, and acute inflammatory arthritis.

There are many types of corticosteroids marketed. The two general categories are short acting and long acting. Short-acting corticosteroids are generally clear in appearance and contain a phosphate salt base. Dexamethasone phosphate (Decadron, Merck Sharp & Dohme, West Point, Penn) is the best example of this group. Long-acting corticosteroids are more commonly used in podiatry. They are milky or cloudy in appearance and contain an acetate salt base. Dexamethasone acetate (Celestone, Schering Corporation, Kenilworth, NJ), is the most common long-acting corticosteroid.

Corticosteroid injections are commonly used for the relief of pain associated with Morton's neuroma and heel spur syndrome. A neuroma is an enlargement of a nerve due to pressure or stretching. The nerve tissue is essentially scarred and inflamed. The most frequently involved nerve is the plantar intermetatarsal nerve to the third intermetatarsal space. Corticosteroid placed on or near the nerve will frequently bring symptomatic relief to the patient. The corticosteroid is injected into the interspace from the dorsal aspect. It is either injected after the interspace has been anesthetized or mixed with a local anesthetic in a syringe.

Heel spur syndrome, also known as plantar fasciitis, can also be treated with corticosteroid injections to reduce inflammation and pain. The pain is primarily located on the plantar medial aspect of

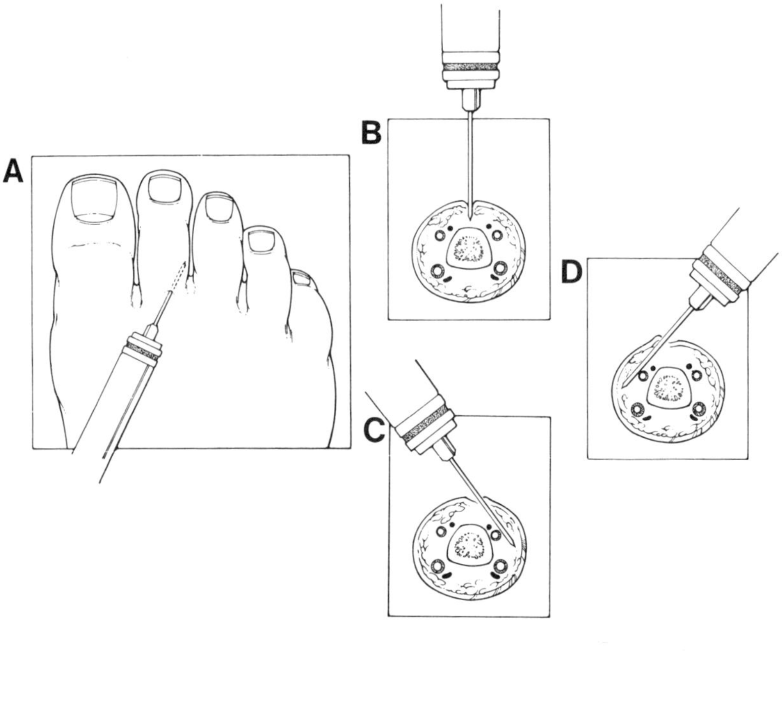

FIG 32–5.
A, the lesser digital block. **B,** entrance into the dorsal aspect of the digit. **C,** extension of the needle down the lateral aspect to the digit, **D,** extension of the needle down the medial aspect of the digit.

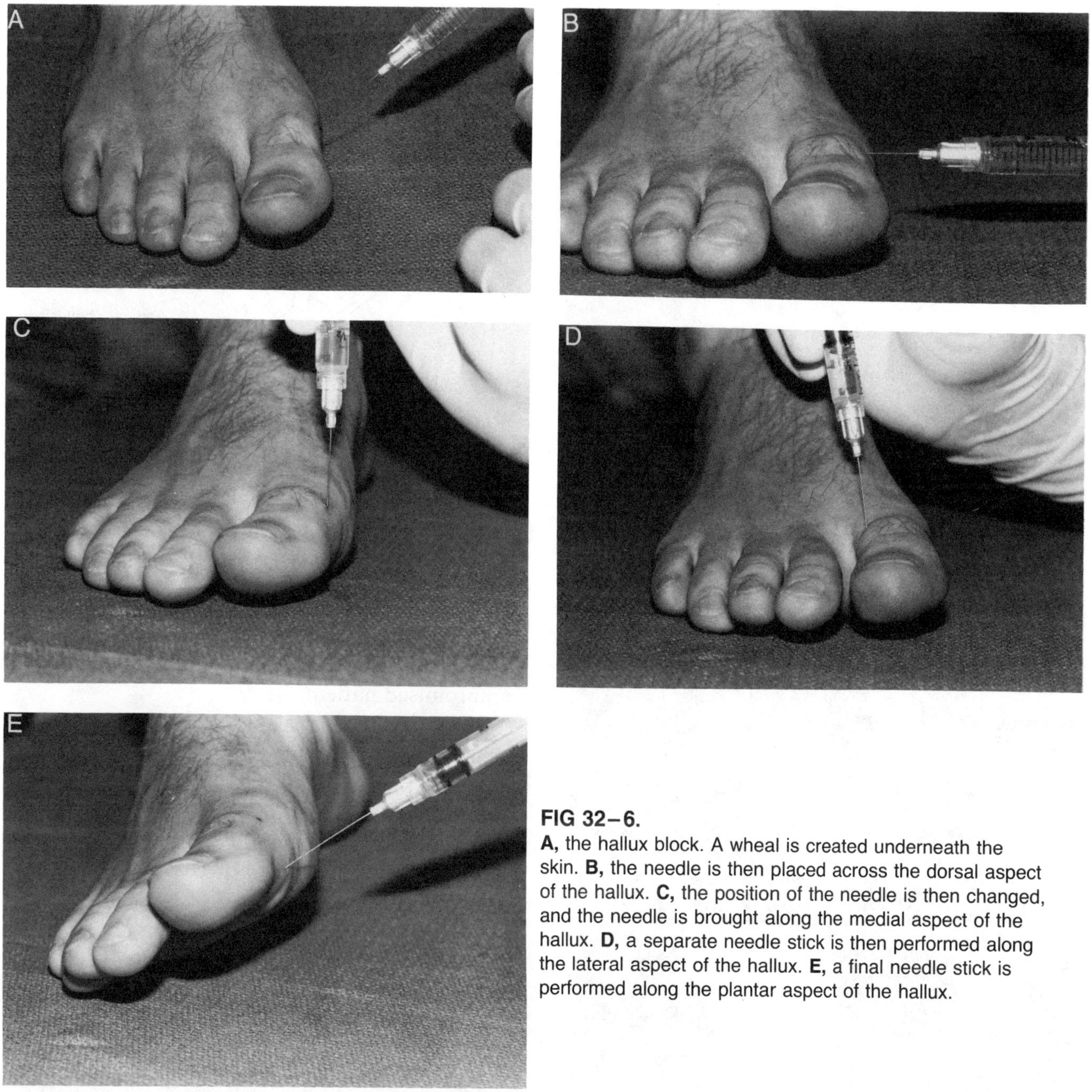

FIG 32–6.
A, the hallux block. A wheal is created underneath the skin. **B,** the needle is then placed across the dorsal aspect of the hallux. **C,** the position of the needle is then changed, and the needle is brought along the medial aspect of the hallux. **D,** a separate needle stick is then performed along the lateral aspect of the hallux. **E,** a final needle stick is performed along the plantar aspect of the hallux.

the heel and is due to an acute inflammation of the insertion of the plantar fascia into the plantar aspect of the calcaneus. The injection is most commonly given from the medial aspect of the heel plantar to the calcaneus (Fig 32–7). The area is first anesthetized, and the needle is left in place. A syringe containing corticosteroid is then placed onto the hub of the needle. The corticosteroid is then injected at the base of the spur. The two ingredients are commonly combined and injected together.

Multiple corticosteroid injections result in tissue atrophy and skin depigmentation. Frequent injections are therefore not recommended. Any more than three corticosteroid injections in one particular area is discouraged.

Intra-articular corticosteroid injections are sometimes performed to relieve acute episodes of

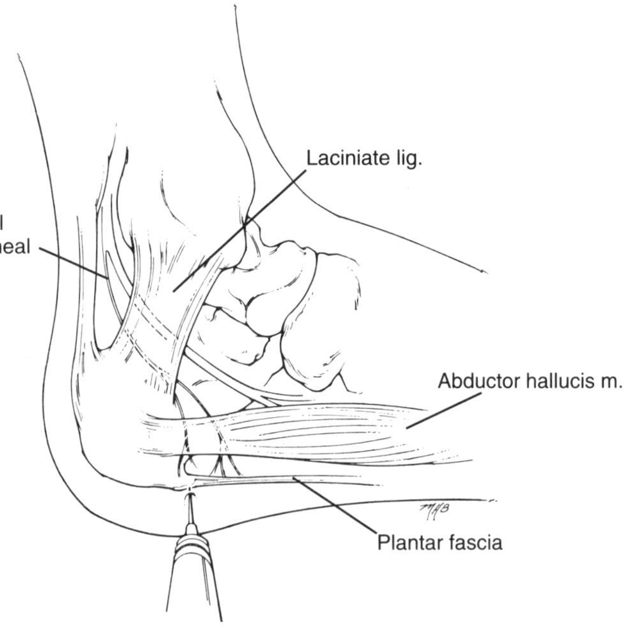

FIG 32–7.
Injection of a heel spur

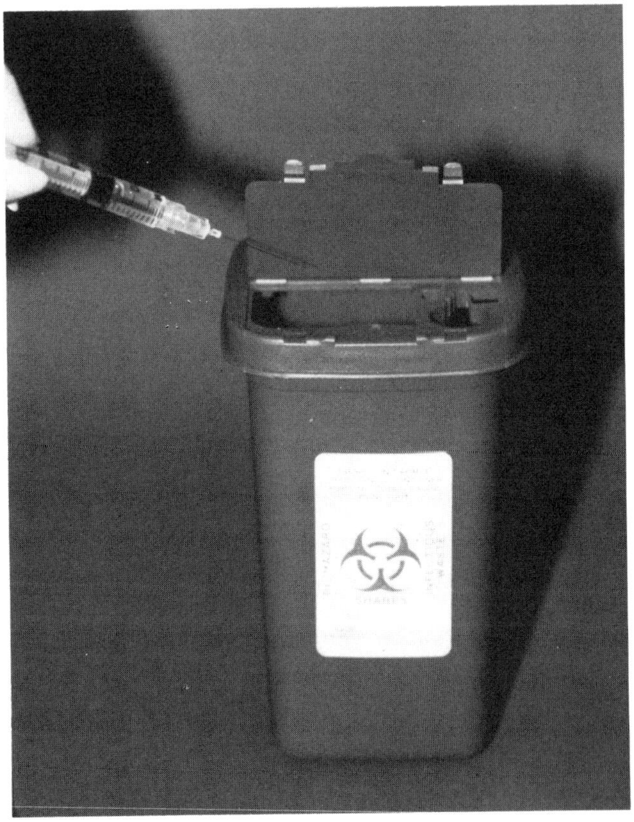

FIG 32–8.
Used needles and syringes should be discarded in approved disposal containers.

arthritis. It is essential to perform an effective sterile preparation of the skin before tapping a joint. The contamination of a joint with bacteria and consequent creation of a septic joint can have a disastrous outcome, especially in a medically compromised patient.

Aspiration of a Synovial Cyst

Synovial cysts, or ganglions, are extravasations of joint capsule or a tendon sheath filled with synovial fluid. When symptomatic they are aspirated. A field or "V" block is performed around the cyst to anesthetize the area. The anesthetic block

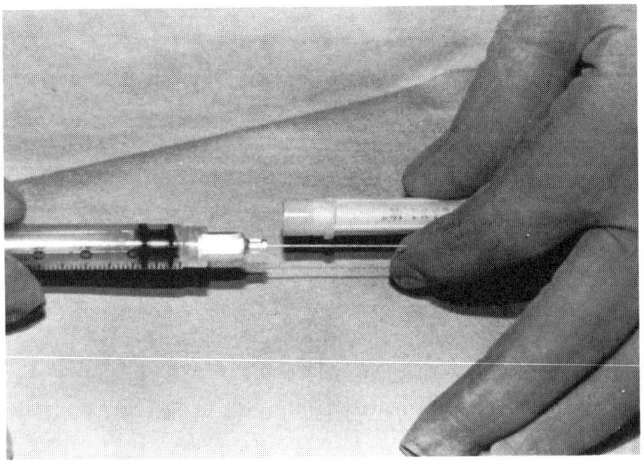

FIG 32–9.
Using both hands to recap a needle can result in a needle stick with a used needle.

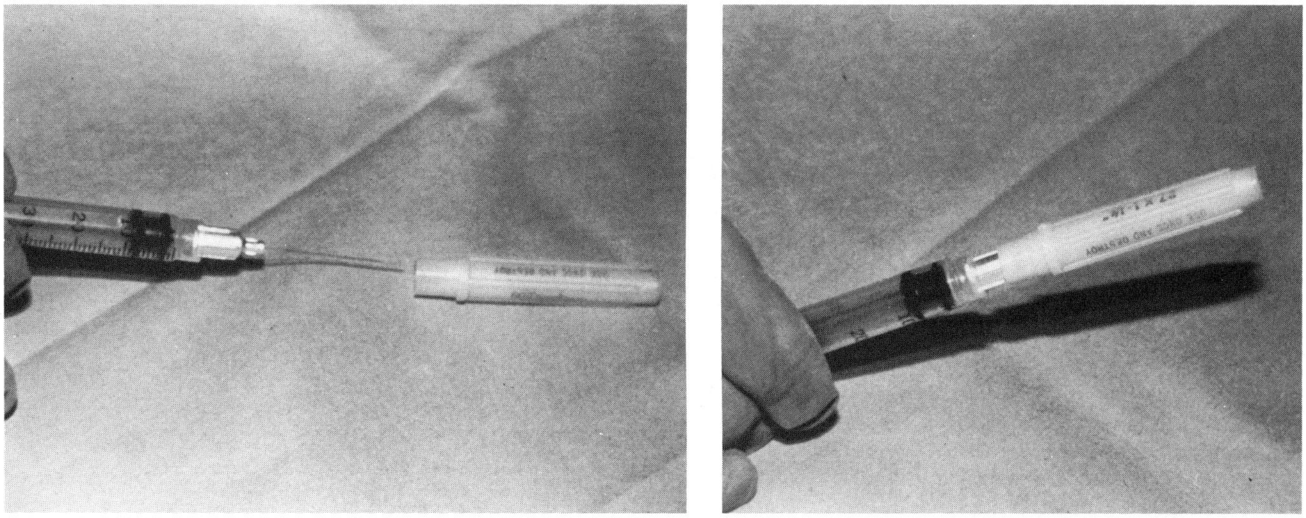

FIG 32–10.
A, if the needle must be recapped, place the cap on a table. **B,** scoop the cap up off of the table with the needle.

is performed with a high gauge needle (27 gauge), and then the cyst is aspirated with a low-gauge needle (20 gauge).

COMPLICATIONS OF INJECTION USE

Injections are an invasive procedure and can create certain complications. Infections, especially after injecting a joint, occasionally occur and must be treated quickly and aggressively to prevent permanent damage. Erythema, edema, pain, and local temperature elevation 48 to 72 hours after the injection are signs of a possible infection. Prevention consists of keeping the injection site as sterile as possible.

Allergic reactions to the injectable such as a rash have been noted and should be carefully monitored.

Toxicity of a local anesthetic is rare but does occasionally occur. Seizures and respiratory arrest are the most severe effects and should be treated with basic supportive measures. (Refer to the chapter on office emergencies.) Care should be taken not to inject a toxic amount of the anesthetic. The recommended maximum dosage differs with each local anesthetic and is reported on the information sheet that comes with each product.

NEEDLE SAFETY AND PROPER DISPOSAL OF NEEDLES AND SYRINGES

The importance of the proper disposal of needles and syringes cannot be stressed enough. Inadvertent needle sticks have been shown to spread diseases such as hepatitis B and acquired immunodeficiency syndrome (AIDS). The Centers for Disease Control recommends that all needles and syringes be placed in properly marked plastic containers immediately after their use (Fig 32–8).

If it is not necessary to recap a needle, the needle should be thrown away in a plastic container. However, when a needle must be recapped, never use both hands (Fig 32–9). It is safer to place the cap on the table and scoop the cap up with the needle (Fig 32–10,A and B). This will minimize the chance of an inadvertent needle stick.

If someone is accidentally stuck with a needle, the site should immediately be cleansed with an antiseptic solution. The medical history of the patient should be reviewed. As a precaution, all employees working directly with patients should be immunized with hepatitis vaccine. If a person is stuck with a needle and has not been immunized, a γ-globulin injection should be performed for immediate immunity. This should be followed with hepatitis vaccine for long-term vaccination.[3]

The podiatric assistant must have a basic understanding of needles, injections, and needle safety in order to effectively aid the podiatrist in daily patient care.

REFERENCES

1. Sarrafian S: *Anatomy of the Foot and Ankle.* Philadelphia, JB Lippincott, 1983, pp 331–332.
2. Mercado AO: *An Atlas of Foot Surgery, Forefoot Surgery.* Oak Park, Ill, Carolando Press, 1979, pp 10–14.

3. Phillips J, Martin D: Surgically acquired diseases, in McGlamry ED (ed): *Reconstructive Surgery of the Foot and Leg, Update '88*. Tucker, Ga, Podiatry Institute Publishing Co, 1988, pp 142–148.

ADDITIONAL REFERENCES

Azarnoff D: *Steroid Therapy*. Philadelphia, WB Saunders Co, 1975, pp 78–94.

Cavaliere R, Bergman R: Anesthesia, in McGlamry ED (ed): *Fundamentals of Foot Surgery*. Baltimore, Williams & Wilkins, 1987, pp 315–333.

Steinbrocker O, Neustadt D: *Aspiration and Injection Therapy in Arthritis and Musculoskeletal Disorders*. New York, Harper & Row Publishers Inc, 1972, pp 1–30, 89–94.

33

Physical Therapy and Rehabilitation

George R. Vito, D.P.M.

I. Therapeutic Exercise
II. Walking Aids
  A. Crutches
III. Physical Therapy Modalities
  A. Electrotherapy
    1. Ultrasound
    2. Phonophoresis
    3. Electrical Stimulation
  B. Hydrotherapy (Whirlpool)

The goals and objectives of the triad of medicine, surgery, and physical therapy are to treat and attempt to reverse the pathology and to effect a cure. Physical therapy should be thought of in the same manner as any other form of therapy with its indications, contraindications, and side effects. The clinician should have a thorough knowledge of the pathology of the disease or condition to be treated and a thorough knowledge of the physiologic effects of the modalities. The clinician should match the modalities to the diseases or conditions in order to reverse, slow down, restore, or maintain function to the best of the patient's ability.[1]

The time of healing and the type of loading that the different structures require for rehabilitation and improvement must be considered.[2] The muscles need repeated contraction with increasing resistance. Ligaments, tendons, and joint capsules need increased tension on the tissues (but not overly prolonged stresses or a supermaximal load). Cartilage and bone require a variation between compression and decompression at different portions of the joint surface with different loads. The vascularity and metabolic rate of the different structures affect their rate of healing. The lower the metabolic rate and the less the vascularity, the more stimulus and more training time that are needed.

With the above factors in mind, a rehabilitation program should be as functional as possible for the foot, ankle, and leg to return to its normal role in the kinetic chain for daily activities. Improvement in functional qualities such as strength, flexibility, power, endurance, and coordination is greatly determined by the number of repetitions (the number of movements of a certain exercise), the amount of load (resistance), and the rest period between sets of repetitions. Starting position, rhythm of contractions, and frequency of training also affect the results of these exercises.[2]

Preoperative evaluation is very important in the overall process of rehabilitation. It gives the physician a baseline of knowledge with which to compare postoperatively. Whether the patient is going to have a triple arthrodesis or a hammertoe procedure, certain measurements and values should be performed and assessed. Measurements of movement of certain joints (termed range of motion) should be performed.

The strength, power, and endurance of the muscles that surround the joint should be measured. Strength can be defined as the maximal amount of force that the joint can move in a certain direction for one maximal contraction. Power is defined as the amount of force that can be generated within a certain time frame, and endurance is the amount of force generated with repetitions until exhaustion is reached. To clarify the previous definitions, to lift 200 lb off the floor once with a maximal effort is a measurement of strength. To lift 200 lb off the floor as many times as you can in 20 seconds is a measurement of power. However, to lift 200 lb off the floor as many times as you can until you can no longer stand is a definition of endurance.

Testing of strength, power, and endurance should be performed on the ankle and knee if midfoot, rearfoot, or ankle surgery is to be performed. This is best tested isokinetically, as compared with isometric or isotonic exercise. Isometric, or static, exercise implies that a muscle contracts without a change in its length. Isotonic exercise describes the type of muscle contraction during which the muscle shortens as tension is developed. Isokinetic exercise is characterized by shortening of the muscle as tension develops through the range of motion, with the speed of motion being held constant by the internal mechanics of the equipment used. Any effort applied by the patient encounters an equal counterforce, or what is often termed "accommodating resistance." In isotonic exercise, a constant amount of weight is applied throughout the entire range of motion, with a varied amount of force and speed. Free weights and universal gym machines are isotonic in nature and can be very harmful to the patient if too much weight is used. Nautilus, Cybex, and Orthotron machines are all isokinetic in nature and provide the patient with safety features not found in isotonic measures (Fig 33–1,A and B).

THERAPEUTIC EXERCISE

The aims of treatment in a rehabilitation program of the surgical patient include resolution of the inflammatory process; restoration of muscle strength, power, endurance, and extensibility; and maintenance of general fitness. Resolution of the inflammatory process is the first phase of rehabilitation and is started as soon as the physician is finished suturing the wound. Compression dress-

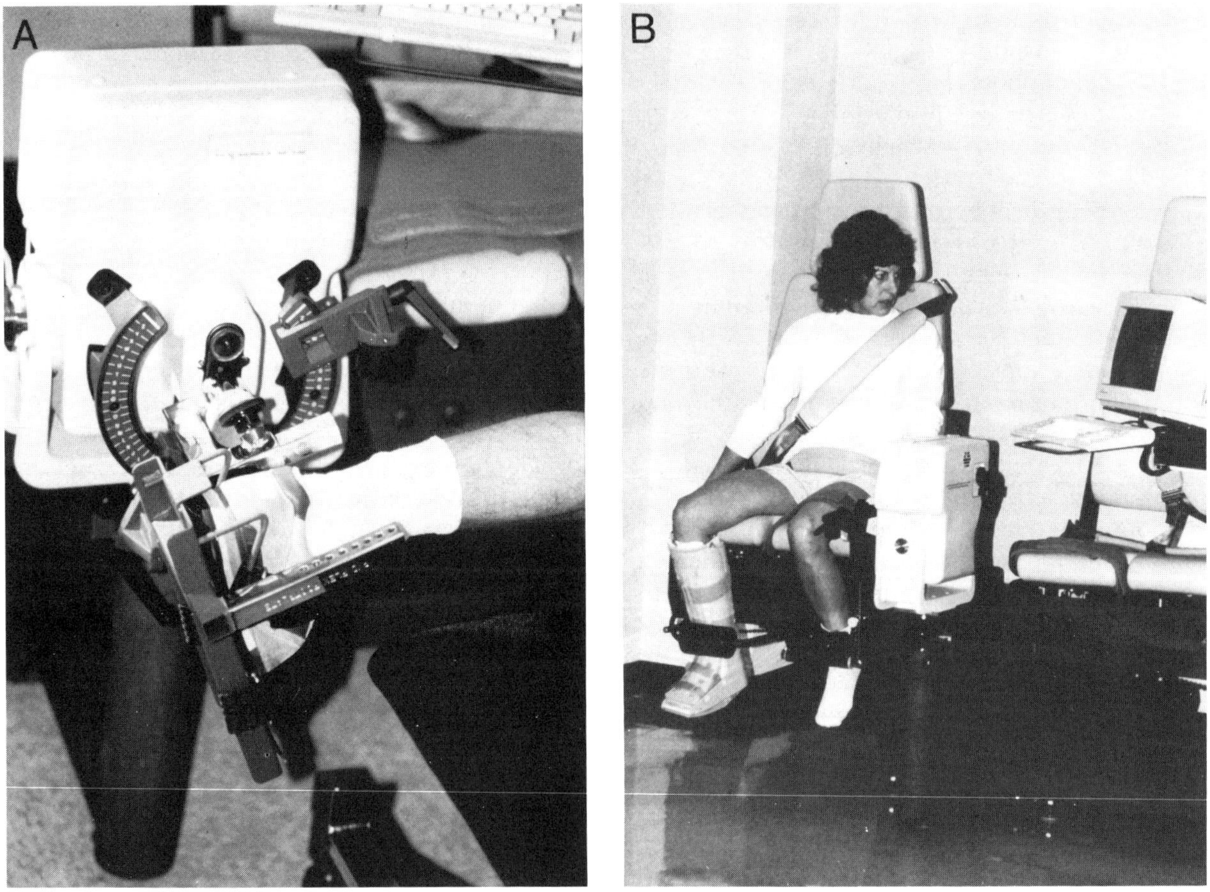

FIG 33–1.
A, isokinetic strength training performed on a Cybex. The motion of plantar flexion and dorsiflexion can be performed in this position. **B,** isokinetic training should be performed on both limbs to maintain strength, power, and endurance.

ings, drains (if needed), ice, and elevation all decrease postoperative edema and inflammation[3, 4] (Fig 33–2).

The second phase of the rehabilitation process is concerned with restoration of joint mobility and proprioception. Initially, passive exercise may be indicated (Fig 33–3,A and B). This form of exercise involves movement of joints and muscles by the physician or therapist without voluntary muscle contraction by the patient. This exercise may be used during periods of rest or immobilization to maintain joint mobility or to re-establish normal joint range.[5] It has been proposed that the continuous generation of proprioceptive impulses from the joint may block the transmission of pain impulses.[6] Passive range of motion continues until a full range of motion is possible for the affected joint. Patients who must be immobilized due to periarticular soft-tissue repair may undergo range-of-motion exercises of the joints above or below the affected area. For example, if a closing base wedge osteotomy is performed on the first metatarsal, the cast should allow movement of the first metatarsophalangeal joint (Fig 33–4). This may be accomplished by extending the cast beyond the hallux plantarly, but not covering the hallux dorsally. Therefore, the cast provides support for the first ray but allows for dorsal first metatarsophalangeal joint range of motion.

Distraction of the joint is the first form of passive range of motion. This provides minimal stress upon the ligaments and soft tissues postoperatively. The joint is distracted coaxially with the

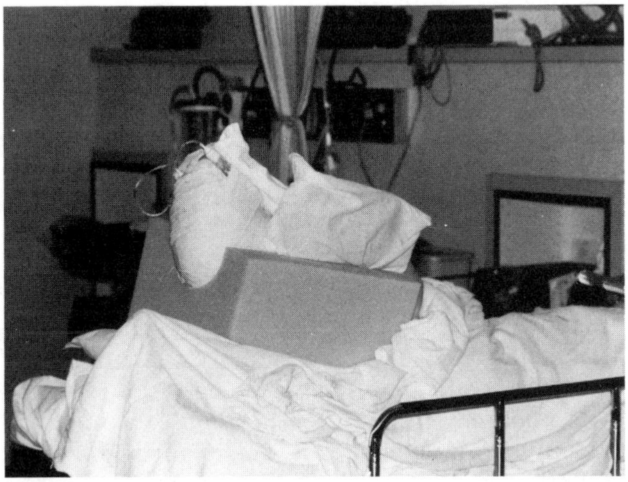

FIG 33–2.
Resolution of the inflammatory process postoperatively can be achieved with ice, elevation, compression, and the use of a closed suction drain.

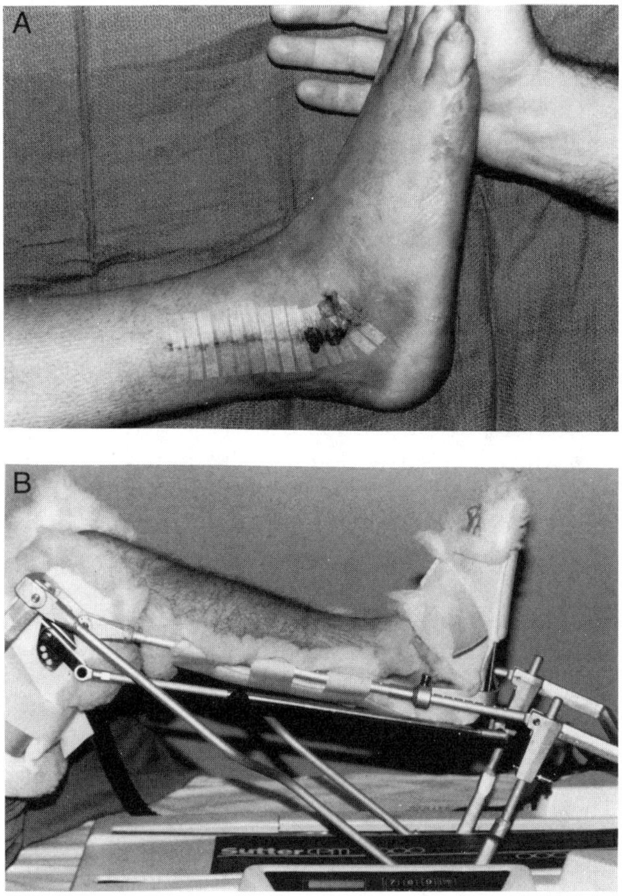

FIG 33–3.
A, manual passive range-of-motion exercises can be performed by the physician as early as 2 days postoperatively. **B,** passive range-of-motion exercises can also be performed by automatic machines with the end range of motions set so that gradual increases in the overall range of motion can be achieved.

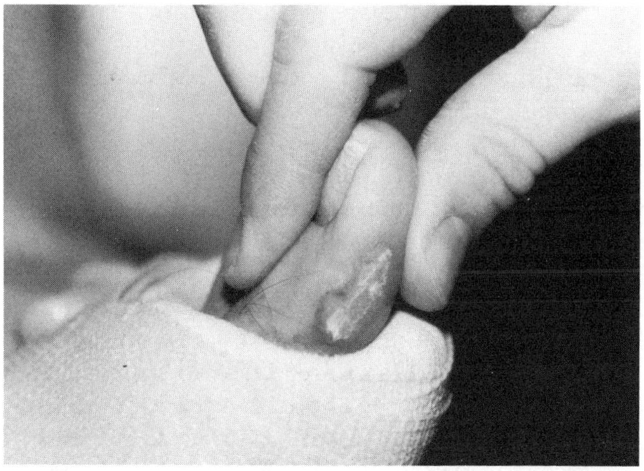

FIG 33–4.
Range of motion of the first metatarsophalangeal joint can be performed even in a below-the-knee cast.

joint. This movement distracts the joint and does not allow the joint capsule to adhere to the joint surface or its surrounding bone. This is performed repeatedly until minimal pain is experienced. The joint is moved dorsally and plantarly and then medially and laterally. This form of exercise is initiated on the first postoperative day. Once the patient can tolerate this activity, the joint is moved in its anatomic range of motion. There may be some mild discomfort, but this will diminish as increased repetitions are achieved. Again, this type of exercise is performed until a full range of motion is achieved.

Active range-of-motion exercises involve voluntary muscle contraction by the patient against gravity to increase muscle strength and function. Simple movements should be attempted initially, followed by more complex circular movements, and then finally "spelling" words with the involved structure. For complex movements of the ankle, have the patient sit on a table with the knee straight and only the ankle extended over the end of the table. With the hallux, have the patient print the entire alphabet in capital letters and perform movements with the entire foot and ankle. These exercises should be performed with the full extent of the joint. Resistive exercises to restore muscular strength, power, and endurance can then be performed.

Strengthening should be the first priority, with concentrated, deliberate, full range-of-motion exercises with weight resistance.[7] This allows for a control of joint function without the danger of overloading the muscles and ligamentous tissues of the joint. Power is then achieved when the joint can fully accept force for a period of time throughout the range of motion without pain. Endurance is the final step to be achieved in total reconditioning and is attained with low resistance but a maximal amount of contraction.

The final stage of rehabilitation consists of walking and running unassisted in a linear fashion. The patient then progresses to angular movements forward and backward. These movements can be performed with the aid of a swimming pool. The water acts to break the force of impact on the involved foot or ankle and also provides resistance, thus helping to regain limb strength. One must remember to be explicit in prescribing therapeutic exercises for patients. State exactly how to perform the exercise and demonstrate the exercise to the patient. State the exact amount of repetitions, sets (number of repetitions), and frequency. Tell the patient when to increase the repetitions or to adjust the resistance of the weights. Identify the muscles and the joints that are involved, thus signifying the purpose of the exercise. Give the patient a specific test of the exercises to be performed.

WALKING AIDS

There are a number of aids available to assist people who have had surgery or who have difficulty in walking. The patient may be completely non–weight bearing, partially weight bearing, or fully weight bearing with assistance, unilaterally or bilaterally.

CRUTCHES

There are three basic types of crutches that are used to reduce weight bearing on one or both legs or to give additional support where the patient's balance may be impaired. Axillary crutches are made of either wood or aluminum and have an axillary pad, a hand piece, and a rubber mold to fit on the bottom of the crutch so that the crutch may grip the ground. The position of the hand piece and the total length of the crutch are usually adjustable. The axillary pad should rest against the chest wall approximately 5 cm below the apex of the axilla, and the hand grip should be adjusted to allow the elbow to be slightly flexed when weight is not being taken. Weight is transmitted down the arm to the hand piece. The elbow is extended. Under no circumstances should the weight be taken through the axillary pad because this could lead to neurapraxia of the radial nerve or brachial plexus. Once the patient is standing with the support of the crutches, make sure that the axillary pads do not press into the axilla.

Elbow crutches and gutter crutches are used less often. These are made from either wood or aluminum. Elbow crutches are usually adjustable in length by means of a press clip or metal button. These crutches are particularly suitable for patients with good balance and strong arms. Weight is transmitted exactly the same way as for axillary crutches. Gutter crutches are used for patients with rheumatoid disease who require some form of support but cannot take weight through hands, wrists, and elbows because of deformity and/or pain.

The physician or therapist should demonstrate crutch walking to the patient and emphasize the important points. In non–weight-bearing ambulation, the patient should always stand with a triangular base (Fig 33–5,A) and the crutches either in front of or behind the weight-bearing leg. To walk, the patient first moves the crutches a little further forward, takes weight down through the crutches, and lifts the foot forward to a position just behind the line of the crutches. Once this is mastered, the patient may progress to lifting the foot forward to a position just in front of the crutches. It is important in certain cases for the patient to progress to shadow walking where the affected leg is moved in a sequence simulating walking but taking no weight (Fig 33–5,B).

There are two methods of partial weight-bearing ambulation using crutches. The first is a progression from shadow walking where no weight is taken through the affected leg to permit a gradual increase of weight to be taken. The crutches and the affected leg are taken forward and put down together. Weight is then taken through the crutches and the affected leg while the unaffected leg is brought forward (Fig 33–6,A). The second method simulates normal walking, and more weight is taken through the affected leg. The right crutch is moved forward, followed by the left leg, and then the left crutch is moved forward, followed by the right leg (Fig 33–6,B).

Walkers are often used to assist a patient in partial weight bearing, similar to crutch walking. Walkers allow more weight to be taken though the leg than do crutches. The most common type is a lightweight frame with four feet that may be adjustable in height. The patient lifts the frame forward, leans on it, and then takes two steps. The patient should take even steps and keep the frame well forward. Ataxic patients who are too unsteady to lift a frame forward may be able to use a frame that can be pushed with wheels.

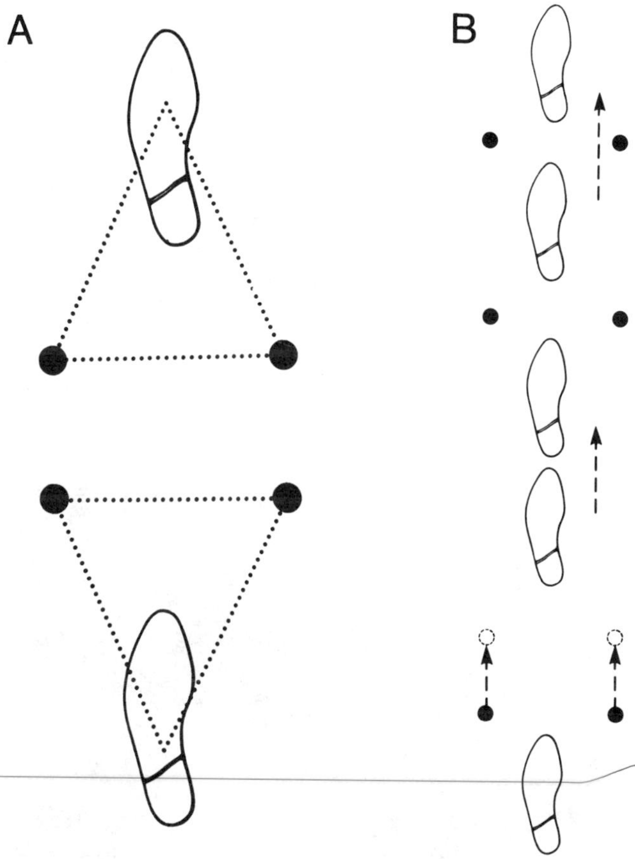

FIG 33–5.
A, a triangular base should be achieved with the crutches in front or behind the weight-bearing leg. **B,** non–weight-bearing ambulation with the use of crutches.

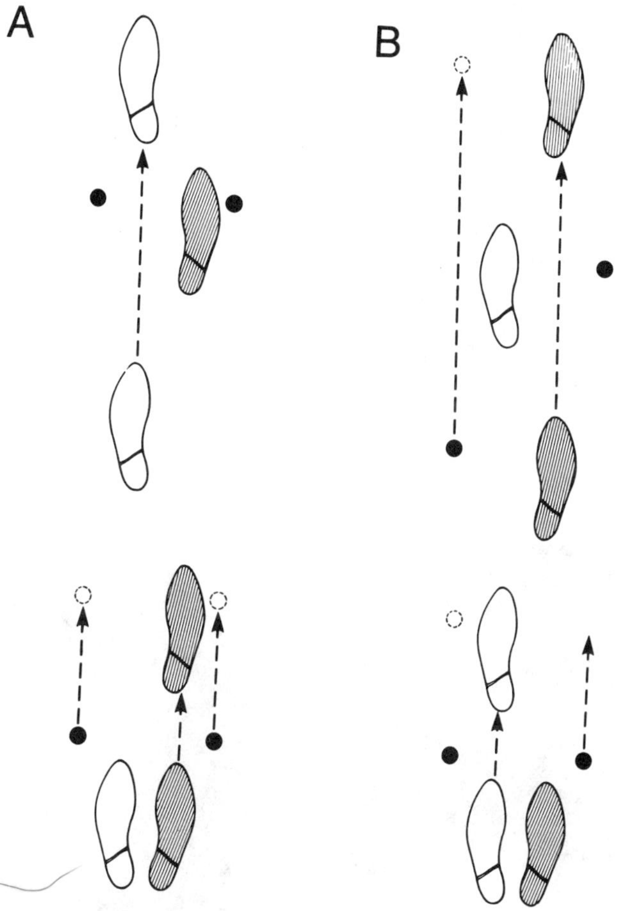

FIG 33–6.
A, partial weight-bearing ambulation with the use of crutches. **B,** a second method of partial weight bearing can be performed by moving the right crutch forward, followed by the left leg. The left crutch is then moved forward, followed by the right leg.

PHYSICAL THERAPY MODALITIES

The use of heat and cold in the rehabilitation process can be valuable tools when applied with a defined rationale, proper technique, and an understanding of the expected outcome. Heat is used primarily to promote healing and in some cases to reduce pain. Cold is most commonly used to reduce swelling, spasm, and spasticity as well as pain. These modalities can be used effectively in combination with each other or alone to produce various desired effects. The response of the body to applications of heat is primarily due to the increase in temperature of the tissues and the duration of temperature elevation. Mild heating that does not exceed 40°C usually produces only mild responses, including relaxation, and initiates moderate increases in blood flow. Localized vigorous heating has a major effect on blood flow and produces substantial increases in vasodilation. A localized increase in temperature increases the metabolic rate, capillary pressure and flow, clearance of metabolites, and oxygenation of tissues. Localized heating of tissue should only be used after acute trauma has subsided (surgery) and when edema has been controlled.[8]

The use of cold therapy is very important in the treatment of the surgical patient. Cold applications minimize the swelling or edema in the acute phase of postoperative rehabilitation (Fig 33–7). Reduction of pain associated with neuromuscular function reduces spasms and spasticity and enhances muscle contraction. Where localized cooling is used, the physiologic responses are initial vasoconstriction, reduction in tissue metabolism, decrease in nerve conduction velocity, reduced response of muscle afferent, secondary vasodilation, and an increase in muscle strength after strength training. The use of cold therapy in the acute phases of inflammatory conditions of surgery are very common. Post-treatment management of the injury site by compression and elevation is necessary to maintain the desired effects of the cold application. Specific caution should be used when cold therapy is applied to ischemic and anesthetic tissues. Its use is specifically contraindicated in several collagenous diseases where rheumatoid conditions may increase the symptoms of pain and joint stiffness. In Raynaud's phenomenon, the application of cold can result in excessive digital arterial spasms, and ischemic necrosis resulting in subsequent amputation and extensive loss of tissue has been reported.[8]

Electrotherapy

The concept of electricity as a therapeutic agent is a recent innovation, and its use has increased in recent years. Although not electrical in nature, ultrasound is often included in discussions on electrotherapy modalities.

Ultrasound

Ultrasound (Fig 33–8) is useful as a therapeutic modality for the reduction of muscular and tendinous spasm. It has also been utilized for pain and other pathologic conditions. Chemical substances may be introduced through the skin by a process called phonophoresis. Ultrasound waves have been reported to penetrate as deep as 4 to 6 cm into the

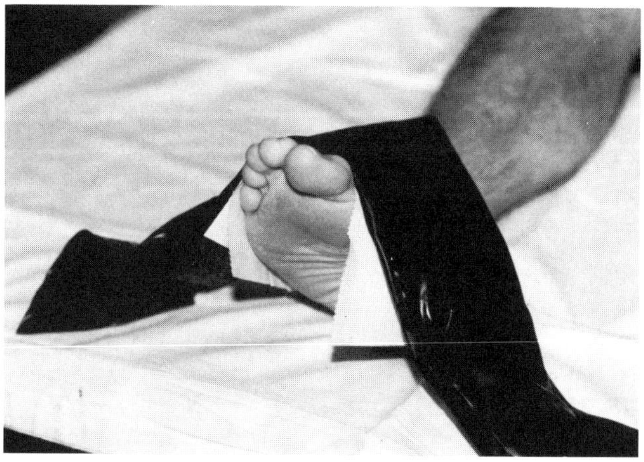

FIG 33–7.
Reduction of edema can be achieved in the rehabilitative phase with the application of cold packs.

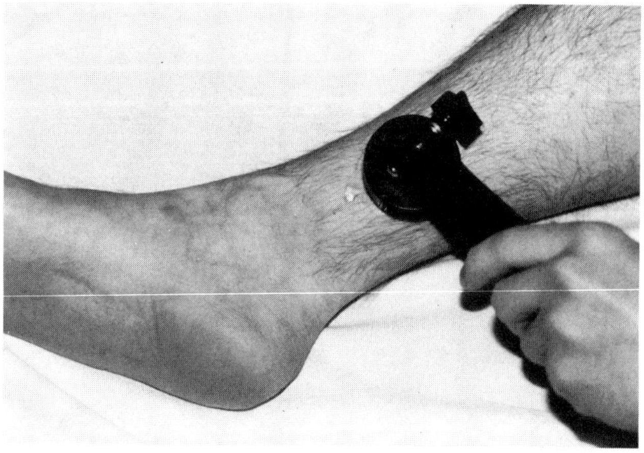

FIG 33–8.
Application of ultrasound to control pain and reduce edema.

tissues. Tissues with a high fluid content such as blood and muscle will absorb sound waves better than will less hydrated tissues. Although seemingly not hydrated, nerve tissue is an excellent conductor of ultrasound waves.

Ultrasound is indicated for spasm in neuromuscular and musculoskeletal conditions such as athletic injuries and postoperative trauma. Ultrasound is rarely used solely for pain management. Contraindications include the growing epiphyses, bony prominences, malignant tumors, acute infections, the pregnant uterus, and ailments of the eye and testicular tissues. Special care must be given to patients with sensory losses and inadequate circulation (diabetics). Metallic implants or surgical fixation materials may cause a problem when using ultrasound. The high-frequency oscillations may disrupt the chemical bonding or cement used with these procedures. Moreover, the interface of metal and tissue may be an ideal site for heat build-up and possible burns. The possible disruption of osteogenic processes in healing fractures suggests extreme caution with the use of ultrasound in and around recent fracture sites.

Mineral oil or an ultrasonic gel or contact medium is used as a coupling agent to create an airtight connection between the ultrasound unit and the foot. Ultrasonography can also be performed underwater. The sonicator (ultrasonic head) is moved slowly but continuously in a circular fashion. The patient should not be able to feel extreme heat. Mild vibratory sensation may be experienced. Ultrasound treatments, depending on the location and diagnosis, take from 3 to 15 minutes.

Phonophoresis

The ability of sound waves to introduce molecules of chemical substances through the skin is a process called phonophoresis. This is a noninvasive procedure. Sound waves generally penetrate 4 to 6 cm; with phonophoresis, there is a limited penetration of molecules of 1 to 2 mm. Skin and systemic reactions with phonophoresis are rare, but practitioners must be aware of the possibilities.[8]

Electrical Stimulation

Electrical stimulation (Fig 33–9) is one of the oldest and most effective modalities used in physical therapy. The terminology of electrical stimulation is very confusing. Nerve stimulation has been differentiated from muscle stimulation in many textbooks. Neuromuscular stimulation (NMS), functional electrical stimulation (FES), electrical muscle stimulation (EMS), and transcutaneous electrical nerve stimulation (TENS) for pain control have been described for different indications and treatment patterns. Only EMS and TENS are commonly used in podiatric medicine. The uses of EMS are as follows:

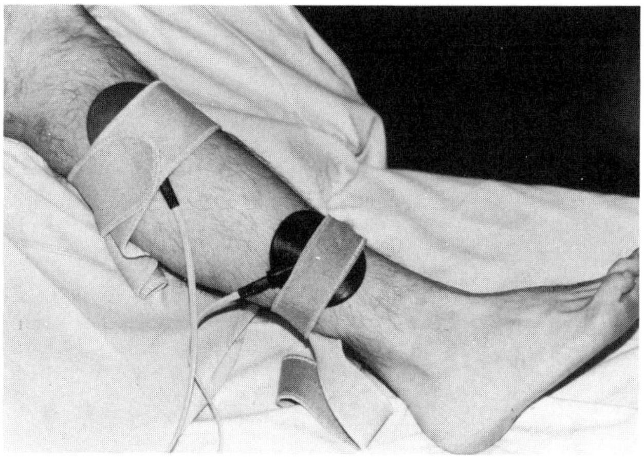

FIG 33–9.
EMS can be performed for muscle re-education.

1. Relaxation of spasm.
2. Monitored contractions of muscles to simulate active exercise.
3. Increased production of endorphins, which is believed to be a consequence of electrical stimulation. This natural, body-generated analgesic is produced normally when the body detects a painful stimulus.
4. Circulatory stimulation by the pumping action of the contracting musculature[8]

TENS (Fig 33–10) has been accepted as a standard modality in the management of both chronic and acute pain. TENS can control pain noninvasively and without narcotics. TENS is a specialized form of electrical stimulation that is designed to reduce pain, in contrast to other forms of electrical stimulation used either to produce muscle contractions or to introduce chemicals into the body. TENS is delivered by a compact portable device that is ideal for patient use at home. In using TENS, an electrical current is applied to the nerve endings in the skin, and this travels toward the brain and blocks transmission of pain from the peripheral nerves. Therefore, stimulating the surface of the skin with electricity overrides the stimulus of pain.

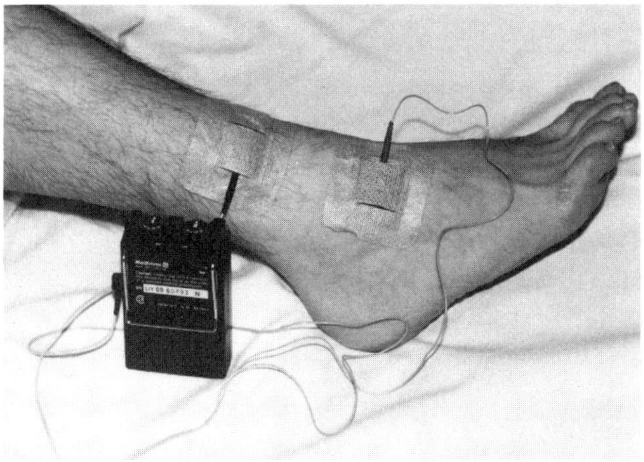

FIG 33–10.
TENS can be used to control muscle spasm and pain.

Hydrotherapy (Whirlpool)

Hydrotherapy uses water as an agent to apply heat with a stimulating mechanical force. Forced air is mixed with water to produce an increase in temperature and an increase in blood flow to the feet and legs. It is contraindicated in patients with phlebitis, peripheral vascular disease, and impaired sensation.

The whirlpool should be filled approximately two thirds full or high enough to cover the injured part. The temperature range of the whirlpool can be anywhere from 85 to 103°F depending upon the diagnosis and therapy. However, the lower end of the temperature range is recommended for patients with diabetes or peripheral vascular disease. Whirlpool therapy may be used for 10 to 20 minutes depending on the diagnosis.

REFERENCES

1. Bruno JP: Some guidelines for the use of physical modalities. *Clin Podiatr* 1984; 1:295–300.
2. Molnar ME: Rehabilitation of the injured ankle. *Clin Sports Med* 1988; 7:193–204.
3. Fox RH, Whyatt HT: Cold induced vasodilation in various areas of the body surface of man. *J Physiol* 1962; 162:289–297.
4. Olson JE, Stravino VD: A review of cryotherapy. *Phys Ther* 1972; 52:840–853.
5. Long JP: Rehabilitation and return to activity after sports injuries. *Primary Care* 1984; 11:137–138.
6. McDonough A: Effects of immobilization and exercise on articular cartilage. A review of literature. *J Orthop Sports Phys Ther* 1981; 3:2–6.
7. Salter R: The biologic concept of continuous passive motion of synovial joints. *Clin Orthop* 1978; 2:292.
8. Kessler RM, Hertling D: *Management of Musculoskeletal Disorders; Physical Therapy Principles and Methods.* Philadelphia, Harper & Row Publishers Inc, 1983.

34

Radiology for the Assistant

Barbara S. Schlefman, D.P.M.

Wilhelm Conrad Roentgen accidentally discovered x-rays on November 8, 1895, in Bavaria while experimenting with a Crookes' tube, a high-voltage cathode ray tube. He noticed that the beam penetrated through objects and cast a fluorescence on a piece of cardboard that had been painted with a barium platinocyanide chemical solution. By placing various objects of varying thickness in front of this invisible beam, he discovered that x-rays had varying penetrating abilities and produced varying images. He was able to view the bones of his hand when he placed it in line with this x-ray beam.

ELECTROMAGNETIC RADIATION

X-rays fall into the electromagnetic spectrum along with visible light, ultraviolet light, radio waves, and other forms of energy waves. The spectrum classifies rays by their wavelength. For example, normal household current has a very long wavelength, while x-ray waves are very short. X-ray waves travel at the speed of light (3×10^{10} cm/sec, or 186,000 miles per second). The beam is invisible to the human eye, has no mass or weight, and is electrically neutral (will not be attracted to a magnet). X-rays are able to penetrate matter or tissue, and they can record an image on photographic film emulsion.

The roentgen (R) is the international unit used for x- and γ-radiation (Fig 34–1). It represents a quantity of x- or γ-radiation that is produced in the air, and it carries an electrostatic unit or quantity of electricity of either sign. In other words, the roentgen is used to describe the production of a certain amount of radiation. The rad (r), or radiation-absorbed dose, is a measurement of the dose absorbed by humans from ionizing radiation that is equivalent to 100 ergs of energy per gram. The roentgen equivalent man (rem), is a unit of dose equal to that quantity of ionizing radiation of any type that produces in humans the same biologic effect as 1 R of x- or γ-rays. It is equal to the absorbed dose, measured in rads, multiplied by the relative biologic effectiveness of the radiation in question. Therefore, the impact of varying strengths of radiation can be compared.

X-RAY TUBE

Every x-ray machine contains an x-ray tube. This tube is a glass envelope containing a cathode and anode (Fig 34–2). An x-ray machine operates on everyday voltage, but a separate line from the

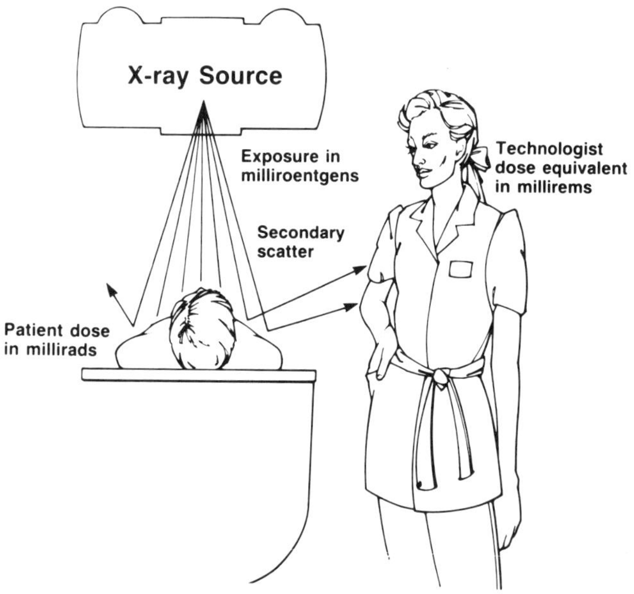

FIG 34–1.
The x-ray source produces the x-rays that are directed at the patient. These rays are either absorbed by the patient, pass through the patient to reach the film, or bounce off the patient and change direction to become secondary scatter radiation that may affect the technologist.

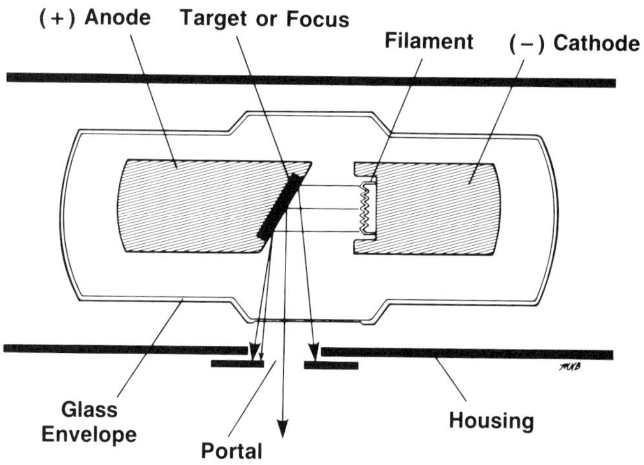

FIG 34–2.
A schematic representation of an x-ray tube.

x-ray room to the breaker box is recommended. The glass envelope is enclosed by a lead or aluminum housing. The cathode is the negative terminal composed of a hot filament made of tungsten with a low-voltage heating current that boils off electrons (incandescence). The greater the filament current, the higher the temperature and the greater the number of electrons emitted. The anode, or target, is a block of copper embedded with a small tungsten button. The electrons produced at the cathode are driven to the anode by a high-voltage difference or high-kilovoltage potential (KVP). The higher the KVP, the faster the electrons will travel. The electrons produced at the cathode are suddenly stopped at the anode, and x-rays are produced. The x-rays are emitted in all directions. Those leaving the porthole or window of the x-ray tube housing constitute the "useful" beam or primary radiation, the center of which is called the central ray (Fig 34–3). This geometric center of an x-ray beam, although invisible, is important when taking an x-ray film. After the primary radiation is emitted from the porthole or diaphragm of the x-ray tube, it is either absorbed by irradiated material or passes through it to become secondary radiation. If the x-ray beam changes direction, it is considered to be secondary scatter radiation. It is usually secondary radiation that affects the film emulsion because the primary beam has passed through or was absorbed by the patient.

RADIATION PROTECTION

Background radiation is produced naturally in the universe from cosmic rays and radioactive

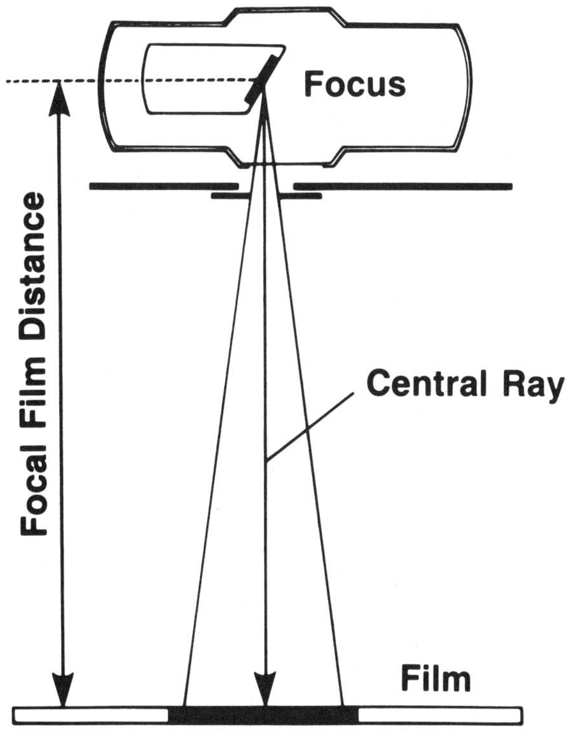

FIG 34–3.
The central ray and focal film distance or target-film distance.

TABLE 34–1.
Average Radiation Dosage

Source	Amount (mrem/yr)
Natural	
Cosmic radiation (sun and stars)—photons and particles emitted by the sun and sources outside of our solar system, even outside our galaxy	50
Internal radiation (from body tissue)—principal importance is ^{3}H, ^{14}C, ^{40}K, ^{226}Ra, and ^{210}Po	25
Terrestrial radiation from the earth, principally uranium and thorium	50
Man-made	
X-rays (medical)	90
Occupational (nuclear power plant workers; mining, refining, and fabrication of nuclear fuel)	20
Fallout	2–15
Environmental	5
Miscellaneous (television receivers, video display terminals, airport surveillance systems, watches)	2
Total	244–257

minerals and isotopes. Man-made background radiation is produced from medical x-rays, nuclear reactors, atomic weapon testing, fallout, and consumer products such as color television sets, watch dials, and smoke detectors. Each person is exposed to approximately 250 mrem per year in daily activities whether or not he has been directly exposed to radiation (see Table 34–1). Approximately half of this exposure is derived from natural sources. The exposure to cosmic radiation increases as one increases distance from the earth, as in an airplane. Internal sources of radiation are attributed to phosphate fertilizers in muscle tissue. Ninety percent of man-made radiation exposure is from medical and dental x-rays.

Biologic Effect

In sufficient amounts, radiation can have biologic effects on the population. Somatic effects are noted in the exposed population and primarily affect rapidly dividing cells. These effects include blood count changes, skin erythema (redness) and ulcerations, sterility, cataracts, cancer, and even death if exposed to high quantities of radiation. Genetic effects are noted in future generations due to chromosomal damage and germ cell changes. These genetic effects include birth abnormalities, childhood leukemia, and fetal death. The total exposure to a fetus throughout pregnancy must not exceed 0.5 rem (500 mrem). Pregnancy should not be interrupted because of exposure to an abdominal or extremity diagnostic x-ray examination. Studies have shown that the possibility of a birth defect following a diagnostic x-ray is extremely small when compared with the natural birth defect rate.

Short-term effects are due to a high exposure dose of radiation. Death can occur within hours after exposure to several thousand rads due to breakdown of the neurologic and cardiovascular systems. This is known as the central nervous system syndrome. At doses above 600 rad, death occurs within 15 to 30 days due to destruction of the gastrointestinal system. At doses greater than 100 rad, the blood-forming organs are affected, and death can ensue. This is known as the hematopoietic syndrome. Exposure to 50 rad or less generally will not show any indication of permanent injury.

Long-term effects manifest themselves many years after exposure to radiation. The increase in the carcinogenic effect is seen in bone and skin cancers, leukemias, and lung cancer. Embryologic and fetal tissues are most sensitive during the second through sixth weeks of human gestation. Embryonic tissue is relatively resistant to damage by radiation during later stages of pregnancy. Cataracts result following several hundred rad of exposure.

Medical x-rays produce varying amounts of radiation exposure to the patient that is usually subdivided into high–, medium–, and low–gonad exposure groups. While irradiation of the hip, pelvis, and lumbar spine falls into the high–gonad exposure group, foot, ankle, and extremity x-rays fall into the low gonad exposure group.

Maximum Permissible Dose

Exactly how much radiation exposure is bad is not really known. The standard used today is the maximum permissible dose (MPD). The cumulative lifetime MPD is $5(N - 18)$ rad, where N is the age. The yearly MPD for employees over 18 years of age exposed to radiation on a regular basis is 5 rad per year or 3 rad per quarter. The MPD to the extremities is much higher: 75 rad per year or 25 rad per quarter. No one under the age of 18 years may be employed as a radiation worker. The MPD to the general public is 1/10 those for employees. Personnel monitoring is performed by the use of a film badge (Fig 34–4). A small piece of x-ray film is held in a plastic holder and worn by each employee. The film reacts only to radiation and not to light. The badge can be worn at the chest or hip level, or two may be worn for more stringent control. If a lead shield is being worn, the film badge should ideally be placed under the shield to monitor the direct radiation to the gonadal area. Again, two badges may be worn, one under and one over the shield, where high exposure and stricter control are expected. The film badge should not be worn by an employee when having personal medical or dental x-ray films taken. The film badge is read monthly, and the accumulated radiation exposure is recorded.

Due to potential genetic effects, a pregnant female should not be irradiated unless the x-ray films are imperative to her well-being and the benefits outweigh the risks. A sign should be posted in the x-ray area warning female patients to inform the technician if there is a possibility that they are pregnant (Fig 34–5). The technician can then warn the patient of the potentially dangerous effect of radiation. Careful shielding to prevent unnecessary exposure is a must. In general, when taking medical x-ray films consider the following public health significance. The probability of any long-term radiation effects occurring to an individual is low, but a real risk does exist. Always consider this risk vs. the possible benefit of the examination. Do not expose a patient to any risk at

FIG 34–4.
A film badge.

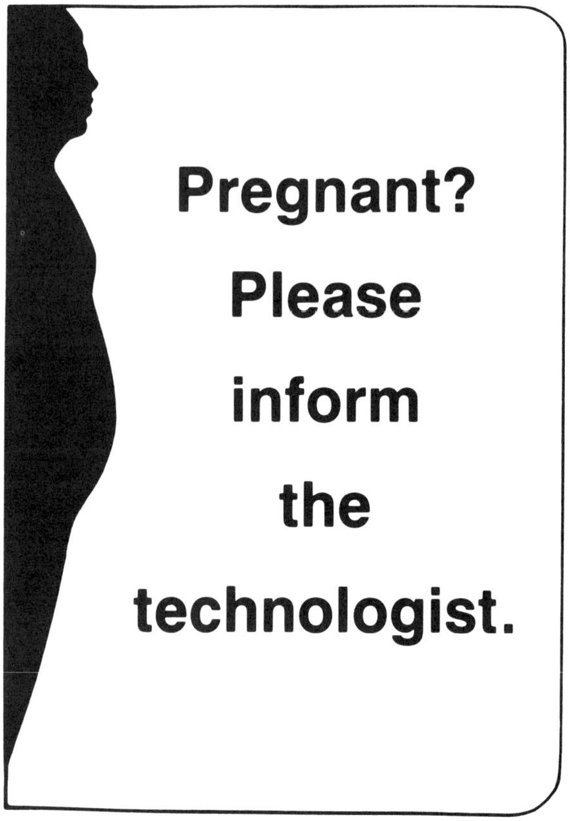

FIG 34–5.
A warning sign for pregnant women.

all if an examination is not needed. If it is needed, do everything possible to minimize the radiation received by the patient. Therefore, reduce the risk by eliminating all unwarranted exposure, and increase the benefits by improving the radiographic film quality.

If the technologist is pregnant, a review of radiation protective measures is imperative. Under normal daily activity, a technologist should receive less than 1,000 mrem annually or less than 100 mrem under a protective lead apron. The fetal dose would then be less than 50 mrem. This is significantly lower then the MPD of 500 mrem (0.5 rems) for the gestational period. Therefore, additional protective measures are not necessary. The use of two film badges, one under the lead shield, and one over the lead shield is recommended.

Protection Mechanisms

Radiation protection should be exercised by all employees. Employees should never hold a patient. If the patient is a child, then the mother or other party with the child should hold and immobilize the child when taking an x-ray film. The only acceptable time for an employee to hold a patient is if the mother is pregnant. If you must hold the child, then make sure that you are wearing a lead apron and gloves. X-ray films should be taken for medical purposes only. Never experiment with office artifacts (i.e., staplers, paper clips, etc.). A lead barrier such as a panel or apron should be utilized (Fig 34–6). A lead-lined glass window is required so that the technician can view the patient during x-ray exposure. Due to the low radiation exposure of the extremities, it is an acceptable standard to stand 6 ft away without a barrier. Gonadal shielding with a minimum of 0.5 mm of lead is required when x-raying the pelvic area. Protective apparel such as gloves and aprons with 0.5-mm-thick lead should be worn by all employees who may be directly exposed to any radiation in order to reduce scatter radiation by 99.9% (Fig 34–7).

Patient immobilization techniques eliminate the necessity of retakes, thereby reducing radiation exposure. Sandbags, tape, and sponges should be utilized where appropriate. Beam restrictive devices such as collimators, cones, cylinders, and diaphragms reduce scatter radiation. These devices are made of radiopaque metal in various sizes to fit the x-ray tube portal. Collimators may be manually attached and slide in or attach in

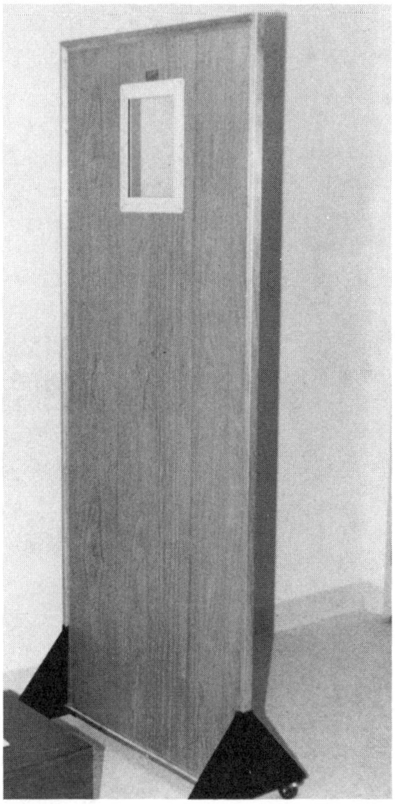

FIG 34–6.
A lead barrier or shield.

various sizes depending on the film and image size. Adjustable collimators contain internal beam limiters that adjust the horizontal and vertical dimensions. Today, federal regulations require adjustable collimators on all new equipment. When using an adjustable collimator, the light beam should never extend past the film or cassette so as to irradiate only the area of clinical interest. The ratio of the x-ray beam area to the film area should be less than one.

Low-energy x-rays contribute little to the diagnostic quality of a radiograph and increase the patient's dose unnecessarily. Filtration of the x-ray beam aims to increase the hardness of the x-ray beam. Aluminum (0.5 mm thick) is housed around the x-ray tube (inherent) to limit soft x-rays that are absorbed by the skin. This allows the passage of hard radiation that penetrates through the body part and records information on an x-ray film. Aluminum can also be placed beneath the porthole (added). The total filtration (inherent plus added) required is dependent on the KVP utilized:

0.5 mm Al = <50 KVP
1.5 mm Al = 50–70 KVP
2.5 mm Al = >70 KVP

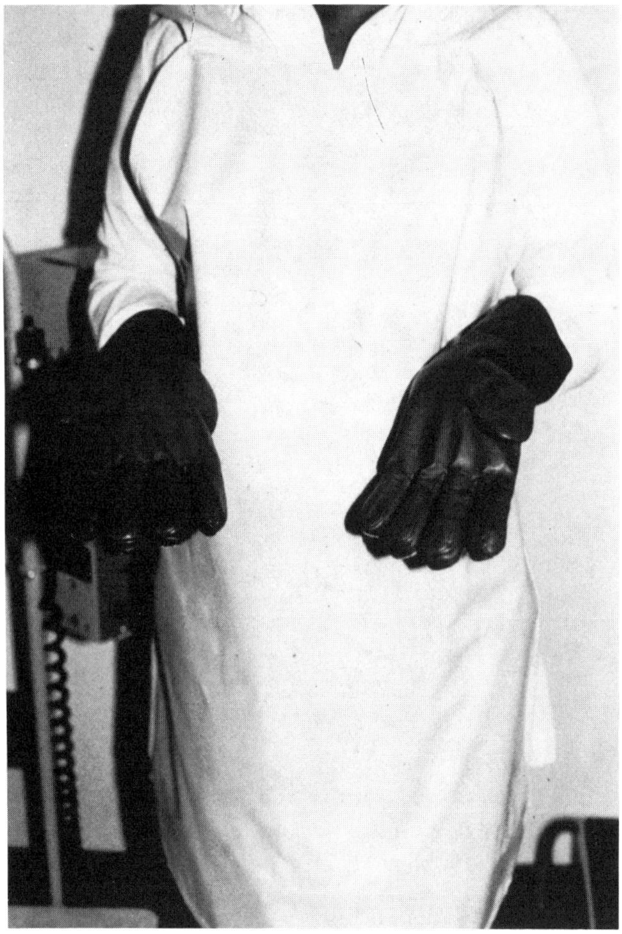

FIG 34–7.
A lead apron and lead gloves.

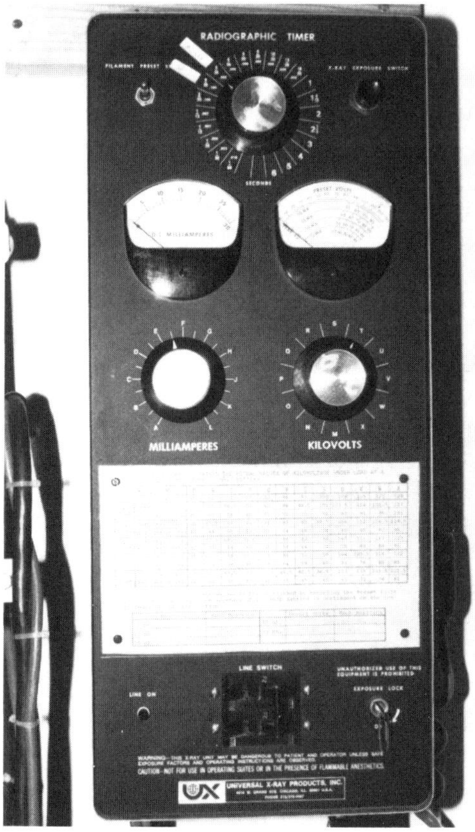

FIG 34–8.
The control panel from an x-ray machine is shown. The top dial controls the time (in seconds), the lower left dial controls the milliamperage, and the lower right dial controls the kilovoltage potential.

Random or excessive exposure should be eliminated. A good history and physical examination of the patient's problem will give information to determine which views are needed. Minimizing exposure time and good darkroom techniques will reduce exposure as well.

BASIC PRINCIPLES OF RADIATION

Intrinsic Factors

Intrinsic factors, milliamperage, the time, and the kilovoltage pertain to the radiographic technique. An understanding of these factors will help one take a better x-ray film (Fig 34–8).

The milliamperage represents the tube current or intensity of the x-ray beam. It is the x-ray exposure rate. It measures the number of electrons that pass from the cathode to the anode, or the *quantity* of the beam. Milliamperage does not affect the penetrating power. The quantity of radiation is directly related to the density on the film, or the amount of film blackening. If the milliamperage is increased, the finished film will appear blacker or darker.

The time, measured in seconds, provides the total exposure rate, or total quantity of radiation. As the time increases, there is increased exposure and increased density or blackening on the film ($mA \times sec = mAs$).

The kilovoltage represents the *quality*, or penetrating ability, of the beam. As the KVP increases, there is an increase in penetration of the photons along with an increase in the amount that penetrates through the body part and reaches the film. Therefore, the KVP also affects the exposure rate as well as the mAs. An increase of 15% in the KVP is the equivalent of doubling the mAs. Greater detail (or greater contrast) on a radiograph is accomplished by decreasing the KVP and increasing the mAs.

Extrinsic Factors

The focal film distance or target-film distance is a very important factor when taking a radiograph (see Fig 34–3). As the distance increases, there is a decrease in penumbra or magnification, and therefore, there is an increase in definition and detail. The intensity of the radiation varies inversely with the square of the distance. The farther the person is from the x-ray source, the less radiation dose per unit he will receive. Therefore, if the distance from the x-ray source is doubled, the radiation intensity is reduced to a fourth of the intensity at the original distance. To get the same amount of blackening on the x-ray film, the exposure would have to be increased four times as much. Either the KVP or mAs can be increased. The accepted focal film distance is 36 to 40 in. Podiatric studies usually utilize a 28-in. focal film distance.

The object-film distance represents the distance of the object being x-rayed to the film. It should be as small as possible to decrease penumbra and increase definition (Fig 34–9). Therefore, the foot should be touching the film where possible.

The focal spot is on the anode and varies in size. A smaller focal spot size results in less penumbra, greater visibility of the umbra (proper image), and greater detail.

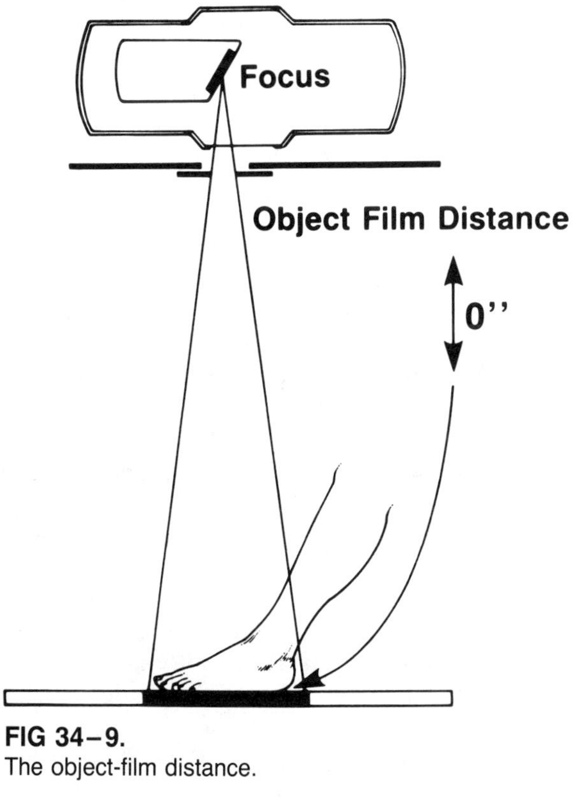

FIG 34–9.
The object-film distance.

Fog represents unwanted density on an x-ray film due to scatter radiation. As the KVP increases, the fog also increases. Fog can be minimized by the use of a grid that absorbs secondary scatter radiation. This grid is only necessary when a high KVP is utilized when x-raying thick body parts. A grid is not necessary for foot roentgenography.

Film, Film Holders, and Screens

X-ray film is an emulsion of silver bromide crystals suspended in a gelatin matrix coated upon a plastic base for support. The base is composed of cellulose acetate or polyester and has a blue-green tint. A subcoating adheres the emulsion to the base. Light and x-rays reduce the silver bromide to black metallic silver during the developing process. The more black silver deposited, the greater the film density, or the greater the blackening.

There are three types of film: screen film, nonscreen film, and industrial film. Screen film is used with cassettes that contain intensifying screens. They are duplitized (coated on both sides). The intensifying screen is sensitive to blue light. Therefore, the amount of x-ray exposure needed is 1/10 to 1/15 of that needed for nonscreen film. Nonscreen film responds to x-rays only and not blue light. It too is duplitized. Greater exposure is needed, but its benefit relies on the fact that greater detail and contrast are obtained. Industrial film has a single layer of emulsion and provides the greatest detail. The film size most appropriate for foot radiographs is 8 × 10 and 10 × 12 in.

Cassettes with intensifying screens or cardboard holders are used to hold the x-ray film while taking an x-ray (Fig 34–10). Cardboard holders provide better definition and higher contrast. The back side of the holder is lined with lead to prevent backscatter. This holder is primarily used for extremity work where a lower technique is used (lower mAs or KVP). Only 2% of the recorded density on a radiograph is due to direct radiation when using intensifying screens. Most is due to light exposure to the two intensifying screens that surround the x-ray film. The cassette is also lead backed.

The screen speed may vary. High- or fast-speed screens contain large crystals, which results in greater penumbra. The smallest amount of radiation is needed to expose the film, but the detail is

FIG 34–10.
An open cassette is viewed. The screen that lines both sides of the cassette is white. The x-ray film is a blue-green tint.

poor. Medium or par screen speed provides somewhat greater detail at the expense of increased radiation exposure. Detail, fine– or slow–screen speed, film provides even greater detail, and finally ultra detail, or very slow speed, screen provides the best detail but requires the greatest amount of radiation exposure when using a screen. Therefore, the faster the film speed, the less radiation exposure needed.

X-ray film also comes in different varieties of "film sensitivity" or "film speed." Films are rated by relative speed numbers, with 1 being a slow speed and 10 being a high speed. High-speed screen film is highly sensitive, and less exposure time is needed. Low-speed screen film requires a greater amount of radiation exposure. The type of x-ray film used is dependent on the type of intensifying screen used in the cassette.

When taking an x-ray film, the primary radiation exits the x-ray tube and penetrates the patient. This produces secondary and scatter radiation. The radiation exits the patient and bombards the intensifying screen of the x-ray film holder. The screen crystals emit light in all directions onto the film, and electromagnetic waves (light and x-rays) react with the silver bromide crystals in the x-ray film emulsion. A latent image is produced, and after development it can be seen with the naked eye.

Film should be stored in a cool dry place. The humidity should be between 40% and 60%. The temperature should ideally be between 50° and 70°F. Film may be refrigerated, but it should stand at room temperature for 24 to 36 hours prior to use. Film should be used before its expiration date. Unused film may be stored in special film bins, or it may be kept in its original cardboard packaging.

Density and Absorption of X-Rays

X-ray films are formed from the differential absorption of ionizing radiation. Dense bone with an increased calcium content absorbs more x-rays, and therefore less x-rays reach the plate. Fewer silver bromide crystals are precipitated, and these are then washed off by the fixer and will appear whiter on an x-ray film. On the other hand, more x-rays pass through less dense tissue such as muscle or fat and reach the x-ray film. More silver bromide crystals are precipitated and not washed off, and this gives that portion of the x-ray film a blacker appearance. Film or plate density is the radiographic measure of the quantity of radiation absorbed by the film due to the deposition of black metallic silver on the x-ray film. A blacker or darker film contains more density than one that is whiter in appearance. Tissue density is the relative ability of tissues to absorb x-rays. An obese person or a thick bone has more density than a thin person or soft-tissue structures. Therefore, radiographic contrast refers to this pattern of different shades of black and white seen on a radiograph due to the differential absorption of x-rays as they pass through body parts of differing densities and thicknesses.

Many factors will affect plate density. A primary consideration is the patient and the thickness of the part to be x-rayed. Consider the age of the patient, his sex, the amount of fat, and his condition (i.e., muscular, dehydrated). If you are x-raying an ankle in a big, strong male, consider increasing your x-ray technique. If you are x-raying the toe of a thin, cachexic female or a child, consider decreasing your x-ray technique. When x-raying through a plaster cast, the technique must be increased. If the cast is wet (less than 24 hours since put on), triple the mAs, or increase the KVP by 14 to 16. If the cast is dry (greater than 24 hours since put on), double the mA·s, or increase the KVP by 10 to 12. When x-raying through a fiberglass cast, the technique should also be increased, but not as much as for a plaster cast.

An increase in the milliamperage or the time will increase plate density. An increase in the KVP will also increase plate density. An increase in the focal film distance will reduce film density. If for some reason the distance is increased, the technique must also be increased to obtain adequate plate density. The density increases as the screen speed increases. Grids, filtration, and collimation, by decreasing scatter radiation, tend to decrease plate density.

Definition and Distortion

Definition describes the sharpness or detail on a radiograph. Definition can be increased by decreasing the focal spot size (radiation source), increasing the focal film distance, and decreasing the object-film distance. Better definition is obtained by using slower-speed screens and film and by decreasing the KVP with an associated increase in the mA·s.

Motion creates a blurred image and decreases definition. A cooperative patient can minimize motion. Immobilization techniques such as tape, sponges, and sandbags may be necessary. By decreasing the time and increasing the milliamperage, the mA·s will remain unchanged, but motion will be minimized. When x-raying children, the time should not exceed 1/10 of a second. Fast-speed intensifying screen, a decreased focal film distance, and an increase in KVP will all allow one to decrease the time, thus minimizing motion.

Distortion is a misrepresentation of the true size and shape of objects. Size distortion occurs due to an increase in the object-film distance. The object-film distance should be as close to zero as possible. Shape distortion occurs due to angulation of the x-ray beam passing through the part. The long axis of the part should be parallel to the film, the tube aligned to the middle of the part, and the central ray at right angles to the plane of interest. Occasionally, we intentionally deviate from these standards, such as when taking an oblique x-ray film. We accept shape distortion in order to get a better or different view of the part in question.

TABLE 34–2.
A Comparison of Developing Time and Developing Temperature

Temperature (°F)	Developing Time (min)
80	1¼
75	1¾
72	2
70	2½
68*	3*
65	3½
63	4

*Recommended.

RADIOGRAPHIC PROCESSING AND THE DARKROOM

The x-rays form a latent image upon hitting the film. It is only through x-ray development that a visual image is produced. There are two main steps to this process: development and fixation. This process can be done by a conventional manual technique or by the use of an automatic processor. The principles are the same for both, only the equipment varies.

A darkroom is needed for x-ray film processing. It should be a totally sealed room with no light leakage. Plumbing is required because both manual and automatic processing requires water. A safelight may be utilized. A safelight is a 7½- to 15-W bulb placed in a box or specially designed holder with a colored filter. The safelight should be tested prior to use by exposing a sheet of x-ray film lightly or briefly to white light. This will cause the film to turn gray. Now cover half the film with cardboard and expose the other half to the safelight for 30 to 60 seconds. Develop the film, and compare the two halves. An improper safelight will produce fog on the film. When an x-ray technician becomes adept at developing x-ray films, a safelight is generally no longer needed.

If an x-ray film is exposed to white light, the film will turn black following development. If an image was previously produced, it will be covered up or erased. If an x-ray film appears clear following development, one can assume that no light or x-ray beam has affected the film emulsion because all the silver was washed off.

Manual x-ray development requires a 2- to 5-gal developing tank depending on the size of the x-ray film being used (Fig 34–11). The main tank is filled with water and has two inserts, one for the developer and one for the fixer. The developer is a

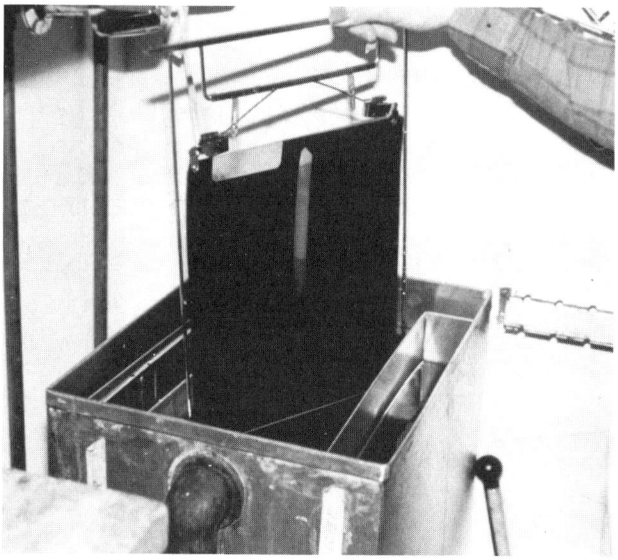

FIG 34–11.
A manual developing tank.

chemical solution that contains a reducing agent (elon or hydroquinone) that reduces the silver bromide crystals to metallic silver, an activator (sodium carbonate) that softens or swells the gelatin, a preserver (sodium sulfite) that preserves the developer, and a restrainer (potassium bromide) that controls the rate of development and prevents reduction of the unexposed grains of silver bromide crystals. The fixer, or hyposulfite, changes the unexposed silver bromide crystals to a soluble salt that is then washed off. The fixer contains neutralizers, preservers, and hardening agents as well.

In manually developing an x-ray film, the film is removed from its cassette in the darkroom, placed on a hanger, and inserted into the developing tank. Make sure that both the developer and fixer have been mixed well to reduce staining. Optimal developing time is 3 minutes at 68°F (60 to 75°F is acceptable). Temperatures cooler than 60°F result in underdevelopment and poorly fixed radiographs. Temperatures above 75°F result in such short developing time that the film emulsion may be damaged, again producing a less-than-satisfactory radiograph. An increase in developing time or developing temperature will cause increased density on the radiograph. Table 34–2 suggests developing times for various temperatures.

Following development, the film is rinsed for 30 second in a "stop bath" of water. This removes the excess developer before the film is placed in the fixer to avoid contamination of the solutions. This water bath also serves to maintain a more constant temperature of the two chemical tanks.

The film is next placed in the fixer. The recommended fixing time is twice the developing time. Therefore, 6 minutes is optimal. It is an acceptable practice to remove the film from the fixer after 3 minutes for viewing. Then replace the film for the remainder of the time.

Following fixation, the film is placed in the water for a final wash. The recommended time is 12 to 20 minutes. This rids the film of any residual chemicals. Again, to save time in an office, it is an acceptable practice to quickly rinse the film, review it with the patient, and then replace it in the water for its full wash. The film is then placed on a drying rack for approximately 30 minutes. It should be stored upright in a properly labeled envelope. X-ray films should be maintained for at least 5 years or, in the case of children, until they reach the age of maturity.

Automatic processors take 90 seconds to 3 minutes to complete the entire process (Fig 34–12). The film automatically advances through the tanks and then runs through a high-powered dryer so that the finished product is fully dry. The uniformity of development obtained from automatic processing is improved due to more constant maintenance of the chemicals. In addition, there is less likelihood of error when using this process. Automatic processors have a replenishing pump that constantly adds the developing and fixing solutions to the tanks to maintain uniformity of development and prevent the chemicals from becoming exhausted.

Labeling of a radiograph is very important and is done prior to the actual developing process so that films are permanently labeled. It is not an accepted practice to add a stick-on label to a fin-

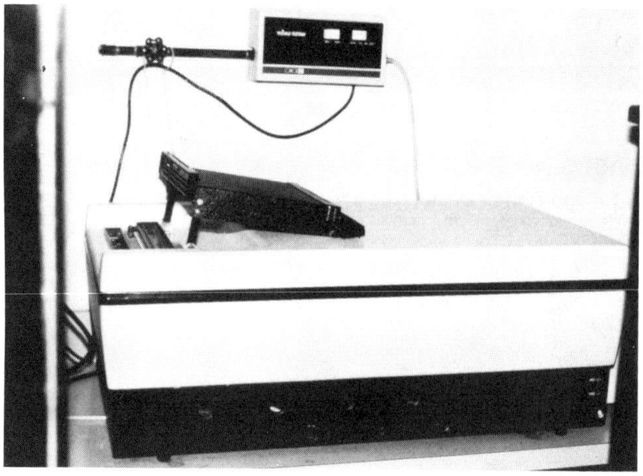

FIG 34–12.
A small automatic processor used in an office environment.

TABLE 34–3.
X-ray Troubleshooting (What to Do If It Didn't Come Out Right)

Problem	Solution
Film clear	Make sure that the cassette was not inserted backwards Make sure that the x-ray is angled directly to the cassette Make sure that the power is on and the circuit breaker is working The machine may need to be serviced
Film too light (underexposure)	Increase the KVP Increase the mAs Decrease the filters Decrease the focal film distance Increase the developing time and temperature Check the strength of the developing solutions
Film too dark (overexposure)	Decrease the KVP Decrease the mAs Decrease the developing time and temperature Check for double exposure of the same film Decrease the focal film distance
Poor film contrast (fog-grey)	Decrease the KVP Increase the collimation because there is too much scatter Check film storage and the age of the film, which may be too old Change chemicals in the developing tanks Decrease the developing temperature Check for light leakage in the darkroom Check the safe light
Distortion	Increase the focal film distance Decrease the object-film distance Check the angulation of the central ray
Poor detail	Increase the focal film distance Decrease the object-film distance Decrease motion Use high-speed, nonscreen film for better detail

ished film. Several methods are available. The patient's name, date of the examination, doctor's name and address, and which side (right or left) being x-rayed must be included. Radiopaque marking tape comes precut or on a roll. This tape adheres to a plastic holder and contains the doctor's name and address. The balance of the information is typed or written with a pen. Other methods include 3 × 5-in. cards that work with ID printers (Fig 34–13) and kits that contain removable lead letters that fit into an ID holder. Handy clip-on markers can be used to identify the right side from the left.

Miscellaneous equipment needed for the darkroom includes a water thermometer, darkroom timer, stainless steel developing hangers, drying rack, and solution agitator. An immersion heater is an extra that maintains the solutions at a constant temperature. Film storage bins are made of lightproof steel. Lead blockers are used to protect the portion of the x-ray film that is not in use at the moment. X-ray illuminators or view boxes aid in visualization of the finished x-ray film. X-ray duplicators are important so that you always

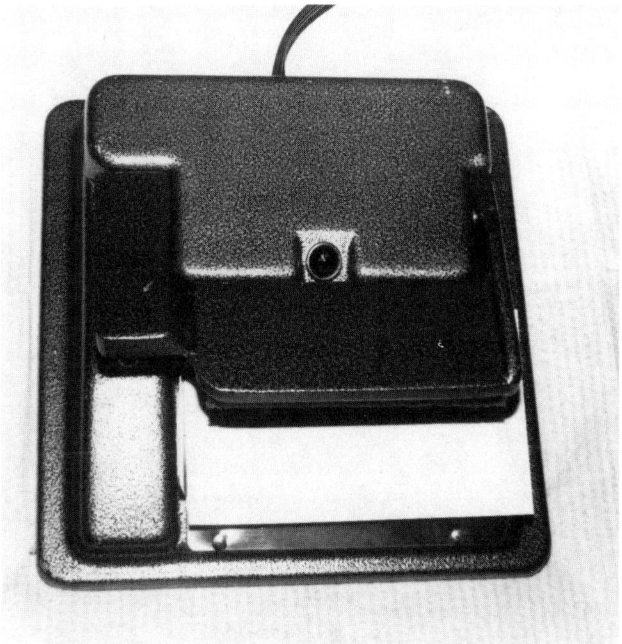

FIG 34–13.
An ID printer.

maintain your original x-ray films (Fig 34–14). Special duplicating film is required.

Film artifacts result from actions before and during development. Fog occurs on a film due to exposure to light, poor chemicals, and old film. Stains occur on the film when the chemicals are oxidized or exhausted or when the developing tanks are corroded. It is mandatory to change the chemicals at least every 2 months. If a large number of x-ray films are taken, the chemicals need to be changed more often because the chemicals are depleted depending on the number of radiographs being taken. Marks and defects occur from fingernails, water droplets, crinkle marks, static marks, and streaking, which is due to failure to agitate the circulating developing and fixing solutions prior to use. Table 34–3 defines solutions to many problems one may have when taking an x-ray film.

The X-Ray Room

Today, with more stringent laws governing the use of x-ray equipment, the planning of the x-ray room is important. The walls lining the x-ray room should be shielded with $\frac{1}{16}$-in. lead. This is not a strict requirement, providing that the x-ray beam is not aimed at a wall where people may be located on the other side. The operator should be able to stand 6 ft away from the equipment and yet be able to view the patient while shooting the x-ray film. A protective barrier with a lead-lined glass opening is advisable.

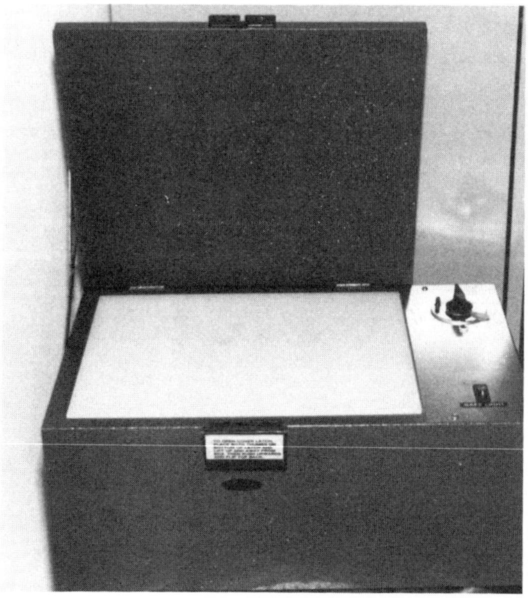

FIG 34–14.
An x-ray duplicator.

X-ray units may be mobile, wall mounted, or floor mounted. Place the machine in the most useful space depending on your floor layout. Some floor-mounted units come with a built-in orthoposer. Some x-ray units come with variable milliamperage settings, and others come with a fixed unit of one or two settings (i.e., 10 or 15 mA for foot x-ray machines). A variable KVP dial as well as time dial is desirable as well.

Many states today require registration of x-ray equipment and special training of office assistants who are involved in taking x-rays films. This is usually handled by the radiologic health section of the State Department of Human Resources or the State Department of Health Services.

RADIOGRAPHIC POSITIONING

Angle and Base of Gait

The angle of gait is the angle that the feet make with the line of progression as the patient walks. Normally it is approximately 10 to 15 degrees abducted (turned out) to this imaginary line of progression. The base of gait is the distance between the two malleoli while the patient walks. Usually it is 2 in. Weight-bearing x-ray films should ideally be taken in the angle and base of gait (Fig 34–15), especially if a biomechanical evaluation is needed. Non–weight-bearing views are taken postoperatively, in the case of trauma, with unstable patients, and also where specialized views negate weight bearing. In order to take angle and base-of-gait x-ray films each foot must be x-rayed separately. Two views may be taken on a 10 × 12-in. film by using a lead blocker to protect half of the film while the other half is being exposed. The patient places one foot in the appropriate position, with the lead blocker covering the other half of the film. The other foot is now placed in the angle and base of gait and the x-ray film taken. The lead blocker is now moved to the other side, and the identical procedure is performed on the opposite foot.

Orthoposer

An orthoposer is a specially constructed platform that is used to take weight-bearing foot and ankle radiographs (Fig 34–16). The orthoposer is elevated above the ground and has a slot whereby an x-ray cassette can be stood upright. The well of the slot is lined with lead. The orthoposer primarily assists in lateral projection radiographs. The

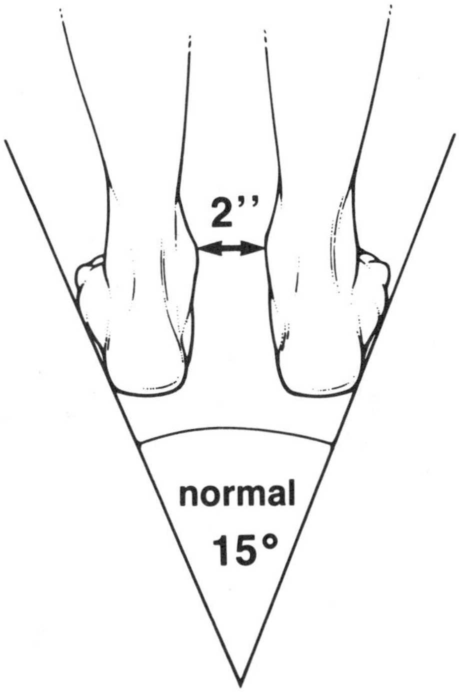

Angle and Base of Gait

FIG 34–15.
The angle and base of gait.

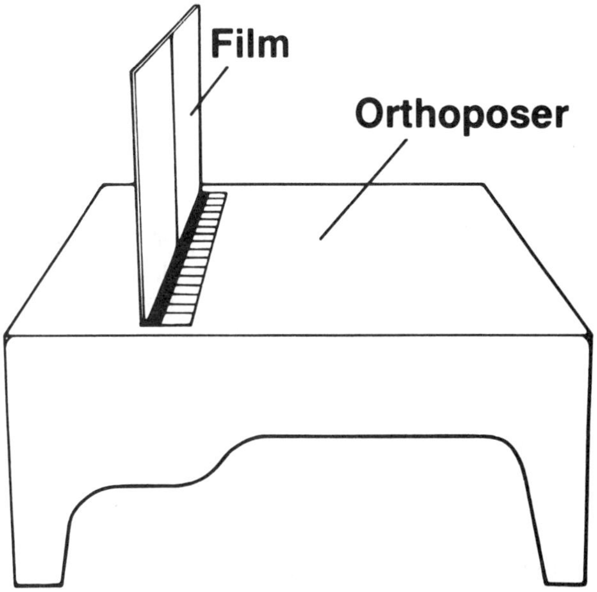

FIG 34–16.
An orthoposer.

difficulty arises when an x-ray tube cannot be lowered enough with the patient standing on the floor and the x-ray beam must be perpendicular to the film. Therefore, elevating the foot off the floor on the orthoposer allows better positioning of the x-ray beam.

It is often important to know what part of the foot is of the utmost importance before actually taking the x-ray film. This is especially important in preoperative and postoperative evaluation. The radiation exposure will be greatest at the central ray and will be less at peripheral areas. Therefore, in evaluating rearfoot pathology, where the structures are more dense, you will want to aim the central ray at the rearfoot as well as increase the exposure time, mAs, or KVP to get increased exposure in order to provide adequate density on the radiograph.

Postoperative radiography also deserves a special note. In critical situations it is best to remove any casts or dressings from the foot. Also remember that it will probably be somewhat uncomfortable for the patient to stand at great lengths. It is best to get everything you need set up first and then bring the patient to the x-ray area. Be careful in situations where the patient is non–weight bearing. Rest the foot on the plate with the patient standing and bearing weight on the opposite foot. Where available, non–weight-bearing x-ray films should be taken on a table top with the patient lying supine.

Intraoperative x-ray films are often taken to ensure adequate surgical technique prior to closure of the surgical site (Fig 34–17). Appropriate shielding of the operating personnel is needed. The patient is usually lying supine, and one person must hold the x-ray plate in the proper position against the patient's foot. The x-ray cassette

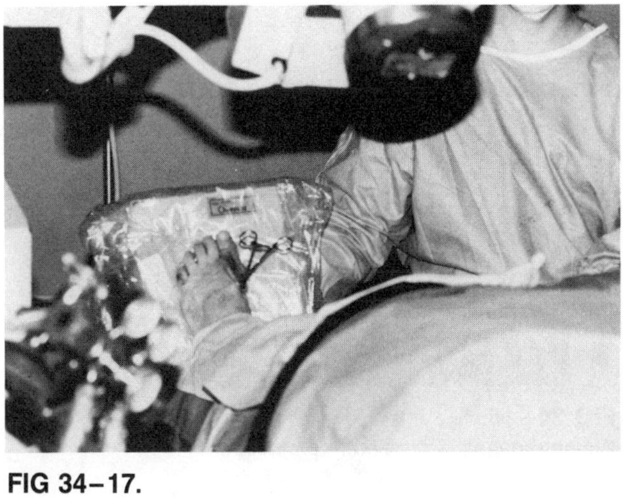

FIG 34–17.
An intraoperative x-ray procedure. The surgeon is standing off to the right, and the x-ray machine is to the left.

is wrapped in a sterile x-ray holder. The person holding the cassette should make sure his hands and body are not in line with direct exposure. The radiographs should be processed immediately so that operative time is not delayed.

A projection is the tube's eye view, or path, of the central ray (i.e. anteroposterior [AP]). A view is the finished radiograph and is opposite to the projection (i.e., posteroanterior [PA]). For full evaluation of a patient, multiple projections are required.

STANDARD RADIOGRAPHIC PROJECTIONS OF THE FOOT*

Dorsoplantar Projection

A dorsoplantar projection is actually an AP projection of the foot; only the terminology is appropriately altered. Where possible the dorsoplantar projection should be taken with weight bearing. An orthoposer or podium will facilitate weight-bearing views. The film should be placed flat on the orthoposer, and the patient should stand on the film. Where angle and base-of-gait x-ray films are desirable, one foot should be exposed at a time, with a lead shield protecting the other half of the plate. The x-ray head is angled 15 degrees from the vertical posteriorly toward the calcaneus (Fig 34–18). The central ray is directed at the navicular (Fig 34–19). When both feet are filmed simultaneously, the central ray is directed equally between the feet.

**The material in this section was reprinted with permission from Schlefman BS: Radiology, in McGlamry ED (ed):* Fundamentals of Foot Surgery. *Baltimore, Williams & Wilkins, 1987, pp 136–148.*

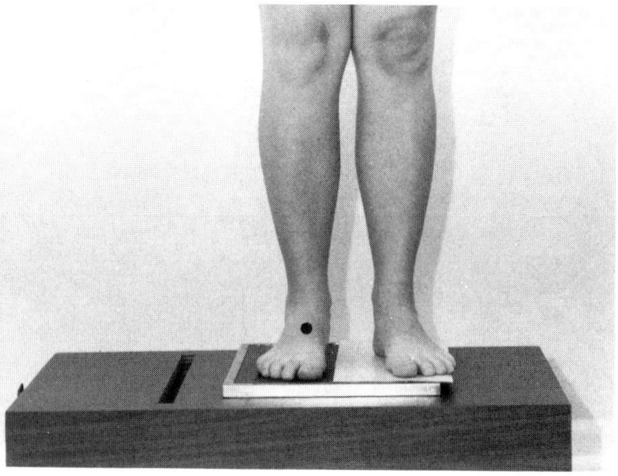

FIG 34–19.
Weight-bearing dorsoplantar projection.

In cases where weight-bearing views are not possible (i.e. trauma, postoperatively, the elderly), a non–weight-bearing dorsoplantar projection is advisable. It is best to place the patient supine with the knee bent and the sole of the foot resting flat on the plate. The tube is angled 15 degrees from the vertical (Fig 34–20).

The dorsoplantar projection allows an accurate

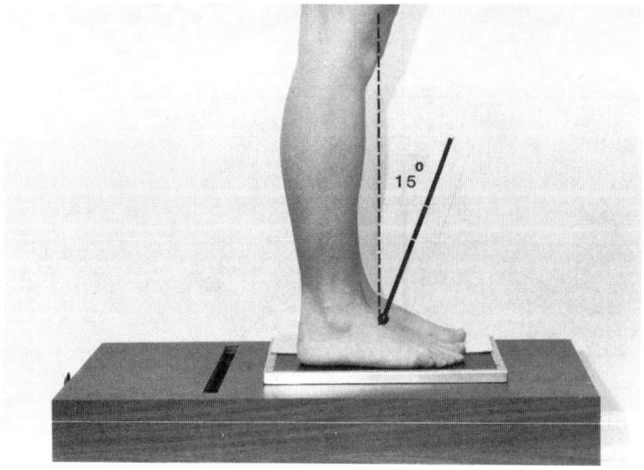

FIG 34–18.
Weight-bearing dorsoplantar projection.

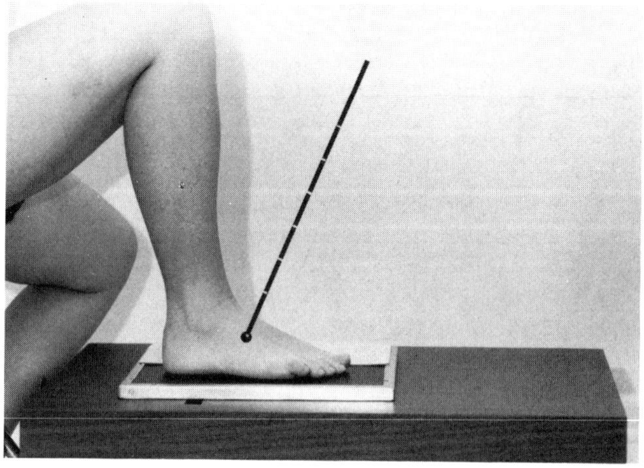

FIG 34–20.
Non–weight-bearing dorsoplantar projection.

representation of the phalanges, metatarsals, navicular, cuboid, medial cuneiform, and to a lesser extent the middle and lateral cuneiforms. The distal portion of the talus and calcaneus as well as the midtarsal joint, Lisfranc's joint, the metatarsophalangeal joints, and the interphalangeal joints may be observed (Fig 34–21).

Often a dorsoplantar projection is taken with lesion markers, a small circular lead or soft wire fixed to the plantar aspect of the foot with tape to precisely locate the position of a questionable lesion in relation to underlying bone (Fig 34–22).

Lateral Projection

The x-ray cassette is placed vertically in the lead-lined well of the orthoposer. The patient places one foot on each side of the film with the medial aspect of the foot in question touching the film. Angle and base of gait x-ray films are easy to obtain with proper positioning. The tube is angled 90 degrees from the vertical, and the central ray is aimed at the first cuneiform (Fig 34–23). This view adequately depicts the talus, calcaneus, cuboid, and to a lesser extent the navicular and medial cuneiform. The metatarsals and phalanges overlap to varying degrees (Fig 34–24). Any digit may be elevated to a plane above the others by a radiolucent object so that the digits may be individually evaluated. This is commonly done with the hallux (Fig 34–25).

In taking a non–weight-bearing lateral view, one places the patient supine on the unaffected

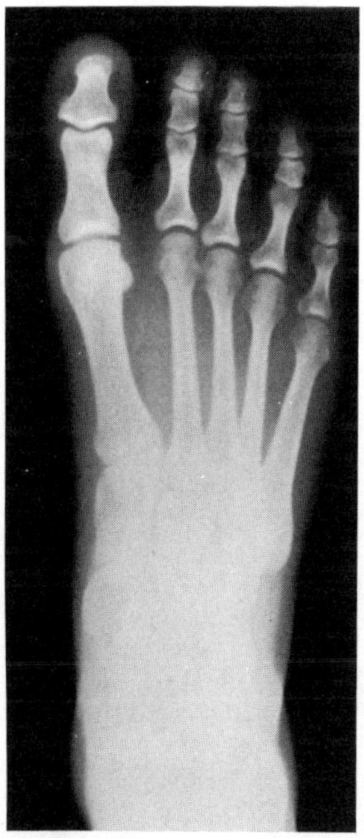

FIG 34–21.
Dorsoplantar view.

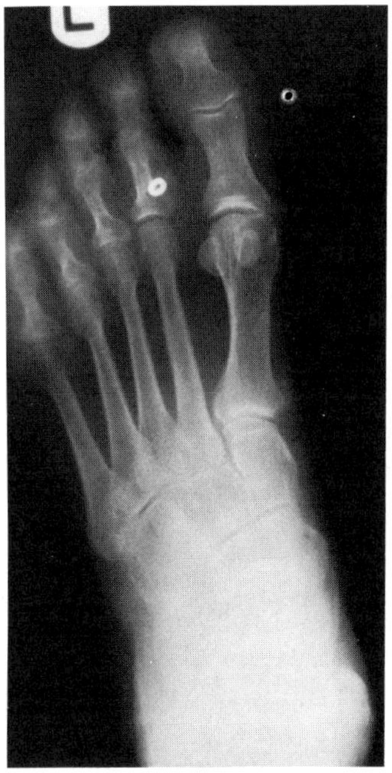

FIG 34–22.
Dorsoplantar view with a lesion marker beneath the second metatarsal head.

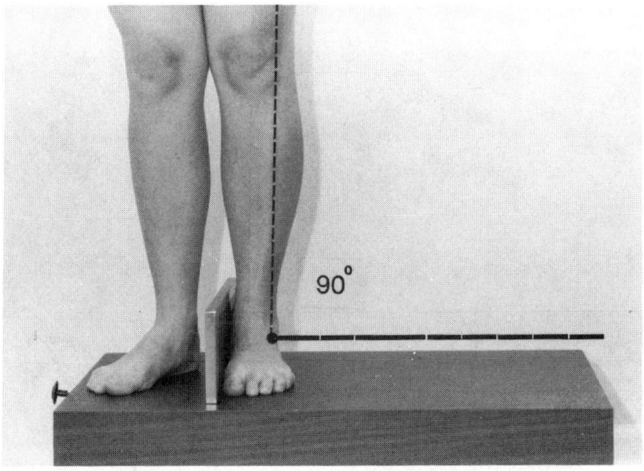

FIG 34–23.
Weight-bearing lateral projection.

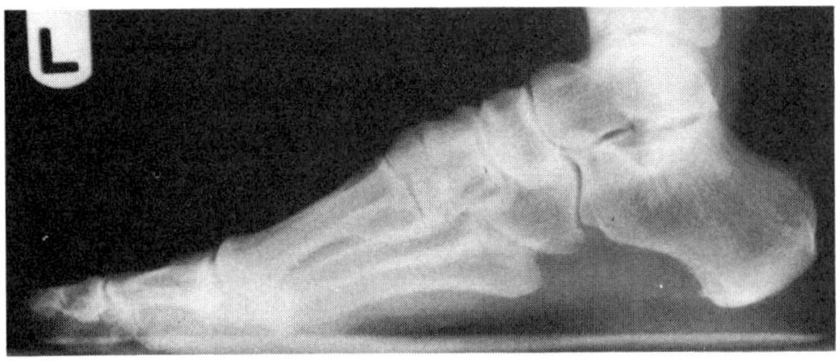

FIG 34–24.
Weight-bearing lateral view. This view adequately depicts the talus, calcaneus, cuboid, and to a lesser extent the navicular and medial cuneiform. The metatarsals and phalanges overlap to varying degrees.

side with the lateral malleolus in contact with the film. The central ray is directed perpendicular to the midpoint of the foot (Fig 34–26).

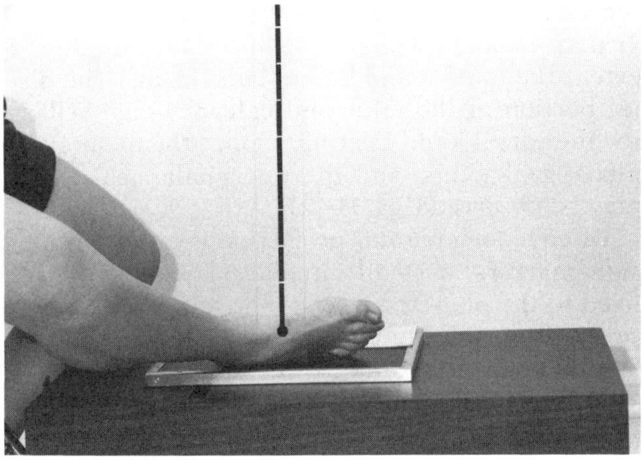

FIG 34–26.
Non–weight-bearing lateral projection. The central ray is directed perpendicular to the midpoint of the foot.

Medial Oblique Projection

There is much disagreement about terminology when discussing medial oblique and lateral oblique projections of the foot. By definition, a projection is defined as the direction the central ray passes through the part. Hence, in a medial oblique projection, the central ray should enter the foot from a medial oblique position. This is in fact not how most orthopedists or radiologists define a medial oblique projection.

For a medial oblique projection the foot is placed on a cassette that is flat on the orthoposer with the medial aspect of the foot against the edge of the film. The central ray is directed 45 degrees from the vertical to the navicular (Fig 34–27). This view is only beneficial for evaluating the most medial structures of the foot including the first and second metatarsals, the first and second cuneiforms, and the tibial and fibular sesamoids (Fig 34–28).

An alternative non–weight-bearing projection involves flexing the knee and adducting it until the plantar aspect of the foot makes a 15-, 30-, 45-, or 60-degree angle with the film. The central ray is directed to the first cuneiform and perpendicular to the film (Fig 34–29).

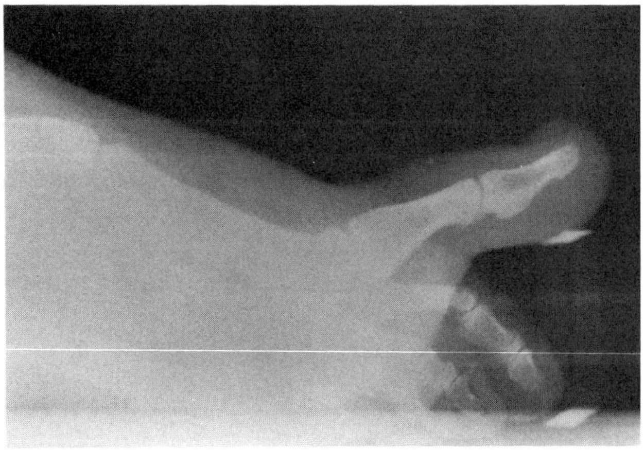

FIG 34–25.
Raised hallux view.

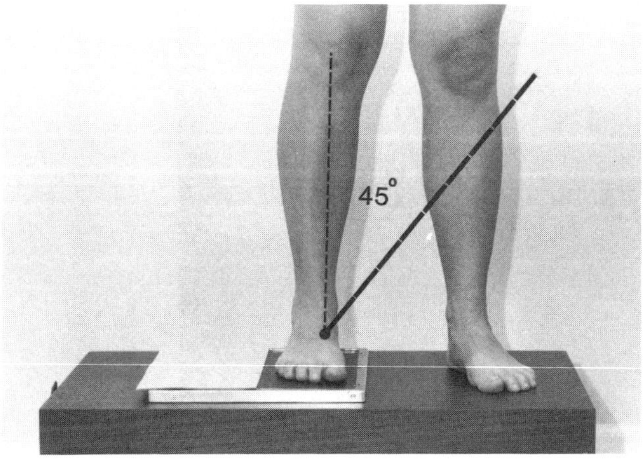

FIG 34–27.
Weight-bearing medial oblique projection.

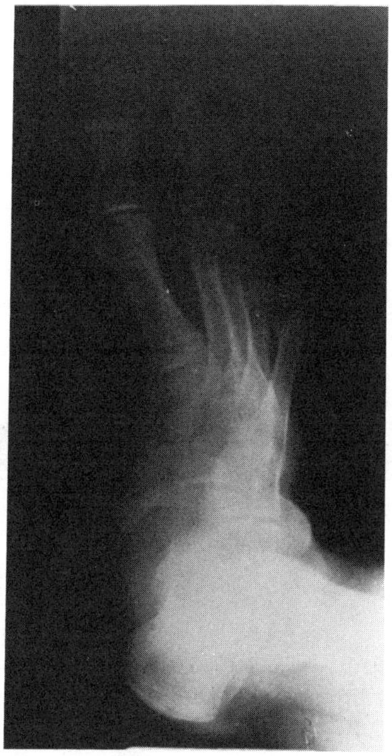

FIG 34–28.
Weight-bearing medial oblique view.

Lateral Oblique Projection

In the weight-bearing projection, the patient stands on the x-ray cassette with the most lateral border of the foot against the edge of the cassette. The tube is angled 45 degrees from the vertical and is aimed at the cuboid bone (Fig 34–30). This is the most common oblique view in podiatric usage. It gives a magnified and distorted presentation of the bones of the foot (Fig 34–31). Variations from the 45-degree angle may be more useful for observing one bone over another bone. A 15-degree oblique projection shows the medial cuneiform, a 30-degree oblique projection shows the lateral cuneiform, and a 60-degree oblique projection shows the cuboid and anterior facet of the talocalcaneal joint.

The non–weight-bearing projection is similar to dorsoplantar projection. With the foot resting on the x-ray plate, the patient adducts the knee until the sole of the foot makes an angle of 30 to 45 degrees with the plane of the film. The central ray is then aimed perpendicular to the film and directed to the third cuneiform (Fig 34–32).

Axial Sesamoid Projection

For an axial sesamoid projection, the film is placed vertically in the slot in the orthoposer, and the patient faces the film with the toes dorsiflexed against the film. The patient then raises up on the heels. The central ray is directed perpendicular to the center of the foot (or the center of the film if both feet are done simultaneously) (Fig 34–33). Many positioning devices have been designed to aid the axial sesamoid projection. An alternative positioning involves placing the patient prone or on hands and knees with the film flat on the x-ray table, the toes dorsiflexed, and the ball of the foot

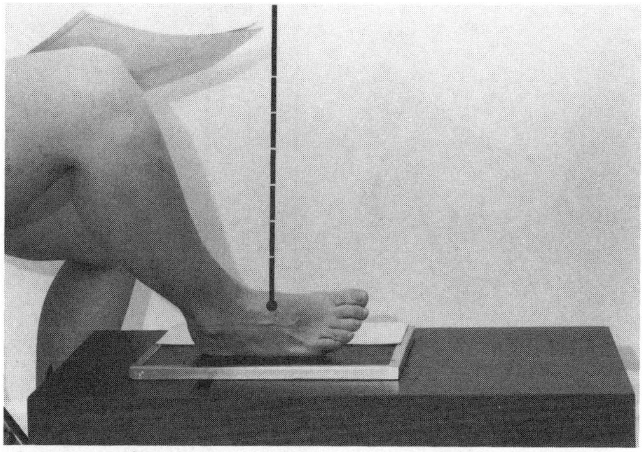

FIG 34–29.
Non–weight-bearing medial oblique projection.

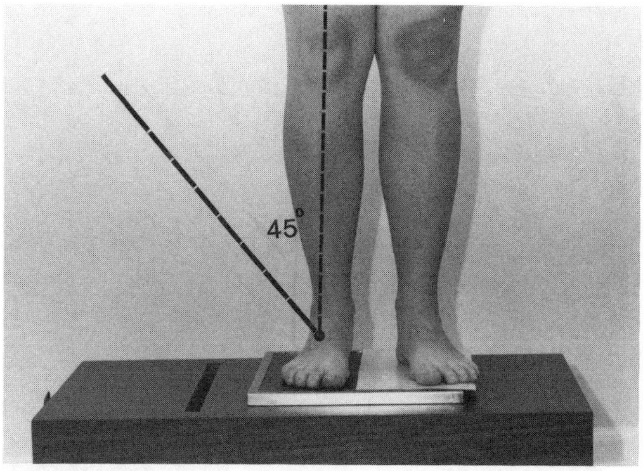

FIG 34–30.
Weight-bearing lateral oblique projection. The tube is angled 45 degrees from the vertical and is aimed at the cuboid bone.

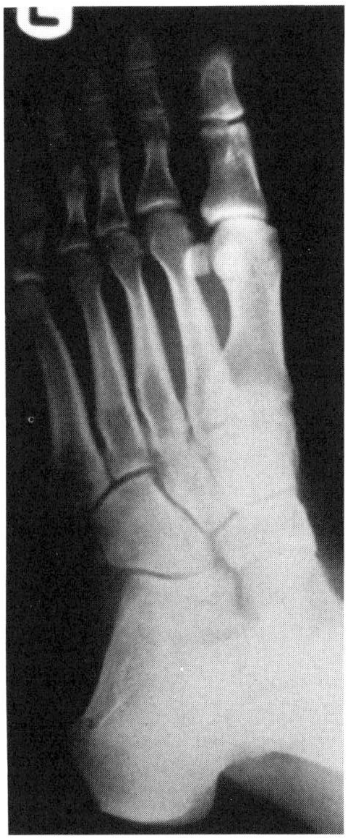

FIG 34–31.
Weight-bearing lateral oblique view. Note the magnified and distorted presentation of the bones of the foot.

placed perpendicular to the horizontal. The central ray is directed vertical to the metatarsophalangeal joints (Fig 34–34). This view is used to evaluate the sesamoid bones and their relationship with the first metatarsal head. It has ques-

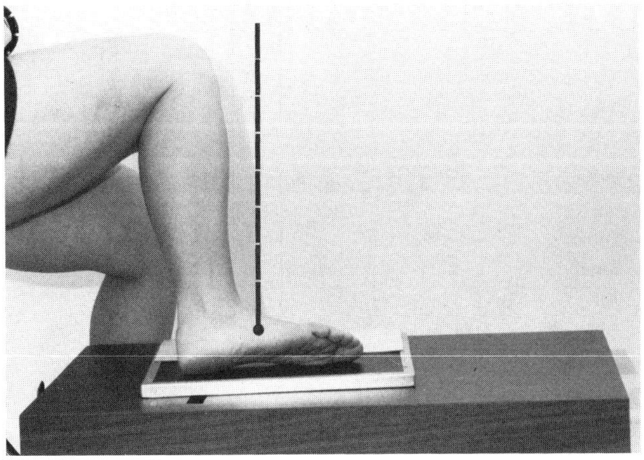

FIG 34–32.
Non–weight-bearing lateral oblique projection.

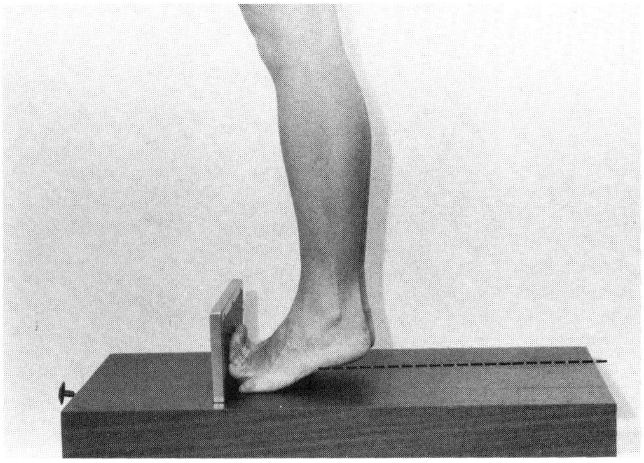

FIG 34–33.
Axial sesamoid projection.

tionable value in evaluating the relative declination of the metatarsal heads in relation to each other (Fig 34–35).

Axial Calcaneal Projections

For axial calcaneal projections, the film is placed flat on the orthoposer, and the patient stands with the heel at the most posterior edge of the film. The central ray is directed at a 45-degree angle to the posterior aspect of the calcaneus (Fig 34–36). An alternative method involves the patient sitting with the leg stretched out over the cassette. The ankle joint is dorsiflexed to 90 de-

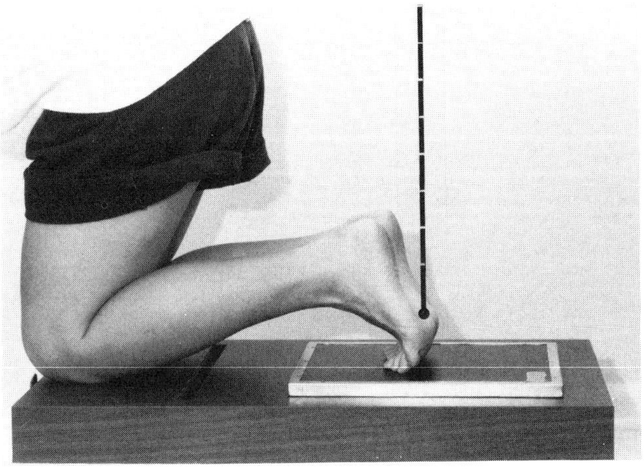

FIG 34–34.
An alternate position for the axial sesamoid projection.

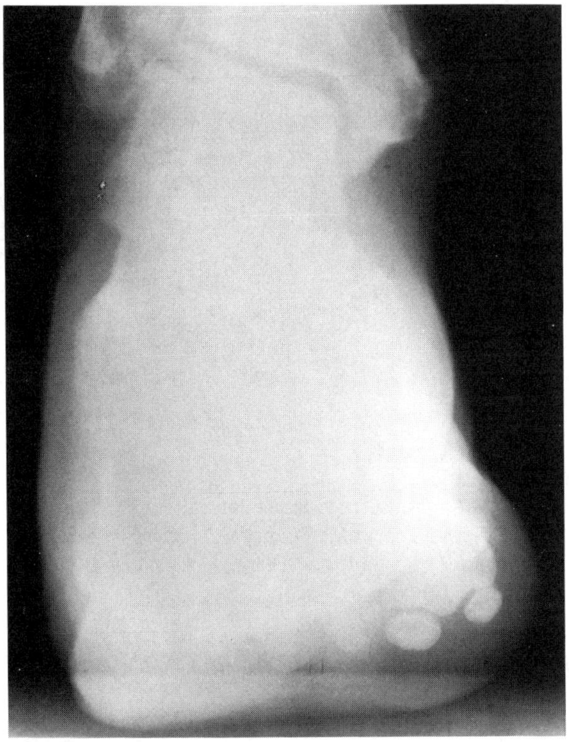

FIG 34–35.
Axial sesamoid view.

grees, and a long piece of gauze looped around the forefoot may be used to aid dorsiflexion. The central ray is directed to the distal plantar aspect of the calcaneus at a 45-degree angle from the vertical (Fig 34–37). This projection is used to examine

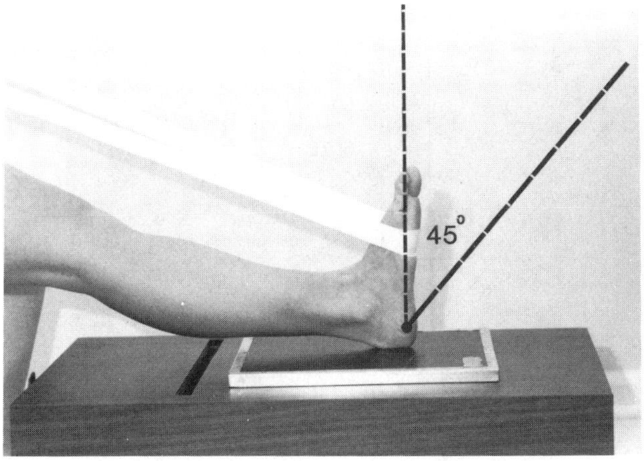

FIG 34–37.
An alternate method for the axial calcaneal projection.

the calcaneus for fractures or possible abnormalities in shape. It is also used to evaluate the position of internal fixation devices used in triple arthrodesis (Fig 34–38).

Harris and Beath Projection (Coalition View)

The Harris and Beath projection is taken similar to the weight-bearing axial calcaneal projection. The main difference is that multiple angles are required to allow visualization of the subtalar joint. A scout lateral x-ray film will allow one to approximate the declination of the posterior facet of the subtalar joint in reference to the weight-bearing plane. Three projections are recom-

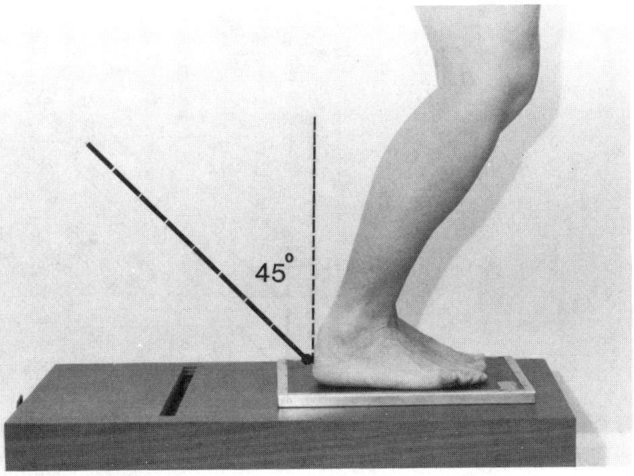

FIG 34–36.
Axial calcaneal projection.

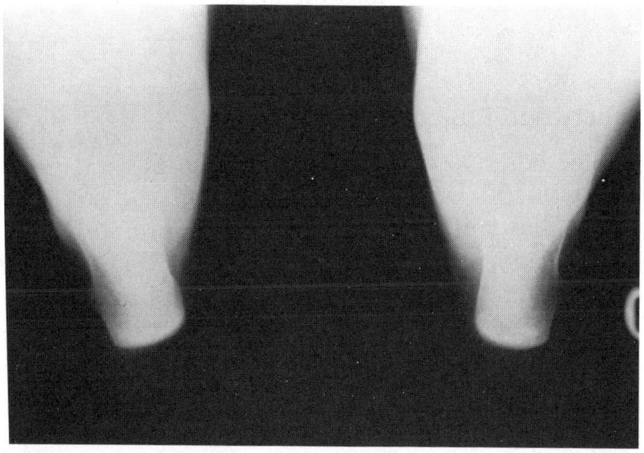

FIG 34–38.
Axial calcaneal view.

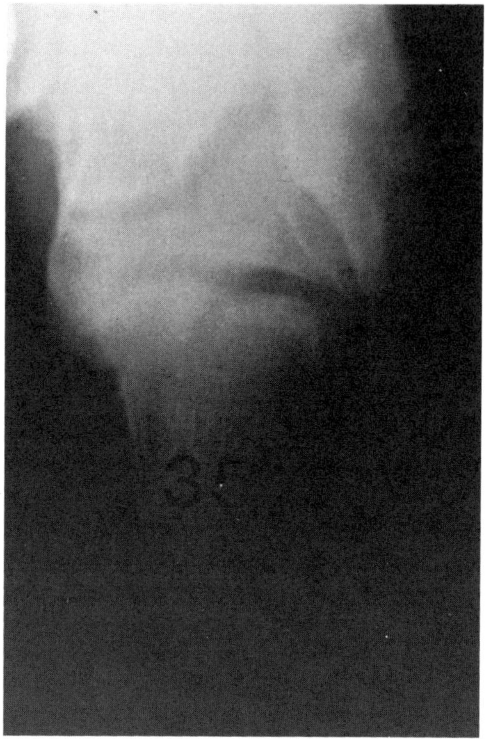

FIG 34–39.
Harris and Beath view at 50 degrees.

mended. One is taken 10 degrees above, 10 degrees below, and at the measured angle (i.e. 30, 40, and 50 degrees if the measured declination is 40 degrees). The patient should flex the knees and ankles slightly before the film is shot. This projection gives an axial view of the calcaneus, the inferior aspect of the talus, as well as the middle and posterior facets of the talocalcaneal articulation (Fig 34–39).

Isherwood Projections

The Isherwood projections consist of three positions to fully visualize the joints of the subtalar joint. The oblique dorsoplantar or oblique lateral view demonstrates the anterior joint (Fig 34–40), the medial oblique axial view demonstrates the middle and posterior joints (Fig 34–41), and the lateral oblique axial view demonstrates the posterior joint in profile (Fig 34–42). A 30- and 45-degree wedge of wood, plaster, or any radiolucent material is needed for positioning. The patient is seated in a chair with the leg extended over the orthoposer or lies supine on a table top.

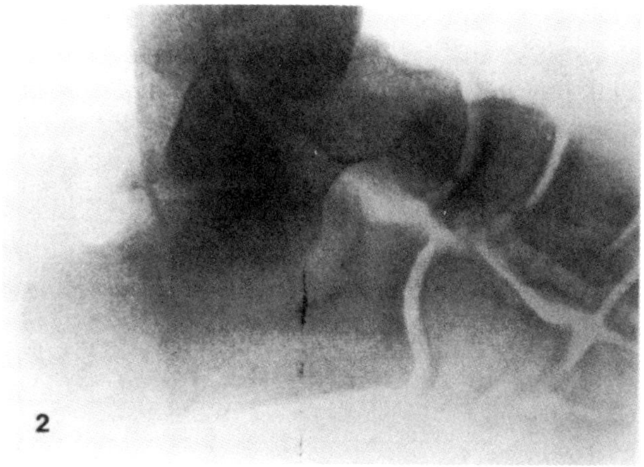

FIG 34–40.
Oblique dorsoplantar or oblique lateral view. (From Schlefman BS: Radiology, in McGlamry ED (ed): *Fundamentals of Foot Surgery.* Baltimore, Williams & Wilkins, 1987, pp 136–148. Used by permission.)

Oblique Dorsoplantar or Oblique Lateral

The foot is positioned on a 45-degree wedge with the medial aspect of the foot resting on the x-ray cassette. The knee is flexed to obtain a 90-degree relationship of the foot to the leg. The central ray is directed vertically to a point 1 in. below and 1 in. anterior to the lateral malleolus (Fig 34–43).

Medial Oblique Axial

The foot is positioned on a 30-degree wedge with the medial aspect of the foot resting on the

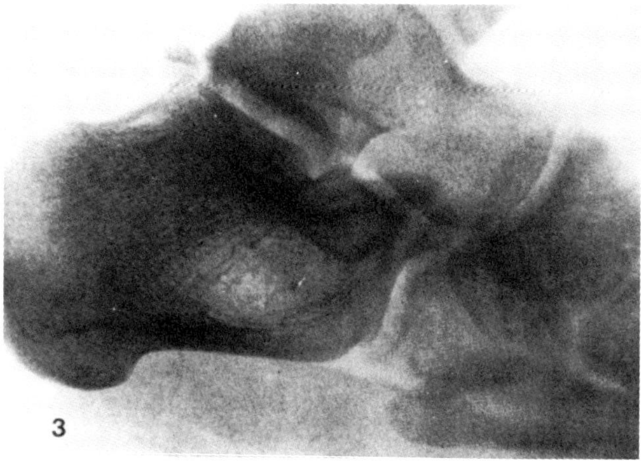

FIG 34–41.
Medial oblique axial view. (From Schlefman BS: Radiology, in McGlamry ED (ed): *Fundamentals of Foot Surgery.* Baltimore, Williams & Wilkins, 1987, pp 136–148. Used by permission.)

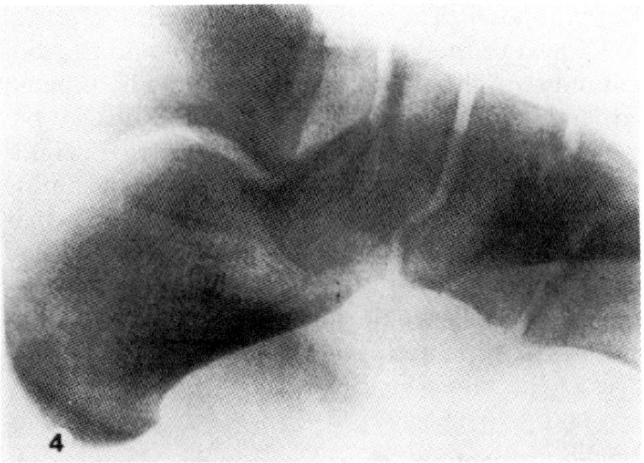

FIG 34–42.
Lateral oblique axial view. (From Schlefman BS: Radiology, in McGlamry ED (ed): *Fundamentals of Foot Surgery.* Baltimore, Williams & Wilkins, 1987, pp 136–148. Used by permission.)

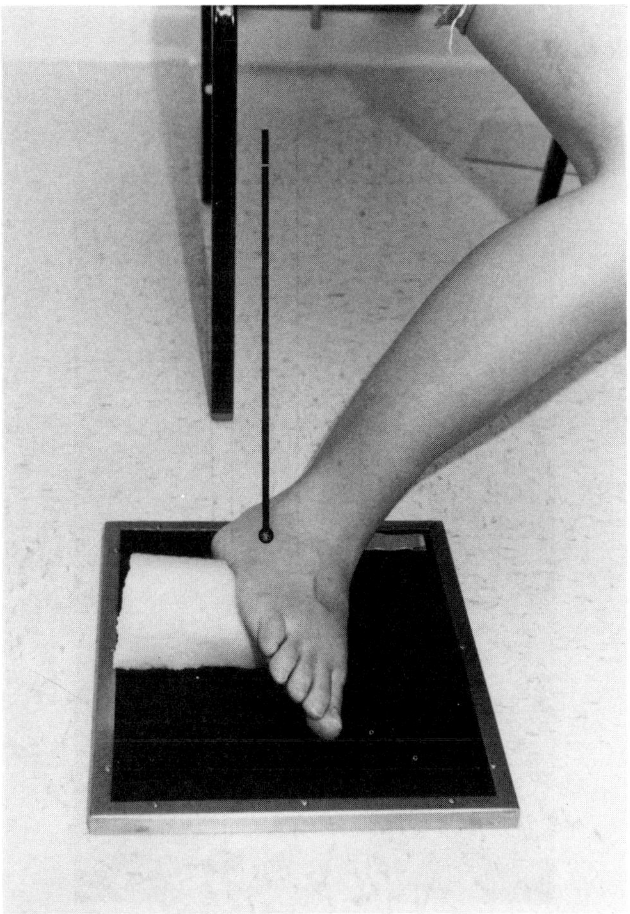

FIG 34–43.
Oblique dorsoplantar or oblique lateral projection.

x-ray cassette. The foot is held in maximum dorsiflexion and inversion with the help of a sling. The central ray is directed to a point 1 in. distal and 1 in. anterior to the lateral malleolus at an angle of 10 degrees cephalad from the vertical (Fig 34–44).

Lateral Oblique Axial

The foot is positioned on a 30-degree wedge with the lateral aspect of the foot resting on the x-ray cassette. The foot is held in maximum dorsiflexion and eversion with the help of a sling. The central ray is directed to a point 1 in. distal to the medial malleolus at an angle of 10 degrees cephalad from the vertical (Fig 34–45).

As one can readily see, positioning is very difficult with the Isherwood projections. The author believes that the benefits derived from these projections are minimal. It is probably better to first take standard radiographic projections (dorsoplantar, oblique, lateral), and if these do not suffice, then advanced techniques such as tomograms and computed tomography (CT) should be used.

STANDARD RADIOGRAPHIC PROJECTIONS OF THE ANKLE*

Anteroposterior Projection

For an AP projection, ankle x-ray films should be taken with the patient weight bearing where practical. The x-ray cassette is held vertically in

**The material in this section was reprinted with permission from Schlefman BS: Radiology, in McGlamry ED (ed):* Fundamentals of Foot Surgery. *Baltimore, Williams & Wilkins, 1987, pp 136–148.*

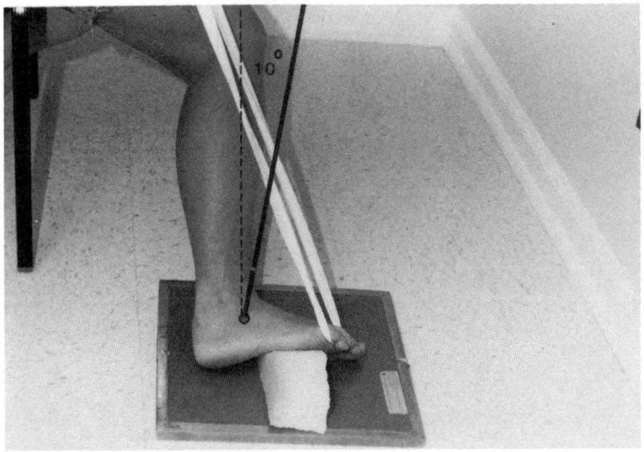

FIG 34–44.
Medial oblique axial projection.

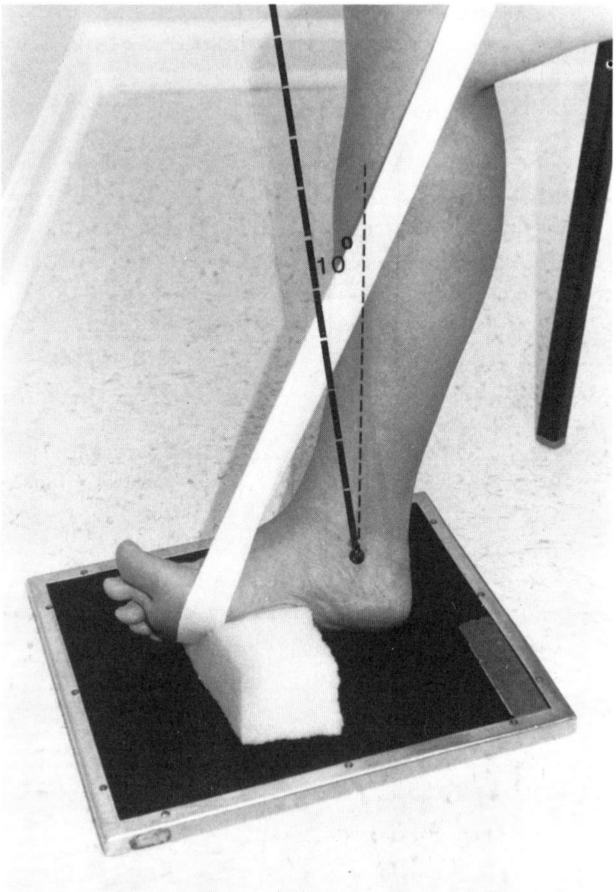

FIG 34–45.
Lateral oblique axial projection.

the orthoposer. The patient stands with the posterior aspect of the heel against the film and the foot pointed straight ahead. The central ray is directed perpendicular to the film and enters midway between the malleoli (Fig 34–46). In the non–weight-bearing projection, the patient is placed supine with the leg extended over the cassette, which is placed flat on the table. The central ray is directed vertically. This projection gives an adequate presentation of the ankle joint, including the distal ends of the tibia and the fibular and trochlear surfaces of the talus (Fig 34–47).

Mortise Projection

The mortise projection is similar to an AP projection with the exception of a 15-degree internal rotation of the leg placing the malleoli on a plane parallel to the film (Fig 34–48). This projection shows a better representation of the lower tibiofibular articulation (Fig 34–49).

Medial Oblique Projection

The medial oblique projection is similar to the AP and mortise projections. The leg is externally

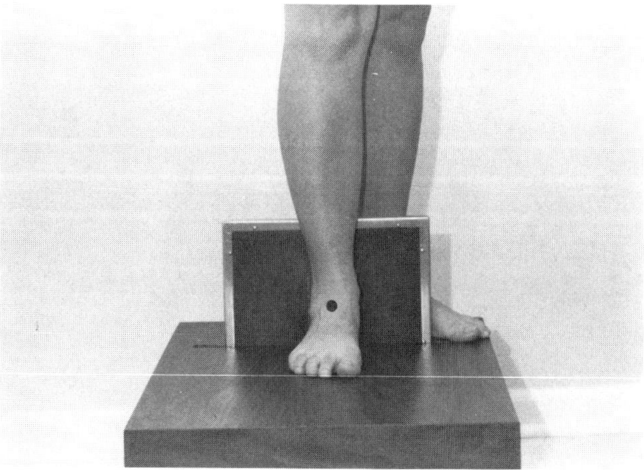

FIG 34–46.
Weight-bearing anteroposterior projection.

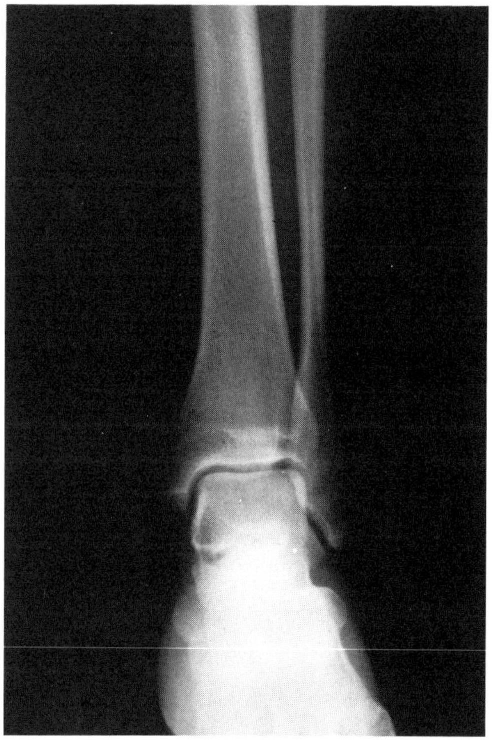

FIG 34–47.
Anteroposterior projection.

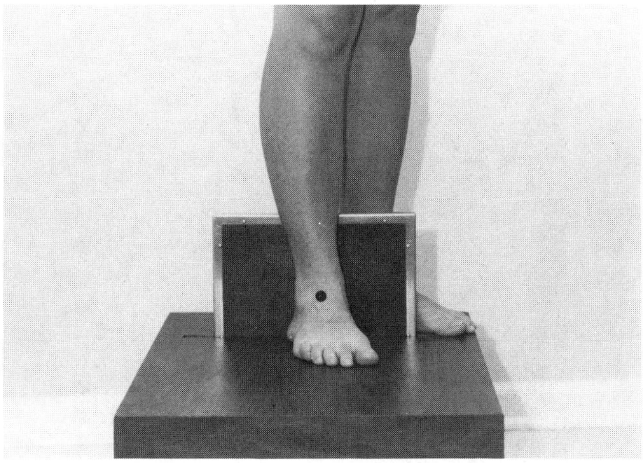

FIG 34–48.
Mortise projection.

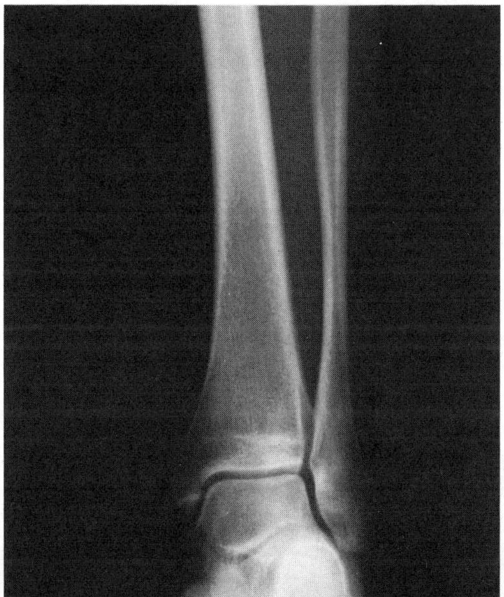

FIG 34–49.
Mortise view.

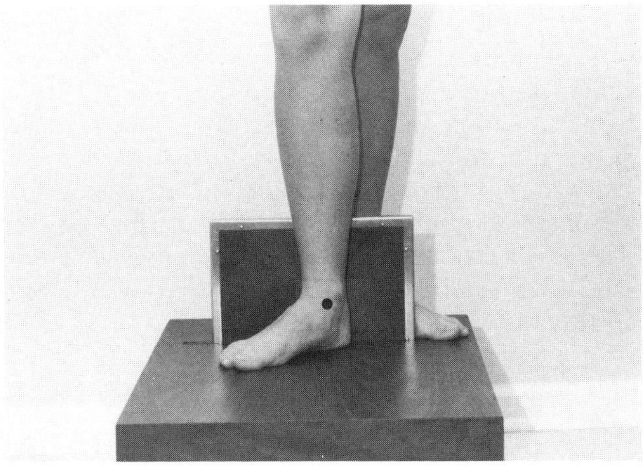

FIG 34–50.
Medial oblique projection.

rotated 45 degrees so that the central ray passes obliquely through the ankle and enters medially (Fig 34–50).

Lateral Oblique Projection

In the lateral oblique projection, the leg is internally rotated approximately 45 degrees (Fig 34–51). This further opens up the tibiofibular syndesmosis. Any variation in degrees of internal or external rotation may be used when examining an ankle for trauma.

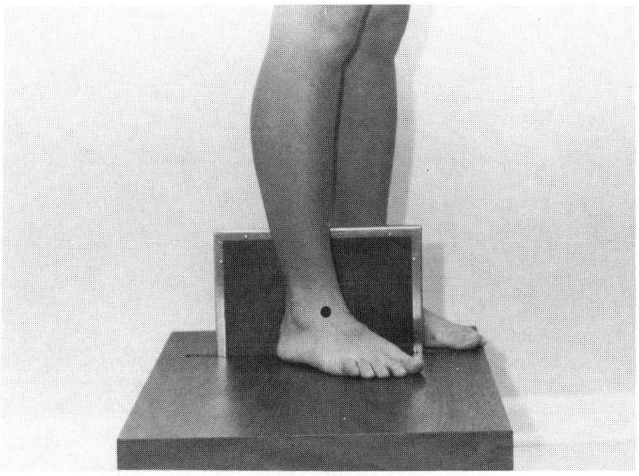

FIG 34–51.
Lateral oblique projection.

Lateral Projection

Like the lateral projection of the foot, the medial aspect of the foot is placed in contact with the x-ray cassette, and the central ray is directed perpendicular to the film. The film is positioned vertically so that more of the ankle and leg is shown at the expense of the toes and forefoot (Fig 34–52). The trochlear surface of the talus and its articulation with the tibia and fibula are visualized well in this view (Fig 34–53).

Stress Dorsiflexion Projection

The stress dorsiflexion projection is similar to the lateral weight-bearing projection of the ankle. The opposite leg is placed forward of the one being irradiated. The patient forcefully flexes the knee and ankle of the affected side to obtain as much dorsiflexion of the foot on the leg as possible (Fig 34–54). This projection is used to demonstrate any anterior ankle impingement as in ankle equinus (Fig 34–55).

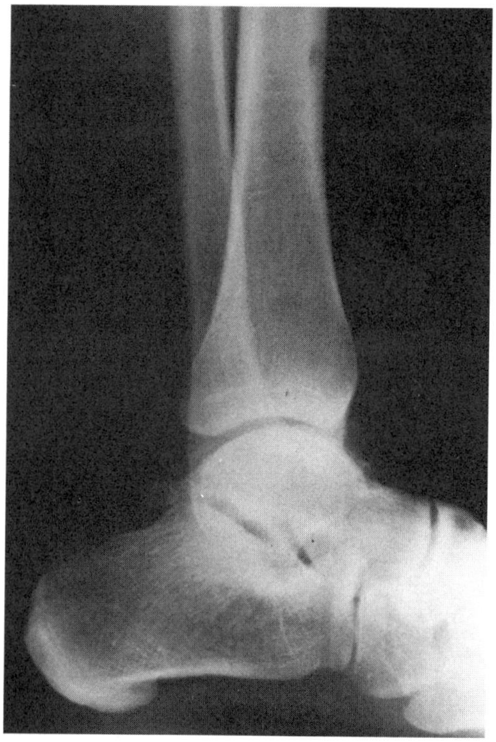

FIG 34–53.
Lateral view.

Inversion Stress Projection

Inversion stress radiographs are usually performed following ankle inversion sprains when no bony pathology is noted on standard ankle radiographs. The patient lies supine on the x-ray table with the leg extended and the foot positioned over the cassette. The examiner stabilizes the lower portion of the leg with one hand while forcefully inverting (supinating) the foot with the other hand. The central ray is directed vertically to the central portion of the ankle joint, and the x-ray film is made at the time when the ankle is held in the most extreme inversion (Fig 34–56).

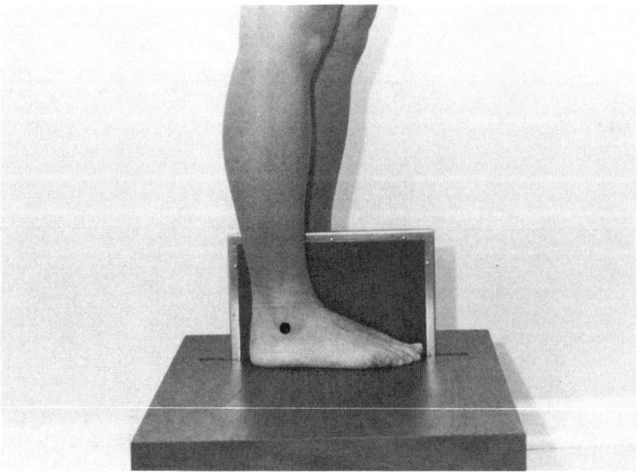

FIG 34–52.
Lateral projection.

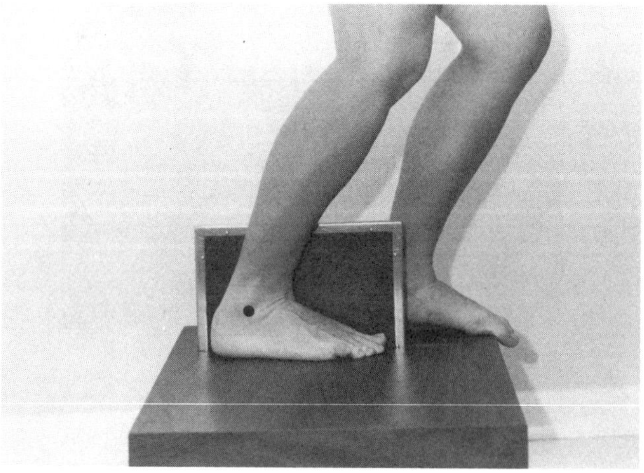

FIG 34–54.
Stress dorsiflexion projection.

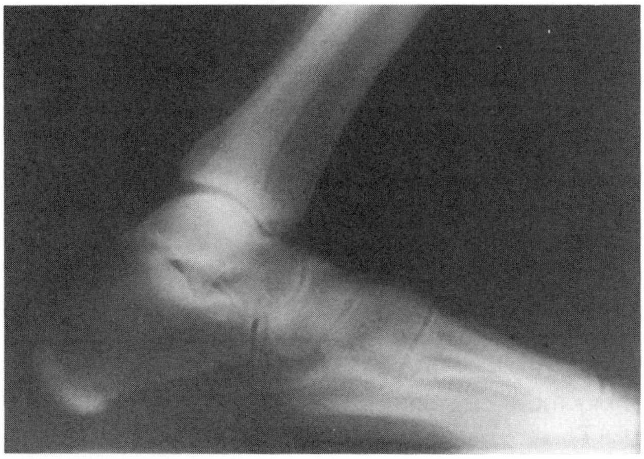

FIG 34–55.
Stress dorsiflexion view.

The examiner's hands should be protected with lead gloves, and a lead apron should be worn. Often the injured area must be anesthetized before examination. This may involve either local infiltration of a local anesthetic or the use of a high common peroneal nerve block. The uninjured side should be examined in a similar fashion for comparison. The tilting of the talus in the ankle mortise is compared (Fig 34–57).

Forced eversion may also be performed to evaluate pathologic conditions of the deltoid ligaments. Talar tilting over 10 degrees seems to be pathologic.

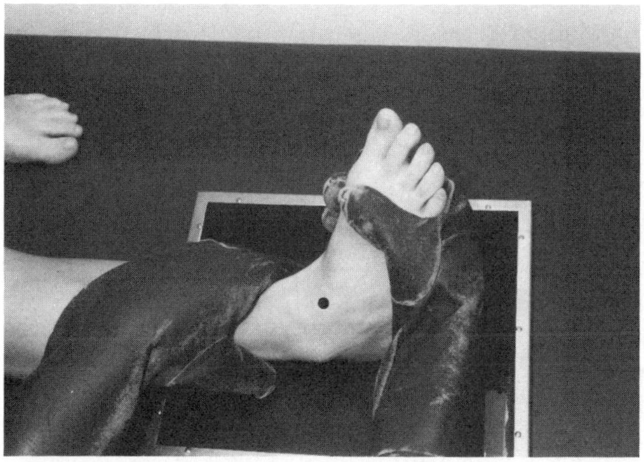

FIG 34–56.
Inversion stress projection.

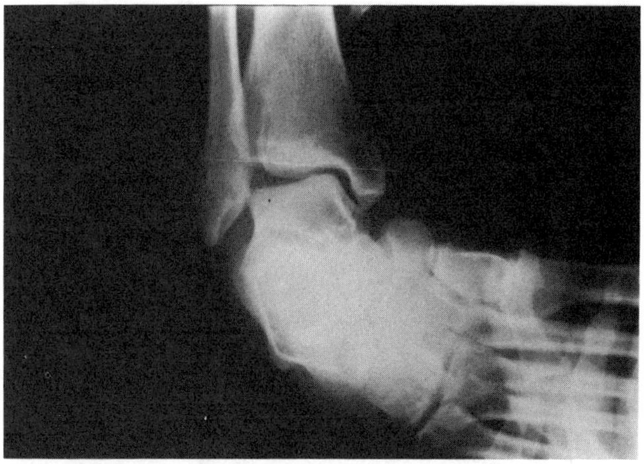

FIG 34–57.
Inversion stress view showing significant talar tilt.

Anterior Drawer Projection (Push-Pull Stress)

Like the inversion stress projection, an anterior drawer projection is taken following ankle trauma where disruption of the soft-tissue structures is suspected. The patient is placed supine with the leg extended and the lateral aspect of the foot placed against the underlying cassette. The examiner places one hand against the anterior aspect of the leg, and the other hand is placed behind the heel. Opposite forces are then applied in an attempt to pull the talus forward out of the ankle mortise. The central ray is directed perpendicular to the film and enters at the medial malleolus (Fig 34–58). Again, the examiner should be shielded, and bilateral views should be taken for comparison.

It is difficult to report on normal or abnormal values. If the talus can be forcefully dislocated anterior to the ankle mortise, then it would appear that some type of ligamentous disruption must have taken place (Fig 34–59,A and B).

SPECIAL RADIOGRAPHIC TECHNIQUES

Nuclear Medicine (Bone Scanning)

Bone scanning developed during the 1940s and early 1950s, and its continued use is seen today. Radiopharmaceuticals are radioactive compounds that are artificially produced and are injected into the patient and then localized in specified organs. A scintillation probe or detector is positioned over the organ, and the emitted γ-photons are con-

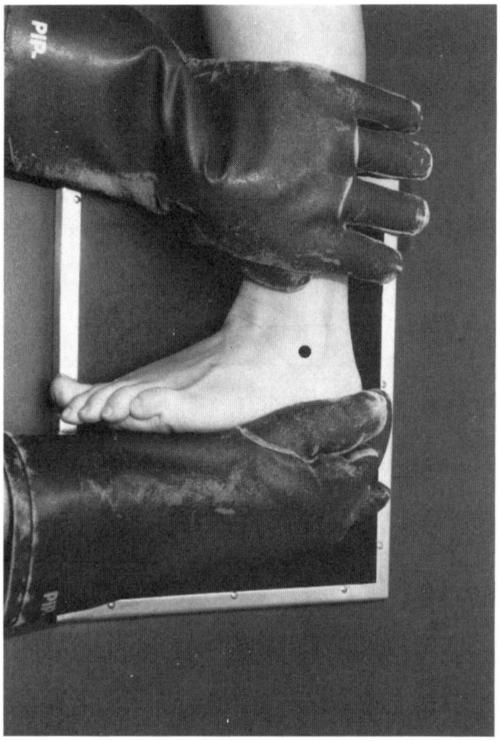

FIG 34–58.
Anterior drawer projection.

verted into visible light and counted. A photomultiplier tube converts the light into an electronic pulse. A two-dimensional photo display unit records the image and the number of counts on film.

The most commonly used imaging agents today are technetium 99m–methylene diphosphate (^{99m}Tc-MDP), gallium 67 citrate (^{67}Ga), and indium 111 oxine white blood cells (^{111}In). ^{99m}Tc-MDP is considered a bone scanning agent because it has a high affinity for bone. Normal radionuclide uptake is seen at areas of tendon insertion, constant stresses and osseous remodeling, and the epiphyseal plates in children. ^{67}Ga is primarily used for evaluation of tumors and inflammatory disorders such as infections. ^{111}In is used to detect acute infections, while ^{67}Ga is used to detect subacute or chronic infections.

Indications for bone imaging include evaluation of metastatic disease, diagnosing benign and malignant lesions, differentiating between osteomyelitis and cellulitis, determining bone viability, diagnosing infarction, aseptic necrosis evaluation, or viewing radiographically difficult-to-see fractures (i.e., stress fractures) and prosthetic joints (for infection or loosening). Osseous healing following either bone grafting or osteotomy procedures may be evaluated. Bone scanning is often used to evaluate pain that is not clearly nonskeletal in origin, especially where the pain is ill defined or diffuse.

Computed Tomography

CT is also known as computerized transverse axial tomography (CTAT), computer-assisted tomography or computerized axial tomography (CAT), reconstructive tomography (RT), and computerized transaxial transmission reconstructive tomography (CTT). Unwanted planes or layers of the body's anatomy are eliminated with the use of the cross-sectional anatomy used in CT. A scanning gantry that houses an x-ray generator and detector system, a data processing system (computer), a viewing console (cathode ray tube), and a storage system (computer) are needed for CT.

The radiation dose of each slice is approximately equivalent to a single conventional x-ray. Slices vary from 1.5 to 5 mm depending on the thickness of the part to be imaged. Podiatric uses of CT include evaluation of the presence and nature of tumors, osteomyelitis, internal bone architecture, and trabecular bone mineralization changes. In the cases of trauma, CT is used to evaluate metatarsal stress fractures and complex fractures of the calcaneus, talus, or midfoot area.

Magnetic Resonance Imaging

Magnetic resonance imaging (MRI) is a fairly new technique that is commonly used today. The average cost of a study is approximately $1,200. The system is similar to CT except that a magnetic gantry is used in lieu of moving x-ray tubes and detectors. Again, a computer and image-handling unit (cathode ray screen) is needed. MRI is a noninvasive technique that is completely harmless to the patient. There is no exposure to ionizing radiation or radioactive isotopes. MRI measures the hydrogen ion content of matter. Water has the highest amount of hydrogen ions. Therefore, MRI measures the water content of the various body tissues. CT measures the specific gravity.

The uses of MRI are increasing daily. Its greatest benefit comes from imaging of the soft tissues such as muscle, tendon, and ligamentous struc-

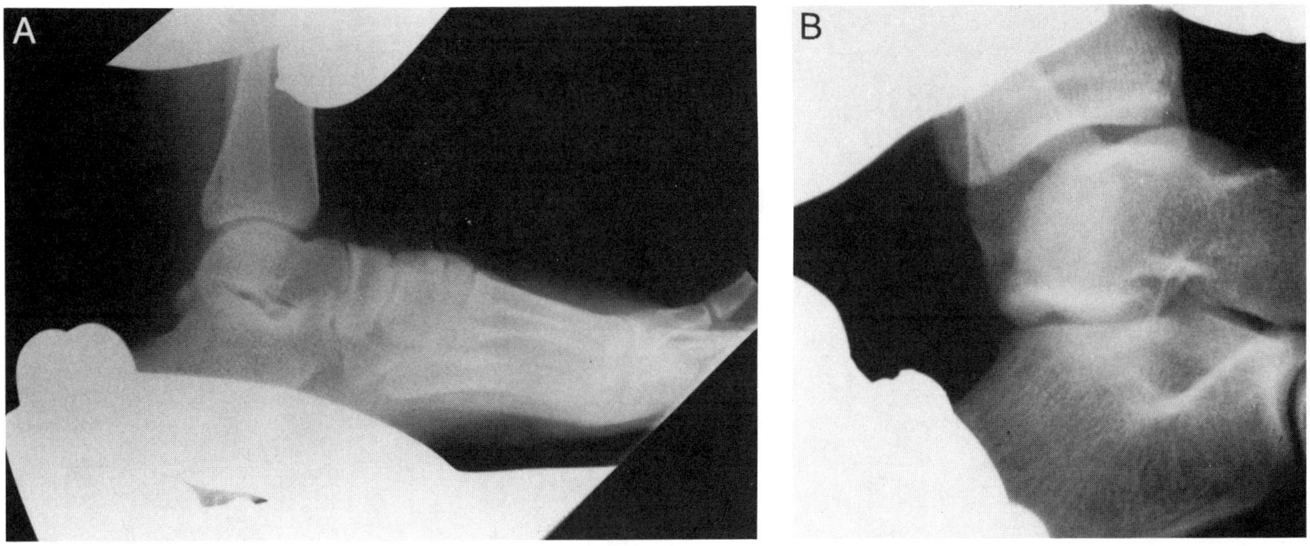

FIG 34–59.
Anterior drawer view showing a comparison of a normal foot **(A)** and abnormal foot **(B).**

tures. MRI can be used to identify stress fractures, nonspecific inflammation in the foot, soft tissue masses including Morton's neuroma, tendonitis or tendon rupture, infections, and bone changes such as osteoporosis, osteonecrosis, and aseptic necrosis. MRI is contraindicated in patients with aneurysm clips or cardiac pacemakers. Caution should be exercised in the scanning of infants, patients requiring monitoring or life support systems, and pregnant females.

BIBLIOGRAPHY

Ballinger PW: *Merrill's Atlas of Radiographic Positions and Radiologic Procedures.* St Louis, CV Mosby Co, 1982, pp 19–32, 38–64.

Benson JM: Radiation safety. *J Fam Pract* 1982; 15:435–439.

Crystal L, Orminski D: Axial views and angle and base of gait. *J Am Podiatr Assoc* 1981; 71:331–332.

Donick II: *Podiatry for the Assistant.* Mt Kisco, NY, Futura Publishing, 1977, pp 203–236.

Donick II: *Podiatry for the Assistant,* ed 2. Baltimore, Williams & Wilkins, 1989, pp 109–127.

Estersohn HS, Wolf KL, Day JC: The podium. *J Am Podiatr Assoc* 1981; 71:222–223.

Gamble FO, Yale I: *Clinical Foot Roentgenology,* ed 2. Huntington, NY, Robert E Krieger Publishing, 1975, pp 324–260.

Isherwood I: A radiologic approach to the subtalar joint. *J Bone Joint Surg [Br]* 1961; 43:566–574.

Kehr LE: Radiology: A simplified axial view. *J Am Podiatr Assoc* 1978; 68:130–131.

Kinsman S, Kroeker R: *Leg-Podiatric Radiology.* Sacramento, Calif, State Department of Health, 1973, pp 89–121.

Pinsky MJ: The Isherwood views: A roentgenologic approach to the subtalar joint. *J Am Podiatr Assoc* 1979; 69:200–206.

Rubenstein JA: X-ray primer. *Podiatr Staff* 1988; 9:25–30.

Schlefman BS: Radiology, in McGlamry ED (ed): *Fundamentals of Foot Surgery.* Baltimore, Williams & Wilkins, 1987, pp 136–148.

Syllabus on Diagnostic X-ray Radiation Protection for Certified X-ray Supervisors and Operators, State of California, Department of Health Services, Radiologic Health Section, 1978.

Throckmorton JK, Gudas CJ: Radiographic axial sesamoid projection in the diagnosis of sesamoid fractures. *J Am Podiatr Assoc* 1978; 68:96–100.

Weissman SD: *Radiology of the Foot.* Baltimore, Williams & Wilkins, 1983, pp 13–37.

35

Postoperative Physiology

Stephen J. Miller, D.P.M.

In order to better understand the purpose and importance of postoperative instructions, it is essential to have knowledge of what is happening to the body physiologically. That knowledge will then allow you to assist the patient in healing quickly and efficiently.

Once the body (lower extremity) has been injured either by surgery or trauma, it reacts immediately by initiating a three-phase healing process. The first phase is not actually healing but rather a cleanup process at the damaged site to remove debris, increase oxygen supply, and establish an environment amenable to tissue repair. The principal activity during this first phase is inflammation, so it is termed the inflammatory or substrate (preparing the substrate) phase.

The inflammatory phase lasts for 3 to 5 days and is gradually replaced by the proliferative or second phase of soft-tissue healing. This phase lasts for about 30 days, during which time the material for repair (primarily collagen) is produced and laid down in the wound. Bone healing takes substantially longer, so the wound must be protected longer.

Pain and swelling are greatest during the inflammatory phase, and the wound is most susceptible to the development of infection during this time. The wound margins are weak and need protection, especially from injury and contamination. As the proliferative phase takes over and the wound gets stronger, the tissues must begin to be mobilized while controlling against excessive swelling.

Whatever the patient can do to assist the wound through these two phases of repair will indeed optimize healing and minimize complications. Management is aimed primarily at controlling postoperative bleeding, preventing excessive swelling, and avoiding infection while protecting the wound and keeping the patient comfortable.

The third phase of wound healing, the remodeling phase, begins in the third week and continues for several months. Remodeling, reorganization, and differentiation occur to bring the wound to its maximum strength.

PHILOSOPHY AND TIMING OF INSTRUCTIONS

Postoperative instructions can help the patients heal quickly and efficiently. With postoperative instructions as the primary tool, patients should be educated to realize that healing is their responsibility and that many things that they can control will enhance their healing.

Once surgery has been planned and performed, the postoperative instructions are probably the most important factor to influence a successful outcome. In fact, the content and delivery of the instructions are so critical that they can be the difference between a happy, informed patient or a stressful lawsuit.

Written postoperative instructions serve to educate patients and save time. They do not replace verbal instructions but reinforce them while providing a hard copy of details that patients can refer to later. Usually, these written instructions are dispensed *after* the surgery, but to better prepare the patient the instructions can be provided *before* the operation. However, because it is easy to misplace paper, it is common practice to dispense postoperative instructions both before and after surgery. As a further medical-legal consideration, the instruction sheet should be signed and dated by the patient as proof that it was received. A copy of the signed instructions should then be placed in the patient chart as part of the permanent record.

VERBAL POSTOPERATIVE INSTRUCTIONS

Verbal instructions from the doctor can have a powerful influence on patient compliance. However, because of anxiety, sedative medication, or pain during the perioperative time, the instructions are often not remembered clearly. The doctor should address two or three important issues for postoperative care and then allow the assistant to expound on the instructions with the written postoperative instruction sheet. The assistant's job, best done when dispensing the written postoperative instructions, is to reinforce the key points, answer any questions, and reassure the patient.

Always address the patient by name, and keep the instructions simple. Do not confuse the patient by bombarding him with too many instructions. Repeat important concerns, such as the need for elevation, and leave the patient with the firm assurance that the doctor and office staff are always available to handle any problems that may arise. Do not mislead patients by informing them that the surgery site will not hurt or that the surgery will give them a perfect foot. The assistant cannot predict the surgical outcome.

WRITTEN POSTOPERATIVE INSTRUCTIONS: NAILS AND WARTS

Wart (verruca) and nail procedures are frequently performed in the office. Therefore, the postoperative management differs from that of a more complex surgical procedure. Separate written instructions for minor procedures should be prepared. These instructions can include a brief explanation of the medical problem and can also be part of the consent form (Fig 35–1).

Following wart or skin lesion surgery, it is important to keep the area dry until the first dressing change because the site is more susceptible to infection during this period. Often, the patient will redress the foot after the first 24 to 48 hours at home. Instructions on home care including soaking, use of topical agents, and bandaging are then needed. If special techniques for removal or destruction such as laser or radiosurgery have been used, appropriate precautions should also be included. Wart surgical sites can bleed profusely postoperatively. It is important for patients to stay non–weight bearing and keep the site elevated, especially for the first 8 to 10 hours. If the site bleeds heavily through the dressing due to insufficient compression, instruct the patient to apply tissue and tape it in place over the dressing. Patients should not remove the original dressing themselves. Additional postoperative instructions for wart surgery should be simple and few in number.

Instructions following nail surgery differ for temporary (partial or total avulsions) or permanent (partial or total chemical matrixectomies) procedures (Figs 35–2 and 35–3). Initial elevation and considerations for excessive bleeding remain the same as for warts. The remaining postoperative nail surgery instructions should delineate how long to retain the initial dressing, when to start soaks, how long to apply antiseptic or medication, and what to do should problems arise. Details are especially important in the soaking instructions. Include information on the solution and how to make it, the temperature and how long to soak, what antiseptic or medication to ap-

VERRUCA EXCISION

We have just surgically removed multiple benign growths (verrucae or papillomas) from your foot. As was explained to you, these are caused by a verruca virus, which is thought to be contagious.

Since they are caused by a virus, these growths may recur as do common colds, which are also caused by a virus. Some people are more susceptible to verrucae (plantar warts) than others. Usually the longer you have had these growths, the more difficult it is to get rid of them.

Follow-up care is just as important as the surgery. We not only observe the healing process but also check for any new growths that may be starting.

To ensure the best possible results with the least amount of discomfort, please follow these instructions:

1. Take the medication as directed.
2. Keep the bandage clean and dry.
3. Avoid strenuous activity for 24 hours.
4. Do not be alarmed if a small amount of blood appears on the bandage. This is to be expected.
5. Report back to our office for necessary redressings when indicated.
6. If any unusual situation arises, plcase call us immediately.

Thank you for following these instructions.

FIG 35–1.
Example of postoperative instructions for verruca excision.

ply, and how to redress the site. Each podiatrist may have slightly different methods for postoperative management. The key is to provide clear instructions with sufficient detail to achieve patient compliance. The instruction sheet should also include phone numbers to call if problems arise, along with space to notate the next appointment date and time.

UNIVERSAL POSTOPERATIVE INSTRUCTIONS

Universal postoperative instructions give general information to the patient. These instructions should be neatly printed on office stationary and should include office phone numbers so that the patient can clarify any instructions if necessary (Fig 35–4). Although each individual office may have slightly different information to include, the general topics that should be covered in these universal instructions are as follows:

Introduction

Start with a simple statement reminding the patients that they have just had surgery and can benefit their own healing process by following these instructions.

Trip Home

The first instruction should direct the patient to keep the foot elevated to avoid excessive swelling, bleeding, and pain.

Weight Bearing

Delineate clearly whether the patient can walk on the affected foot or not. Detail if and when the postoperative shoe should be worn.

INGROWN TOENAIL

This is a common foot problem. Any nail may be affected, but it occurs most often on the great toes. Improper trimming, short shoes, tight hosiery, foot imbalance, injury, and abnormal bone growth beneath the toenail are frequent causes. The nail may curve and cause the edge to press and cut into the tissue margins. Should the skin be broken, bacteria may enter, and a painful, infected (paronychia) ingrown toenail results. This condition requires repeated treatment to ensure recovery, and the more severe and neglected ingrown nails wil require surgery for permanent correction.

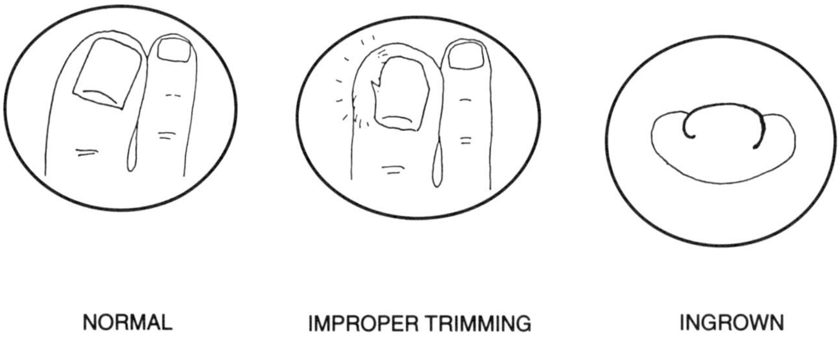

Treatment: (Once, twice daily)

1. Soak the infected ingrown toenail for 30 minutes in a warm solution of Epsom salts and water (1 tbsp per quart in a basin or 1 tsp per 8 oz and apply with a saturated cotton ball over the entire toenail; moisten as necessary).
2. Cleanse entire toe with antiseptic (alcohol, Betadine, or hydrogen peroxide), and dry thoroughly.
3. Cover with a dry, sterile Band-Aid.
4. Additional instructions: ______________________________

____

____

____

____

FIG 35–2.
Instructions for the treatment of an ingrown toenail.

Elevation.

Elevation is the single most important factor that will prevent swelling and keep the patient comfortable. Clearly explain how high and for what period of time the extremity should be elevated. Remind the patient to support the posterior aspect of the knee with a pillow to prevent it from becoming painful (Fig 35–5).

Swelling

Explain how much swelling to expect, and detail the measures to control it such as elevation, ice, and dressing compression.

Ecchymosis

Inform the patient that it can be normal for the skin to take on a bruised appearance and that this is no cause for alarm.

POST–NAIL SURGERY INSTRUCTIONS

(CHEMICAL METHOD)

1. Go straight home and elevate your feet for the rest of the day.
2. A small amount of blood may appear through the dressing. This is normal. If it soaks through and continues to bleed fresh blood, call the office.
3. Keep dressing dry and in place for 24 hours; then remove the bandages, and start foot soaks.
4. Foot soak routine:
   a. Soak in warm water and Epsom salts, (1 to 2 tbs per basin) for 20 minutes per day. (Twice a day for the first week will speed healing.)
   b. Apply one drop of Betadine (dark brown liquid) to each nail edge.
   c. Apply a Band-Aid to cover the toe(s).
5. Avoid direct shoe or slipper pressure to the affected toe(s). Use a postsurgical shoe if necessary.
6. Your nail will continue to drain for 3 to 5 weeks. This is the normal course of healing.
7. If you have any complications such as persistent pain, swelling, or bleeding, please call the doctor at either of the numbers listed above.

SPECIAL INSTRUCTIONS ______________________________

____

____

FIG 35–3.
Postoperative instructions for care following chemical matrixectomy.

Bleeding

Explain that a small amount of blood on the bandage is normal. Instruct the patient what should be done for excessive bleeding (Fig 35–6).

Dressing Care

Firmly order the patient to keep the dressing dry and not to remove it. The patient is not to inspect the wound or poke objects inside the bandage.

Bathing/Showering

State clearly that the patient should not get the foot wet in a bath or shower. Make sure that it is understood that a plastic bag applied over the dressing will leak. If the office has a waterproof dressing cover, offer it to the patient.

Exercise

Explain that gentle, non–weight-bearing exercises will help stimulate circulation and prevent the dangerous formation of blood clots in the veins.

Foot Cradle

Protecting the operated foot from the pressure of bedclothes will add to the patient's comfort and prevent unnecessary trauma. Suggest such things

POSTOPERATIVE FOOT SURGERY INSTRUCTIONS

A surgical procedure has just been performed on your foot. The amount of discomfort will vary from one patient to another. The following instructions are for your benefit in order to help minimize swelling and pain and to ensure good healing. Please follow them.

1. Go directly home, and elevate your feet on the way if possible. Do not sit with your feet down or crossed for any length of time. This causes the feet to swell and become painful.

2. A limited amount of swelling is expected. In some cases, the skin may take on a bruised appearance. This is no cause for alarm.

3. Elevate your feet about 6 in. above hip level by supporting your feet and legs with pillows and with a pillow under your knees.

4. Keep your bandages clean and dry. Do not remove the bandages or inspect the wound. A small amount of blood on the bandage is normal.

5. Cover the foot with a plastic bag, and hang it outside the tub while bathing. NO SHOWERS!!! A standing sponge bath is acceptable.

6. Exercise your legs frequently by bending your knees and ankles to stimulate circulation and speed healing.

7. At night place a cradle made from a cardboard carton at the foot of the bed to protect your foot from the covers.

8. Take your medicine(s) as directed. If they cause a stomach upset, headache, rash, or other abnormal reactions, discontinue their use and call the doctor.

9. Crutches or walkers can be helpful at times to take the weight off the foot when walking or standing.

10. Curtail alcoholic beverages and smoking.

11. Get plenty of rest with the foot elevated, drink plenty of fluids, and eat your regular well-balanced diet.

12. If your bandages become tight and/or your toes become numb or tingling or turn blue, call your doctor.

13. CALL YOUR DOCTOR IMMEDIATELY IF
    - The bandages become overly stained.
    - Your medication does not stop the discomfort.
    - You should bump or injure your feet.
    - You develop a fever.

14. Your next appointment is ____________________ .

15. Other Instructions: ____

____

____

FIG 35–4.
Universal postoperative foot surgery instructions.

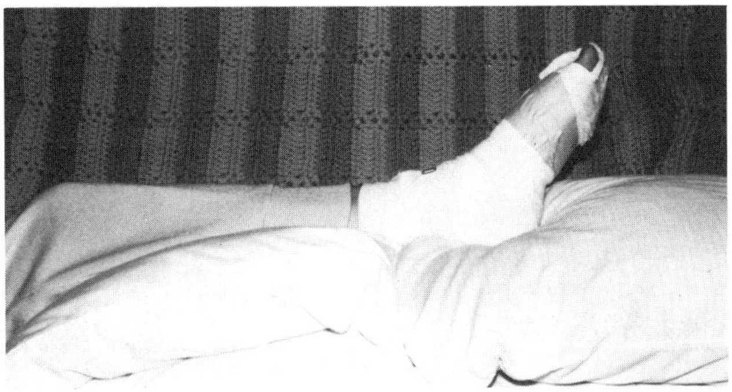

FIG 35–5.
Correct elevation position with the knee flexed and the foot resting on pillows.

as a cardboard box with one side cut out for such a purpose (Fig 35–7).

Pain and Medications

During the early phases, it is important for the patient to take pain medication when the discomfort first begins. Inform the patient that if he waits too long and allows the pain to build up, it becomes more difficult to dissipate. Other medications should be taken as directed with the caution given to call the doctor if any abnormal reactions are experienced.

Crutches/Walkers

The use of assistive devices can be encouraged. If non–weight bearing is ordered, then more specific instructions can be added under "Other Instructions."

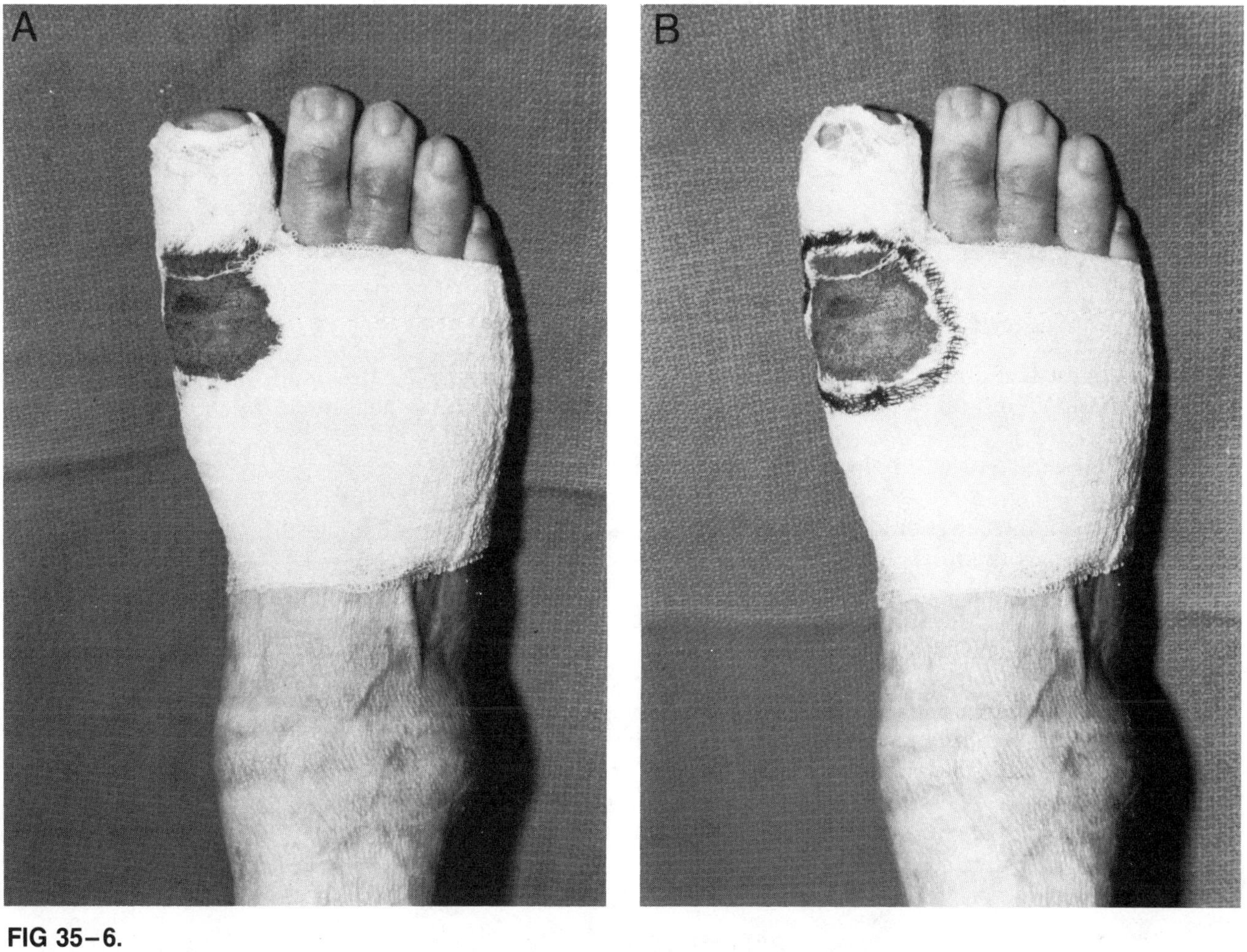

FIG 35–6.
A, bleeding onto the surface of the dressing. **B,** mark the periphery of the area to see whether the blood is extending.

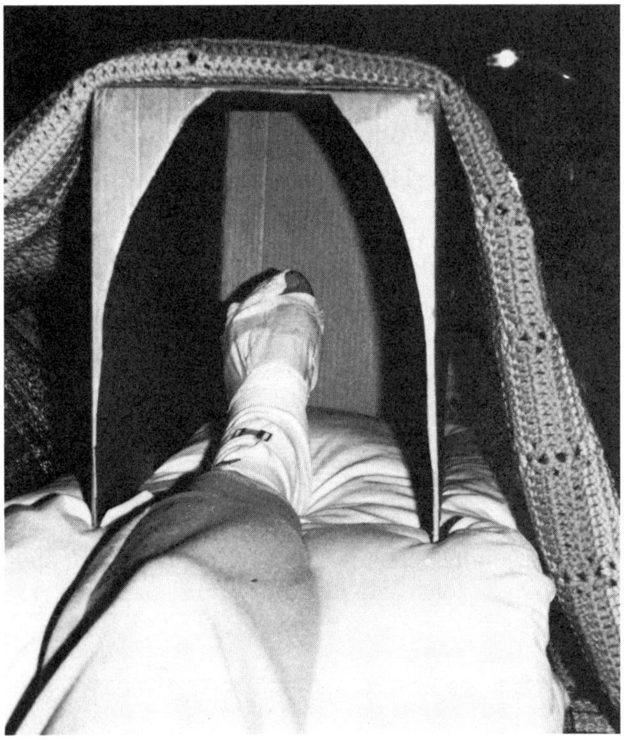

FIG 35–7.
Protecting the postsurgical foot with a homemade "dog-house" box.

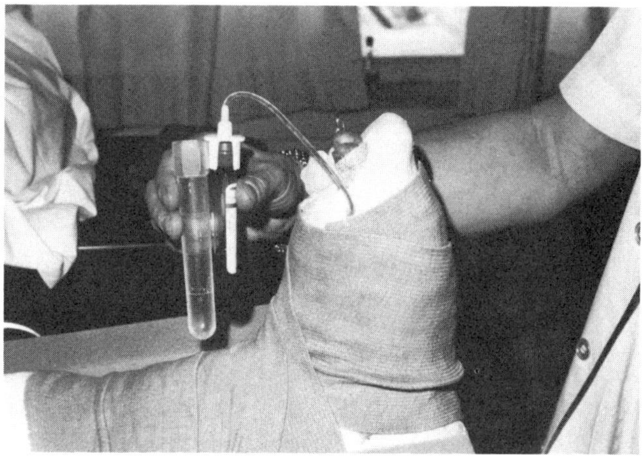

FIG 35–8.
Closed suction drain with a vacuum tube and protective sleeve.

Alcohol/Drugs

Discourage smoking, alcoholic beverages, and nonprescription drugs. This instruction is not only beneficial for healing but has medical-legal implications.

Resting/Recuperation

Include a statement encouraging the patient to rest, drink plenty of fluids, and eat a regular, well-balanced diet.

INSTRUCTIONS FOR SURGICAL DRAIN

Your doctor has placed a CLOSED SUCTION DRAIN in your surgical wound. Its purpose is to remove blood and other fluids from the wound, thus allowing it to heal more quickly.

The following steps will help you to care for your drain at home.

1. The vacuum tube should be changed when it is half full, or every 8 hours if it remains empty. (Sometimes the tubes lose their vacuum or suction.)

2. To change the tube, remove the white plastic top from the tube-stopper (plug). BE CAREFUL NOT TO PULL ON THE CATHETER.

3. Insert the needle in the white plastic top through the stopper of the new tube. You should see the fluid move in the catheter.

4. Place the tube back in the plastic housing, and secure it to the dressing.

5. If the drain does not appear to be working and blood soaks through your bandages, please call your doctor.

FIG 35–9.
Instructions for home management of a closed suction drain.

Tight Dressings/Casts

Numbness, tingling, blue discoloration of the toes, and pain that is unresponsive to pain medication are all indications of a constrictive dressing or cast. This is a dangerous situation. Stoic patients think that these signs are to be expected after surgery. They must be instructed to call the doctor.

When to Call the Doctor

Specific instructions as to when to call the office or doctor will help prevent patient confusion. It is reassuring to know that the doctor is accessible. Make the instructions stand out. Instruct the patient to call the doctor if the bandages become overly stained, the medication does not stop the discomfort, the foot is bumped or injured, or a fever develops.

Next Appointment

Remind the patient of the date and time for the follow-up visit appointment.

Other Instructions

Always leave a few extra lines for special instructions that the assistant or the doctor may wish to impart to the patient.

Special Instructions

Special instructions can be added for special situations or to reinforce an important part of postoperative management. If the instructions are involved, then a separate instruction sheet can be dispensed. A good example of this is when the patient is discharged with a closed suction drainage tube exiting from the wound and dressing (Figs 35–8 and 35–9). It is important to review special written instructions with verbal reinforcement. Other examples for special instructions are external pins, external fixation devices, casts, crutches, and the use of removable walking casts.

Written instructions can save an enormous amount of time in answering most patient questions after surgery. They can be selectively reinforced with verbal instructions from the doctor and staff. Medical-legal problems can be avoided by making sure that the patient is reassured and well-informed. The podiatric medical assistant must see to it that the patient receives and understands the instructions.

36

Complications

Stephen V. Corey, D.P.M.
Richard J. Zirm, D.P.M.

The podiatric assistant plays a pivotal role in dealing with a potential postoperative complication. Many times the assistant will have the first interaction with the patient concerning the problem. It therefore becomes imperative that the assistant recognize a potential problem and initiate steps toward proper care. Delays in diagnosis and treatment can lead to a significant postoperative dilemma.

The following chapter will outline some common postoperative complications and their treatment. The goal is to give the assistant a better understanding of the causes and care of these problems. The assistant, however, should not undertake any of these problems on her own. Following recognition of a problem, the assistant should relay the appropriate information to the surgeon for evaluation.

Postoperative complications can be simple or complex. Complications such as edema, hematoma, wound dehiscence, and infection are all interrelated, which makes the diagnosis extremely difficult at times. Some of these problems can cause greater destruction than others. However, any complication can deter the surgical result.

EDEMA

Edema, or swelling, can be a disturbing and painful process to the patient. Excessive edema can result from a variety of factors ranging from surgical technique to poor patient compliance in following postoperative instructions.

Edema is an accumulation of fluids in the extravascular tissues.[1] This accumulation of interstitial fluid subsequently results in expansion of the tissues. Edema is the result of a disturbance in the equilibrium between intravascular and extravascular fluids that is caused by surgical trauma. A brief understanding of the processes involved in edema production is paramount to the control of edema.

Surgical intervention initiates a series of inflammatory processes that promote fluid accumulation in the tissues. Initially, aggravation and disruption of blood and tissue cells lead to a release of chemical mediators. These chemicals, such as histamine, cause a dilation of the small arterioles and leakage of fluid from the small venules.[2] The result is fluid and protein accumulation in the extravascular tissues. Subsequently, accumulation of proteins within the tissue cause a greater extravascular pressure gradient and an increase in flow of fluid from the intravascular to the extravascular spaces.[2]

The venous and lymphatic systems are responsible for the return of fluids to the central system. The vessels can be significantly compromised during the surgical process. Severance and manipulation of these vessels can result in a decrease in outflow and an increase in fluid accumulation.

Control of Postoperative Edema

Prevention of postoperative edema begins with maintaining the integrity of the vascular and lymphatic system through gentle anatomic dissection and atraumatic surgical technique.[1] The more trauma that occurs during surgery, the greater the local inflammatory reaction. Careful surgical technique with identification, clamping, and ligation of vessels is also of utmost importance in decreasing postoperative edema.

A short-acting corticosteroid such as dexamethasone phosphate can be used intraoperatively to reduce the intensity of the inflammatory phase of healing. By limiting the extent of the early inflammation phase, postoperative edema can be controlled as well.

The principles in controlling edema are recalled by the acronym RICE (rest, ice, compression, elevation).

Resting of the part allows the inflammation to stabilize. Continued irritation from activity results in a progression and escalation of the inflammatory process. A decrease in activity and mobility should also decrease swelling by virtue of a decreased metabolic rate that translates to a decrease in tissue requirements for blood perfusion and nutrients.

Cold application with ice causes a local vascular constriction and a decrease in the leakage of fluids. In addition, cold application has also been shown to suppress the inflammatory process.[3] Ice tends to be more effective in the very early stages of inflammation, usually the first 24 to 48 hours.

Compression obtained from bandages or other devices is paramount in the control of edema. The bandages, when properly applied, allow for physiologic swelling while preventing excessive edema. The dressing should be applied evenly, without constriction. Compression is achieved through the concentric layers. All dressings should begin at the digits and extend proximally, even when the incision is located proximally. Failing to begin the dressing as far distally as possible will result in an accumulation of fluid distal to the bandage. The compression should also be applied in a distal-to-proximal manner. This is to help "milk" the fluid away from the foot in conjunction with the venous and lymphatic system. Any concavity present on the surface of the extremity should be sufficiently padded to allow for even compression.

The benefit of elevation is to facilitate the massive venous and lymphatic drainage. Gravity is used to the advantage of the patient to expedite the proximal flow. The foot should be elevated above the level of the hip or, even better, the heart.

Nonsteroidal anti-inflammatory drugs (NSAIDs) effectively interfere with various aspects of the inflammatory process. These drugs also decrease the perceptive pain of the patient by diminishing swelling. Many different brands of NSAIDs are now available, and the success and tolerance of any NSAID with any certain patient are quite variable. NSAIDs are contraindicated in patients who demonstrate an allergy to aspirin, a hypersensitivity to the drug, gastrointestinal complaints, and hematologic disorders.

Sequelae

Excessive postoperative edema can lead to other complications. Uncontrolled swelling can put a tremendous amount of tension on the skin and the wound (Fig 36–1). In addition to an increase in pain, this excessive tension can lead to

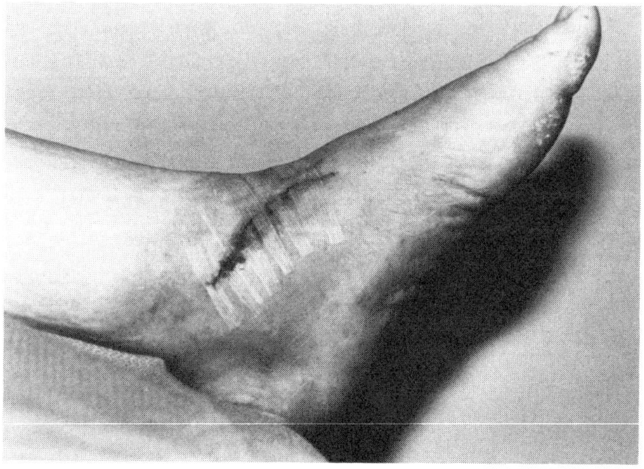

FIG 36–1.
Excessive postoperative edema following a tarsal arthrodesis procedure. Note the tension of the skin and the lack of normal relaxed skin tension lines in addition to peri-incisional erythema.

more complicated problems. The first is separation of the wound edges, or dehiscence, which will be discussed shortly. Blisters may form if the skin can no longer expand in response to the swelling. The chance for developing an infection will increase with fluid accumulation in the postoperative wound. Compromised local tissues bathed in fluid high in protein and nutrients provide an excellent medium for bacterial growth.[1] Therefore, any serious degree of edema should be closely monitored with frequent dressing changes.

A common and difficult problem following lower extremity surgery is to predict the duration of and treat prolonged edema. Elevating the extremity as much as possible is essential. Range-of-motion exercises allow the muscles to indirectly pump lymphatic fluid proximally. Compression therapy can be continued once postoperative dressings are no longer needed. The foot and lower portion of the leg should be circumscribed with a double layer of tubular elastic bandage. Compression support hose that can be fitted to the patient are also available.

Frequent massage of the local tissue helps reduce edema once postoperative tenderness has subsided. Physical therapy modalities including ultrasound, contrast baths, whirlpools, and galvanic stimulation can all be used at this time to combat persistent postoperative edema.

HEMATOMA

Hematoma refers to the collection of blood in the tissues or surgical wound[1] (Fig 36–2). The blood typically migrates between tissue layers or at the incision line. It is caused by leakage from local vessels damaged by blunt trauma, local injury, or surgical dissection. Seroma refers to the localized accumulation of serum. Serum is the clear portion of blood that remains after clotting has removed the fibrinogen and other elements. It leaks into tissues following local damage to the small vessels during the early stages of the inflammatory process.[1]

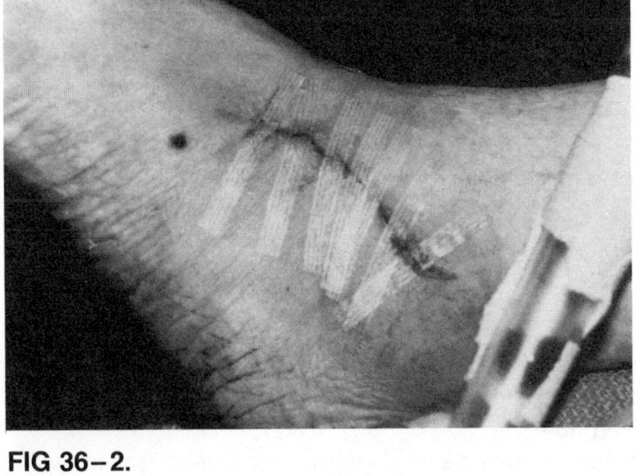

FIG 36–2.
Postoperative hematoma following triple arthrodesis.

The occurrence of a hematoma in the postoperative scenario can lead to infection or long-term swelling and disability. Understanding the cause of this problem will significantly aid in the reduction of its occurrence. Proper management requires prompt recognition and treatment as well as diligent adherence to the principles of healing and wound manipulation.

Prevention

The blood supply lies between the skin and the deep fascia in the subcutaneous tissue layer. Inadequate attention to surgical hemostasis is the primary source of most postoperative hematomas. The importance of the principle of atraumatic and anatomic dissection cannot be overemphasized.

A common cause of hematoma formation occurs when utilizing tourniquets for hemostasis. Because the tourniquet reduces blood flow to the surgical field, severed arteries or veins may not be identified and ligated. A way to prevent this is for the surgeon to release the tourniquet prior to closure to check for any bleeders. Reliance on pressure bandaging to control internal bleeding will often result in hematoma formation. If complete control of bleeding is impossible during surgery, then hemostatic agents may be employed.

Any dead space that persists following closure will allow the accumulation of significant amounts of blood or serum. When a potential dead space exists, a drain should be used to reduce the accumulation of blood. There are many types of drains that can be utilized. The closed suction system seems to be preferred because of continuous drainage without regard to gravity. A sterile Penrose or rubber band drain can also be utilized. These drains are dependent on gravity and need precise placement to be effective. Maceration of the wound where the drain exits can also occur.

Diagnosis

The first clinical indicator of postoperative hematoma is pain. The pain is often severe and out of proportion to the procedure performed. Hematoma often mimics an early wound infection. The body responds almost identically to each with an intense local inflammatory reaction. For this reason, a good rule of thumb is as follows: if a patient is experiencing severe pain that is not well controlled by medication, the wound should be evaluated.

The pain associated with the hematoma is caused by the expansion of the hematoma itself within the tissue combined with an intense local inflammation. The pain and swelling of hematomas are usually manifested within the first 24 hours, whereas an infection will usually present at 48 to 72 hours postoperatively. Upon inspection, the wound may have a localized area of tenderness or redness. The redness associated with a hematoma is usually well localized without the proximal extension seen in infection. Occasionally blood can be seen to ooze from the incision. The clinician must be able to quickly distinguish between hematoma and infection and initiate appropriate treatment.

Sequelae

Aside from pain, hematoma can lead to dehiscence and even frank skin loss if the local circulation is impaired or compromised. Gross tissue edema results from severe pressure causing obstruction of local capillaries, veins, and lymphatics.

The fate of a formed hematoma depends on whether it is a localized, clotted pool of blood or is disseminated diffusely through the tissue planes. A localized hematoma tends to undergo fibroplasia and organize into dense scar tissue.[1] A disseminated hematoma can readily be absorbed by the body in the inflammatory process.

Blood has long been recognized to be an excellent medium for bacterial growth. Therefore, it is of no surprise that hematomas are associated with an increased incidence of infection. The combined presence of a blood and compromised tissue significantly increases the chances for a postoperative infection. Additionally, the presence of hematoma impedes the activity of the local immune system and leads to decreased migration and activity of inflammatory cells to the area.[1]

Management of Hematoma

Initially, when the hematoma is fluctuant and not organized, the blood can simply be expressed through the wound. The simplest technique is applying gentle pressure to the margins of the wound and squeezing out the undesirable fluid accumulations while the patient is anesthetized.

A second technique that can be used before the blood is clotted is aspiration with a syringe. A hypodermic syringe with a large-bore needle (18 or 20 gauge) is inserted and the fluid extracted from the wound (Fig 36–3). Care must be taken while inserting the needle to maintain aseptic techniques. Following either method, a good compressive dressing should be applied.

Pharmacologic agents can be used after the hematoma has organized. Hyaluronidase is a hydrolytic enzyme that breaks down the hematoma when injected locally.[1] The enzyme will remove any local obstruction and allow better diffusion of fluids within the tissues to enhance inflammatory destruction of the hematoma. Streptokinase is a nonenzymatic protein that can function similarly to break up the fibrin network in the clotted blood when injected locally.[1]

When it becomes evident that the size or pressure of a hematoma is compromising wound healing, then it should be evacuated by re-entering the wound. The primary incision may be used for evacuation of the hematoma. Organized clots should be removed with liberal irrigation and all residual bleeders clamped and ligated or electrocoagulated. Closed suction drainage and a course of prophylactic antibiotics can then be employed.

Management of hematoma formation in the later phases can be performed by utilizing several noninvasive techniques. Firm but nonconstructive compression dressings are an effective method to

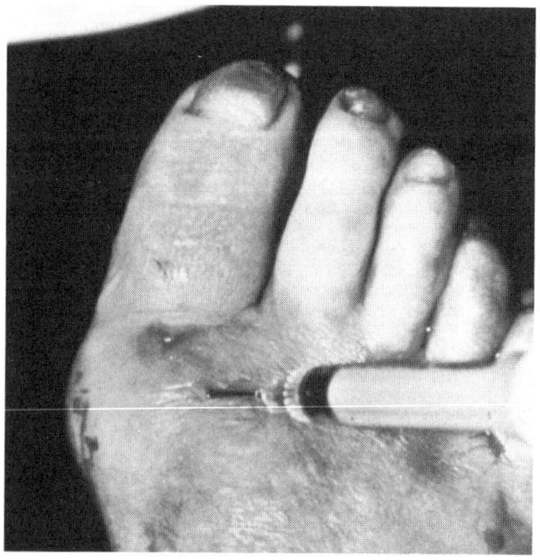

FIG 36–3.
Large-bore needle used to aspirate a first-interspace hematoma.

decrease established hematoma and edema. Application of moist heat will accelerate the enzymatic degradation of an established hematoma. Physical therapy consisting of range-of-motion exercises, massage, and ultrasound all act to break up the fibrin network of the hematoma, and this could decrease the size of the resultant edema and scar tissue.

WOUND DEHISCENCE

Dehiscence is the rupture or gaping of an incision. Wound dehiscence may be partial or complete, depending on the degree of separation of wound edges, postoperative herniation, and evisceration (Fig 36–4).

There are many predisposing factors that may promote dehiscence of a surgical wound. They include faulty closure, use of improper suture material, hematoma or seroma formation, infection, and the presence of necrotic tissue.[4] Rough intraoperative handling of tissue can result in necrosis of the wound edges and lead to dehiscence. Irritation and pressure from a cast are additional causes of wound breakdown. Metabolic disorders such as anemia, protein deficiencies, vitamin C deficiencies, and peripheral vascular disease also may contribute and encourage poor wound healing.[5]

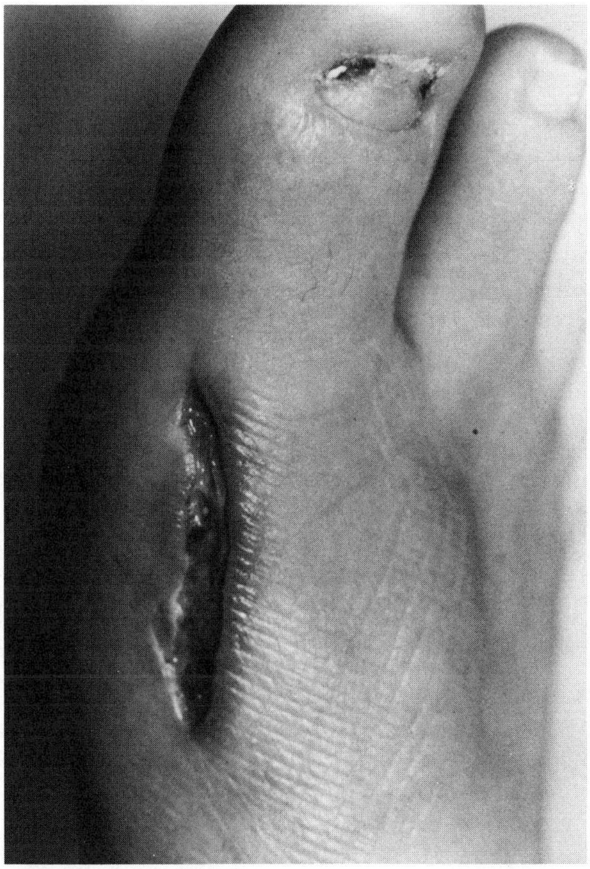

FIG 36–4.
Postoperative wound dehiscence following hallux abducto valgus surgery.

Prevention

A surgical wound should be closed in the same anatomic layers that were created during dissection. Deep fascia and capsule material must be firmly approximated, followed by closure of the superficial fascial layer to prevent a potential dead space from developing. Drains should be utilized whenever excessive fluid is expected. Finally, skin closure must be approximated with the appropriate suture and technique to ensure an even coaptation of the tissues without overlap or steppage. Postoperative hematoma, seroma, and edema should be controlled by taking the appropriate measures. These complications can all lead to a wound dehiscence if not adequately managed.

Dehiscence involving skin edges is often due to faulty suturing. The skin edges may not be well approximated. Sutures that cause improper apposition of the skin edges will result in inadequate wound healing and a weak incision.[4] Occasionally incisions may be closed under excessive tension. The tension can result in gaping of the wound. In order to reduce the tension across the incision, heavy retention sutures with buttresses can be utilized.

Dorsal nonabsorbable sutures should be kept in place for 10 to 14 days. Plantar sutures should be kept in for at least 3 weeks and interdigital sutures for 2 weeks. Of course the strength and resiliency of the incision line should be assessed prior to removing the sutures. A common practice is to remove every other suture at one office visit and wait until the next office appointment to remove the remainder of the sutures, thus allowing the wound to obtain sufficient strength. Steri-Strips can be maintained intact until they fall off at 4 to 5 weeks, especially when they are reinforcing an absorbable suture closure.

Treatment of Wound Dehiscence

The underlying cause of wound dehiscence must be identified and addressed. An incision that has gaped because of a superficial infection should be incised, drained, and cleared before a second attempt at closure is initiated. A wound that has gaped open due to excessive pressure secondary to a hematoma should initially have the hematoma drained. Once the cause of the dehiscence is controlled, the method for reapproximation can be determined.

If cosmesis and time are of no concern, the wound can heal by secondary intention. It is paramount to use sound principles of local wound care to establish a good granular base if healing via secondary intention is planned (Fig 36–5). If the decision to close the wound is by primary intention, a minor surgical procedure will be performed. The procedure consists of sharply freshening up the wound margins and using various suture techniques to primarily close the wound (Fig 36–6). In this case simple interrupted sutures may be reinforced by either horizontal or vertical mattress sutures in order to gain eversion of the wound margins (Fig 36–7). Larger retention sutures with buttresses may be necessary in some cases where the skin has retracted.

INFECTION

Infection is the body's defense system responding to microorganisms (bacteria) invading the surgical site.[6] Although postoperative infections are relatively uncommon (less than 2%), the destruction can be great. Uncontrolled infection could result in the loss of a limb. A quick and accurate diagnosis must be made to reduce the overall damage created by the infection. The best treatment for postoperative infections is prevention by maintaining good sterile technique.

A postoperative infection is the result of an imbalance between the patient's defense system and the microorganisms present.[6] All surgical wounds are exposed to bacteria in varying degrees. This does not mean that every wound will become infected. A certain dose of microorganisms must be present before an infectious process is initiated. The bacteria come from the patient's skin, the air, and foreign bodies. Maintenance of strict aseptic technique in the operating room significantly reduces the quantity of these organisms.

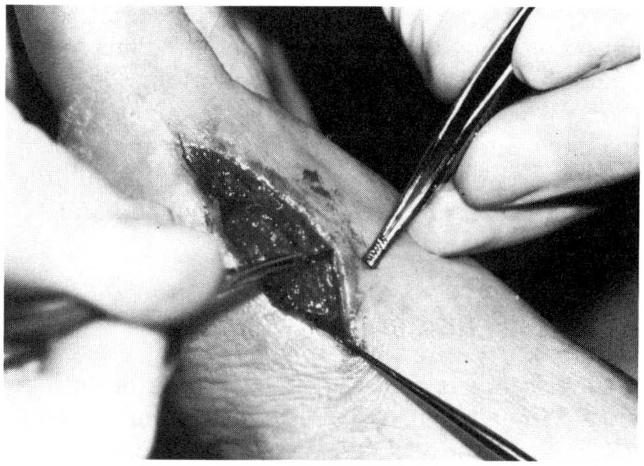

FIG 36–6.
Intraoperative photograph demonstrating debridement of the wound and "freshening" of the wound margins.

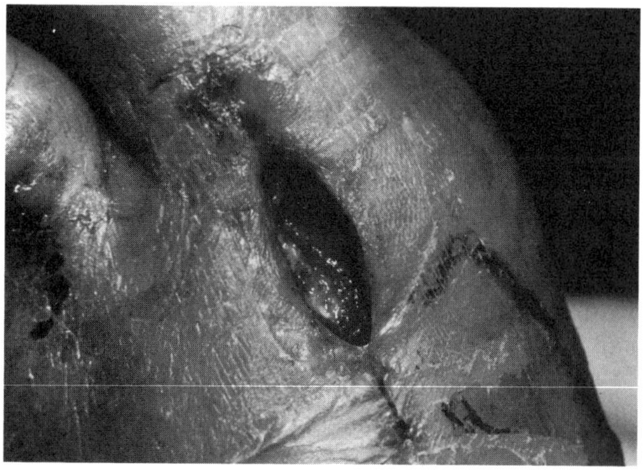

FIG 36–5.
Late-stage wound dehiscence following first-ray surgery. The skin has retracted from the sides of the wound, and the subcutaneous tissue has atrophied.

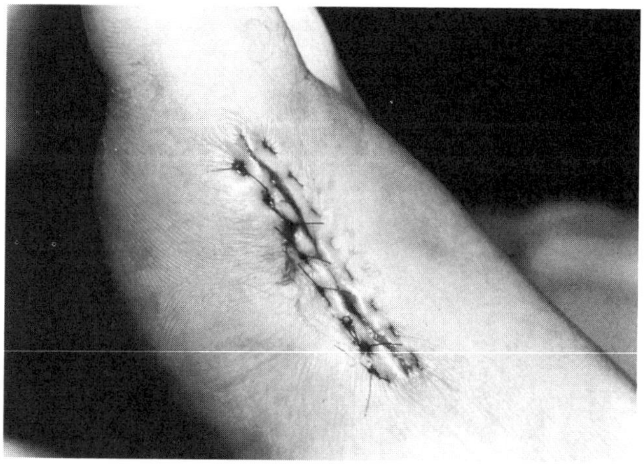

FIG 36–7.
Final appearance of the wound. Note the wound eversion obtained with horizontal mattress sutures.

Diagnosis

The first signs of infection typically occur in the third to seventh postoperative day. However, infections can be seen as early as 24 hours following surgery. The initial complaints are usually fever and an increase in pain. Other generalized signs and symptoms may include chills, nausea, vomiting, malaise, leg pain, and headaches. Once these symptoms are recognized and a postoperative infection is suspected, the operative wound should be evaluated immediately. Delays in the diagnosis and treatment could result in extensive damage. The extent of sequelae is directly related to the speed of diagnosis.

The cardinal signs of inflammation are rubor (red), tumor (swollen), calor (warm), dolor (pain), and functio laesa (loss of function).[2] These signs are observed normally in surgical wounds. The intensity, however, will be exaggerated if an infectious process is present,[6] (Fig 36–8). The redness or cellulitis may be contained within the incision area or progress up the leg. The more aggressive the infection, the quicker the ascending cellulitis. Cellulitis is a diffuse, spreading inflammation of the cutaneous structure and is an extension of the infectious process[6] (Fig 36–9).

Drainage is another indicator of infection. Clear or serous (bloody) drainage is normal. Drainage that is opaque and thick is termed *exudate* and is a sign of infection. Evaluation of the drainage as to its consistency, color, or odor should be performed and documented (Fig 36–10,A and B). Identification of the organism can sometimes be made just

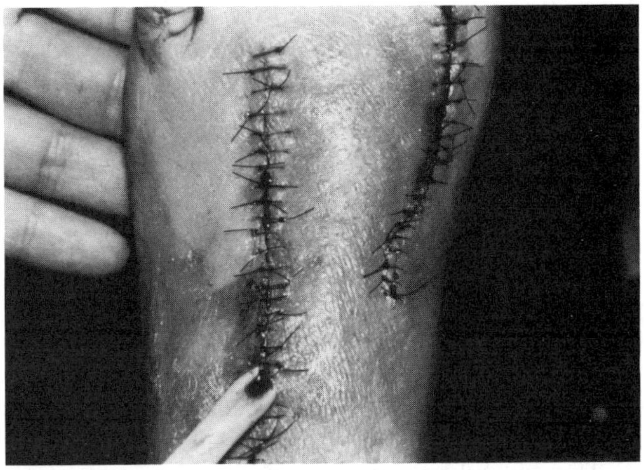

FIG 36–9.
Erythema and edema with an ominous drainage representing a postoperative infection.

A

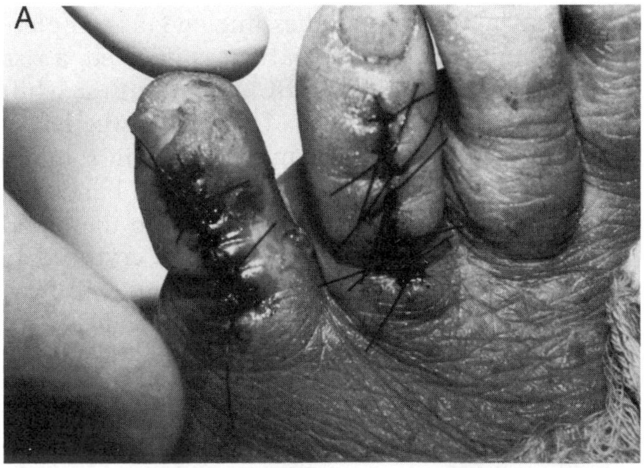

B

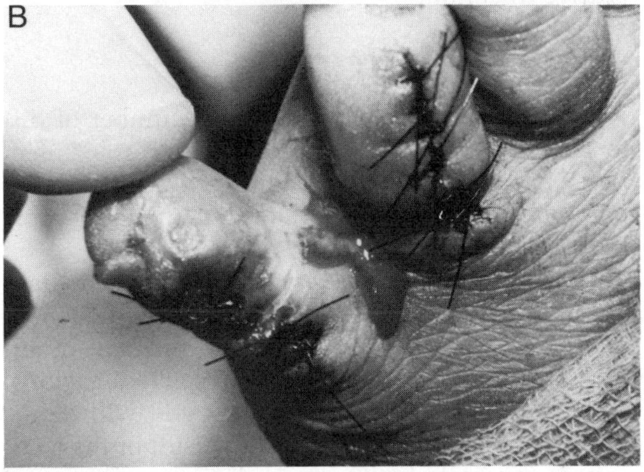

FIG 36–10.
A, postoperative infection following digital surgery. **B,** note the tension of the skin and the purulent drainage expressed from the web space.

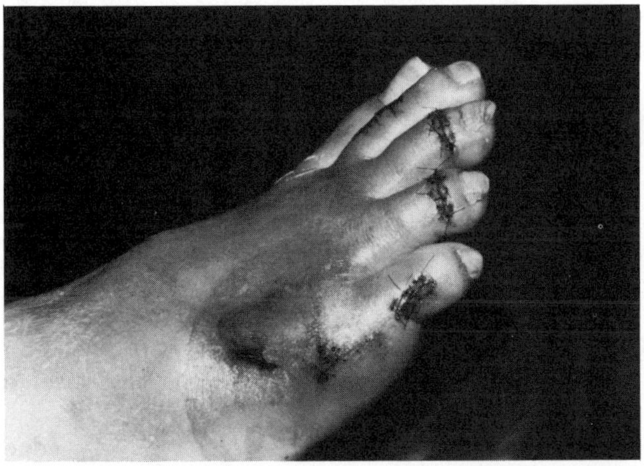

FIG 36–8.
Pain, edema, erythema, and heat, the four cardinal signs, were present in this postoperative infection of a tailor's bunion.

by evaluating the drainage. *Staphylococcus* has a characteristic yellow exudate, while *Pseudomonas* has a greenish appearance. Anaerobic organisms can be identified by their fetid odors.

The clinical examination is followed by the laboratory evaluation. The key to accurate diagnosis and treatment of infections is to obtain a Gram's stain and a culture from the wound. A Gram's stain is an easy and inexpensive test to obtain information on the etiology of the infection. Many organisms can be identified by the staining characteristics (gram-positive vs. gram-negative) and shape (cocci vs. rods). The procedure can easily be performed in the office (Table 36–1).

The careful retrieval of a culture is next. Cultures of the deep wound are preferred. This is usually possible through the incision. One should be careful that the culture swab does not touch the skin to prevent possible contamination from the normal flora.

Other laboratory studies include a complete blood count (CBC). If the patient is infected, a rise in the white blood cell (WBC) count with a "shift to the left" should be seen. The shift to the left is an increased presence of immature WBCs in response to infection. The immature WBC bands are thrown out from the bone marrow into the blood in an effort to fight the infection.[1] The erythrocyte sedimentation rate (ESR) or C-reactive protein presence can also be evaluated. These tests are very sensitive to inflammation but are not specific for infection. Their values can be elevated in any inflammatory process including surgery. Therefore their role is limited in the diagnosis of postoperative infection.

TABLE 36–1.
Gram's Stain Procedure

1. Swab a slide with the specimen
2. Air-dry the slide
3. Apply Gram's crystal violet stain* for 5–10 sec
4. Rinse with tap water
5. Apply Gram's iodine for 10 sec
6. Apply decolorizer† until the runoff clears
7. Rinse with tap water
8. Apply safranin stain‡ for 10 sec
9. Rinse and blot dry

*Purple stain for gram-positive organisms.
†Removes the purple stain from gram-negative organisms.
‡Red stain for gram-negative organisms.

Treatment

An infection can be treated in a number of different ways. The primary goal in treating infections is to eradicate the infection as quickly as possible so as to result in the least amount of morbidity.

Once a postoperative infection has been diagnosed, aggressive local wound care should be initiated. This can range from simple removal of sutures to extension of or additional incisions. Obviously, the extent of the infection will determine the extent of exposure. The result of the local care is complete incision and drainage of infected soft tissue and bone.

The wound should be completely opened so that any purulence can be completely drained. If a seroma or hematoma is encountered, it should also be completely drained. Nonviable or necrotic tissue should be removed. Failure to remove nonviable tissue could give the organism a good medium in which to thrive.

If infection of the bone is suspected, a portion should be sent to the pathologist to evaluate under the microscope. Bone infections are more difficult to eradicate and therefore require extended treatment.

Additionally, any foreign bodies within the wound, including sutures and implants, should be removed. These objects make good areas for the organisms to survive and cause reinfection once treatment with the antibiotics is stopped.

Following complete debridement, the wound is typically left open. The wound undergoes daily packing, debridement, and irrigation. Local wound care should be done under aseptic conditions to prevent additional contamination. The wound can be closed by secondary intention or delayed primary closure once it is clean and two to three negative cultures have been retrieved.

Antibiotic therapy is also initiated. Initial therapy is based on the clinical diagnosis and the results of the Gram's stain. The initial antibiotic begins before the results of the culture and sensitivity are back. Once the culture results are back, the antibiotic therapy is adjusted to the specific organism. Definitive antibiotics are based on the culture and sensitivities and the response to the initial therapy.

The podiatric assistant should have knowledge of the causes and symptoms of postoperative complications. Proper recognition of the symptoms leads to prompt treatment and reduction of morbidity.

REFERENCES

1. Miller SJ: Edema, hematoma, infection, in McGlamry ED (ed): *Comprehensive Textbook of Foot Surgery*. Baltimore, Williams & Wilkins, 1987, pp 1005–1040.
2. Hurley JV: *Acute Inflammation*. New York, Churchill Livingstone Inc, 1983, pp 29–57.
3. Miller SJ: Postoperative management, in McGlamry ED (ed): *Fundamentals of Foot Surgery*. Baltimore, Williams & Wilkins, 1987, pp 294–314.
4. Peacock EE, Winkle WV: *Surgery and Biology of Wound Repair*. Philadelphia, WB Saunders Co, 1970, pp 125–140.
5. Ehrlich HP, Hunt TK: Effects of cortisone and vitamin A on wound healing. *Ann Surg* 1968; 167:324.
6. Downey MS, Lamy CJ: Postoperative infections: General principles and considerations. *Clin Podiatr Med Surg* 1990; 7:405.

37

Concepts of Steam Sterilization

Raymond G. Cavaliere, D.P.M.
Terence M. McElgun, D.P.M.

I. Bacteriology
II. Sterilization and Disinfection
III. Indicators
IV. Preparation Before Autoclaving
V. Wrapping of Materials for Sterilization
VI. Steam Sterilization
VII. Flash Sterilization

"The practice of surgical asepsis is as old as civilization."[1] Hippocrates (460–370 B.C.) realized the importance of hand cleaning before surgery and advocated irrigating wounds with boiling water.[1,2] Galen (A.D. 131–200), the Greek physician, boiled instruments used in treating wounded gladiators. Fracastorius in 1546 described the concept of airborne contamination and believed that diseases were spread either by direct contact, by touching objects touched by an infected individual, or by airborne transmission.

All of these theories were better understood after Anton van Leeuwenhoek developed the microscope in 1683. Through the use of the microscope, bacteria could be studied. It was the studies of Louis Pasteur, the French chemist and microbiologist, that established the validity of the germ theory of disease. He proved that infection was caused by the growth of microorganisms. Pasteur called these microbes "germs" that were carried by the air or spread by direct contact and could be destroyed by heat as well as other means. Pasteur's findings motivated an English surgeon, Lord Joseph Lister (1827–1912), to identify surgical implications for his new germ theory. Lister theorized that he could prevent infection if he could prevent airborne organisms from gaining access to the wound.[1] Lister introduced the use of carbolic acid to achieve antiseptic technique. Through his work on surgical antisepsis, Sir Joseph Lister earned the title of "Father of Antiseptic Surgery."

Further advances in asepsis occurred from 1881 to 1882 when Robert Koch, a German bacteriologist, introduced methods of steam. Koch demonstrated that moist heat was a more effective method of sterilization than dry heat because of its greater penetrating powers. This began the era of antiseptic-aseptic technique. In 1876, heat-resistant bacteria were demonstrated. This led to the introduction of the steam sterilizer by Ernst Von Bergmann.

Surgeons learned that steam itself was inadequate for sterilization. Steam must be under pressure to raise the temperature sufficiently to kill heat-resistant microorganisms.[2] Thus, the autoclave was developed to accomplish that purpose: steam under pressure.

BACTERIOLOGY

A basic knowledge of bacteriology is necessary to understand the goals of autoclaving. Bacteriology is the study of single-celled microorganisms that are measured in microns (bacteria). They are the smallest living things with self-contained metabolic processes. The smallest bacteria are barely visible under an ordinary light microscope. It would take about 30 trillion bacteria of average size to weigh an ounce. Under optimum conditions, bacteria divide on the average of every 20 minutes. Therefore, a single bacterium may produce 1 million new cells in 10 hours.[1]

Bacteria have different shapes, which is useful in classification. The cocci are spherical. Streptococci ("strep") are spherical bacteria that grow in chains. Staphylococci, in addition to being spherical, tend to be clumped like a bunch of grapes. Cocci also grow singly, and some, like the pneumococci, are paired. Bacilli are rod shaped and may occur as a single cell or in chains. Spirilla are corkscrew in shape and always occur as a single cell.

Bacteria that are known to cause disease are classified as pathogenic and as such are harmful to humans. In addition, some bacteria are capable of forming a specialized structure called a spore. The spore enables the organism to survive prolonged exposure to drying, heat, chemical disinfectants, and other adverse conditions. When the proper conditions for growth occur (an open wound during surgery), the spore wall splits, and the bacteria begin to reproduce. Examples of spore-forming bacteria are *Clostridium perfringens*, which produces gas gangrene, and *Clostridium tetani*, which results in tetanus.[1]

The fact that spores are able to resist many unfavorable conditions emphasizes the need for a reliable method of killing them by autoclaving. This is the concept of surgical asepsis.

STERILIZATION AND DISINFECTION

The goal of autoclaving is to produce a sterilized item. By definition, sterilization is the complete destruction of *all* forms of microbial life.[3] This includes the destruction of bacteria, viruses, and spores capable of transmitting major infectious diseases such as hepatitis B, acquired immunodeficiency syndrome (AIDS), herpes, and tuberculosis.

Disinfection, on the other hand, is the process of destroying only certain disease-producing microorganisms. It is an intermediate state designed to eliminate as many microorganisms from the environment as possible. Disinfection is less effective than sterilization since it destroys only some bacteria but does not destroy spores, which are potentially infectious.

Disinfection is accomplished by either physical or chemical means and is designed to lower the number of pathogens so that the host is not unnecessarily challenged. Physical disinfectants include boiling water and ultraviolet radiation. Boiling water cannot kill spores. Heat-resistant bacterial spores can withstand boiling water for many hours of continuous exposure.[2] Also, inactivation of some viruses, such as those associated with hepatitis, is uncertain.

Ultraviolet rays are capable of killing bacteria in air or water. The practical use of ultraviolet rays for disinfection in the office setting is limited because bacteria are in a constant state of motion and may move out of the way of the ultraviolet light before being killed. Also, ultraviolet rays can cause burns of the skin and conjunctivitis of the eyes.

Chemical disinfectants must be proved effective against the bacteria *Staphylococcus aureus*, *Salmonella choleraesuis*, and *Pseudomonas aeruginosa* in order to be labeled for hospital use. An example of a chemical disinfectant is glutaraldehyde. An aqueous solution of 2% activated, buffered glutaraldehyde kills microorganisms by denaturation of protein. This is the agent of choice for disinfecting semicritical instruments between patient uses such as those procedures not involved in direct blood contact or noninfective procedures. Instruments used in the office for debridement of hyperkeratotic tissue and nails would be disinfected between patients with such a solution.

In general, in order to reduce the likelihood that an instrument is contaminated, disinfectants should never be used if the instrument can be sterilized. This is most important when instruments are contaminated with blood. Steam sterilization is more effective and less expensive to use than costly chemical disinfectants.

INDICATORS

Since there exists the possibility that an item has not been sterilized during autoclaving, a system of sterilization controls must be used. There are three types of controls: mechanical devices such as recording and indicating thermometers (Fig 37–1), chemical indicators, and biologic indicators.

A chemical indicator is a paper strip, plastic gauge, or glass vial that contains a dye or chemical that exhibits a physical change when subjected to one or more physical parameters.[4] The physical parameters for steam sterilization include time, temperature, and moisture.[5] One kind of chemical control is a dye-impregnated indicating print, that

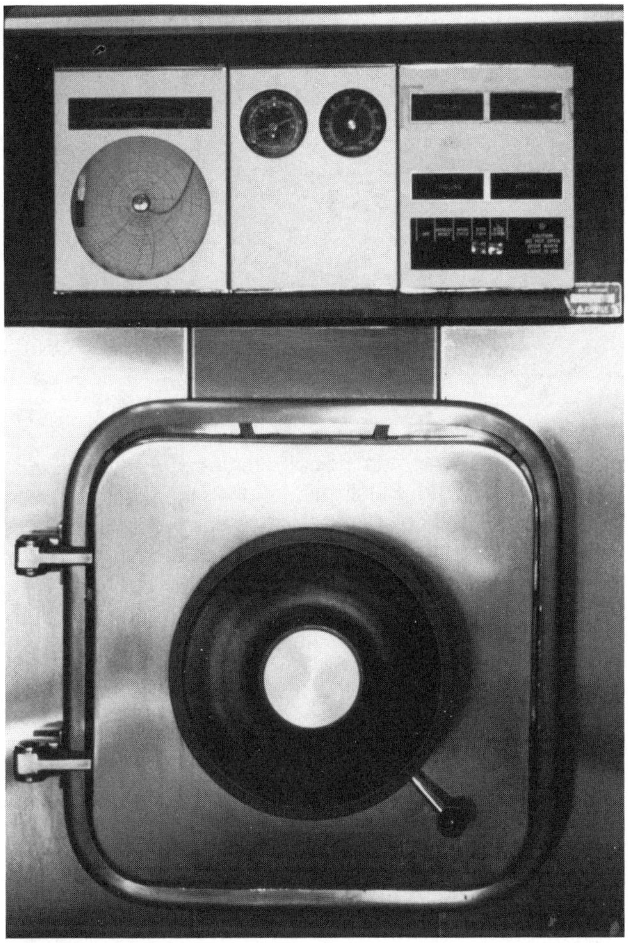

FIG 37–1.
Sophisticated autoclaves that graphically record the temperature and pressure of the autoclaving process are generally found in hospitals.

changes color when steam of a specific temperature is in contact with it for a given length of time[6] (Fig 37–2,A–C).

A heat-sensitive sterilizing tape will develop dark stripe marks indicating that an item has been through the sterilizing process (Fig 37–3,A and B). Chemical indicators show only that the items have been exposed to the physical conditions in the sterilizer and do not prove that sterilization has been achieved.

To ensure that an item has been sterilized, the sterilizing process must be checked by using a biologic indicator such as a spore test. The biologic indicator is a commercially prepared capsule or strip that contains a highly resistant spore-forming microorganism *(Bacillus stearothermophilus)* that is nonpathogenic and does not produce toxins. After the sterilization cycle, the biologic indicator is cultured by a laboratory to verify that total kill is achieved. This is the only reliable method to verify that the sterilization process is actually destroying all of the microorganisms and spores. All of the biologic and chemical indicators are interpreted and stored according to the manufacturer's instructions and specifications.

In an office environment, chemical indicators are a sufficient means of monitoring the steam sterilization process. Sterilization of instruments and dressings depends not only on the autoclaving process but also on their preparation and packing prior to autoclaving.

PREPARATION BEFORE AUTOCLAVING

Prior to sterilization, instruments must be properly cleaned to decrease the bioburden and remove material that may cause staining. Bioburden refers to the amount, type, and resistance level of microbial contamination on an item.[7] Tissue, bone, and blood may contribute to a high bioburden level, but gross debris need not be visible for a bioburden to be present.[8] When the bioburden level is extremely high, a longer exposure to steam may be required. In addition, debris that remains on an instrument may dry and actually protect microorganisms during autoclaving. It is therefore imperative that debris be removed before sterilizing in order to expose the microorganisms to the sterilizing process. The cleaning process prior to sterilization physically removes microbes and organic debris that harbor microorganisms.[2]

In the hospital setting, instruments are cleaned in a washer-sterilizer. This sterilizer is designed to terminally wash and sterilize instruments immediately after an operation is finished.[2] In order for the washer-sterilizer to function at peak efficiency, the bioburden must not be allowed to dry in box locks and serrations of the instruments. Therefore instruments should be soaked and wiped frequently during the surgical procedure.

The washing portion of the washer-sterilizer cycle includes a vigorous agitating detergent bath accomplished by high-velocity jets of steam and air. The detergent lifts the blood and tissue debris from the instrument. This is followed by an inflow of steam into the chamber with simultaneous outflow of water to complete the process.[1]

The preferred mechanical cleaning method for office use is ultrasonic cleaning. In this machine, instruments are immersed in a detergent solution

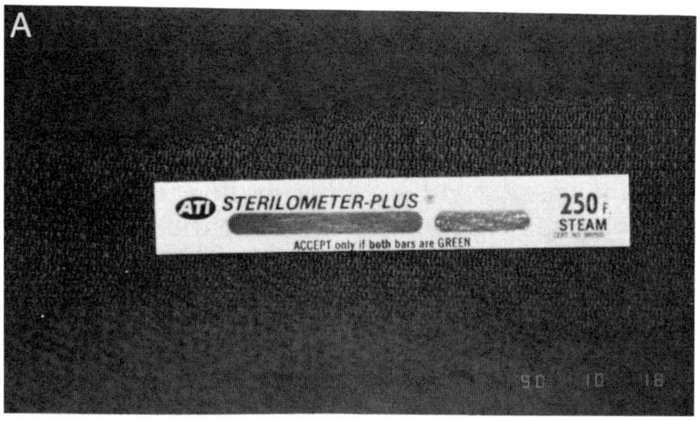

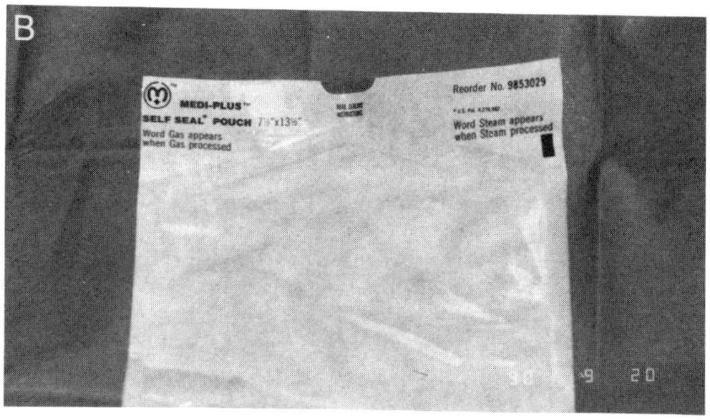

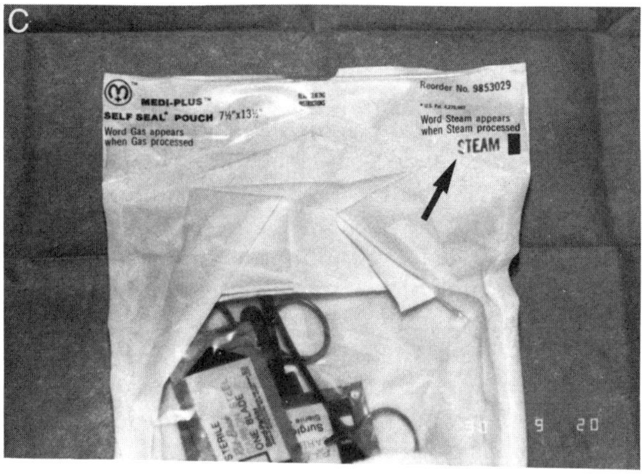

FIG 37–2.
A, a chemical paper strip indicator that is placed within the pack to be sterilized. Sterilization of the inner contents is ensured only if the color indicator has changed. In this case, both bars must be a green color. **B,** sterilization pouch prior to steam autoclaving. Note the lack of an indicator in the top right hand corner of the pouch. **C,** the same pouch after steam autoclaving. The word "steam" appears and indicates that proper sterilization has been completed.

and subjected to energy created by high-frequency sound waves. This creates a process called cavitation. Cavitation occurs when the sound waves create tiny bubbles in the solution. These bubbles collide with the instrument and form small vacuum areas on the instrument surface that dislodge the debris. Instruments should be in their opened position, and a low-sudsing, neutral-pH detergent should be used. Best results are achieved by using distilled, deionized water.[8] Using neutral detergents and distilled, deionized water will ensure longer instrument life.

Dissimilar metals such as stainless steel, copper, and brass should not be mixed together in the ultrasonic cleaner because an ionic transfer may occur between these metals. This results in pitting and etching of the instruments.[1] Plating of the instruments may also occur and result in a dark staining of the instruments.

Cleaning instruments with soap and water while mechanically removing debris with a soft toothbrush or commercial wire brush is also an effective means of mechanical cleaning prior to autoclaving.

Certain metals may require the use of a corrosion inhibitor prior to the steam sterilization process. Stainless steel resists corrosion and therefore should not require a corrosion inhibitor. Carbon steel and other metals that do not have corrosion resistance should be treated prior to autoclaving. A type of corrosion inhibitor is an inorganic oxidizing substance, such as sodium nitrate in a 2% solution; the oxidizer forms a passive oxide layer that minimizes electrolysis. Polar organic compounds such as surgical milk absorb onto the metal surface to form a protective layer.

Instruments should also be lubricated with an antimicrobial water-soluble lubricant and then drained. Lubricants are removed from instruments by detergents used in the washer-sterilizer and ultrasound cleaner.[1] The lubricant forms a protective coating for the instrument that reduces rusting, staining, and corrosion.[1] The lubricant improves instrument function and reduces the amount of bioburden on the instrument. Oil should not be used to lubricate instruments since steam sterilization will not penetrate the oil effectively. The lubricant must be water soluble to permit penetration. The lubricant must also have a neutral pH and contain a high concentration of surfactants to dissolve organic debris on the instrumentation.[1]

WRAPPING OF MATERIALS FOR STERILIZATION

To complete the process prior to autoclaving, a properly cleaned instrument must be assembled in a compact unit, wrapped, secured, and labeled.[6] Basic sets of instruments or trays of instruments for specific operations are prepared for sterilizing after cleaning is completed. Instruments are placed in trays with a perforated bottom to allow adequate penetration of steam around the instruments.[2] Hinged instruments such as hemostats and needle holders must be opened to permit steam penetration on all surfaces. Fragile instruments such as skin hooks require physical protection from damage and may be wrapped in gauze. Plastic and metal containers or foam inserts are sometimes used.[3]

Heavy instruments are placed in the bottom of the tray. Basin sets should be nested so that the smaller basins fit inside the larger ones. An absorbent towel or gauze sponge is placed between basins to permit adequate penetration of steam around all surfaces and prevent condensation between basins. Gauze sponges are not packaged inside basins since steam may not penetrate all surfaces.[2, 3]

Drapes and gowns should be loosely rolled or fan-folded to allow penetration of steam between layers. In general, packs should not exceed 12 × 12 × 20 in. in size and 12 lb in weight. If many items are to be sterilized, then two or more packs are preferred to one overpacked tray. In addition, packs should be strategically placed in the autoclave to ensure proper steam penetration. Never overpack the autoclave (Fig 37–4).

Throughout the sterilizing process, steam must directly contact all surfaces of the instrument and the wrapping material itself.[5] Therefore, the wrapping material must be permeable to steam, and the contents of the package should be arranged in such a way as to expose all surfaces to the steam. In addition, the packaging material cannot allow dust or microbacteria to permeate it after the autoclaving process has taken place. Materials used for packaging are flexible and memory-free to permit aseptic transfer of the contents. Sometimes

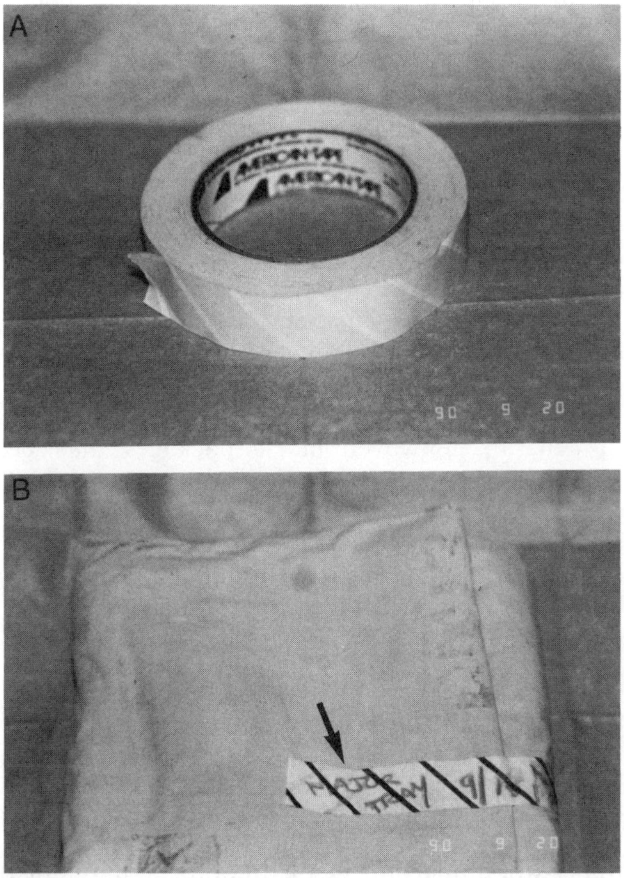

FIG 37–3.
A, heat-sensitive autoclaving tape. Note the oblique clear lines in the tape. **B,** after adequate steam autoclave exposure, dark stripes appear through the tape. These measures are a system of checks to ensure adequate autoclaving technique.

FIG 37–4.
Avoid overpacking surgical trays. Even with the use of a deeply placed chemical indicator, adequate steam penetration of all surgical instruments cannot be ensured.

the packaging material itself may act as a drape when establishing a sterile field.

Materials for wrapping instruments include woven textiles, nonwoven fabric, plastics, paper, metal sterilizing containers, and a variety of paper and plastic combinations[2,3] (Fig 37–5). Steam sterilization cycles are based on the assumption that packages will be wrapped in 140-thread-count muslin, which was the standard sterilization wrap for many years. Higher–thread count materials are beginning to replace 140-count muslin. Many of the 280-thread-count woven wrappers also have a special moisture-resistant treatment.

Nonwoven fabrics are processed cellulose fibers and are intended for single use and therefore must be disposed of after use. The problem with these materials is that condensation occurs on metal surfaces of instrument sets during steam sterilization and may not be removed during drying.

Plastic films such as Weck sterilizing tubing are economical and easy to use for packaging single instruments or small packs. It also permits visualization of the contents, thus eliminating the need for labeling.

There are a variety of paper products that are available for steam sterilization. Paper does have memory and tends to flip back easily, thus contaminating the sterile field. Paper also punctures easily and may tear when removing the tape indicator. When a pack is prepared, it must then be wrapped in a suitable packaging material.

Usually two wrappers sequentially wrapped are used to secure the package contents. The double wrapping protects the inner package from contamination during handling and serves as a dust barrier.[2] The inside wrapper, when opened, may be used in a sterile field.

The wrapper must be properly folded to allow the package to be opened after being sterilized. Proper folding also secures the contents of the package. The two most common methods of wrapping are the "square fold or straight method" (Fig 37–6), which is used to wrap large packs and instrument trays, and the "envelope fold or diagonal method" (Fig 37–7), which is used for small packs and most instrument sets and single items. These methods are more readily explained and easily understood through drawings and practice.

Once the pack is wrapped, it is usually secured with sterilization indicating tape. The tape secures the package and changes color after sterilization to indicate that the package has been exposed to the physical parameters associated with sterilization. Pins, staples, or paper clips should never be used to secure the package. These can penetrate the wrapping and cause contamination to occur. All items and packs should be clearly labeled with the date of sterilization and name of the contents enclosed.[1,3]

After packs are sterilized, they should be stored on clean shelves and protected from moisture and dust. The length of time a package remains sterile after sterilization is referred to as the "shelf life." Loss of sterility of a package is considered to be event related and is dependent in part on the type of material used for packaging and the number of times a package is handled before use. However, in general, nonwoven fabric packages may be stored for 30 days, while paper packages last 8 weeks. Plastic sacks such as Weck sterilization tubing increases the shelf life to 3 months.[1,6] Excessive handling or transportation of a pack to another distant physical location should require resterilization.

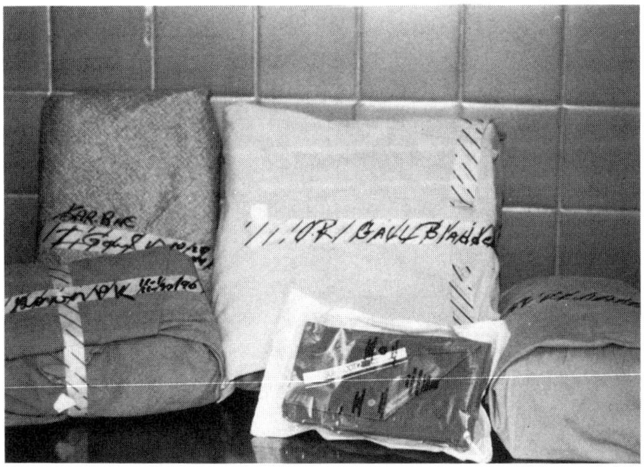

FIG 37–5.
Sterilized packs must be identified and dated to assist in proper retrieval of instruments as well as adherence to the shelf life.

STEAM STERILIZATION

Sterilization by steam under pressure is called autoclaving. Although an increase in pressure and temperature occurs together, it is temperature that is the important factor in autoclaving. Moist heat is the sterilizing agent. The significance of pressure is that it raises the temperature of the steam. The advantages of steam sterilization over other methods of sterilization are many. Steam sterilization is the safest, easiest, and surest method of sterilization. It is also the fastest and

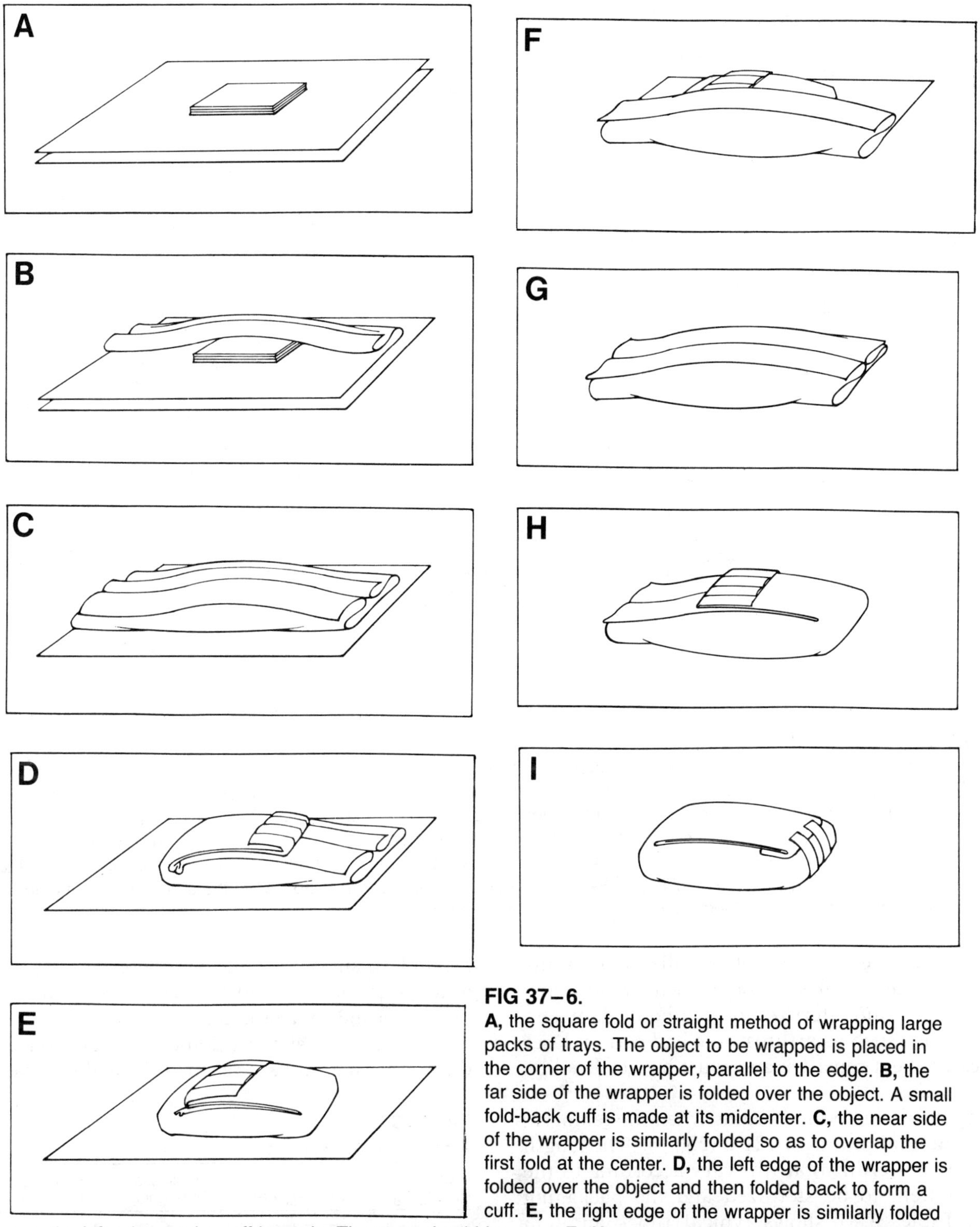

FIG 37–6.
A, the square fold or straight method of wrapping large packs of trays. The object to be wrapped is placed in the corner of the wrapper, parallel to the edge. **B,** the far side of the wrapper is folded over the object. A small fold-back cuff is made at its midcenter. **C,** the near side of the wrapper is similarly folded so as to overlap the first fold at the center. **D,** the left edge of the wrapper is folded over the object and then folded back to form a cuff. **E,** the right edge of the wrapper is similarly folded over the left edge, and a cuff is made. The wrap should be snug. **F–H,** a second outer wrapper is applied in the same manner as the first. **I,** the wrapper edge is secured with chemical indicator tape, identified, and dated. All cuffs will be used to maintain the sterility of the inner wrapper when opening the pack.

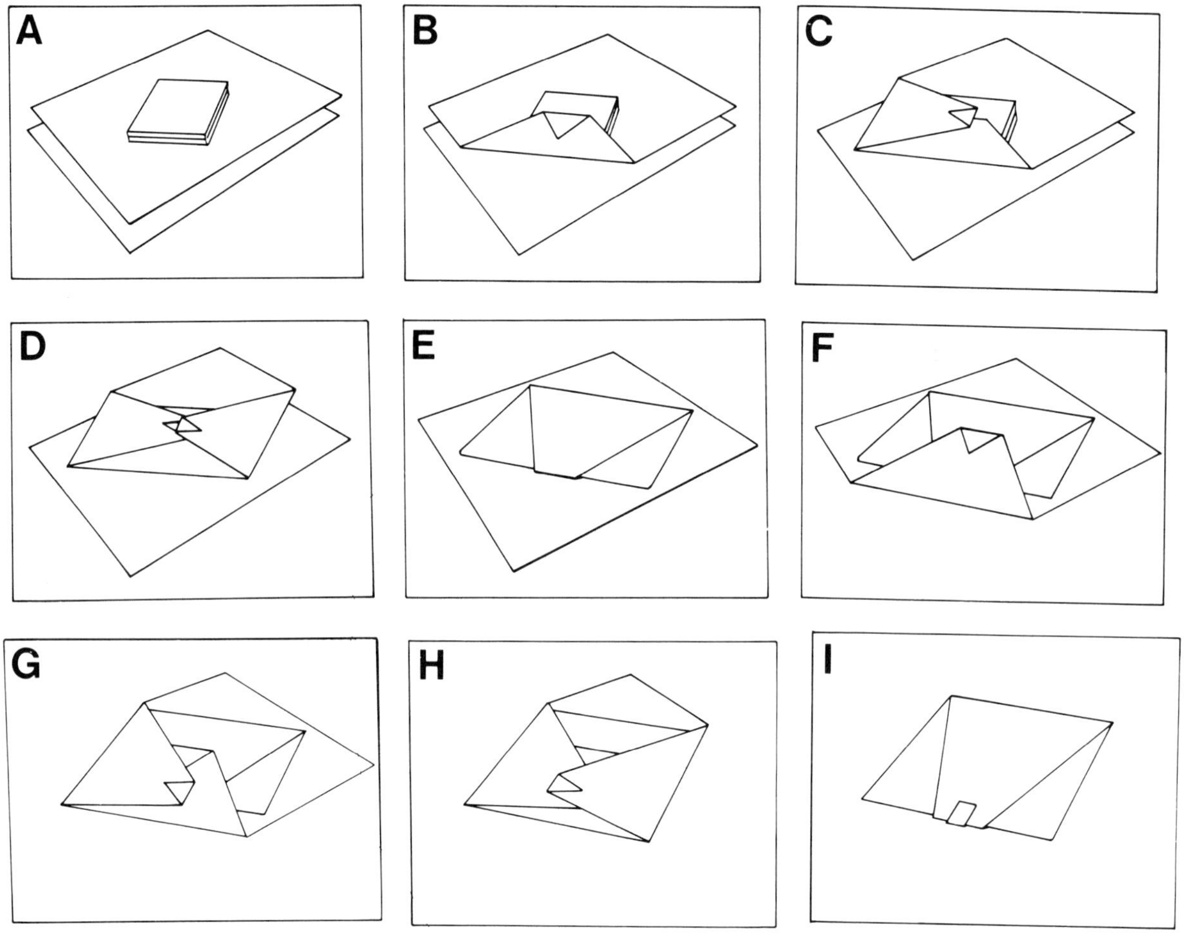

FIG 37–7.
A–I, the envelope fold or diagonal method of wrapping small packs and single instruments. **A,** place the square wrapper diagonally on the table as shown. The object to be wrapped is placed in the center, at right angles to the wrapper. **B,** the bottom corner is folded up to the midline of the object and then folded back to form a cuff. **C** and **D,** a similar fold with formation of a cuff is now performed on the left and right sides of the packed object. Each fold must overlap the previous fold. **E,** the top corner of the wrapper is now folded over the object, and the flap is tucked over the previous left and right folds. A small tab is left visible for easy opening via sterile technique. **F–H,** the second, outer wrapper is applied in the same manner as the first. **I,** the pack is secured with chemical indicator tape, identified, and dated.

least expensive method of sterilization. Many items such as stainless steel can withstand many cycles of steam sterilization without damage.[2] Other items such as arthroscopic and certain laser lenses are heat sensitive and must be sterilized by other means.

The sterilizing period begins when the temperature is at a minimum of 121°C (250°F).[9] The length of time for sterilization will vary according to the type of item to be sterilized and the packaging used. Table 37–1 shows typical times an item must be exposed to achieve sterilization.

The loading of the autoclave is a critical step. Packs and items should be positioned on edge and arranged in the autoclave so that steam can pass around all surfaces. To avoid overcrowding in the autoclave, there should be free space on all sides and at least 3 in. at the top.[6]

Timing of the sterilization cycle begins once the desired temperature is reached throughout the au-

TABLE 37–1.
Average Sterilization Times

Instrument Packaging	Temperature	Sterilization Time (min)	Estimated Total Time (min)
Unwrapped	270°F(132°C)	3	15–23
	250°F(121°C)	15	30–35
Wrapped	270°F(132°C)	15	30–35
	250°F(121°C)	30	45
Packs	250°F(121°C)	30	45

toclave chamber. The time exposure needed varies according to the temperature of the steam and whether the item is wrapped or unwrapped. After the steam cycle is completed, moist packaging must be dried prior to removal from the autoclave chamber. If a warm package is prematurely removed from the autoclave, sudden cooling may occur. This will cause condensation inside the package, thus raising the risk of contamination.

FLASH STERILIZATION

Flash sterilization of an item is used when time does not allow for the routine wrapping, autoclaving, and drying process. The procedure consists of placing an unwrapped instrument in an open, perforated bottom tray and exposing it to 132°C (270°F) steam at a pressure of 27 psi for a minimum of 3 minutes. Flash sterilization should not be used when there is sufficient time to sterilize an item by the conventional autoclaving method. Flash sterilization should be used in an emergency situation such as when an instrument is dropped during a surgical procedure.[8]

Although the flash sterilization process is a safe, effective method to rapidly sterilize instruments, the aseptic transfer of the instrument to the sterile field presents a problem. An instrument in a hot, wet, unwrapped tray is more likely to become contaminated by exposure to dust, debris, and airborne microorganisms during the transfer prior to its use. It is therefore imperative that flash sterilized instruments be directly delivered to their point of use.[8] In addition, flash sterilization is not recommended for implants such as staples, K-wires, plates, screws, and joint replacement prostheses. These materials are intended to stay in the body for extended periods of time and especially cannot be contaminated. Sterilization is not as reliable in the shortened cycle, and this decreases the overall safety factor and provides greater opportunity for trapped air in the chamber, which increases the possibility of contamination.

Office antiseptic techniques as well as surgical asepsis are important aspects of patient care. Through proper understanding of microorganisms and their role in the transference of disease, office personnel can effectively reduce infection.

REFERENCES

1. Groah L: *Operating Room Nursing: Perioperative Practice.* E Norwalk, Conn, Appleton & Lange, 1990, pp 140–195.
2. Kohn M: *Berry and Kohn's Introduction to Operating Room Technique.* New York, McGraw-Hill International Book Co, 1986, pp 122–143.
3. *Training Manual for Central Service Technicians.* Washington, DC, American Hospital Association, 1986, pp 113–133.
4. Strzelecki L, Nelson J: Evaluation of closed container flash sterilization system. *Orthop Nurs* 1987; 8:21–24.
5. Perkins J: *Principles and Methods of Sterilization in Health Sciences,* ed 2. Springfield, Ill, Charles C Thomas Publishers, 1969, p 111.
6. Henderson V: *Textbook of the Principles and Practice of Nursing.* New York, MacMillan Publishing Co Inc, 1978, pp 881–885, 1406–1412.
7. Kneedler JA, Dodge GH: *Perioperative Patient Care: The Nursing Perspective,* ed 2. Cambridge, Mass, Blackwell Scientific Publications Inc, 1987, p 228.
8. Fogg DM: Criteria for flash sterilization. *AORN J* 1989; 50:888–892.
9. Bolding B: Steam sterilization systems: How they work (Part I). *Can Operat Room Nurs J* 1988; 3:9–10.

ADDITIONAL REFERENCE

Howie J: Upgrading surgeons: Autoclaves—A personal recollection. *J Infect* 1988; 16:231–234.

38

Basic Pharamcology for Podiatric Medicine

Mickey D. Stapp, B.S. (Pharm.)

I. Antibacterial Drugs (Antibiotics)
  A. β-Lactams (Penicillins and Cephalosporins)
  B. Aminoglycosides
  C. Sulfonamides
  D. Tetracyclines
  E. Quinolones
  F. Erythromycins
  G. Antiseptics
  H. Miscellaneous Antibacterials
II. Antifungal Agents
III. Antigout Agents
IV. Antianxiety Agents
V. Antiparasitics
VI. Hemorheologic Agents
VII. Analgesics
VIII. Nonsteroidal Anti-inflammatory Agents
IX. Sedative/Hypnotic Agents
X. Muscle Relaxants
XI. Keratolytic Agents
XII. Debriding Agents
XIII. Corticosteroids
XIV. Local Anesthetic Agents
XV. Antidiabetic Agents
XVI. The Prescription

Medical pharmacology can be defined as the study of the properties, uses, and actions of drugs to prevent, diagnose, and treat diseases.[1] A drug can be defined as any chemical agent that affects living tissue.[2] This chapter will familiarize the reader with the basic pharmacology of the medications most often prescribed by the podiatric physician. Also included will be those agents used in the office practice and one additional class, the antidiabetic drugs, normally not prescribed by the podiatric physician. This chapter will also cover prescription writing and prescription abbreviations.

ANTIBACTERIAL DRUGS (ANTIBIOTICS)

Antibacterial drugs are those that kill (bactericidal) or inhibit the growth of (bacteriostatic) susceptible pathogenic bacteria. These drugs are often prescribed in podiatric medicine for various infections of the lower extremity. Antibacterials can be subdivided into eight major groups depending on their chemical similarities and antimicrobial spectrum. These eight groups are β-lactams (penicillins and cephalosporins), aminoglycosides, sulfonamides, tetracyclines, quinolones, erythromycins, antiseptics, and miscellaneous.

β-Lactams (Penicillins and Cephalosporins)

β-Lactam antibiotics include the penicillin family and the cephalosporin family (Table 38–1). (Drug manufacturers and addresses can be found in Appendix 38–1.) β-Lactam is the name given to the ring within the chemical structures of all members of this subgroup. The significance of this common structure is unclear regarding the action of the antibiotic, but it is clinically significant regarding cross sensitivity (i.e., those allergic to penicillins are at a greater risk to exhibit allergic sensitivity to some cephalosporins).[3] In addition, drugs from both families can be inactivated by an

TABLE 38–1.
Antibacterial Drugs (Antibiotics)

Generic	Tradename
PENICILLINS	
Penicillin V potassium	Pen-Vee K, V-cillin K
Ampicillin	Amcill, Omnipen, Polycillin
Amoxicillin	Amoxil, Polymox
Amoxicillin/clavulanic acid	Augmentin
PENICILLINASE-RESISTANT PENICILLINS	
Oxacillin	Prostaphlin, Bactocill
Dicloxacillin	Dynapen, Pathocil
CEPHALOSPORINS	
Cephalexin	Keflex
Cefaclor	Ceclor
Cefadroxil	Duricef, Ultracef
Cephradine	Velosef
Cefuroxime	Ceftin
Cefixime	Suprax
AMINOGLYCOSIDES	
Topicals	
Gentamicin sulfate	Garamycin Cream/Ointment
Injectables	
Amikacin	Amikin
Gentamicin	Garamycin
Tobramycin	Nebcin
SULFONAMIDES	
Sulfamethoxazole/trimethoprim	Bactrim, Septra
Silver sulfadiazine	Silvadene Cream
Mafenide	Sulfamylon Cream
TETRACYCLINES	
Tetracycline	Achromycin, Sumycin
Doxycycline	Doryx, Vibramycin
Minocycline	Minocin
QUINOLONES	
Ciprofloxacin	Cipro
ERYTHROMYCINS	
Erythromycin base	ERYC, E-Mycin, Ery-Tab, PCE
Erythromycin estolate	Ilosone
Erythromycin ethylsuccinate	E.E.S., EryPed, Pediamycin
Erythromycin stearate	Erythrocin Stearate
ANTISEPTICS	
Povidone-iodine	Betadine*
Hexachlorophene	pHisoHex
Chlorhexidine gluconate	Hibiclens*
MISCELLANEOUS ANTIBACTERIALS	
Rifampin	Rifadin
Metronidazole	Flagyl, Metrogel
Neomycin, polymyxin B	Neosporin Cream*
Bacitracin/neomycin/polymyxin	Neosporin Ointment*

*Over the counter.

enzyme, β-lactamase or penicillinase, that is produced by some resistant bacteria. Clavulanic acid is an agent used in conjunction with some members of the β-lactams to inhibit penicillinase, thereby expanding the spectrum of activity.

Antibiotics of the β-lactam group primarily are bactericidal by inhibiting the synthesis of the bacterial cell wall. Those that can be taken orally are reliable agents for the treatment of many common infections caused by penicillin-sensitive organisms such as streptococci, staphylococci, and pneumococci. A careful history must be taken whenever a drug from this group might be prescribed to determine the possibility of an allergic reaction. The patient should be carefully questioned regarding previous use of penicillin or related drugs and any adverse reaction that may have occurred.

Aminoglycosides

The second group of antibacterial drugs is the aminoglycosides. (see Table 38–1). The majority of this class of drugs can only be used intravenously (IV) because they are poorly absorbed from the gastrointestinal tract. They are also generally reserved for serious aerobic gram-negative bacterial infections, and serum levels must be monitored closely due to the associated ototoxicity and nephrotoxicity.[4] Two of the aminoglycosides, gentamicin and neomycin, are prescribed and used in the office as topical antibiotics. Both are bactericidal by inhibiting the protein synthesis of susceptible bacteria. These topical preparations have been widely used as antibacterial agents for mild superficial skin infections caused by susceptible staphylococci, streptococci, and gram-negative organisms.[5]

Sulfonamides

The third group of antibacterial drugs is the sulfonamides (see Table 38–1). They are structural analogues of para-aminobenzoic acid (PABA), a substance required by many microorganisms for the production of folic acid. Sulfonamides compete with the bacterial cell for PABA, thus inhibiting the production of folic acid and the growth of the microorganism. Host cells (in humans) are unaffected because they do not synthesize folic acid but attain it from the diet.[3] The majority of the sulfonamides are used effectively for the treatment of urinary tract infections and as an adjunct in the treatment of many other infections. Few are routinely used in the practice of podiatric medicine. A sulfonamide preparation may be used as an adjunct to other antibiotics in serious or polymicrobial infections. Two sulfonamides are used topically in the treatment of burns. A thorough history must be taken regarding past allergy to sulfonamides before any therapy with one of these agents is initiated.

Tetracyclines

The fourth group of antibacterial drugs is the tetracyclines (see Table 38–1). These agents are bacteriostatic by inhibiting protein synthesis only in multiplying organisms. Tetracyclines have a wide spectrum of activity against both gram-positive and gram-negative bacteria. Their clinical use has diminished since their introduction due to the emergence of many resistant pathogenic strains. Tetracyclines are generally reserved for the treatment of acne, rickettsial diseases, *Haemophilus influenzae,* and chlamydiae.[6] One important consideration if the use of a tetracycline is contemplated is the avoidance of any food or medicinal product that contains calcium, magnesium, aluminum, or iron. These agents chelate the tetracycline and prevent absorption. Thus, dairy products and antacids must be avoided. One way to prevent this chelation is to take the prescribed tetracycline antibiotic 1 hour before or 2 hours after taking any other product or food containing one of these chelating agents.

Another important consideration is that tetracyclines may cause an increased sensitivity to sunlight, and a patient taking these medications should be cautioned and advised to use an appropriate sunscreen. Most importantly, tetracyclines should never be given to pregnant or nursing women or to children under the age of 12 years because these drugs may permanently discolor developing teeth.[6]

Quinolones

The fifth group of antibacterial agents is a relatively new class of antibiotics called the quinolones (see Table 38–1). These bactericidal agents work to prevent protein synthesis of the bacteria by inhibiting a specific enzyme necessary for DNA replication. Only one agent of this class, ciprofloxacin, is routinely used in the practice of podiatry. Because of good oral absorption and good bone penetration, this agent offers a means of treating osteomyelitis on an outpatient basis. This agent may also be very efficacious in the treatment of skin and soft-tissue infections once treated only with parenteral medications. Susceptible organisms are predominantly gram-negative bacteria, but some gram-positive bacteria are susceptible as well.[7] Resistance to ciprofloxacin is rapidly developing by organisms such as *Staphylococcus aureus* and *Pseudomonas aeruginosa* with just a few years of clinical use.

Ciprofloxacin should be taken with food, but the concomitant use of antacids should be avoided.[8] Quinolones, including ciprofloxacin, should not be prescribed for children less than 18 years old due to the possibility of deforming immature cartilage.[9]

Erythromycins

The sixth group of antibacterial drugs is the erythromycins (see Table 38–1). The erythromycins are bacteriostatic macrolide antibiotics that block protein synthesis. Erythromycin is used to treat mild to moderate infections caused by susceptible streptococci, anaerobic cocci, and mycoplasmas. It is especially useful as an alternative to patients allergic to penicillin. Erythromycin is available as a base, as esters (estolate and ethylsuccinate), and as a salt (stearate). Generally, all erythromycins are better absorbed if taken on an empty stomach, 1 hour before or 2 hours after meals.[5] The most common side effects are abdominal distress, cramping, and pain, as well as nausea and vomiting.[3] If the patient experiences these side effects, the medication may be given with food in an attempt to prevent further discomfort.

Antiseptics

The seventh group of antibacterial agents is generally used as bacteriostatic skin cleansers and preoperative surgical scrubs (see Table 38–1). The iodine-containing preparations are also used as microbicides to kill gram-positive and gram-negative bacteria, viruses, fungi, and yeasts.[10] Hypersensitivity to iodine is relatively common, and all patients must be questioned as to a possible allergy, including an allergy to shellfish, since these foods contain a high content of iodine.[11]

Miscellaneous Antibacterials

The final group of antibacterial agents is a miscellaneous group (see Table 38–1). This group contains the drug rifampin, which is generally used in the treatment of tuberculosis but which may also be used as an adjunct in the treatment of chronic *Staphylococcus* osteomyelitis.[5] This group also contains metronidazole, a bacteriocidal agent used in the treatment of trichomoniasis, amebiasis, giardiasis, and serious anaerobic infections.[12] An important consideration with the use of metronidazole is the avoidance of all alcohol and alcohol-containing medicinal preparations during therapy and for 72 hours after therapy. This drug has a serious reaction with alcohol that causes severe nausea and vomiting.[13] Two other drugs that may be used topically for superficial skin infections are bacitracin and polymyxin B. Bacitracin may be used alone or in combination with other agents, while polymyxin B is used only in combination with other agents.

ANTIFUNGAL AGENTS

Antifungal preparations are also often prescribed in podiatric medicine (Table 38–2). A topical preparation might be prescribed for the treatment of a superficial fungal infection, i.e., tinea pedis or cutaneous dermatophyte infection. In the case of a more deep-seated fungal infection, i.e., onychomycosis or a recalcitrant cutaneous dermatophyte infection, an oral preparation might be prescribed. For the treatment of a systemic fungal infection, one involving vital organs such as the lungs, more ambitious IV therapy might be required. Antifungal agents generally work by one of two mechanisms, by interfering with the synthesis of the cell membrane or by disrupting the cell membrane of the fungus.[5] Without the cell membrane, the fungus loses vital cellular constituents, ultimately leading to its death. Griseofulvin, an oral antifungal agent, works by a different mechanism of action. It inhibits the growth (fungistatic) of the fungus rather than killing it (fungicidal). Griseofulvin stops cellular division within the fungus and thus only affects young, active cells.[14]

When topical antifungal medications are prescribed, the patient should be instructed in what manner, how often, and for how long to use the medication. Patients receiving oral antifungal medications must understand the extended length of time necessary for the more serious infections, possibly as long as 1 year of treatment. Since the oral antifungal medications are potentially hepatoxic and require periodic blood tests, the patient's probable compliance must be assessed before these medications are prescribed. The treatment of systemic fungal infections is beyond the realm of podiatric medicine and hence will not be discussed in this chapter.

TABLE 38–2.
Antifungals

Generic	Tradename
TOPICAL ANTIFUNGALS	
Cetyl pyridinium chloride, triacetin, chloroxylenol, and other ingredients	Fungoid Tincture
Fuchsin, phenol, resorcinol, acetone, and alcohol	Castellani Paint
Resorcinol, salicylic acid, and other ingredients	Fungi-Nail*
Clotrimazole	Lotrimin, Lotrimin AF,* Mycelex
Miconazole	Monistat-Derm, Micatin*
Nystatin	Mycostatin, Nilstat
Naftifine	Naftin
Ketoconazole	Nizoral
Haloprogin	Halotex
Ciclopirox	Loprox
Econazole	Spectazole
Tolnaftate	Tinactin*
ORAL ANTIFUNGALS	
Griseofulvin	Grifulvin V, Fulvicin P/G
Ketoconazole	Nizoral

*Over the counter.

ANTIGOUT AGENTS

Gout is a metabolic condition characterized by hyperuricemia with resultant deposition of sodium urate crystals in tissues, joints, and the kidneys.[15] This condition is often first diagnosed by the podiatric physician because the first and most common site of crystal deposition is in the first metatarsophalangeal joint. This deposition results in acute inflammation and sometimes excruciating pain.

Colchicine is one drug that is used in the treatment of active gout to reduce the acute inflammatory response. Colchicine's mechanism of action is not fully understood, but it does appear to inhibit the migration of neutrophils and phagocytosis of the urate crystals, which ultimately causes the inflammatory episode and the associated pain. Colchicine may cause nausea, vomiting, and diarrhea, and in large doses it is potentially toxic. This drug is dosed every 1 to 2 hours until the pain is relieved or until gastrointestinal side effects develop.[16] The nonsteroidal anti-inflammatory drugs

TABLE 38–3.
Agents Used in Podiatry

Generic	Tradename
ANTIGOUT PREPARATIONS	
Colchicine	Various manufacturers
Probenecid	Benemid
Allopurinol	Zyloprim, Lopurin
ANTIANXIETY AGENTS	
Histamine antagonist agents	
Diphenhydramine	Benadryl*
Hydroxyzine HCl	Atarax
Hydroxyzine pamoate	Vistaril
Benzodiazepine	
Diazepam	Valium†
Lorazepam	Ativan†
Alprazolam	Xanax†
Chlorazepate	Tranxene†
Oxazepam	Serax†
Chlordiazepoxide	Librium†
ANTIPARASITICS	
Thiabendazole	Mintezol Suspension or Tablets
HEMORHEOLOGIC AGENTS	
Pentoxifylline	Trental

*Over the counter.
†Controlled, Schedule IV.

(NSAIDs) are commonly used in the treatment of acute gout. They will be discussed later.

Two other drugs, probenecid and allopurinol, are indicated for the prevention of recurrent attacks. Probenecid works by blocking the renal tubular reabsorption of uric acid, thus increasing renal excretion and decreasing serum uric acid levels. Allopurinol works by inhibiting an enzyme necessary for uric acid production (Table 38–3).

ANTIANXIETY AGENTS

Antianxiety agents, sometimes called mild tranquilizers, are occasionally used in podiatric medicine (see Table 38–3). These antianxiety agents are indicated for the short-term treatment of moderate anxiety and muscle tension. Two classes of drugs are used most often today, the histamine antagonists and the benzodiazepines. The histamine antagonists act as antihistamines, antianxiety agents, antiemetics, and sedatives.[17] The benzodiazepines are the most widely prescribed drugs on the market today. The benzodiazepines are the first class of drugs discussed that are classed as controlled substances.

Such drugs come under the jurisdiction of the Controlled Substances Act and are divided into five schedules based on their potential for abuse. Schedule I drugs have a high potential for abuse and no accepted medical use in the United States. Schedule II drugs have a high potential for abuse and may lead to severe psychological or physical dependencies. Schedule III drugs have a lower potential for abuse than those in schedules I and II. Schedule IV drugs have a low potential for abuse and may lead to limited physical or psychological dependence. Schedule V drugs have the lowest abuse potential of the controlled substances and consist of preparations containing limited quantities of certain narcotic drugs, generally for antitussive and antidiarrheal purposes.[18]

Benzodiazepines are used most widely as antianxiety agents, but under certain conditions they may also be used as muscle relaxants and anticonvulsants.[19] The pharmacologic action of the histamine antagonists and the benzodiazepines is not fully understood, only that they act on the central nervous system (CNS). The major side effect of both of these classes of antianxiety agents is sedation. The patients for whom these medications are prescribed must be cautioned of this as well as the concurrent use of alcohol because this will potentiate the CNS depressant effect.

ANTIPARASITICS

Antiparasitics are rarely prescribed by podiatric physicians. One indication for an antiparasitic preparation is in the treatment of cutaneous larva migrans (creeping eruption). These are raised, erythematous, serpiginous (snakelike) lesions confined to the skin. Larvae of nematodes, usually a dog or cat hookworm, penetrate the skin and migrate underneath the epidermis. This condition is treated with topical or systemic thiabendazole[20] (see Table 38–3).

HEMORHEOLOGIC AGENTS

Pentoxifylline is the only hemorheologic agent used in podiatric medicine today (see Table 38–3). This agent is indicated for the treatment of intermittent claudication in patients with chronic occlusive arterial disease.[21] The mechanism of action of pentoxifylline is not fully understood, but this agent does act to lower blood viscosity and improve red blood cell flexibility, thereby improving blood flow and increasing oxygen delivery to the tissues.

The effects of this medication may be seen in 2 to 4 weeks, but treatment should be continued for 8 weeks before the drug is determined nonefficacious and treatment is discontinued.[22] Pentoxifylline is chemically related to the methylxanthines and should be used with caution in patients who have exhibited intolerance or hypersensitivity to caffeine, theophylline, and theobromine (found in chocolate).[21]

ANALGESICS

Analgesics are drugs used to relieve or decrease pain. Analgesics are often described as narcotic or nonnarcotic analgesics (Table 38–4). Medically, a narcotic is defined as a substance that induces sleep or stupor. Legally, a narcotic is defined as a dependency-producing drug limited to prescription.[23] Today, the term *narcotic analgesic* refers to those agents derived from or chemically related to opium. Those drugs derived directly from opium are termed *opiates*. Those drugs chemically derived from opiates or synthetically produced to resemble opiates are termed *opioids*.

Nonnarcotic analgesics are commonly used today as single agents or in combination with other agents. Nonnarcotic analgesics are combined with narcotic analgesics in some preparations, each potentiating the analgesic effect of the other. Nonnarcotic analgesics include aspirin, acetaminophen, and some of the NSAIDs, which will be discussed separately.

Aspirin (acetylsalicylic acid) has many actions including analgesia, anti-inflammatory effects, antipyresis, and inhibition of platelet aggregation.[16] Aspirin works by inhibiting prostaglandin synthesis. Prostaglandins are natural chemicals that occur in the body and play a major role in the inflammatory process and the pain associated with inflammation. Aspirin is indicated as an analgesic for mild to moderate pain as a single agent and, when combined with other narcotic analgesics, for moderate to severe pain. Aspirin has a tendency to cause gastrointestinal side effects ranging from nausea and vomiting to ulceration of the stomach and duodenum.[24] During the history and physical examination, many patients will claim to have an allergy to aspirin. In reality, the majority of these are not true hypersensitivities, but an intolerance to the medication in the form of gastrointestinal upset.[25] In an attempt to minimize the gastrointestinal upset associated with aspirin, it may be enterically coated so that it is absorbed in the small intestine and not in the stomach. Due to the delayed absorption of the enteric-coated aspirin, it is not indicated for the relief of acute pain. Aspirin may also be buffered, in which case small amounts of antacids are added, in an attempt to decrease the gastrointestinal irritation and upset.[16]

A major consideration with aspirin therapy is

TABLE 38–4.
Analgesics

Generic	Tradename
NONNARCOTIC ANALGESICS	
Aspirin	Bayer,* Empirin,* Zorprin
Aspirin, enteric coated	Ecotrin*
Aspirin, buffered	Bufferin,* Ascriptin,* Alka-Seltzer*
Aspirin/caffeine	Anacin*
Aspirin/butalbital/caffeine	Fiorinal
Aspirin/acetaminophen/caffeine	Excedrin*
Acetaminophen	Tylenol,* Datril,* Tempra,* Panadol*
Acetaminophen/butalbital/caffeine	Fioricet
OPIATE NARCOTIC ANALGESICS	
Morphine	M.S. Contin†
Codeine	Various manufacturers†
OPIOID NARCOTIC ANALGESICS	
Hydromorphone	Dilaudid†
Oxymorphone	Numorphan†
Meperidine	Demerol
Levorphanol	Levo-Dromoran†
Methadone	Dolophine†
Propoxyphene	Darvon‡
NONNARCOTIC AND NARCOTIC COMBINATIONS	
Oxycodone/aspirin	Percodan†
Oxycodone/acetaminophen	Percocet, Tylox†
Hydrocodone/acetaminophen	Lortab, Anexsia, Vicodin, Norcet‡
Propoxyphene/aspirin	Darvon Compound‡
Propoxyphene/acetaminophen	Darvocet‡
Aspirin/butalbital/caffeine/codeine	Fiorinal with Codeine‡
Aspirin/codeine	Empirin with Codeine‡
Aspirin/dihydrocodeine/caffeine	Synalgos DC‡
Acetaminophen/codeine	Tylenol with Codeine, Phenaphen with Codeine‡

*Over the counter.
†Controlled, Section II.
‡Controlled, Section III.

Reye's syndrome. Reye's syndrome is characterized by an encephalopathy and fatty degeneration of the liver that develops in children with chickenpox or influenza who are being treated with aspirin.[26] Many cases of aspirin-associated Reye's syndrome have been fatal. Aspirin is also contraindicated in patients receiving anticoagulant therapy such as warfarin (Coumadin). Due to the antiplatelet effect of aspirin, serious bleeding complications may result if administered with anticoagulants.[27] It is best to avoid administering and prescribing aspirin-containing products to children less than 16 years old and to patients receiving any anticoagulant therapy. A safer alternative for these circumstances is acetaminophen.

Acetaminophen has analgesic and antipyretic actions but lacks the anti-inflammatory and antiplatelet actions of aspirin. Acetaminophen's analgesic mechanism of action is unknown. Acetaminophen, like aspirin, is used alone for mild to moderate pain and, in combination with narcotic analgesics, for moderate to severe pain. Acetaminophen is relatively free of side effects in therapeutic doses. In large overdosages, acetaminophen is hepatotoxic.[16]

Narcotic analgesics are often prescribed by podiatric physicians to alleviate moderate to severe pain preoperatively, postoperatively, or following trauma. Narcotics act in the CNS to cause release of the body's natural analgesics (enkephalins and endorphins) which results in alteration in the perception of and response to pain.[23] Again, because these drugs act in the CNS, the major side effect is sedation, and the patient should be well-informed of this effect and the additive effect that the concurrent use of alcohol and other CNS depressants may have. Patients taking narcotic analgesics may also experience nausea, vomiting, and constipation. One preparation, meperidine and promethazine HCl (Mepergan), a combination of a narcotic analgesic and a phenothiazine derivative, possesses antihistaminic, sedative, and antiemetic actions. This combination offers an alternative for patients experiencing nausea and vomiting from other narcotic analgesics.

All narcotic analgesics depress respiration in therapeutic doses. Therefore, these drugs must be used with caution in patients with asthma, emphysema, and other obstructive pulmonary conditions.[28] Narcotic analgesics can induce both physiological and psychologic dependency with long-term use. Tolerance, when a patient needs an increased dosage to achieve the same therapeutic effect, can develop with just 2 weeks of regular use of narcotic analgesics.[23] These medications must be strictly controlled, given to those patients absolutely requiring their use, and generally administered only after nonnarcotic analgesics have been unsuccessful.

NONSTEROIDAL ANTI-INFLAMMATORY AGENTS

Inflammation is a natural process of the human body. The process of inflammation is an attempt to neutralize, destroy, and prevent further dissemination of foreign or noxious agents. It also helps to establish necessary conditions for repair and resolution of the pathologic activity. NSAIDs are indicated when the inflammatory process may be having a deleterious effect on the patient.[24] In general, NSAIDs are indicated for acute bouts of chronic inflammation, including rheumatoid arthritis and osteoarthritis. This class of drugs works through the same mechanism as aspirin; in fact, aspirin is included in this class as well as nonnarcotic analgesics. NSAIDs inhibit cyclo-oxygenase, an enzyme necessary for the formation of prostaglandins. Some of the NSAIDs also have mild analgesic and antipyretic actions.[16] These agents are used predominantly in the practice of podiatric medicine for varied inflammatory conditions.

NSAIDs are classified by chemical groups (Table 38–5). The different chemical classes are important when one agent from one chemical class is found to be nonefficacious or to cause unwanted effects. An agent from a different chemical class may then be tried, but not another agent from the same chemical class as the first agent.

The most frequently encountered side effects of the NSAIDs, nausea, vomiting, and diarrhea, are due to gastrointestinal irritation. Patients taking a nonsteroidal anti-inflammatory agent should be instructed to take the medication with food or milk. Another important side effect of NSAID therapy is sodium and fluid retention. This side effect presents as an important drug interaction between NSAIDs and diuretics. NSAIDs appear to inhibit the diuresis and antihypertensive effect of the diuretics. One should be alert for evidence of a reduced diuretic response, and if increasing the dose of the diuretic fails to achieve the desired response, then a different NSAID, possibly from a different chemical class, might be considered.[27]

TABLE 38–5.
Nonsteroidal Anti-inflammatory Agents

Generic	Tradename
SALICYLATE NSAIDs	
Salisalate	Disalcid
Choline magnesium trisalicylate	Trilisate
Diflunisal	Dolobid
INDOLE NSAIDs	
Indomethacin	Indocin
Sulindac	Clinoril
Tolmetin sulfate	Tolectin
PROPIONIC ACID NSAIDs	
Ibuprofen	Motrin, Rufen, Advil,* Nuprin,* Medipren,* Motrin IB*
Fenoprofen	Nalfon
Naproxen	Anaprox, Naprosyn
Ketoprofen	Orudis
Flurbiprofen	Ansaid
FENAMIC ACID NSAIDs	
Meclofenamate	Meclomen
PHENYLACETIC ACID NSAIDs	
Diclofenac	Voltaren
OXICAM NSAIDs	
Piroxicam	Feldene
PYRAZOLONE NSAIDs	
Phenylbutazone	Butazolidin

*Over the counter.

An adverse effect of the NSAIDs is renal dysfunction. It is believed, since the kidneys are key organs in the synthesis of prostaglandins, that the decreased prostaglandin synthesis caused through the mechanism of action of NSAIDs may initiate nephritis, renal injury, and acute renal failure. Therefore, these agents must be used with caution in patients with chronic renal failure and renal insufficiency.[24] NSAIDs are also associated with gastrointestinal bleeding, ulceration, and perforation. This class of drugs must also be used with caution in patients with a history of peptic ulcer disease. If the patient is taking a medication for a peptic ulcer, either stomach or duodenal, the risks vs. benefits must be carefully weighed before NSAID therapy is undertaken. Two such peptic ulcer medications are cimetidine (Tagamet) and ranitidine (Zantac). A new medication is available to prevent peptic ulceration. Used concurrently with the NSAIDs, misoprostol (Cytotec) will reduce the occurrence of gastric ulcers (but not duodenal ulcers) associated with NSAID therapy.[29] The use of misoprostol is probably most effective in patients with past peptic ulcers and not for preventing those NSAID-associated ulcers in patients with no history of peptic ulcer.[30]

SEDATIVE/HYPNOTIC AGENTS

Sedative and hypnotic drugs are occasionally used by the podiatric physician when injury or postoperative pain might temporarily disrupt the normal sleeping patterns (Table 38–6). A sedative drug is one that produces a state of drowsiness. A hypnotic drug is one that induces sleep.

The benzodiazepines, previously discussed with the antianxiety agents, are the safest and most commonly used, although barbiturates, chloral hydrate, the histamine antagonists, and other classes are occasionally used. These agents should only be used for a short period of time, until the condition causing the interruption of sleep is resolved. Chronic use should be avoided because dependency may develop and alteration of normal

TABLE 38–6.
Sedative-Hypnotics and Muscle Relaxants

Generic	Tradename
SEDATIVE-HYPNOTIC AGENTS	
Benzodiazepine hypnotics	
Flurazepam	Dalmane*
Temazepam	Restoril*
Triazolam	Halcion*
Benzodiazepine sedatives	
Lorazepam	Ativan*
Oxazepam	Serax*
Barbiturate hypnotics	
Secobarbital	Seconal†
Pentobarbital	Nembutal†
Butabarbital	Butisol‡
Phenobarbital	Luminal*
Histamine antagonist sedatives	
Hydroxyzine	Atarax, Vistaril
Miscellaneous hypnotics	
Glutethimide	Doriden‡
Methyprylon	Noludar‡
Chloral hydrate	Noctec*
SKELETAL MUSCLE RELAXANTS	
Carisoprodol	Soma
Carisoprodol/aspirin	Soma Compound
Chlorzoxazone	Parafon, Parafon Forte
Metaxalone	Skelaxin
Methocarbamol	Robaxin
Methocarbamol/aspirin	Robaxisal
Orphenadrine	Norflex
Cyclobenzaprine	Flexeril

*Controlled, Schedule IV.
†Controlled, Schedule II.
‡Controlled, Schedule III.

sleeping patterns can occur.[23] Alcohol should be avoided while taking these medications. An overdosage of hypnotic agents can lead to respiratory depression and death. These agents have been frequently used in suicide attempts, and therefore only small quantities should be prescribed at a time.

MUSCLE RELAXANTS

Skeletal muscle relaxants are indicated for pain and muscle spasm associated with acute musculoskeletal conditions (see Table 38–6). Four of these agents, carisoprodol, chlorzoxazone, metaxalone, and methocarbamol, work at the level of the spinal cord to inhibit multisynaptic neurons involved in producing and maintaining skeletal muscle spasm. These same four agents may also help increase mobility of the involved muscles. These agents may have a variety of side effects ranging from light-headedness, drowsiness, and dizziness to nausea, vomiting, and anorexia.

Another agent for muscle relaxation is orphenadrine citrate. This agent does not have direct relaxation effects on skeletal muscle. Instead, it acts in the brainstem or on motor centers of the cerebrum to block facilitory function through an anticholinergic action. The side effects associated with the use of orphenadrine are a result of this anticholinergic action and include dry mouth, urinary retention, tachycardia, and palpitations.

A final agent in the class of skeletal muscle relaxants is cyclobenzaprine. This agent acts at the level of the brainstem to decrease motor activity, thereby decreasing muscle spasm, but without interfering with muscle function. This agent also has some anticholinergic side effects such as dry mouth along with drowsiness and dizziness.[31] All patients prescribed a muscle relaxant must be advised of the sedative properties and advised against the use of alcohol while receiving this therapy.

KERATOLYTIC AGENTS

Keratolytics are used to mechanically remove epidermal cells. These medicinal products are frequently used in the podiatric office. All preparations consist of salicylic acid in varying concentrations as the active ingredient (Table 38–7). Mild concentrations of salicylic acid may be used in the removal of hyperkeratotic skin, verrucae, and psoriasis. Stronger concentrations should only be used on verrucae, and contact with other tissue should be avoided. Keratolytics, especially the stronger agents, are contraindicated in diabetic patients or patients with peripheral vascular disease.[8]

TABLE 38–7.
Keratolytic Agents and Wound Debriders

Generic	Tradename
MILD KERATOLYTICS	
Salicylic acid, 6%	Keralyt Gel, Hydrisalic Acid
STRONG KERATOLYTICS	
Salicylic acid, 17%	Occlusal Solution
Salicylic acid, 26%	Occlusal HP Solution
Salicylic acid, 16.7%, and lactic acid, 16.7%	Duofilm, Salactic Film
WOUND DEBRIDERS	
Dextran beads	Debrisan
Collagenase	Santyl
Sutilains	Travase
Trypsin	Granulex
Fibrinolysin/ deoxyribonuclease	Elase

DEBRIDING AGENTS

Wound debriders are used to speed the healing process of ulcers, traumatic and surgical wounds, and burns (see Table 38–7). Wounds do not heal well in the presence of tissue debris or exudate. It is therefore beneficial to mechanically or chemically debride the wound.

Wound debriders are routinely used in the podiatric practice and are occasionally prescribed to be used on an outpatient basis. One such method of debridement is with the use of hydrophilic beads of dextran that absorb exudates, plasma proteins, fibrinogen, and bacteria. Another method is the use of proteolytic enzymes. These act to dissolve protein, exudate, and other debris. These proteolytic enzymes are usually applied to an already-cleaned, affected area. These enzymatic agents are pH sensitive, and caution must be used so as not to follow their use with heavy metal irrigations such as Borrow's solution or antiseptics containing iodine (Betadine) or silver.[32]

CORTICOSTEROIDS

Another class of medicinal agents used in the podiatric office is the corticosteroids (Table 38–8).

TABLE 38–8.
Corticosteroids

Generic	Tradename
ORAL AND INJECTABLE GLUCOCORTICOIDS	
Betamethasone	Celestone
Dexamethasone	Decadron, Hexadrol
Hydrocortisone	Solu-Cortef, Hydrocortone
Methylprednisolone	Medrol, Solu-Medrol
Prednisolone	Delta-Cortef, Meticortelone
Prednisone	Deltasone, Meticorten, Orasone
Triamcinolone	Aristocort, Kenacort, Kenalog
TOPICAL GLUCOCORTICOIDS	
Alclometasone	Aclovate
Amcinonide	Cyclocort
Betamethasone	Diprolene, Diprosone, Valisone
Clobetasol	Temovate
Desonide	Tridesilon
Desoximetasone	Topicort
Fluocinonide	Lidex
Halcinonide	Halog
Hydrocortisone	Hytone, Lanacort,* Cortaid,* Caldecort*
Triamcinolone	Aristocort, Kenalog

*Over the counter.

Corticosteroids are natural hormones produced by the body in the adrenal glands. Mineralocorticoids and glucocorticoids are both included in the term *corticosteroids.* Mineralocorticoids mainly affect fluid and electrolyte balance in the kidney, thereby maintaining blood volume and blood pressure. These agents are not utilized in the practice of podiatric medicine. Glucocorticoids act throughout the entire body and exert their effect on metabolism to maintain blood sugar levels, inhibit inflammation, and suppress the immune response. Glucocorticoids are used in podiatric medicine for their potent anti-inflammatory action. They may be utilized in rheumatic disorders such as rheumatoid arthritis, psoriatic arthritis, gout, and bursitis. Glucocorticoids may also be utilized in collagen diseases like systemic lupus erythematosus and dermatologic conditions ranging from contact dermatitis to erythema multiforme.[33]

Many synthetic glucocorticoids (commonly called steroids) are available in oral, topical, and injectable dosage forms. All three types of dosage forms are used in podiatry. Whenever the therapeutic use of a glucocorticoid agent is contemplated, the benefits vs. the potential risks must be evaluated. It must also be realized that these agents only treat the symptoms, or suppress the symptoms and are not curative. These drugs are very potent and can have many toxic effects. Toxic effects can result from too rapid withdrawal and from continued use of large doses. Acute adrenal insufficiency results from too rapid withdrawal of glucocorticoids after prolonged therapy. Toxic effects resulting from prolonged therapy at high doses include muscle wasting, abnormal fat distribution causing "moon face" or "buffalo hump," edema, hirsutism, thinning of skin and hair, infertility, striae, osteoporosis, and peptic ulcer formation.[34]

Due to the serious potential problems associated with the use of glucocorticoids, special consideration must be given to the manner in which this therapy is prescribed. First, these agents should only be used after a safer therapy for the same indication has been considered, such as an NSAID. Second, if the condition is dermatologic in origin, then a topical steroid therapy might be attempted. Topical glucocorticoids are generally safer than the oral or injectable dosage forms, but they too are absorbed systemically and can produce the same toxic effects.[34]

The lowest possible therapeutic dose must be used when prescribing an oral regimen, and then an alternate day therapy or a tapering-dose therapy must also be utilized. The alternate-day therapy consists of a double dosage on one day and then no drug on the following day. This every-other-day therapy allows for the re-establishment of a more normal hormone activity on the "off"-steroid day. The alternate-day therapy should only be instituted after the condition being treated has been controlled with daily-dose therapy.[35] The tapering-dose therapy consists of a reduction in dose each day, or every few days, until the chosen end of therapy. The rate at which the dosage should be decreased and the length of time required to taper the dose vary with the drug, its dosage, and the duration of its use. This therapy prevents an abrupt withdrawal that may cause a life-threatening acute adrenal insufficiency.[36]

Glucocorticoid drugs have many drug interactions. Since glucocorticoids cause sodium and fluid retention, they can also inhibit the diuresis and the antihypertensive effects of diuretics. Another interaction is an increased tendency for gastric ulceration when taken concurrently with other ulcerogenic drugs because glucocorticoids have ulcerogenic potential. The use of such a combination must be questioned and thoroughly evaluated, and patients receiving such combinations should be watched closely.[27]

LOCAL ANESTHETIC AGENTS

The next class of drugs, local anesthetics, is limited to office use and not prescribed for the patient (Table 38–9). Local anesthetic agents work by preventing the generation and conduction of nerve impulses. This class of drugs is used to produce a loss of sensation in a specific area of the body without a loss of consciousness. Local anesthetic drugs are used every day in podiatric practice for minor and major surgical procedures, joint manipulations, and postoperative pain management. There are two types of local anesthetics classed by their chemical structure, the ester group and the amide group.

The ester group of local anesthetics are metabolized by an enzyme in the blood and therefore have a short duration of action. The esters are metabolized to PABA, which is an allergen to some patients. If a patient claims to have an allergy to PABA (found in many sunscreens) or to local anesthetics, then an agent from the amide group of local anesthetics should be administered. The amides are metabolized in the liver and therefore generally have a longer duration of action.[37] The amide agents have a lesser likelihood of hypersensitivity reactions than the ester agents do. The amide agents contain preservatives in the multiple-dose vials that may be responsible for an allergic reaction.[38]

Desirable characteristics of a local anesthetic include low systemic toxicity, short onset time, sufficient duration of action for the procedure, and anesthetic action confined to nerve tissue in the desired location. An agent often added to local anesthetics to help achieve some of these ideal characteristics is epinephrine. Epinephrine acts as a vasoconstrictor to minimize the systemic spread, slow metabolism of the anesthetic to increase the duration, and aid in keeping the anesthetic localized.[39] Side effects of local anesthetic agents are minimal if used correctly, but nausea, vomiting, tachycardia, and syncope can occur.[23] Toxic reactions can be avoided if maximum doses and proper administration techniques are observed.

TABLE 38–9.
Local Anesthetics and Antidiabetic Agents

Generic	Tradename
ESTER GROUP LOCAL ANESTHETICS	
Procaine	Novocain
Tetracaine	Pontocaine
AMIDE GROUP LOCAL ANESTHETICS	
Lidocaine	Xylocaine
Bupivicaine	Marcaine, Sensorcaine
Etidocaine	Duranest
Mepivacaine	Carbocaine
Prilocaine	Citanest
ANTIDIABETIC AGENTS	
Sulfonylureas	
Acetohexamide	Dymelor
Chlorpropamide	Diabinase
Tolazamide	Tolinase
Tolbutamide	Orinase
Glyburide	Micronase, Diabeta
Glipizide	Glucotrol

ANTIDIABETIC AGENTS

The final class of drugs is neither used in the podiatry office nor routinely prescribed by the podiatric physician. This class, the antidiabetic drugs, must be familiar to the assistant because the diabetic patient is an important aspect in the practice of podiatric medicine. The antidiabetic class of drugs includes insulin and sulfonylureas (see Table 38–9). Insulin is indicated for use in patients with the inability to manufacture and secrete endogenous insulin. Insulin therapy acts as a substitute for the patient's deficient natural insulin. It is given subcutaneously once or twice daily. The sulfonylureas, also called oral hypoglycemics, are indicated for the patient whose capacity to secrete insulin from the pancreas is only partially impaired. Sulfonylureas act by stimulating the release of natural insulin from the pancreas.

THE PRESCRIPTION

The prescription is an extension of each physician's health care plan for the patient. Prescriptions are a physician's orders for the medications that he feels are beneficial and necessary in the treatment of the patient. The podiatric physician must also feel that these medications can be administered properly and safely by the patient or his guardian without medical supervision. Prescriptions from the podiatric physician may also be orders for physical therapy, various braces, orthotic devices, and shoe gear. These are beyond the scope of this chapter.

A prescription is constructed of many different components, each giving vital information to the pharmacist who ultimately relays selected parts of this information to the patient (Fig 38–1). The first component part of the prescription is the pa-

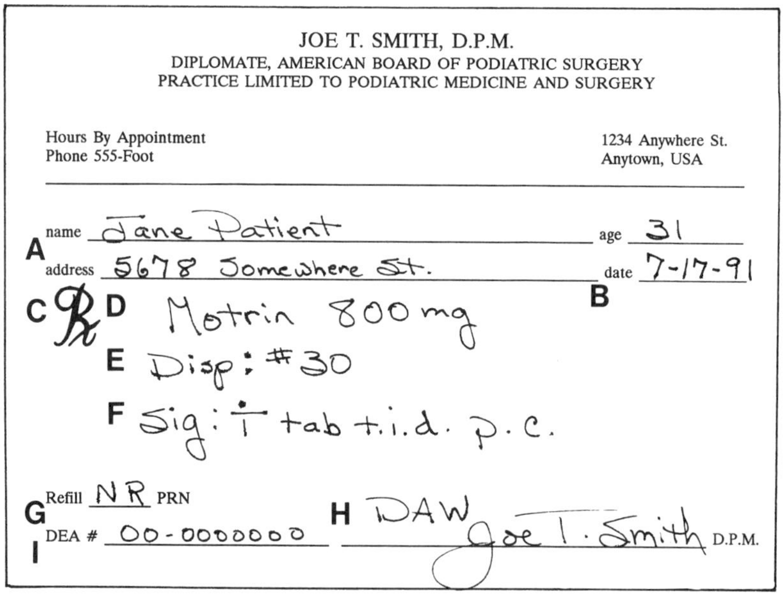
JOE T. SMITH, D.P.M.
DIPLOMATE, AMERICAN BOARD OF PODIATRIC SURGERY
PRACTICE LIMITED TO PODIATRIC MEDICINE AND SURGERY

Hours By Appointment
Phone 555-Foot

1234 Anywhere St.
Anytown, USA

A name Jane Patient age 31
address 5678 Somewhere St. date 7-17-91 B

C ℞ D Motrin 800 mg
E Disp: #30
F Sig: ī tab t.i.d. p.c.

G Refill NR PRN
I DEA # 00-0000000
H DAW Joe T. Smith D.P.M.

FIG 38–1.
The components of a prescription. **A,** patient information; **B,** date written; **C,** superscription; **D,** inscription; **E,** subscription; **F,** signatura; **G,** refill information; **H,** substitution information; **I,** physician's DEA number and signature.

tient information. The patient's name on each written prescription is an absolute necessity. The patient's address is required in many states, especially if the prescription is written for a controlled or scheduled substance. The patient's age is usually not required if the prescription is for an adult, but if written for an infant, child, or a geriatric patient, age is very important and offers the pharmacist a means of double checking the prescribed dose, strength, and medication.

The next part of the prescription is the date written. This is important since many states limit the life of a written prescription according to the date written. Other states limit the life of a prescription according to the first date actually filled. Nonscheduled medications generally have a life of 1 year, and scheduled medications, Class II through V, have a life of only 6 months.

The next four components make up the heart of the prescription and include the superscription, inscription, subscription, and signatura. The superscription is the abbreviation "Rx," which stands for recipe and is Latin for "take thou"; often this may be preprinted on the prescription blank. Following the superscription is the inscription, which includes the name and strength or dosage of each medicinal agent. Generally only one agent is written per prescription blank, unless a compounded prescription, one consisting of two or more ingredients that must be prepared by the pharmacist, is prescribed. Below the inscription is the subscription, which are directions to the pharmacist. Such directions might include "dispense 30 tablets" or "prepare an ointment of. . . ." The quantity of medication is included in the subscription. If the prescription is written for a controlled or scheduled medication, the quantity should be written numerically, followed by either Roman numerals or spelling out of the numbers, enclosed in parentheses. Below the subscription on the prescription blank is the signatura, which is abbreviated "Sig" and means in Latin, to write. The signatura are instructions for the patient that are necessary for self-administration; the pharmacist will include these on the label of the dispensing container. For example, the signatura might include such patient instructions as, "i cap q8h or t.i.d."

The last three components of the prescription are the refill information, substitution information, and the prescriber's signature and proper Drug Enforcement Agency (DEA) registration number. The refill information is generally preprinted, and the physician or assistant writing the prescription simply fills in a number if the physician desires for the patient to have refills. If the physician does not desire a refill on a particular medication, the word "no" or the letters "NR" for no refill should be written in the blank provided. The number 0 can easily be altered to another number or another digit inserted in front. A blank space at the refill information allows the patient to write a number of refills. The word "no" and the letters NR are much more difficult to alter.

The substitution information varies greatly from state to state. If the physician desires the brand name of a particular medication over the generic form, he must so indicate according to the

TABLE 38–10.
Prescription Abbreviations

aa	of each	p.c.	after meals
a	before	p.o.	by mouth
a.c.	before meals	p.r.n.	as needed, when required
ad lib	as much as wanted	q.s.a.d.	a sufficient amount, up to
b.i.d.	twice daily	q.d.	every day
c	with	q.h.	every hour
caps	capsules	q.4.h.	every 4 hours
g	gram	q.i.d.	4 times a day
gr	grain	q.o.d.	every other day
gtt	drop	ss	one half
h	hour	s	without
h.s.	hour of sleep, at bedtime	stat	now, immediately
M.	mix	tabs	tablets
No.	number	t.i.d.	3 times a day
oz.	ounce	tinct.	tincture
p	after	ung.	ointment

specific laws of his practicing state. Substitution laws may vary, with some states requiring only the initials DAW (dispense as written), to the words "medically necessary" in the physician's own handwriting and not preprinted or stamped being required by state law.

The physician's signature and DEA registration number are generally placed last on the prescription blank. If the podiatric medical assistant writes the prescription, be sure that the podiatric physician signs it afterward and provides a final check. If the physician's name is not preprinted on the prescription blank, the physician should also print his name legibly underneath the signature. If a scheduled medication is prescribed, the physician's DEA registration number must be on the prescription. It is the physician's personal preference as to whether the DEA registration number be preprinted on the prescription blank or whether he must write it for each scheduled medication he prescribes.[40]

Prescription abbreviations are generally used in the signatura component of the prescription. The pharmacist, once presented with the written prescription, then "translates" these abbreviations into everyday terminology as the patient's instructions on the label of the dispensing container. It is important for the physician to use "accepted" abbreviations so that the relay of information from the physician to pharmacist to patient is not lost or altered in the "translation" process. Some of the standard prescription abbreviations are shown in Table 38–10.

This chapter presents a basic pharmacology of the majority of classes of drugs seen in podiatric medicine. With a basic knowledge of pharmacology as well as an understanding of the prescription form and its contents, the podiatric medical assistant will develop a greater appreciation for the medical treatment of podiatric conditions and diseases. The assistant will then become a more active participant in the patient's treatment and well-being.

REFERENCES

1. Katzung BG: Introduction, in Katzung BG (ed): *Basic and Clinical Pharmacology.* San Mateo, Calif, Appleton & Lange, 1989, p 1.
2. Benet LZ, Sheiner LB: Introduction, in Goodman LS, Gilman A, Rall TW, et al (eds): *The Pharmacological Basis of Therapeutics.* New York, Macmillan Publishing Co Inc, 1985, p 1.
3. Spencer RT: Major antimicrobial drugs, in Spencer RT, Nichols LW, Lipkin GB, et al (eds): *Clinical Pharmacology and Nursing Management.* Philadelphia, JB Lippincott, 1989, pp 201–225.
4. Jawetz E: Aminoglycosides and polymyxins, in Katzung BG (ed): *Basic and Clinical Pharmacology.* San Mateo, Calif, Appleton & Lange, 1989, p 571.
5. Sande MA, Mandell GL: Antimicrobial agents, in Goodman LS, Gilman A, Rall TW, et al (eds): *The Pharmacological Basis of Therapeutics.* New York, Macmillan Publishing Co Inc, 1985, pp 1072–1228.
6. Marcinko DE: *Protocol Manual for Podiatric Infections.* Nashville, Tenn, Podiatry Insurance Company of America, 1986, p 1.
7. LeFrock JL: Use of ciprofloxacin in podiatric medicine. *J Am Podiatr Med Assoc* 1989; 79:497–499.
8. *Physicians' Desk Reference,* ed 44. Oradell, NJ, Medical Economics Company, 1990, pp 999, 2057.
9. Corey SV: Oral antibiotics, in DiNapoli DR (ed): *Reconstructive Surgery of the Foot and Leg: Update 90.* Tucker, Ga, Podiatry Institute Publishing Co, 1990, p 103.
10. Harvey SC: Antiseptics and disinfectants; fungi-

cides; ectoparasiticides, in Goodman LS, Gilman A, Rall TW, (eds): *The Pharmacological Basis of Therapeutics.* New York, Macmillan Publishing Co Inc, 1985, pp 964–966.
11. Hamilton EMN, Whitney EN, Sizer FS: *Nutrition: Concepts and Controversies.* St Paul, Minn, West, 1985, pp 291–293.
12. Spencer RT: Drugs used to treat rickettsiae, protozoa, helminths, and ectoparasites, in Spencer RT, Nichols LW, Lipkin GB, et al (eds): *Clinical Pharmacology and Nursing Management.* Philadelphia, JB Lippincott, 1989, p 284.
13. Webster LT Jr: Drugs used in the chemotherapy of protozoal infections, in Goodman LS, Gilman A, Rall TW, et al (eds): *The Pharmacological Basis of Therapeutics.* New York, Macmillan Publishing Co Inc, 1985, p 1054.
14. Spencer RT: Drugs used to treat infections caused by viruses and fungi, in Spencer RT, Nichols LW, Lipkin GB, et al: (eds): *Clinical Pharmacology and Nursing Management.* Philadelphia, JB Lippincott, 1989, p 261.
15. Levy LA: Arthritis, in Levy LA, Hetherington VJ (eds): *Principles and Practice of Podiatric Medicine.* New York, Churchill Livingstone Inc, 1990, pp 371–372.
16. Flower RJ, Moncada S, Vane JR: Drug therapy of inflammation, in Goodman LS, Gilman A, Rall TW, et al (eds): *The Pharmacological Basis of Therapeutics.* New York, Macmillan Publishing Co Inc, 1985, pp 680–709.
17. Douglas WW: Histamine and 5-hydroxytryptamine (serotonin) and their antagonists, in Goodman LS, Gilman A, Rall TW, et al (eds): *The Pharmacological Basis of Therapeutics.* New York, Macmillan Publishing Co Inc, 1985, pp 620–624.
18. Simonsmeier LM, Fink JL III: Laws governing pharmacy, in Osol A, Chase GD, Gennaro AR, et al (eds): *Remington's Pharmaceutical Sciences.* Easton, Penn, Mack Printing, 1980, pp 1858–1859.
19. Baldessarini RJ: Drugs and the Treatment of Psychiatric Disorders, in Goodman LS, Gilman A, Rall TW, (eds): *The Pharmacological Basis of Therapeutics.* New York, Macmillan Publishing Co Inc, 1985, pp 436–437.
20. Peterson PK, Dahl MV: *Dermatologic Manifestations of Infectious Diseases.* Kalamazoo, Mich, Upjohn, 1987, p 40.
21. Rall TW: Central nervous system stimulants, in Goodman LS, Gilman A, Rall TW, et al: (eds): *The Pharmocological Basis of Therapeutics.* New York, Macmillan Publishing Co Inc, 1985, pp 590–598.
22. Olin BR: *Facts and Comparisons.* Philadelphia, JB Lippincott, 1990, p 89.
23. Spencer RT: Central nervous system depressants, in Spencer RT, Nichols LW, Lipkin GB, et al (eds): *Clinical Pharmacology and Nursing Management.* Philadelphia, JB Lippincott, 1989, pp 437–463.
24. Nichols LW: Anti-inflammatory and related agents, in Spencer RT, Nichols LW, Lipkin GB, et al (eds): *Clinical Pharmacology and Nursing Management.* Philadelphia, JB Lippincott, 1989, pp 318–335.
25. Dahl SL, Katcher BS: Rheumatic diseases, in Katcher BS, Young LY, Koda-Kimble MA (eds): *Applied Therapeutics: The Clinical Use of Drugs.* Spokane, Wash, Applied Therapeutics, 1983, p 1421.
26. Littlefield LC: Fever, in Katcher BS, Young LY, Koda-Kimble MA (eds): *Applied Therapeutics: The Clinical Use of Drugs.* Spokane, Wash, Applied Therapeutics, 1983, pp 79–80.
27. Hansten PD: *Drug Interactions.* Philadelphia, Lea & Febiger, 1985, pp 94–321.
28. Evens RP, DuBe J: Pain, in Katcher BS, Young LY, Koda-Kimble MA (eds): *Applied Therapeutics: The Clinical Use of Drugs.* Spokane, Wash, Applied Therapeutics, 1983, pp 60–61.
29. Bennett RW: Treatment strategies for osteo and rheumatoid arthritis. *US Pharmacist* 1990; 6:37.
30. Edelson JT, Tosteson AN: Cost-effectiveness of misoprostol for prophylaxis against nonsteroidal anti-inflammatory drug–induced gastrointestinal tract bleeding. *JAMA* 1990; 264:41–47.
31. Nichols LW: Drugs affecting the musculoskeletal system: Skeletal muscle relaxants and antispastic agents, in Spencer RT, Nichols LW, Lipkin GB, et al (eds): *Clinical Pharmacology and Nursing Management.* Philadelphia, JB Lippincott, 1989, pp 897–901.
32. Spencer RT: Agents used in debridement of wounds, in Spencer RT, Nichols LW, Lipkin GB, et al (eds): *Clinical Pharmacology and Nursing Management.* Philadelphia, JB Lippincott, 1989, pp 311–312.
33. Goldfien A: Adrenocorticosteroid and adrenocortical antagonists, in Katzung BG (ed): *Basic and Clinical Pharmacology.* San Mateo, Calif, Appleton & Lange, 1989, p 485.
34. Haynes RC, Murad F: Adrenocorticotropic hormone: adrenocortical steroids and their synthetic analogs; inhibitors of adrenocortical steroid biosynthesis, in Goodman LS, Gilman A, Rall TW, et al (eds): *The Pharmacological Basis of Therapeutics.* New York, Macmillan Publishing Co Inc, 1985, pp 1475–1483.
35. Kishi DT: Disorders of the adrenals, in Katcher BS, Young LY, Koda-Kimble MA (eds): *Applied Therapeutics: The Clinical Use of Drugs.* Spokane, Wash, Applied Therapeutics, 1983, pp 1282–1283.
36. Spencer RT: Steroid hormones and their antagonists, in Spencer RT, Nichols LW, Lipkin GB, et al (eds): *Clinical Pharmacology and Nursing Management.* Philadelphia, JB Lippincott, 1989, p 722.
37. Hondeghem LM, Miller RD: Local anesthetics, in Katzung BG (ed): *Basic and Clinical Pharmacology.* San Mateo, Calif, Appleton & Lange, 1989, pp 317–321.
38. Duncan GS: Regional and local anesthesia, in Levy LA, Hetherington VJ (eds): *Principles and Practice of Podiatric Medicine.* New York, Churchill Livingston Inc, 1990, p 799.
39. Ritchie JM, Greene NM: Local anesthetics, in Goodman LS, Gilman A, Rall TW, et al (eds): *The Pharmacological Basis of Therapeutics.* New York, Macmillan Publishing Co Inc, 1985, p 313.
40. Ansel HC: The prescription, in Osol A (ed): *Remington's Pharmaceutical Sciences.* Easton, Penn, Mack Publishing Co, 1980, pp 1715–1720.

APPENDIX 38–1.
Manufacturer References

Manufacturer	Drug
Abbott Laboratories Abbott Park, IL 60064	Ery-tab, PCE, E.E.S., EryPed, Erythrocin Stearate, Tranxene, Nembutal
Astra Pharmaceutical Products Westboro, MA 01581	Xylocaine, Sensorcaine, Duranest, Citanest
Beecham Laboratories Bristol, TN 37620	Amoxil, Augmentin, Bactocill, Anexsia
Boots Pharmaceuticals, Inc. Shreveport, LA 71106	Lopurin, Zoprin, Rufen
Bristol Laboratories Evansville, IN 47721	Polycillin, Polymox, Prostaphlin, Dynapen, Ultracef, Bufferin, Excedrin, Datril, Nuprin
Burroughs Wellcome Co. Research Triangle Park, NC 27709	Neosporin, Septra, Zyloprim, Empirin, Empirin with Codeine
Carnrick Labs, Inc. Cedar Knolls, NJ 07927	Skelaxin
Combes, Inc. White Plains, NY 10604	Lanacort
Curatek Pharmaceuticals Elk Grove Village, IL 60007	Metrogel
Dermik Laboratories, Inc. Blue Bell, PA 19422	Hytone
Dista Products Company Indianapolis, IN 46285	Keflex, Ilosone, Nalfon
Du Pont Pharmaceuticals, Inc. Manati, PR 00701	Hycodan, Numorphan, Percodan, Percocet, Coumadin
Fisons Corporation Bedford, MA 01730	Caldecort
Flint Laboratories, Inc. Deerfield, IL 60015	Travase
Geigy Pharmaceuticals Ardsley, NY 10502	Butazolidin, Voltaren
Genderm Corporation Northbrook, IL 60062	Occlusal, Occlusal HP
Glaxo Inc. Research Park, NC 27709	Ceftin, Zantac, Aclovate, Temovate
Glenbrook Laboratories New York, NY 10016	Bayer, Panadol
Herbert Laboratories Irvine, CA 92715	Naftin
Dow B. Hickman, Inc. Sugar Land, TX 77487	Granulex
Hoechst-Roussel Pharmaceuticals, Inc. Somerville, NJ 08876	Loprox, Trental, Topicort, Diabeta
Janssen Pharmaceutica, Inc. Piscataway, NJ 08854	Nizoral
Johnson & Johnson Patient Care New Brunswick, NJ 08903	Debrisan
Knoll Pharmaceuticals Whippany, NJ 07981	Dilaudid, Vicodin, Santyl
Kramer Pharmacal, Inc. Miami, FL 33174	Fungi-Nail
Lederle Laboratories Wayne, NJ 07470	Suprax, Achromycin, Minocin, Nilstat, Aristocort, Cyclocort
Eli Lilly and Company Indianapolis, IN 46285	V-cillin K, Ceclor, Dolophine, Darvon, Darvon-Compound, Darvocet, Dymelor
Marion Laboratories, Inc. Kansas City, MO 64137	Silvadene
McNeil Pharmaceutical Spring House, PA 19477	Tylenol, Tylenol with Codeine, Tolectin, Medipren, Parafon,
Mead Johnson Laboratories Evansville, IN 47721	Duricef, Tempra

(Continued.).

APPENDIX 38–1 (cont.).

Manufacturer	Drug
Merck, Sharp & Dohme West Point, PA 19486	Benemid, Mintezol, Dolobid, Indocin, Clinoril, Flexeril, Decadron, Hydrocortone
Merrel Dow Pharmaceuticals, Inc. Cincinnati, OH 45215	Rifadin
Miles, Inc., Pharmaceutical Division West Haven, CT 06516	Cipro, Mycelex, Alka-Seltzer, Tridesilon
Organon, Inc. West Orange, NJ 07052	Hexadrol
Ortho Pharmaceutical Corp. Raritan, NJ 08869	Monistat-Derm, Micatin, Spectazole, Grifulvin V
Parke-Davis Morris Plains, NJ 07950	Amcill, ERYC, Benadryl, Meclomen, Elase, Doryx
Pedinol Pharmacal, Inc. Farmingdale, NY 11735	Fungoid Tincture, Castellani Paint, Hydrisalic Acid, Salactic Film
Pfizer Laboratories Division New York, NY 10017	Vibramycin, Vistaril, Feldene, Diabinese
Princeton Pharmaceutical Products Princeton, NJ 08543	Halog
The Purdue Frederick Company Norwalk, CT 06856	Betadine, MS Contin, Trilisate
Reid-Rowell Marietta, GA 30062	Orasone
Riker Laboratories, Inc. St. Paul, MN 55144	Disalcid, Norflex
A.H. Robins Company Richmond, VA 23220	Phenaphen with Codeine, Robaxin, Robaxisal
Roche Laboratories Nutley, NJ 07110	Bactrim, Valium, Librium, Levo-Dromoran, Dalmane, Noludar
Roerig New York, NY 10017	Atarax, Glucotrol
Rorer Pharmaceutical Corp. Fort Washington, PA 19034	Ascriptin, Doriden
Ross Laboratories Columbus, OH 43216	Pediamycin
Russ Pharmaceuticals, Inc. Birmingham, AL 35216	Lortab
Sandoz Pharmaceuticals Corp. East Hanover, NJ 07936	Fiorinal, Fioricet, Fiorinal with Codeine, Restoril
Schering Corporation Kenilworth, NJ 07033	Garamycin, Lotrimin, Lotrimin AF, Tinactin, Fulvicin P/G, Celestone, Meticortelone, Meticorten, Diprolene, Diprosone, Valisone
Searle Pharmaceuticals, Inc. Chicago, IL 60680	Flagyl, Cytotec
Smith, Kline, and French Labs Philadelphia, PA 19101	Ecotrin, Tagamet
E.R. Squibb and Sons, Inc. Princeton, NJ 08543	Velocef, Sumycin, Mycostatin, Noctec, Kenacort, Kenalog
Stiefel Laboratories, Inc. Coral Gables, FL 33134	Duofilm
Stuart Pharmaceuticals Wilmington, DE 19897	Hibiclens
Syntex Laboratories, Inc. Palo Alto, CA 94303	Anaprox, Naprosyn, Lidex
The Upjohn Company Kalamazoo, MI 49001	E-Mycin, Xanax, Motrin, Motrin-IB, Ansaid, Halcion, Solu-Cortef, Medrol, Solu-Medrol, Delta-Cortef, Deltasone, Cortaid, Tolinase, Orinase, Micronase
Wallace Laboratories Cranbury, NJ 08512	Butisol, Soma, Soma Compound
Westwood Pharmaceuticals, Inc. Buffalo, NY 14213	Halotex, Keralyt
Whitehall Laboratories, Inc. New York, NY 10017	Anacin, Advil
Winthrop Pharmaceuticals New York, NY 10016	Sulfamylon, pHisoHex, Demerol, Luminal, Novocain, Pontocaine, Marcaine, Carbocaine
Wyeth Laboratories Philadelphia, PA 19101	Pen-Vee K, Omnipen, Pathocil, Ativan, Serax, Mepergan, Synalgos-DC, Orudis, Seconal

39

Office Emergencies

D. Scot Malay, D.P.M.
Laurence G. Rubin, D.P.M.

Office emergencies should not be a common occurrence; however, when they do arise, the patient requires prompt and thorough attention. The patient's life may depend on your response, and familiarity with specific protocols is necessary to ensure rapid and efficient execution of the procedures required to remedy the emergency at hand. Preparation, organization, and good communication within the office will make emergency situations easier to handle and more likely to result in a favorable outcome.

Emergency situations can often be avoided or more rapidly treated by knowing the patient's medical history and physical status. For example, an appropriate emergency response may be executed more rapidly by knowing that the diabetic patient being treated may lose consciousness secondary to hypoglycemia (low blood sugar) or that an epileptic may experience a seizure secondary to mild hypoxia (lack of oxygen) or local anesthetic overdosage. Proper patient education and preparation will often assist in avoiding potentially dangerous situations related to everyday office procedures and techniques. Essentially all routine procedures should be performed with standard precautionary measures such as aspirating for blood reflux (indicating intravascular positioning of the needle) while infiltrating local anesthetic solutions, avoiding the administration of medications to which the patient may be hypersensitive, and allowing the patient to recline in the Trendelenburg position (heart above the level of the head) while undergoing injection therapy or other potentially painful or anxiety-inducing treatment.

It is not uncommon for the podiatric assistant to be the first person to identify a potentially harmful or emergency situation in the office and to initiate the proper therapeutic protocol. It is therefore very important for all of the members of the office staff to know their distinct duties in response to the sudden and urgent occasion for action. It is important for office personnel to have a functional understanding of basic cardiac life support and other emergency techniques, equipment, and medications and that an overall emergency protocol be established and practiced by the entire staff. It is highly recommended that all office personnel be certified in basic cardiac life support, which consists primarily of airway management and cardiopulmonary resuscitation (CPR). Certification courses are regularly available at local hospitals and through a variety of organizations such as the American Heart Association and the American Red Cross. If only one person is on the scene of the emergency, that person should immediately call for help. If two people are on the scene together, one should stay with the patient, and the other should summon assistance. As soon as possible, the local emergency medical service should be notified so that the patient, once stabilized, can be transported to a hospital for continued care. It is useful to know the estimated time of arrival of the emergency medical service and the estimated time required to get the patient to the hospital emergency room. In certain office arrangements, it may be possible to organize an emergency response team consisting of multidisciplinary members, much like the "code team" at a hospital.

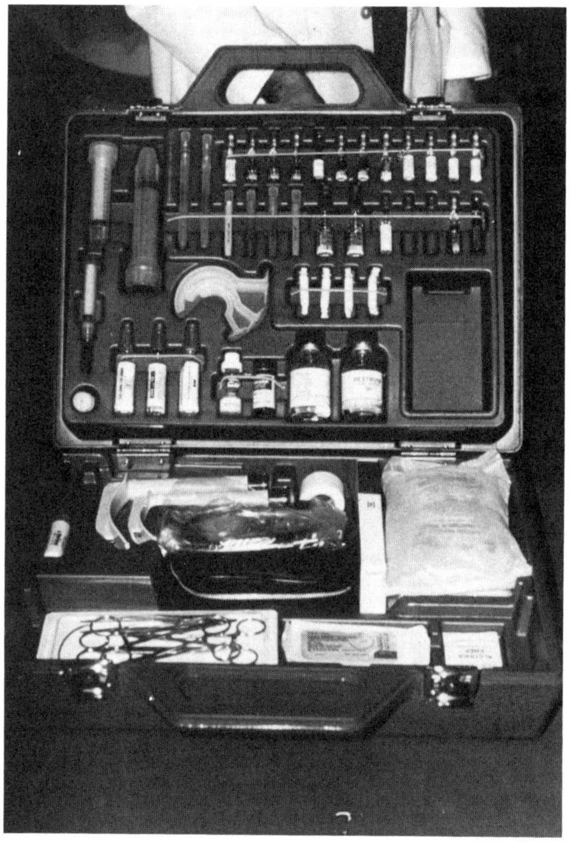

FIG 39–1.
Commercially available office emergency drug and equipment kit.

EMERGENCY EQUIPMENT AND MEDICATIONS

It is necessary to maintain and have available certain specialized equipment and medications in order to adequately respond to the wide variety of office emergencies that may arise. Certain items are considered essential, such as oxygen and epinephrine; however, the exact list of equipment and medications kept in any office should correlate with the practitioner's knowledge and experience using these agents. Administration of all emergency medications must be performed with caution because certain side effects can be devastating. Moreover, medications should be available in the proper dosages so that administration is not delayed. It is also important to have a written list of proper dosages for both adults and children (adult dosages are listed for most of the medications described in this text). Complete emergency kits are commercially available (Fig 39–1) and can be ordered with just basic components or loaded with a wide variety of supplies.

All emergency medications and equipment should be kept in a designated location and should be easily accessible and transportable to every other area of the office. Keep in mind that emergencies are not limited to treatment rooms but may occur in the waiting room, rest rooms, or business areas, as well as outside the office proper while still on the premises. Emergency supplies should be periodically checked at regular docu-

TABLE 39–1.
Recommended Emergency Equipment

Self-inflating resuscitation bag with clear mask (Fig 39–2)
Airways: oral, nasopharyngeal
Water-based lubricant for airways and tubes
Cricothyreotomy set (10–14 gauge lumen) (Fig 39–3)
Portable oxygen unit, mask, and nasal cannula (Fig 39–4)
Tongue blades (to retract the tongue and clear the airway)
Aspiration bulb or suction and catheters
Flashlight
Sphygmomanometer
Stethoscope
Paper bag
Tourniquet (rubber and pneumatic)
Alcohol swabs for cleansing the skin
Tape for securing intravenous lines and airways
Intravenous access and fluid administration sets (assorted catheters—including 16 gauge; syringes and butterfly needles; and tubing)

TABLE 39–2.
Recommended Emergency Medications

Oxygen
Intravenous fluids (normal saline or lactated Ringer's)
Aromatic spirits of ammonia ampules
Aqueous epinephrine (1:1,000 and 1:10,000 solutions)
Nitroglycerin (0.4- or 0.6-mg tablets)
Diazepam (10–20 mg)
Midazolam (5 mg)
Phenytoin (50 mg/mL in 2-mL ampules)
Diphenhydramine (25 mg injectable, 50 mg oral)
Dexamethasone phosphate (4 mg/mL)
Albuterol aerosol for oral inhalation
Naloxone (0.4 mg/mL in 1-mL ampules)
50% dextrose solution (ampule, D_{50})
Candy or juice
Epinephrine 1:1,000 (three 1-mL vials)

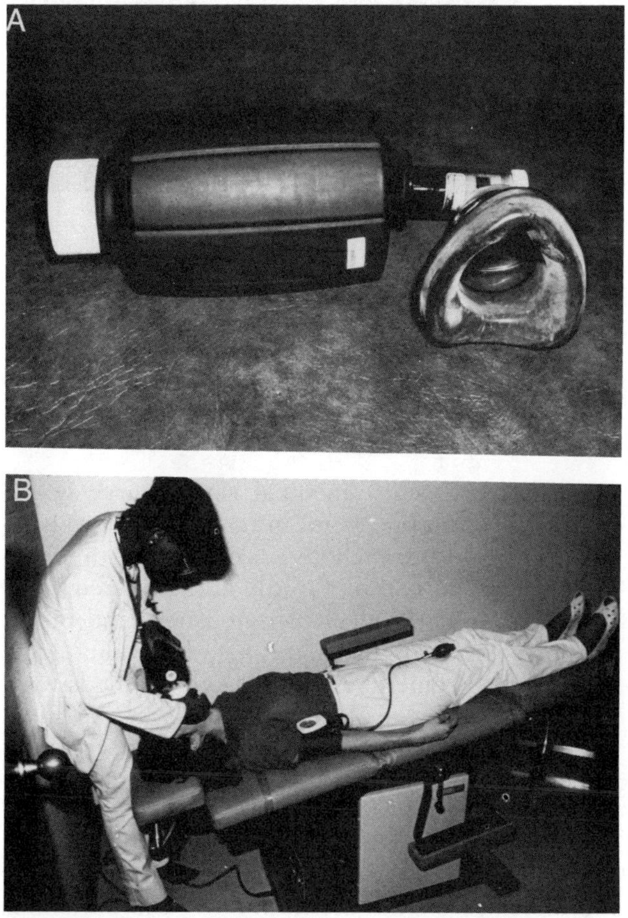

FIG 39–2.
A, a self-inflating resuscitation bag (modification of the Ambu bag) with a clear mask for emergency ventilation of the patient. **B,** depiction of the resuscitation bag in use. The mask is clear so that vomitus can be visualized and suctioned away by the rescuer.

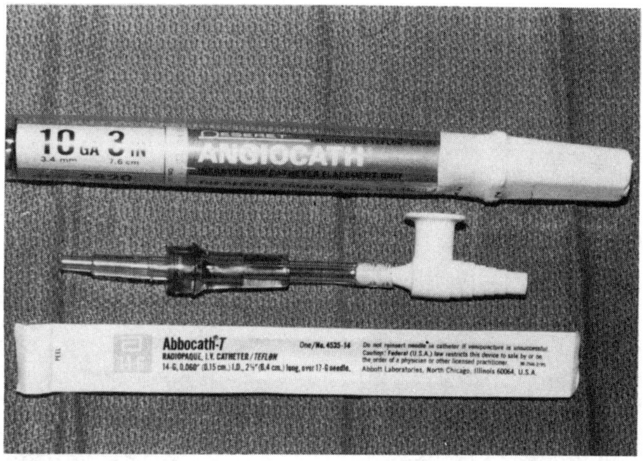

FIG 39–3.
Makeshift cricothyreotomy set for emergency airway management.

mented intervals to ensure that the equipment is in proper working order and that the shelf life of the medications has not expired. It is highly recommended that a detailed list of the equipment (Table 39–1), dosages and medications (Table 39–2), and basic procedures be kept readily available.

GENERAL RESPONSE AND ASSESSMENT

Once it has been determined that an office emergency is in progress, the patient's condition must be accurately evaluated and appropriate therapy initiated. If possible, all information pertaining to diagnostic and therapeutic measures should be recorded. It is particularly important to record the time of administration and dosages of medications given to the patient. Moreover, it is important to rapidly notify the local emergency medical service (ambulance) at the earliest possible moment, and the stabilized patient should almost always be transported to the emergency room as soon as possible. Many adverse reactions and emergency medical situations can develop into prolonged abnormal conditions, and the patient may require continued care in the emergency room or intensive care unit.

In any office emergency, basic life support is the highest priority and attention should be paid to the ABCs of CPR: *a*irway, *b*reathing, and *c*irculation.[1] The patient should be placed in the supine position against a hard surface, and constricting clothing should be loosened or removed. Vital signs must be measured and recorded, including

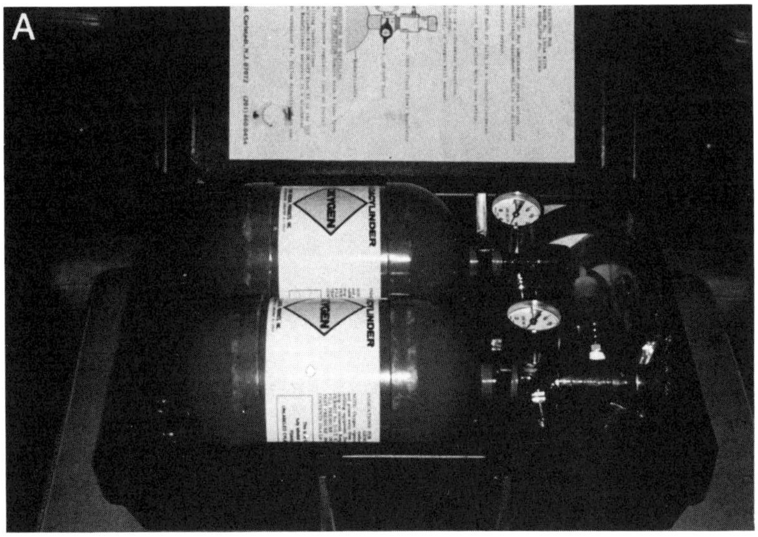

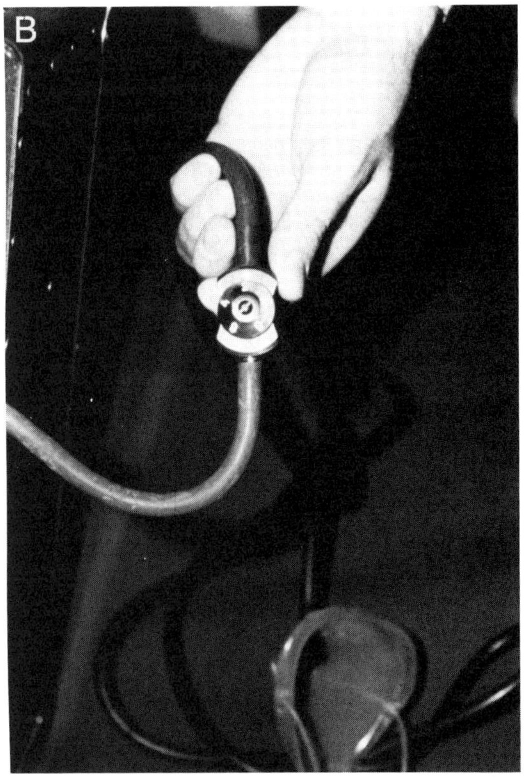

FIG 39–4.
A, oxygen tanks for office emergency use. **B,** oxygen supply hose with a regulator and clear face mask. In most office emergencies, oxygen should be administered at a rate of 6 to 8-L/min.

blood pressure, pulse, and respiration rates. Respirations can be evaluated by looking, listening, and feeling for the patient's breath or chest wall motion. Establishment of an airway[2] may be necessary if the patient is not breathing and is generally achieved upon proper head and neck positioning and removal of any foreign objects from the mouth or upper airway. The Heimlich maneuver or chest thrusts can be used to clear the airway of any persistent obstruction.[3]

If necessary, an artificial airway should be inserted by using either the oral, nasopharyngeal, or endotracheal methods. If the patient does not display spontaneous breathing after an airway has been established, then artificial respiration (rescue breathing) must be initiated and maintained at a rate of about one ventilation (breath) every 1 to 1.5 seconds. The patient's pulse should be determined by checking the radial, femoral, or carotid arteries. If a pulse cannot be palpated at any of these sites, then a Doppler ultrasound device can be used, if it is available, for more accurate assessment. If the pulse is absent, then manual cardiac massage should be performed in conjunction with rescue breathing (Table 39–3).[4, 5] It can be useful to apply transducers to the patient's chest and obtain an electrocardiogram; however, this is not typically available in most podiatric office settings

TABLE 39–3.
Rescue Breathing and Cardiac Massage

Number of Rescuers	Chest Compressions (80–100/min)	Ventilations (1–1.5 sec/Breath)
1	15	2
2	5	1

until the emergency medical service arrives. Finally, it is often beneficial in the emergency situation to obtain intravenous access so that medications and fluids can be rapidly administered.[6]

The patient's level of consciousness and pupillary response to light should also be evaluated. A good way to remember the various methods used to determine level of consciousness is the mnemonic AVPU: A—the patient is ***a***lert and oriented to person, place, and time; V—the patient only responds to ***v***erbal stimuli (able to react in some fashion to the examiner's voice); P—the patient only responds to ***p***ainful stimuli (firmly rubbing the knuckles on the sternum); U—the patient is ***u***nresponsive to any stimulus. A flashlight can be used to determine the pupillary response to light in an effort to rapidly assess the central nervous system. The pupil should constrict in response to light shown directly into the eye or indirectly by shining light into the opposite eye (consensual response). Failure to elicit reflex pupillary constriction in response to light shown into either eye of the unconscious patient is an ominous sign and generally indicates profound central nervous system hypoxia or injury.

COMMON OFFICE EMERGENCIES

Syncope

Syncope, or fainting, is perhaps the most common office emergency encountered in the typical podiatric practice. Fortunately, this is usually a benign situation that responds readily to appropriate therapeutic intervention and is easily preventable in most cases. The condition can be harmful to the patient, however, and prompt attention should be directed to determining the cause and rectifying the situation.

The most common form encountered in the office is vasovagal syncope and occurs secondary to a strong emotional response (e.g., anxiety or fear) and/or pain. In simple physiologic terms, this results in an automatic response by the nervous system that leads to overstimulation of the heart by the vagus nerve, which in turn decreases both the rate of cardiac contraction and the amount of blood pumped by the heart. This drop in cardiac output decreases blood flow to the brain, and transient cerebral ischemia ensues. In response to decreased cerebral oxygenation, the body automatically compensates by constricting blood vessels in the extremities, abdomen, and pelvis in an effort to shift blood flow to the brain. The same automatic response that causes peripheral blood vessels to constrict simultaneously stimulates the sweat glands in the skin. As a result, the patient feels cool and clammy. If cerebral hypoxia persists, the patient will eventually lose consciousness and typically fall to the ground. This generally places the heart at the same level as the brain, thereby making it easier for the heart to supply oxygenated blood to the brain and thus resulting in spontaneous recovery from syncope.

A good example of vasovagal syncope is illustrated by the very anxious patient undergoing injection therapy. This patient will commonly warn you that he is predisposed to fainting and often states that he "usually passes out when he gets a needle."

Other causes of syncope include metabolic disturbances such as hypoglycemia or organic brain lesions (defects in the actual brain tissue) caused by cerebral vascular disease or related to epilepsy.

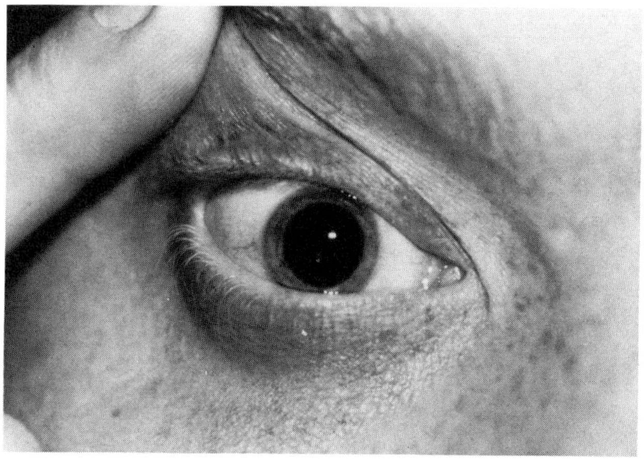

FIG 39–5.
Pupillary mydriasis (full dilation).

These disorders are not benign and require careful neurologic evaluation and treatment.

The signs and symptoms of syncope include pallor and diaphoresis, and the patient appears pale, cold, and clammy. The patient will often exhibit mydriasis (Fig 39–5), hypotension, and reflex tachycardia, followed by loss of consciousness. At this point the patient may fall to the ground and injure himself on hard or sharp objects. Less often, tremor and seizure will be seen if cerebral blood flow remains abnormally diminished. Generally, the patient will spontaneously regain consciousness once the brain is placed at a level equivalent to or below that of the heart. After regaining consciousness, the patient may complain of nausea and display residual anxiety.

Treatment consists of measures directed toward maximizing cerebral circulation and protecting the patient from injury related to falling against the floor or other hard objects. The patient should be placed in the supine position with his legs elevated (Fig 39–6). This is known as the Trendelenburg position and is a standard technique used whenever cerebral oxygenation is considered to be decreased. If the patient is just a little "lightheaded," sitting with the head between the legs is often all that is needed to enhance blood flow to the brain. All tight-fitting or constrictive clothing should be loosened or removed, and as always, a patent airway must be established and maintained throughout the entire incident. Moreover, the patient's head should be turned to the side so that any vomitus can be easily evacuated from the mouth without being aspirated into the upper respiratory system. Aspiration of gastric contents into the respiratory system can cause severe air-

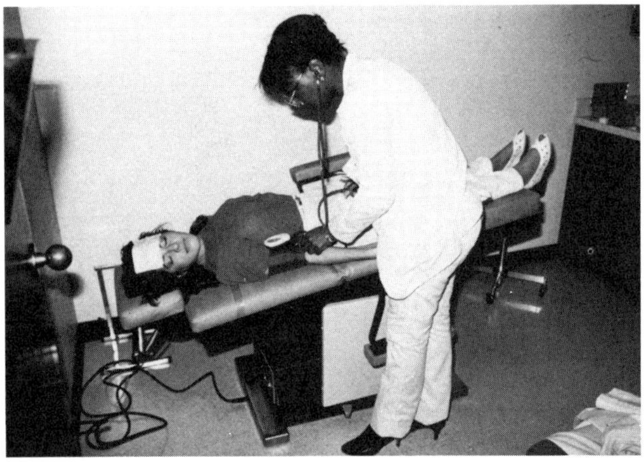

FIG 39–6.
The Trendelenburg position places the patient's heart above the level of the brain in an effort to maximize cerebral blood flow and oxygenation. This can be harmful to certain patients suffering from cardiac disease because the lower extremities are elevated above the heart, thereby increasing venous return to the heart and cardiac work load.

way occlusion, inflammation, and pneumonitis, thereby preventing effective respiration and requiring specific treatment and hospitalization.

Adjunctive measures include the administration of oxygen at 2 to 4 L/min via mask or nasal canula. Aromatic spirits of ammonia can also be used to help revive the victim because the vapor irritates the nasal mucosa, thereby stimulating the patient. Cool compresses such as a paper towel or a cloth moistened with cold water should be applied to the face and neck and are especially helpful in preventing syncope in the anxious patient. The patient should also be reassured that he is safe and that he has experienced a common problem that readily responds to simple treatment. Vital signs should be measured and recorded every few minutes until the patient has fully recovered. It is also important to provide the patient with privacy since he may be embarrassed by the event.

Hypersensitivity Reactions

Hypersensitivity reactions occur in a variety of forms and levels of severity ranging from mild skin rash to cardiovascular collapse and death.[7,8] The onset of the reaction is also variable and may occur immediately or several hours following introduction of an allergen, which is a foreign substance to which the individual's immune system is sensitive. The basic allergic or hypersensitivity reaction involves the introduction of a foreign substance to the immune system, such as a protein or molecular component of a drug. The foreign substance is termed an antigen and stimulates the production of antibodies that identify and neutralize the alien matter. In some instances, the foreign substance only becomes recognized as antigenic once it attaches to certain carrier proteins that already exist within the body. In this case, the foreign substance is known as a hapten, and it is the hapten-protein complex that is immunogenic and stimulates specific antibody production.

Antibodies circulate throughout the body and are the main components of the immune system responsible for recognizing antigens. Antibodies are also known as immunoglobulin, and IgE is primarily responsible for hypersensitivity reactions. Antibodies are produced by white blood cells in response to an initial exposure to an antigen, after which the body is said to be sensitized with respect to the specific foreign substance. Once produced, antibodies become situated along the outer membrane of a particular type of white blood cell known as the mast cell. Inside the mast cell are granules that contain a variety of biochemicals, most notably histamine. Upon exposure to antigen, the antibodies bind to the antigen, which in turn alters the mast cell and induces degranulation, or release of histamine from within the mast cell granules. Histamine is a very potent biochemical that can adversely interact with many tissues within the body and result in abnormal changes such as severe vasodilation, shift of fluid from within the blood vessels to the interstitial spaces outside of the vessels, profound swelling, constriction of the passages of the airway, and other potentially harmful responses that constitute the hypersensitivity reaction.

Initial exposure to an antigen does not necessarily result in a hypersensitivity reaction; however, subsequent exposure to the foreign substance, after enough antibody has been produced and stored within the tissues, can elicit a full-blown anaphylactic response. Anaphylaxis is the result of the body's immune system overreacting, or going "beyond protection," in response to the presence of an antigen. Certain antigens do not require previous exposure to elicit an adverse hypersensitivity or anaphylactoid reaction. Certain antibiotics, nonsteroidal anti-inflammatory drugs (NSAIDs), and other therapeutic agents have been known to effect anaphylactoid reactions occasionally resulting in the victim's death without these agents ever having been previously administered to the patient. It is important to realize that only a minute amount of antigen is required to elicit a hypersensitivity reaction, unlike a toxic reaction to a drug or chemical which usually requires substantial overdosage.

Clinically, the signs and symptoms of anaphylaxis and anaphylactoid reactions are identical, as are the emergency measures used to treat the patient having the hypersensitivity reaction. In most cases, an adverse allergic response can be avoided by ascertaining whether or not the patient relates any food or drug allergies that result in the development of a skin rash or difficulty in breathing.

Anaphylactic and anaphylactoid reactions can be manifested in varying degrees of severity ranging from skin rash to severe shock, and the clinical presentation often involves overlapping signs and symptoms. Proper treatment varies according to the signs and symptoms displayed by the patient.

Urticarial Rash

The mildest level of involvement is the urticarial rash (Fig 39–7), which presents as erythematous wheals or hives with associated pruritus (itching). This simply means that the skin appears red and swollen, perhaps with vesicles or even blisters, in conjunction with itching. The appearance is very similar to that of a severe sunburn. If the patient displays no evidence of shortness of breath or difficulty in breathing and the blood pressure and heart rate remain normal, then treatment of the urticarial rash should consist of withdrawing the suspected allergen in conjunction with the administration of appropriate medications. Allergen withdrawal may not always be possible, especially if the offending substance was ingested by or administered to the patient hours earlier. However, if the hypersensitivity reaction occurs during or soon after injection therapy, then infiltration of the offending agent should be stopped, or the injection site should be separated from further uptake into the systemic circulation by means of tourniquet application or subcutaneous infiltration of a vasoconstrictor such as 0.2 to 0.3 cc of 1:1,000 epinephrine in a ring around the injection site. Furthermore, diphenhydramine, 25 to 50 mg, should be administered orally or 50 mg injected intramuscularly if the patient cannot take oral medication. The patient should be observed and vital signs monitored until the rash and pruritus subside. Dexamethasone, 4 to 8 mg, can also be administered intramuscularly; however, this is not useful in the acute setting and is only recommended for its potentially beneficial effects that occur hours later should the reaction be severe and persistent. This is also a good time to obtain intravenous access (Fig 39–8) if this has not already been achieved. Should the hypersensitivity reaction progress and the patient develop significant hypotension, the vessels of the arms and legs will constrict and make it difficult to obtain peripheral intravenous access at a later time during the course of the reaction. The intravenous line can be maintained by slowly infusing lactated Ringer's solution or normal saline. If necessary,

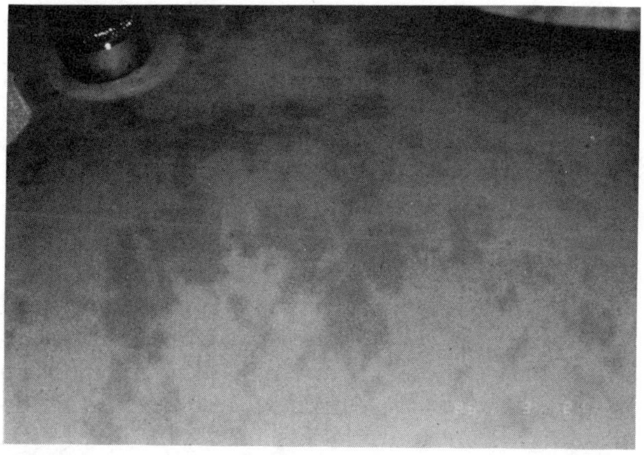

FIG 39–7.
Splotchy, irregular, erythematous (red) urticarial rash on the chest of a patient following antibiotic administration.

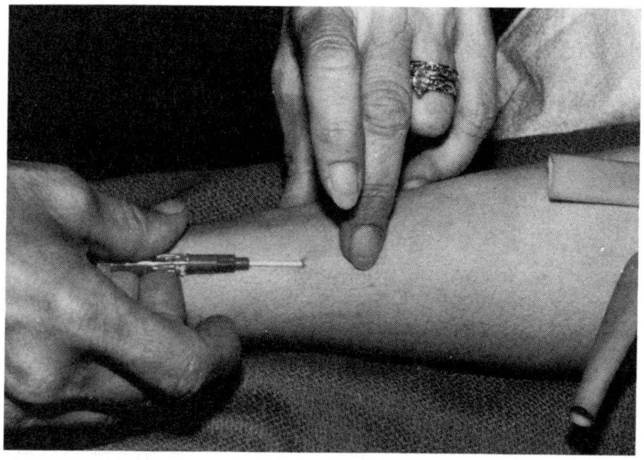

FIG 39–8.
Obtaining peripheral intravenous access in the forearm with an 18-gauge catheter.

the stabilized patient should be transported to the hospital for further monitoring and treatment.

Angioneurotic Edema

Angioneurotic edema represents the next level of severity of hypersensitivity reaction and presents as swelling of the mucus membranes that particularly affects the eyelids, cheeks, lips, pharynx, and larynx, generally in conjunction with an urticarial rash. Hoarseness and stridor may develop secondary to laryngeal edema and can also effect upper airway obstruction. Furthermore, wheezing may develop in response to lower airway edema and bronchospasm, and the patient may become cyanotic if respiration is significantly impaired. Treatment is similar to those measures used to counter an urticarial rash; however, administration of epinephrine in conjunction with higher dosages of diphenhydramine is recommended.

Epinephrine, 0.2 to 0.5 cc of a 1:1,000 solution (1 mg/mL), should be given subcutaneously every 5 to 15 minutes if the reaction is severe. Care must be taken to monitor the patient's blood pressure, heart rate, and respirations whenever epinephrine is administered, particularly in the elderly. This agent directly increases peripheral vasoconstriction, the heart rate, and the strength of cardiac contraction, and this results in increased blood pressure and cardiac output. These effects can be detrimental to any patient with ischemic heart disease and/or hypertension and may result in angina or myocardial infarction. Moreover, patients who have a history of cardiovascular disease may be regularly medicated with β-adrenergic blocking agents, are especially susceptible to the α-adrenergic stimulatory effects of epinephrine, and may experience profound peripheral vasoconstriction and an increased heart rate. Patients suffering from angioneurotic edema should also receive oxygen via mask or nasal cannula; diphenhydramine, 50 to 75 mg administered intramuscularly; and 8 mg of dexamethasone. Moreover, intravenous access should be established and maintained. Once stabilized, the patient should be transported to the hospital for further monitoring and treatment.

Asthmatic Attack

Occasionally, bronchospasm (lower airway constriction) and edema are the main clinicopathologic entities encountered in a hypersensitivity reaction. When this occurs, the patient is said to be suffering from an asthmatic attack. An asthmatic attack, however, need not necessarily be related to an allergic or hypersensitivity reaction caused by an extrinsic substance and may arise secondary to anxiety, fear, or other strong emotional events. Clinical examination of the patient suffering from an asthmatic attack reveals wheezing secondary to bronchospasm and dyspnea (difficulty in breathing), and an associated flush that progresses to cyanosis may develop. If the patient has a past history of asthma, he will probably recognize the onset of the reaction and counter the pathologic progression with the use of a prescription aerosol bronchodilator. Typically the patient will get into a comfortable position, loosen tight clothing, and take a puff or two on his inhaler.

If the attack is caused by an extrinsic substance, then treatment should consist of eliminating further exposure to the allergen and administration of epinephrine, 0.3 to 0.5 cc of a 1:1,000 mixture (1 mg/mL) given subcutaneously every 5 to 15 minutes up to three doses. Once again, epinephrine should be used with caution because it can increase the blood pressure and heart rate and result in angina. After administering the initial dose of epinephrine, an aerosol bronchodilator such as albuterol can also be administered if wheezing and bronchospasm persist. Oxygen should be delivered via mask or nasal cannula, and intravenous access should also be established and maintained. Once stabilized, the asthmatic patient should be transported to the hospital for further evaluation and treatment as necessary.

Anaphylactic Shock

Anaphylactic shock is a rapidly progressive, life-threatening malady that requires prompt recognition and immediate treatment. Symptoms generally appear between 1 and 30 minutes after exposure to the causative antigen. Anaphylaxis may result in the patient's death within 5 minutes of the onset of symptoms. The patient will usually experience pruritus, urticaria, and/or angioedema with a cutaneous flush and perioral and periorbital edema. Laryngospasm can effect stridor, and auscultation of the lungs reveals wheezing secondary to bronchospasm. Patients will often complain of light-headedness, weakness, and a sense of impending doom and may lose consciousness. Vital signs will usually demonstrate hypotension, tachycardia, and tachypnea.

The causative allergen must be immediately withdrawn, and definitive treatment is initiated as soon as possible. The patient should be placed into a supine or Trendelenburg position and the airway evaluated for patency and maintained. Airway management may require placement of an oral or nasopharyngeal device or the use of an endotracheal tube. Cardiopulmonary resuscitation may be required. Epinephrine is the drug of choice for anaphylactic shock, and 0.3 to 0.5 cc of a 1:1,000 mixture (1 mg/mL) should be administered subcutaneously every 15 minutes as needed. It is also important to obtain intravenous access as soon as possible and to administer lactated Ringer's solution or normal saline as rapidly as possible (wide open). Oxygen should be delivered via mask or nasal cannula at 6 L/min. Moreover, diphenhydramine should be administered at 25 mg intravenously or 50 mg intramuscularly in conjunction with 8 mg of dexamethasone intramuscularly. Vitals signs must be continuously monitored and the patient transported to the hospital as soon as possible.

Hyperventilation

Hyperventilation typically occurs in response to a high level of anxiety and is associated with rapid and shallow breathing. The combination of rapid and shallow breathing results in excessive loss of carbon dioxide, which in turn alters the body's acid-base equilibrium (pH). When excessive amounts of carbon dioxide are blown off by the lungs, the pH level of the blood rises, and this condition is known as respiratory alkalosis. The patient will display tachypnea (rapid breathing), often in conjunction with apprehension, and complaints of chest tightness and shortness of breath. The patient may also experience palpitations, epigastric distress, blurred vision, and vertigo. Paresthesias such as numbness, tingling, or a pins-and-needles sensation may also affect the extremities, particularly the arms and hands. Progressive alkalosis can also disrupt calcium metabolism, and in severe cases, tetany with carpopedal (wrist and foot) spasm may be experienced.

The initial treatment of hyperventilation is relatively simple and consists of reassuring and comforting the patient while simultaneously having him breathe into a paper bag (Fig 39–9). The exhaled air in the paper bag will have a higher concentration of carbon dioxide than room air. Rebreathing expired carbon dioxide can effectively counter respiratory alkalosis and raise the level of carbon dioxide in the bloodstream, thereby lowering the body's pH and normalizing the acid-base balance. The pathologic event should subside after a few minutes of rebreathing as long as the patient becomes calm and relaxed. In severe cases it may be beneficial to sedate the patient in an effort to alleviate high anxiety, and this can be achieved with the administration of diazepam, 5 mg orally or 2 mg intravenously, or midazolam, 1 mg intravenously.

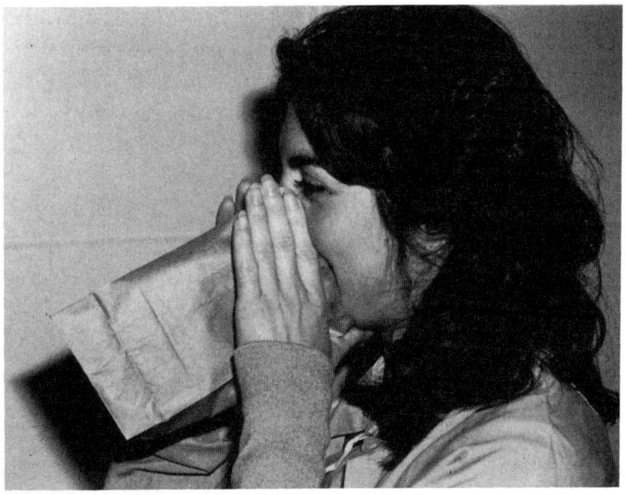

FIG 39–9.
Rebreathing into a brown paper bag to lower blood pH and counter the effects of hyperventilation.

Seizure

Seizures encountered in the office setting are usually related to pre-existing epilepsy or drug toxicity such as occurs following the overdosage of certain local anesthetic solutions. In the case of a patient suffering from grand mal epilepsy, the seizure is often preceded by an aura such as a flash of light or another distinct sensation. These patients will exhibit overt signs of central nervous system overstimulation and muscular spasm (grand mal epilepsy), and they will typically lose consciousness during the seizure and fall to the floor. It is not uncommon for seizure victims to sustain an injury when they lose consciousness and fall in an uncontrolled fashion or collide with a hard object in the room. Once on the ground, the patient will experience profound muscular contraction and lie in a stiff position for several minutes, often followed by synchronous body movements related to repeated muscular relaxation and contraction. The patient may become hypoxic during the seizure and may appear slightly pale or cyanotic (bluish). There is often a loss of bowel and bladder control during the seizure, and many patients experience postictal (the period following a seizure) amnesia and aphasia and are unable to remember the event or express themselves verbally afterward.

The emergency management of patients undergoing a seizure evolves primarily around protecting the victim from injury during the brief event and monitoring them afterward. One of the most important points to remember is that the patient can sustain serious injury if he loses consciousness and falls against a hard or sharp object. In an effort to avoid injury, the patient should be supported and gently guided to the floor, and the seizure should be allowed to run its course without restraint. It is not advisable to try and place any object into the patient's mouth once the jaw has contracted shut because this can cause injury to the tongue, mouth, and dentition and may result in bleeding that can occlude the airway. Eyeglasses and tight clothing should be removed or loosened. Once the seizure has subsided, the mouth should be checked for vomitus or hemorrhage and the head turned to the side for clearing the mouth as necessary. The postictal patient will also appear exhausted and will require rest for several hours. It may be beneficial to provide oxygen via nasal cannula in certain individuals, particularly the elderly or patients with pre-existing cardiovascular disease. The patient should be transported to the hospital for evaluation and further monitoring and treatment as deemed necessary.

If the seizure does not subside after several minutes or if the patient seems to pass from one seizure to another without regaining consciousness in between, a condition known as status epilepticus, then antiseizure medication should be administered. Diazepam, 5 to 10 mg administered intravenously via slow push, or dilantin, 300 mg intravenously, can be used to arrest a seizure. It is generally difficult to administer medications intravenously when the patient is undergoing a seizure, and this typically requires stabilizing one of the patient's arms during the time necessary to infuse the drug. Phenytoin should be administered if 20 to 30 mg of diazepam have failed to stop the event. You should be prepared to assist and support the patient's respiration following the administration of these agents, because they can inhibit breathing at dosages necessary to eradicate a seizure. It can be useful to administer oxygen via mask or nasal cannula. Moreover, if the seizure itself becomes prolonged and the patient becomes severely anoxic or suffers from respiratory or cardiopulmonary arrest, then basic life support must be initiated in the form of respiratory or cardiopulmonary resuscitation.

If the seizure is caused by acute drug toxicity, the outward appearance of the patient is essentially the same as if the seizure were caused by long-standing epilepsy. If drug overdosage is the cause, then administration of the drug must be stopped immediately. Once again, the most important aspect of treatment is to protect the patient from injuring himself during the seizure. Unfortunately, drug-related seizures tend to be more protracted events in comparison to the brief episodes associated with epilepsy, and antiseizure medications are often required in an effort to stop the seizure. The remainder of the treatment is identical to that for grand mal epilepsy.

Insulin Shock

Insulin shock occurs secondary to hypoglycemia (low blood sugar), which can be caused by an inadequate supply of available carbohydrate or hyperinsulinism (too much insulin in the tissues). Insulin is a hormone secreted by the pancreas and is responsible for the regulation of carbohydrate (sugar), amino acid, and lipid metabolism. An insulin deficiency results in excessive levels of blood glucose and diabetes mellitus. Excessive insulin levels result in hypoglycemia and may inhibit proper brain function since glucose is a primary nutrient, along with oxygen, required by the central nervous system. It is not uncommon for insulin-dependent diabetic patients to develop insulin shock after taking their morning insulin dosage and failing to properly eat breakfast. This can create a relatively high insulin level in the presence of an inadequate amount of readily available carbohydrate, with resultant hypoglycemia and clinical evidence of insulin shock. It is therefore very important to know which of your diabetic patients require insulin for proper metabolic control and to suspect insulin shock should they display the typical signs and symptoms of this disorder.

Patients suffering from insulin shock usually appear confused, nervous, and anxious. Diaphoresis (profuse perspiration) and tachycardia (rapid heart rate) are often associated with this condition, and the skin becomes cool and moist. The patient may also complain of nausea. If left untreated, insulin shock can lead to unconsciousness, convulsions, and coma secondary to inadequate glucose levels in the central nervous system.

Treatment of insulin shock consists primarily of increasing the blood sugar content. If the patient is conscious, he can be given candy, orange juice, or sugar and water. If the patient is unconscious, then one ampule (50 cc) of 50% dextrose should be administered intravenously. Intravenous administration of 5% dextrose in water (D_5W) should also be maintained at a slow drip infusion rate, and the patient should be transported to the hospital emergency room for observation and continued treatment as necessary.

Diabetic Ketoacidosis

Diabetic ketoacidosis is caused by a very high bold glucose level, usually greater than 300 mg/100 mL of serum. This condition typically occurs in a previously undiagnosed diabetic individual or a poorly controlled patient with diabetes mellitus. In this case, acidosis occurs when the body's acid-base balance shifts toward the acid range because of an overproduction of metabolic acids related to abnormal carbohydrate metabolism and excessive production of ketones in the tissues and fluids of the body. This may occur if a diabetic patient fails to properly administer his insulin and monitor dietary carbohydrate intake.

Nausea and vomiting are common symptoms of diabetic ketoacidosis, and the patient will often complain of extreme thirst and a dry mouth. The patient will often display labored breathing (dyspnea) as the body's respiratory system automatically attempts to blow off excessive acid in an effort to compensate for the acidosis. The patient's breath will usually have an acetone aroma. Exhaling excessive acid is, however, rather ineffective in the presence of ketoacidosis because the metabolic acids are nonvolatile and stable in the bloodstream. The patient may also complain of pain and tenderness in the abdomen. The metabolic imbalance also results in depletion of sodium and potassium, and hypotension may develop. These patients may lose consciousness and are at risk for multisystem failure, particularly serious renal failure, and even death secondary to metabolic acidosis if the condition persists untreated.

Emergency treatment of suspected diabetic ketoacidosis involves rapid intravenous administration of normal saline. Rapid assessment of the blood glucose level can be made by means of the finger stick method. Although this method can be somewhat inaccurate, it is usually adequate and can be very useful in the office setting. If the patient knows his usual dose of insulin and can indicate that he has missed a dose or has not been using the medication, insulin should be administered subcutaneously or intravenously in the appropriate dosage (the patient's regular dosage). A typical initial dose of insulin in the emergency situation is 50 units administered intravenously and 50 units administered subcutaneously. The patient must be transported to the hospital emergency room as soon as possible for accurate metabolic monitoring and control.

Airway Obstruction

In the office setting, airway obstruction usually occurs secondary to the presence of a foreign body or vomitus lodged in the oropharynx (upper portion of the throat) or larynx (upper portion of the windpipe that contains the vocal cords). The tongue can block the airway if it is retracted against the posterior portion of the oral cavity and epiglottis, thereby occluding the oropharynx. The signs of airway obstruction are choking; violent respiratory effort; retractions in the spaces of the supraclavicular, suprasternal, and intercostal areas; and cyanosis. Cyanosis appears as a bluish discoloration, particularly of the skin and mucous membranes, and is caused by the presence of oxygen-depleted hemoglobin in the bloodstream. If the airway remains obstructed beyond even a short period of time, respiratory arrest may ensue. The absence of breathing, in turn, can result in cardiac arrest. It is therefore extremely important to notify the emergency medical service as soon as the diagnosis of airway obstruction is made because the condition may persist and the patient can progress to cardiopulmonary arrest and die.

Proper treatment of airway obstruction varies with the degree of patient symptomatology. If the patient can speak, even though he is choking, this indicates that he is still exchanging air and should be allowed to attempt to alleviate the condition on his own. If the patient continues to choke and displays progressive cyanosis or loss of consciousness or if respiratory arrest develops, then the Heimlich maneuver (subdiaphragmatic abdominal thrusts) or chest thrusts and manual clearing of the airway should be attempted. Upon clearing the airway, supplemental oxygen should be delivered via mask or nasal cannula if the patient displays spontaneous breathing. Rescue breathing at a ventilation rate of one breath every 1 to 1.5 seconds or CPR (see Table 39–3) may be necessary if either respiratory arrest or cardiopulmonary arrest, respectively, are present following establishment of a patent airway. If the airway remains obstructed, then the Heimlich maneuver must be repeated until a patent passage is obtained and airflow restored. The patient should be transported by the emergency medical service to the hospital emergency room as soon as possible.

In rare instances, it may be necessary to perform an emergency cricothyreotomy in an attempt to save the life of a patient suffering from respiratory and/or cardiopulmonary arrest secondary to airway obstruction. This technique, however, can itself be harmful to the patient if performed improperly and requires special training that is available through most hospital continuing education services. The technique is performed by piercing the cricoid and thyroid cartilages below the patient's larynx (voice box) with a large-bore needle such as a 10-gauge indwelling catheter (see Fig 39–3). This will provide a passage for airflow below the area of obstruction. Once the cartilage has been perforated, the needle is replaced with the flexible catheter, which is connected to an oxygen source and Ambu bag; CPR is implemented as necessary and the patient is transported to the emergency room.

Respiratory Arrest

As mentioned above, airway obstruction can lead to respiratory arrest. Cessation of breathing can also occur secondary to drug toxicity and is often caused by narcotic and barbiturate overdosage. Once again, the symptoms are an absence of breathing and cyanosis. The patient can become comatose after a few minutes if breathing is not restored. Clinically speaking, the cardinal triad for narcotic or barbiturate toxicity is miosis (contraction of the pupil of the eye), unconsciousness, and severely depressed breathing in the form of a diminished respiratory rate or apnea (cessation of breathing). Death may ensue if treatment is not initiated.

Whenever respiratory arrest is diagnosed, patency of the airway must be evaluated. The emergency treatment of airway obstruction has been previously discussed. If the cause of respiratory arrest does not appear to be related to airway obstruction, then the possibility of drug toxicity must be considered. The actual diagnosis of drug overdosage is made by means of analysis of the blood serum for evidence of the drug. Emergency treatment consists of ventilating the patient with an Ambu bag connected to 100% oxygen and intravenous administration of 0.4 to 2 mg of naloxone hydrochloride every 2 to 3 minutes up to 10 mg. Naloxone hydrochloride is a narcotic antagonist that functions to compete with circulating narcotic for drug receptor sites in the tissues. The patient should be transported to the hospital emergency room as soon as possible.

Pulmonary Thromboembolism

A pulmonary embolism can occur when a thrombus (blood clot) mobilizes from the larger veins of the lower extremity, usually in the calf or thigh, to the blood vessels supplying the lungs. Blood can coagulate, or clot, within the veins of the lower extremity for a variety of different reasons. Any pathologic condition that decreases the blood flow in the lower extremity, thereby creating the condition of venous stasis, can predispose the patient to venous thrombosis. Coagulation of venous blood, or clotting of the blood within the vein, may occur secondary to significant soft-tissue trauma, fractures, venous insufficiency and varicose veins (poorly functioning veins), phlebitis (inflamed veins), or immobilization of the extremity and decreased patient activity. In fact, postoperative patients at bed rest or any patient immobilized in a short or long leg cast are at risk of developing venous thrombosis and subsequent pulmonary embolism. Other factors that increase the risk of developing venous thrombosis include tobacco smoking, obesity, the use of birth control pills, a history of previous venous thrombosis and pulmonary embolism, and the presence of abdominal or pelvic malignancy.

Once a clot forms inside a lower extremity vein, all or any part of the thrombus can break lose and flow with the blood returning to the heart. The free-flowing clot is termed an embolism. The embolism can pass easily and rapidly through the large veins in the thigh, pelvis, abdomen, and thorax and then through the right side of the heart and into the large pulmonary artery. As the pulmonary artery branches into smaller-vessels supplying blood to both lungs and the distinct segments of each lung, the embolism may become lodged within the smaller diameter arteries and, once again, become a stationary thrombus that occludes blood flow into the lung tissue beyond the blockage. A single large embolism or multiple smaller emboli can rapidly block blood flow to the lung and result in serious damage to the functional tissues of the lung. If enough of the pulmonary vasculature becomes occluded, respiration will be impeded, and the patient may die in a very short period of time.

The patient suffering from an acute pulmonary embolism will display a rapid onset of chest and/or back pain, shortness of breath, tachypnea (rapid breathing), tachycardia (rapid heart rate), dyspnea (labored breathing), and hypotension and relate a sense of impending doom. The patient may also display hemoptysis (coughing up blood) and an elevated temperature. After a few minutes, cyanosis will develop secondary to hypoxia (decreased oxygen in the tissues), and depending upon the severity of the embolism, the patient may eventually lose consciousness and die.

The emergency treatment of an acute pulmonary embolism occurring in the office setting primarily involves the administration of 100% oxygen via mask at a rate of 6 L/min. The patient should also have all clothing loosened and be placed in a semi-erect position as long as he remains conscious. Vital signs should be monitored and recorded, and the emergency medical service should be notified immediately. If possible, intravenous access should be achieved and maintained for subsequent use as needed. If the patient loses consciousness, he should be placed in the Trendelenburg position, and CPR should be administered as deemed necessary. Unfortunately, severe occlusion of the pulmonary vasculature can prevent adequate gas exchange in the lungs and inhibit effective respiration despite appropriate administration of oxygen and CPR. The patient should be transported to the hospital emergency room and appropriate heparin therapy administered as soon as possible.

Because of the rapidly devastating nature of a large pulmonary embolism, even prompt recognition of the condition does not always allow enough time to adequately treat the victim. For this reason, the mainstay of treatment for a pulmonary embolism evolves around prevention of the development of lower extremity venous thrombosis. It is important to ask every surgical candidate, or any patient requiring cast immobilization or bed rest, whether he has a history of venous thrombosis or pulmonary embolism. Moreover, it is crucial to minimize the duration of bed rest and to try to establish early postoperative out-of-bed activity and range-of-motion exercises. If the patient must remain non–weight bearing in a cast, then a daily regimen of gentle massage of the proximal aspect of the calf musculature and alternating dorsiflexion–plantar flexion exercises of the toes and metatarsophalangeal joints may be helpful in preventing thrombosis in the veins of the leg.

Patients at bed rest should also wear antiembolism stockings to provide a gradient of foot and calf compression, perform daily range-of-motion exercises, and refrain from smoking and the use of birth control pills. Certain medications such as aspirin may be useful in preventing the formation of blood clots in the veins of the lower extremities; however, proper anticoagulant therapy for patients at high risk of developing thrombosis generally involves the administration of heparin or sodium warfarin.

Angina Pectoris

Angina pectoris is a painful condition that most commonly occurs secondary to coronary artery disease and myocardial ischemia (diminished blood flow to the musculature of the heart). The condition is often precipitated by physical stress or anxiety and should be anticipated in any patient with a history of cardiovascular disease, including hypertension. The patient suffering from angina pectoris will typically complain of crushing or burning substernal chest pain, often associated with feelings of suffocation, shortness of breath, and impending doom. Anginal pain can radiate to the chin or jaw or into either arm, most commonly the left. The pain typically lasts for only 3 to 5 minutes before subsiding, and the symptoms can be mistaken for those of severe indigestion. Tachycardia may be present; however, the patient's vital signs usually remain stable during the event. If the patient does not rest or receive treatment, the condition may progress to myocardial infarction, and actual ischemic necrosis of the heart musculature may develop. There exists a variant form of angina pectoris known as Prinzmetal's angina in which the painful attacks occur while the patient is at rest.

The office emergency management of angina pectoris consists of placing the patient in a semirecumbent position and administering 100% oxygen via mask or nasal cannula at a rate of 6 L/min. A nitroglycerin capsule (0.4 to 0.6 mg) should be administered sublingually and can be repeated twice at 5-minute intervals if the symptoms persist. Nitroglycerin temporarily decreases the work load of the myocardium (heart musculature), thereby decreasing the heart's oxygen requirement, while simultaneously increasing collateral blood flow to the heart musculature. Many patients with a history of angina pectoris will use nitroglycerin in either capsular or transdermal ointment form for prophylaxis and treatment of the painful condition. All tight or constricting clothing should be loosened, and the patient should be reassured in an effort to calm him down and help relieve anxiety. Vital signs should be monitored and recorded, and the patient should be transported to the hospital emergency room for further evaluation and treatment as necessary. If the patient has a history of cardiovascular disease, then his cardiologist should be contacted regarding the situation.

Myocardial Infarction

Myocardial infarction is most commonly caused by coronary artery disease; however, it has also been linked to cocaine abuse. The symptoms can be similar to those associated with angina pectoris, but they generally persist beyond 3 to 5 minutes. The patient will usually experience crushing or burning chest pain, often described as a feeling of having something very heavy placed upon the chest. The pain is usually localized to the substernal region and can radiate to the jaw, back, shoulders, or arms. Once again, radiating pain most commonly affects the left upper extremity. Diaphoresis (profuse perspiration), nausea, weakness, and cyanosis may develop. Moreover, the patient may become overwhelmed with a sense of impending doom. Myocardial infarction can lead to severe cardiac dysrhythmia and even cardiac arrest. This condition must be distinguished from angina pectoris and severe indigestion.

The treatment of myocardial infarction in the office setting requires rapid intervention and transport of the stabilized patient to the hospital emergency room. The initial treatment is the same as that described for angina pectoris. The patient should be placed in a semirecumbent position and all constricting clothing loosened or removed. Pure oxygen should be delivered via mask or nasal cannula at 6 L/min, and sublingual nitroglycerin (0.4 to 0.6 mg) should be administered. An intravenous line should be initiated with a 16- to 18-gauge catheter, and 2 to 5 mg of morphine sulfate can be slowly administered at 5- to 10-minute intervals. Morphine displays beneficial effects on the blood vessels and ischemic heart via a variety of different mechanisms and also effects pain relief. Meperidine, 10 to 20 mg intravenously, can be used if morphine is not available. The intravenous line should be maintained by using D_5W or lactated Ringer's solution administered slowly (approximately 42 drops per minute to keep the vein open). Vital signs must be monitored closely because cardiac arrest may ensue, and the patient should be transported to an emergency facility as soon as possible. If available, the patient should be connected to an electrocardiograph for evaluation of the electrical activity of the myocardium. However, this is generally not available until the emergency medical service arrives.

Cardiac Arrest

Both myocardial infarction and respiratory arrest can lead to the development of cardiac arrest. The signs of cardiac arrest include unresponsiveness, apnea, and the absence of a pulse. Moreover, the victim will display cyanosis as well as fully dilated pupils that are fixed (unresponsive to light).

The treatment of cardiac arrest consists of the techniques of basic cardiac life support. This entails the establishment of an airway and initiation of cardiopulmonary resuscitation (see Table 39–3). CPR should be started immediately and continued until a pulse and blood pressure become measurable and breathing resumes. The specific techniques of basic life support should be understood and practiced by those members of the office staff who encounter patients. Regular certification should be maintained. The patient should be transported to the hospital emergency room as soon as possible.

Local Anesthetic Toxicity

Local anesthetic agents are used on a daily basis in the practice of podiatric medicine and surgery. Commonly used local anesthetics include lidocaine, mepivacaine, and procaine. The local anesthetic is typically supplied in solution with some form of chemical preservative and may also be used in conjunction with a peripheral vasoconstrictor such as epinephrine. Local infiltration of these agents into the subcutaneous tissue creates a loss of sensation to the part without affecting the patient's level of consciousness or central control of vital functions. Proper infiltration of a local anesthetic solution about a peripheral nerve will block impulse conduction along the nerve cell, thereby creating anesthesia in the tissues distal to the level of infiltration.

Following infiltration, a local anesthetic is metabolized by enzymes in the surrounding tissues or the liver and then excreted by the kidneys. The addition of epinephrine to the anesthetic solution decreases the rate of metabolism, thereby prolonging the local anesthetic effect, while simultaneously decreasing systemic absorption of the agent, thereby diminishing the likelihood of a generalized toxic reaction. In most instances, only a small amount of local anesthetic is required to effectively provide anesthesia, and there are strict guidelines (see the drug's package insert) denoting the maximum amount of a particular agent that can be safely infiltrated before the likelihood of systemic toxicity becomes great. It is important to know the guidelines pertaining to the toxic dosage for the particular local anesthetic agents used in your office. Certain conditions including pseudocholinesterase (the tissue enzyme responsible for metabolizing local anesthetics such as procaine) deficiency and hepatic or renal disease can predispose the patient to local anesthetic toxicity by decreasing the rate of metabolism and excretion of these agents.

There are three basic adverse reactions related to the use of local anesthetic agents. These include vasovagal syncope (described above), hypersensitivity (described above) to the local anesthetic or the preservatives in the solution, and systemic toxicity[9, 10] related to absorption of an excessive amount of the agent into the bloodstream. Overdosage usually occurs secondary to intravascular infiltration of the agent and results in rapid systemic uptake. Infiltration of an excessive amount of the agent into any tissue, particularly fat or muscle, can also result in systemic toxicity.

Local anesthetic toxicity affects both the central nervous system and the cardiovascular system. The initial signs and symptoms include nervousness and anxiety, vertigo, blurred vision, tinnitus (ringing in the ears), tremors, and drowsiness. As the toxicity progresses, the patient may develop central nervous system excitation (due to a loss of inhibitory control) and a seizure, eventually followed by central nervous depression and loss of consciousness with subsequent respiratory depression and arrest. If the systemic overdosage occurs rapidly (intravascular injection), the initial signs of central nervous system dysfunction may be bypassed, and the victim may develop a seizure right away. The cardiovascular effects of local anesthetic toxicity occur simultaneously with the central nervous system changes and include peripheral vasodilatation and hypotension, bradycardia (slowing heart rate), weak cardiac contraction, and subsequent cardiac arrest.

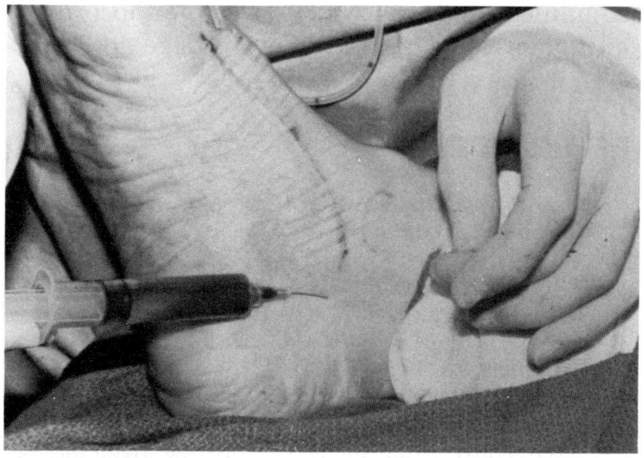

FIG 39–10.
Aspiration of blood into the syringe while administering a posterior tibial nerve block. This is indicative of intravascular placement of the needle into the posterior tibial artery or an accompanying vein. When this occurs, the needle should be repositioned in an effort to avoid intravascular injection of the local anesthetic solution and a toxic reaction to the drug.

Emergency management of local anesthetic toxicity in the office setting involves supportive measures as described in the sections above for the management of the patient experiencing a seizure or respiratory and/or cardiac arrest. It is also important to prevent further uptake of the agent from the site of injection either by means of tourniquet application or local infiltration of vasoconstrictor around the original site of local anesthetic injection. Prevention of local anesthetic toxicity is a crucial aspect of everyday office practice and involves knowledge of the patient's medical history, strict adherence to recommended dosage guidelines, and technical factors such as aspirating for blood during anesthetic infiltration. Aspiration of a large amount of blood into the syringe is indicative of intravascular placement of the needle (Fig 39–10). Moreover, the use of local anesthetic agents mandates the availability of emergency equipment and drugs such as oxygen in order to adequately manage a toxic overdosage.

REFERENCES

1. Grauer K, Cavallaro DL: *ACLS: Certification Preparation and A Comprehensive Review,* ed 2. St Louis, CV Mosby Co, 1987, pp 231–243.
2. Allo MD, Miller CF: Airway management, in Zuidema GD, Rutherford RB, Ballinger WF (eds): *The Management of Trauma,* ed 4. Philadelphia, WB Saunders Co, 1985, pp 379–384.
3. Lebovics R: Diseases of the upper respiratory tract, in Wilson JD, Braunwald E, Isselbacher KJ, et al (eds): *Harrison's Principles of Internal Medicine,* ed 12. New York, McGraw-Hill International Book Co, 1991, p 1101.
4. Myerburg RJ, Castellanos A: Cardiovascular collapse, cardiac arrest, and sudden death, in Wilson JD, Braunwald E, Isselbacher KJ, et al (eds): *Harrison's Principles of Internal Medicine,* ed 12. New York, McGraw-Hill International Book Co, 1991, pp 240–242.
5. Gay WA: Cardiac arrest and resuscitation, in Shines GT (ed): *Principles of Trauma Care,* ed 3. New York, McGraw-Hill International Book Co, 1985, pp 57–61.
6. Grauer K, Cavallaro DL: *ACLS: Certification Preparation and A Comprehensive Review,* ed 2. St Louis, CV Mosby Co, 1987, pp 203–216.
7. Fath JJ, Cerra FB: The therapy of anaphylactic shock. *Drug Intell Clin Pharmacol* 1984; 18:14–21.
8. Costa A: Anaphylactic shock. *Postgrad Med* 1988; 83:368–373.
9. Covino BG: Local anesthesia (part 1). *N Engl J Med* 1972; 286:975–983.
10. Covino BG: Local anesthesia (part 2). *N Engl J Med* 1972; 286:1035–1042.

Index